CELEBRITY ACCESS

THE DIRECTORY

1997-1998 6th EDITION

Edited by Thomas and Catherine Burford

CELEBRITY ACCESS PUBLICATIONS

Burford, Thomas G.
   Celebrity access: the directory/Thomas G. Burford.-- 1997-1998 rev. ed.-- Mill Valley, Calif. : Celebrity Access Publications, c1997.
   p. cm.
   ISSN: 1057-9427
   "Or how and where to write the rich and famous"-- Cover.
   Includes index.
   ISBN: 0-9619758-5-7

1. Motion picture actors and actresses--Directories. 2. Entertainers--Directories. 3. Celebrities--Directories. 4. Sports--Directories 5. Autographs--collectors and collecting. I. Title.

PN2285.B79 1997   791.4'092
                        QBI95-20033

Cover design by Veronica Denny
Book design/editing by Catherine Burford

CONTENTS

SPECIAL DEDICATION

The dictionary describes a gentleman, as a man whose conduct conforms to a high standard of propriety and correct behavior.

James Maitland Stewart, born May 20, 1908; Indiana, PA. America's much loved Hollywood box office draw, with his often copied shy, stammering style. Acting in classics such as: "The Philadelphia Story" (Oscar 1947), "Vertigo," and "It's a Wonderful Life," he went to the top and stayed there.

Charisma, is a term used in Hollywood used to describe star quality, and Stewart had it from the beginning. Not only did it translate well on screen, but it's truly the man off screen. Jimmy's fans, never forget how well he has treated them over the years. Until recently, he answered all his own fan mail. A huge job. Someone like Jimmy, who is known and loved the world over, receives thousands of requests for autographs regularly.

I once asked him why he consistently answered all his own fan mail. His answer from the heart was, "I'll never forget the fact, that through fan support over the years, I have achieved the level of stardom which I have." Impressive to say the least.

You won't see his name listed in this directory. After many years of faithful service to his fans, he's decided to retire from the time consuming fan mail duties. He's earned the right to step back a million times over. God bless you Jimmy, we love you.

Benjamin Franklin Johnson, Jr., born June 13, 1918, died April 8, 1996; Pawhuska, OK. Ben will be remembered for the many western roles he played in films such as: "Fort Apache," "She Wore a Yellow Ribbon," and "The Last Picture Show" (Oscar 1971). Ben once told me that "The Wild Bunch" was his favorite work because it set a new standard for how westerns would be made and perceived in the future, by the audience.

I really liked Ben. A cowboy's cowboy. We met many years ago, and I knew immediately I would admire and enjoy the company of this man. Armed with a story, and a great sense of humor, he would spin tales of the good old days of film making. I was enriched by them. Ben always had time for a fan and camera. He never thought of himself as a major star, being the humble man he was, he always thought of himself as a cowboy.

A gentleman always. We had some great times hanging out together over the years, and a lot of laughs. You treated me as a friend. I'll miss you Ben, we all will.

ACKNOWLEDGMENTS

I would like to thank all those who gave me support, friendship, and encouragement -- Catherine Burford for her intensive work on this book, locating the many mistakes and correcting them, and especially for again reformatting *The Directory* to make it better than it has ever been. To my good friends Janice and Wayne Racek. The following people have all contributed greatly with researching, verifying, and reverifying thousands of new addresses. The quality and quantity of new information sent by these people was superb this time. They are to be commended for a lot of time and effort in this project. Roger Adams, Anthony Alfiero, Michael Andersen, Lawrence Edge, Terri & Robert Farrell, Robert Hopper, Shawn Jackson, Roger Kranich, Roger Label, Hartriono Sastrowardoyo, Paris Stachtiaris, Michael Stevens, Reggie Turner, Dennis Vance, John Walsh, and Joe Wormall. Welcome to newcomers "The Infamous" Ron Cote, and Ben & Dora Sweeney.

A special thanks to my associates in the writing/publishing business: Michael Andersen, Jim Wiggins, Roger Christensen, Jim Weaver, Michael Johnson, Jeffrey Morey, and Jurgen Schwarz. These are very special people. We all publish or contribute to a form of directory, and we are now, more actively sharing information on updates and changes. This gives us all a better, and more accurate product for our readers. They all contributed freely, and this shared effort is to be applauded.

On a personal note, thanks to Linda Kay for the referrals, and Allen Stenhouse sends inspiration with his submissions. His letters always cheered me up. And finally Amber Klapholz, for much needed data entry, Brandon Kemp and Jeff Brandon for scheduling to free me up.

And thank you, to all who helped by sending in "good" addresses for *The Directory*, and informing me of the ones which were no longer current. Without them, this book wouldn't have as much useful information as it does. These thoughtful people sent in address return labels from their envelopes, and postal "Return to Sender" labels with the address, which had come back undelivered. We encourage everyone's help!

If we've forgotten anyone, it was truly unintentional. So, to all of you, my thanks. I hope for continued friendship.

INTRODUCTION

Philography, or in common parlance, autograph collecting, is an almost perfect hobby -- it can be done at home in your spare time, it requires no expensive equipment, and takes up a minimum of space. Receiving your first response will not only be very exciting, it will easily make your investment in this book well worth while. **Warning!** This book is only intended for you to have fun writing your favorite stars, do not go visit them. We do not list or identify home addresses, so these people may have their well deserved privacy. You may find that if you attempt to visit these addresses you may very well be arrested for trespassing, invasion of privacy, or held by private security. Respect the individuals privacy. These addresses are mostly business addresses, and will not allow access to the general public.

Most of the addresses listed in this book are of well-known actors and actresses, however, there are also entries for selected people in politics, science, and the arts. The book is **not** cluttered with the addresses of corporations and fan clubs: they are listed only if they have a personal connection with a celebrity.

This book is one of the best philography tools you can get your hands on. It includes information beyond that offered by any other books in this field. In addition to providing the expected "good" addresses, this book provides "Alternate and Forwarded" addresses as secondary listings, and our individual descriptive notes and "V Date", which indicates when a response was returned from that celebrity. You will find our chapters informative and our reference section truly unique.

Thomas Burford

AUTOGRAPH CARE AND PRESERVATION
by Joe Kraus

There is probably nothing more exciting for an autograph collector than to finally obtain that one long-sought-after piece. At the same time, there is nothing more depressing than to find a similar prize destroyed because it did not receive proper care. While there is no magic wand to create the elusive autograph or document you are seeking, there is help at hand to preserve and care for the autographs already in your collection.

Benjamin Franklin may have summed up the necessity of proper care in one statement. "For want of a nail," he said, "the shoe was lost; for want of a shoe the horse was lost; and for want of a horse the rider was lost; being overtaken and slain by the enemy, all for want of care about a horseshoe nail."

Collectors have many choices in how and where to store and preserve autographs. These can range anywhere from a bank vault to a shoe box placed under the foot of a bed. But it seems as soon as a collector thinks he or she has done it the way he or she wants, someone comes along with a new idea. Then it is out with the old, and in with the new. In the end it doesn't matter a great deal what you do, for what works for one person may not work all that well for another. Because of this one shouldn't dwell so much on what **to** do, but rather what **not** to do.

Do not, for instance, ever use paper clips, rubber bands, glue, staples, or tape on your autographs, not even around the corners of the paper. And never laminate your autographs. Never use varnish or shellac, or spray anything over an autograph -- even the advertised plastic sprays which are said to protect documents. The value of such sprayed material is lost, not to mention the long-term damage to the autographed item. Do not ever use the kind of "stick-'em-down album" that you see in five-and-dime and camera supply stores. Again, while it may seem that this is the answer to all your problems, your autographs can in time become permanently stuck, and in addition, the acid sometimes goes right through the paper of the photograph or document, appearing as yellow lines on the surface. Rather, place your collection into three-ring binders, between acetate sheets. Clear plastics can pose a danger, as many plastics are acidic. One way to spot a danger is to rub your fingers over the sheets. If they feel oily -- stay away. Don't ever leave your autographs exposed to sunlight regardless whether you are outside, or inside with direct light reaching your collection. The light, in time, will fade your signatures. Be concerned as well with extremes of heat or cold, and with wet or damp places, as these may cause your collection to warp, mildew or even melt!

Always be concerned about floods or fires. For storage, find a waterproof and fireproof container and store your albums within the house or other similar location, not in a garage, attic, or basement. But even within a house, place your collection on a shelf or in a closet, not on the floor. If you store autographs in three-ring binders, place them on a shelf as you would a book, not face down with other heavy albums on top. The pressure could cause certain inks, such as the dry erase and metallic marker types, to lift off. Give each album space and room to breathe. Remember also, that there are many pests, such as insects, worms, and mice or rats, which can, given the opportunity, damage or completely destroy your collection.

Another concern is burglary. While most burglars would not know what to do with an autograph collection, it still might get taken just as a curiosity. Do what you would do with any other valuable. Photographing or videotaping is the most common and accurate method used, and is recommended by insurance companies. It is best, as well, to keep a running record of your collection should part or all of it be destroyed, damaged or stolen. Most homeowners' or renters' insurance policies have provisions in which you can list your collection. Insurance firms, however, are highly skeptical of the exaggerated prices many collectors place on these types of valuables. An updated letter from an acknowledged dealer on his/her letterhead will be needed for your files and the insurance firm's records. This letter should give a general description of your collection and place a value on it.

Bank vaults, while many think them secure, might cause another problem. Ventilation is essential. Keeping your manuscripts and autographs in an airless environment can be harmful. Store autographs in a clean, dry place where air can freely circulate.

Should you frame autographs and hang them on your wall, make sure they hang well away from direct sunlight. Also make sure they are matted, not under straight glass. A mat will keep the autograph away from the glass and safe from sticking against the glass.

Mats should be acid free and for mounting use only acid-free tape. Glass in frames should be non glare document glass. Plexiglass UF-3 filters out ultraviolet rays. This will prevent much of the fading that you could get from using regular glass.

Before framing an item, however, it is best to encapsulate it. Encapsulation is the process in which autographs are sealed at all four edges between two pieces of acid-free Mylar (bonded together using acid-free adhesive backings such as polyester transparent tape). What this does is form a protective envelope around your autograph. Over this place your mat.

Exercise care and caution when handling autographs. Protect them from tears or creasing, greasy fingers or spilled soda pop. In short, use good common sense and your autographs will remain in excellent repair.

Joe Kraus is currently editor/publisher of <u>Child Stars Magazine</u> in Stockton, CA. He is a former editor of the <u>U.A.C.C./Pen & Quill Magazine</u> and former editor/owner of <u>Autograph Collectors Magazine</u>.

AN OPEN LETTER TO FANS
by Yvonne Craig

One evening, whilst sitting at dinner with Tom, we began talking about fans and what I liked about hearing from them, what worked, and what was intrusive or frightening about encounters with them. It was then that Tom suggested that I write it down and he'd put it in his book. So, though I wouldn't presume to speak for all actors on this subject, perhaps I can give you some guidelines which might apply to others as well.

1) I am always gratified to hear from fans especially since the bulk of my work was done rather a while back. When I was shooting "Batman" I received no fan mail personally and must assume that either Fox Studios or ABC-TV was intercepting and answering it for me. I currently answer all requests for autographs personally as I believe do most of us "oldies but goodies" actors who are not actively involved in shooting a series at this time. However, because I have a busy life and try to allocate just a few hours a month to this task, it is impossible for me to answer extensive questions. It also helps if fans will send a S.A.S.E. for my reply, and if they enclose a photo they'd like signed, all the better. Reminder: when you request an 8X10 photo from any celebrity, please send an envelope that will accommodate it. I can't tell you how often I receive a request for a signed photo accompanied by a S.A.S.E. that is letter size! Also if you want it personalized (I do so unless specifically requested not to), you need to mention that person's name. For instance I get letters saying "I was such a "Batman" fan and now my daughter is as well. Could you send her a photo and one for me?" They then sign their name which means they get a personalized photo but their daughter does not because I don't know what the child's name is. Disappointment! Also, after giving it a lot of thought, I recently decided not to respond to any more post cards which are pre-printed so that they read: "Dear --- (this is filled in with my name by the sender) I have been a fan of yours for a long time. Please send an autographed photo. Sincerely," or one which contains an obvious formula like: "I've been a big fan of yours for so long. You are the best there's ever been. Can I have an autograph?" This sort of formula on a card could apply to anyone, is easy to spot, and is probably sent out to a number of people at the same time. Finally, many stars give their autograph with ease through the mail, and I'm sure a simple "thank you" would be appreciated if they used their own photo, postage, and envelope.

2) Some of us do personal appearances, and that's a perfect time to ask those questions you wanted to have answered by mail. I usually allocate time during any personal appearance for just such a "Question & Answer" period. It lasts at least an hour each day of the appearance. I find that often the same people raise their hands again and again, but

I have to assume they're asking things about which the more timid are equally interested so I kind of go with whatever happens. What I really hate is to get up and say "Does anyone have anything they'd like to ask?" and be met by a sea of implacable faces, with no raised hands. This is where I just have to wing it in regard to what you guys might find interesting, only to be met as I leave the stage by sixteen people who DO have questions but were too shy to speak up.

3) The following are some guidelines that you might keep in mind:

a. Most performers are as shy or shyer than you are. We use acting as a means to creatively overcome this but the condition still exists. So its very uncomfortable to have someone whisper and point in our direction but very nice to have that person come up and say "I enjoyed you in -----".

b. It's flattering to have someone write a note of appreciation to you via normal channels -- that is to say via the address you find in this book or through SAG, AFTRA, AEA, or our manager or agent. It is unnerving to have someone track you down and/or show up at your home uninvited. We all tend to be a bit paranoid since the murder of Rebecca Shaeffer.

c. We are generally NOT like the characters we play. It's good to be convincing as a character but less fun when someone physically accosts you for some misdeed of a character you've been successfully portraying.

4) I guess the most important thing to keep in mind when dealing with celebrities is actually what you keep in mind in life in general: Treat others as you'd like to be treated. But bear in mind that what I'm saying is from a relatively "low profile" point of view. I'm sure if this chapter were being written by Cher or Madonna or Bruce Willis there would be more than a few lines directed at crowds infringing on one's space as well as how not to ask for autographs during someone's dinner or while in the Ladies/Mens room. However: Treat others as you'd like to be treated still should cover it.

Yvonne Craig is an actress, well-known for her role as "Batgirl" in the popular television show "Batman," which aired in the late 1960's. She has appeared in numerous films, including "The Young Land," "It Happened at the World's Fair," "Kissin' Cousins," "By Love Possessed," "One Spy Too Many," and "In Like Flint." She has also made many guest appearances on TV series. She currently resides and works in the Los Angeles Area.

CONTACTING CELEBRITIES THROUGH THE MAIL
by Thomas Burford

Celebrities! We place them on pedestals, and often forget that they are people with feelings and emotions like the rest of humanity. For autograph collectors, this is an especially important point to remember. When you write to your favorite stars, remember to treat them with intelligence and dignity.

A "truly authentic" autograph is the one which is obtained by you "in person". This kind of contact also leaves you with the memory of meeting the celebrity in person and having a unique one-on-one experience. If you are fortunate enough meet a celebrity in person, remember that he or she is entitled to a private life just as you and I are. Before approaching a celebrity, think about where you are. Because of someone's complete lack of manners, a very famous movie star now refuses to sign for anyone after being asked for an autograph in a rest room. There is a time and place for everything, and that was certainly neither the time nor place.

If you see that a celebrity is trying to remain inconspicuous, he or she may not appreciate your intrusion, and you may not get your autograph. But if you approach stars calmly, without drawing attention to them, (they will appreciate your doing this) and politely ask them to sign something, they probably will. If you have a clean plain-white unfolded card or piece of paper, use it. These make the best examples for framing. Most fans are caught off guard, so any reasonable article to sign on will do in a pinch. Many stars have told me in interviews they don't like paper and pen thrust into their faces, so please use good manners. They also dislike intrusions during meals or when with family.

Since the chances of finding stars in person are slim for most of us, we must rely heavily on the mail. The rest of this article will be devoted to giving the best instruction we can for learning the proper way to collect autographs by mail.

Our most powerful tool for increasing the chance of an autograph is the "self-addressed-stamped-envelope" or S.A.S.E., as it is most commonly referred to. The S.A.S.E. must have enough postage to insure its return without expecting the celebrity to pay any of it for you. This should accompany any letter you send. Your address should be printed clearly on the envelope if you expect any kind of a response. A complete address and zip code is critical on **anything** you mail. Remember to always put your address on your envelope, on your S.A.S.E., on your letterhead, and on whatever photo you send so it doesn't get mixed up with someone else's. (When writing on any photo's reverse surface, use only the slightest pressure, as the pen may leave an impression which could show through on the front surface.) A celebrity will frequently return your S.A.S.E. with your request as their way of "saying thank you for remembering". The size of your S.A.S.E. will be decided by what your request is. If you send a 4x5 inch index card, your S.A.S.E. should be large enough for it to be returned without having to fold it in any way. If you send a photograph, include a S.A.S.E large enough, and with enough postage for it to be returned in the best possible condition. To further insure that any damage will be minimal, we also recommend the use some sort of cardboard backing between which the photograph can be inserted. This gives your photograph a certain amount of rigidity while passing through the mail.

Some stars will send signed photos without any S.A.S.E. or photographs sent to them. These stars are becoming fewer and fewer every day. Because of the enormous cost involved for photos, postage, envelopes (and secretaries' salaries!), and the fact that the bonanza days of studios and their contract players are long gone, your contributions will be needed more in days to come. **Do not send anything return-receipt requested, certified, or by any other way in which a celebrity would have to sign or take responsibility for. The item will almost certainly be refused.**

The response/return time for your request will vary, and depends on many factors. How current is the address at which you are writing the celebrity? Perhaps the individual has moved (and stars move with great frequency). The mail may need to forwarded, or perhaps there **is** no forwarding address. Celebrities are generally very busy people. The individual may be away on vacation, living at his or her summer or winter home, out on a movie location, on the road with a concert tour or stage production, or is perhaps ill. The possibilities are endless. All these could be reasons for slowing the response to an autograph request. The reason could also be that the photographs were mislaid, misfiled, sent to a wrong address, or even temporarily lost. We have known of cases in which items have been returned after an elapse of two years. Whatever the reason, **they are not responsible** for anything you send. By following this advice you may be surprised to find an occasional extra photo tucked into your envelope -- some of the stars are very generous this way. We should further mention, for those of you who will be writing to people overseas, to purchase an I.R.C. (International Reply Coupon). These are used to exchange for postage in foreign countries. You should be able to purchase the coupons at your own Postal Main Branch, and they are fairly inexpensive. Two to four are usually enough.

Writing a good letter to a celebrity could make the difference between a minimal response and the response you've always wanted. When writing you should be polite, patient, and respectful. It never hurts to say "please", and "thank you". You might even consider **not** being over familiar with a celebrity by calling him or her by first name. In our opinion, your letter should be hand written and on clean paper. (Please do type the letter if your handwriting is hard to read!) One should be as original as possible, for the celebrities have seen every possible type of fan letter you could imagine. A sure fire way of having your mail thrown in the garbage is to photocopy a letter, and hand-write the name of the person you are writing to at the beginning. This also applies to letters printed on computers, form letters (these are obvious), and envelopes with the address on an address label. The later appears to be part of a mailing service or list to them.

The letter should be short and to the point. Usually one page on one side until you know the celebrity wishes to continue writing to you in the future. Long letters may never be completely read if the celebrity isn't interested in personally responding. Since in most cases a secretary or assistant screens the mail, the content and length may decide if the celebrity ever sees it. Don't expect a personal response from the celebrity, as there are so many requests from fans it is not possible to attend to them all. You may however be one of the chosen few to receive that one-in-a-million letter. Sometimes persistence has paid off. After several letters to a hard to reach person, she finally responded. This doesn't always work and it could backfire on you. Be careful and courteous in each letter so as not to upset the celebrity. If the purpose of the letter is an autograph get right to the point in the first paragraph. (You can mention how you would prefer an authentic autograph from the individual, but time will tell whether your request will be honored.) This gives the celebrity the option of fulfilling your request and reading the rest of the letter later. An intelligent letter is always recommended. Don't talk about collecting a lot of stars, as the individual should be the center of attention in the letter, not other celebrities. The rest of the letter should be used to show the celebrity your knowledge of him or her, and his or her career. This is where you would also critique, praise, or comment. But if you are rude or disrespectful you can expect you mail to go unanswered, and the items you sent may be thrown away or even torn up and returned.

Many celebrities don't answer their mail personally. It is frequently answered by secretaries, agents, and fan mail services on the behalf of the celebrity, with all good intentions. But it is disheartening to fans to discover that their autographs were signed by someone other than the celebrity. There are also other types of items sent out by the celebrities' offices which are explained in greater detail in another chapter. Some of these are, photos with signature stamps, mechanical signatures, and signature imprints. More celebrities are sending these every day. Regardless what is sent, **save everything** for someday it will be collectable, and will be your direct contact with your past. It will be fun in a few years to look back on these items to see the changes. You may find some surprises.

What should you send? We have several do's and don'ts. Don't ask for more than one photo and send no more than three for signing. If your have asked for a free photo from a celebrity be aware that some offices keep track of what they send out. They may write and tell you they already honored your request months before. Most celebrities will automatically inscribe a photo to the requester. Should you want one as a gift for a friend it is not unusual to request one signed to your friend. If you want an un-inscribed photo you may run into problems as the celebrity may suspect you want it for other reasons. It is not a good idea to send gifts of food for obvious reasons, but tokens of appreciation are sometimes accepted. Don't send money unless you are asked to formally order an item from them which you want. The celebrities who do send photos send whatever they happen to have on hand. It could be rude to make an unreasonable request for a specific item. You may however mention that you are looking for a particular item and ask if they could tell you where you could find one. When you send anything for an autograph (ie. books, album covers, first day covers, and sheet music) don't over wrap it. They won't fight it to open it. Don't send anything you can't afford to loose. If you have a rare or hard to get item, you should keep it, as it could disappear quickly and mysteriously. We suggest you keep records of what you mail out, when you mailed it, and any follow-up letters you may have sent. Occasionally the celebrity will try to help you locate a lost item if you can furnish specific information on when, where, and what you lost.

Reference material with the history of films and celebrity biographies, as well as books on autograph collecting, can be found at your local library and book stores. We have included a reference section in this book to help you locate clubs, papers, and magazines which promote autograph collecting and interests in film, sports, and other areas. Many of these publications print facsimiles of signatures to help you identify ones you may receive in the mail. If you require further authentication there are several dealers who advertise in these publications and would be willing to help you. I highly recommend that you check on the reputation of any dealer before sending off your prize possession. A reputable dealer won't mind the inquiry. Many are members of fine organizations that have an ethics board and work to protect the integrity of autograph collecting.

A final note on our Postal System. Though the Post Office tries to do its best to move our mail, it does occasionally make mistakes. We have seen letters returned from addresses we know were and are good. Agencies which represent celebrities often make many of the cancellations you see on your return mail. These labels are just like the ones the Post Office uses when mail is undeliverable. Since you won't know who stamped your letter with one of these we recommend checking the address again along with any information you can decipher on the envelope. Sometimes the Post Office will attach a yellow "Return To Sender" sticker on the envelope. Always read this carefully. Most will have a forwarding address on them, even though the forwarding order has expired.

There are many reasons why one would collect autographs and we will always encourage novices to not be disappointed with failure the first few attempts. We have all suffered setbacks at one time or another, and we are still always looking forward. Autograph collecting is so widely diversified in its different fields, and virtually cost free to begin (it requires no special equipment), that it is fun, educational, and rewarding.

All the best of luck.

(The following is an actual letter from a dedicated fan to a celebrity; it is an example of an effective bit of letter-writing. Only the names and film titles have been changed.)

Dear Mr. Smith,

I had to write after seeing "Hollywood Back Door" again. You were so cool throughout the film. I've often wanted to write for an autographed photo but I've never been sure whether you would personally see my letter. I've had disappointment in the past with secretaries signing photos, and even mechanically produced signatures. As a true fan I realize major celebrities with busy schedules, like you must have, sometimes do not have the luxury of answering everyone that writes. I hope I am one of the lucky ones.

The film that touched my heart more than anything else you have ever done was "Blue Windows". Everyone around me was crying when it appeared you had died in the last scene. I have to confess when I saw your face reappear, I too was standing on my seat in applause. What a fine and happy ending. I've been trying so hard to find and see everything you've made. You are the best.

I've searched for a long time for photos from "Burford's Dozen" to send you for signing, but so far no luck. In the mean time, I've enclosed a couple 3" x 5" index cards with a self addressed, stamped envelope for your convenience. Would you kindly sign them for me? I would like to thank you in advance for any consideration you may show me.

Respectfully Yours,

John Doe

AUTOGRAPHS, HANDWRITING, AND FORGERY
by Dr. Michael Zanoni

Handwriting and signatures are representations of ideas and identity that convey a person's uniqueness. Possessing the original signature of some significant individual is to have a powerful symbol of all which that person has accomplished.

The collector of contemporary autographs faces very different questions regarding authenticity than does the antiquarian. Very old writings were all executed by hand using instruments and paper which are relatively distinct as to era. The collector of old writings has many signs, symptoms and clues to reveal simulated or forged documents. But the collector of modern writings, particularly the beginning hobbyist, is confronted with numerous sources and methods of simulation.

Handwriting is executed by a combination of conscious and unconscious processes. This is why handwriting takes on unique characteristics. The person who tries to simulate another's signature must consciously execute the appearance and letter-forms of the handwriting. Unless the simulator has specific artistic talent, attempts to replicate another's signature will introduce various defects which are readily apparent.

Since many years of observation, training, and experience are required to become an expert handwriting examiner, this short article cannot prepare someone to render opinions about authenticity. But the information presented will assist in the evaluation and selection process performed by every autograph collector.

SIMPLE FORGERIES

Sometimes called "normal writing simulations", these are situations where someone executes another's signature using their own normal handwriting. You may also hear these called "secretarial signatures" in the situation where a public figure or celebrity has one person whose job it is to sign photos and comply with requests for autographs. These signatures will appear very natural and lifelike because they are, in fact, natural writing. In order to differentiate between secretarial and genuine autographs, one must have access to several samples of known writings. But even this can be difficult, since many public figures have more than one person providing secretarial autographs!

TRACED FORGERIES

There are several ways of producing a traced forgery, and all will show similar symptoms. The simplest way of making a tracing is by the use of light shining through the paper. The paper which is to bear the forged signature is placed over a genuine signature. These are then placed on a light-box or a window, and the image of the genuine signature is traced over. The tracing may be done with a pen, in which case the forger has only one opportunity to make a correct replica. Or the tracing may be done very lightly with a pencil. In this case, additional attempts at producing an acceptable replica can be made. The thin pencil line is then later traced over with ink. A third way of producing a traced forgery is particularly popular with photographs. A photocopy of a genuine signature is placed over the photo which is to carry the replica writing. A fine point ball-pen or pencil is used to trace over the genuine signature. The pressure creates an indentation in the emulsion of the photograph. This indentation is then traced over with a pen, giving the appearance that a ball-pen was used to sign a genuine signature.

Even the best traced forgeries will show the common characteristic of "lifelessness" when compared to genuine writings. When compared to original signatures, tracings generally do not show the dynamic qualities of original writings. Other symptoms and signs may also be observed. Tracings are executed slowly, therefore the ink line will appear uniform and perhaps even heavy. There may be many pen-lifts not present in a genuine signature. Loops and curved lines will often show what is called "deviation from the anticipated curve". This is when the line diverts or wavers from the form or direction one would assume it to normally take. This deviation occurs when the forger carefully tries to follow the pattern signature, but is unable to see the full sweep of the original writing because the hand or pen is in the field of view. Tracings first made with a pencil and then inked over will show the shiny remains of pencil graphite when examined under low magnification. Inked impressions on photographic emulsions will often show either parallel and conflicting impressions if inked with a ball-pen, or may show illogical impressions when inked over with a fiber tip or nibbed pen. But be careful about mistaking the tremor of age and disability for the carefully contrived appearance of a traced forgery.

ARTISTIC FORGERIES

These simulations are the most difficult to identify. They involve what is essentially a drawing of a signature. The forger studies and practices replicating genuine writing. The simpler and more angular the writing, he easier it is to produce an acceptable replica. Also, the closer the genuine writing is to the manner of writing of the forger, the easier it is to produce a simulation. Detection of a good artistic forgery may require examination of dozens of known signatures. In these cases, the examiner often looks for subtle variations between the known and questioned signatures where the forger's personal writing style may not have been completely suppressed.

IMPRESSIONING DEVICES

So-called "rubber stamp" impressions may be made by a rubber-like latex substance, from a silkscreen process in which ink is forced through a pattern embossed on a fabric strip, or by a porous plastic that delivers ink by capillary action.

Signatures produced by "rubber-stamps" are often readily identified, but in some cases (particularly on photographs) careful examination is required to be certain.

Rubber stamps on paper are often readily detectable. Under magnification, one can see the evenness of the ink, the lack of shading, and the absence of any stroke characteristics introduced by changed pen angle. There may also be marks from places where the rubber backing holding the impressioning typeface has not been fully cut away. Sometimes, there will be a "splotchy" appearance to the ink like due to the typeface being worn, dirty, or from the ink being moist. You may also notice that a pattern from the fabric or sponge surface of the stamp-pad has carried over to the signature.

In replica signatures made with porous surface stamps there will not be the usual characteristics of a fabric pattern, but the giveaway is often the even nature of the ink line and under magnification one may sometimes note that the ink line is composed of numerous dots and not a smoothly flowing line.

It is often difficult to determine if a signature on a photograph has been produced by a stamp replication process. On a matte surface print the stamped signature may lose its conspicuous characteristics. On glossy surface photos, particularly with water-soluble inks on older non-resin coated paper, it is possible for the glazed surface of the paper to lose its glossy characteristics and have the rubber stamp appear as if it is pressed down into the emulsion such as would occur with a ball pen. The signs to look for here are the even nature of the ink line and a total lack of embossing and the reverse of the photo.

PHOTOGRAPHS OF AUTOGRAPHED PHOTOGRAPHS

A common problem for autograph collectors is the autographed photograph which is in reality a photograph of an autographed photograph. (Try saying _that_ real fast!) This situation arises when a celebrity places an actual autograph on a picture, which is then re-photographed to make a large number of prints. Quite often, the actual autograph will include some phrase or wording, such as "Yours forever" or "Thanks for your interest and support". It may be that an actual autograph appears on a photograph of another photograph with further wording. But it is very common to find photographs of autographed photographs that have an apparently original dedication or inscription above a signature that is actually part of the photographic image. Someone may have obtained a promotional photo containing a signature, and then placed an inscription above the photographic signature. If the inscription has a writing style similar to the signature, one could easily assume that all writings were by the celebrity.

LITHOGRAPHED SIGNATURES

This is a problem very similar to photographs of autographed photographs. It is not uncommon for a celebrity to utilize promotional pictures that are reproduced by offset or lithographic processes, and are not truly photographs. Quite often, a fan may obtain a genuine autograph on one of these pictures. But equally often, the reproduction also contains a signature of the celebrity which is difficult to differentiate from an actual writing produced by a fiber tipped pen. Careful examination under magnification may be required to determine whether the signature is written or placed there by the printing press. A genuine signature will usually have at least one place where lines cross and the ink has some changed characteristic (more or less shiny, slightly different color, edge of ink line noticeable) not present in a printed signature. Experience is a good teacher in these cases.

THE AUTOPEN

This is a mechanical device that produces a replica of a genuine signature by following a template. These are used in situations where a signature must appear on literally hundreds of documents daily. Generally, autopen signatures have a consistent and almost lifeless line quality with little or no shading. The ink may be fiber tip or rolling ball. These are normally seen in modern governmental appointment certificates and routine politically bases correspondence. Some celebrities also use autopen devices, although they are more common in political and governmental usage. The concept of the autopen goes back to the pantograph-like devices popular in the early 1800's for making duplicate correspondence.

PHOTOCOPIES

Development of the electrostatic photocopy machine revolutionized business operations and added another method for producing replica signatures. This is especially the case since the increased popularity of the fiber-tipped pens. Differentiation between an original signature and a photocopy of an original signature can be difficult. Generally, the best photocopy is on paper having a smooth surface and low rag content (cotton) content. A photocopied signature on textured 100% rag content bond paper will probably be readily identifiable under low magnification as a photocopy. But the same signature copied onto paper specifically manufactured for photocopy use may be almost indistinguishable from an original signature executed with black fiber tip pen. This is one area where experience and observation are the best teachers. There are several slightly different processes for bonding the copy toner to the paper, therefore the product of different manufacturers should be examined to gain experience. Some processes will make the writing line appear like it is melted and sitting into the paper surface. It is also easy to confuse the microscopic splatter made by a fiber-tip pen as it forms looping strokes with excess photocopy toner that has been fused onto the paper near the writing line.

Photocopied signatures are often seen on personal letters purportedly written by celebrities. A secretary will type some brief personal text and then run the letter through a photocopy machine to add a replica of a genuine signature.

EQUIPMENT

The examination of most writings, and the detection of the more common varieties of forgery, requires very little equipment. The most useful tool is a magnifier of the type used for examining 35mm slides. These can be obtained at most camera stores for less than ten dollars. This viewer consists of a transparent round plastic base which supports a lens of about 8 power. The viewer rests directly upon the surface to be examined, thus does not require focusing. A small pen-light is sometimes useful to provide oblique illumination when examining indentations in paper.

A second type of useful optical tool is the pocket microscope. This is a device smaller than a pack of cigarettes which consists of a battery powered illuminating lamp and a compound lens assembly of about 40 power. These are available from Radio Shack for less than ten dollars. This device is useful for examining lines in detail, determination of the type of writing instrument used, and for inspection of suspicious signatures for half-tone dots (which would indicate that it had been made by printing press rather than pen).

Very little other equipment is required, and seldom (if ever) will an autograph collector need something that magnifies more than 40 times. But overall, the best piece of equipment is experience.

+ PRINTING, WRITING, & DOCUMENT RELATED CHRONOLOGY +

This chronology was prepared for use by scholars, collectors, document examiners, and archivists. Where possible, secondary source citations have been identified. In cases where dates differed greatly between two references, resolution has been attempted by examining how progress fits within other events. When multiple sources cite dates within a range or are very close in time, "c." for circa has been used. In any summary presentation depending almost entirely upon research by others, it is unavoidable that errors and inaccuracies may be perpetuated. Therefore, this chronology should be regarded merely as data. Much more research, compilation, and verification needs to be done before anything of this nature can be called authoritative. Therefore, readers are asked to provide me with further data and references appropriate for ongoing compilation. And of course, identification of errors will be most appreciated. Previous versions of this chronology have circulated widely.

c.2600 B.C.E.	Ink invented in China (Tien-Tcheu) (8).
c.1580 B.C.E.	Eighteenth Dynasty Egypt: carbon inks used, red & green mineral dyes used in writing (2).
c.900 B.C.E.	Money printed with woodcuts in China (4).
c.332-30 B.C.E.	Seal impression in red ink on document from Ptolemaic period (2).
c.250 B.C.E.	Romans write with slit metal reed (-stilus-) upon leaves (-folia-) (1).
46 B.C.E.	First year of Julian epoch
c.100 C.E.	Romans use sepia (from squid) as ink; also used red & green dyes (8)
c.600s	First bound books and introduction of quill pens (7)
863	Oldest printed book known (China)
c.900s	Paper manufacturing introduced in Spain by Moslems (4)
1020	Beginning of gradual transition from carbon to iron-tannin inks (8)
1041	Printing by movable type in China (4)
1049	Oldest known manuscript on cotton paper in England (7)
c.1050	Iron-tannin inks in common usage (8)
c.1100	Paper manufacturing introduced in Sicily (3)
c.1100	Gothic lettering appears: flourishes, hairlines and hooks (2)
1131	English government records written on paper rolls. Discontinued 1833 (2)
c.1147	Printing with woodcuts in Europe (2)
c.1190	Commercial papermaking appears in France and Germany (2)
c.1200	Paper manufacturing introduced in Italy (4)
c.1200-50	Paper made from linen used in Europe (2)
1282	Earliest known water-mark (7)
c.1300	Paper manufacturing introduced in France (4)
1307	Names of paper makers first incorporated into water-marks (3)
c.1400	Introduction of alum-tanned white pigskin bindings (7)
c.1440	Printing by movable type in Europe (Gutenberg) (3)
1445-1500	Laid paper comes into use

1454	First dated publication produced with movable type (7)
1457	First book bearing the name of the printer (7)
1461	First illustrated book (woodcut) (4)
1463	First book with a title page (7)
1464	First printing press in Italy (at Subiaco) (3)
1465	Earliest blotting paper (7)
c.1470	Increase in bound books produced; vellum & leather principally (7)
1470	First book with pagination and headlines (7)
1472	First book with printed signatures to guide the binder (7)
c.1474	First book printed in English (William Caxton) (7,4)
1483	First double water-mark (7)
1500	Introduction of the small octavo (7)
c.1500s	Blotting paper referred to in text as if it is well known
c.1500s	Formulas for iron-tannin inks given in domestic encyclopedias (8)
1536	First book printed on American continent (in Mexico) (10)
1540	First copper-plate engraving used in book illustration in England (11)
c.1545	Introduction of italic typeface (by Manutius in Italy) (4)
c.1545	Mineral oil and resin first used in printing inks (8)
c.1554	Modern sealing wax of shellac and resin. Previously, sealing wax made of beeswax alone or beeswax with resin. Red seals colored with vermilion, green with verdigris, brown & black with verdigris & organic material (4)
c.1560	Discovery of graphite; earlier pencils made of lead or lead alloy (6)
1560	Introduction of the sextodecimo (7)
1565	First known illustration in a book of a wood-encased pencil using graphite instead of lead metal (12)
1570	Introduction of thin papers (7)
c.1574	Numerous recipes available for colored sealing wax from resin (4)
c.1575	First gold tooling (7)
1580	Introduction of modern forms of i,j,u,v (7)
c.1580	First pasteboards (7)
1582	Gregorian Calendar partially adopted by Catholic nations in Europe (Oct. 4, 1582 followed by Oct. 15, 1582). Lutheran states in Germany did not adopt until 1700, England and the Colonies in 1752.
1586	Poland adopts Gregorian calendar
1587	Hungary adopts Gregorian calendar
c.1600	Copper plate illustration replaces crude woodcuts (7)
c.1600	Introduction of red morocco bindings (7)
1650	Wood covers used for binding (7)
1670	Introduction of the Hollander beater for making pulp (7)
1700	German Lutheran states adopt Gregorian calendar.
c.1700-50	Handwriting still executed by printing individual letters (5)
1720	Perfection of vignette illustration (7)
1734	Caslon type introduced (7)
c.1750	First cloth backed paper, used only for maps (7)

c.1750	Gradual disappearance of vellum for binding. Introduction of millboard covered with calfskin or marbled paper (7)
c.1750	First wove paper in England after re-discovery by John Baskerville (7,8)
1752	Gregorian calendar finally adopted in England and the Colonies. (Many Colonial and Revolutionary-era documents bear double dates, labeled "Old Style" and "New Style" so that people could use whichever system was accustomed).
c.1763	Logwood inks probably first introduced (5,7,8)
1770	Indigo first used in inks (Eisler) (8)
1780	Revival of the woodcut (7)
1780	Steel pens invented (7)
1796	First embossed binding (7)
1796	First lithographic machine (7)
1799	Prior to this year, all paper was handmade (5,6)
1799	First papermaking machine used in France (4)
1800	Blotting paper in general use in England (7)
1800	Straw first used in England to make book paper (6,7)
c.1803	Metal pens first placed on the market (7)
1807	First papermaking machine used in England (4)
c.1816	Colored inks first made in England using pigments (4)
c.1820	Linen canvas first used instead of parchment to hold the back of the book into the cover (7)
c.1820	Introduction of straight grained morocco bindings (7)
1820	Invention of modern metal nibbed pen (7)
1825	Binding cloth generally available (7)
1825	First permanent photographic image (Niepece) (7)
1826	Patent granted in Italy for manufacture of paper from wood pulp (4)
c.1830	First linen cover. Beginning of era of poor leather bindings (7)
1830	Title printed on paper labels which were stuck on cloth (7)
1833	England discontinues writing government records on rolls of paper (2)
1832	First stamping on cloth (7)
c.1835	Decoration by machinery introduced (7)
1834-36	Introduction of iron-tannin inks containing indigo (Stephens) (5)
1839	Invention of photography (Daguerre)
1840	Titles often stamped on cloth (7)
1840	Paper manufactured from mechanical wood pulp (Keller's process) (4,6)
c. 1840	Christmas card reportedly engraved by Daniel Aikman in Scotland (14)
1845	Linen board cover in common use (7)
1845	Common practice to trim edges of books (7)
1846	Earliest known book printed in San Francisco (10)
1846	Lithographed and hand colored Christmas card printed by Summerley (Henry Cole) in London. (14)
1848	Commercial production of logwood ink with potassium chromate added (5)

c.1850	Straw in common use in England to make paper (4)
1850-1865	First "handwriting revolution" in U.S. (5)
1852	Invention of photogravure (7)
1854	Earliest known book printed in Los Angeles (10)
1855	Cotton first used as cover for binding boards (7)
1856	Discovery of first coal-tar dye (Perkins mauve) (6)
1856	Alizarine inks patented (Leonhardi) (8)
1859	Logwood inks produced using alum (5,6)
c.1860	Esparto used in England for papermaking (6)
1860	Beginning of custom of paring calf binding leathers to the thickness of the paper (7)
1860	Handwriting copybooks by Spencer and Payson, Dunton & Scribner. Beginning of second 19th century U.S. handwriting revolution(modified round hand forms) (5)
1861	Introduction of the synthetic indigo for inks in England (6)
1861	Earliest known book printed in San Jose (10)
1864	Patent on first capillary fed ink fountain-pen (Waterman) (9)
1867	Commercial production of ink with nigrosine (5)
1867	First patent for sulfite process of making wood pulp (5)
1868-72	Invention of typewriter (Sholes) (9,5)
c.1870-80	General use of mechanical wood pulp in papermaking
1870	Spencerian or Payson, Dunton & Scribner handwriting copybook systems adopted by most U.S. schools (5)
1873	Handwritten capital "J" with rounded top comes into common use through Spencerian copybook. Not adopted by P,D & S until 1876 (5)
1874-76	Typewriter first commercially available (5,9)
1878	Invention of stylographic pen (7)
1878	Malachite green dye discovered (6)
1878-79	First shift-key on typewriter (5,9)
c.1880-90	General use of cellulose wood pulp in papermaking (5,6)
1881	Cole's 1846 Christmas card reprinted by chromolithography by De La Rue and many sold (14)
1885	Invention of the half-tone process (Ives) (7)
1896	Capital letters on Smith Premier typewriter made narrower (5)
1890-1900	Development and introduction of vertical handwriting in U.S. (5)
1898	First patent on ball-point writing instrument; not in general use and few were produced (9)
1903	First Arabic typewriters in Egypt (6)
1905	First offset litho press (7)
1936	Ball-point pen ("Rolpen") manufactured in Czechoslovakia. About 25,000 produced until production stopped in 1939. Sales confined to European continent. (9)
1939	Biro obtains French patent on ball-point pen (9)
c.1943	Biro begins manufacture of ball-point pens in Argentina (9)
1945	First large-scale commercial sale of ball-point pens in U.S. (9)
1955	First "liquid lead" pencil marketed by Scripto (9)

1957	Proportional spacing introduced on IBM Executive and Remington Statesman typewriters (9)
c. 1962	Pentell introduces fiber or porous tip pen in Japan (13)
c. 1968	Pressurized ballpoint pen inks developed for use by astronauts (13)
c. 1968	Rolling ball marker introduced in Japan (13)

REFERENCE CITATIONS

1. Schlegal, A.W., -Lectures on Dramatic Art and Literature-, p. 202. (Secondary source: cited by Durant, -Caesar and Christ-, p.73)
2. Durant, -Caesar and Christ-
3. Durant, -The Renaissance-, p.318
4. Durant, -The Reformation-, p.157-160
5. Osborn, Albert. -Questioned Documents-, Boyd Print Co., 1929
6. Lucas, A. -Forensic Chemistry and Scientific Criminal Investigation-, Edward Arnold, London, 1931
7. Benjamin, Mary. -A Key to Collecting-, Dover, 1946. (Secondary source citations, primarily from following: Sadlier, Michael. -Evolution of Publisher's Binding Styles-, 1930 and Grant, Julius. -Books and Documents; Dating, Permanence and Preservation-, Grafton, London, 1937.)
8. -Encyclopedia Britannica-, 1911, "Inks".
9. Conway, James. -Evidential Documents-, Charles C. Thomas 1959.
10. Durury, Clifford. -California Imprints, 1846-1876-, privately printed, 1970
11. Uden, Grant. -Understanding Book Collecting-, Antique Collectors Club, 1983.
12. Petroski, Henry. -The Pencil-, Knopf 1989.
13. Saferstein, Richard (ed.), Forensic Science Handbook, Prentice-Hall, New Jersey, 1968.
14. Chase, Ernest Dudley, -The Romance of Greeting Cards-, University Press, Boston, Mass., 1926.

+ + + + + + +

Explicit leuc totum; Pro Christo da mihi potum
---European monastic scribe, c. 1350 C.E.

TRANSLATION: "The work is finished; for Christ's sake get me my beer"

Compiled by Michael M. Zanoni, Ph.D.
Box 369
San Carlos CA 94070
(415) 473-9635

Dr. Michael Zanoni is a licensed private investigator in San Mateo County, California. He has testified in court as an expert many times about handwriting, forgeries and questioned documents.

THE DIRECTORY

TIPS TO REMEMBER

This book is intended entertainment/amusement only.We assume no responsibility for addresses which change or become invalid, items lost in the mail, or who responds to your correspondence. We provide the best contact addresses we can find for you to write these celebrities.

1.   **DON'T VISIT THESE ADDRESSES.** These addresses were intended for correspondence only, as a means for you to contact the celebrity by mail. Uninvited visitors may be unwelcome.

2.   **DON'T MAIL WHAT YOU CAN'T AFFORD TO LOOSE.** Many fans send letters, gifts, and other personal items. Frequently these are lost in the mails. You will also find, celebrities don't usually sign for mail which makes them personally responsible for the items.

3.   **STARS HAVE FREQUENT ADDRESS CHANGES.** Generalizing, the more famous or younger the star, the more they will have address changes. New homes, agents, fan clubs, and contacts are common. These addresses will expire quickly. We have therefore listed alternate and forwarding addresses to aid you. If you have some returned letters due to "Forwarding order expired," read the yellow postal label carefully. Many times a new forwarding address will be imprinted there. If you are creating a mailing list from our book, you must test the addresses first before doing a more expensive mailing. We are not responsible for your results.

4.   **YES WE MAKE OCCASIONAL MISTAKES.** During the proofing or research, unfortunately we may miss a listing which is misspelled, or assigned an incorrect occupation. Since we don't always hear of all who pass away, we make a great attempt to find and remove as many of these listings as possible.

5.   **CELEBRITIES DON'T ALWAYS ANSWER THEIR OWN MAIL.** Many times an authorized agent, employee, secretary, or fan service will screen the mail first, and sometimes answer on the celebrities behalf. Because of the incredible amount of fan mail these days, assistants are common place in the industry.

Celebrities are usually very gracious, and love to hear from their fans. They should be treated respectfully when you write them. If you have a request of them, be patient. They are generally very busy, and they will respond when they have time. Remember to say please and thank you. A little respect can go a long way. Don't request the unreasonable. Celebrities have seen all the mail scams, so be honest and sincere.

HOW TO USE THIS BOOK

(Except for Address #1 these are examples only)

Burford, Thomas
20 Sunnyside Ave
Suite A241
Mill Valley, CA 94941
Actor/Writer <----------

V:**04/06/91**<------------

The **primary addresses** are identified by the listing of the celebrity's claim to fame located here.

This is the "**V**" **verification** date. This date is when we last made contact with the celebrity, or his/her representative at this address, or we received a response.

327 Main St
Smalltown, CA 94999
Alternate <----------------

Sometimes the celebrity has more than one address (i.e., his/her home, East or West Coast, or overseas agents, publicists, etc.). This address would be a second choice if the celebrity is away from his/her primary address.

192 Center Ave
Sun City, CA 99099
Forwarded <--------------

Mail is occasionally **forwarded** from one agency or home to another. This is a third address at which one might locate the celebrity.

A

A&E Network
235 E 45th St
New York, NY 10017
Network HQ *V: 02/02/96*

1800 Century Park E #450
Los Angeles, CA 90067
Alternate *V: 11/11/96*

ABC Film/Tape Library
1717 DeSales St NW
Washington, DC 20036
Archive *V: 02/02/96*

ABC-TV
c/o Viewer Services
77 W 66th St
New York, NY 10023
Production Office *V: 03/20/96*

4151 Prospect Ave
Los Angeles, CA 90027
Alternate *V: 02/03/96*

ABC-TV News
1926 Broadway
New York, NY 10023
Production Office *V: 02/03/96*

147 Columbus Ave
New York, NY 10023
Alternate *V: 02/03/96*

AFH Management
5724 W 3rd St #509
Los Angeles, CA 90036
Talent Agency *V: 02/07/96*

AFTRA
6922 Hollywood Bl 8th Fl
Hollywood, CA 90028
Actors Union *V: 02/03/96*

ALL MY CHILDREN
ABC-TV
320 W 66th St
New York, NY 10023
Production Office *V: 04/04/96*

ALMOST PERFECT
Paramount Television
5555 Melrose Ave
Hollywood, CA 90038
Production Office *V: 10/23/96*

AMERICA'S FUNNIEST HOME VIDEOS
Vin Di Bona-Mail
12233 W Olympic Bl/#270 Bldg G
Los Angeles, CA 90064
Production Office *V: 01/10/96*

Vin Di Bona/Tapes Only
PO Box 4333
Hollywood, CA 90078
Alternate *V: 02/15/96*

AMERICA'S FUNNIEST PEOPLE
Vin Di Bona
12233 W Olympic Bl
Ste 270, Bldg G
Los Angeles, CA 90064
Production Office *V: 02/19/96*

AMERICA'S MOST WANTED
c/o Fox TV
5746 Sunset Bl
Los Angeles, CA 90069
Production Office *V: 01/20/96*

AMERICA'S TALKING
c/o CNBC/Charles Grodin
965 5th Ave
New York, NY 10021
Production Office *V: 01/09/96*

c/o Charles Grodin
2200 Fletcher Ave
Ft Lee, NJ 07024
Alternate *V: 01/21/96*

AMERICAN GOTHIC
Paramount Television
5555 Melrose Avenue
Hollywood, CA 90038
Production Office *V: 10/23/96*

AMPAS
8949 Wilshire Bl
Beverly Hills, CA 90211
Academy Office *V: 03/17/96*

ANOTHER WORLD
NBC-TV
79 Madison Ave 5th Fl
New York, NY 10016
Production Office *V: 03/04/96*

ARSENIO HALL SHOW
ABC-TV
77 W 66th St
New York, NY 10023
Audience Services *V: 01/13/97*

AS THE WORLD TURNS
Proctor & Gamble
524 W 57th St
New York, NY 10019
Production Office *V: 02/16/96*

ASA
4430 Fountain Ave-Suite A
Hollywood, CA 90029
Talent Agency *V: 11/11/96*

Aaron, Henry Hank
PO Box 4064
Atlanta, GA 30302
Baseball Star *V: 03/01/96*

Aaron Spelling Productions
1041 N Formosa Ave
W Hollywood, CA 90046
Production Office *V: 02/03/96*

Abbott, Diahnne
460 W 46th Ave
Los Angeles, CA 90065
Actress *V: 02/03/96*

Abbott, John
6424 Ivarene Ave
Los Angeles, CA 00068
Actor *V: 01/12/96*

Abbott, Philip
c/o Nelson
5400 Shirley Ave
Tarzana, CA 91356
Actor *V: 05/06/96*

Abdul, Paula
30 W 21st St
New York, NY 10010
Singer *V: 01/21/96*

14755 Ventura Bl #1-700
Sherman Oaks, CA 91403
Alternate *V: 10/23/96*

14046 Aubrey Rd
Beverly Hills, CA 90210
Forwarded *V: 02/13/96*

Abdul-Jabbar, Kareem
Amstel-Eisenstadt-Frasier
6310 San Vicente Bl #401
Los Angeles, CA 90048
Basketball Star *V: 12/01/96*

1436 Summitridge Dr
Beverly Hills, CA 90210-2246
Alternate *V: 04/02/96*

Abrams, Rita
Mill Valley Music
15 Emerson Dr
Mill VAlley, CA 94941
Songwriter *V: 01/12/96*

Abrams Artists
9200 Sunset Bl #625
Los Angeles, CA 90069
Talent Agency *V: 01/05/96*

Abrams-Rubaloff-Lawrence
8075 West 3rd St #303
Los Angeles, CA 90048
Talent Agency *V: 01/05/96*

Abzug, Bella
2 Fifth Ave
New York, NY 10011
Politician *V: 02/04/96*

Academy Entertainment
9250 Wilshire Bl
Beverly Hills, CA 90212
Production Office *V: 02/03/96*

Academy Magazine
PO Box 5465
San Jose, CA 95150
Publisher *V: 02/03/96*

Ackerman, Forrest
2495 Glendower Ave
Los Angeles, CA 90027
Publisher *V: 02/03/96*

Ackroyd, David
273 N Many Lakes Dr
Kalispell, MT 59901-8344
Actor *V: 08/29/96*

Acme Talent
6310 San Vicente Bl #520
Los Angeles, CA 90048
Talent Agency *V: 02/07/96*

Acton, Loren
Lockheed
3251 Hanover St
Palo Alto, CA 94304-1191
Astronaut *V: 04/18/96*

Actors Equity Association
6430 Sunset Bl #1002
Los Angeles, CA 90028
Actors Union *V: 02/03/96*

Adair, Deborah
Kohner Agency
9300 Wilshire Bl #555
Beverly Hills, CA 90212
Actress V: 12/11/96

1605 Lindamere Pl
Los Angeles, CA 90077
Alternate V: 09/10/96

Adams, Cindy
1050 Fifth Ave
New York, NY 10028
Actress V: 05/05/96

Adams, Don
2160 Century Park E
Los Angeles, CA 90067
Actor V: 09/14/96

Adams, Edie
8040 Ocean Terrace
Los Angeles, CA 90046
Actress V: 02/03/96

Adams, Julie
5915 Corbin Ave
Tarzana, CA 91356
Actress V: 02/04/96

20th Century Artists
15315 Magnolia Bl #429
Sherman Oaks, CA 91403
Alternate V: 12/15/96

2446 N Commonwealth Ave
Los Angeles, CA 90027
Alternate V: 04/12/96

Kohner Agency
9300 Wilshire Bl #555
Beverly Hills, CA 90212
Forwarded V: 02/12/96

Adams, Mason
Kohner Agency
9300 Wilshire Bl #555
Beverly Hills, CA 90212
Actor V: 12/11/96

Adams, Maud
2791 Ellison Dr
Beverly Hills, CA 90210
Actress V: 01/21/96

Adderly, Nat
11806 N 56th St
Tampa, FL 33617
Musician V: 02/01/96

Adjani, Isabelle
Assoc Des Amis-BP 166
Paris Cedex 11 75523, France
Actress V: 10/23/96

Presse 1-Adjani-BP 475-07
F-75327 Paris, France
Alternate V: 02/28/96

2 Rue Gaston de St Paul
75016 Paris, France
Forwarded V: 04/21/96

Adler, Lou
3969 Villa Costera
Malibu, CA 90265
Actor V: 03/14/96

Adorf, Mario
Perlacher Strassa 28
8022 Grunwald, Germany
Actor V: 01/10/96

Agar, John
639 N Hollywood Way
Burbank, CA 91505
Actor V: 01/12/96

Agassi, Andre
8921 Andre Dr
Las Vegas, NV 89113
Tennis Star V: 02/01/96

6739 Tara Ave
Las Vegas, NV 89102
Forwarded V: 11/10/96

Agence Artistiques
Georges Beaume/Guy Bonnet
4 rue de Ponthieu
F-75008 Paris France
Talent Agency V: 02/03/96

Agence Cineart
Cineart/Nainchrik
31 avenue Champs Elysees
F-75008 Paris, France
Talent Agency V: 02/03/96

Agences Associate
c/o Georges Baume
201 rue Faubourg St Honore
Paris F-75008, France
Talent Agency V: 01/20/96

Agency for Performing Arts
9000 Sunset Bl #1200
Los Angeles, CA 90069
Talent Agency V: 02/03/96

Agentur Mattes
Merzstrasse 14
8000 Munchen 81, Germany
Talent Agency V: 02/03/96

Agentur Paltz
Ortlindestrasse 6/X
8000 Munchen 81, Germany
Talent Agency V: 02/03/96

Agentur Ute Nicolai
Schorlemerallee 16
1000 Berlin 33, Germany
Talent Agency V: 02/03/96

Agutter, Jenny
6884 Camrose Dr
Los Angeles, CA 90068
Actress V: 02/02/96

388/396 Oxford St
London W1 9HE, England
Alternate V: 02/21/96

Cach Haunes
Parracombe, Barnscape
N Devon, England
Forwarded V: 01/05/96

Aiello, Danny
195 Surrey Ct
Ramsey, NJ 07466
Actor V: 02/01/96

Aimee Entertainment
15000 Ventura Bl #340
Sherman Oaks, CA 91403
Talent Agency V: 01/02/96

Akers, Thomas D
NASA/LBJ Space Center
Houston, TX 77058
Astronaut V: 07/03/96

Akyroyd, Dan
9200 Sunset Bl #428
Los Angeles, CA 90069
Actor V: 01/30/96

Alabama
PO Box 529
Ft Payne, AL 35967
Musical Group V: 07/03/96

Wm Morris Agency
818 19th Ave South
Nashville, TN 37203
Forwarded V: 02/02/96

Alaimo, Marc
8485 Melrose Pl #E
Los Angeles, CA 90069
Actor V: 01/17/97

Albee, Edward
PO Box 697
Montauk, NY 11954
Writer V: 01/13/97

Alberghetti, Anna Maria
10333 Chrysanthemum Lane
Los Angeles, CA 90077
Singer V: 01/11/96

Albert, Eddie
719 Amalfi Dr
Pacific Palisades, CA 90272
Actor V: 03/02/96

Gold/Marshak
3500 W Olive Ave
Burbank, CA 91505
Alternate V: 02/23/96

Albert, Edward
Hawks Ranch/27320 Winding Way
Malibu, CA 90265
Actor V: 08/08/96

Albright, Lola
PO Box 250070
Glendale, CA 91225
Actress V: 01/11/96

213 N Valley #136
Burbank, CA 91505
Alternate V: 01/22/96

Alcaide, Chris
502 N Cerritos Rd
Palm Springs, CA 92262
Actor V: 11/11/96

Alda, Alan
c/o UTA
15315 Magnolia Bl #429
Sherman Oaks, CA 91403
Actor V: 12/15/96

Alden, Ginger
4152 Royal Crest Pl
Memphis, TN 38138
Actress V: 03/02/96

Alderman, Darrell
PO Box 71007
Madison Heights, MI 48071
Drag Racer V: 10/23/96

Aldred, Sophie
London Management
235-241 Regent St
London W1A 2JT, England
Actress V: 01/11/96

Aldrin, Buzz
Starcraft Enterprises
233 Emerald Bay
Laguna Beach, CA 92651
Astronaut V: 11/10/96

Alexander, Jane
Morris Agency
1350 Ave of the Americas
New York, NY 10019
Actress V: 01/11/96

Nat'l Endowment for Arts
1100 Pennsylvania Ave NW
Washington, DC 20506
Alternate V: 01/27/96

The Lansburgh
425 8th St NW
Washington, DC 20004
Forwarded V: 08/08/96

Alexander, Jason
6230-A Wilshire Bl #103
Los Angeles, CA 90048-5104
Actor V: 11/01/96

Alexis, Kim
345 N Maple Dr #185
Beverly Hills, CA 90210
Actress V: 02/09/96

300 Park Ave South
New York, NY 10010
Alternate V: 10/23/96

Alfonso, Kristian
Metro Talent Agency
4526 Wilshire Bl
Los Angeles, CA 90010
Actress V: 12/11/96

1873 Sunset Plaza
Los Angeles, CA 90069
Alternate V: 11/10/96

30450 Passageway Pl
Agoura Hills, CA 91301
Forwarded V: 10/23/96

Ali, Muhammad
PO Box 187
Berrien Springs, MI 49103
Boxing Star V: 02/02/96

Ali Akbar Khan
215 W End Ave
San Rafael, CA 94941
Musician V: 11/11/96

Alien Productions
8660 Hayden Pl
Culver City, CA 90230
Production Office V: 11/11/96

All Girls Prodroductions
500 S Buena Vista St
Burbank, CA 91521
Production Office V: 11/11/96

Allen, Andrew M
NASA/LBJ Space Center
Houston, TX 77058
Astronaut V: 11/11/96

Allen, Chad
6489 Cavalleri Rd #204
Malibu, CA 90265-4019
Actor V: 11/10/96

c/o Lazarri
12049 Smokey Ln
Cerritos, CA 90710
Forwarded V: 01/11/96

Allen, Debbie
607 Marguerite Ave
Santa Monica, CA 90403
Singer V: 03/02/96

2265 Westwood Bl #469
Los Angeles, CA 90064-2019
Forwarded V: 03/01/96

Allen, Ginger Lynn
Sciowitz-Clay-Rose
1680 Vine St #614
Los Angeles, CA 9028-8832
Actress V: 01/10/96

Allen, Joseph P
NASA/LBJ Space Center
Houston, TX 77058
Astronaut V: 11/11/96

Allen, Karen
Innovative Artists
1999 Ave of the Stars #2850
Los Angeles, CA 90067
Actress V: 12/12/96

PO Box 237
Monterey, MA 01245
Alternate V: 03/11/96

Allen, Nancy
Buckwald & Associates
9229 Sunset Bl #710
Los Angeles, CA 90069
Actress V: 12/06/96

9150 Wilshire Bl #205
Beverly Hills, CA 90212
Alternate V: 01/15/96

Allen, Rex
Lone Star Ranch
Box 1111
Sonoita, AZ 85637
Actor V: 01/11/96

PO Box 430
Sonoita, AZ 85637-0430
Alternate V: 01/11/96

Allen, Sian Barbara
1622 Sierra Bonita Ave
Los Angeles, CA 90046
Actress V: 01/19/96

Allen, Stan
7380 S Eastern Ave #124-179
Las Vegas, NV 89123
Magician V: 02/01/96

Allen, Steve
c/o Meadowlane
15201 Burbank Bl-#B
Van Nuys, CA 91411
Producer V: 11/11/96

16185 Woodvale Rd
Encino, CA 91436
Alternate V: 11/11/96

Allen, Tim
9601 Wilshire Bl #620
Beverly Hills, CA 90210
Actor V: 11/01/96

7461 Beverly Bl #400
Los Angeles, CA 90036
Alternate V: 09/14/96

Allen, Tim, Cont.
1122 S Robertson Bl #15
Los Angeles, CA 90035
Forwarded V: 04/12/96

Allen, Woody
930 5th Ave
New York, NY 10018
Producer V: 11/11/96

Rollins & Jaffe
130 W 57th St
New York, NY 10019
Alternate V: 01/22/96

Allen Jr, Rex
128 Pine Oak Dr
Hendersonville, TN 37075
Singer V: 10/23/96

Allen Talent Agency
260 S Beverly Dr-2nd Fl
Beverly Hills, CA 90212
Talent Agency V: 11/11/96

Alley, Kirstie
c/o Wolf/Kasteler
1033 Gayley Ave #208
Los Angeles, CA 90024
Actress V: 11/11/96

Alliance Talent
9171 Wilshire Bl #441
Beverly Hills, CA 90210
Talent Agency V: 11/11/96

Allison, Bobby
Rt 1 Box 365
Austinville, VA 24312
NASCAR Driver V: 01/11/96

5254 Pit Road South
Harrisburg, NC 28075
Alternate V: 01/11/96

140 Church St
Hueytown, AL 35020
Forwarded V: 01/11/96

Allison, Donnie
140 Church St
Hueytown, AL 35020
NASCAR Driver V: 01/11/96

Allyson, June
1651 Foothill Rd
Ojai, CA 93020
Actress V: 09/11/96

Alonzo, Maria Conchita
c/o UTA
15315 Magnolia Bl #429
Sherman Oaks, CA 91403
Actress V: 12/15/96

PO Box 537
Beverly Hills, CA 90213
Alternate V: 02/13/96

Alt, Carol
Kohner Agency
9300 Wilshire Bl #555
Beverly Hills, CA 90212
Actress V: 02/12/96

163 John St
Greenwich, CT 06831-8514
Alternate V: 08/16/96

Altman, Jeff
5065 Calvin Ave
Tarzana, CA 91356
Actor V: 01/11/97

Altman, Robert
Sandcastle 5 Prod
502 Park Ave #15-G
New York, NY 10022
Director V: 02/01/96

Alvarado Agency
8455 Beverly Bl #406
Los Angeles, CA 90048
Talent Agency V: 11/04/96

Amanpour, Christine
CNN America
1050 Techwood Dr NW
Atlanta, GA 30318
Correspondant V: 01/12/96

Amato, Joe
Amato Racing
PO Box 404
Pittston, PA 18640
Drag Racer V: 10/23/96

Amblin Entertainment
100 Universal Plaza
Bungalow 477
Universal City, CA 91608
Production Office V: 01/01/96

Ambrosio/Mortimer
9150 Wilshire Bl #175
Beverly Hills, CA 90212
Talent Agency V: 02/25/96

Ament, Jeff
Curtis Mgmt
207 1/2 1st Ave S #300
Seattle, WA 98104
Guitarist V: 10/23/96

American Cinematographer
PO Box 2230
Hollywood, CA 90078
Publisher V: 11/01/96

American Film Institute
2021 N Western Ave
Los Angeles, CA 90027
Institute Office V: 11/21/96

American Film Magazine
1515 Broadway 15th Fl
New York, NY 10036-5702
Publisher V: 01/23/96

American Guild/Variety Artists
4741 Laurel Canyon Bl #208
N Hollywood, CA 91607
Actors Union V: 11/21/96

American Horse, George
15010 Ventura Bl #219
Sherman Oaks, CA 91403
Actor V: 01/01/96

526 S Reese Pl
Burbank, CA 91506
Alternate V: 01/22/96

American League HQ
350 Park Ave
New York, NY 10022
Production Office V: 11/22/96

American Movie Classics
150 Crossways Park West
Woodbury, NY 11797
Network HQ V: 04/02/96

Working Media
162 Columbus Ave
Boston, MA 02116
Alternate V: 02/22/96

Ames, Ed
1457 Claridge Dr
Beverly Hills, CA 90210
Actor V: 11/11/96

Ames, Rachel
303 S Crescent Heights Bl
Los Angeles, CA 90048
Actress V: 11/01/96

Amos, John
Artists Agency
10000 Santa Monica Bl #305
Los Angeles, CA 90067
Actor V: 12/03/96

Step & One Half Prod
PO Box 587
Califon, NJ 07830
Alternate V: 11/01/96

Amsel/Eisenstadt/Frazier
6310 San Vincente Bl #401
Los Angeles, CA 90048
Talent Agency V: 01/01/96

Ana-Alicia
9744 Wilshire Bl #308
Beverly Hills, CA 90212
Actress V: 11/11/96

SDB Partners
1801 Ave of the Stars #902
Los Angeles, CA 90067
Alternate V: 12/13/96

1148 4th St #206
Santa Monica, CA 90403-5049
Forwarded V: 08/29/96

Anders, William A
NASA/LBJ Space Center
Houston, TX 77058
Astronaut V: 11/03/96

Andersen, Greta
3281 Devon Circle
Huntington Beach, CA 92647
Olympian V: 11/11/96

Anderson, Bill
PO Box 888
Hermitage, TN 37076
Singer V: 01/12/96

Anderson, Ernest
4141 Knobhill Dr
Sherman Oaks, CA 91403-4620
Actor V: 01/15/96

Anderson, Gerry
G A Magazine
332 Lytham Rd
Blackpool FY4 1DW, England
Director V: 10/23/96

11 William Rd
London NW1 3ER, England
Alternate V: 02/26/96

Anderson, Gillian
Wm Morris Agency
151 El Camino
Beverly Hills, CA 90212
Actress V: 12/12/96

The X Files Office
110-555 Brooks Bank Ave #10
N Vancouver, BC V7J 3S5, Canada
Alternate V: 11/01/96

Anderson, Herbert
6351 Gloria Dr
Huntington Beach, CA 92647-4224
Actor V: 01/10/96

Anderson, John
c/o Roberts
PO Box 2977
Hendersonville, TN 37077
Singer V: 02/02/96

Anderson, Lois
The Studio
50 Catalpa Ave
Mill Valley, CA 94941
Artist V: 11/01/96

Anderson, Loni
Metro Talent Agency
4526 Wilshire Bl
Los Angeles, CA 90010
Actress V: 12/11/96

Sandy Hook Productions
20652 Lassen #98
Chatsworth, CA 91311
Forwarded V: 02/04/96

Anderson, Lynn
4925 Tyne Valley Bl
Nashville, TN 37220
Singer V: 11/11/96

c/o Garner
38 Music Square E #218
Nashville, TN 37203
Alternate V: 02/02/96

Anderson, Melissa Sue
1558 Will Geer Rd
Topanga Canyon, CA 90290-4238
Actress V: 08/29/96

Anderson, Melody
Kohner Agency
9300 Wilshire Bl-#555
Beverly Hills, CA 90212
Actress V: 02/12/96

Anderson, Michael J
c/o Paul Burford
52 Yorkminster Rd
North York, Ontario
Canada M2P 1M3
Director V: 05/06/96

Anderson, Pamela
31342 Mulholland Hwy
Malibu, CA 90265-2701
Actress V: 02/07/97

Mazella Entertainment
345 N Maple Dr #185
Beverly Hills, CA 90210
Alternate V:05/09/96

8730 Sunset Bl #220
W Hollywood, CA 90069
Forwarded V: 11/06/96

Anderson, Richard
10120 Cielo Dr
Beverly Hills, CA 90210
Actor V: 03/02/96

Anderson, Richard Dean
c/o ICM
8942 Wilshire Bl
Beverly Hills, CA 90211
Actor V: 12/11/96

Wolf/Kasteller
1033 Gayley Ave #208
Los Angeles, CA 90024
Alternate V: 06/21/96

1828 Courtney Ave
Los Angeles, CA 90046
Forwarded V: 04/12/96

Anderson, Terry
Pinewood Studios, Iverheath
Buchs SL0 0NH, England
Producer V: 02/09/96

Andersson, Bibi
Tykovagen 28
Lidingo 18161 Sweden
Actress V: 10/24/96

Andress, Ursula
c/o IPO
Via F Siacci 38
I-00197 Rome, Italy
Actress V: 03/14/96

Via Nomentana 60
00161 Rome, Italy
Alternate V: 01/27/96

Andretti, John
PO Box 34156
Indianapolis, IN 46234
Race Driver V: 10/10/96

Yarborough Motorsports
9617 Dixie River Rd
Charlotte, NC 28208
Alternate V: 10/23/96

Andretti, Mario
53 Victory Ln
Nazareth, PA 18064
Race Driver V: 02/21/96

Andrews, Anthony
Paradigm Agency
10100 Santa Monica Bl-25th Fl
Los Angeles, CA 90067
Actor V: 12/13/96

Peters/Dunlap/Fraser
Chelsea Harbour, Lots Rd
London SW10 0XF, England
Alternate V: 02/23/96

Andrews, Julie
PO Box 666
Beverly Hills, CA 90213
Actress V: 01/11/96

Andrews, Maxene
14200 Carriage Oak Ln
Auburn, CA 95603
Singer V: 04/04/96

Andrews, Patti
c/o Weschler
9823 Aldea Ave
Northridge, CA 91354
Singer V: 01/11/96

Andrews, Tige
4914 Encino Terrace
Encino, CA 91316
Actor V: 01/11/96

Angel City Talent
1680 Vine St #716
Los Angeles, CA 90028
Talent Agency V: 02/07/96

Angelou, Maya
3240 Valley Rd
Winston Salem, NC 27106-2504
Writer V: 08/29/96

Angelyne
1136 N Larabee
Los Angeles, CA 90069
Actress V: 04/02/96

PO Box 3864
Beverly Hills, CA 90212
Alternate V: 03/03/96

Animation Magazine
PO Box 25547
Los Angeles, CA 90025
Publisher V: 01/21/96

Aniston, Jennifer
9830 Wilshire Bl
Beverly Hills, CA 90212
Actress V: 09/14/96

5750 Wilshire Bl #580
Los Angeles, CA 90036
Alternate V: 10/23/96

Anka, Paul
10573 W Pico Bl #159
Los Angeles, CA 90064-2348
Composer V: 12/14/96

12078 Summit Circle
Beverly Hills, CA 90210
Alternate V: 02/06/96

Ann-Margret
2707 Benedict Canyon Rd
Beverly Hills, CA 90210
Actress V: 01/11/96

435 N Bedford Dr #1000
Beverly Hills, CA 90210
Alternate V: 02/18/96

5664 Cahuenga Bl #336
N Hollywood, CA 91601
Forwarded V: 04/12/96

Annabella
1 Rue Pierret
92200 Neuilly France
Actress V: 03/14/96

Annis, Francesca
2 Vicarage Ct
London W8, England
Actress V: 01/21/96

Ansara, Michael
4624 Park Mirasol
Calabasas, CA 91302
Actor V: 01/17/97

Anspach, Susan
2369 Beach Ave
Venice, CA 90291-4602
Actress V: 11/01/96

Answer Fan
1112 First St #134
Coronado, CA 92118
Fan Service V: 01/20/96

Ant
733 N Seward Ave
Los Angeles, CA 90036
Actor V: 12/09/96

Ant, Adam
2452 Meadow Valley Terrace
Los Angeles, CA 90039
Singer V: 04/13/96

Anthony, Lysette
Gersh Agency
232 N Canon Dr
Beverly Hills, CA 90210
Actress V: 12/09/96

Anton, Susan
16830 Ventura Bl #300
Encino, CA 91436-1715
Actress V: 11/10/96

8942 Wilshire Bl
Beverly Hills, CA 90211
Alternate V: 01/13/97

Antonelli, Laura
62 Via del Pelligrino
00186 Rome, Italy
Actress V: 02/01/96

Anwar, Gabrielle
9560 Wilshire Bl #560
Beverly Hills, CA 90212
Actress V: 10/23/96

Apodaca Agency
2049 Century Park E #1200
Century City, CA 90067
Talent Agency V: 01/01/96

Apodaca/Munro Agency
13801 Ventura Bl
Sherman Oaks, CA 91423
Talent Agency V: 02/07/96

Applegate, Christina
20411 Chapter Dr
Woodland Hills, CA 91364-5612
Actress V: 02/21/96

Applegate, Christina, Cont.
PO Box 900
Beverly Hills, CA 90213
Alternate V: 02/04/96

9055 Hollywood Hills Bl
Los Angeles, CA 90046
Forwarded V: 04/12/96

Apt, Jerome
NASA/LBJ Space Center
Houston, TX 77058
Astronaut V: 11/22/96

Archer, Anne
13201 Old Oak Lane
Los Angeles, CA 90049-2501
Actress V: 06/01/96

Archer, Dave
PO Box 150180
San Rafael, CA 94915
Artist V: 11/08/96

Swanson Gallery
3040 Larkin St
San Francisco, CA 94109
Alternate V: 12/12/96

Archive Photos
530 W 25th St-6th Fl
New York, NY 10001
Archives V: 02/27/96

Ard, Sam
Ard Racing
Rt 11, Box 162
Asheboro, NC 27203
NASCAR Owner V: 03/14/96

Arista Films
16027 Ventura Bl #305
Encino, CA 91436
Production Office V: 02/21/96

Arista Records
6 W 57th St
New York, NY 10019
Production Office V: 01/21/96

Arkin, Adam
2372 Veteran Ave
Los Angeles, CA 90064
Actor V: 10/23/96

Innovative Artists
1999 Ave of the Stars #2850
Los Angeles, CA 90067
Alternate V: 02/02/96

Arkin, Alan
c/o ICM
40 W 57th St
New York, NY 10019
Actor V: 01/30/96

151 El Camino Dr
Beverly Hills, CA 90212
Forwarded V: 04/12/96

Arliss, Dimitra
Music Assn of Aspin
PO Box AA
Aspen, CO 81612-7428
Actress V: 11/01/96

Armani, Giorgio
650 Fifth Ave
New York, NY 10019
Designer V: 05/14/96

Armatrading, Joan
Running Dog Mgmt
Lower Hampton Rd-Sudbury
Middlesex TW16 5PR, England
Singer V: 05/24/96

Armed Forces TV/Radio
10888 La Tuna Canyon Rd
Sun Valley, CA 91352-2098
Production Office V: 02/01/96

Armstrong, Garner Ted
Church of God Int'l
PO Box 2530
Tyler, TX 75710
Evangelist V: 02/15/96

Armstrong, Neil
PO Box 436-Rte 123
Lebanon, OH 45036
Astronaut V: 04/02/96

Armstrong, RG
3856 Reklaw Dr
Studio City, CA 91604
Actor V: 02/01/96

Armstrong, Tom
King Features
235 East 45th St
New York, NY 10017
Cartoonist V: 02/03/96

Arnaz, Lucie
RR 3-Flintrock Ridge Rd
Katonah, NY 10536-9803
Actress V: 03/11/96

Arnaz Jr, Desi
c/o Success
12626 Ojai Rd
Santa Paula, CA 93060
Actor V: 02/20/96

525 Hotel Plaza
Boulder City, NV 89005
Alternate V: 01/11/97

Arngrim, Alison
Moore Artists
1551 S Robertson Bl
Los Angeles, CA 90035
Actress V: 12/12/96

PO Box 46891
Los Angeles, CA 90046-0841
Alternate V: 01/20/96

Arnold, Debbie
12 Cambridge Park
East Twickenham
Middlesex TW1 2PF, England
Actress V: 04/23/96

Arnold, Eddy
PO Box 97
Brentwood, TN 37027
Singer V: 02/01/96

Arnold, Tom
PO Box 15458
Beverly Hills, CA 90209-1458
Actor V: 03/14/96

Wm Morris Agency
151 El Camino Dr
Beverly Hills, CA 90212
Alternate V: 01/14/96

Arquette, Patricia
c/o Cage
8033 W Sunset Bl #52
Los Angeles, CA 90046-2427
Actress V: 08/29/96

c/o UTA
9560 Wishire Bl #500
Beverly Hills, CA 90212
Alternate V: 10/10/96

Arquette, Rosanna
c/o ICM
8942 Wilshire Bl
Beverly Hills, CA 90211
Actress V: 12/11/96

Arrington, Buddy
1811 Volusia Ave
Daytona Beach, FL 32015
NASCAR Driver V: 03/02/96

Arthur, Bea
2000 Old Ranch Rd
Los Angeles, CA 90049
Actress V: 02/20/96

Arthur Associates
9363 Wilshire Bl #212
Beverly Hills, CA 90210
Talent Agency V: 02/08/96

Artist Management
4340 Campus Dr #210
Newport Beach, CA 92660
Talent Agency V: 05/21/96

835-5th Ave #4
San Diego, CA 92101
Alternate V: 02/15/96

Artist Network
8438 Melrose Pl
Los Angeles, CA 90069
Talent Agency V: 02/23/96

Artists Agency
10000 Santa Monica Bl #305
Los Angeles, CA 90067
Talent Agency V: 02/23/96

Artists Group
10100 Santa Monica Bl #2490
Los Angeles, CA 90067
Talent Agency V: 02/07/96

Artmedia
10 Ave Georges-V
F-75008 Paris, France
Talent Agency V: 02/27/96

Arvesen, Nina
950 Lake St #2
Venice, CA 90291-2861
Actress V: 11/01/96

Ashbrook, Dana
7019 Melrose Ave #332
Los Angeles, CA 90038
Actress V: 01/15/97

Ashbrook, Daphne
Innovative Artists
1999 Ave of the Stars #2850
Los Angeles, CA 90067
Actress V: 12/11/96

Ashby, Linden
c/o APA
9000 Sunset Bl #1200
Los Angeles, CA 90069
Actor V: 01/15/97

Ashenfelter, Horace
100 Hawthorne Ave
Glen Ridge, NJ 07028
Olympian V: 01/13/97

Ashford, Evelyn
818 Plantation Lane
Walnut, CA 91789
Olympian V: 01/13/97

Ashley, Elizabeth
1223 N Ogden Dr
Los Angeles, CA 90046-4706
Actress V: 03/02/96

Ashley, Jennifer
11130 Huston St #6
N Hollywood, CA 91601
Actress V: 10/23/96

Ashley, John
18067 Lake Encino Dr
Encino, CA 91316-4433
Actor V: 03/12/96

Askin, Leon
Kjar Agency
10643 Riverside Dr
Toluca, CA 91602
Actor V: 12/11/96

PO Box 847
Beverly Hills, CA 90213
Alternate V: 03/02/96

Asner, Ed
PO Box 7407
Studio City, CA 91064
Actor V: 10/23/96

c/o Paradigm
10100 Santa Monica Bl-25th Fl
Los Angeles, CA 90067
Alternate V: 02/02/96

Assante, Armand
Creative Artists Agency
9830 Wilshire Bl
Beverly Hills, CA 90212
Actor V: 12/07/96

Astin, John
c/o Schechter
9300 Wilshire Bl #410
Beverly Hills, CA 90212
Actor V: 02/21/96

Astin, Sean
c/o Byron Ltd
4354 Laurel Canyon Bl #301
Studio City, CA 91604
Actor V: 02/08/96

5824 Norwich Ave
Van Nuys, CA 91411
Alternate V: 09/08/96

Atherton, William
5102 San Feliciano Dr
Woodland Hills, CA 91364
Actor V: 01/22/96

Atkins, Chet
c/o Clyde Records
1707 Grand Ave
Nashville, TN 37212
Guitarist V: 01/15/96

1013 17th St South
Nashville, TN 37212
Alternate V: 01/12/96

Atkins, Chris
6934 Bevis Ave
Van Nuys, CA 91405-3844
Actor V: 08/29/96

7072 Park Manor Ave
N Hollywood, CA 91605
Alternate V: 10/23/96

Atkins, Tom
c/o Paradigm
10100 Santa Monica Bl-25th Fl
Los Angeles, CA 90067
Actor V: 03/17/96

Atkins & Associates
303 S Crescent Heights Bl
Los Angeles, CA 90048
Talent Agency V: 01/02/96

Atkinson, Rowan
c/o Jones
47 Dean St
London W1, England
Actor V: 06/03/96

Atlanta Braves
PO Box 4064
Atlanta-Fulton County Stadium
Atlanta, GA 30302
Team Office V: 01/21/96

Atlanta Falcons
Suwanee Road & I-85
Suwanee, GA 30174
Team Office V: 02/07/96

Atlanta Hawks
One CNN Center #405
Atlanta, GA 30303
Team Office V: 02/15/96

Atlantic Records
9229 Sunset Bl #710
Los Angeles, CA 90069-2474
Production Office V: 01/02/96

Attenborough, Richard
Old Friars, Richmond Green
Surrey, England
Director V: 01/14/96

Auberjonois, Rene
Rosenberg Office
8428 Melrose Pl-Suite C
Los Angeles, CA 90069
Actor V: 12/13/96

Oracle/Wilcox
2604B El Camino Real #377
Carlsbad, CA 92008
Alternate V: 01/14/96

448 S Arden Bl
Los Angeles, CA 90020
Alternate V: 02/02/96

Paramount TV/ST-DS9
5555 Melrose Ave
Los Angeles, CA 90038
Forwarded V: 01/21/96

Audie Murphy Nat'l FC
SH Smith
8313 Snug Hill Lane
Potomac, MD 20854
Fan Service V: 03/15/96

Audie Murphy Research Found.
18008 Saratoga Way #516
Santa Calrita, CA 91351
Organization V: 01/25/97

Auel, Jean M
PO Box 430
Sherwood, OR 97140
Author V: 05/21/96

Auermann, Nadja
c/o Elite
111 E 22nd St
New York, NY 10010
Model V: 01/14/96

Via San Viottore 40
20123 Milan Italy
Alternate V: 10/18/96

Auger, Claudine
Wm Morris
151 S El Camino
Beverly Hills, CA 90212
Actress V: 08/20/96

Aumont, Jean-Pierre
4 Allee des Brouillards
F-75018 Paris France
Actor V: 06/07/96

Aung San Suu Kyi
Nat'l League for Democracy
54-56 University Ave
Rangoon, Myanmar
Peacemaker V: 03/14/96

Austin, Teri
Kohner Agency
9300 Wilshire Bl #555
Beverly Hills, CA 90212
Actress V: 12/11/96

4245 Laurel Grove Ave
Studio City, CA 91604
Alternate V: 02/03/96

Austin, Tracy
c/o Advantage
1751 Pinnacle Dr #1500
McLean, VA 22102-3833
Tennis Star V: 08/29/96

Auton, Buster
NASCAR
1811 Volusia Ave
Daytona Beach, FL 32015
NASCAR Official V: 03/14/96

Autry, Alan
Shapira & Associates
15301 Ventura Bl #345
Sherman Oaks, CA 91403
Actor V: 12/14/96

Autry, Gene
4383 Colfax Ave
Studio City, CA 91604
Actor V: 02/03/96

Avalon, Frankie
8942 Wilshire Bl
Beverly Hills, CA 90211
Actor V: 12/11/96

6311 De Soto Ave #1
Woodland Hills, CA 91367
Alternate V: 05/25/96

5513 S Rim St
Westlake Village, CA 91362-5234
Forwarded V: 04/12/96

Avdeyev, Sergei
141/160 Svyosdny Gorodok
Moskovskoi Oblasti, Russia
Cosmonaut V: 09/08/96

Avedon, Richard
407 E 75th St
New York, NY 10021
Photographer V: 11/01/96

Avery, James
Abrams Artists
9200 Sunset Bl #625
Los Angeles, CA 90069
Actor V: 12/01/96

Avery, Margaret
10000 Santa Monica Bl #305
Los Angeles, CA 90067
Actress V: 02/15/96

Axton, Hoyt
c/o Stern
11755 Wilshire Bl #2320
Los Angeles, CA 90025
Singer V: 01/12/96

PO Box 976
Hendersonville, TN 37075
Alternate V: 02/02/96

103 Bedford St #102
Hamilton, MT 59840-2816
Alternate V: 07/14/96

Aykroyd, Dan
c/o CAA
9830 Wilshire Bl
Beverly Hills, CA 90212
Actor V: 12/15/96

Aykroyd, Dan, Cont.
7708 Woodrow Wilson Dr
Los Angeles, CA 90046
Alternate V: 09/08/96

8455 Beverly Bl
Los Angeles, CA 90048-3416
Forwarded V: 01/03/97

Azinger, Paul
390 N Orange Ave #2600
Orlando, FL 32801
Golf Star V: 01/13/97

Aznavour, Charles
12 Chemin du Chateau Blanc
1231 Conches, Switzerland
Singer V: 10/23/96

Azumazeki Stable
c/o Sumo Sensei
4-6-4 Higashi Komagata
Ryogoku, Tokyo, Japan
Wrestling School V: 01/04/96

Azzara, Candice
c/o Shapira
15301 Ventura Bl #345
Sherman Oaks, CA 91403
Actress V: 02/15/96

BABYLON 5
8615 Tamarack Ave
Sun Valley, CA 91352
Production Office V: 02/07/96

BAYWATCH
Fan Mail
5433 Beethoven St
Los Angeles, CA 90066
Production Office V: 09/14/96

BAYWATCH NIGHTS
WB-TV
1438 N Gower
Hollywood, CA 90028
Audience Services V: 04/12/96

BBC-TV Center
Wood Lane
London, W12 8QT England
Network HQ V: 02/27/96

BEFORE THEY WERE STARS
1438 N Gower St-Box 30
Hollywood, CA 90028
Production Office V: 11/11/96

BEVERLY HILLS, 90210
Fox-TV
PO Box 900
Beverly Hills, CA 90213
Production Office V: 12/15/96

PO Box 884044
San Francisco, CA 94188
Forwarded V: 05/02/96

BLESS THIS HOUSE
WarnerTV/Bldg 136 - Rm 113
300 Television Plaza
Burbank, CA 91505
Production Office V: 10/23/96

BOLD AND THE BEAUTIFUL
7800 Beverly Bl #3371
Los Angeles, CA 90036
Production Office V: 11/01/96

BONNIE HUNT SHOW
Worldwide Pants Inc
7716 Beverly Bl-East Bldg #258
Los Angles, CA 90036
Production Office V: 10/23/96

BOP-LA
1467 N Tamarind Ave
Los Angeles, CA 90028
Talent Agency V: 06/04/96

BOSTON COMMON
NBC-TV
30 Rockefeller Plaza
New York, NY 10112
Production Office V: 12/15/96

BOY MEETS WORLD
Jacobs Prods-Anim Bldg 2A-7
500 South Buena Vista
Burbank, CA 91521-1701
Production Office V: 10/23/96

Jacobs Prod/KTLA Studios
5842 Sunset Bl/ Prod Bldg 11
Los Angeles, CA 90028
Alternate V: 11/11/96

c/o ABC-TV
77 W 66th St
New York, NY 10023
Forwarded V: 12/15/96

BROTHERLY LOVE
c/o WB-TV
1438 N Gower
Hollywood, CA 90028
Production Office V: 12/15/96

BUFFY THE VAMPIRE KILLER
WB-TV
1438 N Gower
Hollywood, CA 90028
Audience Services V: 01/13/97

BURNING ZONE
Universal TV
100 Universal City Plaza
Universal City, CA 91608
Production Office V: 10/23/96

UPN-TV
5555 Melrose Ave-Marathon 1200
Los Angeles, CA 90038
Alternate V: 11/11/96

Babcock, Barbara
Paradigm Agency
10100 Santa Monica Bl-25th Fl
Los Angeles, CA 90067
Actress V: 12/13/96

530 W California Bl
Pasadena, CA 91105-1636
Alternate V: 01/11/97

Babilonia, Tai
13889 Valley Vista Bl
Sherman Oaks, CA 91423-4662
Ice Skater V: 08/29/96

Bacall, Lauren
1 W 72nd St #43
New York, NY 10023
Actress V: 09/03/96

Bach, Barbara
2029 Century Park E #1690
Los Angeles, CA 90067
Actress V: 03/14/96

Bach, Catherine
CNA Associates
1801 Ave of the Stars #1250
Los Angeles, CA 90067
Actress V: 02/12/96

Bacharach, Burt
10 Ocean Park Bl #4
Santa Monica, CA 90405-3556
Composer V: 04/02/96

Bachardy, Don
145 Adelaide Dr.
Santa Monica, CA 90402
Artist V: 11/14/96

Bacon, Kevin
c/o CAA
9830 Wilshire Bl
Beverly Hills, CA 90212
Actor V: 11/27/96

Badgley Conner
9229 Sunset Bl #311
Los Angeles, CA 90069
Talent Agency V: 04/04/96

Badham, John
288 Hot Springs Rd
Montecito, CA 93108-2441
Film Director V: 08/29/96

Baer, Parley
4967 Bilmoor Ave
Tarzana, CA 91356
Actor V: 03/13/96

Baer Jr, Max
10433 Wilshire Bl #103
Los Angeles, CA 90024-4613
Actor V: 03/13/96

Baez, Joan
PO Box 1026
Menlo Park, CA 94026
Singer V: 03/12/96

Baggetta, Vincent
3928 Madelia Ave
Sherman Oaks, CA 91403
Actor V: 03/11/96

Bagian, James P
1653 E Maple Rd
Troy, MI 48083
Astronaut V: 03/03/96

Baier/Kleinman
3575 Cahuenga Bl #500
Los Angeles, CA 90068
Talent Agency V: 02/03/96

Bailey, F Lee
Smith Co Inc
1275 K St NW #800
Washington, DC 20005
Lawyer V: 03/02/96

1400 Centerpark Bl
W Palm Beach, FL 33401
Alternate V: 02/13/96

Bailey, GW
c/o Writers & Artists
924 Westwood Bl #900
Los Angeles, CA 90024
Actor V: 03/11/96

Bain, Barbara
Artists Agency
10000 Santa Monica Bl #305
Los Angeles, CA 90067
Actress V: 12/02/96

Bain, Conrad
Innovative Artists
1999 Ave of the Stars #2850
Los Angeles, CA 90067
Actor V: 02/12/96

Baio, Scott
3130 Dona Sarita Pl
Studio City, CA 91604
Actor V: 01/20/96

4333 Foreman Ave
Toluca Lake, CA 91602-2909
Alternate V: 01/12/96

Baiul, Oksana
Int'l Skating Center
1375 Hopmeadow St-POB 577
Simsbury, CT 06070
Ice Skater V: 12/07/96

c/o Bob Young
PO Box 719
Simsbury, CT 06070
Alternate V: 02/07/96

Baker, Brenda
Agency For Performing Arts
9000 Sunset Bl #1200
Los Angeles, CA 90069
Actress V: 12/02/96

Baker, Buck
NC Motor Speedway
PO Box 500
Rockingham, NC 28379
NASCAR Driver V: 07/06/96

Baker, Buddy
NASCAR
1811 Volusia Ave
Daytona Beach, FL 32015
NASCAR Driver V: 11/01/96

Baker, Carroll
Abrams Artists
9200 Sunset Bl #625
Los Angeles, CA 90069
Actress V: 12/01/96

630 Masselin Ave #221
Los Angeles, CA 90036
Alternate V: 01/15/96

Baker, Colin
Grafton House 42/43
2-3 Golden Square
London W1R 3AD, England
Actor V: 02/06/96

Baker, Diane
PO Box 480492
Los Angeles, CA 90048
Actress V: 04/04/96

2733 Outpost Dr
Los Angeles, CA 90068-2061
Alternate V: 01/12/96

283 Baywood Dr
Newport Beach, CA 92660-7133
Alternate V: 07/14/96

2585 La Paloma Ct
Thousand Oaks, CA 91360
Forwarded V: 02/02/96

8877 Tulare Drive #314-D
Huntington Beach, CA 92646
Forwarded V: 11/01/96

Baker, Ellen S
NASA/LBJ Space Center
Houston, TX 77058
Astronaut V: 11/01/96

Baker, James
555-13th St NW #500-E
Washington, DC 20004
Politician V: 05/06/96

Baker, Joe Don
Artists Agency
10000 Santa Monica Bl #305
Los Angeles, CA 90067
Actor V: 12/03/96

Baker, Kenny
51 Mulgrave Ave
Ashton-Preston
Lanos PR2 1HJ, England
Actor V: 01/13/97

Baker, Lisa
PO Box 8522
Midland, TX 79708
Playmate V: 01/13/97

Baker, Mark Linn
2625 6th St #2
Santa Monica, CA 90405-4431
Actor V: 08/29/96

Baker, Michael A
NASA/LBJ Space Center
Houston, TX 77058
Astronaut V: 04/27/96

Baker, Tom
London Management
235/241 Regent St
London, W1A 2JR England
Actor V: 02/14/96

Burnett/Suite 42
Grafton House-2 Golden Sq
London, W1 England
Alternate V: 03/21/96

Bakula, Scott
15300 Ventura Bl #315
Sherman Oaks, CA 91403-3139
Actor V: 08/29/96

812 El Camino Rd
Santa Monica, CA 90405-4431
Alternate V: 08/29/96

c/o UTA
9560 Wilshire Bl #500
Beverly Hills, CA 90212
Forwarded V: 04/01/96

Balding, Rebecca
c/o Sanders
8831 Sunset Bl #304
Los Angeles, CA 90069
Actress V: 02/12/96

Baldwin, Adam
Gersh Agency
232 N Canon Dr
Beverly Hills, CA 90210
Actor V: 12/09/96

Baldwin, Alec
c/o CAA
9830 Wilshire Bl
Beverly Hills, CA 90212
Actor V: 01/14/96

Baldwin, Alec, *Cont.*
Wolf/Kasteller
1033 Gayley Ave #208
Los Angeles, CA 90024
Alternate V: 02/02/96

4833 Don Juan Place
Woodland Hills, CA 91367
Alternate V: 11/01/96

Wolf-Kasteller
132 S Rodeo Dr #300
Beverly Hills, CA 90212-2403
Forwarded V: 08/29/96

Baldwin, Stephen
PO Box 447
Camillus, NY 13031
Actor V: 01/14/96

Baldwin, William
c/o CAA
9830 Wilshire Bl
Beverly Hills, CA 90212
Actor V: 02/02/96

Baldwin Talent
500 S Sepulveda Bl-4th Fl
Los Angeles, CA 90049
Talent Agency V: 02/07/96

Bale, Christian
Wm Morris Agency
151 El Camino
Beverly Hills, CA 90212
Actor V: 12/12/96

c/o Pine Files
6-A Wyndham Place
London W1H 1TN, England
Alternate V: 01/01/96

Balk, Fairuza
Paul Kohner
9300 Wilshire Bl #555
Beverly Hills, CA 90211-2382
Actress V: 03/14/96

Ball Talent
4342 Lankershim Bl
Universal City, CA 91602
Talent Agency V: 02/09/96

Ballantine, Carl
Tisherman Agency
6767 Forest Lawn Dr #115
Los Angeles, CA 90068
Actor V: 12/15/96

Ballantine, Sara
Talent Group
6300 Wilshire Bl #2110
Los Angeles, CA 90048
Actress V: 12/15/96

Ballard, Dr Robert
Mystic Oceano
Mystic, CT 06355
Scientist V: 01/07/96

Oceanographic Institute
Woods Hole, MA 02543
Alternate V: 02/21/96

Ballard, Kaye
Craig Agency
8485 Melrose Place-Suite E
Los Angeles, CA 90069
Actress V: 12/08/96

Ballestros, Serviano
Ruiz Zorrilla 16-20J
39009 Santander, Spain
Golfer V: 01/22/96

Baltimore Orioles
Oriole Park
333 W Camden St
Baltimore, MD 21201
Team Office V: 07/21/96

Bancroft, Anne
2301 La Mesa Dr
Santa Monica, CA 90405
Actress V: 02/03/96

c/o ICM
8942 Wilshire Bl
Beverly Hills, CA 90211
Alternate V: 02/15/96

Banderas, Antonio
Creative Artists Agency
9830 Wilshire Bl
Beverly Hills, CA 90212
Actor V: 12/07/96

201 S Rockingham Ave
Los Angeles, CA 90049
Alternate V: 11/01/96

Bandy, Moe
American Theatre
PO Box 1987
Branson, MO 65616
Singer V: 02/02/96

Banks, Carl
Washington Redskins
21300 Redskin Park Dr
Ashburn, VA 22011
Football Star V: 01/27/96

Banks, Jonathan
Innovative Artists
1999 Ave of the Stars #2850
Los Angeles, CA 90067
Actor V: 12/11/96

909 Euclid St #8
Santa Monica, CA 90403
Alternate V: 01/12/96

Banks, Tyra
PO Box 36-E 18th St
Los Angeles, CA 90053
Model V: 11/01/96

c/o IMG
170 Fifth Ave 10th Fl
New York, NY 10010
Alternate V: 11/01/96

Banks, Willie
Portland Beavers
PO Box 4108
Salt Lake City, UT 84110-4108
Baseball Star V: 01/01/96

Bannock, Russell G
11 Doncliffe Dr
Toronto, Ont, Canada M4N 2E5
War Hero V: 07/21/96

Bannon, Jack
Gage Group
9255 Sunset Bl #515
Los Angeles, CA 90069
Actor V: 02/13/96

Barbeau, Adrienne
Gage Group
9255 Sunset Bl #515
Los Angeles, CA 90069
Actress V: 12/08/96

Baranski, Christine
ICM
40 W 57th St
New York, NY 10010
Actress V: 11/20/96

Barber, Glynis
Buckwald & Associates
9229 Sunset Bl #710
Los Angeles, CA 90069
Actress V: 12/06/96

c/o Billy Marsh
19 Denmark St
London WC2H 8NA, England
Alternate V: 06/06/96

Barber, Miller
PO Box 2202
Sherman, TX 75091
Golf Star V: 01/02/97

Barbera, Joseph R
12003 Briarville Ln
Studio City, CA 91604-4106
Producer V: 11/10/96

Barbi, Shane & Sia
29196 Heathercliff-#216/410
Malibu, CA 90265
Models V: 09/04/96

Barbieri, Paula
c/o Elite Models
111 E 22nd St #200
New York, NY 90024
Model V: 11/18/96

Bardot, Brigitte
La Madrique
83990 St Tropez, France
Actress V: 06/01/96

45 rue Vineuse
75116 Paris, France
Alternate V: 11/01/96

Bare, Bobby
BB Entertainment
PO Box 2422
Hendersonville, TN 37077
Singer V: 02/02/96

Bare Facts
Craig Hosoda
PO Box 3255
Santa Clara, CA 95055
Video Guide V: 12/10/96

Barkdoll, Phil
NASCAR
1811 Volusia Ave
Daytona Beach, FL 32015
NASCAR Driver V: 06/06/96

Barker, Bob
Goodson Productions
5750 Wilshire Bl
Los Angeles, CA 90036-3697
TV Host V: 07/03/96

1851 Outpost Dr
Los Angeles, CA 90069
Alternate V: 11/11/96

Barker, Ronnie
c/o Zahl
57 Great Cumberland Place
London W1H 7LJ, England
Actor V: 11/18/96

Barker Productions
c/o Bob Barker
9201 Wilshire Bl #201
Beverly Hills, CA 90210
Production Office V: 03/17/96

Barkley, Charles
Phoenix Suns
201 E Jefferson St
Phoenix, AZ 85004-2400
Basketball Star V: 11/01/96

Phoenix Suns
2910 N Central Ave
Phoenix, AZ 85012
Alternate V: 01/14/96

4615 E Caron
Phoenix, AZ 85028
Forwarded V: 04/12/96

Barks, Carl
Barks Studios
PO Box 524
Grants Pass, OR 97526
Cartoonist V: 02/01/96

Barnes, Clive
New York Post
210 South St
New York, NY 10002
Critic V: 01/27/96

Barnes, Joanna
2160 Century Park E #2101-N
Los Angeles, CA 90067
Actress V: 01/22/96

Barnes, Priscilla
7461 Beverly Bl-Ste 400
Los Angeles, CA 90036
Actress V: 01/21/96

Barnes, Pricilla, Cont.
c/o Rosenerg
8428 Melrose Pl- Suite C
Los Angeles, CA 90069
Forwarded V: 02/12/96

Baron, Blaire
c/o Schecter
9300 Wilshire Bl #410
Beverly Hills, CA 90212
Actress V: 02/23/96

Barrett, Rona
PO Box 1410
Beverly Hills, CA 90213
Columnist V: 03/13/96

Barrie, Barbara
1999 Ave of the Stars #2850
Los Angeles, CA 90067
Actress V: 02/26/96

15 W 72nd St-Suite 2-A
New York, NY 10023-3428
Alternate V: 11/01/96

Barry, Daniel T
NASA/LBJ Space Center
Houston, TX 77058
Astronaut V: 02/02/96

Barry, Gene
Artists Agency
10000 Santa Monica Bl #305
Los Angeles, CA 90067
Actor V: 12/03/96

c/o Green
10390 Santa Monica Bl
Los Angeles, CA 90025
Alternate V: 01/18/96

Barry, Patricia
Buckwald & Associates
9229 Sunset Bl #710
Los Angeles, CA 90069
Actress V: 12/06/96

Barrymore, Drew
3960 Laurel Canyon Bl #159
Studio City, CA 91604
Actress V: 01/31/96

7985 Santa Monica Bl #109150
W Hollywood, CA 90046-5186
Alternate V: 01/31/96

9560 Wilshire Bl-Ste 500
Beverly Hills, CA 90212
Forwarded V: 01/14/96

Barrymore, Drew, Cont.
612 N Sepulveda Bl #10
Los Angeles, CA 90049
Forwarded V: 02/01/96

Bartel, Paul
7860 Fareholm Dr
Los Angeles, CA 90046
Actor V: 01/27/96

Bartell, Harry
365 Strawberry Lane
Ashland, OR 97520
Radio Star V: 01/31/96

Bartolo, Sal
422 Border St
E Boston, MA 02128
Football Star V: 01/13/97

Barty, Billy
Artists Group
10100 Santa Monica Bl #2490
Los Angeles, CA 90067
Actor V: 12/04/96

4502 Farmdale Ave
N Hollywood, CA 91602
Alternate V: 01/14/96

Baryshnikov, Mikhail
Creative Artists Agency
9830 Wilshire Bl
Beverly Hills, CA 90212
Ballet Star V: 12/07/96

Baseball Commissioner
350 Park Ave
New York, NY 10022
Team Office V: 03/19/96

Baseline
838 Broadway
New York, NY 10003
Publisher V: 03/30/96

Basinger, Kim
c/o CAA
9830 Wilshire Bl
Beverly Hills, CA 90212
Actress V: 10/10/96

Bassett, Angela
c/o ICM
8942 Wilshire Bl
Beverly Hills, CA 90211
Actress V: 12/11/96

Bassett, Angela, Cont.
6427 1/2 Troost Ave
N Hollywood, CA 91606
Alternate V: 01/22/96

Bassey, Jennifer
Artists Group
10100 Santa Monica Bl #2490
Los Angeles, CA 90067
Actress V: 02/12/96

Bassey, Shirley
Villa Capricorn
55 Via Campione
6816 Bissone, Switzerland
Singer V: 04/01/96

Bassinger, Kim
955 S Carillo Dr #200
Los Angeles, CA 90048
Actress V: 09/03/96

Bateman, Jason
2623 2nd St
Santa Monica, CA 90402
Actor V: 01/11/96

c/o ICM
8942 Wishire Bl
Beverly Hills, CA 90211
Alternate V: 01/13/97

Bateman, Justine
Creative Artists Agency
9830 Wilshire Bl
Beverly Hills, CA 90212
Actress V: 12/07/96

Bates, Alan
122 Hamilton Terrace
London, NW8 England
Actor V: 03/29/96

Bates, Kathy
c/o Smith & Associates
121 N San Vicente Bl
Beverly Hills, CA 90211
Actress V: 12/15/96

Batliner, Gerard
Am Schragen Weg 2
FL-9490 Vaduz, Liechtenstein
Politician V: 02/15/96

Bauer, Jaime Lyn
Kjar Agency
10643 Riverside Dr
Toluca, CA 91602
Actress V: 12/11/96

Bauer, Michelle
PO Box 480265
Los Angeles, CA 90048
Actress V: 11/01/96

16032 Sherman Way #73
Van Nuys, CA 91406
Alternate V: 01/-12/96

Bauman, Jon 'Bowzer'
3168 Oakshire Dr
Los Angeles, CA 90067
Singer V: 03/07/96

Bauman-Hiller Agency
5750 Wilshire Bl #512
Los Angeles, CA 90036
Talent Agency V: 11/11/96

Baxter, Meredith
Wm Morris Agency
151 El Camino Dr
Beverly Hills, CA 90212
Actress V: 03/07/96

Int'l FC
1018 Fairview Ave
Lombard, IL 60148
Alternate V: 01/07/96

Baye, Nathalie
Artmedia
10 Ave George V
75008 ^Paris France
Actress V: 05/12/96

Baylor, Elgin
2480 Briarcrest Rd
Beverly Hills, CA 90210-1820
Basketball Star V: 08/29/96

Baywatch Beach Club
c/o FC
PO Box 69249
Los Angeles, CA 90069
Fan Services V: 11/01/96

Beach Boys
4860 San Jacinto Circle W
Fallbrook, CA 92028
Musical Group V: 11/01/96

Beacham, Stephanie
1131 Alta Loma Rd-Ste 517
W Hollywood, CA 90069-2435
Actress V: 08/29/96

Beacham, Stephanie, Cont.
PO Box 6446
Malibu, CA 90264
Alternate V: 02/01/96

Gersh Agency
232 N Canon Dr
Beverly Hills, CA 90210
Forwarded V: 02/12/96

Beal, John
205 W 54th St
New York, NY 10009
Actor V: 05/22/96

Beals, Jennifer
Wm Morris Agency
151 El Camino
Beverly Hills, CA 90212
Actress V: 12/12/96

335 N Maple Dr #250
Beverly Hills, CA 90210
Alternate V: 10/23/96

Robinson Entertainment
10683 Santa Monica Bl
Los Angeles, CA 90025-7449
Forwarded V: 03/14/96

Bean, Alan
NASA/LBJ Space Center
Houston, TX 77058
Astronaut V: 07/03/96

26 Sugarberry Circle
Houston, TX 77024
Alternate V: 03/30/96

Bean, Orson
9255 Sunset Bl #515
Los Angeles, CA 90069
Actor V: 02/13/96

444 Carrell Canal
Venice, CA 90271
Alternate V: 10/23/96

Bearse, Amanda
4177 Klump Ave
N Hollywood, CA 91602
Actress V: 03/08/96

Beart, Emmanuelle
Artmedia
10 Ave George-V
F-75008 Paris, France
Actress V: 02/12/96

Beasley, Allyce
147 N Windsor Bl
Los Angeles, CA 90004-3815
Actress V: 08/29/96

Beatty, Ned
2706 N Beachwood Dr
Los Angeles, CA 90027
Actor V: 01/14/96

Beatty, Warren
c/o CAA
9830 Wilshire Bl
Beverly Hills, CA 90212
Actor V: 03/11/96

13671 Mulholland Dr
Beverly Hills, CA 90210
Forwarded V: 01/20/96

Beauvais, Garcelle
957 N Cole Ave
Los Angeles, CA 90038
Actress V: 01/13/97

Beck, Jeff
11 Old Square, Lincolns Inn
London WC2, England
Singer V: 06/13/96

Beck, Marilyn
PO Box 11079
Beverly Hills, CA 90213
Columnist V: 03/10/96

2132 El Roble Ln
Beverly Hills, CA 90210
Forwarded V: 03/10/96

Becker, Boris
Le Rocca Bella
24 Ave Princess Grace
Monte Carlo, Monaco
Tennis Star V: 02/10/96

Bedelia, Bonnie
1021 Georgina Ave
Santa Monica, CA 90402
Actress V: 04/24/96

Beghe, Jason
400 S Beverly Dr #216
Beverly Hills, CA 90212
Actor V: 01/11/97

Begley Jr, Ed
Agency For Performing Arts
9000 Sunset Bl #1200
Los Angeles, CA 90069
Actor V: 12/02/96

Sterling/Winters
1900 Ave of the Stars #1640
Los Angeles, CA 90067
Alternate V: 01/31/96

3850 Mound View Ave
Studio City, CA 91604
Forwarded V: 03/09/96

Belafonte, Harry
151 El Camino Dr
Beverly Hills, CA 90212
Singer V: 03/18/96

Belafonte, Shari
Kohner Agency
9300 Wilshire Bl #555
Beverly Hills, CA 90212
Actress V: 02/14/96

Belford, Christina
Paradigm Agency
10100 Santa Monica Bl-25th Fl
Los Angeles, CA 90067
Actress V: 02/12/96

SDB Partners
1801 Ave of the Stars #902
Los Angeles, CA 90067
Alternate V: 12/13/96

Belfrage Agency
Julien Belfrage
68 St James St
London SW1A 1PH, England
Talent Agency V: 01/20/96

Belita
Rose Cottage
42-46 Crabtree Lane
London SW6 6LW, England
Actress V: 01/04/96

Bell, Catherine
Ambrosio/Mortimer
9150 Wilshire Bl #175
Beverly Hills, CA 90212
Actress V: 01/15/97

Bell, Greg
831 W Miami Ave
Logansport, IN 46947-2543
Actor V: 08/29/96

Beller, Kathleen
Paradigm Agency
10100 Santa Monica Bl-25th Fl
Los Angeles, CA 90067
Actress V: 12/13/96

Bello, Maria
Gersh Agency
232 N Canon Dr Dr
Beverly Hills, CA 90210
Actress V: 12/15/96

Belmondo, Jean-Paul
9 rue des St Peres
75007 Paris, France
Actor V: 01/01/96

77 Ave Donvert Rochefort
75016 Paris, France
Alternate V: 07/24/96

Artmedia
10 Ave George V
Paris, 75008 France
Forwarded V: 03/21/96

Cerito Films
5 rue Clemont-Marot
F-75008 Paris, France
Forwarded V: 01/17/96

Beltran, Robert
924 Westwood Bl #900
Los Angeles, CA 90024
Actor V: 02/15/96

Belucci, Monica
Elite Model Mgmt
111 E 22nd St #200
New York, NY 10010
Model V: 11/01/96

Belushi, James
8033 Sunset Bl-Suite 88
Los Angeles, CA 90046
Actor V: 01/31/96

9830 Wilshire Bl
Beverly Hills, CA 90212
Alternate V: 05/21/96

Belzar, Richard
Agency For Performing Arts
9000 Sunset Bl #1200
Los Angeles, CA 90069
Actor V: 12/02/96

Ben & Jerry's Ice Cream
Rt 100, PO Box 240
Waterbury, VT 05676
Corporation V: 01/12/96

Benatar, Pat
14755 Ventura Bl #1-710
Sherman Oaks, CA 91403
Singer V: 01/20/96

Benavidez, Roy
1700 Byrne St
El Campo, TX 77437
War Hero V: 06/07/96

Bench, Johnny
105 E 4th St #800
Cincinnati, OH 45202
Baseball Star V: 01/18/96

Benchley, Peter
Elihu Island
Stonington, CT 06378
Author V: 02/09/96

35 Boudinot St
Princeton, NJ 08540
Alternate V: 05/04/96

Bendix, Simone
Joy Jameson Ltd
2/19 The Plaza-535 Kings Rd
London SW10 OSZ, England
Actress V: 11/01/96

Benedict, Dirk
PO Box 634
Bigfork, MT 59911-0634
Actor V: 11/10/96

1637 Wellesley Dr
Santa Monica, CA 90406
Alternate V: 05/21/96

Benedict, Paul
84 Rockland Place
Newton, MA 02164-1234
Actor V: 11/10/96

Benigni, Roberto
Via Traversa 44
Vergaglio, Prato, Italy
Actor V: 01/27/96

Benjamin, Richard
Gersh Agency
232 N Canon Dr
Beverly Hills, CA 90210
Actor V: 03/20/96

Bennett, Bruce
2702 Forrester Rd
Los Angeles, CA 90024
Actor V: 06/14/96

Bennett, Hywell
c/o James Sharkey
15 Golden Sq-3rd Floor
London W1R 3AG, England
Actor V: 01/02/96

Bennett, Tony
Wm Morris Agency
151 El Camino Dr
Beverly Hills, CA 90212
Singer V: 01/14/96

101 W 55th St
New York, NY 10019
Alternate V: 01/11/96

Bennett Agency
6404 Hollywood Bl #316
Los Angeles, CA 90028
Talent Agency V: 02/01/96

Benning, Annette
Traubner/Flynn
2029 Century Park E-#300
Los Angeles, CA 90067-2900
Actress V: 08/08/96

c/o CAA
9830 Wilshire Bl
Beverly Hills, CA 90212
Alternate V: 01/14/96

Benoit, David
Fitzgerald/Hartley/Simmons
50 W Main St
Ventura, CA 93001
Jazz Musician V: 01/01/96

Benson, George
Fritz Mgmt
648 N Robertson Bl
Los Angeles, CA 90069
Musician V: 01/01/96

Benson, Robby
PO Box 1305
Woodland Hills, CA 91365
Actor V: 01/01/96

c/o Bresler
15760 Ventura Bl #1730
Encino, CA 91346
Alternate V: 01/15/96

Benson Agency
8360 Melrose Ave #203
Los Angeles, CA 90069
Talent Agency V: 03/22/96

Benton, Barbi
40 N 4th St
Carbondale, CO 81623-2012
Actress V: 08/08/96

Berenger, Tom
853-7th Ave #9A
New York, NY 10019
Actor V: 01/27/96

c/o CAA
9830 Wilshire Bl
Beverly Hills, CA 90212
Alternate V: 09/03/96

Berg, Patty
PO Box 9227
Ft Meyers, FL 33902
Golfer V: 07/02/96

Bergen, Candice
Wm Morris Agency
151 El Camino Dr
Beverly Hills, CA 90212
Actress V: 01/14/96

'Murphy Brown'
Bldg 3A-Rm 21
4000 Warner Blvd
Burbank, CA 91522
Forwarded V: 02/12/96

Bergen, Polly
Wm Morris Agency
151 El Camino
Beverly Hills, CA 90212
Actress V: 12/12/96

11342 Dona Lisa Dr
Studio City, CA 91604-4315
Alternate V: 01/20/96

Berger, Helmut
Pundterplatz 6
80803 Munich, Germany
Actor V: 01/12/96

Berger, Senta
Robert-Koch Strasse 10
12621 Grunewald, Germany
Actress V: 01/11/96

Bergere, Lee
2385 Century Hill
Los Angeles, CA 90067
Actor V: 03/04/96

32 Beach Plum Way
Hampton, NH 03842-1637
Alternate V: 08/29/96

Bergin, Patrick
Allied Vision/Avon House
360-366 Oxford St
London W1N 9HA, England
Actor V: 02/08/96

Bergman, Ingmar
Svenska Filminstitutet
Box 27126
Stockholm S-10252, Sweden
Director V: 11/01/96

Berkley, Elizabeth
c/o CAA
9830 Wishire Bl
Beverly Hills, CA 90212
Actress V: 02/12/96

c/o MTA
4526 Wilshire Bl
Los Angeles, CA 90010
Alternate V: 10/10/96

Berle, Milton
10750 Wilshire Bl #1003
Los Angeles, CA 90024-4470
Actor V: 03/03/96

Media Artists
8383 Wilshire Bl #954
Beverly Hills, CA 90211
Alternate V: 12/11/96

Berman, Shelley
268 Bell Canyon Rd
Bell Canyon, CA 91307
Actor V: 02/01/96

c/o APA
9000 Sunset Bl #1200
Los Angeles, CA 90069
Alternate V: 12/02/96

Bernard, Crystal
14014 Aubrey Rd
Beverly Hills, CA 90210
Actress V: 10/23/96

Bernard, Crystal, Cont.
Creative Artists Agency
9830 Wilshire Bl
Beverly Hills, CA 90212
Alternate V: 12/07/96

Cedar Mgmt
10866 Wilshire Bl #1200
Los Angeles, CA 90024
Forwarded V: 01/22/96

Bernsen, Collin
9744 Wilshire Bl #308
Beverly Hills, CA 90212
Actor V: 03/03/96

Bernsen, Corbin
3690 Goodland Ave
Studio City, CA 91604-2310
Actor V: 08/29/96

c/o ICM
8942 Wilshire Bl
Beverly Hills, CA 90211
Alternate V: 12/11/96

2114 Kew Dr
Los Angeles, CA 90046
Forwarded V: 02/02/96

Bernstein, Kenny
1105 Seminole
Richardson, TX 95080
Race Driver V: 12/12/96

Berra, Yogi
19 Highland Ave
Montclair, NJ 07042
Baseball Star V: 01/08/96

Berry, Chuck
c/o Berry Park
691 Buckner Road
Wentzville, MO 63385
Musician V: 06/14/96

Berry, Halle
4173 Tattershall Dr
Decatur, GA 30034
Actress V: 02/01/96

8721 Sunset Bl
Los Angeles, CA 90069
Alternate V: 01/20/96

c/o CAA
9830 Wilshire Bl
Beverly Hills, CA 90212
Alternate V: 09/03/96

Berry, Halle, Cont.
Wm Morris Agency
151 El Camino Dr
Beverly Hills, CA 90212
Forwarded V: 01/14/96

Berry, Ken
4704 N Cahuenga Bl
N Hollywood, CA 91602
Actor V: 04/04/96

c/o Cosden
3518 Cahuenga Bl W #216
Los Angeles, CA 90068
Alternate V: 02/26/96

Berry, Ray
David Berry
6405 Shady Brook Lane #2273
Dallas, TX 75206-1308
Football Star V: 01/10/97

Berryman, Michael
RR3-Box 117A
Clarksville AR 72830-9325
Actor V: 08/29/96

Media Artists
8383 Wilshire Bl #954
Beverly Hills, CA 90211
Alternate V: 12/11/96

Bertinelli, Valerie
PO Box 1984
Studio City, CA 91614
Actress V: 04/30/96

12700 Ventura Bl #100
Studio City, CA 91604
Alternate V: 10/23/96

Wm Morris Agency
151 El Camino
Beverly Hills, CA 90212
Alternate V: 12/12/96

9255 W Sunset Bl #1010
W Hollywood, CA 90069-3309
Forwarded V: 01/12/96

Bertolucci, Bernardo
Via Della Lungara 3
00165 Rome, Italy
Director V: 02/01/96

Bertuccelli, Jean-Louis
9 Rue Benard
Paris 75014, France
Director V: 10/23/96

Berwanger, Jay
1245 Warren Ave
Downers Grove, IL 60515
Football Star V: 04/04/96

Berzon Agency
336 E 17th St
Costa Mesa, CA 92627
Talent Agency V: 02/28/96

Bess, Gordon
King Features
235 East 45th St
New York, NY 10017
Cartoonist V: 03/14/96

Bessie Loo Agency
8235 Santa Monica Bl #202
Los Angeles, CA 91604
Talent Agency V: 01/21/96

Best, Pete
8 Hymans Green
West Derby
Liverpool 12, England
Actor V: 03/02/96

Bestwicke, Martine
131 S Sycamore Ave
Los Angeles, CA 90036
Actress V: 11/27/96

Goldey Company
116 N Robertson #700
Los Angeles, CA 90048
Alternate V: 12/10/96

Bettenhausen, Tony
5234 Wilton Wood Ct
Indianapolis, IN 46254
Race Driver V: 03/11/96

Bey, Turhan
Paradisgasse Ave 47
Vienna 1190 XIX, Austria7
Actor V: 03/03/96

Beyer, Troy
Wm Morris Agency
151 El Camino Dr
Beverly Hills, CA 90212
Actress V: 02/12/96

Beymer, Richard
1818 N Fuller Ave
Los Angeles, CA 90046
TV Host V: 01/22/96

Bialik, Mayim
1529 N Cahuenga Bl #19
Los Angles, CA 90028
Actress V: 04/02/96

Biehn, Michael
11220 Valley Spring Ln
N Hollywood, CA 91602-2611
Actor V: 08/29/96

3737 Deervale Dr
Sherman Oaks, CA 91403
Alternate V: 10/23/96

Bierschwale, Eddie
NASCAR
1811 Volusia Ave
Daytona Beach, FL 32015
NASCAR Driver V: 03/02/96

Biggs, Richard
728 W 28th St
Los Angeles, CA 90007
Actor V: 03/04/96

Biggs-Dawson, Roxann
5750 Wilshire Bl #512
Los Angeles, CA 90036
Actress V: 02/15/96

Innovative Artists
1999 Ave of the Stars #2850
Los Angeles, CA 90067
Alternate V: 12/11/96

Bigley Agency
6442 Coldwater Canyon #211
N Hollywood, CA 91606
Talent Agency V: 01/12/96

Bikel, Theodore
94 Honey Hill Rd
Georgetown, CT 06829
Actor V: 02/09/96

Metro Talent Agency
4526 Wilshire Bl
Los Angeles, CA 90010
Alternate V: 12/11/96

1131 Alta Loma Rd
Los Angeles, CA 90069
Forwarded V: 03/04/96

Billboard
PO Box 2071
Mahopac, NY 10541-9855
Publisher V: 03/21/96

Billingsley, Barbara
PO Box 1320
Santa Monica, CA 90406
Actress V: 02/01/96

c/o Cosden
3518 Cahuenga Bl W #216
Los Angeles, CA 90068
Forwarded V: 03/03/96

Billingsley, Ray
King Features
216 E 45th St
New York, NY 10017
Cartoonist V: 03/11/96

Binoche, Juliette
Agency Marceline Lenoir
99 Blvd Marlesherbes
75008 Paris France
Actress V: 12/07/96

Biondi, Matthew
1404 Rimer Dr
Moraga, CA 94556
Olympian V: 01/02/97

Bird, Larry
6278 N Federal Hwy #296
Ft Lauderdale, FL 33308-1908
Basketball Star V: 01/01/96

501 Hibiscus Dr
Hallendale, FL 33009
Alternate V: 11/27/96

Boston Celtics
151 Merrimac St
Boston, MA 02114-4714
Forwarded V: 01/12/96

Birkin, Jane
28 Rue de la Tour
75016 Paris France
Actress V: 09/10/96

Birney, David
20 Ocean Park Bl #118
Santa Monica, CA 90405
Actor V: 03/05/96

Kohner Agency
9300 Wilshire Bl #555
Beverly Hills, CA 90212
Alternate V: 12/11/96

Bishop, Joey
534 Via Lido Nord
Newport, CA 92663
Actor V: 06/06/96

Bisset, Jacqueline
1815 Benedict Canyon Dr
Beverly Hills, CA 90210
Actress V: 06/02/96

Bissett, Josie
8942 Wilshire Bl
Beverly Hills, CA 90211
Actress V: 12/11/96

8033 Sunset Bl #4048
Los Angeles, CA 90046-4247
Alternate V: 01/13/97

10350 Wilshire Bl #502
Los Angeles, CA 90024
Forwarded V: 10/23/96

Bjorn, Anna
Kohner Agency
9300 Wilshire Bl #555
Beverly Hills, CA 90212-3211
Model V: 11/01/96

Black, Cilla
Regent House
235-241 Regent St
London W1V 3AU, England
Actress V: 10/03/96

Black, Clint
Moress/Nanas/Shea
1209 16th Ave South
Nashville, TN 37212
Singer V: 02/02/96

PO Box 299386
Houston, TX 77299
Alternate V: 01/16/96

8033 Sunset Bl #2641
Los Angeles, CA 90046-2427
Forwarded V: 03/06/96

Black Entertainment TV
1232 31st St
Washington, DC 20007
Production Office V: 01/31/96

Blackman, Honor
Michael Ladkin
11 Southwick Mews
London W2 1JG, England
Alternate V: 02/04/96

Blackstone Jr, Harry
16530 Ventura Bl #310
Encino, CA 91436-4550
Magician V: 08/29/96

Blackwell, Ewell
80 Ariel Loop
Hendersonville, NC 28792
Baseball Star V: 05/14/96

Blades, Rubin
Wm Morris Agency
151 El Camino Dr
Los Angeles, CA 90212
Actor V: 03/02/96

1187 Coast Village Rd #1
Montecito, CA 93108-2761
Alternate V: 08/29/96

Blaha, John E
NASA/LBJ Space Center
Hoston, TX 77058
Astronaut V: 12/11/96

Blair, Betsy
11 Chalcot Gardens
Englands Lane
London, NW3 4YB England
Actress V: 04/24/96

Blair, Bonnie
306 White Pine Road
Delafield, WI 53018-1124
Actress V: 10/23/96

1907 W Springfield
Champaign, IL 61820
Alternate V: 01/31/96

Blair, Janet
21650 Burbank Bl #107
Woodland Hills, CA 91367-6471
Actress V: 11/10/96

Blair, Linda
c/o LBFC
8033 Sunset Bl-Suite 204
Los Angeles, CA 90046
Actress V: 12/15/96

Artists Group
10100 Santa Monica Bl #2490
Los Angeles, CA 90067
Forwarded V: 2/1/96

4165 Kraft Ave
Studio City, CA 91604-3039
Forwarded V: 11/10/96

Blake, Robert
Breezy Productions
11604 Dilling St #6
N Hollywood, CA 91604
Actor V: 06/14/96

Blake, Stephanie
First Artists
10000 Riverside Dr #6
Toluca Lake, CA 91602
Actress V: 02/22/96

Blake, Susan
News Center 4
1001 Van Ness Ave
San Francisco, CA 94109
Journalist V: 02/10/96

Blake Agency
415 N Camden Dr #121
Beverly Hills, CA 90210
Talent Agency V: 11/11/96

Blakely, Susan
421 N Rodeo Dr #15-111
Beverly Hills, CA 90210
Actress V: 10/23/96

416 N Oakhurst Dr #305
Beverly Hills, CA 90210
Alternate V: 02/28/96

Blanc, Noel
702 N Rodeo Dr
Beverly Hills, CA 90210
Celebrity V: 01/13/97

Bland, Bobby Blues
108 N Auburndale #1010
Memphis, TN 38104
Singer V: 09/09/96

Blanda, George
1513 Stonegate Rd
LaGrange Park, IL 60525
Football Star V: 05/03/96

Bledsoe, Tempestt
Innovative Artists
1999 Ave of the Stars #2850
Los Angeles, CA 90067
Actress V: 02/12/96

Bleeth, Yasmine
247 S Beverly Dr #102
Beverly Hills, CA 90212
Actress V: 05/06/96

Bleeth, Yasmine, Cont.
10460 Queens Bl #10-C
Forest Hills, NY 11375
Alternate V: 10/23/96

Bliss, Lucille
Smurfette Society
845 Noe St #3
San Francisco, CA 94114
Actress V: 04/22/96

Cavaleri & Associates
405 Riverside Dr #200
Burbanks, CA 91506
Alternate V: 12/07/96

Bloom, Brian
11 Croydon Ct
Dix Hills, NY 11746
Actor V: 05/04/96

Bloom, Claire
c/o Van Gelder
18-21 Jermyn St
London SW1Y 6HP, England
Actress V: 02/02/96

Bloom, Lindsay
PO Box 412
Weldon, CA 93283-0412
Actress V: 01/12/96

3907 W Alameda Ave #101
Burbank, CA 91505
Alternate V: 02/25/96

Bloom Agency
Michael Bloom
9255 Sunset Blvd #710
Los Angeles, CA 90069
Talent Agency V: 02/23/96

Blount, Lisa
Wm Morris Agency
151 El Camino
Beverly Hills, CA 90212
Actress V: 12/12/96

Stevens Mgmt
7473 Mulholland Dr
Los Angeles, CA 90046
Alternate V: 02/01/96

Blount, Mel
RR 1-Box 91
Claysville, PA 15323
Football Star V: 03/17/96

Blue, Vida
PO Box 1449
Pleasanton, CA 94566
Baseball Star V: 01/20/96

Blues Traveler
PO Box 1128
New York, NY 10101
Musical Group V: 01/13/97

Bluford Jr, Guion S
NASA/LBJ Space Center
Hoston, TX 77058
Astronaut V: 06/06/96

NYMA Inc
7501 Greenway Center Dr
Greenbelt, MD 20770
Alternate V: 10/23/96

Blyth, Ann
PO Box 9754
Rancho Santa Fe, CA 92067
Actress V: 04/02/96

Bobbit, John Wayne
7226 Westpark Ave
Las Vegas, NV 89117-4626
Personality V: 01/12/96

Bobko, Karol J
NASA/LBJ Space Center
Houston, TX 77058
Astronaut V: 03/03/96

Bochco, Steven
694 Amalfi Dr
Pacific Palisades, CA 90272
Producer V: 02/25/96

Bochner, Lloyd
42 Haldeman Rd
Santa Monica, CA 90402
Actor V: 06/14/96

Bodemann, Joe
Bodemann GmbH
Meinholz 1
3174 Meine, Germany
Animal Trainer V: 03/20/96

Bodine, Geoff
c/o Geoff Bodine Racing
6007 Victory Lane
Harrisburg, NC 28075
NASCAR Driver V: 03/02/96

Bodine, Todd
NASCAR
1811 Volusia Ave
Daytona Beach, FL 32015
NASCAR Driver V: 03/14/96

Boeing Company
Historical Archives m/s 1R-24
PO Box 3707
Seattle, WA 98124-2207
Archive V: 03/20/96

Boesak, Dr Allen
PO Box 316
Kasselsvlei 7533
South Africa
Politician V: 02/12/96

Bellville South
Cape Town, South Africa
Alternate V: 04/22/96

Bogarde, Dirk
Jonathan Alteras
27 Floral St
London C2E 9DP, England
Actor V: 11/01/96

c/o ICM
76 Oxford St
London W1N 0AX, England
Alternate V: 11/01/96

Bogdanovich, Peter
12451 Mulholland Dr
Beverly Hills, CA 90210-1336
Director V: 01/21/96

Boggs, Wade
6006 Windham Place
Tampa, FL 33647-1149
Baseball Star V: 01/10/96

Boggus, Suzy
33 Music Sq W-2nd Fl #110
Nashville, TN 37203-3326
Singer V: 01/12/96

Bogosian, Eric
230 Elizabeth St
New York, NY 10012
Actor V: 01/21/96

145 Hudson St-#95W
New York, NY 10013-2103
Alternate V: 03/14/96

Bohay, Heidi
48 Main St
S Bound Brook, NJ 08880
Actress V: 10/03/96

Bohm, Uwe
ZBF Agentur
Leopoldstrasse 19
8000 Munchen 40, Germany
Actor V: 02/11/96

Boitano, Brian
101 First St #370
Los Altos, CA 94022
Ice Skater V: 01/20/96

Bolden Jr, Charles F
NASA/LBJ Space Center
Hoston, TX 77058
Astronaut V: 06/06/96

Boldon, Ato
PO Box 3703
Santa Cruz, Trinidad
West Indies
Olympian V: 01/13/97

Bolle, Frank
King Features
216 E 45th St
New York, NY 10017
Cartoonist V: 03/11/96

Bollettieri, Nick
5500 34th St
W Bradenton, FL 34210
Tennis Coach V: 11/01/96

Bolling, Tiffany
c/o Casares
12483 Braddock Dr
Los Angeles, CA 90066
Actress V: 02/25/96

10653 Riverside Dr
Toluca Lake, CA 91602
Alternate V: 03/02/96

Bologna, Joseph
16830 Ventura Bl #326
Encino, CA 991436
Actor V: 06/14/96

415 N Camden Dr #121
Beverly Hills, CA 90210
Alternate V: 02/12/96

Bolton, Michael
c/o Levin
130 W 57th St #10-B
New York, NY 10019
Singer V: 10/10/96

MB Foundation
PO Box 936
Branford, CT 06405
Alternate V: 01/07/96

201 W 85th St #15A
New York, NY 10024
Forwarded V: 02/26/96

c/o Fan Emporium
PO Box 679
Branford, CT 06405
Forwarded V: 01/07/96

Bombeck, Erma
The LA Times
Times Mirror Square
Los Angeles, CA 90053
Author V: 02/16/96

Bon Jovi
Bon Jovi Mgmt
250 W 57th St #603
New York, NY 10107
Singer V: 10/23/96

Bonaduce, Danny
5740 Sunnycrest Dr
W Bloomfield, MI 48323-3069
Actor V: 01/10/97

Bond, Julian
361 Westview Drive SW
Atlanta, GA 30310
Politician V: 03/10/96

Bond, Steve
14050 Marquosas Way
Marina del Ray, CA 90292
Actor V: 11/01/96

Bond, Tommy 'Butch'
14704 Road 36
Madera, CA 93638
Actor V: 09/09/96

Bonerz, Peter
3637 Lowry Road
Los Angeles, CA 90027
Actor V: 06/14/96

Bonet, Lisa
Progressive Artists
400 S Beverly Dr #216
Beverly Hills, CA 90212
Actress V: 12/13/96

22764 Chamera Lane
Topanga, CA 90290
Alternate V: 02/26/96

Bonham-Carter, Helena
18/21 Jeromy St
London SW1Y 6HB, England
Actress V: 03/15/96

Bonnett, Neil
NASCAR
1811 Volusia Ave
Daytona Beach, FL 32015
NASCAR Announcer V: 03/02/96

Bonnie Black Talent
4660 Cahuenga Bl-#306
Toluka Lake, CA 91602
Talent Agency V: 11/11/96

Bono, Chastity
11825 Kling St
N Hollywood, CA 91607-4009
Celebrity V: 11/01/96

4453 Stern Ave
Sherman Oaks, CA 91423
Alternate V: 02/26/96

PO Box 960
Beverly Hills, CA 90212-0960
Forwarded V: 01/11/97

Bono, Sonny
1700 N Indian Dr
Palm Springs, CA 92262
Politician V: 04/02/96

1555 E Palm Canyon Dr #G101
Palm Springs, CA 92264
Alternate V: 01/13/97

Bonsall, Brian
Rosson Agency
11712 Moorpark St #216
Studio City, CA 91604
Actor V: 05/06/96

Boone, Debby
4334 Kester Ave
Sherman Oaks, CA 91423
Singer V: 02/28/96

Boone, Pat
904 N Beverly Dr
Beverly Hills, CA 90210
Singer V: 01/31/96

Boosler, Elayne
11061 Wrightwood Lane
Studio City, CA 91604
Actress V: 04/14/96

Booth, George
PO Box 1539
Stony Brook, NY 11790
Cartoonist V: 01/21/96

Boothe, Powers
23629 Long Valley Rd
Hidden Hills, CA 91302
Actor V: 03/01/96

Bop Magazine
3500 West Olive Ave #850
Burbank, CA 91505
Publisher V: 02/10/96

Borge, Victor
Fieldpoint Park
Greenwich, CT 06830
Comedy Star V: 03/04/96

Gurtman & Murtha
162 W 56th St
New York, NY 10019
Alternate V: 01/31/96

Borgman, Jim
King Features
216 E 45th St
New York, NY 10017
Cartoonist V: 03/11/96

Borinstein-Oreck-Bogart
8271 Melrose Ave #110
Los Angeles, CA 90046
Talent Agency V: 04/27/96

Boris Karloff Enterprises
Sarah Karloff
PO Box 2424
Rancho Mirage, CA 92270
Friends of Karloff V: 01/20/96

Borman, Frank
NASA/LBJ Space Center
Houston, TX 77058
Astronaut V: 11/20/96

Borman, Frank, Cont.
205 W Boutz Rd
Bldg 4/Suite 4
Las Cruces, NM 88003
Forwarded V: 05/04/96

Bosley, Tom
Burton Moss Agency
8827 Beverly Bl #L
Los Angeles, CA 90048
Actor V: 12/01/96

Bosson, Barbara
694 Amalfi Dr
Pacific Palisades, CA 90272
Actress V: 03/02/96

Paradigm Agency
10100 Santa Monica Bl-25th Fl
Los Angeles, CA 90067
Alternate V: 12/13/96

Bostick, Richard
Sabco Racing
PO Box 560579
Charlotte, NC 27317
NASCAR Crew V: 03/26/96

Boston Bruins
Boston Garden
150 Causeway St
Boston, MA 02114
Team Office V: 01/31/96

Boston Celtics
151 Merrimac St
Boston, MA 02114
Team Office V: 02/15/96

Boston Red Sox
Fenway Park
24 Yawkey Way
Boston, MA 02215
Team Office V: 02/01/96

Bostwick, Barry
2770 Hutton Dr
Beverly Hills, CA 90210
Actor V: 11/11/96

Gersh Agency
232 N Canon Dr
Beverly Hills, CA 90210
Alternate V: 12/09/96

Bosworth, Brian
10000 Santa Monica Bl #305
Los Angeles, CA 90067
Actor V: 12/03/96

Bottoms, Sam
4719 Willowcrest Ave
N Hollywood, CA 91602
Actor V: 02/04/96

c/o Badgley Connor
9229 Sunset Bl #311
Los Angeles, CA 90069
Alternate V: 12/04/96

Bottoms, Timothy
Bresler/Kelly
15760 Ventura Bl #1730
Encino, CA 91436
Actor V: 12/06/96

532 Hot Springs Road
Santa Barbara, CA 93108
Alternate V: 06/14/96

Bow, Chuck
1811 Volusia Ave
Daytona Beach, FL 32015
NASCAR Driver V: 03/02/96

Bowe, Riddick
2025 Pennsylvania Ave NW #619
Washington, DC 20006
Boxing Star V: 11/01/96

Bower, Antoinette
1529 N Beverly Glen
Los Angeles, CA 90077
Actress V: 01/10/97

Bowerman, Bill
1 Bowerman Dr
Beaverton, OR 97005
Track Coach V: 01/13/97

Bowersox, Kenneth D
NASA/LBJ Space Center
Houston, TX 77058
Astronaut V: 06/06/96

Bowie, David
641 5th Ave #22Q
New York, NY 10022
Musician V: 06/06/96

Bowman, Christopher
5653 Kester Ave
Van Nuys, CA 91411
Actor V: 02/11/96

Boxcar Willie
HCR 1 Box 708-5
Branson, MO 65616
Singer V: 01/20/96

Boxer, Barbara
307 Cannon House Office Bldg
Washington, DC 20515
Politician V: 10/04/96

Boxleitner, Bruce
24500 John Colter Rd
Hidden Hills, CA 91302
Actor V: 03/21/96

PO Box 5513
Sherman Oaks, CA 91403
Alternate V: 07/03/96

151 El Camino Dr
Beverly Hills, CA 90212
Forwarded V: 02/05/96

Babylon Productions
8615 Tamarack Ave
Sun Valley, CA 91352
Forwarded V: 01/14/96

Boy George
7 Pepys Court
84 The Chase, Clapham
London SW4 0NF, England
Singer V: 05/06/96

Boyle, Lara Flynn
606 N Larchmont Bl #309
Los Angeles, CA 90004
Actress V: 03/03/96

Boyle, Peter
40 W 57th St
New York, NY 10019
Actor V: 02/23/96

Innovative Artists
1999 Ave of the Stars #2850
Los Angeles, CA 90067
Alternate V: 12/11/96

Boyz II Men
Motown Records
5750 Wilshire Bl #300
Los Angeles, CA 90036-3697
Musical Group V: 08/29/96

Brabham, Jack
33 Central Rd, Worcester Park
Surrey KT4 8EG England
Race Driver V: 02/13/96

Bracco, Lorraine
130 W 57th St #5E
New York, NY 10019
Actress V: 10/23/96

Bracken, Eddie
18 Fulton St
Weehauken, NJ 07087
Actor V: 03/21/96

Bradley, Ed
524 W 57th St
New York, NY 10019
Journalist V: 02/23/96

Bradley, James
1555 Riverside Dr #4
Glendale, CA 91201
Actor V: 02/27/96

Bradley, Tom
605 S Irving Bl
New York, NY 90005
Politician V: 02/23/96

Bradshaw, Terry
c/o TBFC
8911 Shady Lane Dr
Shreveport, LA 71118
Football Star V: 10/26/96

Rt 1-Box 227
Gordonville, TX 76245
Alternate V: 01/12/96

PO Box 1607
Shreveport, LA 71165
Alternate V: 06/13/96

Brady, Charles E
NASA/LBJ Space Center
Houston, TX 77058
Astronaut V: 02/02/96

Braeden, Eric
13723 Romany Drive
Pacific Palisades, CA 90272
Actor V: 06/14/96

Braga, Sonia
295 Greenwich St #11B
New York, NY 10007-1053
Actress V: 06/17/96

Branagh, Kenneth
302-308 Regent St
London W1R 5AL, England
Actor V: 10/23/96

Wm Morris Agency
151 El Camino Dr
Beverly Hills, CA 90212
Alternate V: 01/14/96

Brand, Vance D
NASA/LBJ Space Center
Houston, TX 77058
Astronaut V: 03/03/96

Brand Model & Talent
17941 Skypark Circle-Suite F
Irvine, CA 92714
Talent Agency V: 11/11/96

Brandauer, Klaus Maria
Fischerndorf 76
8992 Altausse, Austria
Actor V: 06/06/96

Brandenstein, Daniel C
NASA/LBJ Space Center
Houston, TX 77058
Astronaut V: 03/03/96

Brandis, Jonathan
Gersh Agency
232 N Canon Dr
Beverly Hills, CA 90210
Actor V: 01/10/96

Brando, Marlon
c/o ICM
8942 Wilshire Bl
Beverly Hills, CA 90211
Actor V: 1/15/96

1 E 62nd St
New York, NY 10021
Alternate V: 12/28/96

Brandt, Volker
Fasanenstrasse 29
1000 Berlin 15, Germany
Actor V: 02/11/96

Brandywine, Marcia
743 Huntley Dr
Los Angeles, CA 90069
Actress V: 03/05/96

Branigan, Laura
310 E 65th St
New York, NY 10021
Singer V: 10/10/96

1700 Broadway #500
New York, NY 10019
Alternate V: 03/13/96

Braverman, Bart
524 N Laurel Ave
Los Angeles, CA 900482
Actor V: 02/21/96

Bravo Network
150 Crossways Park West
Woodbury, NY 11797
Production Office V: 11/11/96

Bregman, Martin
Bregman Productions
641 Lexington Ave
New York, NY 10022
Producer V: 01/20/96

Bregman Productions
Martin Bregman
Universal Studios
Universal City, CA 91608
Production Office V: 03/17/96

Bremer, Lucille
925 North Rd
Belmont, CA 94002-2031
Actress V: 01/12/96

Brennan, Eileen
c/o Shapira
15301 Ventura Bl #345
Sherman Oaks, CA 91403
Actress V: 02/12/96

Brennan, Melissa
6520 Platt Ave #634
West Hills, CA 91307-3218
Actress V: 11/01/96

Brenner, Dori
Innovative Artists
1999 Ave of the Stars #2850
Los Angeles, CA 90067
Actress V: 02/12/96

Bresee, Bobbie
PO Box 1222
Los Angeles, CA 90078
Actress V: 02/24/96

Bresler/Kelly & Assoc
15760 Ventura Bl #1730
Encino, CA 91436
Talent Agency V: 05/13/96

Brest, Martin
831 Paseo Miramar
Pacific Palisades, CA 90272
Director V: 02/21/96

Brett, George
PO Box 419969
Kansas City, MO 64141
Baseball Star V: 12/05/96

Brewer, Teresa
394 Pinebrook Pl
New Rochelle, NY 10803
Singer V: 05/13/96

Brewis Agency
12429 Laurel Terrace Dr
Studio City, CA 91604
Talent Agency V: 06/13/96

Brialy, Jean-Claude
Theatres Boufles/Parisian
4 rue Monsigny
75002 Paris, France
Actor V: 12/14/96

Brice, Pierre
Olga Horstig-Primuz
78 ave Champs-Elysees
F-75008 Paris, France
Actor V: 12/17/96

Brickell, Beth
PO Box 26
Paron, AR 72122-0026
Actress V: 01/21/96

Brickman, Morrie
King Features
235 East 45th St
New York, NY 10017
Cartoonist V: 12/17/96

Bridges, Beau
5525 N Jed Smith Rd
Hidden Hills, CA 91302
Actor V: 02/11/96

Creative Artists Agency
9830 Wilshire Bl
Beverly Hills, CA 90212
Alternate V: 12/07/96

Bridges, Jeff
c/o CAA
9830 Wilshire Bl
Beverly Hills, CA 90212
Actor V: 01/02/96

11661 San Vicente Bl #910
Los Angeles, CA 90049
Alternate V: 09/09/96

985 Hot Springs Rd
Montecito, CA 93108
Forwarded V: 01/15/96

Bridges, Lloyd
Wm Morris Agency
151 El Camino Dr
Beverly Hills, CA 90212
Actor V: 03/09/96

225 Loring Ave
Los Angeles, CA 90024
Alternate V: 03/12/96

Bridges Jr, Roy D
6510th Test Wing/CC
Edwards AFB, CA 93523-5000
Astronaut V: 12/17/96

NASA/LBJ Space Center
Houston, TX 77058
Alternate V: 03/03/96

Briers, Richard
c/o Hamilton
24 Denmark St
London WC2H 8NA, England
Actor V: 12/20/96

Briggs, Joe Bob
PO Box 2002
Dallas, TX 75221
Critic V: 01/20/96

Brill, Charlie
3635 Wrightwood Dr
Studio City, CA 91604
Actor V: 02/20/96

Brimley, Wilford
B-7 Ranch, 1000 North
Nehi, VT 84043
Actor V: 11/01/96

Blake Agency
415 N Camden Dr #121
Beverly Hills, CA 90210
Alternate V: 12/06/96

Brinegar, Paul
17322 Halsey St
Granada Hill, CA 91344
Actor V: 12/04/96

Brinkley, Christie
Wm Morris Agency
151 El Camino
Beverly Hills, CA 90212
Model V: 01/14/96

2124 Broadway #104
New York, NY 10023-1722
Alternate V: 11/01/96

Brinkley, Christie, Cont.
CB Inc
459 Columbus Ave #200
New York, NY 10024
Alternate V: 11/01/96

344 E 59th St
New York, NY 10022
Forwarded V: 11/11/96

Brinkley, David
NBC News
1717 DeSales St NW
Washington, DC 20036-4401
Commentator V: 02/21/96

British Ambassador
British Govt Offices
845 3rd Ave
New York, NY 10022
Politician V: 03/11/96

Britt, Mai
PO Box 525
Zephyr Cove, NV 89448
Actress V: 01/02/96

Brittany, Morgan
Agency For Performing Arts
9000 Sunset Bl #1200
Los Angeles, CA 90069
Actress V: 12/02/96

3434 Cornell Rd
Agoura Hills, CA 91301
Alternate V: 03/02/96

Britton, Tony
c/o Agency
388-396 Oxford St
London W1 9HE, England
Actor V: 03/20/96

Broderick, Beth
Kohner Agency
9300 Wilshire Bl #555
Beverly Hills, CA 90212-3211
Actress V: 03/14/96

Broderick, Matthew
c/o CAA
9830 Wilshire Bl
Beverly Hills, CA 90212
Actor V: 01/14/96

17 Charleston St
New York, NY 10014
Alternate V: 03/14/96

Brody, Lane
PO Box 24775
Nashville, TN 37202
Singer V: 01/17/97

Brokaw, Tom
NBC-TV
30 Rockefeller Plaza
New York, NY 10112
Correspondant V: 01/14/96

Brolin, James
c/o Selnick
PO Box 56927
Sherman Oaks, CA 91413-1927
Actor V: 11/01/96

August Entertainment
838 N Fairfax Ave
Los Angeles, CA 90046
Alternate V: 01/14/96

Brolin, Josh
c/o Selznick
PO Box 56924
Sherman Oaks, CA 91413-1927
Actor V: 11/10/96

Bromfield, John
PO Box 2655
Lake Havasu City, AZ 86405-2655
Actor V: 11/01/96

Bron, Eleanor
Schoen Agency
606 N Larchmont Bl #309
Los Angeles, CA 90004
Actress V: 12/13/96

Bronson, Charles
3210 Retreat Ct
Malibu, CA 90263
Actor V: 01/31/96

PO Box 2644
Malibu, CA 90265
Alternate V: 02/02/96

Wm Morris Agency
151 El Camino Dr
Beverly Hills, CA 90212
Forwarded V: 02/26/96

Brookes, Jacqueline
Wm Morris Agency
151 El Camino Dr
Beverly Hills, CA 90212
Actress V: 12/12/96

Brookins, Gary
King Features
235 East 45th St
New York, NY 10017
Cartoonist V: 03/02/96

Brooks, Albert
Scotti Brothers
2114 Pico Bl
Santa Monica, CA 90405
Actor V: 04/04/96

1880 Century Park E #900
Los Angeles, CA 90067
Alternate V: 01/03/97

Brooks, Avery
c/o Cunningham
10635 Santa Monica Bl #130
Los Angeles, CA 90025
Actor V: 01/20/96

Star Trek-DS9
5555 Melrose Ave
Hollywood, CA 90036
Alternate V: 02/23/96

Innovative Artists
1999 Ave of the Stars #2850
Los Angeles, CA 90067
Forwarded V: 02/23/96

LC Productions
PO Box 93-1198
Los Angeles, CA 90093
Forwarded V: 01/31/96

Brooks, Foster
315 S Beverly Dr #216
Los Angeles, CA 90036
Actor V: 01/11/97

Brooks, Garth
New Generation
128 15th Ave N
Nashville, TN 37203
Singer V: 02/28/96

1109 17th Ave S
Nashville, TN 37212
Alternate V: 05/21/96

Brooks, Mel
c/o CAA
9830 Wilshire Bl
Beverly Hills, CA 90212
Producer V: 01/14/96

Brooks, Mel, Cont.
2301 La Mesa Dr
Santa Monica, CA 90405
Alternate V: 02/24/96

Brooksfilm
PO Box 900
Beverly Hills, CA 90213
Forwarded V: 02/22/96

Brooks, Rand
662 Juniper Pl
Franklin Lakes, NJ 07417
Actor V: 02/01/96

Brooks, Randi
11726 San Vicente Bl #900
Beverly Hills, CA 90212
Actress V: 02/24/96

Brooks & Dunn
PO Box 120669
Nashville, CA 37212-0669
Musical Group V: 11/01/96

Brophy, Kevin
15010 Hamlin St
Van Nuys, CA 91411
Actor V: 02/03/96

Brosnan, Pierce
Creative Artists Agency
9830 Wilshire Bl
Beverly Hills, CA 90212
Actor V: 12/07/96

Int'l FC
23852 PC Hwy #007
Malibu, CA 90265
Alternate V: 11/01/96

UA/Monroe House
40-42 King St
London WC2E 8JS, England
Forwarded V: 02/10/96

Eon Productions
2 South Audley St
London W1Y 6AJ, England
Forwarded V: 02/26/96

Brothers, Dr Joyce
Wm Morris Agency
151 El Camino
Beverly Hills, CA 90212
Psychologist V: 12/12/96

1530 Palisades Ave
Ft Lee, NJ 07024
Alternate V: 03/06/96

Brothers Four
1221 Scott Rd
Burbank, CA 91504
Musical Group V: 10/23/96

Broussard, Rebecca
15760 Ventura Bl #1730
Encino, CA 91436
Actress V: 02/12/96

Brown, Blair
c/o ICM
8942 Wilshire Bl
Beverly Hills, CA 90211
Actress V: 12/11/96

Brown, Bobby
1324 Thomas Pl
Fort Worth, TX 76107
Singer V: 11/18/96

3358 Peachtree Rd NE
Atlanta, GA 30326
Alternate V: 02/25/96

Brown, Bryan
Creative Artists Agency
9830 Wilshire Bl
Beverly Hills, CA 90212
Actor V: 12/07/96

Brown, Clancy
Paradigm Agency
10100 Santa Monica Bl-25th Fl
Los Angeles, CA 90067
Actor V: 12/13/96

Brown, Danny J
PO Box 1531
Tampa, FL 33801
War Hero V: 03/17/96

Brown, Dee
c/o Boston Celtics
Boston Gardens
Boston, MA 02114
Basketball Star V: 03/01/96

Brown, Georg Stanford
2565 Greenvalley Rd
Los Angeles, CA 90046-1437
Actor V: 11/10/96

c/o Schechter
9300 Wilshire Bl #410
Beverly Hills, CA 90212
Alternate V: 03/01/96

Brown, Helen Gurley
One West 81st St #22D
New York, NY 10024
Author V: 03/06/96

Brown, James
1217 W Medical Park Rd
Augusta, GA 30909
Singer V: 01/21/96

Alfie Entertainment
6290 Sunset Bl #900
Hollywood, CA 90028
Alternate V: 01/21/96

Brown, Jerry
We The People
200 Harrison St
Oakland, CA 94607
Politician V: 01/13/97

Brown, Julie
Wm Morris Agency
151 El Camino
Beverly Hills, CA 90212
Actress V: 12/12/96

Brown, Julie Caitlan
Amsel/Eisenstadt & Frazier
6310 San Vicente Bl #401
Los Angeles, CA 90048
Actress V: 12/15/96

Brown, Kimberlin
c/o Pelzer
9220 Sunset Bl #230
Los Angeles, CA 90069
Actress V: 10/23/96

Brown, Les
1417 Capri Dr
Pacific Palisades, CA 90272-2706
Band Conductor V: 01/12/96

Brown, Mark N
NASA/LBJ Space Center
Hoston, TX 77058
Astronaut V: 06/06/94

Brown, Olivia
5856 College Ave #139
Oakland, CA 94618
Actress V: 04/20/96

Brown, Peter
House of Representatives
9911 Pico Bl #1060
Los Angeles, CA 90035
Actor V: 12/10/96

Brown, Peter, Cont.
852 Cypress Ave
Hermosa Beach, CA 90254
Alternate V: 02/19/96

Brown, Ruth
600 W 165th St #4H
New York, NY 10032
Singer V: 02/19/96

Brown, Sawyer
4219 Hillsboro Rd #318
Nashville, TN 37215
Singing Group V: 11/01/96

Brown Jr, Curtis L
NASA/LBJ Space Center
Houston, TX 77058
Astronaut V: 02/02/96

Browne, Chance
King Features
216 E 45th St
New York, NY 10017
Cartoonist V: 03/11/96

Browne, Dick
King Features
235 E 45th St
New York, NY 10017
Cartoonist V: 06/03/96

Browne, Jackson
c/o CAA
9830 Wilshire Bl
Beverly Hills, CA 90212
Singer V: 01/14/96

12746 Kling St
Studio City, CA 91604-1125
Alternate V: 11/01/96

3208 Cahuenga Bl W #108
Los Angeles, CA 90068
Alternate V: 01/15/96

Browne, Roscoe Lee
c/o Smith
121 N San Vicente Bl
Beverly Hills, CA 90211
Actor V: 02/10/96

Brubeck, Dave
221 Millstone Road
Wilton, CT 06807
Composer V: 11/01/96

Bruni, Carla
10 Place de la Concorde
Paris F-75008 France
Model V: 11/01/96

Brunt, Jennifer
c/o Elite
111 East 22nd St
New York, NY 10010
Model V: 01/20/96

Bryan, Zackery Ty
Innovative Artists
1999 Ave of the Stars #2850
Los Angeles, CA 90067
Actor V: 12/11/96

Bucha, Paul W
8 Autumn Ridge Rd
S Salem, NY 10590-9801
War Hero V: 02/01/96

Buchanan, Jensen
196 Columbia Heights
Brooklyn, NY 11021
Actress V: 09/09/96

Buchholz, Horst
Clavdoiras
CH-7078 Lenzerheide
Switzerland
Actor V: 03/17/96

Buchli, Jim
NASA/LBJ Space Center
Hoston, TX 77058
Astronaut V: 06/07/96

Buchwald & Associates
9229 Sunset Bl #710
Los Angeles, CA 90069
Talent Agency V: 07/20/96

Buckley, Betty
Wm Morris
151 El Camino
Beverly Hills, CA 90212
Actress V: 11/27/96

Buckley, William F
National Review
150 E 35th St
New York, NY 10016
Author V: 05/12/96

Budge, Don
PO Box 789
Dingmans Ferry, PA 18328
Tennis Star V: 02/17/96

Buena Vista
500 S Buena Vista St #5064
Burbank, CA 91521
Production Office V: 11/01/96

Buffalo Bills
One Bills Dr
Orchard Park, NY 14127
Team Office V: 05/15/96

Buffalo Sabres
Memorial Auditorium
Buffalo, NY 14202
Team Office V: 01/31/96

Buffett, Jimmy
HK Mgmt
80 Universal City Plaza #401
Universal City, CA 91608
Singer V: 10/23/96

Margaritaville
424 A Flemming St
Keywest, FL 33040
Alternate V: 11/01/96

500 Duval St Suite B
Key West, FL 33040-6553
Forwarded V: 02/17/96

Bujold, Genevieve
27258 Pacific Coast Hwy
Malibu, CA 90265
Actress V: 06/21/96

Bull, John S
NASA/LBJ Space Center
Houston, TX 77058
Astronaut V: 03/03/96

Bull, Richard
750 N Rush St #3401
Chicago, IL 60611-2543
Actor V: 11/01/96

651 N Wilcox #3G
Los Angeles, CA 90036
Alternate V: 02/17/96

Bullock, Dona
Artists Agency
10000 Santa Monica Bl #305
Los Angeles, CA 90067
Actress V: 11/01/96

Bullock, Jim J
201 S Mansfield Ave
Los Angeles, CA 90036-3016
Actor V: 01/12/96

Bullock, Jim J. Cont.
1015 Kings Rd #215
Los Angeles, CA 90069
Forwarded V: 02/20/96

Bullock, Sandra
c/o UTA
9560 Wilshire Bl-Ste 500
Beverly Hills, CA 90212
Actress V: 12/01/96

335 N Maple Dr #270
Beverly Hills, CA 90212
Alternate V: 11/01/96

368 N Gardner St
Los Angeles, CA 90036
Forwarded V: 11/01/96

Bunning, Jim
30 Winston Hill Rd
Ft Thomas, KY 41076
Baseball Star V: 01/20/96

Burbage, Cornell
PL Dunbar High School
1600 Man O War Bl
Lexington, KY 40513
Football Star V: 01/13/97

Burbank Studios
4000 Warner Bl
Burbank, CA 91522
Production Office V: 03/17/96

Burdon, Eric
Blumenauer Artists
11846 Balboa Ave #204
Granada Hills, CA 91344
Singer V: 05/06/96

Burford, Chris
PO Box 5168
Walnut Creek, CA 94596
Football Star V: 02/15/96

377 2nd Tee Dr
Incline Village, NV 89451
Alternate V: 02/16/96

Burford, Thomas
20 Sunnyside Ave-Suite A241
Mill Valley, CA 94941-1928
Publisher V: 01/01/97

Burger, Eugene
1260 N Dearborn Pkwy #105
Chicago, IL 60610
Magician V: 04/17/96

Burghoff, Gary
9911 W Pico Bl #1200
Los Angeles, CA 90035
Actor V: 01/15/96

Burke, Alfred
c/o Jameson
219 The Plaza-535 Kings Rd
London SW10 0SZ, England
Actor V: 03/20/96

Burke, Delta
427 N Canon Dr #215
Beverly Hills, CA 90210
Actress V: 12/10/96

1290 Inverness Dr
Pasadena, CA 91103
Alternate V: 03/02/96

Burke, Paul
2217 Avenida Caballeros
Palm Springs, CA 92262
Actor V: 05/22/96

Burke, Sean
Hartford Whalers
1 Civic Center Dr
Hartford, CT 06103
Hockey Star V: 04/05/96

Burkett Talent
12 Hughes St Suite D-100
Irvine, CA 92718
Talent Agency V: 07/20/96

Burkley, Dennis
5145 Costello Ave
Sherman Oaks, CA 91403
Actor V: 02/15/96

Burnett, Carol
PO Box 1298
S Pasadena, CA 91031-1298
Actress V: 02/12/96

General Delivery
Kapalua Estates
Lahaina, HI 96761
Forwarded V: 06/19/96

Burns, Gere
232 N Canon Dr
Beverly Hills, CA 90210
Actor V: 12/09/96

PO Box 3596
Mammoth Lakes, CA 93546-3596
Alternate V: 03/14/96

Bursch, Daniel W
NASA/LBJ Space Center
Houston, TX 77058
Astronaut V: 03/03/96

Burstyn, Ellen
Creative Artists Agency
9830 Wilshire Bl
Beverly Hills, CA 90212
Actress V: 12/07/96

PO Box 217
Palisades, NY 10964-0217
Alternate V: 12/02/96

Burton, LeVar
Star Trek
TNG Paramount
5555 Melrose Ave
Hollywood, CA 90038
Actor V: 09/03/96

13417 Inwood Dr
Sherman Oaks, CA 91423
Alternate V: 04/01/96

Peaceful Warrior
13601 Ventura Bl #209
Sherman Oaks, CA 91432
Forwarded V: 12/03/95

Burton, Tim
837 E Sunrise Bl-Suite G
Long Beach, CA 90806-3250
Director V: 09/09/96

Burton, Wendell
6526 Costello Dr
Van Nuys, CA 91401
Actor V: 02/16/96

Burton Agency
1450 Belfast Dr
Los Angeles, CA 90069
Talent Agency V: 11/21/96

Busey, Gary
18424 Coastline Dr
Malibu, CA 90265
Actor V: 11/01/96

c/o Moress
12424 Wilshire Bl #840
Los Angeles, CA 90025
Alternate V: 02/12/96

Busfield, Timothy
Wm Morris
151 El Camino
Beverly Hills, CA 90212
Actor V: 01/14/96

2416 G St-Suite D
Sacramento, CA 95816
Alternate V: 09/09/96

Bush, Barbara
PO Box 79798
Houston, TX 77279-9798
Former 1st Lady V: 01/30/96

1000 Memorial Dr
Houston, TX 77024
Alternate V: 01/30/96

9 West Oak Dr
Houston, TX 77056
Alternate V: 01/30/96

Bush, George
PO Box 79798
Houston, TX 77279-9798
Former President V: 02/04/96

1000 Memorial Dr
Houston, TX 77024
Alternate V: 03/04/96

9 West Oak Dr
Houston, TX 77056
Alternate V: 03/04/96

PO Box 12404
Austin, TX 78711
Forwarded V: 01/12/97

Buthelezi, Mangosuthu G
Private Bag XO1, Ulundi 3838
Kwazulu, South Africa
Politician V: 01/02/96

Butler, Brett
c/o ICM
8942 Wilshire Bl
Beverly Hills, CA 90211
Actress V: 01/14/96

PO Box 5617
Beverly Hills, CA 90213
Alternate V: 01/12/96

Butler, Dean
6220 Rodgerton Dr
Los Angeles, CA 90068
Actor V: 02/16/96

Buttons, Red
778 Tortuosa Way
Los Angeles, CA 90077
Actor V: 02/22/96

Buzzi, Ruth
Amsel/Eisenstadt
6310 San Vicente Bl #407
Los Angeles, CA 90048
Actress V: 02/20/96

2309 Malaga Rd
Los Angeles, CA 90068
Alternate V: 01/13/97

Byner, John
5863 Ramirez Canyon Rd
Malibu, CA 90265
Actor V: 06/20/96

Pecoraro Productions
3680 Madrid St
Las Vegas, NV 89121
Alternate V: 09/09/96

Byrd, Charlie
764 Fairview Ave E
Annapolis, MD 21403
Musician V: 01/15/96

Byrne, David
7964 Willow Glen Rd
Los Angeles, CA 90046
Singer V: 02/16/96

Byrnes, Edd
PO Box 1623
Beverly Hills, CA 90213
Actor V: 06/20/96

Byrnes, Jim
Cannell Productions
7083 Hollywood Bl
Hollywood, CA 90028
Actor V: 03/23/96

C

C I Inc Talent
843 N Sycamore Ave
Los Angeles, CA 90038
Talent Agency V: 03/22/94

C'est La Vie
7507 Sunset Bl #201
Los Angeles, CA 90046
Talent Agency V: 02/28/96

C-Span
400 N Capitol St NW #650
Washington, DC 20001
Network HQ V: 10/04/96

CALIFORNIA DREAMS
NBC Studios
3000 W Alemeda
Burbank, CA 91523
Production Office V: 01/20/96

CAN'T HURRY LOVE
CBS Ent Prod/TriStar TV
4024 Radford Ave-Bldg 9
Studio City, CA 91604
Production Office V: 10/23/96

CAROLINE IN THE CITY
NBC-TV
30 Rockefeller Plaza
New York, NY 10112
Production Office V: 12/15/96

CARYL&MARILYN:REAL FRIENDS
Sunset Blvd Theatre
6230 Sunset Bl
Hollywood, CA 90028
Production Office V: 11/11/96

CBC-TV
Box 500, Station A
Toronto, Ontario, M5W 1E6 Canada
Production Office V: 02/09/96

CBN Cable Network
CBN Center
Virginia Beach, VA 23463
Network HQ V: 03/01/96

CBS NEWS
CBS Broadcast Center
524 West 57th St
New York, NY 10019
Production Office V: 10/23/96

CBS STORYBREAK
CBS-TV
7800 Beverly Bl
Los Angeles, CA 90036
Production Office V: 03/12/96

CBS-TV
c/o Programming
51 W 52nd St
New York, NY 10019
Production Office V: 03/01/96

CBS-TV, Cont.
c/o Programming
7800 Beverly Bl
Los Angeles, CA 90036
Alternate V: 03/01/96

CBS/MTM Studios
4024 Radford
Studio City, CA 91604
Production Office V: 03/17/96

CED
10635 Santa Monica Bl #130
Los Angles, CA 90025
Talent Agency V: 11/11/96

CENTRAL PARK WEST
CBS-TV
41 E 11th St-6th Fl
New York, NY 10003
Production Office V: 10/23/96

CHARLIE GRACE
WB-Network
4000 Warner Bl
Burbank, CA 91522
Production Office V: 01/14/96

CHICAGO HOPE
Audience Services
PO Box 900
Beverly Hills, CA 90213
Production Office V: 12/15/96

CBS-TV
51 W 52nd St
New York, NY 10019
Alternate V: 12/15/96

CHICAGO SONS
NBC-TV
30 Rockefeller Plaza
New York, NY 10112
Audience Services V: 01/13/97

CLUELESS
Paramount Studios
5555 Melrose Ave/Modular Bldg #213
Los Angeles, CA 90035
Production Office V: 11/11/96

CNA & Associates
1801 Ave of the Stars #1250
Los Angeles, CA 90067
Talent Agency V: 02/01/96

CNBC
2200 Fletcher Ave
Ft Lee, NJ 07024
Production Office V: 12/15/96

CNI Cable News Int'l
25 Rue de Ponthieu
Paris 75098, France
Production Office V: 01/13/96

CNN Headline News
One CNN Center/POB 105366
Atlanta, GA 30348-5366
Production Office V: 01/14/96

COACH
Bungalow 78 Producers Bldg 78
100 Universal City Plaza
Universal City, CA 91608
Production Office V: 10/23/96

ABC-TV
77 W 66th St
New York, NY 10023
Alternate V: 12/15/96

COLUMBO
Universal TV
10201 W Pico Bl
Los Angeles, CA 90035
Production Office V: 12/15/96

Universal TV
70 Universal Plaza
Universal City, CA 91608
Alternate V: 01/16/96

COMMISH
Cannell Film
555 Brooksbank Ave
N Vancouver, BC V7J 3S5 Canada
Production Office V: 01/16/96

COMMON LAW
Warner TV
1438 N Gower
Hollywood, CA 90028
Viewer Services V: 11/11/96

COPS
Fox TV
5746 Sunset Bl
Los Angeles, CA 90069
Production Office V: 01/20/95

WB-TV
1438 N Gower
Hollywood, CA 90028
Audience Services V: 04/12/96

COSBY
CBS-TV
51 W 52nd St
New York, NY 10019
Viewer Services V: 11/11/96

Kaufman Astoria Studios
34-12 36th St
Queens, NY 11106
Alternate V: 12/15/96

COURTHOUSE
Columbia TV-Gable Bldg
10202 W Washington Bl-1st Fl
Culver City, CA 90232
Production Office V: 10/23/96

CRISIS CENTER
NBC-TV
30 Rockefeller Plaza
New York, NY 10112
Audience Services V: 01/13/97

CTV-TV
42 Charles St E
PO Box 740124
Toronto, Ont, M4Y 1T5 Canada
Production Office V: 02/09/96

CURRENT AFFAIR
30 Rockefeller Plaza
New York, NY 10112
Production Office V: 11/20/96

CYBILL
YBYL Productions
4024 Radford Ave, Bld 1, Rm 110
Studio City, CA 91604
Production Office V: 03/12/96

CBS-TV
51 W 52nd St
New York, NY 10019
Alternate V: 12/15/96

Caan, James
2029 Century Park E
Suite 500
Los Angeles, CA 90067
Actor V: 04/15/96

Cabana, Robert D
NASA/LBJ Space Center
Hoston, TX 77058
Astronaut V: 06/20/96

Cabin Fever Entertainment
100 W Putnam Ave
Greenwich, CT 06830
Production Office V: 12/10/96

Cable News Network WTBS
6430 Sunset Bl-6th Fl
Los Angeles, CA 90028
Production Office V: 03/17/96

Cable News WTBS
One CNN Center
PO Box 105366
Atlanta, GA 30348
Network HQ V: 03/01/96

Cadell, Ava
8033 Sunset Bl #661
Los Angeles, CA 90046
Actress V: 10/23/96

Cady, Frank
c/o Greenvine
110 E 9th St #C-1005
Los Angeles, CA 90079
Actor V: 06/14/96

Caesar, Sid
1910 Loma Vista Drive
Beverly Hills, CA 90210
Comedy Star V: 12/14/96

Cage, Nicholas
8033 W Sunset Bl #52
Los Angeles, CA 90046-2427
Actor V: 08/29/96

5647 Tryon
Los Angeles, CA 90068
Alternate V: 11/01/96

Cain, Dean
9830 Wilshire Bl
Beverly Hills, CA 90212
Actor V: 01/14/96

Centre Films
1103 N El Centro Ave
Los Angeles, CA 90038-2805
Alternate V: 11/10/96

1643 12th St #1
Santa Monica, CA 90404-3709
Alternate V: 11/01/96

11718 Barrington Ct #513
Los Angeles, CA 90049-2930
Forwarded V: 08/29/96

Caine, Michael
Rectory Farm House
N Stoke, Oxfordshire, England
Actor V: 12/20/96

Caine, Michael, Cont.
Allied Vision/Avon House
360-366 Oxford St
London W1N 9HA, England
Alternate V: 02/08/96

8942 Wilshire Bl
Beverly Hills, CA 90211
Forwarded V: 01/14/96

Calabro, Thomas
4109 Wilkinson Ave
Studio City, CA 91604
Actor V: 01/11/97

Calcavecchia, Mark
1005 Alamanda Dr
N Palm Beach, FL 33408
Golf Star V: 01/13/97

Caldwell, John
King Features
235 E 45th St
New York, NY 10017
Cartoonist V: 02/14/96

Caldwell, Zoe
Whitehead-Stevens
1501 Broadway
New York, NY 10036
Actress V: 10/23/96

Calfa, Don
c/o Sindell
8271 Melrose Ave #202
Los Angeles, CA 90046
Actor V: 03/20/96

Calgary Flames
Olympic Saddledome
PO Box 1540-Station M
Calgary, Alb, Canada T2P 3B9
Team Office V: 01/31/96

California Angels
PO Box 2000
Anaheim Stadium
Anaheim, CA 92803
Team Office V: 05/15/96

Call, Brandon
5918 Van Nuys Bl
Van Nuys, CA 91401
Actor V: 02/20/96

Callahan, John
342 N Alfred St
Los Angeles, CA 90048
Actor V: 02/19/96

Callan, Michael
1730 Camden Ave #201
Los Angeles, CA 90025
Actor V: 03/03/96

Calloway, Vanessa Bell
Gersh Agency
232 N Canon Dr
Beverly Hills, CA 90210
Actress V: 01/15/97

Calvert, Phylis
Argyll Lodge/Towersy
Thames, Oxon, England
Actress V: 06/20/96

Calvet, Corinne
Pacific Plaza Towers
1431 Ocean Ave #109
Santa Monica, CA 90401
Actress V: 11/01/96

Camacho, Hector "Macho"
4751 Yardarm Ln
Boynton Beach, FL 33436-1983
Boxing Star V: 01/12/96

Star Rd-Box 113
Clewiston, FL 33440
Alternate V: 01/31/96

Camden Talent
822 S Robertson Bl #200
Los Angeles, CA 90035
Talent Agency V: 12/12/96

Camel, Marvin
18331 Mansel Ave
Redondo Beach, CA 90278
Boxing Star V: 12/14/96

Cameron, Kenneth D
NASA/LBJ Space Center
Hoston, TX 77058
Astronaut V: 02/20/96

Cameron, Kirk
PO Box 8665
Calabasas, CA 91372-8665
Actor V: 11/10/96

c/o UTA
9560 Wilshire Bl-5th Fl
Beverly Hills, CA 90212
Alternate V: 03/01/96

23548 Calabasas Rd-#204
Calabasas, CA 91302
Forwarded V: 02/03/96

Cameron & Associates
8369 Sausalito Ave-Suite A
West Hills, CA 91304
Talent Agency V: 11/11/96

Camp, Colleen
Gersh Agency
232 N Canon Dr
Beverly Hills, CA 90210
Actress V: 12/09/96

2050 Fairburn Ave
Los Angeles, CA 90025-5914
Alternate V: 02/03/96

Campaneris, Bert
PO Box 8232
Scottsdale, AZ 85252
Baseball Star V: 01/20/96

Campbell, Bruce
14431 Ventura Bl #120
Sherman Oaks, CA 91423
Actor V: 01/20/96

212 Bell Canyon Rd
Bell Canyon, CA 91307-1110
Alternate V: 03/14/96

2508 Carmen Crest Dr
Los Angeles, CA 90068
Forwarded V: 11/11/96

5314 Alcove Ave
N Hollywood, CA 91607
Forwarded V: 03/15/96

Campbell, Glen
3500 E Lincoln Dr #6
Phoenix, AZ 85018-1010
Singer V: 12/15/96

Campbell, Naomi
Women Inc
107 Green St
New York, NY 10012
Model V: 01/07/96

Campbell, Neve
Performance Unlimited
3-2401 Cliffe St #201
Courtney, BC, Canada V9N 2L5
Actress V: 01/13/97

2700 Nielson Way #1235
Santa Monica, CA 90405
Alternate V: 11/11/96

Campbell, William
Dade/Shultz & Associates
11846 Ventura Bl #100
Studio City, CA 91064
Actor V: 12/08/96

21502 Velicata St
Woodland Hills, CA 91364
Alternate V: 03/13/96

Campion, Jane
Linstead Associates
9-13 Bronte Rd
Bondi Junction NSW
2022 Australia
Director V: 12/07/96

Canadian Broadcasting Corp
1500 Bronson Ave
Box 8478
Ottawa, Ont K1G 3J5, Canada
Archive V: 03/20/96

Canelli, Rick
c/o Chesrown Chevrolet
7300 Broadway
Denver, CO 80221
NASCAR Driver V: 03/26/96

Caninenberg, Hans
Maria-Eich-Strasse 43
8032 Grafelfing, Germany
Actor V: 01/19/96

Cannell, Steven J
7083 Hollywood Bl
Hollywood, CA 90028
Producer V: 12/02/96

Cannell Productions
Stephen J Cannell
7083 Hollywood Bl
Hollywood, CA 90028
Production Office V: 12/17/96

Cannon, Dyan
c/o APA
9000 Sunset Bl #1200
Los Angeles, CA 90069
Actress V: 12/02/96

8033 W Sunset Bl #254
Los Angeles, CA 90046
Alternate V: 02/02/96

Cannon/Warner Brothers
4000 Warner Bl
Burbank, CA 91522
Production Office V: 12/10/96

Canova, Diana
c/o APA
9000 Sunset Bl #1200
Los Angeles, CA 90069
Actress V: 12/02/96

Capitol Artists
8383 Wilshire Bl-Suite 954
Beverly Hills, CA 90211
Talent Agency V: 11/11/96

Capitol Cities/ABC TV
77 W 66th St
New York, NY 10023
Production Office V: 12/10/96

Capriati, Jennifer
5435 Blue Heron Ln
Wesley Chaple, FL 33543-4441
Tennis Star V: 08/29/96

Capshaw, Kate
PO Box 869
Pacific Palisades, CA 90272
Actress V: 02/12/96

Captain & Tennille
PO Box 608
Zephyr Cove, NV 89448
Musical Group V: 10/23/96

Carbajal, Michael
914 E Filmore
Phoenix, AZ 85006
Boxing Star V: 01/10/97

Cardinale, Claudia
Via Flaminia 17km
Rome, Italy
Actress V: 01/17/96

Career Artists Int'l
11030 Ventura Bl Ste 3
Studio City, CA 91604
Talent Agency V: 06/06/96

Carelli, Rick
Chesrown Chevrolet
7300 N Broadway
Denver, CO 80221
Race Driver V: 03/12/96

Carey, Drew
c/o APA
9000 Sunset Bl #1200
Los Angeles, CA 90069
Actor V: 09/01/96

Carey, Drew, Cont.
Sutton/Barth & Vennari
145 S Fairfax Ave #310
Los Angeles, CA 90036
Alternate V: 12/15/96

Carey, Mariah
Horizon Entertainment
130 W 57th St-Suite 12B
New York, NY 10019
Singer V: 02/02/96

c/o Mottola
238 E 67th St
New York, NY 10021
Alternate V: 01/03/96

Carey Jr, Harry
Craig Agency
8485 Melrose Place-Suite E
Los Angeles, CA 90069
Actor V: 12/08/96

PO Box 3256
Durango, CO 81302
Alternate V: 02/02/96

Carlin, George
901 Bringham Ave
Los Angeles, CA 90049
Actor V: 01/14/96

Carlisle, Belinda
3575 W Cahenga Bl #470
Los Angeles, CA 90068
Singer V: 03/03/96

Carlson, Linda
Bauman/Hiller
5750 Wilshire Bl #512
Los Angeles, CA 90036
Actress V: 01/13/96

Carlton, Larry
3308 S Hall Rd
Franklin, TN 37064
Guitarist V: 01/12/96

Carlton, Steve
PO Box 736
Durango, CO 81302
Baseball Star V: 12/01/96

Carmichael, Ian
London Mgmt
235 Regent St
London W1, England
Actor V: 02/28/96

Carne, Judy
c/o Palmeri
PO Box 1442
New York, NY 10274-1442
Actress V: 03/14/96

c/o Palmeri
22 Jones St #2F
New York, NY 10014-4142
Alternate V: 01/21/96

Carnes, Kim
2031 Old Natchez Terrace
Franklin, TN 37064-1902
Singer V: 11/10/96

Carney, Art
RR 20-PO Box 911
Westbrook, CT 06498
Actor V: 03/03/96

143 Kingfisher Ln
Westbrook, CT 06498
Alternate V: 08/08/96

Carolco Films
8800 Sunset Bl
Los Angeles, CA 90069
Production Office V: 03/17/96

Carolco TV
8439 Sunset Bl
Los Angeles, CA 90069
Production Office V: 03/17/96

Caron, Leslie
6 rue de Bellechasse
Paris F-75007, France
Actress V: 11/01/96

Blake Agency
415 N Camden Dr #121
Beverly Hills, CA 90210
Alternate V: 12/06/96

Carothers, Veronica
2718 Nipomo Ave
Long Beach, CA 90815-1542
Actress V: 03/14/96

Carouthers, AJ
2210 The Terrace
Los Angeles, CA 90049
Screen Writer V: 10/23/96

Carpenter, Charisma
9300 Wilshire Bl #410
Beverly Hills, CA 90212
Actress V: 01/15/97

Carpenter, John
c/o ICM
8942 Wilshire Bl
Beverly Hills, CA 90211
Director V: 05/06/96

8532 Hollywood Bl
Los Angeles, CA 90046
Alternate V: 10/23/96

Carpenter, Mary-Chapin
Studio One Artists
7010 Westmoreland Ave #100
Takoma Park, MD 20912
Singer V: 01/21/96

Carpenter, Richard
9386 Raviller Dr
Downey, CA 90240
Singer V: 01/20/96

Carpenter, Scott
NASA/LBJ Space Center
Houston, TX 77058
Astronaut V: 03/03/96

Carr, Gerald P
NASA/LBJ Space Center
Houston, TX 77058
Astronaut V: 03/03/96

Carradine, David
Gold/Marshak & Associates
3500 W Olive Ave #1400
Burbank, CA 91505
Actor V: 12/10/96

9753 La Tuna Canyon Rd
Sun Valley, CA 91352
Alternate V: 10/03/96

Carradine, Keith
Wm Morris Agency
151 El Camino
Beverly Hills, CA 90212
Actor V: 12/12/96

355 S Grand Ave #4150
Los Angeles, CA 90071
Alternate V: 11/10/96

Carradine, Robert
1999 Ave of the Stars #2850
Los Angeles, CA 90067
Actor V: 12/11/96

355 S Grand Ave #4150
Los Angeles, CA 90071
Alternate V: 04/04/96

Carrera, Barbara
2220 Ave of the Stars #2804
Los Angeles, CA 90067-5653
Actress V: 08/29/96

Gold/Marshak & Associates
3500 W Olive Ave #1400
Burbank, CA 91505
Alternate V: 12/10/96

Carrere, Tia
8228 W Sunset Bl-3rd Fl
Los Angeles, CA 90046-2428
Actress V: 03/14/96

816 N La Cienega Bl #8638
W Hollywood, CA 90069
Alternate V: 03/04/96

c/o UTA
9560 Wilshire Bl-5th Fl
Beverly Hills, CA 90212
Forwarded V: 02/12/96

Carrey, Jim
c/o UTA
9560 Wilshire Bl #500
Beverly Hills, CA 90212
Actor V: 01/14/96

c/o Bartel
PO Box 57593
Sherman Oaks, CA 91403
Alternate V: 11/01/96

7920 Marine View Ave #250
Los Angeles, CA 90046
Forwarded V: 01/08/96

Carrier, Larry
Bristol Int'l Raceway
PO Box 3966
Bristol, TN 37625
NASCAR Official V: 03/02/96

Carroll, Diahann
Wm Morris Agency
151 El Camino
Beverly Hills, CA 90212
Actress V: 12/12/96

PO Box 2999
Beverly Hills, CA 90213
Alternate V: 03/13/96

Carroll Agency
139 N San Fernando Rd #A
Burbank, CA 91502
Talent Agency V: 02/07/96

Carruthers, Kitty
22 E 71st St
New York, NY 10021
Ice Skater V: 01/20/96

Carson, Johnny
Carson Productions
PO Box 5474
Santa Monica, CA 90409
Producer V: 01/14/96

6962 Wildlife Rd
Malibu, CA 90265
Alternate V: 02/03/96

Carson Productions
5300 Melrose Ave-#309E
Burbank, CA 90038
Production Office V: 03/17/96

Carter, Dixie
244 W 54th St #707
New York, NY 10019
Actress V: 02/10/96

Carter, Don
13600 SW 88th St
Miami, FL 33186
Bowler V: 06/12/96

Carter, Jack
1023 Chevy Chase Dr
Beverly Hills, CA 90210
Actor V: 06/06/96

Carter, Lynda
Wm Morris Agency
151 El Camino
Beverly Hills, CA 90212
Actress V: 12/12/96

9200 Harrington Dr
Potomac, MD 20854
Alternate V: 05/04/96

Carter, Nell
Wm Morris Agency
151 El Camino
Beverly Hills, CA 90212
Actress V: 12/12/96

Direct Mgmt Grp
947 N La Cienega Bl #G
Los Angeles, CA 90069
Alternate V: 11/29/96

Carter, Rosalynn
1 Woodland Dr
Plains, GA 31780
Former 1st Lady V: 03/01/96

Carter, TK
Ambrosio & Mortimer
9150 Wilshire Bl #175
Beverly Hills, CA 90212
Actor V: 12/01/96

Carter, Thomas
10958 Strathmore Dr
Los Angeles, CA 90024
Actor V: 02/16/96

Carter Jr, James Earl
Carter Center
One Copenhill
Atlanta, GA 30307-1498
Former President V: 03/10/96

1 Woodland Dr
Plains, GA 31780
Alternate V: 02/02/96

Carter-Cash, June
711 Summerfield Dr
Hendersonville, TN 37075
Singer V: 03/24/96

c/o PR
PO Box 508
Hendersonville, TN 37075
Alternate V: 02/02/96

Carteris, Gabrielle
c/o ICM
8942 Wilshire Bl
Beverly Hills, CA 90211
Actress V: 12/11/96

Cartland, Barbara
Camfield Place
Hatfield, Herts, England
Author V: 02/15/96

Cartoon Art Museum
665 Third St-5th Fl
San Francisco, CA 94107
Museum V: 11/02/96

Cartoon Network
One CNN Center
PO Box 105366
Atlanta, GA 30348
Production Office V: 12/15/96

Cartwright, Angela
Gilly Talent
8721 Sunset Bl #103
Los Angeles, CA 90069
Actress V: 02/12/96

Haeggstrom Office
6404 Wilshire Bl #1100
Los Angeles, CA 90048
Alternate V: 12/10/96

4330 Backman St
N Hollywood, CA 91602
Alternate V: 02/21/96

10112 Riverside Dr
Toluca Lake, CA 91602
Forwarded V: 01/11/97

Cartwright, Nancy
Artists Group
10100 Santa Monica Bl #2490
Los Angeles, CA 90067
Actress V: 12/03/96

Cartwright, Veronica
Wm Morris Agency
151 El Camino
Beverly Hills, CA 90212
Actress V: 12/12/96

4342 Bakman Ave
N Hollywood, CA 91602
Alternate V: 02/12/96

12754 Sarah St
Studio City, CA 91604
Alternate V: 11/01/96

12725-H Ventura Bl
Studio City, CA 91604
Forwarded V: 03/15/96

Caruso, Anthony
c/o Moss
733 N Seward St
Los Angeles, CA 90038
Actor V: 02/26/96

Caruso, David
c/o UTA
9560 Wilshire Bl #500
Beverly Hills, CA 90212
Actor V: 01/14/96

Carvey, Dana
8942 Wilshire Bl
Beverly Hills, CA 90211
Actor V: 01/14/96

Carvey, Dana, Cont.
17333 Ranco St
Encino, CA 91316
Alternate V: 09/01/96

Casablanca Productions
8544 Sunset Bl
Los Angeles, CA 90069
Production Office V: 03/17/96

Casares, Maria
8 Rue Asseline
Paris 75014, France
Actress V: 03/01/96

Casella, Max
Innovative Artists
1999 Ave of the Stars #2850
Los Angeles, CA 90067
Actor V: 12/11/96

Casey, Bernie
Ambrosio & Mortimer
9150 Wilshire Bl #175
Beverly Hills, CA 90212
Actor V: 12/01/96

Cash, Johnny
House of Cash
711 Summerfield Dr
Hendersonville, TN 37075
Singer V: 12/11/96

700 E Main St
Hendersonville, TN 37075-2609
Alternate V: 01/12/96

c/o APA
9000 Sunset Bl #1200
Los Angeles, CA 90069
Forwarded V: 01/14/96

Cash, Rosanne
c/o Side One
1775 Broadway-7th Fl
New York, NY 10019
Singer V: 02/02/96

Casper, Billy
14 Quiet Meadow Ln
Mapleton, UT 84663
Golfer V: 12/11/96

PO Box 1088
Chula Vista, CA 91912
Alternate V: 10/03/96

Casper, John H
NASA/LBJ Space Center
Hoston, TX 77058
Astronaut V: 06/06/96

Cassel, Jean-Pierre
388-396 Oxford St
London W1, England
Actor V: 03/10/96

Cassevettes, Nick
22223 Buena Venture St
Woodland Hills, CA 91364
Actor V: 03/09/96

Cassidy, David
Wm Morris
1350 Ave of the Americas
New York, NY 10012
Actor V: 12/12/94

4155 Witzel Dr
Sherman Oaks, CA 91423
Alternate V: 11/10/96

Cassidy, Joanna
Innovative Artists
1999 Ave of the Stars #2850
Los Angeles, CA 90067
Actress V: 02/12/96

230 S Irving Bl
Los Angeles, CA 90004-3810
Alternate V: 06/22/96

2530 Outpost Dr
Los Angeles, CA 90068
Forwarded V: 03/15/96

Cassidy, Shaun
8484 Wilshire Bl #500
Beverly Hills, CA 90212
Actor V: 11/01/96

Casson, Mel
King Features
216 E 45th St
New York, NY 10017
Cartoonist V: 03/11/96

Casting Society of America
6565 Sunset Bl #306
Los Angeles, CA 90028
Production Office V: 11/11/96

Castle Rock
335 N Maple Dr #135
Beverly Hills, CA 90210
Production Office V: 11/11/96

Castle-Hill Talent
1101 S Orlando
Los Angeles, CA 90035
Talent Agency V: 02/07/96

Cates, Phoebe
1636 3rd Ave #309
New York, NY 10128-3622
Actress V: 01/12/96

45 W 67th St Ste 7-B
New York, NY 10023
Alternate V: 12/23/96

9560 Wilshire Bl #500
Beverly Hills, CA 90212
Forwarded V: 03/15/96

Catlett, Mary Jo
4375 Farmdale Ave
N Hollywood, CA 91604
Actress V: 09/21/96

Cattrall, Kim
Wm Morris Agency
151 El Camino
Beverly Hills, CA 90212
Actress V: 12/12/96

616 Lorna Lane
Los Angeles, CA 90049
Alternate V: 02/01/96

Caulfield, Maxwell
4036 Foothill Rd
Carpenteria, CA 90313
Actor V: 01/13/96

4770 9th St-Suite B
Carpenteria, CA 93013
Alternate V: 11/10/96

Cavaleri & Associates
405 Riverside Dr #200
Burbank, CA 91506
Talent Agency V: 06/13/96

Caveny, Michael
572 Prospect Bl
Pasadena, CA 91103
Magician V: 01/18/96

Cavett, Dick
Wm Morris Agency
151 El Camino
Beverly Hills, CA 90212
TV Host V: 12/12/96

Cavett, Dick, Cont.
2200 Fletcher Ave
Ft Lee, NJ 07024
Alternate V: 02/03/96

Celebrity Access Publications
20 Sunnyside Ave-Suite #A241
Mill Valley, CA 94941-1928
Publisher V: 03/29/96

Celebrity Look-Alikes
Ron Smith
2600 Cumberland Pkwy
Atlanta, GA 30339
Talent Agency V: 01/20/96

Celebrity Mail Service
932 N Curson Ave #5
Los Angeles, CA 90046
Fan Mail V: 11/11/96

Celentano, Adriano
Viale Carso 63
I-00195 Rome, Italy
Actor V: 01/17/96

Cenker, Bob
RCA Astro-Space Division
PO Box 800
Princeton, NJ 08543-0800
Astronaut V: 06/12/96

Century Artists
1148-4th St #206
Santa Monica, CA 90403
Talent Agency V: 11/11/96

Century Home Video
2688 S La Cienega Bl
Los Angeles, CA 90034
Production Office V: 12/10/96

Cernan, Eugene A
NASA/LBJ Space Center
Houston, TX 77058
Astronaut V: 03/03/96

Cey, Ron
22714 Creole Rd
Woodland Hills, CA 91364
Baseball Star V: 12/31/96

Chadwick, Florence
PO Box 3407
La Jolla, CA 92038-3407
Swimming Star V: 11/11/96

Chaio, Leroy
NASA/LBJ Space Center
Houston, TX 77058
Astronaut V: 03/03/96

Chakiris, George
7266 Clinton St
Los Angeles, CA 90036
Actor V: 02/03/96

Chamberlain, Richard
c/o CAA
9830 Wilshire Bl
Beverly Hills, CA 90210
Actor V: 02/23/96

3711 Roundtop Dr
Honolulu, HI 96822
Forwarded V: 02/02/96

Chamberlain, Wilt
15216 Antelo Pl
Los Angeles, CA 90024
Basketball Star V: 12/12/96

Chambers, Marilyn
5627 Sepulvida Bl #214
Van Nuys, CA 91411
Adult Films V: 02/02/96

Champine, Robert
204 Tipton Ave
Newport News, VA 23606
Test Pilot V: 02/09/96

Chan, Jackie
1001 Nagatani-Mansion
26 Banchi, Sakamachi
Shinjuhu, Tokyo 160, Japan
Actor V: 11/01/96

145 Waterloo Rd
Kowloon, Hong Kong
Alternate V: 11/01/96

Chandler, John
c/o BDP
10637 Burbank Bl
N Hollywood, CA 91601
Actor V: 03/08/96

Chandler, Kyle
Schoen & Associates
606 N Larchmont Bl #309
Los Angeles, CA 90004
Actor V: 12/15/96

Chang-Diaz, Franklin R
NASA/LBJ Space Center
Hoston, TX 77058
Astronaut V: 06/06/96

Channing, Stockard
c/o ICM
8942 Wilshire Bl
Beverly Hills, CA 90211
Actress V: 12/11/96

c/o PF
10345 W Olympic Bl #200
Los Angeles, CA 90064
Forwarded V: 11/01/96

Chao, Rosalind
c/o Paradigm
10100 Santa Monica Bl-25th Fl
Los Angeles, CA 90067
Actress V: 11/11/96

924 Westwood Bl #900
Los Angeles, CA 90024
Alternate V: 04/02/96

c/o PTA
200 W 57th St #900
New York, NY 10019
Forwarded V: 02/12/96

Chaplin, Geraldine
Wm Morris Agency
31/32 Soho Square
London W1V 5DG, England
Actress V: 03/14/96

Chaplin, Mike
NASCAR
1811 Volusia Ave
Daytona Beach, FL 32015
NASCAR Official V: 03/14/96

Chapman, Mark Lindsay
Ambrosio/Mortimer
9150 Wilshire Bl #175
Beverly Hills, CA 90212
Actor V: 01/17/96

Chapman, Philip K
NASA/LBJ Space Center
Houston, TX 77058
Astronaut V: 03/03/96

Charbonneau, Patricia
c/o Paradigm
10100 Santa Monica Bl-25th Fl
Los Angeles, CA 90067
Actress V: 02/12/96

Charisse, Cyd
10724 Wilshire Bl #1406
Los Angeles, CA 90024
Actress V: 01/04/96

Charles, Ray
2107 W Washington Bl #200
Los Angeles, CA 90018
Singer V: 06/05/96

4863 Southridge Ave
Los Angeles, CA 90008
Alternate V: 03/06/96

Charles Agency
11950 Ventura Bl #3
Studio City, CA 91604
Talent Agency V: 11/11/96

Charleson, Leslie
2314 Live Oak Dr E
Los Angeles, CA 90068
Actress V: 03/01/96

Charlotte Hornets
100 Hive Drive
Charlotte, NC 28217
Team Office V: 02/15/96

Charo
Wm Morris
151 El Camino
Beverly Hills, CA 90212
Actress V: 04/04/96

Charo's Restaurant & Bar
North Shore-PO Box 1007
Hanalei, Kauai, HI 96714
Alternate V: 11/11/96

Charter Management
8200 Wilshire Bl #218
Beverly Hills, CA 90211
Talent Agency V: 02/20/96

Chartoff, Melanie
Artists Agency
10000 Santa Monica Bl #305
Los Angeles, CA 90067
Actress V: 02/12/96

444 S Roxbury Dr #A
Beverly Hills, CA 90212
Alternate V: 03/08/96

Chartoff-Winkler Productions
10125 W Washington Bl
Culver City, CA 90230
Production Office V: 03/17/96

Chase, Chevy
c/o CAA
9830 Wilshire Bl
Beverly Hills, CA 90212
Actor V: 01/14/96

PO Box 257
Bedford, NY 10506-0257
Alternate V: 01/12/96

Chasin Agency
8899 Beverly Bl #713
Los Angeles, CA 90048-2412
Talent Agency V: 01/07/96

Chateau/Billings Agency
5657 Wilshire Bl #340
Los Angeles, CA 90036
Talent Agency V: 02/07/96

Chaves, Richard
Media Artists
8383 Wilshire Bl #954
Bevrly Hills, CA 90211
Actor V: 02/01/96

Cheatham, Maree
8391 Beverly Bl #244
Los Angeles, CA 90048
Actress V: 01/13/97

Checa, Maria
Playboy Enterprises
2112 Broadway St
Santa Monica, CA 90404-2912
Model V: 01/12/96

Checker, Chubby
PO Box 160
Birchrunville, PA 19421
Singer V: 11/01/96

1646 Hilltop Rd
Birchrunville, PA 19421
Alternate V: 11/10/96

Evans & Schulman
11 Delmar Ct
Brigantine, NJ 08203
Forwarded V: 02/03/96

c/o DeLauro
1756 Broadway/#22-J
New York, NY 10019
Forwarded V: 05/06/96

Cheek, Molly
13038 Landale St
Studio City, CA 91604-1005
Actress V: 03/14/96

3690 Goodland Ave
Studio City, CA 91604-2310
Alternate V: 01/21/96

Cheli, Maurizio
NASA/LBJ Space Center
Houston, TX 77058
Astronaut V: 02/02/96

Chen, Joan
2601 Filbert St
San Francisco, CA 94123-3215
Actress V: 03/17/96

7900 Willow Glen Rd
Los Angeles, CA 90046
Alternate V: 11/11/96

Cher
PO Box 960
Beverly Hills, CA 90213-0960
Actress V: 01/21/96

c/o Cher News
PO Box 2310
Beverly Hills, CA 90213
Alternate V: 11/01/96

Chestnut, Mark
PO Box 120544
Nashville, TN 37212
Singer V: 01/21/96

Cheung, George Kee
Sutton/Barth & Vennari
145 S Fairfax Ave #310
Los Angeles, CA 90036
Actor V: 12/15/96

Gage Group
9255 Sunset Bl #515
Los Angeles, CA 90069
Alternate V: 03/08/96

Chiao, Leroy
NASA/LBJ Space Center
Houston, TX 77058
Astronaut V: 02/02/96

Chicago Bears
Halas Hall
250 N Washington Rd
Lake Forest, IL 60045
Team Office V: 05/15/96

Chicago Blackhawks
Chicago Stadium
1800 W Madison St
Chicago, IL 60612
Team Office V: 01/31/96

Chicago Bulls
One Magnificent Mile
980 N Michigan Ave #1600
Chicago, IL 60611
Team Office V: 02/15/96

Chicago Cubs
1060 W Addison St
Wrigley Field
Chicago, IL 60613
Team Office V: 02/01/96

Chicago Historical Society
Prints & Photographs
Clark St at North Ave
Chicago, IL 60614
Archive V: 03/18/96

Chicago White Sox
333 W 35th St
Comiskey Park
Chicago, IL 60616
Team Office V: 02/01/96

Child, Julia
103 Irving St
Cambridge, MA 02138
Chef V: 03/09/96

Childress, Richard
Childress Racing
PO Box 1189-Industrial Dr
Welcome, NC 27374
NASCAR Owner V: 05/05/96

Chiles, Lois
Ambrosio & Mortimer
9150 Wilshire Bl #175
Beverly Hills, CA 90212
Actress V: 12/01/96

644 San Lorenzo
Santa Monica, CA 90402
Alternate V: 03/03/96

Chilton, Kevin P
NASA/LBJ Space Center
Houston, TX 77058
Astronaut V: 03/03/96

Cho, Margaret
Wm Morris Agency
151 El Camino
Beverly Hills, CA 90212
Actress V: 02/12/96

Chokachi, David
Wm Morris Agency
151 El Camino
Beverly Hills, CA 90212
Actor V: 12/15/96

Chong, Rae Dawn
Metro Talent Agency
4526 Wilshire Bl
Los Angeles, CA 90010
Actress V: 12/11/96

824 Moraga Dr
Los Angeles, CA 90049
Alternate V: 02/20/96

1491 Stone Canyon Rd
Los Angeles, CA 90024
Alternate V: 11/01/96

Chong, Tommy
1625 Casale Rd
Pacific Palisades, CA 90272
Actor V: 03/10/96

Chopra, Deepak
Sharp Institute
973-B Lomas Santa Fe
Solano Beach, CA 92075
Author V: 01/14/96

Christensen, Helena
Agence Gaulthier
62 bd Sebastopol
Paris F-75003, France
Model V: 11/01/96

Christensen's Directory
PO Box 900189
San Diego, CA 92190
Publisher V: 01/21/96

Christian, Claudia
Kohner Agency
9300 Wilshire Bl #555
Beverly Hills, CA 90212
Actress V: 12/11/96

14431 Ventura Bl #260
Sherman Oaks, CA 91423
Alternate V: 10/23/96

Christie, Julie
23 Linden Gardens
London W2, England
Actress V: 09/01/96

Christie, Lou
Dartmouth Mgmt
228 W 71st St #1E
New York, NY 10023
Singer V: 11/29/96

Christine, Andrew
King Features
216 E 45th St
New York, NY 10017
Cartoonist V: 03/11/96

Christopher, Dennis
2026 1/2 Argyle
Los Angeles, CA 90028
Actor V: 10/23/96

175 5th Ave #2413
New York, NY 10010
Alternate V: 02/08/96

Christopher, Warren
Dept of State
2201 C St NW
Washington, DC 20520
Politician V: 01/31/96

Christopher, William
Artists Group
10100 Santa Monica Bl #2490
Los Angeles, CA 90067
Actor V: 12/04/96

PO Box 50698
Pasadena, CA 91105-0698
Alternate V: 11/11/96

Chung, Connie
Geller Media Mgmt
250 W 57th St #213
New York, NY 10019
Correspondant V: 01/14/96

Cilton, Kevin P
NASA/LBJ Space Center
Hoston, TX 77058
Astronaut V: 06/05/96

Cincinnati Bengals
200 Riverfront Stadium
Cincinnati, OH 45202
Team Office V: 05/15/96

Cincinnati Reds
100 Riverfront Stadium
Cincinnati, OH 45202
Team Office V: 02/15/96

Cine-Media Int'l
PO Box 7005
Long Beach, CA 90807
Production Office V: 03/17/96

Cinefantastic
PO Box 270
Oak Park, IL 60303
Publisher V: 01/02/96

Cinema Talent
2609 Wyoming Ave-Suite A
Los Angeles, CA 90048
Talent Agency V: 11/11/96

Cinemax
1100 Ave of the Americas
New York, NY 10036
Network HQ V: 03/01/96

2049 Century Park E #1400
Los Angeles, CA 90067
Alternate V: 03/17/96

Circle Talent Associates
433 N Camden Dr #400
Beverly Hills, CA 90210
Talent Agency V: 06/06/96

Clampett Productions
729 Seward St
Hollywood, CA 90038
Production Office V: 03/17/96

Clancy, Tom
PO Box 800
Huntington, MD 10639
Author V: 09/06/96

Clapton, Eric
c/o CAA
9830 Wilshire Bl
Beverly Hills, CA 90212
Singer V: 01/14/96

18 Harley House
Regents Park
London NW1, England
Alternate V: 09/06/96

Clark, Anthony
4933 W Craig Rd #268
Las Vegas, NV 89130
Magician V: 08/01/96

Clark, Candy
5 Briarhill Rd
Montclair, NJ 07042
Actress V: 10/23/96

Epstein/Wyckoff
280 S Beverly Dr #400
Beverly Hills, CA 90212
Alternate V: 12/08/96

Clark, Dick
Dick Clark Productions
3003 W Olive
Burbank, CA 91505
TV Host V: 12/11/96

Clark, Matt
Kohner Agency
9300 Wilshire Bl #555
Beverly Hills, CA 90212
Actor V: 12/11/96

1199 Park Ave #15D
New York, NY 10128
Alternate V: 05/06/96

Clark, Petula
15 Cheminbelle Fonte Coligny
Geneva, Switzerland
Singer V: 02/13/96

235 Regent St
London W1R 7AG, England
Alternate V: 02/26/96

Clark, Ramsey
36 E 12th St
New York, NY 10003
Musician V: 03/05/96

Clark, Roy
1800 Forrest Bl
Tulsa, OK 74114
Singer V: 10/23/96

c/o Clark Productions
3225 S Norwood Ave
Tulsa, OK 74135
Alternate V: 01/22/96

Clark, Susan
Bauman & Hiller
5750 Wilshire Bl #512
Los Angeles, CA 90036
Actress V: 12/05/96

7943 Woodrow Wilson Dr
Los Angeles, CA 90046
Alternate V: 09/19/96

Clark, Will
1000 Papworth Ave
Metairie, LA 70005
Baseball Star V: 11/29/96

Clark Company,
13415 Ventura Bl #3
Sherman Oaks, CA 91423
Talent Agency V: 07/20/96

Clark Gable Foundation
PO Box 65
Cadiz, OH 43907
Fan Service V: 01/21/96

Clarkson, Lana
LA Talent
8335 Sunset Bl
Los Angeles, CA 90069
Actress V: 11/01/96

Clary, Robert
1001 Sundial Ln
Beverly Hills, CA 90210
Actor V: 06/01/96

Clay, Andrew
c/o Silverstein
836 N La Cienega Bl #202
W Hollywood, CA 90069-4708
Actor V: 08/29/96

c/o Silverstein
6 Green Hill Rd
Harvard, MA 01451
Alternate V: 11/15/96

Clayburgh, Jill
PO Box 18
Lakeville, CT 06039-0018
Actress V: 01/08/96

Cleave, Mary L
NASA/LBJ Space Center
Hoston, TX 77058
Astronaut V: 06/01/96

Cleese, John
Mayday Mgmt
68-A Delancy St/Camden Town
London NW1 7RY, England
Actor V: 06/01/96

Cleghorne, Ellen
9150 Wilshire Bl #350
Beverly Hills, CA 90210
Actress V: 01/03/97

Clements, Ronald F
Walt Disney Productions
500 S Buena Vista St
Burbank, CA 91521
Animator V: 10/23/96

Clervoy, Jean-Francois
NASA/LBJ Space Center
Houston, TX 77058
Astronaut V: 02/02/96

Cleveland Browns
Cleveland Stadium
Cleveland, OH 44114
Team Office V: 05/15/96

Cleveland Cavaliers
PO Box 5000
Richfield, OH 44286-5000
Team Office V: 02/15/96

Cleveland Cavaliers
The Coliseum
2923 Streetsboro Rd
Richfield, OH 44286
Alterante V: 11/11/96

Cleveland Indians
Gateway Stadium
Cleveland, OH 44114
Team Office V: 02/15/96

Clifford, Clark
Clifford & Warnke
815 Commonwealth Ave NW
Washington, DC 20006
Politician V: 05/22/96

Clifford, Michael R
NASA/LBJ Space Center
Houston, TX 77058
Astronaut V: 03/03/96

Clinton, Hillary Rodham
The White House
1600 Pennsylvania Ave
Washington, DC 20515
First Lady V: 02/02/96

Clinton, William Jefferson
The White House
1600 Pennsylvania Ave
Washington, DC 20515
President USA V: 12/02/96

1800 Center St
Little Rock, AR 72206
Alternate V: 12/02/96

Clooney, George
Wm Morris Agency
151 El Camino
Beverly Hills, CA 90212
Actor V: 12/12/96

8817 Lookout Mtn Ave
Los Angeles, CA 90046-1819
Alternate V: 08/29/96

Close, Glenn
Creative Artists Agency
9830 Wilshire Bl
Beverly Hills, CA 90212
Actress V: 12/07/96

Cluka, Scott
c/o Childress
PO Box 1189-Industrial Dr
Welcome, NC 27374
NASCAR Crew V: 03/12/96

Coast to Coast Talent
4942 Vineland Ave #200
N Hollywood, CA 91601
Talent Agency V: 03/22/96

Coates, Kim
Paradigm Talent
10100 Santa Monica Bl-25th Fl
Los Angeles, CA 90067
Actor V: 01/13/97

Coates, Phyllis
PO Box 1969
Boyes Hot Springs, CA 95476
Actress V: 11/20/96

c/o Star
4555 Mariota Ave
Toluca Lake, CA 91602
Alternate V: 02/12/96

Coats, Michael L
NASA/LBJ Space Center
Houston, TX 77058
Astronaut V: 03/03/96

Cobb, Julie
SDB Partners
1801 Ave of the Stars #902
Los Angeles, CA 90067
Actress V: 02/12/96

Coburn, James
Shapira & Associates
15301 Ventura Bl #345
Sherman Oaks, CA 91403
Actor V: 12/14/96

Coburn, James, Cont.
Special Artists
335 N Maple Dr #360
Beverly Hills, CA 90210
Alternate V: 01/13/96

1601 Schuyler Rd
Beverly Hills, CA 90210-2543
Alternate V: 06/22/96

Coca, Imogene
Joyce Agency
370 Harrison Ave
Harrison, NY 10528
Actress V: 11/27/96

Cockrell, Kenneth D
NASA/LBJ Space Center
Houston, TX 77058
Astronaut V: 03/03/96

Cody, Iron Eyes
4470 Sunset Dr #503
Los Angeles, CA 90027
Actor V: 09/08/96

Coe, David Allen
PO Box 1387
Goodlettsville, TN 37070-1387
Singer V: 11/10/96

c/o Manager
PO Box 609
Branson, MO 65616
Forwarded V: 02/02/96

Coelho, Susie
Gold/Marshak
3500 W Olive Ave
Burbank, CA 91505
Actress V: 02/12/96

Cohen, Alexander
25 W 54th St #5F
New York, NY 10019-5411
Producer V: 03/03/96

Cohen, Leonard
c/o Premiere
3 E 54th St #1400
New York, NY 10022
Poet V: 11/29/96

Colbert, Robert
151 Ocean Park Bl
Santa Monica, CA 90405
Actor V: 03/03/96

Cole, Dennis
2160 Century Park E #1712
Los Angeles, CA 90067
Actor V: 03/03/96

Cole, Gary
c/o ICM
8942 Wilshire Bl
Beverly Hills, CA 90211
Actor V: 12/11/96

3855 Berry Dr
Studio City, CA 91604
Alternate V: 05/04/96

Cole, Michael
6332 Costello Ave
Van Nuys, CA 91401-2209
Actor V: 03/17/96

Cole, Natalie
Wm Morris Agency
151 El Camino Dr
Beverly Hills, CA 90212
Singer V: 01/14/96

c/o Cleary Mgmt
1801 Ave of the Stars #1105
Los Angeles, CA 90067
Alternate V: 12/01/96

Coleman, Dabney
9200 Sunset Bl #428
Los Angeles, CA 90069
Actor V: 01/21/96

360 N Kenter Ave
Los Angeles, CA 90049
Alternate V: 09/02/96

Coleman, Gary
4710 Don Miguel Dr
Los Angeles, CA 90008
Actor V: 12/01/96

Collins, Eileen M
NASA/LBJ Space Center
Houston, TX 77058
Astronaut V: 03/03/96

Collins, Gary
2751 Hutton Dr
Beverly Hills, CA 90210
Actor V: 01/17/97

Collins, Jackie
PO Box 10581
Burbank, CA 91510-0581
Author V: 01/12/96

Collins, Jackie, Cont.
710 N Foothill Rd
Beverly Hills, CA 90210
Forwarded V: 05/21/96

13701 Riverside Dr #608
Sherman Oaks, CA 91423
Forwarded V: 03/03/96

Collins, Joan
15363 Mulholland Dr
Los Angeles, CA 90077-1622
Actress V: 02/10/96

1196 Cabrillo Dr
Beverly Hills, CA 90210
Alternate V: 09/06/96

16 Bulbecks Walks
S Woodham Ferrers-Clemsford
Essex CM3 5ZN, England
Forwarded V: 12/15/96

Collins, Michael
NASA/LBJ Space Center
Houston, TX 77058
Astronaut V: 03/03/96

Collins, Stephen
Wm Morris Agency
151 El Camino
Beverly Hills, CA 90212
Actor V: 12/12/96

21 E 90th St #10A
New York, NY 10128
Alternate V: 02/15/96

12960 Brentwood Terrace
Los Angeles, CA 90049-4841
Forwarded V: 01/12/96

Colorado Rockies
1700 Broadway #2100
Denver, CO 80290
Team Office V: 02/15/96

Colours Agency
8344 1/2 West Third St
Los Angeles, CA 90048
Talent Agency V: 02/28/96

Colter, Jessie
1117 17th Ave S
Nashville, TN 37212
Singer V: 06/23/96

Columbia Pictures
Columbia Plaza N #417
Burbank, CA 91505
Production Office V: 03/17/96

Columbia Pictures (TV)
Sunset Gower Studio
1438 N Gower St
Hollywood, CA 90028-8394
Production Office V: 11/11/96

Columbini, Aldo
PO Box 3006
Granada Hills, CA 91394
Magician V: 06/27/96

Comaneci, Nadia
2325 Westwood Dr
Norman, OK 73069
Olympian V: 11/01/96

Combs, Holly Marie
Bresler/Kelly
15760 Ventura Bl #1730
Encino, CA 91436
Actress V: 12/06/96

Combs, Jeffrey
Stone Manners Talent
8091 Selma Ave
Los Angeles, CA 90068
Actor V: 12/15/96

Combs, Rodney
NASCAR
1811 Volusia Ave
Daytona Beach, FL 32015
NASCAR Driver V: 03/02/96

Comedy Central
1775 Broadway
New York, NY 10019
Production Office V: 02/02/96

Commercials Unlimited
9601 Wilshire Bl #620
Beverly Hills, CA 90210
Talent Agency V: 12/12/96

Como, Perry
305 Northern Bl #35-A
Great Neck, NY 11021
Singer V: 04/12/96

Compton, Joyce
23388 Mulholland Dr
Woodland Hills, CA 91364
Actress V: 03/05/96

Conaway, Jeff
3162 Durand Dr
Los Angeles, CA 90068-1614
Actor V: 11/10/96

Confederate Railroad
Assoc Talent
818 19th Ave S
Nashville, TN 37203
Musical Group V: 11/01/96

Conforte, Gino
Amsel/Eisenstadt
6310 San Vicente Bl #407
Los Angeles, CA 90048
Actor V: 02/28/96

Conley, Darlene
1840 S Beverly Glen Bl #501
Los Angeles, CA 90025-0728
Actress V: 11/10/96

Conley, Joe
PO Box 6487
Thousand Oaks, CA 91359
Actor V: 02/03/96

Conn, Didi
14820 Valley Vista Bl
Sherman Oaks, CA 91403
Actress V: 11/29/96

House of Representatives
9911 Pico Bl #1060
Los Angeles, CA 90035
Alternate V: 02/12/96

Connelly, Jennifer
8942 Wilshire Bl
Beverly Hills, CA 90211
Actress V: 01/15/96

Connery, Jason
c/o Jamison
The Plaza-219/555 Kings Rd
London SW10 0SZ, England
Actor V: 02/08/96

Connery, Sean
c/o CAA
9830 Wilshire Bl
Beverly Hills, CA 90212
Actor V: 01/14/96

Casa Malibu, Fuente del Rodeo
Andalucia La Nueva, Malaga
Spain
Alternate V: 01/07/96

Connery, Sean, Cont.
c/o Capitol
15 Portland Place
London W1N 3AA, England
Forwarded V: 02/09/96

Connick Jr, Harry
c/o CAA
9830 Wilshire Bl
Beverly Hills, CA 90212
Singer V: 03/04/96

c/o HCFC
260 Brookline St #200
Cambridge, MA 02139
Alternate V: 12/03/96

3 Hastings Square
Cambridge, MA 02139-4724
Forwarded V: 03/30/96

Connors, Carol
1709 Ferrari Dr
Beverly Hills, CA 90210
Composer V: 06/14/96

Connors, Mike
c/o ICM
8942 Wilshire Bl
Beverly Hills, CA 90211
Actor V: 02/04/96

Conrad, Christian
16746 Addison St
Encino, CA 91436-1056
Actor V: 06/22/96

Conrad, Kimberly
10236 Charing Cross Rd
Los Angeles, CA 90077
Model V: 10/23/96

Conrad, Paul
c/o Times/Mirror
Times Mirror Square
Los Angeles, CA 90053
Cartoonist V: 07/23/96

Conrad, Robert
Shapira & Associates
15301 Ventura Bl #345
Sherman Oaks, CA 91403
Actress V: 12/14/96

Conrad Jr, Charles
McDonnell Douglas
5301 Bolsa Ave
Huntington Beach, CA 92647
Astronaut V: 12/01/96

Considine, Tim
506 N Alpine Dr
Beverly Hills, CA 90210-3316
Actress V: 11/10/96

Conte, John
75600 Beryl Dr
Indian Wells, CA 92260
Actor V: 01/24/96

Contemporary Artists
1427 3rd St-Promenade #205
Santa Monica, CA 90401
Talent Agency V: 07/23/96

Converse, Peggy
2525 Briarcrest Rd
Beverly Hills, CA 90210
Actress V: 11/27/96

Conway, Gary
PO Box 5617
San Angelo, TX 76902
Actor V: 12/01/96

Conway, Tim
Conway Entertainment
PO Box 17047
Encino, CA 91416-7047
Actor V: 12/03/96

425 S Beverly Dr
Beverly Hills, CA 91316
Alternate V: 03/23/96

Cook, Barry
Sabco Racing
5901 Orr Rd
Charlotte, NC 28213
NASCAR Crew V: 03/26/96

Cooke, Alistair
Nassau Point
Cutchogue, NY 11935
Author V: 09/04/96

Coolidge, Rita
11684 Ventura Bl #858
Studio City, CA 91604
Singer V: 10/23/96

9595 Wilshire Bl #1020
Beverly Hills, CA 90212
Alternate V: 03/03/96

Cooper, Henry
36 Brampton Grove
London NW4 England
Boxer V: 10/23/96

Cooper, Jackie
9621 Royalton Dr
Beverly Hills, CA 90210
Actor V: 02/01/96

Cooper Jr, L Gordon
NASA/LBJ Space Center
Houston, TX 77058
Astronaut V: 03/03/96

Cope, Derrike
4428 Taggart Creek Rd
Charlotte, NC 28208
NASCAR Driver V: 03/12/96

Cope, Dick
Whitcomb Racing
9201 Garrison Rd
Charlotte, NC 28208
NASCAR Driver V: 03/02/96

Copley, Teri
18435 San Fernando Mission Bl
Granda Hills, CA 91344
Actress V: 02/02/96

4334 Matilija Ave #217
Sheramn Oaks, CA 91423-3660
Alternate V: 01/10/97

Copperfield, David
9017 Wilshire Bl #500
Beverly Hills, CA 90210
Magician V: 01/14/96

11777 San Vicente Bl #601
Los Angeles, CA 90049
Alternate V: 03/17/96

515 Post Oak Bl #300
Houston, TX 77027
Forwarded V: 01/13/97

Coppola, Alicia
Wm Morris
151 El Camino
Beverly Hills, CA 90212
Actress V: 05/06/96

Coppola, Francis Ford
Zeotrope Studios
916 Kearny St
San Francisco, CA 94133
Director V: 02/01/96

c/o CAA
9830 Wilshire Bl
Beverly Hills, CA 90212
Alternate V: 01/14/96

Coralie Agency
4789 Vineland #100
N Hollywood, CA 91602
Talent Agency V: 04/27/96

Corbett, Gretchen
3500 W Olive Ave #1400
Burbank, CA 91505
Actress V: 02/10/96

c/o Connor
9229 Sunset Bl #311
Los Angeles, CA 90069
Alternate V: 02/12/96

Corbett, John
Creative Artists Agency
9830 Wilshire Bl
Beverly Hills, CA 90212
Actor V: 12/07/96

Corbin, Barry
2117 Greta Ln
Ft Worth, TX 76120-5201
Actor V: 01/12/96

4519 Tyrone Ave
Sherman Oaks, CA 91423-2628
Alternate V: 01/12/96

Metro Talent Agency
4526 Wilshire Bl
Los Angeles, CA 90010
Alternate V: 12/11/96

Corby, Ellen
9024 Harratt St
Los Angeles, CA 90069
Actress V: 01/02/96

Corday, Mara
PO Box 800393
Valencia, CA 91380
Actress V: 05/06/96

Corey, Jeff
Bauman/Hiller
5750 Wilshire Bl #512
Los Angeles, CA 90036
Actor V: 03/09/96

Corley, Pat
Artists Group
10100 Santa Monica Bl #2490
Los Angeles, CA 90067
Actor V: 02/25/96

Cornell, Lydia
142 S Bedford Dr
Beverly Hills, CA 90212
Actress V: 07/14/96

Cornett, Leanza
c/o ET
5555 Melrose Ave
Hollywood, CA 90038
Commentator V: 01/20/96

Corsaut, Aneta
4312 Agnes Ave
Studio City, CA 91604
Actress V: 06/16/96

Cort, Bud
Pakula & King Agency
9229 Sunset Bl #315
Los Angeles, CA 90069
Actor V: 12/12/96

Cortese, Dan
15250 Ventura Bl #900
Sherman Oaks, CA 91403-3221
Actor V: 06/22/96

Cosby, Bill
c/o SAH
PO Box 4049
Santa Monica, CA 90411-4049
Actor V: 11/10/96

Wm Morris Agency
151 El Camino Dr
Beverly Hills, CA 90212
Forwarded V: 02/03/96

Cosden Agency
3518 Cahuenga Bl West #216
Los Angeles, CA 90068
Talent Agency V: 11/11/96

Costa, Bob
NBC-TV
30 Rockefeller Pl
New York, NY 10012
Commentator V: 10/23/96

Costa, Mary
3340 Kingston Pike-Unit 1
Knoxville, TN 37191-4674
Singer V: 11/10/96

Costner, Kevin
c/o CAA
9830 Wilshire Bl
Beverly Hills, CA 90212
Actor V: 03/11/96

Costner, Kevin, Cont.
PO Box 275
Montrose, CA 91021
Alternate V: 02/02/96

2806 Nichols Canyon
Los Angeles, CA 90046
Forwarded V: 01/02/96

Coulier, David
9150 Wilshire Bl #350
Beverly Hills, CA 90212-3427
Actor V: 11/10/96

Coulson, Catherine
PO Box 158
Ashland, OR 97520
Actress V: 01/13/96

Country Fever Magazine
9171 Wilshire Bl #300
Beverly Hills, CA 91505
Publisher V: 02/10/96

Country Weekly Magazine
600 East Coast Ave
Lantana, FL 33462
Publisher V: 02/10/96

Couric, Katie
NBC-TV
30 Rockefeller Plaza #304
New York, NY 10112
Correspondant V: 01/07/96

Court TV
600 Third Ave-2nd Fl
New York, NY 10016
Production Office V: 12/15/96

Cousy, Bob
427 Salisbury St
Worcester, MA 01609
Basketball Star V: 04/12/96

Covey, Richard O
NASA/LBJ Space Center
Houston, TX 77058
Astronaut V: 03/03/96

Cowper, Nicola
Brunskill Management
169 Queens Gate #A8
London SW7 5EH, England
Actress V: 02/04/96

Cox, Courtney
Creative Artists Agency
9830 Wilshire Bl
Beverly Hills, CA 90212
Actress V: 12/07/96

Cox, Jimmy
PO Box 85619
Mt Lemmon, AZ 85619
Actor V: 12/12/96

Cox, Jimmy
NASCAR
1811 Volusia Ave
Daytona Beach, FL 32015
NASCAR Official V: 03/14/96

Craddock, Billy Crash
3007 Old Martinsville Rd
Greensboro, NC 27455
Singer V: 01/12/96

Craig, Jenny
445 Marine View Ave #300
Del Mar, CA 92014-3950
Entrepreneur V: 01/08/96

Craig, Jim
36 N Main St
N Easton, MA 02356
Hockey Star V: 01/31/96

Craig, Michael
Chatto & Linnit
Coventry St
London W1 England
Actor V: 03/09/96

Craig, Roger
271 Vista Verde Way
Portolla Valley, CA 94028
Football Star V: 09/06/96

Craig, Yvonne
PO Box 827
Pacific Palisades, CA 90272
Actress V: 03/17/96

Media Artists
8383 Wilshire Bl #954
Beverly Hills, CA 90211
Alternate V: 03/02/96

Craig Agency
8485 Melrose Place-Suite E
Los Angeles, CA 90069
Talent Agency V: 05/13/96

Crain, Jeanne
1029 Arbolado Rd
Santa Barbara, CA 93103-2037
Actress V: 08/29/96

Cramer, Floyd
c/o Purcell
210 E 51st St
New York, NY 10022
Singer V: 02/02/96

Cramer, Stepfanie
Kohner Agency
9300 Wilshire Bl #555
Beverly Hills, CA 90212
Actress V: 12/11/96

Crampton, Barbara
501 S Beverly Dr-3rd Fl
Beverly Hills, CA 90212-4512
Actress V: 10/23/96

House of Representatives
9911 Pico Bl #1060
Los Angeles, CA 90035
Alternate V: 12/10/96

501 S Beverly Dr #300
Beverly Hills, CA 90212
Alternate V: 11/27/96

Craven, Gemma
41 Hazelbury Rd
London SW6, England
Actress V: 01/24/96

Craven, Ricky
c/o Craven
PO Box 748
Statesville, NC 28687
NASCAR Driver V: 02/08/96

Craven, Wes
1000 W Washington Bl #3011
Culver City, CA 90232
Director V: 11/01/96

Crawford, Cindy
c/o Elite
111 E 22nd St #200
New York, NY 10010
Model V: 11/15/96

26 E 10th St-Penthouse
New York, NY 10003
Alternate V: 02/21/96

Crawford, Cindy, Cont.
Wm Morris
151 El Camino Dr
Beverly Hills, CA 90212
Forwarded V: 01/14/96

Wolf/Kasteler
132 S Rodeo Dr #300
Beverly Hills, CA 90212
Forwarded V: 11/01/96

Crawford, Johnny
Crawford Entertainment
PO Box 1851
Los Angeles, CA 90078
Actor V: 01/08/96

Crawford, Michael
c/o ICM
76 Oxford St
London W1N 0AX, England
Alternate V: 03/03/96

Crawford, William
PO Box 4
Palmer Lake, CO 80133-0004
War Hero V: 02/09/96

Creative Artists Agency
9830 Wilshire Bl
Beverly Hills, CA 90212
Talent Agency V: 06/13/96

Creatures At Large Press
c/o John Stanley
PO Box 687
Pacifica, CA 94044
Publisher V: 01/20/96

Crenna, Richard
Creative Artists Agency
9830 Wilshire Bl
Beverly Hills, CA 90212
Actor V: 12/07/96

3941 Valley Meadow Rd
Encino, CA 91436
Alternate V: 03/11/96

Crews, John R
1324 SW 54th St
Oklahoma City, OK 73119
War Hero V: 02/09/96

Cribbins, Bernard
c/o Salmon
59 Frith St
London W1V 5TA, England
Actor V: 01/17/96

Crippen, Robert L
NASA/LBJ Space Center
Houston, TX 77058
Astronaut V: 03/03/96

Crisp, Quentin
46 E 3rd St
New York, NY 10003
Author V: 06/02/96

Cristal, Linda
9129 Hazen Dr
Beverly Hills, CA 90210
Actress V: 02/02/96

Criton, Michael
433 N Camden Dr #500
Beverl Hills, CA 90210
Author V: 01/11/97

Critters of the Cinema
44400 N Shaffer Rd
Lake Hughes, CA 93532
Animal Talent V: 02/26/96

Cromwell, James
SDB Partners
1801 Ave of the Stars #902
Los Angeles, CA 90067
Actor V: 12/13/96

Cronkite, Walter
519 E 84th Ave
New York, NY 10028
Journalist V: 01/02/97

Cronyn, Hume
c/o ICM
8942 Wilshire Bl
Beverly Hills, CA 90211
Actor V: 12/11/96

63-23 Carlton St
Rego Park, NY 11374
Alternate V: 03/10/96

c/o ICM
8942 Wilshire Bl
Beverly Hills, CA 90211
Forwarded V: 03/02/95

Crosby, Cathy Lee
1223 Wilshire Bl #404
Santa Monica, CA 90403-5400
Actress V: 03/19/96

Crosby, David
c/o CAA
9830 Wilshire Bl
Beverly Hills, CA 90212
Singer V: 02/10/96

Crosby, Denise
c/o MTA
4526 Wilshire Bl
Los Angeles, CA 90010
Actress V: 02/12/96

ST-TNG/Paramount TV
5555 Melrose Ave
Los Angeles, CA 91522
Alternate V: 01/07/96

43-B St
Venice, CA 90291
Alternate V: 11/01/96

935 Embury St
Pacific Palisades, CA 90272
Forwarded V: 07/03/96

Crosby, Mary
Gold/Marshak
3500 W Olive Ave #1400
Burbank, CA 91505
Actress V: 12/10/96

5454 Gentry Ave
N Hollywood, CA 91606
Alternate V: 07/01/96

Crosby, Norm
1400 Londonderry
Los Angeles, CA 90069
Actor V: 07/01/96

9200 Sunset Bl #428
Los Angeles, CA 90069
Alternate V: 01/21/96

Cross, Ben
29 Burlington Gardens
London W4, England
Actor V: 04/14/96

Crossfield, Scott
12100 Thoroughbred Rd
Herndon, VA 22071
Test Pilot V: 04/01/96

Crow, Sheryl
Wm Morris
151 El Camino Dr
Beverly Hills, CA 90212
Singer V: 01/14/96

Crow & Associates
1010 Hammond St #102
W Hollywood, CA 90069
Talent Agency V: 11/11/96

Cruise, Tom
c/o CAA
9830 Wilshire Bl
Beverly Hills, CA 90212
Actor V: 02/01/96

Odin Productions
4400 Coldwater Canyon Ave #220
Studio City, CA 91604
Alternate V: 02/26/96

Crumb, Robert
Fantagraphics
7563 Lake City Way
Seattle, WA 98115
Cartonist V: 09/06/96

Cryer, John
9560 Wilshrie Bl #500
Beverly Hills, CA 90212
Actor V: 10/23/96

Cryer, Jon
Paradigm Agency
10100 Santa Monica Bl-25th Fl
Los Angeles, CA 90067
Actor V: 12/13/96

Crystal, Billy
9830 Wilshire Bl
Beverly Hills, CA 90212
Actor V: 01/03/97

Culbertson Jr, Frank L
NASA/LBJ Space Center
Hoston, TX 77058
Astronaut V: 04/02/94

Culkin, Macaulay
Wm Morris
151 El Camino
Beverly Hills, CA 90212
Actor V: 06/14/96

40 W 57th St
New York, NY 10019
Alternate V: 03/19/96

Cullen, Brett
Gersh Agency
232 N Canon Dr
Beverly Hills, CA 90210
Actor V: 01/15/97

Cullum, Mark
King Features
216 E 45th St
New York, NY 10017
Cartoonist V: 03/11/96

Culp, Robert
Ambrosio & Mortimer
9150 Wilshire Bl #175
Beverly Hills, CA 90212
Actor V: 12/01/96

357 Crown Dr
Los Angeles, CA 90049
Alternate V: 02/03/96

Cumber Attractions Agency
6363 Sunset Bl #807
Hollywood, CA 90028
Talent Agency V: 06/13/96

Cummings, Quinn
c/o Smith
121 N San Vicente Bl
Beverly Hills, CA 90211
Actress V: 02/12/96

Cummins, Gregory Scott
c/o Schiowitz
1680 N Vine St #614
Los Angeles, CA 90028
Actor V: 03/14/96

Cunningham, Walter
NASA/LBJ Space Center
Houston, TX 77058
Astronaut V: 03/03/96

Cuomo, Mario
c/o FOMC
845 3rd Ave-20th Fl
New York, NY 10022
Politician V: 01/07/96

Curb, Michael
3907 W Alameda Ave #2
Burbank, CA 91505-4332
Producer V: 02/01/96

Curry, Tim
c/o UTA
9560 Wilshire Bl-5th Fl
Beverly Hills, CA 90212
Actor V: 01/24/96

26666 Aberdeen Ave
Los Angeles, CA 90027
Forwarded V: 03/12/96

Curtin, Jane
PO Box 1070
Sharon, CT 06069-1070
Actress V: 11/10/96

Curtis, Jamie Lee
c/o CAA
9830 Wilshire Bl
Beverly Hills, CA 90212
Actress V: 01/14/96

PO Box 2358
Running Springs, CA 92382
Alternate V: 01/02/96

Curtis, Keene
c/o Schoen
606 N Larchmont Bl #309
Los Angeles, CA 90004
Actor V: 02/20/96

Curtis, Robin
House of Representatives
9911 Pico Bl #1060
Los Angeles, CA 90035
Actress V: 12/10/96

Curtis, Tony
PO Box 15577
Honolulu, HI 96830-5577
Actor V: 04/21/96

11831 Folkstone Lane
Los Angeles, CA 90077
Forwarded V: 02/19/96

Cusack, Ann
Innovative Artists
1999 Ave of the Stars #2850
Los Angeles, CA 90067
Actress V: 12/11/96

Cusack, John
838 Sheridan
Evanston, IL 60202
Actor V: 11/23/96

Cypher, Jon
424 Manzanita Ave
Ventura, CA 93003-1147
Actor V: 12/12/96

Pakula & King Agency
9229 Sunset Bl #315
Los Angeles, CA 90069
Alternate V: 12/12/96

Cyrus, Billy Ray
PO Box 121854
Nashville, NY 37212-1854
Singer V: 11/30/96

c/o McFadden
818 18th Ave S
Nashville, TN 37203-3219
Alternate V: 02/02/96

D

D'Abo, Maryam
Gage Group
9255 Sunset Bl #515
Los Angeles, CA 90069
Actress V: 12/08/96

Kohner Agency
9300 Wilshire Bl #555
Beverly Hills, CA 90212
Forwarded V: 05/12/96

D'Abo, Olivia
c/o ICM
8942 Wilshire Bl
Beverly Hills, CA 90211
Actress V: 02/08/96

335 N Maple Drive #360
Beverly Hills, CA 90210
Forwarded V: 03/03/96

D'Angelo, Beverly
8033 Sunset Bl #247
Los Angeles, CA 90046-2427
Actress V: 02/03/96

D'Arbanville, Patti
444 E 66th St #6-KK
New York, NY 10021
Actress V: 08/08/96

Abrahms Artists
9200 Sunset Bl #625
Los Angeles, CA 90069
Alternate V: 02/12/96

D'Errico, Donna
Rael Company
9255 Sunset Bl #425
Los Angeles, CA 90069
Actress V: 12/15/96

D'Rivera, Paquito
Havana-NY Music Co
PO Box 777
Union City, NJ 07087
Saxophonist V: 10/23/96

DANGEROUS CURVES
11811 W Olympic Bl
Los Angeles, CA 90064
Production Office V: 03/18/96

DANGEROUS MINDS
Disney Studios
500 S Buena Vista Bl
Burbank, CA 91521-0668
Production Office V: 11/11/96

ABC-TV
77 W 66th St
New York, NY 10023
Alternate V: 11/11/96

DARK JUSTICE
Lorimar TV
9644 Lurline Ave
Chatsworth, CA 91311
Production Office V: 01/16/96

DARK SKIES
NBC-TV
30 Rockefeller Plaza
New York, NY 10112
Viewer Services V: 11/11/96

DATELINE NBC
NBC News
30 Rockefeller Plaza
New York, NY 10112
Production Office V: 02/09/96

DAVE'S WORLD
CBS-TV
51 W 52nd St
New York, NY 10019
Production Office V: 12/15/96

DAVE'S WORLD
CBS-TV
4024 Radford Ave-Bldg 7
Studio City, CA 91604
Alternate V: 01/16/96

DAVIS RULES
Carsey-Warner
4024 Radford Ave #3
Studio City, CA 90604
Production Office V: 01/20/96

DAY ONE
147 Columbus Ave-8th Fl
New York, NY 10023
Production Office V: 01/21/96

DAYS OF OUR LIVES
NBC-TV Burbank
3000 W Alameda Ave
Burbank, CA 91523
Production Office V: 03/26/96

DH Talent
1800 N Highland Ave #300
Los Angeles, CA 90028
Talent Agency V: 02/02/96

DIAGNOSIS MURDER
Viacom Productions
10 Universal City Plz- 32nd Fl
Universal City, CA 91608-1009
Production Office V: 03/12/96

CBS-TV
51 W 52nd St
New York, NY 10019
Alternate V: 12/15/96

DIFFERENT WORLD
Carsey-Warner
4024 Radford Ave #3
Studio City, CA 90604
Production Office V: 01/20/96

DOUBLE RUSH
CBS-TV/Schukovsky-English
4024 Radford Ave
Studio City, CA 91604
Production Office V: 03/12/96

DR QUINN: MEDICINE WOMAN
CBS Entertainment
4024 Radford Ave
Building 1-Room 115
Studio City, CA 91604
Production Office V: 03/14/96

CBS-TV
51 W 52nd St
New York, NY 10019
Alternate V: 12/15/96

DREW CAREY SHOW
ABC-TV
77 W 66th St
New York, NY 10023
Production Office V: 12/15/96

Drew Carey Show, Cont.
WB-TV
4000 Warner Bl
Burbank, CA 91522
Alternate V: 01/14/96

DREXELL'S CLASS
FOX-TV
PO Box 900
Beverly Hills, CA 90213
Production Office V: 01/20/96

DUE SOUTH
Alliance Communications
940 Lansdowne Ave, Bldg 15-3rd Fl
Toronto, Ont, Canada M6H 4G9
Production Office V: 03/12/96

DWEEBS
Warner TV
6767 Forest Lawn Dr #100
Los Angeles, CA 90068
Production Office V: 10/23/96

DZA Talent
8981 Sunset Bl #204
Los Angeles, CA 90069
Talent Agency V: 11/11/96

Dade/Schultz Associates
11846 Ventura Bl #100
Studio City, CA 91604
Talent Agency V: 03/13/96

Dafoe, Willem
c/o CAA
9830 Wilshire Bl
Beverly Hills, CA 90212
Actor V: 03/17/96

33 Wooster St #200
New York, NY 10013
Alternate V: 07/21/96

Dahl, Arlene
PO Box 116
Sparkhill, NY 10976
Actress V: 11/01/96

Dailey, Bill
1331 Park Ave SW #802
Albuquerque, NM 87104
Actor V: 05/20/96

Daily, Janet
Janbill Ltd-SR#4
Box 2197
Branson, MO 65616
Author V: 06/05/96

Dalai Lama
Thekchen Choling, McLeod Gundi
Kangra District, Himachal
Pradesh, India
Reigious Leader V: 03/17/96

Dale, Jim
26 Pembridge Villas
London, W11 England
Actor V: 01/11/96

Hutton Mgmt
200 Fulham Rd
London SW10, England
Alternate V: 02/28/96

Dallas Cowboys
Cowboys Center
One Cowboys Parkway
Irving, TX 75063-4999
Team Office V: 06/12/96

Dallas Mavericks
Reunion Arena
777 Sports St
Dallas, TX 75207
Team Office V: 02/15/96

Dallas Stars
North Texas Ice Arena
10101 Cowboys Pkwy
Irving, TX 75063
Team Office V: 01/31/96

Dallenbach, Wally
Roush Racing
PO Box 1089
Liberty, NC 27298
NASCAR Driver V: 07/07/96

Dallesandro, Joe
4400 Ambrose Ave
Los Angeles, CA 90027
Actor V: 10/23/96

Dallis, Nick
King Features
235 E 45th St
New York, NY 10017
Cartoonist V: 05/02/96

Dalton, Abby
4755 Park Encino Ln
Sherman Oaks, CA 92403
Actress V: 10/23/96

Dalton, Lacy J
915 Millbury Ave
La Puente, CA 91646
Singer V: 01/13/97

Dalton, Timothy
Sharkey Associates
21 Golden Square
London W1R 3PA, England
Actor V: 06/01/96

Daltry, Roger
Trinifold Mgmt
Harley House/22 Marylebone Rd
London NW1 4PR, England
Singer V: 10/18/96

Daly, John
3710 Classic St
Memphis, TN 38125
Golfer V: 12/01/96

Daly, Tyne
Kohner Agency
9300 Wilshire Bl #555
Beverly Hills, CA 90212
Actress V: 12/11/96

700 N Westknoll Dr #302
Los Angeles, CA 90069
Alternate V: 01/14/96

Damon, Stuart
367 N Van Ness
Los Angeles, CA 90004
Actor V: 06/15/96

Dance, Charles
1311 N California St
Burbank, CA 91505
Actor V: 05/03/96

Danes, Claire
924 Westwood Bl #900
Los Angeles, CA 90024
Actress V: 01/14/97

Dangerfield, Rodney
530 E 76th St
New York, NY 10021
Actor V: 04/06/96

Paper Clip Productions
1888 Century Park E
Los Angeles, CA 90067
Forwarded V: 06/22/96

Daniels, Charlie
c/o Corlew
17060 Central Pike
Lebanon, TN 37087
Singer V: 02/02/96

Daniels, Jeff
PMK Public Relations
1776 Broadway #800
New York, NY 10019
Actor V: 10/23/96

c/o ICM
8942 Wilshire Bl
Beverly Hills, CA 90211
Alternate V: 02/08/96

Daniels, William
Artists Agency
10000 Santa Monica Bl #305
Los Angeles, CA 90067
Actor V: 12/03/96

Danner, Blythe
8942 Wilshire Bl
Beverly Hills, CA 90211
Actress V: 10/23/96

304 21st St
Santa Monica, CA 90402
Alternate V: 04/04/96

Danning, Sybil
611 S Catalina St #220
Los Angeles, CA 90005-1728
Actress V: 08/29/96

Danson, Ted
c/o CAA
9830 Wilshire Bl
Beverly Hills, CA 90212
Actor V: 01/14/96

132 S Rodeo Dr #300
Beverly Hills, CA 90212
Alternate V: 01/15/96

Danza, Tony
25000 Malibu Rd
Malibu, CA 90265
Actor V: 10/10/96

Sony Studios/DLean Bldg
10202 W Washington Bl
Culver City, CA 90232-3195
Forwarded V: 03/14/96

Darkow, John
King Features
216 E 45th St
New York, NY 10017
Cartoonist V: 03/11/96

Darren, James
PO Box 1088
Beverly Hills, CA 90213
Actor V: 06/15/96

Darrieux, Danielle
1 rue Alfred de Vingnu
Paris F-75008, France
Actress V: 03/14/96

Darrow, Henry
Schechter Agency
9300 Wilshire Bl #410
Beverly Hills, CA 90210
Actor V: 12/13/96

Kohner Agency
9300 Wilshire Bl #555
Beverly Hills, CA 90212
Alternate V: 01/02/96

Davenport, Jim
1016 Hewitt Dr
San Carlos, CA 94070
Baseball Star V: 12/10/96

Davenport, Nigel
Leading Artists
60 Saint James St
London SW1, England
Actor V: 04/02/96

2 Conduit St
London W1, England
Alternate V: 02/28/96

Davenport, Willie
714 Millgate Place
Baton Rouge, LA 70808
Olympian V: 10/23/96

Davi, Robert
Innovative Artists
1999 Ave of the Stars #2850
Los Angeles, CA 90067
Actor V: 12/11/96

David, Hal
12420 Ridge Rd
Los Angeles, CA 90049
Composer V: 03/02/96

Davidovitch, Lolita
c/o ICM
8942 Wilshire Bl
Beverly Hills, CA 90211
Actress V: 02/12/96

Davidson, Jaye
c/o ICM
8942 Wilshire Bl
Beverly Hills, CA 90211
Actor V: 01/14/96

Davidson, John
21243 Ventura Bl #101
Woodland Hills, CA 91364
Actor V: 03/02/96

1567 Spinnaker Dr
PO Box 213/189
Ventura Harbor, CA 93001
Alternate V: 01/22/96

6051 Spring Valley Rd
Hidden Hills, CA 91302
Forwarded V: 01/09/97

Davidson, Tommy
Wm Morris Agency
151 El Camino Dr
Beverly Hills, CA 90212
Actor V: 02/25/96

Davies, John Rhys
CCA Mgmt
4 Court Lodge, 48 Slone Sq
London SW 1, England
Actor V: 01/17/96

Davis, Ann B
Artists Group
10100 Santa Monica Bl #2490
Los Angeles, CA 90067
Actress V: 02/05/96

1427 Beaver Rd
Ambridge, PA 15003
Alternate V: 03/19/96

Davis, Clifton
Artists Group
10100 Santa Monica Bl #2490
Los Angeles, CA 90067
Actor V: 12/04/96

11431 Ventura Bl #275
Sherman Oaks, CA 91423-2606
Alternate V: 01/21/96

Davis, Eric
Klasy/Csupo
1258 N Highland Ave
Hollywood, CA 90038
Cartoonist V: 02/04/96

Davis, Gail
10615 Moorpark
N Hollywood, CA 91602
Actress V: 02/10/96

Davis, Geena
13160 Mulholland Dr
Beverly Hills, CA 90210
Actress V: 10/23/96

6201 Sunset Bl #7
Los Angeles, CA 90028
Alternate V: 02/01/96

c/o CAA
9830 Wilshire Bl
Beverly Hills, CA 90212
Forwarded V: 03/11/96

Davis, Glenn
47-650 Eisenhower Dr
LaQuinta, CA 92253
Football Star V: 04/03/96

Davis, Jeff
NASCAR
1811 Volusia Ave
Daytona Beach, FL 32015
NASCAR Driver V: 03/26/96

Davis, Judy
Colin Friels
129 Bourke St
Woollomooloo, Sydney
NSW 2011, Australia
Actress V: 03/02/96

Prince of Wales Theatre
Coventry St
London W1, England
Alternate V: 02/28/96

Davis, Mac
c/o MTA
4526 Wilshire Bl
Los Angeles, CA 90010
Singer V: 02/15/96

Davis, N Jan
NASA/LBJ Space Center
Hoston, TX 77058
Astronaut V: 06/06/96

Davis, Ossie
Artists Agency
10000 Santa Monica Bl #305
Los Angeles, CA 90067
Actor V: 12/03/96

Davis, Sammy L
RR22 Box 80A
Flat Rock, IL 62427
War Hero V: 02/01/96

Davis, Skeeter
c/o Taylor
48 Music Square E
Nashville, TN 37203
Singer V: 02/02/96

508 Seward Rd
Brentwood, TN 37027
Alternate V: 04/20/96

Davis Talent
515 N La Cienega Bl
Los Angeles, CA 90048
Talent Agency V: 11/11/96

Davison, Bruce
Wm Morris Agency
151 El Camino Dr
Beverly Hills, CA 90212
Actor V: 02/06/96

Davison, Peter
c/o Van Gelder
18/12 Jermyn St
London SW1V 6HP, England
Actor V: 01/02/96

c/o Conway
Eagle House, 109 Jermyn St
London SW1 6HB, England
Alternate V: 01/17/96

Dawber, Pam
c/o ICM
8942 Wilshire Bl
Beverly Hills, CA 90211
Actress V: 12/11/96

Wings Inc
2236 Encinitas Bl-Suite A
Encinitas, CA 92024
Forwarded V: 02/12/96

Dawson, Andre
6295 SW 58th Pl
Miami, FL 33143
Baseball Star V: 05/01/96

Dawson, Richard
1117 Angelo Dr
Beverly Hills, CA 90210
Actor V: 03/21/96

Day, Doris
PO Box 223163
Carmel, CA 93922
Actress V: 03/21/96

PO Box 8509
Universal City, CA 91608
Alternate V: 03/30/96

Day George, Lynda
10310 Riverside Dr #104
N Hollywood, CA 91602-2457
Actress V: 05/13/96

Day-Lewis, Daniel
Alister Reid
65 Connaught St
London W2, England
Actor V: 02/03/96

Wm Morris Agency
151 El Camino
Beverly Hills, CA 90212
Alternate V: 12/17/96

Julian Belfrage
60 St James St
London SW1, England
Forwarded V: 06/16/96

Dayne, Taylor
PO Box 476
Rockville Centre, NY 11571
Singer V: 03/21/96

De Haven, Gloria
88 Central Park West #12-G
New York, New York 10023
Actress V: 10/23/96

De Mornay, Rebecca
c/o JPM
760 N La Cienega Bl #200
Los Angeles, CA 90069
Actress V: 10/23/96

DeCamp, Rosemary
317 Camino de los Colinas
Redondo Beach, CA 90277
Actress V: 01/13/97

DeCordova, Fred
1875 Carla Ridge
Beverly Hills, CA 90210
Producer V: 02/21/96

Carson Productions
3000 W Alemeda Ave
Burbank, CA 91523
Alternate V: 05/16/96

DeForest, Calvert
c/o Ed Sullivan Theatre
1697 Broadway
New York, NY 10019
Actor V: 03/04/96

UN Productions
130 Engle St
Englewood, NJ 07631
Alternate V: 04/01/96

DeGeneres, Ellen
c/o UTA
15315 Magnolia Bl #429
Sherman Oaks, CA 91403
Actress V: 12/15/96

DeHaven, Gloria
88 Central Park West #12G
New York, NY 10023
Actress V: 01/19/96

73 Devonshire Rd
Cedar Grove, NJ 07009
Alternate V: 03/15/96

DeHavilland, Olivia
Boite Postal 156-16
Paris Cedex 16-75764, France
Actress V: 01/31/96

3 Rue Benouville
Paris, 751116 France
Alternate V: 06/02/96

DeLancie, John
SDB Partners
1801 Ave of the Stars #902
Los Angeles, CA 90067
Actor V: 12/13/96

1313 Brunswick Ave
S Pasadena, CA 91030
Alternate V: 04/02/96

DeLorenzo, Michael
Borinstein/Oreck & Bogart
8271 Melrose Ave #110
Los Angeles, CA 90046
Actor V: 12/06/96

DeLuise, Dom
1186 Corsica Dr
Pacific Palasides, CA 90272
Actor V: 09/09/96

Artists Group
10100 Santa Monica Bl #2490
Los Angeles, CA 90067
Alternate V: 01/31/96

DeLuise, Michael
1186 Corsica Dr
Pacific Palisades, CA 90272
Actor V: 09/06/96

DeLuise, Peter
Premiere Artists Agency
8899 Beverly Bl #510
Los Angeles, CA 90048
Actor V: 12/13/96

1223 Wilshire Bl #411
Santa Monica, CA 90403
Alternate V: 02/20/96

DeNiro, Robert
c/o CAA
9830 Wilshire Bl
Beverly Hills, CA 90212
Actor V: 01/14/96

9544 Hidden Valley Pl
Beverly Hills, CA 90210
Alternate V: 03/17/96

375 Greenwich St
New York, NY 10013
Forwarded V: 07/01/96

110 Hudson St
New York, NY 10018
Forwarded V: 03/15/96

DePalma, Brian
270 N Canon Dr #1195
Beverly Hills, CA 90210-5323
Producer V: 03/15/96

DeShannon, Jackie
7626 Sunnywood Ln
Los Angeles, CA 90046
Singer V: 05/06/96

DeVito, Danny
PO Box 491246
Los Angeles, CA 90049-9246
Actor V: 01/09/96

c/o CAA
9830 Wilshire Bl
Beverly Hills, CA 90212
Alternate V: 01/14/96

31020 Broadbeach Rd
Malibu, CA 90265
Forwarded V: 01/31/96

DeWitt, Joyce
1250 6th St #403
Santa Monica, CA 90401
Actress V: 08/08/96

DeYoung, Cliff
2143 Colby Ave
Los Angeles, CA 90025-6207
Actor V: 01/12/96

Dean, Billy
c/o CMS
1106 16th Ave South
Nashville, TN 37212
Singer V: 01/31/96

Dean, Eddie
32161 Sailview Ln
Westlake Village, CA 91361
Actor V: 02/19/96

Corriganville
PO Box 3688
Simi Valley, CA 93093
Alternate V: 12/12/94

Dee, Frances
Rt 3-Box 375
Camarillo, CA 93010
Actress V: 05/01/96

Dee, Ruby
PO Box 1318
New York, NY 10802
Actress V: 05/15/96

Dee, Sandra
The Agency
1800 Ave of the Stars #400
Los Angeles, CA 90067
Actress V: 05/15/96

8960 Cynthia St #306
Los Angeles, CA 90069-4446
Alternate V: 03/05/96

Dees, Rick
KITTS AM/FM Radio
3400 W Riverside Dr #800
Burbak, CA 91505-4671
Celebrity V: 06/22/96

Delaney, Delvene
Showcase #4
5 Alexander St-PO Box 951
Crows Nest 2065, Austrailia
Actress V: 07/03/96

Delaney, Kim
Gersh Agency
232 N Canon Dr
Beverly Hills, CA 90210
Actress V: 12/09/96

4724 Poe Ave
Woodland Hills, CA 91364-4656
Alternate V: 03/19/96

Delany, Dana
c/o ICM
8942 Wilshire Bl
Beverly Hills, CA 90211
Actress V: 12/11/96

2522 Beverly Ave
Santa Monica, CA 90405
Alternate V: 10/23/96

Delon, Alain
Adel Productions
4 rue Chambiges-3rd Fl
F-75008 Paris, France
Actor V: 01/17/96

Dench, Dame Judith
60 Saint James St
London SW1, England
Actress V: 03/12/96

Deneuve, Catherine
Alain Sarde
78 Champs-Elysees
Paris 75008, France
Actress V: 11/11/96

76 Rue Bonaparte
Paris 75016, France
Alternate V: 03/01/96

40 Rue Francois
Paris 75008, France
Forwarded V: 02/02/96

Dennehy, Brian
Smith & Associates
121 N San Vicente Bl
Beverly Hills, CA 90211
Actor V: 12/15/96

Dennison, Michael
c/o Agency
388 Oxford St
London W1, England
Actor V: 02/28/96

Densmore, John
49 Halderman Rd
Santa Monica, CA 90402
Musician V: 11/29/96

Denton, Christa
SDB Partners
1801 Ave of the Stars #902
Los Angeles, CA 90067
Actress V: 12/13/96

Denver, Bob
General Delivery-Box 269
Princeton, WV 24740
Actor V: 11/01/96

Denver, John
300 South Spring St
Aspen, CO 81611
Singer V: 01/31/96

PO Box 1587
Aspen, CO 81612
Alternate V: 07/03/96

Denver Broncos
5700 Logan St
Denver, CO 80216
Team Office V: 05/15/96

Denver Nuggets
1635 Clay St
Denver, CO 80204
Team Office V: 02/15/96

PO Box 4658
Denver, CO 80204-1799
Alternate V: 11/11/96

Depardieu, Gerard
c/o Gaumont
30 Ave Charles de Gaul
Neuilly-sur-Seine 92260, France
Actor V: 11/11/96

Depardieu, Gerard, Cont.
Penta Int'l
8 Queen St
London W1X 7PH, England
Alternate V: 02/09/96

DD Productions
10 ave George-V
F-75008 Paris France
Alternate V: 01/17/96

Depp, Johnny
c/o ICM
8942 Wilshire Bl
Beverly Hills, CA 90211
Actor V: 01/02/96

Derek, Bo
3275 Monticiello
Santa Ynez, CA 93460
Actress V: 06/01/96

Nu-Image
110 N Doheny
Beverly Hills, CA 90211
Forwarded V: 01/20/94

Derek, John
3275 Monticiello
Santa Ynez, CA 93460
Actor V: 11/01/96

Dern, Bruce
Creative Artists Agency
9830 Wilshire Bl
Beverly Hills, CA 90212
Actor V: 12/07/96

23430 Malibu Colony Dr
Malibu, CA 90265
Alternate V: 01/28/96

Dern, Laura
2401 Main St
Santa Monica, CA 90405-3515
Actress V: 12/15/96

760 N La Cienega Bl
Los Angeles, CA 90069
Alternate V: 03/02/96

Derrick, Coleman
New Jersey Nets
Meadowlands Arena
E Rutherford, NJ 07073
Basketball Star V: 04/05/96

Desiderio, Robert
3960 Laurel Canyon #280
Studio City, CA 91604
Actor V: 03/03/96

Details Magazine
350 Madison Ave
New York, NY 10017
Publisher V: 02/10/96

Detmers, Maruschka
Myriam Bru
80 ave Charles de Gaulle
F-92200 Neuilly s/s France
Actress V: 01/17/96

Detroit Lions
1200 Featherstone Rd
Pontiac, MI 48342
Team Office V: 05/15/96

Detroit Pistons
Palace of Auburn Hills
2 Championship Dr
Auburn Hills, MI 48057
Team Office V: 02/15/96

Detroit Red Wings
Joe Louis Sports Arena
600 Civic Center Dr
Detroit, MI 48225
Team Office V: 01/31/96

Detroit Tigers
Tiger Stadium
2121 Trumbull Ave
Detroit, MI 48216
Team Office V: 02/15/96

Devane, William
9000 Sunset Bl #1200
Los Angeles, CA 90069
Actor V: 01/15/96

Devroe Agency
6311 Romaine St
Los Angeles, CA 90038
Talent Agency V: 02/07/96

Dey, Susan
c/o ICM
8942 Wilshire Bl
Beverly Hills, CA 90211
Actress V: 12/11/96

Litke/Gale/Madder
10390 Santa Monica Bl #300
Los Angeles, CA 90025
Forwarded V: 10/10/96

DiCaprio, Leonardo
Gold/Marshak
3500 W Olive Ave #1400
Burbank, CA 91505
Actor V: 02/03/96

c/o CAA
9830 Wilshire Bl
Beverly Hills, CA 90212
Alternate V: 01/14/96

405 S Beverly Dr #500
Beverly Hills, CA 90212
Alternate V: 12/15/96

DiMaggio, Joe
c/o Engleberg
3230 Sterling Rd
Hollywood, FL 33021
Baseball Star V: 02/08/96

DiMucci, Dion
3099 NW 63rd St
Boca Raton, FL 33496-3309
Singer V: 01/21/96

DiPreta, Tony
King Features
235 E 45th St
New York, NY 10017
Cartoonist V: 01/04/96

Diamond, Neil
161 S Mapleton Dr
Los Angeles, CA 90077
Singer V: 03/03/96

Diamont, Don
15045 Sheriew Pl
Sherman Oaks, 91403
Actor V: 02/12/96

Diaz, Cameron
351 N Ogden Dr #7
Los Angeles, CA 90036
Actress V: 10/10/96

Dicenzo, George
Stone Hollow Farm
Rt 1, Box 728
Pipersville, PA 18947
Actor V: 01/12/96

Dick, Douglas
604 Gretna Green Way
Los Angeles, CA 90049
Actor V: 05/13/96

Dick Clark Productions
3003 W Olive
Burbank, CA 91505
Production Office V: 12/01/94

Dickerson, Eddie
c/o Penske
6 Knob Hill Rd
Mooresville, NC 28256
NASCAR Crew V: 03/12/96

Dickinson, Angie
Blake Agency
415 N Camden Dr #121
Beverly Hills, CA 90210
Actress V: 12/06/96

9580 Lime Orchard Rd
Beverly Hills, CA 90210
Alternate V: 10/04/96

Dickinson, Sandra
Howes & Prior
66 Berkeley House, Hay Hill
London W1X 7LH, England
Actress V: 02/04/96

Diddley, Bo
4426 Sorrel Lane SW
Albuquerque, NM 87105-6341
Musician V: 05/02/96

Dierkop, Charles
c/o BDP
10637 Burbank Bl
N Hollywood, CA 91601
Actor V: 01/31/96

Diffre, Joe
Image Management
27 Music Square E
Nashville, TN 37203
Singer V: 11/01/96

Diller, Phyllis
Loeb & Loeb
345 Park Ave
New York, NY 10154-0004
Actress V: 03/14/96

163 S Rockingham Rd
Los Angeles, CA 90049
Alternate V: 05/13/96

Dillman, Bradford
Artists Group
10100 Santa Monica Bl #2490
Los Angeles, CA 90067
Actor V: 12/04/96

Dillman, Bradford, Cont.
770 Hot Springs
Santa Barbara, CA 93103
Alternate V: 05/12/96

Dillon, Denny
c/o ICM
8942 Wilshire Bl
Beverly Hills, CA 90211
Actress V: 12/11/96

Dillon, Matt
49 W 9th St
New York, NY 10011
Actor V: 01/15/96

Dillon, Melinda
Innovative Artists
1999 Ave of the Stars #2850
Los Angeles, CA 90067
Actress V: 12/11/96

Dion, Celine
CP 65
Repentigny
Quebec J6A 5H7, Canada
Singer V: 11/01/96

Dion, Colleen
Abrams Artists
9200 Sunset Bl #625
Los Angeles, CA 90069
Actress V: 05/06/96

Directors Guild
7920 Sunset Bl
Los Angeles, CA 90046
Guild Office V: 01/12/96

Discovery Channel
7700 Wisconsin Ave
Bethesda, MD 20814-3522
Network HQ V: 03/01/96

Disney, Roy E
500 S Buena Vista St
Burbank, CA 91521-6018
Producer V: 03/03/96

Disney Adventures
500 S Buena Vista St
The Burbank Center #100
Burbank, CA 91521-6018
Publisher V: 02/10/96

Disney Channel
3800 W Alameda Ave
Burbank, CA 91505
Network HQ V: 03/01/96

Disney Company
500 S Buena Vista St
Burbank, CA 91521-6018
Production Office V: 12/12/96

Disney Company Archives
c/o D Smith
500 S Buena Vista St
Burbank, CA 91521-6018
Archive V: 03/10/96

Disney Imagineering
1401 Flower St
Glendale, CA 91201
Production Office V: 03/17/96

Disney Productions Ltd
European Offices
31-32 Soho Square
London W1, England
Production Office V: 03/01/96

Ditka, Mike
11 Warrington Dr
Lake Bluff, IL 60044
Football Star V: 10/23/96

Dixon, Craig
10630 Wellworth Ave
Los Angeles, CA 90024
Olympian V: 10/23/96

Dixon, Donna
8955 Norma Pl
Los Angeles, CA 90069
Actress V: 02/10/96

7708 Woodrow Wilson Ave
Los Angeles, CA 90046
Forwarded V: 01/19/96

Dixon, Ivan
2268 Maiden Lane
Altadena, CA 91001
Actor V: 03/05/96

Dobson, Kevin
PO Box 5617
Beverly Hills, CA 90210
Actor V: 01/13/97

Dodson, Barry
Sabco Racing
5901 Orr Rd
Charlotte, NC 27213
NASCAR Crew V: 02/08/96

Doherty, Shannen
Wm Morris Agency
151 El Camino Dr
Beverly Hills, CA 90212
Actress V: 01/14/96

Dohm, Gaby
Trogerstrasse 17
8000 Munchen 80
Germany
Actress V: 02/23/96

Dolby, Ray
Dolby Labs
100 Potrero Ave
San Francisco, CA 94103-4813
Inventor V: 04/16/96

Dolenz, Ami
Innovative Artists
1999 Ave of the Stars #2850
Los Angeles, CA 90067
Actress V: 02/10/96

RP Marcurri
10600 Holman Ave #1
Los Angeles, CA 90024
Forwarded V: 03/04/96

Dolenz, Mickey
c/o APA
9000 Sunset Bl #1200
Los Angeles, CA 90069
Actor V: 12/02/96

c/o Cameran
8369 Sausalito Ave-Suite A
West Hills, CA 91304
Alternate V: 02/26/96

c/o Agent
8A Brunswick Gardens
London W8, England
Forwarded V: 05/16/96

Domingo, Placido
150 Central Park S
New York, NY 10019
Opera Star V: 10/23/96

Domino, Fats
New Orleans Ent
3530 rue Delphine
New Orleans, LA 70131
Singer V: 02/13/96

Donahue, Elinor
House of Representatives
9911 Pico Bl #1060
Los Angeles, CA 90035
Actress V: 02/12/96

4525 Lemp Ave
N Hollywood, CA 91602
Alternate V: 05/14/96

Donahue, Phil
420 E 54th St #22-F
New York, NY 10022
Commentator V: 11/29/96

c/o NBC-TV
30 Rockefeller Plaza
New York, NY 10112
Alternate V: 01/14/96

Donlavey, Junie
5011 Midlothian Turnpike
Richmond, VA 23224
NASCAR Driver V: 03/02/96

Donner, Robert
c/o Klass
144 S Beverly Dr
Beverly Hills, CA 90212
Actor V: 02/26/96

Donner/Shuler Agency
Richard Donner
4000 Warner Bl-Bldg 102
Burbank, CA 91522
Production Office V: 03/17/96

Donohoe, Amanda
Wm Morris Agency
151 El Camino Dr
Beverly Hills, CA 90212
TV Host V: 02/17/96

Donovan, Art
1512 Jeffers Rd
Baltimore, MD 21204
Football Star V: 04/04/96

Donovan (Leitch)
PO Box 472
London SW7 2QB, England
Singer V: 03/21/96

8528 Walnut Dr
Los Angeles, CA 90046
Alternate V: 01/24/96

Doohan, James
DoFame Inc
PO Box 2800
Redmond, WA 98073
Actor V: 11/01/96

PO Box 1100
Burbank, CA 91507
Alternate V: 02/02/96

Stevens Talent
3518 W Cahuenga Bl #301
Los Angeles, CA 90068
Forwarded V: 12/15/96

Dooley, Paul
Camden ITG
822 S Robertson Bl #200
Los Angeles, CA 90035
Actor V: 02/21/96

Doran, Ann
3939 Walnut Ave
Carmichael, CA 95608-2191
Actress V: 01/20/96

Dorff, Stephen
Booth Schut
11350 Ventura Bl #206
Studio City, CA 91604
Actor V: 11/10/96

Dorn, Michael
Star Trek-TNG Paramount
5555 Melrose Ave
Hollywood, CA 90038
Actor V: 04/19/96

3751 Multiview Dr
Los Angeles, CA 90068
Alternate V: 01/12/96

Dotter, Bobby
NASCAR
1811 Volusia Ave
Daytona Beach, FL 32015
NASCAR Driver V: 03/14/96

Douglas, Donna
PO Box 49455
Los Angeles, CA 90049
Actress V: 04/21/96

Douglas, Illeana
Creative Artists Agency
9830 Wilshire Bl
Beverly Hills, CA 90212
Actress V: 12/07/96

Douglas, James Buster
465 Waterbury Ct-Suite A
Gahanna, OH 43230-5312
Boxing Star V: 08/29/96

James "Buster" Douglas Fan Club
PO Box 15912
Coumbus, OH 43215
Alternate V: 01/22/97

Douglas, Kirk
Creative Artists Agency
9830 Wilshire Bl
Beverly Hills, CA 90212
Actor V: 12/07/96

805 N Rexford
Beverly Hills, CA 90210
Alternate V: 03/14/96

Douglas, Michael
936 Hot Springs Rd
Montecito, CA 93108
Actor V: 03/15/96

PO Box 49054
Los Angeles, CA 90049-9054
Alternate V: 12/14/96

Dourif, Brad
c/o ICM
8942 Wilshire Bl
Beverly Hills, CA 90211
Actor V: 12/11/96

PO Box 3762
Beverly Hills, CA 90212
Alternate V: 04/06/96

Dove, Billie
Thunderbird Country Club
70612 Hwy 111
Rancho Mirage, CA 92270
Actress V: 01/24/96

Down, Lesley-Anne
Artists Group
10100 Santa Monica Bl #2490
Los Angeles, CA 90067
Actress V: 12/03/96

Downey, Roma
c/o Gersh Agency
232 N Canon Dr Dr
Beverly Hills, CA 90210
Actress V: 12/15/96

Downey Jr, Robert
1350 1/2 N Harper Ave
Los Angeles, CA 90046
Actor *V: 10/23/96*

c/o CAA
9830 Wilshire Bl
Beverly Hills, CA 90212
Alternate *V: 01/14/96*

29169 Heathercliff Rd #216533
Malibu, CA 90265
Forwarded *V: 05/03/96*

Downs, Hugh
c/o ABC News
157 Columbus Ave
New York, NY 10023
Commentator *V: 08/07/96*

Doyle, David
House of Representatives
9911 Pico Bl #1060
Los Angeles, CA 90035
Actor *V: 02/15/96*

Doyle, Jerry
Henderson & Hogan
247 S Beverly Dr #102
Bevery Hills, CA 90210
Actor *V: 12/10/96*

14431 Ventura Bl #260
Sherman Oaks, CA 91423
Alternate *V: 01/15/96*

8615 Tamarack
Sun Valley, CA 91352
Forwarded *V: 11/01/96*

Doyle-Murray, Brian
Abrams Artists
9200 Sunset Bl #625
Los Angeles, CA 90069
Actor *V: 12/01/96*

555 W 57th St #1230
New York, NY 10019
Alternate *V: 10/23/96*

Dr Demento
c/o KMET
5746 Sunset Bl
Los Angeles, CA 90028
Radio Star *V: 03/05/96*

Drago, Billy
Buckwald & Associates
9229 Sunset Bl #710
Los Angeles, CA 90069
Actor *V: 12/06/96*

Drake, Frances
1511 Summit Ridge Dr
Beverly hills, Ca 90210
Actress *V: 06/15/96*

Drake, Larry
Gersh Agency
232 N Canon Dr
Beverly Hills, CA 90210
Actor *V: 12/09/96*

Dravecky, Dave
19995 Chisholm Trail
Monument, CO 80132
Baseball Star *V: 02/02/96*

DreamWorks SKG
Executive Office
100 Universal City Plaza
Universal City, CA 91608
Producer *V: 01/14/96*

Drescher, Fran
Gersh Agency
232 N Canon Dr
Beverly Hills, CA 90210
Actress *V: 12/09/96*

2400 Whitman Pl
Los Angles, CA 90068
Alternate *V: 10/23/96*

Dreyfuss, Richard
c/o ICM
8942 Wilshire Bl
Beverly Hills, CA 90211
Actor *V: 12/15/96*

2809 Nicholas Canyon Rd
Los Angeles, CA 90046
Alternate *V: 02/28/96*

241 Central Park W
New York, NY 10024
Forwarded *V: 01/09/97*

Dru, Joanne
Janie Jackson
1459 Carla Ridge Dr
Beverly Hills, CA 90210
Actress *V: 06/01/96*

Drury, James
PO Box 899
Cypress, TX 77429-0899
Actor V: 08/28/96

12755 Mill Ridge #622
Cypress, TX 77429
Alternate V: 03/02/96

Dryer, Fred
4117 Radford Ave
Studio City, CA 91604-2105
Actor V: 01/09/96

The Agency
1800 Ave of the Stars #400
Los Angeles, CA 90067
Alternate V: 02/21/96

Duchovny, David
c/o ICM
8942 Wilshire Bl
Beverly Hills, CA 90211
Actor V: 12/11/96

110-555 Brooks Bank Bl #10
N Vancouver V7J 3S5, Canada
Alternate V: 01/14/96

Dudikoff, Michael
Craig Agency
8485 Melrose Place-Suite E
Los Angeles, CA 90069
Actor V: 12/08/96

1608 Via Zurita
Palos Verde, CA 90274
Alternate V: 02/01/96

Duffy, Julia
c/o ICM
8942 Wilshire Bl
Beverly Hills, CA 90211
Actress V: 12/11/96

c/o Lacey
5699 Kanan Rd #285
Agoura, CA 91301
Forwarded V: 04/22/96

Duffy, Patrick
Writers & Artists
924 Westwood Bl #900
Los Angeles, CA 90024
Actor V: 12/15/96

Dugan, Dennis
228 N Layton Dr
Los Angeles, CA 90049
Actor V: 06/06/96

c/o CAA
9830 Wilshire Bl
Beverly Hills, CA 90212
Alternate V: 02/02/96

Dukakis, Olympia
222 Upper Mountain Rd
Montclair, NJ 07043
Actress V: 02/20/96

Duke, Patty
2950 E Mettleton Rd
Coeur D'Alene, ID 83814
Actress V: 10/23/96

Duke Jr, Charles M
280 Lakeview
New Braunfels, TX 78130
Astronaut V: 03/17/96

PO Box 310345
New Braunfels, TX 78131-0345
Alternate V: 05/14/96

NASA/LBJ Space Center
Hoston, TX 77058
Forwarded V: 01/19/96

Dukes, David
255 S Lorraine Bl
Los Angeles, CA 90004
Actor V: 04/05/96

c/o ICM
8942 Wilshire Bl
Beverly Hills, CA 90211
Alternate V: 08/08/96

Dukes, Michael
5151 Collins Ave #522
Maimi Beach, FL 33140
Boxer V: 09/06/96

Dullea, Keir
320 Flemming Lane
Fairfield, CT 06430
Actor V: 02/09/96

c/o BDP
10637 Burbank Bl
N Hollywood, CA 91601
Forwarded V: 02/02/96

Dumas, Jerry
King Features
235 E 45th St
New York, NY 10017
Cartoonist V: 06/01/96

Dunagin, Ralph
King Features
235 E 45th St
New York, NY 10017
Cartoonist V: 07/26/96

Dunaway, Faye
8721 Beverly Bl-2nd Fl
Los Angeles, CA 90048-1803
Actress V: 03/14/96

PO Box 15778
Beverly Hills, CA 90209
Forwarded V: 10/23/96

Dunbar, Bonnie J
NASA/LBJ Space Center
Hoston, TX 77058
Astronaut V: 01/19/96

Duncan, Sandy
44 W 77th St
New York, NY 10024-5150
Actress V: 01/08/96

10390 Santa Monica Bl #300
Los Angles, CA 90025
Alternate V: 10/23/96

Dundee, Angelo
11264 Pines Bl
Hollywood, FL 33026-4101
Boxing Star V: 03/14/96

Dunn, Bob
King Features
235 E 45th St
New York, NY 10017
Cartoonist V: 03/19/96

Dunn, Nora
Smith & Associates
121 N San Vicente Bl
Beverly Hills, CA 90211
Actress V: 12/15/96

Dunne, Griffin
445 Park Ave #701
New York, NY 10022
Actor V: 03/12/96

Dunne, Holly
PO Box 2525
Hendersonville, TN 37077-2525
Singer V: 08/08/96

Dunst, Kirsten
Iris Burton Agency
PO Box 15306
Beverly Hills, CA 90209
Actress V: 10/23/96

Durbin, Deanna
BP 767
75123 Paris Cedex-03
France
Actress V: 11/01/96

Durkin Artists
127 Broadway #210
Santa Monica, CA 90401
Talent Agency V: 01/17/96

Durning, Charles
Paradigm Agency
10100 Santa Monica Bl-25th Fl
Los Angeles, CA 90067
Actor V: 12/13/96

10590 Wilshire Bl #506
Los Angeles, CA 90024
Alternate V: 01/11/97

Durst, Will
Worst of Durst
2107 Van Ness Ave #303
San Francisco, CA 94109-2536
Comedy Star V: 11/01/96

Durton, Jeff
Roush Racing
122 Knob Hill Rd
Mooresville, NC 28115
NASCAR Driver V: 10/23/96

Dussalt, Nancy
12211 Iredell St
Studio City, CA 91604
Actress V: 01/24/96

Duvall, Shelley
Gersh Agency
232 N Canon Dr
Beverly Hills, CA 90210
Actress V: 12/09/96

12445 Viewcrest Rd
Studio City, CA 91604
Alternate V: 11/01/96

Duvall, Shelley, Cont.
9595 Wilshire Bl #505
Beverly Hills, CA 90212
Forwarded V: 02/11/96

Dylan, Bob
PO Box 264
New York, NY 10003
Singer V: 01/19/96

PO Box 870-Cooper Station
New York, NY 10276
Alternate V: 08/01/96

Dysart, Richard
Writers & Artists
924 Westwood Bl #900
Los Angeles, CA 90024
Actor V: 12/15/96

654 Copeland Ct
Santa Monica, CA 90405
Alternate V: 04/06/96

Writers & Artists
11726 San Vicente Bl
Los Angeles, CA 90049
Forwarded V: 01/17/96

Dzundza, George
Gersh Agency
232 N Cannon Dr
Beverly Hills, CA 90210
Actor V: 04/02/96

E

E-Entertainment TV
5670 Wilshire Bl-2nd Fl
Los Angeles, CA 90036
Production Office V: 12/10/96

EARLY EDITION
CBS-TV
51 W 52nd St
New York, NY 10019
Viewer Services V: 11/11/96

Chicago Studio City
5660 W Taylor St
Chicago, IL 60644
Alternate V: 12/15/96

ELLEN
Walt Disney Studios
500 S Buena Vista St
Animation Bl #3D
Burbank, CA 91521-1844
Production Office V: 01/14/96

ABC-TV
77 W 66th St
New York, NY 10023
Alternate V: 12/15/96

EMPTY NEST
Witt/Thomas
846 N Cahuenga Bl
Hollywood, CA 90038
Production Office V: 01/20/96

ENTERTAINMENT TONIGHT
5555 Melrose Ave-Mae West Bldg
Los Angeles, CA 90038
Production Office V: 02/10/96

EQUAL JUSTICE
c/o Orion
1888 Century Park East
Los Angeles, CA 90067
Production Office V: 12/18/96

ER
Warner-TV
4000 Warner Brothers Bl
Producers Bldg 1, Rm 204
Burbank, CA 91505
Production Office V: 04/04/96

ESPN
ESPN Plaza
9665 Wilshire Bl #800
Beverly Hills, CA 90212
Production Office V: 03/17/96

ESPN Plaza
935 Middle St
Bristol, CT 06010-7454
Alternate V: 03/01/96

EVERYBODY LOVES RAYMOND
Worldwide Pants
1040 N Las Palmas-Bldg 24
Los Angeles, CA 90038
Production Office V: 12/15/96

EZ STREETS
CBS-TV
51 W 52nd St
New York, NY 10019
Viewer Services V: 11/11/96

Earles, H Clay
Martinsville Speedway
PO Box 3311
Martinsville, VA 24115
NASCAR Official V: 06/06/96

Earnhardt, Dale
Childress Racing
PO Box 1189, Industrial Dr
Welcome, NC 27374
NASCAR Driver V: 03/02/96

Rt 8, Box 463
Mooresville, NC 28115
Alternate V: 07/07/96

Earp, Wyatt
Media Artists
8383 Wilshire Bl #954
Beverly Hills, CA 90211
Actor V: 01/12/96

Eastiwich, Rawly
224 Chestnut St
Maddonfield, NJ 08033
Baseball Star V: 01/20/96

Eastman, Ben
RFD-RT #2
Hotchkiss, CO 81419
Olympian V: 10/23/96

Eastman, Kevin
Ninja Turtles
PO Box 417
Haydenville, CA MA 01039
Cartoonist V: 09/11/96

Easton, Robert
Kohner Agency
9300 Wilshire Bl #555
Beverly Hills, CA 90212
Actor V: 01/23/96

Easton, Sheena
Wm Morris Agency
151 El Camino Dr
Beverly Hills, CA 90212
Singer V: 02/01/96

Easton, William
Kohner Agency
9300 Wilshire Bl #555
Beverly Hills, CA 90212
Actor V: 12/11/96

Eastwood, Alison
Agence Gaulthier
62 bd Sebastopol
Paris F-75003 France
Model V: 11/01/96

Eastwood, Clint
PO Box 4366
Carmel, CA 93921
Actor V: 02/02/96

4000 Warner Bl #16
Burbank, CA 91522
Forwarded V: 02/02/96

Wm Morris Agency
151 El Camino Dr
Beverly Hills, CA 90212
Forwarded V: 01/14/96

Eber, Jose
9465 Wilshire Bl #606
Beverly Hills, CA 90212
Designer V: 01/02/97

Ebersole, Christine
Gersh Agency
232 N Canon Dr
Beverly Hills, CA 90210
Actress V: 12/09/96

1244-A 11th St
Santa Monica, CA 90401
Alternate V: 02/12/96

20 W 90 St-Suite A
New York, NY 10024
Forwarded V: 06/22/96

Ebert, Roger
c/o Ephraim
108 W Grand
Chicago, IL 60610
Film Critic V: 01/14/96

PO Box 146366
Chicago, IL 60614-6300
Alternate V: 04/04/96

Ebony Magazine
c/o Johnson
820 S Michigan Ave
Chicago, IL 60605
Publisher V: 02/10/96

Ebsen, Buddy
605 Via Horquilla
Palos Verdes Estates CA 90274
Actor *V: 12/07/96*

Borinstein/Oreck
8271 Melrose Ave #110
Los Angeles, CA 90046
Alternate *V: 01/02/96*

Eckersley, Dennis
263 Morse Rd
Sudbury, MA 01778
Baseball Star *V: 02/03/96*

Eckholdt, Steven
2275 N Gower
Los Angeles, CA 90068-2948
Actor *V: 01/11/97*

Eden, Barbara
c/o Eicholtz
9816 Denbigh
Beverly Hills, CA 90210
Actress *V: 03/01/96*

PO Box 57593
Sherman Oaks, CA 91403
Alternate *V: 01/14/96*

Edgland, Ty
PO Box 120964
Nashville, TN 37212-0964
Singer *V: 11/01/96*

Edmonton Oilers
Northlands Coliseum
Edmonton, Alberta, Canada T5B 4M9
Team Office *V: 02/01/96*

Edney, Beattie
c/o Equity
8 Harley St
London, W1N 2AB, England
Actress *V: 01/03/96*

Edwards, Anthony
NBC-TV
30 Rockefeller Plaza
New York, NY 10112
Actor *V: 01/14/96*

3373 Ley Dr
Los Angeles, CA 90027
Alternate *V: 10/23/96*

Edwards, Blake
11777 San Vicente Bl #501
Los Angeles, CA 90049
Producer *V: 11/11/96*

Edwards, Jennifer
526 Tuallitan Rd
Los Angeles, CA 90049-1943
Actress *V: 03/21/96*

Edwards, Stephanie
8075 W 3rd St #303
Los Angeles, CA 90048
Actress *V: 10/23/96*

Efendi Talent Agency
1923 1/2 Westwood Bl #3
Los Angeles, CA 90025
Talent Agency *V: 12/12/96*

Eggar, Samantha
Craig Agency
8485 Melrose Pl #E
Los Angeles, CA 90069
Actress *V: 02/12/96*

Eggert, Nicole
c/o UTA
15315 Magnolia Bl #429
Sherman Oaks, CA 91403
Actress *V: 12/15/96*

20591 Queens Park
Huntington Beach, CA 92646
Alternate *V: 02/23/96*

Eichhorn, Lisa
19 W 44th St #1000
New York, NY 10036
Actress *V: 02/21/96*

Eikenberry, Jill
Wm Morris Agency
151 El Camino
Beverly Hills, CA 90212
Actress *V: 02/12/96*

Eisman, Hy
King Features
235 E 45th St
New York, NY 10017
Cartoonist *V: 07/03/96*

Eisner, Michael D
500 S Buena Vista St
Burbank, CA 91521
Producer *V: 06/15/96*

Ekberg, Anita
c/o Video 3
Via Della Giuliana 38
Roma D-80802 Italy
Actress V: 11/01/96

Ekland, Britt
Sindell & Associates
8271 Melrose Ave #202
Los Angeles, CA 90069
Actress V: 12/14/96

16830 Ventura Bl #501
Encino, CA 91436-1717
Alternate V: 08/08/96

El Fadil, Saddig
Star Trek-DS9
5555 Melrose Ave
Hollywood, CA 90036
Actor V: 02/23/96

Dr's Exchange
PO Box 12254
La Crescenta, CA 91224-0954
Forwarded V: 01/14/96

Elam, Jack
Shapira & Associates
15301 Ventura Bl #345
Sherman Oaks, CA 91403
Actor V: 12/14/96

PO Box 5718
Santa Barbara, CA 93150
Alternate V: 11/01/96

Eleniak, Erika
DeLottie/Touche
2029 Century Park E #300
Los Angeles, CA 90067-2904
Actress V: 03/11/96

Wm Morris Agency
151 El Camino
Beverly Hills, CA 90212
Alternate V: 12/12/96

Elfman, Jenna
Studio Center
4024 Radford Ave
Studio City, CA 91604
Actress V: 11/11/96

Slessinger & Associates
8730 Sunset Bl-Suite 220 W
Los Angeles, CA 90069
Alternate V: 12/15/96

Elise, Christine
400 S Beverly Dr #216
Beverly Hills, CA 90212
Actress V: 01/13/97

Elite Model Mgmt
345 North Maple Dr #397
Beverly Hills, CA 90210
Talent Agency V: 02/02/96

Elizondo, Hector
Wm Morris Agency
151 El Camino
Beverly Hills, CA 90212
Actor V: 12/12/96

Elk, Jim
Dade/Schultz
11846 Ventura Bl #100
Studio City, CA 91604
Actor V: 01/31/96

Ellerbee, Linda
King Features
216 E 45th St
New York, NY 10017
Author V: 03/11/96

Lucky Duck Productions
96 Morton St #600
New York, NY 10014
Alternate V: 02/23/96

Elliot, Alison
Innovative Artists
1999 Ave of the Stars #2850
Los Angeles, CA 90067
Actress V: 12/15/96

Elliot, Win
14 October Rd
Weston, CT 06883
Radio Star V: 03/11/96

Elliott, Bill
Johnson & Associates
Rt 2, Box 162
Rhonda, NC 28670
NASCAR Driver V: 03/02/96

PO Box 435
Dawsonville, GA 30534
Alternate V: 11/20/96

Elliott, Chris
563 N Bronson Ave
Los Angeles, CA 90004
Actor V: 01/03/97

Elliott, David James
c/o UTA
9560 Wilshire Bl-5th Fl
Beverly Hills, CA 90212
Actor V: 01/15/97

Elliott, Sam
33050 Pacific Coast Hwy
Malibu, CA 90265
Actor V: 06/15/96

Ellis, Janet
Arlington Entertainment
1/3 Charlotte St
London W1P 1HD, England
Actress V: 02/04/96

Ellis Talent Group
6025 Sepulveda Bl #201
Van Nuys, CA 91411
Talent Agency V: 07/23/96

Ellison, Harlan
Kilimajaro Group
PO Box 55548
Sherman Oaks, CA 91413-0548
Author V: 02/26/96

Elrod, Jack
7240 Hunter's Branch Dr NE
Atlanta, GA 30328
Cartoonist V: 11/01/96

Elvira
Panacea Entertainment
2705 Glendower Ave
Los Angeles, CA 90027
Personality V: 01/21/96

Cassandra Peterson
PO Box 38246
Hollywood, CA 90038
Alternate V: 03/01/96

Ely, Ron
4146 Mariposa Dr
Santa Barbara, CA 93110
Actor V: 07/07/96

Emberg, Kelly
1608 N Poinsettia
Manhattan Beach, CA 90266
Model V: 02/23/96

Emerald Artists
6565 Sunset Bl #312
Hollywood, CA 90068
Talent Agency V: 02/02/96

Encore
2200 Fletcher Ave
Ft Lee, NJ 07024
Production Office V: 12/15/96

5445 DTC Parkway #600
Englewood, CO 80111
Alternate V: 12/15/96

England, Anthony W
NASA/LBJ Space Center
Houston, TX 77058
Astronaut V: 03/03/96

England, Ty
PO Box 120964
Nashville, TN 37212-0964
Singer V: 11/01/96

Engle, Joe H
NASA/LBJ Space Center
Houston, TX 77058
Astronaut V: 03/03/96

Englund, Robert
Abrams Artists
9200 Sunset Bl #625
Los Angeles, CA 90069
Actor V: 12/01/96

2029 Pinehurst Rd
Los Angeles, CA 90068-3731
Alternate V: 03/05/96

Ensign, Michael
Abrams Artists
9200 Sunset Bl #625
Los Angeles, CA 90069
Actor V: 01/17/96

Entertainment Network
11111 Santa Monica Bl #1210
Los Angeles, CA 90025
Production Office V: 03/17/96

Entertainment Weekly
1675 Broadway
New York, NY 10019
Publisher V: 03/01/96

Ephron, Nora
8942 Wilshire Bl
Beverly Hills, CA 90211
Director V: 01/14/96

Epstein & Wycoff
280 S Beverly Dr #400
Beverly Hills, CA 90212
Talent Agency V: 04/27/96

Erdman, Richard
c/o Moss
733 N Seward St-PH
Los Angeles, CA 90038
Actor V: 03/13/96

Ermey, R Lee
c/o MTA
4526 Wilshire Bl
Los Angeles, CA 90010
Actor V: 02/20/96

Metro Talent Agency
4526 Wilshire Bl
Los Angeles, CA 90010
Alternate V: 12/11/96

Erskine, Carl
6214 S Madison Ave
Anderson, IN 46013
Baseball Star V: 01/20/96

Erving, Julius
PO Box 25040
Southwark Station
Philadelphia, PA 19147
Basketball Star V: 01/15/96

Erwin, Bill
Dade/Schultz
11846 Ventura Bl #100
Studio City, CA 91604
Actor V: 02/02/96

Eskelson, Dana
CBS-Audience Services
51 W 52nd St
New York, NY 10019
Actress V: 12/12/96

Estefan, Gloria
Estefan Enterprises
6205 SW 40th St
Miami, FL 33155
Singer V: 04/03/96

Int'l FC
PO Box 4447
Miami, FL 33269
Forwarded V: 02/28/96

Estes, Rob
c/o ICM
8942 Wilshire Bl
Beverly Hills, CA 90211
Actor V: 12/15/96

Estevez, Emilio
PO Box 4041
Malibu, CA 90264-4041
Actor V: 05/06/96

31725 Sea Level Dr
Malibu, CA 90265
Alternate V: 03/17/96

Estevez, Ramon
837 Ocean Ave #101
Santa Monica, CA 90402
Actor V: 01/20/96

Estrada, Eric
3768 Eureka Dr
Studio City, CA 91604
Actor V: 03/19/96

Eubanks, Bob
5900 Highridge Rd
Hidden Hills, CA 91302
TV Host V: 01/13/97

Evangelista, Linda
c/o Elite
8 Bis rue Le Cuirot
75014 Paris, France
Model V: 12/01/96

Evans, Andrea
310 W 72nd St #7G
New York, NY 10023
Actress V: 08/30/96

Artists Group
10100 Santa Monica Bl #2490
Los Angeles, CA 90067
Alternate V: 02/12/96

Evans, George
King Features
235 E 45th St
New York, NY 10017
Cartoonist V: 06/26/96

Evans, Greg
King Features
235 E 45th St
New York, NY 10017
Cartoonist V: 02/13/96

Evans, Linda
Wm Morris Agency
151 El Camino
Beverly Hills, CA 90212
Actress V: 12/12/96

Evans, Linda, Cont.
6714 Villa Madera Dr SW
Tacoma, WA 98499
Alternate V: 03/30/96

167 S Canon Dr
Beverly Hills, CA 90212
Forwarded V: 02/17/96

Evans, Troy
Ambrosio/Mortimer
9150 Wilshire Bl #175
Beverly Hills, CA 90212
Actor V: 01/31/96

Everest, Pete
12440 E Barbary Coast Rd
Tucson, AZ 85749
Test Pilot V: 01/31/96

Everest Jr, Frank K
12440 E Barbary Coast Rd
Tucson, AZ 85749
Test Pilot V: 10/23/96

Everett, Chad
Artists Group
10100 Santa Monica Bl #2490
Los Angeles, CA 90067
Actor V: 12/04/96

5472 Island Forest Pl
Westlake Village, CA 91312-5406
Alternate V: 02/21/96

Everhart, Angie
Next Model Mgmt
23 Watts St-6th Fl
New York, NY 10013-1639
Model V: 03/14/96

Everly, Don
PO Box 120725
Nashville, TN 37212
Singer V: 10/23/96

Everly, Phil
10414 Camarillo St
N Hollywood, CA 91602
Singer V: 10/23/96

Everson, Cory
Cory Power
690-A Los Angeles Ave #115
Simi Valley, CA 93065
Fitness Expert V: 01/09/96

Everson, Cory, Cont.
c/o ACS
233 12th St #805
Columbus, OH 31901
Forwarded V: 03/09/96

ESPN 'Gotta Sweat'
ESPN Plaza
Bristol, CT 06010-7454
Forwarded V: 01/09/96

Evert, Chris
Evert Ent/IMG
7200 W Camino Real #310
Boca Raton, FL 33433-5537
Tennis Star V: 02/28/96

701 NE 12th Ave
Ft Lauderdale, FL 33304
Alternate V: 02/20/96

F

FACE TO FACE
CBS Broadcast Center
524 W 57th St
New York, NY 10019
Production Office V: 06/15/96

FAMILY MATTERS
Warner Bros-TV
4000 Warner Bl
Burbank, CA 91522
Production Office V: 01/16/96

FAMILY MATTERS
ABC-TV
77 W 66th St
New York, NY 10023
Alternate V: 12/15/96

FBI-UNTOLD STORIES
100 Universal Plaza #447
Universal City, CA 91608
Production Office V: 03/19/96

FEDS
Wolf Films/Universal
100 Universal City Plaza
Universal City, CA 91608
Production Office V: 12/15/96

FEDS
CBS-TV
51 W 52nd St
New York, NY 10019
Audience Services V: 01/13/97

FIRED UP
NBC-TV
30 Rockefeller Plaza
New York, NY 10112
Audience Services V: 01/13/97

FOREVER KNIGHT
Tri-Star Television
7 Curity Avenue-2nd Fl
Toronto, Ontario, Canada M4Y 1W5
Production Office V: 03/18/96

48 HOURS
CBS Broadcast Center
48 Hours
524 W 57th St
New York, NY 10019
Production Office V: 06/15/96

FOX-TV
PO Box 900
Beverly Hills, CA 90213
Production Office V: 01/21/96

5746 Sunset Bl
Hollywood, CA 90028
Alternate V: 03/18/96

205 E 67th St
New York, NY 10021
Alternate V: 02/27/96

10201 W Pico Bl
Los Angeles, CA 90035
Forwarded V: 03/11/96

FPA
12701 Moorpark #205
Studio City, CA 91604
Talent Agency V: 05/13/96

FRASIER
Paramount Studios
5555 Melrose Ave/Studio 25
Los Angeles, CA 90038
Production Office V: 01/20/96

NBC-TV
30 Rockefeller Plaza
New York, NY 10112
Alternate V: 12/15/96

FRESH PRINCE OF BEL-AIR
NBC Productions
3000 W Alameda Ave-Studio 11
Burbank, CA 91523
Production Office V: 11/11/96

NBC Productions
330 Bob Hope Dr
Burbank, CA 91523
Alternate V: 01/20/96

FRIENDS
Warner TV
300 S Television Plaza
Bl 136 Ste 266
Burbank, CA 91050
Production Office V: 11/20/96

NBC-TV
30 Rockefeller Plaza
New York, NY 10112
Alternate V: 12/15/96

FULL HOUSE
Warner Bros TV
4000 Warner Bl
Burbank, CA 91522
Production Office V: 01/16/96

FXM
PO Box 900
Beverly Hills, CA 90213-0900
Production Office V: 12/15/96

Fabares, Shelley
PO Box 6010-826
Sherman Oaks, CA 91413
Actress V: 01/31/96

Fabian, Ava
Playboy Studio West
2112 Broadway St
Santa Monica, CA 90404-2912
Model V: 11/10/96

Fabian, John M
NASA/LBJ Space Center
Houston, TX 77058
Astronaut V: 03/03/96

Fabio
PO Box 4
Inwood, NY 11696
Model V: 11/01/96

c/o Richman
9777 Wilshire Bl #915
Beverly Hills, CA 90212
Alternate V: 01/14/96

Fabray, Nanette
Writers & Artists
924 Westwood Bl #900
Los Angeles, CA 90024
Actress V: 12/15/96

14360 Sunset Bl
Pacific Palisades, CA 90272
Alternate V: 04/04/96

Face, Roy
608 Della Dr #5-F
N Versailles, PA 15137
Baseball Star V: 01/20/96

Fagerbakke, Bill
1500 Will Geer Rd
Topanga, CA 90290-4238
Actor V: 11/10/96

Faherty, Tim
King Features
216 E 45th St
New York, NY 10017
Cartoonist V: 03/11/96

Fairbanks Jr, Douglas
The Inverness Corp
545 Madison Ave
New York, NY 10022
Actor V: 05/02/96

Fairchild, Morgan
Shapira & Associates
15301 Ventura Bl #345
Sherman Oaks, CA 91403
Actress V: 12/13/96

2424 Bowmont Dr
Beverly Hills, CA 90210-1811
Alternate V: 01/12/96

Falk, Lee
King Features
235 E 45th St
New York, NY 10017
Cartoonist V: 06/25/96

Falk, Peter
100 Universal City Pl
Bldg #507-Suite 1B
Universal City, CA 91608
Actor V: 11/01/96

1004 N Roxbury Dr
Beverly Hills, CA 90210
Alternate V: 09/23/96

Falwell, Jerry L
Liberty Baptist Fellowship
3765 Candler's Mountain Rd
Lynchburg, VA 24506
Religious Leader V: 10/23/96

Family Channel
2877 Guardian Lane
PO Box 2050
Virginia Beach, VA 23450-2050
Production Office V: 01/12/96

Family Communications
4802 5th Ave
Pittsburgh, PA 15213
Production Office V: 01/21/96

Faracy, Stephanie
8765 Lookout Mtn Rd
Los Angeles, CA 90046
Actress V: 02/23/96

Farentino, Debra
Innovative Artists
1999 Ave of the Stars #2850
Los Angeles, CA 90067
Actress V: 02/12/96

10390 Santa Monica Bl #300
Los Angeles, CA 90025
Forwarded V: 03/15/96

Farentino, James
1340 Londonderry Pl
Los Angeles, CA 90069
Actor V: 03/17/96

Fargo, Donna
Prima-Donna
PO Box 150527
Nashville, TN 37215
Singer V: 02/02/96

Farina, Dennis
c/o Geddes
1201 Greenacre Ave
Los Angeles, CA 90046-5707
Actor V: 11/10/96

Farley, Chris
9150 Wilshire Bl #350
Beverly Hills, CA 90212
Actor V: 09/11/96

Farnsworth, Richard
20th Century Artists
15315 Magnolia Bl #429
Sherman Oaks, CA 91403
Actor V: 12/15/96

Farnsworth, Richard, Cont.
Diamond 'D' Ranch
Box 215
Lincoln, NM 88338-0215
Alternate V: 01/07/96

Farr, Jamie
Artists Group
10100 Santa Monica Bl #2490
Los Angeles, CA 90067
Actor V: 12/04/96

99 Buckshin Rd
Bell Canyon
Canoga Park, CA 91307
Alternate V: 02/02/96

53 Ranchero
Bell Canyon, CA 91307
Forwarded V: 10/23/96

Farrell, Cirroc
20th Century Artists
14724 Ventura Bl-5th Fl
Sherman Oaks, CA 91403
Actor V: 02/23/96

Farrell, Mike
Paradigm Agency
10100 Santa Monica Bl-25th Fl
Los Angeles, CA 90067
Actor V: 12/13/96

PO Box 6010-826
Sherman Oaks, CA 91413
Alternate V: 04/03/96

Farrell, Sharon
1619 Oak Dr
Topanga, CA 90290
Actress V: 06/09/96

Farrell, Terry
Buckwald & Associates
9229 Sunset Bl #710
Los Angeles, CA 90069
Actress V: 12/06/96

Kohner Agency
9300 Wilshire Bl #555
Beverly Hills, CA 90212
Alternate V: 02/12/96

Star Trek-DS9
5555 Melrose Ave
Hollywood, CA 90036
Alternate V: 02/23/96

Farrell, Tommy
5225 Riverton Ave
N Hollywood, CA 91601
Actor V: 02/12/96

Farrell/Coulter Talent
PO Box 15189
N Hollywood, CA 91615
Talent Agency V: 11/11/96

Farrow, Mia
Wm Morris
151 El Camino Dr
Beverly Hills, CA 90212
Actress V: 01/14/96

124 Henry Sanford Rd
Bridewater, CT 06752-1213
Alternate V: 11/10/96

Faustino, David
Artists Agency
10000 Santa Monica Bl #305
Los Angeles, CA 90067
Actor V: 12/03/96

1806 N Maple St
Burbank, CA 91505
Alternate V: 03/03/96

Fawcett, Farrah
c/o HAA
8033 Sunset Bl-#F
Los Angeles, CA 4059A
Actress V: 10/23/96

3130 Antelo Rd
Los Angeles, CA 90077
Alternate V: 06/06/96

9507 Heather Rd
Beverly Hills, CA 90210-1739
Alternate V: 01/12/96

Faye, Alice
49400 JFK Trail
Palm Desert, CA 92260
Actress V: 05/05/96

Fedewa, Tim
NASCAR
1811 Volusia Ave
Daytona Beach, FL 32015
NASCAR Driver V: 03/14/96

Feinstein, Diane
30 Presidio Terrace
San Francisco, CA 94118
Politician V: 03/14/96

Feldman, Corey
3209 Tareco Dr
Los Angeles, CA 90068-1525
Actor V: 11/10/96

c/o Dobson
1917 1/2 Westwood Bl #2
Los Angeles, CA 90025
Alternate V: 11/10/96

2138 N Cahuenga Bl
Hollywood, CA 90068
Alternate V: 11/10/96

Feldon, Barbara
14 E 74th St
New York, NY 10021
Actress V: 10/10/96

Creative Artists Agency
9830 Wilshire Bl
Beverly Hills, CA 90212
Alternate V: 02/12/96

Fell, Norman
4335 Marina City Dr
Marina del Rey, CA 90292
Actor V: 01/20/96

Feller, Bob
Ro-An-Fel Inc
Box 157
Gates Mill, OH 44040
Baseball Star V: 04/16/96

Fenn, Sherilyn
3758 Regal Vista Dr
Sherman Oaks, CA 91403
Actress V: 02/02/96

Ferrar-Maziroff Agency
8430 Santa Monica Bl #220
Los Angeles, CA 90069
Talent Agency V: 03/13/96

Ferrare, Cristina
Shapira & Associates
15301 Ventura Bl #345
Sherman Oaks, CA 91403
Actress V: 12/13/96

1280 Stone Canyon Rd
Los Angeles, CA 90077
Alternate V: 01/23/96

Ferratti, Rebecca
9242 Beverly Bl
Beverly Hills, CA 90210
Playmate V: 01/13/97

Ferratti, Rebecca, Cont.
Edge Comic Company
15301 Bitner Pl
Moopark, CA 93021
Alternate V: 01/02/97

c/o MIM
9255 Sunset Bl-Suite 727
Los Angeles, CA 90069
Forwarded V: 01/02/97

Ferrell, Conchata
1335 Seward St
Los Angeles, CA 90028
Actress V: 05/13/96

Paradigm Agency
10100 Santa Monica Bl-25th Fl
Los Angeles, CA 90067
Alternate V: 12/13/96

Ferreol, Andrea
Writers & Artists
924 Westwood Bl #900
Los Angeles, CA 90024
Actress V: 02/12/96

Ferrigno, Lou
Craig Agency
8485 Melrose Place-Suite E
Los Angeles, CA 90069
Fitness Expert V: 12/08/96

621 17th St
Santa Monica, CA 90402
Alternate V: 03/07/96

Craig Agency
8485 Melrose Place #E
Los Angeles, CA 90069
Alternate V: 03/17/96

PO Box 1671
Santa Monica, CA 90406
Alternate V: 11/01/96

Fidrych, Mark
171 Crescent St #B
Shresbury, MA 01545
Baseball Star V: 01/20/96

Field, Sally
PO Box 492417
Los Angeles, CA 90049
Actress V: 01/11/97

9830 Wilshire Bl
Beverly Hills, CA 90212
Alternate V: 01/14/96

Field, Shirley Ann
c/o Buchwald
9229 Sunset Bl #710
Los Angeles, CA 90069
Actress V: 02/12/96

Fielder, John
c/o ICM
8942 Wilshire Bl
Beverly Hills, CA 90211
Actor V: 02/01/96

225 Adams St #10-B
Brooklyn, NY 11201
Alternate V: 01/12/97

Fields, Debbie
Mrs Fields Cookies
333 Main St-PO Box 4000
Park City, UT 84060-4000
Entrepreneur V: 01/09/96

Fields, Holly
Shapira & Associates
15301 Ventura Bl #345
Sherman Oaks, CA 91403
Actress V: 12/14/96

c/o Borinstein
8271 Melrose Ave #110
Los Angeles, CA 90046
Forwarded V: 02/01/96

Fields Talent
3325 Wilshire Bl #749
Los Angeles, CA 90010
Talent Agency V: 03/29/96

Fiennes, Ralph
c/o CAA
9830 Wilshire Bl
Beverly Hills, CA 90212
Actor V: 01/14/96

Larry Dalzell
17 Broad Ct #12
London WC2B 5QN, England
Alternate V: 11/11/96

Fierstein, Harvey
Innovative Artists
1999 Ave of the Stars #2850
Los Angeles, CA 90067
Actor V: 12/11/96

15 Hawthorne Rd
Ridgefield, CT 06877
Alternate V: 02/08/96

Fierstein, Harvey, Cont.
c/o AGF
30 W 21st St #700
New York, NY 10010
Alternate V: 09/11/96

c/o Gersh
232 N Canon Dr
Beverly Hills, CA 90210
Forwarded V: 02/22/96

Film Artists Associates
7080 Hollywood Bl #1118
Hollywood, CA 90028
Talent Agency V: 03/29/96

Film Arts Foundation
Videotape Library
346 9th St-2nd Fl
San Francisco, CA 94103
Archive V: 03/14/96

Film Threat Magazine
9171 Wilshire Bl #300
Beverly Hills, CA 91505
Publisher V: 02/10/96

Financial News Network
6701 Center Dr W
W Los Angeles, CA 90045
Production Office V: 03/17/96

Fingers, Rollie
4944 Smith Canyon Ct
San Diego, CA 92126
Baseball Star V: 01/13/97

Finkel, Fyvush
Silver/Massetti
8730 Sunset Bl #480
Los Angeles, CA 90069
Actor V: 12/14/96

PO Box 900
Beverly Hills, CA 90213
Alternate V: 01/09/96

Finney, Albert
39 Seymour Walk
London, SW10 England
Actor V: 02/23/96

25 Dover St
London W1, England
Alternate V: 02/18/96

388 Oxford St
London W1 England
Alternate V: 01/19/96

Fiorentino, Linda
c/o CAA
9830 Wilshire Bl
Beverly Hills, CA 90212
Actress V: 01/14/96

c/o UTA
9560 Wishire Bl #500
Beverly Hills, CA 90212
Alternate V: 01/10/96

First Artists Agency
10000 Riverside Dr #10
Toluca Lake, CA 91602
Talent Agency V: 03/17/96

Firth, Peter
Froggert Mgmt
4 Windmill St
London W1, England
Actor V: 02/28/96

Fischer, Helmut
Kaiserplatz 5
8000 Munchen 40, Germany
Actor V: 02/23/96

Fishburne, Lawrence
10100 Santa Monica Bl-25th Fl
Los Angeles, CA 90067
Actor V: 01/14/96

c/o Sugland
5200 Lankersham Bl #260
N Hollywood, CA 91601
Alternate V: 01/02/96

Fisher, Anna L
NASA/LBJ Space Center
Hoston, TX 77058
Astronaut V: 01/19/96

Fisher, Carrie
9830 Wilshire Bl
Beverly Hills, CA 90212
Actress V: 01/14/96

7985 Santa Monica Bl #109-336
Los Angeles, CA 90046
Alternate V: 03/03/96

1700 Coldwater Canyon
Beverly Hills, CA 90210
Forwarded V: 03/15/96

Fisher, Eddie
1000 N Point St #1802
San Francisco, CA 94109
Singer V: 03/19/96

Fisher, Frances
IFA Talent
8730 Sunset Bl #490
Los Angeles, CA 90069
Actress V: 12/11/96

Fisher, Gail
1150 S Hayworth Ave
Los Angeles, CA 90035
Actress V: 04/01/96

Fisher, Joely
c/o UTA
15315 Magnolia Bl #429
Sherman Oaks, CA 91403
Actress V: 12/15/96

Fisher, William F
NASA-LBJ Space Center
Houston, TX 77058
Astronaut V: 03/03/96

Fitzgerald, Geraldine
50 E 79th St
New York, NY 10021
Actress V: 04/01/96

Flagg, Fannie
1520 Willina Ln
Montecito, CA 93108
Actress V: 04/12/96

Flanery, Sean Patrick
185 San Felipe Ave
San Francisco, CA 94127
Actor V: 12/01/96

Flannery, Susan
Gersh Agency
232 N Canon Dr
Beverly Hills, CA 90210
Actress V: 10/23/96

Fleetwood, Mick
2899 Agoura Rd #582
Westlake Village, CA 91367
Musician V: 10/23/96

Fleming, Peggy
16387 Aztec Ridge
Los Gatos, CA 95030
Olympian V: 02/21/96

Fleming, Rhonda
10281 Century Woods Dr
Los Angeles, CA 90067
Actress V: 01/15/96

Fletcher, Louise
1520 Camden Ave #105
Los Angeles, CA 90025
Actress V: 03/02/96

c/o Buchwald
9229 Sunset Bl #710
Los Angeles, CA 90069
Alternate V: 02/12/96

Flick East-West Talents
9057 Nemo St-#A
W Hollywood, CA 90069
Talent Agency V: 03/29/96

Flock, Tim
Charlotte Speedway
PO Box 600
Concord, NC 28026-0600
NASCAR Driver V: 03/02/96

Flood, Curt
4139 Cloverdale Ave
Los Angeles, CA 90008
Baseball Star V: 06/15/96

Flores, Tom
Seattle Seahawks
11220 NE 53rd St
Kirkland, WA 98033
Football Star V: 12/10/96

Florida Marlins
100 NE 3rd Ave-3rd Fl
Ft Lauderdale, FL 33301
Team Office V: 02/15/96

Florida Panthers
100 NE 3rd St-10th Fl
Fort Lauderdale, FL 33301
Team Office V: 01/31/96

Flowers (Webb), Gennifer
13834 Magnolia Bl
Sherman Oaks, CA 91423-1202
Celebrity V: 01/12/96

Floyd, Ray
1 Erieview Plaza #1300
Cleveland, OH 44114
Golfer V: 01/20/96

Flynn, Barbara
Markham & Froggatt
Julian House-4 Windmill St
London W1, England
Actress V: 02/04/96

Flynn, Colleen
Wm Morris Agency
151 El Camino
Beverly Hills, CA 90212
Actress V: 01/15/97

Foale, C Michael
NASA/LBJ Space Center
Hoston, TX 77058
Astronaut V: 01/31/96

Foch, Nina
Wm Morris Agency
151 El Camino Dr
Beverly Hills, CA 90212
Actress V: 02/12/96

Fogelberg, Dan
PO Box 2399
Pagosa Springs, CO 81147
Singer V: 01/09/96

Folger, Franklin
King Features
235 E 45th St
New York, NY 10017
Cartoonist V: 03/27/96

Fonda, Bridget
9560 Wilshire Bl #500
Beverly Hills, CA 90212
Actress V: 03/02/94

Indian Hill Ranch
Livingston, MT 59047
Forwarded V: 05/01/96

Fonda, Jane
1 CNN Center NW-#1080
Atlanta, GA 30303
Actress V: 02/10/96

c/o CAA
9830 Wilshire Bl
Beverly Hills, CA 90212
Alternate V: 01/14/96

Fonda, Peter
Indian Hill Ranch
Rt 38, Box 2024
Livingston, MT 59047
Actor V: 03/19/96

Fong, Kam
1088 Bishop St #406
Honolulu, HI 96813
Actor V: 02/20/96

Fontaine, Joan
Villa Fontana
229 A Lower Walden Rd
Carmel Highlands, CA 93923
Actress V: 03/01/96

PO Box 222600
Carmel, CA 93922
Alternate V: 09/06/96

Fontaine Agency
9255 Sunset Bl
Los Angeles, CA 90069
Talent Agency V: 03/29/96

Football Hall of Fame
2121 George Hallas Dr NW
Canton, OH 44708
Museum V: 03/17/96

Ford, Betty
40365 Sand Dune Rd
Rancho Mirage, CA 92270
Former 1st Lady V: 06/05/96

Ford, Faith
c/o UTA
9560 Wilshire Bl-5th Fl
Beverly Hills, CA 90212
Actress V: 02/12/96

Ford, Gerald
40365 Sand Dune Rd
Rancho Mirage, CA 92270
Former President V: 01/31/96

PO Box 927
Rancho Mirage, CA 92270
Alternate V: 04/20/96

Ford, Harrison
3555 N Moose Wilson Rd
Jackson Hole, WY 83001
Actor V: 02/02/96

Pat McQueeney
10279 Century Woods Dr
Los Angeles, CA 90067
Alternate V: 01/14/96

Ford, Lita
128 Sinclair Ave #3
Gardena, CA 91206
Singer V: 01/11/96

Ford Model Agency
344 E 59th St
New York, NY 10022
Talent Agency V: 12/10/96

Foreman, Deborah
Artists Group
10100 Santa Monica Bl #2490
Los Angeles, CA 90067
Actress V: 02/12/96

Foreman, George
7639 Pine Oak Dr
Humble, TX 77397-1438
Boxing Star V: 01/15/96

Youth Center
2202 Lone Oak
Houston, TX 77093
Alternate V: 05/22/96

Formesa, Fern
5018 N 61st Ave
Glendale, AZ 85301
Actress V: 01/21/96

Forrest, Frederic
Artists Group
10100 Santa Monica Bl #2490
Los Angeles, CA 90067
Actor V: 12/04/96

4121 Wilshire Bl
Los Angeles, CA 90010
Alternate V: 09/04/96

Forrest, Helen
1870 Camino del Cielo
Glendale, CA 91208
Singer V: 04/01/96

Forrest, Sally
1125 Angelo Dr
Beverly Hills, CA 90210
Actress V: 07/19/96

Forrest, Steve
Amstel-Eisenstadt-Frasier
6310 San Vicente Bl #401
Los Angeles, CA 90048
Actor V: 12/01/96

Forslund, Constance
Ambrioso/Mortimer
9150 Wilshire Bl #175
Beverly Hills, CA 90212
Actress V: 02/12/96

Forsyth, Rosemary
1591 Benedict Canyon Rd
Beverly Hills, CA 90210
Actress V: 04/01/96

Forsythe, John
Paradigm Agency
10100 Santa Monica Bl-25th Fl
Los Angeles, CA 90067
Actor V: 12/13/96

3849 Roblar Ave
Santa Ynez, CA 93460
Alternate V: 06/15/96

Forsythe, William
c/o UTA
15315 Magnolia Bl #429
Sherman Oaks, CA 91403
Actor V: 12/15/96

Forte, Fabian
6671 Sunset Bl #1502
Hollywood, CA 90028
Singer V: 02/11/96

Foss, Joe
PO Box 566
Scottsdale, AZ 85252
War Hero V: 01/31/96

Fosse, Ray
7950 W Bates Rd
Tracy, CA 95376
Baseball Star V: 01/20/96

Foster, Jim
Daytona Int'l Speedway
PO Box 2801
Daytona Beach, FL 32115-2801
NASCAR Official V: 03/19/96

Foster, Jodie
c/o ICM
8942 Wilshire Bl
Beverly Hills, CA 90211
Alternate V: 01/21/96

Foster, Meg
Schoen Agency
606 N Larchmont Bl #309
Los Angeles, CA 90004
Actress V: 12/13/96

Four Freshman
PO Box 93534
Las Vegas, NV 89193-3534
Singing Group V: 01/09/96

Fox, Bernard
Coast to Coast Talent
4942 Vineland Ave #200
N Hollywood, CA 91601
Actor V: 12/07/96

Fox, Michael J
c/o CAA
9830 Wilshire Bl
Beverly Hills, CA 90212
Actor V: 01/14/96

3960 Laurel Canyon Bl
Studio City, CA 91604
Alternate V: 10/23/96

Fox, Samantha
11 Mt Pleasant Villa
London W1 4HH, England
Actress V: 08/08/96

Fox, Vivica
ABC-TV
77 W 66th St
New York, NY 10023
Actress V: 01/10/97

250 W 57th St #2223
New York, NY 10019
Alternate V: 01/15/97

Foxworth, Robert
Writers & Artists
924 Westwood Bl #900
Los Angeles, CA 90024
Actor V: 12/15/96

c/o Krisbo
9720 Wilshire Bl #300
Beverly Hils, CA 90210
Alternate V: 09/04/96

Foxworthy, Jeff
8380 Melrose #310
Los Angeles, CA 90069
Actor V: 11/01/96

Foxx, Jamie
Creative Artists Agency
9830 Wilshire Bl
Beverly Hills, CA 90212
Actor V: 12/07/96

Foyt, AJ
6415 Toledo St
Houston, TX 77008
Race Driver V: 05/15/96

10306 S Post Oak Rd
Houston, TX 77035
Alternate V: 03/14/96

Frakes, Jonathan
Star Trek TNG Paramount
5555 Melrose Ave
Hollywood, CA 90038
Actor V: 03/04/96

5062 Calvin Ave
Tarzana, CA 91356
Alternate V: 01/13/96

Paradigm Agency
10100 Santa Monica Bl-25th Fl
Los Angeles, CA 90067
Alterante V: 12/13/96

9033 Briarcrest Dr
Beverly Hills, CA 90210
Forwarded V: 03/19/96

Frampton, Peter
234 S Tower Dr-#1
Beverly Hills, CA 90211-3431
Singer V: 11/10/96

7411 Center Bay Dr
N Bay Village, FL 33141-4013
Alternate V: 01/15/96

Franciosa, Tony
567 Tigertail Rd
Los Angeles, CA 90024
Actor V: 06/15/96

Francis, Anne
Henderson & Hogan Agency
247 S Beverly Dr #102
Bevery Hills, CA 90210
Actress V: 12/10/96

PO Box 5417
Santa Barbara, CA 93103
Alternate V: 06/01/96

Francis, Genie
Paradigm Agency
10100 Santa Monica Bl-25th Fl
Los Angeles, CA 90067
Actress V: 12/13/96

9033 Briarcrest Dr
Beverly Hills, CA 90210
Forwarded V: 02/03/96

Frank, Clinton
28 Bridlewood Rd
Northbrock, IL 60062
Football Star V: 02/17/96

Frank, Larry
832 Fork Shoals Rd
Greenville, SC 29605
NASCAR Driver V: 03/14/96

Frank, Phil
SF Chronicle/Features
901 Mission St
San Francisco, CA 94103
Cartoonist V: 05/11/96

Franklin, Aretha
Wm Morris
151 El Camino Dr
Beverly Hills, CA 90212
Singer V: 01/14/96

8450 Linwood St
Detroit, MI 48206
Alternate V: 04/12/96

Franklin, Bonnie
Bauman & Hiller
5750 Wilshire Bl #512
Los Angeles, CA 90036
Actress V: 12/05/96

448 W 44th St
New York, NY 10036
Alternate V: 04/13/96

Franklyn, Sabina
Michael Ladkin
2A Warwick Place N
London SW1V 1QW, England
Actress V: 02/04/96

Franks, Michael
Les Schwartz
9220 Sunset Bl #320
Los Angeles, CA 90069
Singer V: 12/01/96

Frann, Mary
Artists Group
10100 Santa Monica Bl #2490
Los Angeles, CA 90067
Actress V: 12/03/96

11635 Santa Monica Bl #130
Los Angles, CA 90025-4900
Alternate V: 10/23/96

Franz, Dennis
Paradigm Agency
10100 Santa Monica Bl-25th Fl
Los Angeles, CA 90067
Actor V: 12/13/96

Franz, Dennis, Cont.
Paradigm Agency
200 W 57th St-Ste 900
New York, NY 10019
Alternate V: 01/14/96

11805 Bellagio Rd
Los Angeles, CA 90049
Forwarded V: 02/06/96

Fraser, Brendan
2210 Wilshire Bl #513
Santa Monica, CA 90403
Actor V: 10/23/96

Fraser, Gretchen
5023 236th Pl SE
Woodinville, WA 98072-8610
Skier V: 11/01/96

Fratianne, Linda
15691 Borges Ct
Moorpark, CA 93021-3229
Actress V: 06/22/96

Frazer, Liz
42/43 Grafton House
2/3 Golden Square
London W1, England
Actress V: 05/28/96

Frazier, Joe
2917 N Broad St
Philadelphia, PA 19132
Boxing Star V: 10/04/96

Frazier, Walt
400 Central Park W #7-W
New York, NY 19925-5833
Basketball Star V: 01/07/97

Freberg, Stan
10450 Wilshire Bl #1-A
Los Angeles, CA 90024-4612
Comedy Star V: 11/10/96

Freed Company
2029 Century Park E #600
Los Angeles, CA 90067
Talent Agency V: 02/02/96

Freehan, Bill
4248 Sunningdale
Bloomfield Hills, MI 48013
Baseball Star V: 01/20/96

Freeman, Kathleen
Henderson & Hogan Agency
247 S Beverly Dr #102
Bevery Hills, CA 90210
Actress V: 12/10/96

6247 Orion Ave
Van Nuys, CA 91411
Alternate V: 04/16/96

Freeman, Morgan
Wm Morris
151 El Camino Dr
Beverly Hills, CA 90212
Actor V: 01/02/96

2472 Broadway-#227
New York, NY 10025-7449
Alternate V: 03/14/96

Frehm, Walter
King Features
235 E 45th St
New York, NY 10017
Cartoonist V: 04/12/96

French, Leigh
1850 N Vista St
Los Angeles, CA 90046
Actress V: 04/01/96

Frewer, Matt
Paradigm Agency
10100 Santa Monica Bl-25th Fl
Los Angeles, CA 90067
Actor V: 12/13/96

6670 Wildlife Rd
Malibu, CA 90265
Forwarded V: 03/15/96

Frey, Glen
29623 Louis Ave
Santa Clarita, CA 91351-1336
Actor V: 11/01/96

5020 Brent Knoll Ln
Suwanee, GA 30174-1376
Singer V: 01/12/96

Fricke, Janie
PO Box 7998
Lancaster, TX 75146
Singer V: 01/06/96

Frid, Jonathan
175 5th Ave #2517
New York, NY 10010
Actor V: 03/22/96

Fries Agency
6381 Hollywood Bl #600
Hollywood, CA 90028
Talent Agency V: 02/07/96

Frye, Soliel Moon
PO Box 5164
Glendale, CA 91201
Actress V: 01/11/96

Fujioka, John
Garrick Int'l
8831 Sunset Bl #402
Los Angeles, CA 90069
Actor V: 12/08/96

Fuller, Kurt
Gage Group
9255 Sunset Bl #515
Los Angeles, CA 90069
Actor V: 12/08/96

Fuller, Robert
Tisherman Agency
6767 Forest Lawn Dr #115
Los Angeles, CA 90068
Actor V: 12/15/96

Fullerton, Charles G
Ames Research
PO Box 273
Edwards AFB, CA 93523
Astronaut V: 03/17/96

NASA/LBJ Space Center
Houston, TX 77058
Forwarded V: 03/03/96

Funicello, Annette
16202 Sandy Lane
Encino, CA 91316
Actress V: 08/12/96

Funt, Allen
PO Box 827
Monterey, CA 93942-0827
Producer V: 08/28/96

Furlan, Mira
Ambrosio & Mortimer
9150 Wilshire Bl #175
Beverly Hills, CA 90212
Actress V: 12/01/96

14431 Ventura Bl #200
Sherman Oaks, CA 91423
Alternate V: 01/13/97

Furlong, Edward
Michaels & Wolfe
333 S Beverly Dr #201
Beverly Hills, CA 90212
Actor V: 11/01/96

Innovative Artists
1999 Ave of the Stars #2850
Los Angeles, CA 90067
Alternate V: 12/11/96

Furst, Stephen
Artists Agency
10000 Santa Monica Bl #305
Los Angeles, CA 90067
Actor V: 03/17/96

3900 Huntercrest Ct
Moorpark, CA 93021
Alternate V: 02/15/96

Future Agency
8929 S Sepulveda Bl #208
Los Angeles, CA 90045
Talent Agency V: 11/11/96

G

GENERAL HOSPITAL
ABC-TV
4151 Prospect Ave
Hollywood, CA 90027
Production Office V: 06/15/96

GERALDO
30 Rockefeller Plaza
New York, NY 10112
Production Office V: 11/20/96

GOOD MORNING AMERICA
ABC News
147 Columbus Ave
New York, NY 10023
Production Office V: 03/19/96

GOODE BEHAVIOR
UPN-TV/Trailer33
5555 Melrose Ave-Marathon 1200
Los Angeles, CA 90038
Viewer Services V: 11/11/96

GRACE UNDER FIRE
CBS-MTM Studios
4024 Radford Ave
Studio City, CA 91604
Production Office V: 01/20/96

GRACE UNDER FIRE, Cont.
c/o ABC-TV
77 W 66th St
New York, NY 10023
Alternate V: 12/15/96

GUIDING LIGHT
NY Production Center
222 E 44th St
New York, NY 10017
Production Office V: 03/18/96

GUN
ABC-TV
77 W 66th St
New York, NY 10023
Audience Services V: 01/13/97

Gable, John Clark
Scagnetti Agency
5118 Vineland Ave #102
N Hollywood, CA 91601
Actor V: 12/13/96

Gabor, Zsa Zsa
1001 Belair Rd
Los Angeles, CA 90077
Actress V: 02/11/96

Kal Ross
8721 Sunset Bl
Los Angeles, CA 90069
Alternate V: 01/14/96

Gabriel, Juan
Ventura Productions
11003 Rooks Rd
Pico Rivera, CA 90660
Singer V: 10/23/96

Gabriel, Peter
c/o Probono
132 Liverpool Rd
London N1 1B2, England
Singer V: 03/14/96

Gailforce Management
81-83 Walton St
London SW3 2HP, England
Alternate V: 02/11/96

PO Box 35
Bath, Avon, England
Forwarded V: 02/01/96

Gabrielle, Monique
Purrfect Productions
PO Box 430
Newbury Park, CA 91320
Actress V: 11/20/96

Gabrielle, Monique, Cont.
Gerler Agency
3349 Cahuenga Bl West #1
Los Angeles, CA 90068
Alternate V: 12/08/96

PO Box 57781
Sherman Oaks, CA 91413-2791
Forwarded V: 03/15/96

Gage Group
9255 Sunset Bl #515
Los Angeles, CA 90069
Talent Agency V: 02/23/96

Gagnier, Holly
Paradigm Agency
10100 Santa Monica Bl-25th Fl
Los Angeles, CA 90067
Actress V: 12/13/96

Gail, Max
PO Box 4160
Malibu, CA 90265
Actor V: 01/10/96

29451 Bluewater Rd
Malibu, CA 90265
Alternate V: 07/03/96

Galavision
605 3rd Ave-12th Fl
New York, NY 10158
Production Office V: 12/15/96

Gallagher
14984 Roan Ct
W Palm Beach, FL 33414
Comedian V: 10/23/96

Gallagher, Megan
Gersh Agency
232 N Canon Dr
Beverly Hills, CA 90210
Actress V: 12/09/96

442 Landfair Ave
Los Angeles, CA 90024
Alternate V: 01/27/96

Gallagher, Peter
171 W 71st St #3-A
New York, NY 10023
Actor V: 08/17/96

Gallo, Ernest
600 Yosemite Bl
Modesto, CA 95354
Wine Master V: 02/01/96

Galloway, Don
J Miller
1800 Century Park E #300
Los Angeles, CA 90067-1506
Actor V: 06/22/96

Box 786
Cedar Glen, CA 92321
Alternate V: 10/23/96

Gam, Rita
180 W 58th St #8B
New York, NY 10018
Actress V: 05/01/96

Gamble, Ed
King Features
216 E 45th St
New York, NY 10017
Cartoonist V: 03/11/96

Gant, Harry
Jackson Racing
PO Box 726
Arden, NC 28705
NASCAR Driver V: 03/02/96

Garagiola, Joe
6221 E Huntress Dr
Paradise Valley, AZ 85253
Baseball Star V: 07/13/96

Garcia, Andy
c/o ICM
8942 Wilshire Bl
Beverly Hills, CA 90211
Actor V: 01/14/96

Gardner, Dale A
NASA/LBJ Space Center
Hoston, TX 77058
Astronaut V: 01/19/96

Gardner, Guy S
NASA/LBJ Space Center
Houston, TX 77058
Astronaut V: 03/03/96

Gardner, Randy
8730 Sunset Bl-6th Fl
Los Angeles, CA 90069
Ice Skater V: 01/02/96

4640 Glencoe Ave #6
Marina del Rey, CA 90292
Alternate V: 06/15/96

Garland, Beverly
Slessinger & Associates
8730 Sunset Bl #220 W
Los Angeles, CA 90069
Actress V: 12/14/96

8014 Briar Summit Dr
Los Angeles, CA 90064
Alternate V: 09/07/96

Beverly Garland Interiors
4222 Vineland Ave
N Hollywood, CA 91602
Forwarded V: 01/09/96

Garlits, Don
13700 SW 16th Ave
Ocala, FL 32676
Drag Racer V: 12/12/96

Garneau, Marc
NASA/LBJ Space Center
Houston, TX 77058
Astronaut V: 02/02/96

Garner, James
c/o ICM
8942 Wilshire Bl
Beverly Hills, CA 90211
Actor V: 01/14/96

33 Oakmont Dr
Los Angeles, CA 90049
Alternate V: 02/14/96

Warner Brothers
4000 Warner Bl
Burbank, CA 91522
Forwarded V: 03/09/96

Garner, Phil
c/o Brewers
201 S 46th St
Milwaukee, WI 53214
Baseball Star V: 01/21/96

Garofalo, Janeane
c/o UTA
9560 Wilshire Bl-Ste 500
Beverly Hills, CA 90212
Actress V: 01/14/96

c/o UTA
15315 Magnolia Bl #429
Sherman Oaks, CA 91403
Forwarded V: 12/15/96

Garr, Teri
9150 Wilshire Bl #350
Beverly Hills, CA 90212-3427
Actress V: 10/23/96

Garrett, Betty
3231 Oakdell Rd
Studio City, CA 91604
Actress V: 01/11/96

Garrett Agency
6525 Sunset Bl-5th Fl
Los Angeles, CA 90028
Talent Agency V: 03/17/96

Garrick International
8831 Sunset Bl #402
Los Angeles, CA 90069
Talent Agency V: 03/16/96

Garriott, Owen
NASA/LBJ Space Center
Hoston, TX 77058
Astronaut V: 01/19/96

Garth, Jennie
c/o ICM
8942 Wilshire Bl
Beverly Hills, CA 90211
Actress V: 12/11/96

PO Box 5792
Sherman Oaks, CA 91413
Alternate V: 12/01/96

Garver, Kathy
c/o Stars
777 Davis St
San Francisco, CA 94111
Actress V: 01/31/96

Cosden Agency
3518 Cahuenga Bl West #216
Los Angeles, CA 90068
Alternate V: 12/08/96

Garvey, Steve
11822 Kearsarge St
Los Angeles, CA 90048
Baseball Star V: 06/09/96

Gascoine, Jill
Marina Martin
6A Danbury St
London N1 8JU, England
Actress V: 02/04/96

Gava, Cassandra
PO Box 69588
W Hollywood, CA 90046
Actress V: 01/09/96

Gavin, John
10263 Century Woods Dr
Los Angeles, CA 90067-6312
Actor V: 02/02/96

Gayle, Crystal
Gayle Entertainment
51 Music Square E
Nashville, TN 37203
Singer V: 02/02/96

Gaylord, Scott
1451 Depen
Lakewood, CO 80214
Race Driver V: 05/21/96

Gazzara, Ben
1080 Madison Ave
New York, NY 10028
Actor V: 02/03/96

Artists Group
10100 Santa Monica Bl #2490
Los Angeles, CA 90067
Alternate V: 01/12/96

Geary, Anthony
R Katz
345 N Maple Dr #235
Beverly Hills, CA 90210
Actor V: 01/14/96

7010 Pacific View Dr
Los Angeles, CA 90068
Alternate V: 01/12/96

Geary, Cynthia
Wm Morris Agency
151 El Camino Dr
Beverly Hills, CA 90212
Actress V: 02/12/96

21121 Foxtail
Mission Viejo, CA 90212
Alternate V: 10/23/96

Geddes Agency
1201 Greenacre Bl
W Hollywood, CA 90046
Talent Agency V: 03/29/96

Geeson, Judy
Silver/Kass/Massetti
8730 Sunset Bl #480
Los Angeles, CA 90069
Actress V: 02/12/96

c/o MLR
200 Fulham Rd
London SW10, England
Alternate V: 02/28/96

Geffen, David
Geffen Records
9130 Sunset Bl
Los Angeles, CA 90069
Producer V: 02/03/96

DreamWorks SKG
100 Universal City Plaza
Universal City, CA 91608
Alternate V: 01/14/96

Gelbart, Larry
807 N Alpine Dr
Beverly Hills, CA 90210
Producer V: 03/10/96

Geldof, Bob
Davington Priory
Faversham, Kent England
Singer V: 03/23/96

Gelff Talent
16133 Ventura Bl #700
Encino, CA 91436
Talent Agency V: 03/17/96

Gellar, Sara Michelle
Paradigm Agency
10100 Santa Monica Bl-25th Fl
Los Angeles, CA 90067
Actress V: 01/15/97

Gemar, Charles D
NASA/LBJ Space Center
Hoston, TX 77058
Astronaut V: 01/31/96

Genesis
Information Service
PO Box 107
London N6 5RU, England
Musical Group V: 05/14/96

Hit & Run Music
25 Ives St
London SW3, England
Alternate V: 02/11/96

George
John F Kennedy Jr
1633 Broadway-41st Fl
New York, NY 10019
Publication V: 01/14/96

George, Phyllis
Cave Hill Ln-Box 4308
Lexington, KY 40511
Actress V: 04/05/96

George, Susan
520 Washington Bl #187
Marina del Rey, CA 90292
Actress V: 02/02/96

PO Box 428
Maidenhead
Berkshire, 5L6 4EW England
Forwarded V: 02/01/96

George, Wally
14155 Magnolia Bl #127
Sherman Oaks, CA 91423
Commentator V: 02/12/96

PO Box 787
Los Angeles, CA 90028
Alternate V: 02/01/96

Gerard, Gil
c/o Schechter
9300 Wilshire Bl #102
N Hollywood, CA 90212
Actor V: 01/06/96

16947 Adlon Rd
Encino, CA 91436-3812
Alternate V: 10/23/96

Gere, Richard
9696 Culver Bl #203
Culver City, CA 90232
Actor V: 10/23/96

26 E 10th St #PH
New York, NY 10003
Alternate V: 01/02/96

c/o ICM
8942 Wilshire Bl
Beverly Hills, CA 90211
Forwarded V: 03/11/96

Star Mail
PO Box 69842
Hollywood, CA 90069
Forwarded V: 01/10/96

Gerler Agency
3349 Cahuenga Bl W #1
Los Angeles, CA 90068
Talent Agency V: 03/29/96

Gernhardt, Michael L
NASA/LBJ Space Center
Houston, TX 77058
Astronaut V: 02/02/96

Gerrold, David
9420 Reseda Bl #804
Northridge, CA 91324-2932
Author V: 01/20/96

Gersh Agency
232 N Canon Dr
Beverly Hills, CA 90210
Talent Agency V: 08/08/96

Gertz, Jami
c/o ICM
8942 Wilshire Bl
Beverly Hills, CA 90211
Actress V: 02/12/96

Getty, Estelle
1240 N Wetherly Dr
Los Angeles, CA 90069-1816
Actress V: 01/12/96

11601 Wilshire Bl #400
Los Angeles, CA 90025
Alternate V: 02/02/96

68-85 218th St
Bayside, NY 11364
Forwarded V: 02/03/96

Ghostley, Alice
c/o APA
9000 Sunset Bl #1200
Los Angeles, CA 90069
Actress V: 12/02/96

3800 Reklaw Dr
N Hollywood, CA 91604
Alternate V: 03/30/96

Giannini, Giancarlo
c/o Squillante
Via Della Guiliana 101
Rome, Italy
Actor V: 02/28/96

Via Salaria 292
Rome 0199, Italy
Alternate V: 02/09/96

Gibb, Cynthia
2422 Cedar Ave
Long Beach, CA 90806
Actress V: 10/23/96

Gibb, Don
Artists Group
10100 Santa Monica Bl #2490
Los Angeles, CA 90067
Actor V: 12/04/96

c/o Craig
8485 Melrose Place #E
Los Angeles, CA 90069
Alternate V: 02/21/96

Gibbons, Billy
Lone Wolf Mgmt
PO Box 16390
Austin, TX 78716
Musician V: 10/23/96

Gibbons, Leeza
PO Box 4321
Hollywood, CA 90078
TV Hostess V: 10/23/96

1760 N Courtney Ave
Los Angeles, CA 90046
Alternate V: 08/08/96

Gibbs, Joe
9900 Twin Lakes Parkway
Charlotte, NC 28269
NASCAR Driver V: 10/23/96

Gibbs, Marla
Artists Group
10100 Santa Monica Bl #2490
Los Angeles, CA 90067
Actress V: 12/04/96

4310 Degnan Bl
Los Angeles, CA 90008
Alternate V: 04/04/94

2323 W Martin Luther King Bl
Los Angeles, CA 90008
Forwarded V: 02/16/96

Gibson, Debbie
PO Box 568
Merrick, NY 11566
Singer V: 01/14/96

1684 Sterling Ave
Merrick, NY 11566
Alternate V: 01/12/96

Gibson, Debbie, Cont.
300 Main St #201
Huntington, NY 11743
Forwarded V: 03/23/96

Gibson, Don
Opryland Music
65 Music Square W
Nashville, TN 37203
Actor V: 02/02/96

Gibson, Edward G
NASA/LBJ Space Center
Houston, TX 77058
Astronaut V: 03/03/96

Gibson, Mel
c/o ICM
8942 Wilshire Bl
Beverly Hills, CA 90211
Actor V: 03/11/96

Warner Brothers
4000 Warner Bl
Burbank, CA 91522
Forwarded V: 03/09/96

Gibson, Robert L
NASA/LBJ Space Center
Houston, TX 77058
Astronaut V: 03/03/96

Gielgud, John
South Pavillion
Wotton Underwood, Bucks
Aylesbury HP18, England
Actor V: 05/01/96

Giella, Joe
King Features
216 E 45th St
New York, NY 10017
Cartoonist V: 03/11/96

Gifford, Frank
108 Cedar Cliff Rd
Riverside, CT 06878-2606
Football Star V: 01/13/96

Gifford, Kathie Lee
108 Cedar Cliff Rd
Riverside, CT 06878-2606
TV Hostess V: 01/13/96

Gilbert, Lewis
Clement House
99 Aldwych
London WC2B 4JY, England
Actor V: 02/28/96

Gilbert, Melissa
PO Box 57593
Sherman Oaks, CA 91403
Actress V: 01/10/96

Wm Morris Agency
151 El Camino Dr
Beverly Hills, CA 90212
Alternate V: 01/14/96

23991 Mulholland Dr #458
Woodland Hills, CA 91354
Alternate V: 03/13/96

5664 Cahuenga Bl-Ste 431
N Hollywood, CA 91601
Forwarded V: 01/20/96

Gilbert, Sara
16254 High Valley Dr
Encino, CA 91346
Actress V: 03/15/96

Gilberto, Astrud
Int'l Music Network
112 Washington St
Marblehead, MA 01945
Singer V: 12/01/96

Gilead,
'Bodies in Motion'
PO Box 10622
Honolulu, HI 96816-0622
Fitness Expert V: 01/10/96

Giles, Nancy
PO Box 16153
Beverly Hills, CA 90209-2153
Actress V: 01/21/96

Gill, Vince
Fitzgerald/Hartley
50 W Main St
Ventura, CA 93001
Singer V: 02/02/96

Wm Morris Agency
151 El Camino Dr
Beverly Hills, CA 90212
Alternate V: 01/14/96

Fitzgerald/Hartley
1908 Wedgewood Ave
Nashville, TN 37212
Alternate V: 11/01/96

2325 Crestmoor Rd
Nashville, TN 37215
Forwarded V: 01/09/97

Gilla Roos Agency
9744 Wilshire Bl #203
Beverly Hills, CA 90212
Talent Agency V: 03/29/96

Gillard, Starr
6525 Sunset Bl #303
Hollywood, CA 90028
Actress V: 01/21/96

Gillatt, John
King Features
216 E 45th St
New York, NY 10017
Cartoonist V: 03/11/96

Gilley, Mickey
Interest Inc
PO Box 1242
Pasadena, TX 77501
Singer V: 03/26/96

3455 W Hwy 76
Branson, MO 65616
Alternate V: 01/12/97

Gilliam, Terry
The Old Hall
South Grove, Highgate
London N6 England
Actor V: 03/23/96

Gilliland, Butch
Anaheim Racing
313 N Anaheim Bl
Anaheim, CA 92805
Race Driver V: 03/12/96

Gillman, Sid
2968 Playa Rd
Carlsbad, CA 92009
Football Star V: 05/24/96

Gilmore, David
43 Portland Rd
London W11 4LJ, England
Singer V: 12/01/96

Ginsberg, Allen
City Lights
261 Columbus Ave
San Francisco, CA 94133
Poet V: 02/11/96

Ginty, Robert
16133 Ventura Bl #800
Encino, CA 91436
Actor V: 03/12/96

Ginty, Robert, Cont.
c/o ICM
8942 Wilshire Bl
Beverly Hills, CA 90211
Forwarded V: 01/16/96

Giradot, Annie
Editions Laffont
6 Place Saint-Sulpice
75002 Paris, France
Actress V: 12/14/96

Gish, Annabeth
25663 Buckthorne Dr
Calabasas, CA 91302-2202
Actress V: 08/28/96

Giusti, Dave
524 Claire Dr
Pittsburgh, PA 15241
Baseball Star V: 01/20/96

Givens, Robin
885 3rd Ave #2900
New York, NY 10022-4834
Actress V: 12/16/96

8818 Thrasher Ave
Los Angeles, CA 90069
Alternate V: 01/27/96

Gersh Agency
232 N Canon Dr
Beverl Hills, CA 90210
Forwarded V: 03/10/96

Glaser, Paul Michael
317 Georgina Ave
Santa Monica, CA 90402
Actor V: 06/15/96

Interscope Communications
10900 Wilshire Bl-Ste 1400
Los Angeles, CA 90024
Alternate V: 03/14/96

Gleason, Paul
9229 Sunset Bl #710
Los Angeles, CA 90069
Actor V: 01/21/96

Stone Manners Talent
8091 Selma Ave
Los Angeles, CA 90068
Alternate V: 12/15/96

Glenn, John
503 Hart Senate Office Bldg
Washington, DC 20510
Astronaut V: 11/25/96

NASA/LBJ Space Center
Houston, TX 77058
Alternate V: 03/03/96

Glenn, Scott
126 E De Vargas St #1902
Santa Fe, NM 87501
Actor V: 03/04/96

Box 1018
Ketchum, ID 83340
Alternate V: 11/01/96

c/o ICM
8942 Wilshire Bl
Beverly Hills, CA 90211
Alternate V: 03/04/96

Gless, Sharon
Wm Morris Agency
151 El Camino Dr
Beverly Hills, CA 90212
Actress V: 02/03/96

4709 Teesdale Ave
Studio City, CA 91604-1117
Alternate V: 07/01/94

Hurwitz Associates
427 N Canon Dr #215
Beverly Hills, CA 90210
Alternate V: 12/10/96

PO Box 48005
Los Angeles, CA 90048-0005
Forwarded V: 08/28/96

Global Pictures
4774 Melrose Ave
Hollywood, CA 90029
Production Office V: 03/17/96

Globe Magazine
5401 NW Broken Sound Bl
Boca Raton, FL 33487
Publisher V: 02/10/96

Glover, Crispin
3573 Carnation Ave
Los Angeless, CA 90026
Actor V: 03/15/96

Glover, Danny
41 Sutter St #1648
San Francisco, CA 94104-4903
Actor V: 01/31/96

Glover, John
2417 Micheltorena St
Los Angeles, CA 90039
Actor V: 04/06/96

8942 Wilshire Bl
Beverly Hills, CA 90211
Alternate V: 06/15/96

Goddard, Anna Marie
Playboy Enterprises
2112 Broadway St
Santa Monica, CA 90404-2912
Model V: 03/14/96

Godwin, Linda M
NASA/LBJ Space Center
Hoston, TX 77058
Astronaut V: 01/19/96

Going, Joanna
Wm Morris Agency
151 El Camino Dr
Beverly Hills, CA 90212
Actress V: 02/12/96

Bloom Agency
9200 Sunset Bl #710
Los Angeles, CA 90069
Alternate V: 02/03/96

Gold, Missy
Gold Agency
3500 W Olive Ave #1400
Burbank, CA 91505
Actress V: 03/02/96

937 N Vista St
Los Angeles, CA 90046
Forwarded V: 12/15/96

Gold, Tracy
Gold Agency
3500 W Olive Ave #1400
Burbank, CA 91505
Actress V: 03/02/96

12631 Addison St
N Hollywood, CA 91607
Alternate V: 02/03/96

Gold & Marshak
3500 W Olive #1400
Burbank, CA 91505
Talent Agency V: 03/17/96

Goldberg, Eric
Disney Animation
500 S Buena Vista St
Burbank, CA 91521
Animator V: 09/12/96

Goldberg, Whoopi
Whoop Inc
5555 Melrose Ave-Wilder 114
Los Angeles, CA 90038
Actress V: 11/01/96

Addis/Wexler
955 Carrillo Dr-3rd Fl
Los Angeles, CA 90048
Alternate V: 03/17/96

Goldblum, Jeff
c/o ICM
8942 Wilshire Bl
Beverly Hills, CA 90211
Actor V: 01/14/96

8033 Sunset Bl #367
Los Angeles, CA 90046
Forwarded V: 03/23/96

Golden, William Lee
Golden Eagle
168 Hickory Heights Dr
Hendersonville, TN 37075
Singer V: 02/02/96

Golden State Warriors
Oakland Coliseum Arena
Nimitz Fwy & Hegenberger Rd
Oakland, CA 94621
Team Office V: 02/15/96

Oakland Coliseum Arena
7000 Coliseum Way
Oakland, CA 94621-1918
Alterante V: 11/11/96

Goldey Company
116 N Robertson #700
Los Angeles, CA 90048
Talent Agency V: 02/02/96

Goldhor, David
Eagle Eye
4019 Tujunga Ave
Studio City, CA 91604
Director V: 01/21/96

Goldoni, Lelia
15459 Wyandotte St
Van Nuys, CA 91405
Actress V: 02/15/96

Goldrup, Ray
2383 Broderick
West Jordan, UT 84084
Author V: 12/18/96

Goldsboro, Bobby
Stephany Mgmt
1021 Preston Dr
Nashville, TN 37206
Singer V: 02/02/96

Goldsmith, Paul
1148 Vivian Lane
Munster, IN 46321
NASCAR Driver V: 03/02/96

Goldwater, John
8 White Birch Lane
Scarsdale, NY 10583
Cartoonist V: 12/01/96

Goldwyn Company
10203 Santa Monica Bl #500
Los Angeles, CA 90067
Production Office V: 03/17/96

Golino, Valeria
8033 W Sunset Bl #419
Los Angeles, CA 90046-2427
Actress V: 03/14/96

Creative Artists Agency
9830 Wilshire Bl
Beverly Hills, CA 90212
Alternate V: 12/07/96

c/o Mickelson
1707 Clearview Dr
Beverly Hills, CA 90210
Alternate V: 01/11/96

8036 Woodrow Wilson Dr
Los Angeles, CA 90046
Alternate V: 01/21/96

Golonka, Arlene
17849 Duncan St
Reseda, CA 91335
Actress V: 01/12/96

Silver/Kass/Massetti
8730 Sunset Bl #480
Los Angeles, CA 90069
Alternate V: 02/26/96

1835 Pandora Ave #3
Los Angeles, CA 90025
Forwarded V: 04/21/96

Gonshaw, Francesca
Greg Mellard
12 D'Arblay St-2nd Fl
London W1V 3FP, England
Actress V: 02/04/96

Gonzalez, Gonzalez
c/o Grady
4444 Lankershim Bl #207
N Hollywood, CA 91602
Actor V: 02/15/96

Goodall, Caroline
James Sharkey
15 Golden Square-3rd Fl
London W1RV 3AG, England
Actress V: 02/04/96

Goodman, Dody
Webb Enterprises
13834 Magnolia Bl
Sherman Oaks, CA 91423
Actress V: 12/15/96

Goodman, John
Creative Artists Agency
9830 Wilshire Bl
Beverly Hills, CA 90212
Actor V: 12/07/96

Goodson Productions
Customer Relations
5757 Wilshire Bl #5750
Los Angeles, CA 90036
Production Office V: 03/17/96

Goolagong, Evonne
80 Dutroon Ave.
Roseville NSW Australia
Tennis Star V: 10/23/96

Gordeeva, Ekaterina
Int'l Skating Center
1375 Hopmeadow St
Simsbury, CT 06070
Olympian V: 01/09/96

Gordon, Barry
c/o SDB
1801 Ave of the Stars #902
Los Angeles, CA 90067
Actor V: 01/31/96

Gordon, Cecil
Travis Racing
PO Box 588, Hwy 16 N
Denver, NC 28037
NASCAR Crew V: 02/08/96

c/o Childress
PO Box 1189 Industrial Dr
Welcome, NC 27374
Alternate V: 03/12/96

Gordon, Don
2095 Linda Flora Rd
Los Angeles, CA 90077
Actor V: 06/16/96

c/o Acme
6310 San Vicente Bl #520
Los Angeles, CA 90048
Alternate V: 02/26/96

Gordon, Hannah
Hutton Mgmt
200 Fulham Rd
London SW10 9PN, England
Actress V: 02/04/96

Gordon, Jeff
Hendrick Motor Sports
5325 Stowe Lane-PO Box 9
Harrisburg, NC 28075
NASCAR Driver V: 03/02/96

Gordon, Leo V
Gerler/Stevens
3349 Cahuenga Bl #2
Los Angeles, CA 90068
Actor V: 01/21/96

Gerler Agency
3349 Cahuenga Bl West #1
Los Angeles, CA 90068
Actor V: 12/08/96

Gordon Company
260 S Beverly Dr #308
Beverly Hills, CA 90212
Talent Agency V: 03/20/96

Gordon Jr, Richard F
NASA/LBJ Space Center
Houston, TX 77058
Astronaut V: 03/03/96

Gore, Al
Office of the Vice-President
Washington, DC 20510-0011
Vice-President USA V: 10/04/96

Gore, Al, Cont.
The Admiral House
34th & Massachuttes Ave
Washington, DC 20005
Alternate V: 02/23/96

Gore, Lesley
141 Vernon Ave
Patterson, NJ 07503
Singer V: 03/03/96

170 E 77th St #2-A
New York, NY 10021-1912
Alternate V: 02/15/96

Gore, Tipper
The Admiral House
34th & Massachuttes Ave
Washington, DC 20005
VP Wife V: 02/23/96

Gorme, Eydie
Stage 2 Productions
PO Box 5140
Beverly Hills, CA 90210
Singer V: 03/07/96

Gorrell, Bob
King Features
235 E 45th St
New York, NY 10017
Cartoonist V: 02/13/96

Gorshin, Frank
72 Cross Way
Westport, CT 06880
Actor V: 10/23/96

c/o Webb
7500 Devista Dr
Los Angeles, CA 90046
Alternate V: 02/26/96

Gossage, Rick 'Goose'
35 Marland Dr
Colorado Springs, CO 80906
Baseball Star V: 04/13/96

Gossett Jr, Louis
c/o Logo Entertainment
6100 Wilshire Bl-Suite 1400
Los Angeles, CA 90048
Actor V: 01/11/97

c/o CAA
9830 Wilshire Bl
Beverly Hills, CA 90210
Alternate V: 01/17/96

Gossett Jr., Louis, Cont.
PO Box 6187
Malibu, CA 90265
Alternate V: 01/21/96

5916 Bonsall Dr
Malibu, CA 90265
Forwarded V: 02/02/96

Gough, Michael
Torleigh Green Lane
Ashmore, Salisbury
Wiltshire SP5 5AQ, England
Actor V: 03/17/96

Gould, Elliott
21250 Califa #201
Woodland Hills, CA 91367
Actor V: 01/27/96

Gould, Harold
603 Ocean Ave #4-East
Santa Monica, CA 90402
Actor V: 12/14/96

Goulet, Robert
Rogo & Rove
2700 E Sunset Rd #C-27
Las Vegas, NV 89120-3506
Singer V: 11/01/96

3110 Monte Rosa Ave
Las Vegas, NV 89102
Alternate V: 01/12/96

Grabe, Ronald J
NASA/LBJ Space Center
Hoston, TX 77058
Astronaut V: 01/31/96

Graceland Estates
3734 Elvis Presley Bl
Memphis, TN 38116
Presley Home V: 10/19/96

PO Box 16508
Memphis, TN 38186-0508
Alternate V: 01/13/96

Grady, Don
150 E Olive Ave #304
Burbank, CA 91502
Actor V: 03/02/96

4537 Simpson Ave
N Hollywood, CA 91607
Alternate V: 03/17/96

Grady Agency
4444 Lankershim Bl #207
N Hollywood, CA 91602
Talent Agency V: 11/11/96

Graf, Steffi
Polo Club of Boca Raton
5400 Champion Bl
Boca Raton, FL 33496
Tennis Star V: 01/17/96

6831 Bruel
Bei Manheim, Germany
Alternate V: 03/02/96

Graff, Ilene
11455 Sunshine Terrace
Studio City, CA 91604
Actress V: 02/15/96

Graham, Gary
c/o MTA
4526 Wilshire Bl
Los Angeles, CA 90010
Actor V: 03/14/96

Graham, Gary
Metro Talent Agency
4526 Wilshire Bl
Los Angeles, CA 90010
Actor V: 12/11/96

Grahn, Nancy
Premiere Artists
8899 Sunset Bl #102
Los Angeles, CA 90048
Actress V: 02/12/96

Grammer, Kelsey
Artists Agency
10000 Santa Monica Bl #305
Los Angeles, CA 90067
Actor V: 01/11/96

Artists Agency
10000 Santa Monica Bl #305
Los Angeles, CA 90067
Alternate V: 12/03/96

Paramount TV
5555 Melrose Ave
Los Angeles, CA 90038
Alternate V: 01/14/96

Grandpa Jones
PO Box 854
Goodlettsville, TN 37072
Comedian V: 01/17/97

Granger, Farley
18 W 72nd St #25
New York, NY 10023
Actor V: 02/22/96

Grant, Amy
PO Box 50701
Nashville, TN 37205
Singer V: 01/14/96

9 Music Square S #214
Nashville, TN 37203-3211
Alternate V: 01/31/96

Reverston Farm, Moran Rd
Franklin, TN 37064
Alternate V: 02/07/96

c/o CAA
9830 Wilshire Bl
Beverly Hills, CA 90212
Forwarded V: 02/12/96

Grant, Deborah
Wm Morris
151 El Camino Dr
Beverly Hills, CA 90212
Actress V: 02/12/96

Grant, Gogi
10323 Alamo #202
Los Angeles, CA 90064
Singer V: 02/03/96

Grant, Hugh
c/o CAA
9830 Wilshire Bl
Beverly Hills, CA 90212
Actor V: 01/14/96

Box 786
Cedar Glenn, CA 92321
Alternate V: 10/23/96

c/o ICM
Oxford House-76 Oxford St
London W1N OAX, England
Forwarded V: 11/01/96

Grant, Jennifer
Karg/Weissenbach & Assoc
329 N Wetherly Dr #101
Beverly Hills, CA 90211
Actress V: 12/15/96

Grant, Lee
610 West End Ave #7B
New York, NY 10024
Actress V: 01/10/97

Grant, Lee, Cont.
Artists Group
10100 Santa Monica Bl #2490
Los Angeles, CA 90067
Alternate V: 12/03/96

Grant, Mickie
250 W 94th St #6-G
New York, NY 10025
Actress V: 04/06/96

Grant, Rodney A
Geddes Agency
1201 Greenacre Bl
W Hollywood, CA 90046
Actor V: 12/08/96

Grave Line Tours
PO Box 931694
Hollywood, CA A 90039
Production Office V: 02/10/96

Graveline, Duane E
NASA/LBJ Space Center
Houston, TX 77058
Astronaut V: 03/03/96

Graves, Peter
c/o Stern
11755 Wilshire Bl #2320
Los Angeles, CA 90025
Actor V: 01/21/96

660 E Channel Rd
Santa Monica, CA 90402
Alternate V: 09/09/96

Graves, Teresa
3437 W 78th Pl
Los Angeles, CA 90043
Actress V: 01/20/96

Gray, Billy
19612 Grandview Dr
Topanga Canyon, CA 90290
Actor V: 01/15/96

Gray, Coleen
1432 N Kemwood St
Burbank, CA 91505
Actress V: 02/02/96

Gray, Dulcie
c/o Agency
388 Oxford St
London W1, England
Actress V: 02/28/96

Gray, Erin
c/o Schechter
9300 Wilshire Bl #410
Beverly Hills, CA 900212
Actress V: 02/12/96

c/o EG Produtions
12423 Ventura Ct
Studio City, CA 91604
Alternate V: 11/11/96

10921 Alta View Dr
Studio City, CA 91604
Forwarded V: 03/18/96

Gray, Linda
PO Box 1370
Santa Clarita, CA 91386
Actress V: 02/12/96

PO Box 5064
Sherman Oaks, CA 91403
Alternate V: 01/13/97

Grayson, Katheryn
Hill Associates
6430 Variel Ave #101
Woodland Hills, CA 91367
Actress V: 09/12/96

Webb Agency
7500 Devista Dr
Los Angeles, CA 90046
Forwarded V: 02/12/96

Green, Al
PO Box 456
Millington, TN 38083-0456
Singer V: 08/28/96

Green, Brian Austin
Artists Agency
10000 Santa Monica Bl #305
Los Angeles, CA 90067
Actor V: 12/03/96

11333 Moorpark St-#27
Studio City, CA 91602
Alternate V: 11/10/96

Green Bay Packers
1265 Lombardi Ave
Green Bay, WI 54303
Team Office V: 05/15/96

Greene, Graham
59 Don Valley Dr
Toronto M4K 2J1, Ontario, Canada
Actor V: 01/02/96

Greene, Graham, *Cont.*
Smith & Associates
121 N San Vicente Bl
Beverly Hills, CA 90211
Alternate V: 12/15/96

Greene, Melanie
8904 Wonderland Ave
Los Angeles, CA 90046-1854
Actress V: 01/31/96

Greene, Michele
c/o MTA
4526 Wilshire Bl
Los Angeles, CA 90010
Actress V: 02/12/96

Greenwood, Bruce
Gersh Agency
232 N Canon Dr
Beverly Hills, CA 90210
Actor V: 12/09/96

Greenwood, LC
329 S Dallas Ave
Pittsburg, PA 15235
Football Star V: 05/11/96

Greenwood, Lee
c/o Bentley
1311 Elm Hill Pike
Nashville, TN 37210
Singer V: 02/02/96

Greer, Dabbs
284 S Madison #102
Pasadena, CA 91101
Actor V: 04/05/96

Dade/Schultz
11846 Ventura Bl #100
Studio City, CA 91604
Forwarded V: 02/26/96

Gregory, Frederick D
NASA-LBJ Space Center
Houston, TX 77058
Astronaut V: 03/03/96

Gregory, James
55 Cathedral Rock Dr #33
Sedona, AZ 85336
Actor V: 03/01/96

Gregory, Mary
c/o Lovell
1350 N Highland Ave #24
Los Angeles, CA 90028
Actress V: 02/12/96

Gregory, William G
NASA/LBJ Space Center
Houston, TX 77058
Astronaut V: 03/03/96

Greico, Richard
2934 1/2 N Beverly Glen Cir #252
Los Angeles, CA 90077-1724
Actor V: 01/21/96

Greist, Kim
Innovative Artists
1999 Ave of the Stars #2850
Los Angeles, CA 90067
Actress V: 12/11/96

Gretzky, Wayne
9100 Wilshire Bl #1000W
Beverly Hills, CA 90212-3413
Hockey Star V: 01/12/96

14135 Beresford Dr
Beverly Hills, CA 90210
Alternate V: 09/12/96

401 S Prairie Ave
Inglewood, CA 90301
Alternate V: 10/23/96

c/o LA Kings/The Forum
3900 W Manchester Bl
Inglewood, CA 90306
Alternate V: 01/14/96

c/o LA Kings
PO Box 10
Inglewood, CA 90306
Forwarded V: 03/07/96

Grey, Jennifer
c/o CAA
9830 Wilshire Bl
Beverly Hills, CA 90212
Actress V: 02/12/96

Grey, Joel
Gelfand Company
1880 Century Park E #900
Los Angeles, CA 90067
Actor V: 01/02/96

Innovative Artists
1999 Ave of the Stars #2850
Los Angeles, CA 90067
Alternate V: 12/11/96

Grey, Virginia
15101 Magnolia Bl #54
Sherman Oaks, CA 91403
Actress V: 03/23/96

Grieco, Richard
Creative Artists Agency
9830 Wilshire Bl
Beverly Hills, CA 90212
Actor V: 12/07/96

2934 1/2 N Beverly Glen Circle
Los Angeles, CA 90077-1724
Alternate V: 01/31/96

975 Kapiolani Bl
Honolulu, HI 96814
Forwarded V: 11/01/96

Grier, Pam
c/o APA
9000 Sunset Bl #1200
Los Angeles, CA 90069
Actress V: 02/12/96

3790 S Roslyn Way
Denver, CO 80037
Alternate V: 01/02/96

PO Box 370958
Denver, CO 80237-0958
Alternate V: 10/23/96

Grier, Rosey
11656 Montana Ave #301
Los Angeles, CA 90049
Actor V: 02/10/96

1977 S Vermont Ave #200
Los Angeles, CA 90007
Alternate V: 04/13/94

Griese, Bob
3250 Mary St
Miami, FL 33133
Football Star V: 09/17/96

Griffey Jr, Ken
1420 NW Gilman Bl #2717
Issawuah, WA 98027
Baseball Star V: 10/23/96

Griffey Sr, Ken
5385 Cross Bridge Rd
West Chester, OH 45069
Baseball Star V: 01/15/96

Griffin, Merv
9876 Wilshire Bl
Beverly Hills, CA 90210
TV Host V: 10/23/96

Griffith, Andy
PO Box 1968
Manteo, NC 27954-1968
Actor V: 04/04/96

Griffith, Bill
King Features
235 E 45th St
New York, NY 10017
Cartoonist V: 02/19/96

Griffith, James
Film Atrists
7080 Hollywood Bl #704
Los Angeles, CA 90028
Actor V: 06/09/96

Griffith, Ken
c/o Agency
388 Oxford St
London W1, England
Actor V: 02/28/96

Griffith, Melanie
201 S Rockingham Ave
Los Angeles, CA 90049-3635
Actress V: 11/01/96

231 N Orchard Dr
Burbank, CA 91506
Alternate V: 03/13/96

Griffith-Joyner, Florence
Flo-Jo Int'l
27758 Santa Margarita #385
Mission Viejo, CA 92691
Olympian V: 01/03/96

11444 W Olympic-10th Fl
Los Angeles, CA 90064
Forwarded V: 02/03/96

Griffiths, Ken
c/o Agency
388 Oxford St
London W1 9HE, England
Actor V: 01/02/96

Grimes, Gary
10637 Burbank Bl
N Hollywood, CA 91601
Actor V: 03/17/96

Grimes, Tammy
Gage Group
9255 Sunset Bl #515
Los Angeles, CA 90069
Actress V: 02/12/96

Grinkov, Sergei
Int'l Skating Center
1375 Hopmeadow St
Simsbury, CT 06070
Olympian V: 01/09/96

Grisham, John
Garon-Brook
101 W 55th St
New York, NY 10019
Author V: 01/14/96

Grissom, Steve
NASCAR
1811 Volusia Ave
Daytona Beach, FL 32015
NASCAR Driver V: 03/02/96

Grizzard, George
400 E 54th St Bl #200
New York, NY 10022
Actor V: 01/13/97

Groat, Dick
320 Beech St
Pittsburgh, PA 15218
Baseball Star V: 04/18/96

Grodenchik, Max
Rom's Bar/C Peters
5016 Lakecrest Dr
Charlotte, NC 28215
Actor V: 01/14/96

Grodin, Charles
CNBC/America's Talking
965 5th Ave
New York, NY 10021
Actor V: 01/09/96

187 Chestnut Hill Rd
Wilton, CT 96897
Alternate V: 09/13/96

9560 Wilshire Bl #500
Beverly Hills, CA 90212
Alternate V: 04/05/96

c/o MGM
10000 W Washington Bl
Culver City, CA 90232
Forwarded V: 03/20/96

Groening, Matt
Fox TV
10201 W Pico Bl #206-6
Los Angeles, CA 90035
Cartoonist V: 03/03/96

Groh, David
301 N Canon #305
Beverly Hills, CA 90210
Actor V: 11/29/96

Groom, Sam
140 Riverside Dr #16-0
New York, NY 10024
Actor V: 04/06/96

Gross, Mary
Schoen Agency
606 N Larchmont Bl #309
Los Angeles, CA 90004
Actress V: 12/13/96

Gross, Paul
Screencenture VII
940 Lansdowns Ave-Bldg 15
Toronto, Ont, Canada M6H 4C9
Actor V: 01/20/96

Grout, James
Crouch & Salmon
59 Frith St
London W1V 5TA, England
Actor V: 03/17/96

Groza, Lou
906 Terminal Tower Bldg
Cleveland, OH 44113
Football Star V: 03/17/96

Gruner, Wolfgang
Westendallee 57
1000 Berlin 19, Germany
Actor V: 01/19/96

Grunsfield, John M
NASA/LBJ Space Center
Houston, TX 77058
Astronaut V: 02/02/96

Guest, Christopher
Box 2358
Running Springs, CA 92382
Actor V: 01/03/97

Guest, Lance
2269 La Granada Dr
Los Angeles, CA 90068-2723
Actor V: 02/18/96

Gugino, Carla
Wm Morris Agency
151 El Camino
Beverly Hills, CA 90212
Actress V: 12/15/96

Guilbert, Ann
57570 Wilshire Bl-PH 5
Los Angeles, CA 90036
Actress V: 04/18/96

Guillaume, Robert
Conteeth Entertainment
15250 Ventura Bl
Sherman Oaks, CA 91403
Actor V: 01/31/96

11963 Crest Pl
Beverly Hills, CA 90210-1321
Alternate V: 01/10/96

Guinness, Alec
London Mgmt
235-241 Regent St
London W1A 2JT, England
Actor V: 03/17/96

Kettlebrook Meadows
Steep Marsh
Petersfield
Hampshire, England
Alternate V: 05/01/96

Guisewite, Cathy
4900 Main St
Kansas City, MO 64112
Cartoonist V: 06/16/96

Guitar World Magazine
1115 Broadway
New York, NY 10010
Publisher V: 02/10/96

Gulliver, Dorothy
28792 Lajos Ln
Valley Center, CA 92082
Actress V: 04/18/96

Gunn, Anna
2267 Alcyona Dr
Los Angeles, CA 90068-2804
Actress V: 01/31/96

Gunthor, Werner
Rue de Chateau 25
CH-2520 La Neuveville
Switzerland
Skier V: 01/19/96

Gutensohn, Katherin
Oberfeldweg 12
8203 Oberaudorf, Germany
Skier V: 02/11/96

Guthrie, Arlo
The Farm
Washington, MA 01223
Singer V: 03/12/96

Rolling Blunder Review
PO Box 657
Housatonic, MA 01236-0657
Alternate V: 03/30/96

Rising Son Records
Blunderton Pike
Washington, MA 01223
Forwarded V: 02/18/96

Gutierrez, Sidney M
NASA/LBJ Space Center
Hoston, TX 77058
Astronaut V: 01/31/96

Guttenberg, Steve
15237 Sunset Bl #48
Pacific Palisades, CA 90272
Actor V: 01/31/96

Wm Morris
151 El Camino Dr
Beverly Hills, CA 90212
Alternate V: 06/06/96

Guy, Jasmine
Innovative Artists
1999 Ave of the Stars #2850
Los Angeles, CA 90067
Actress V: 12/11/96

Gwynne, Anne
4350 Colfax #2
Studio City, CA 91604
Actress V: 01/31/96

H

HANGIN' WITH MR COOPER
WB-TV
4000 Warner Bl
Burbank, CA 91522
Production Office V: 01/16/96

HARD COPY
WB-TV
1438 N Gower
Hollywood, CA 90028
Audience Services V: 04/12/96

Hard Copy/Paramount
5555 Melrose Ave/Mae West Bldg
Hollywood, CA 90038-3197
Alternate V: 01/31/96

30 Rockefeller Plaza
New York, NY 10112
Alternate V: 11/20/96

HARDBALL
CBS Studios
4024 Radford Ave
Studio City, CA 91604
Production Office V: 01/20/96

HBO & HBO Pictures
1100 Ave of the Americas
New York, NY 10036
Production Office V: 01/12/96

HEARTS ARE WILD
Lorimar TV
300 S Lorimar Plaza
Burbank, CA 91505
Production Office V: 01/20/96

HERCULES
WB-TV
1438 N Gower
Hollywood, CA 90028
Audience Services V: 04/12/96

HIGH INCIDENT
Dreamworks TV/Bldg 477
100 Universal City Plaza
Universal City, CA 91608
Production Office V: 11/11/96

ABC-TV
77 W 66th St
New York, NY 10023
Alternate V: 12/15/96

HIGH SOCIETY
Warner Bros TV
300 Television Plaza, Bldg 137
Burbank, CA 91505
Production Office V: 10/23/96

HIGHLANDER
WB-TV
1438 N Gower
Hollywood, CA 90028
Audience Services V: 04/12/96

HOME IMPROVEMENT
Disney/Windancer
500 S Buena Vista St
Burbank, CA 91521-2215
Production Office V: 11/20/96

ABC-TV
77 W 66th St
New York, NY 10023
Alternate V: 12/15/96

HOMEBOYS IN OUTER SPACE
Walt Disney TV
500 S Buena Vista-Bldg 21
Burbank, CA 91521
Production Office V: 10/23/96

UPN-TV
5555 Melrose Ave-Marathon 1200
Los Angeles, CA 90038
Alternate V: 11/11/96

HOMICIDE
NBC-TV
30 Rockefeller Plaza
New York, NY 10112
Production Office V: 12/15/96

HRH Prince Albert
Palais de Monaco
98015 Monte Carlo 518, Monaco
Royalty V: 02/20/96

Place du Musee
MC 98000, Monaco
Alternate V: 02/20/96

HRH Prince Harry
His Royal Highness
Buckingham Palace
London SW1A 1AA, England
Royalty V: 03/11/96

HRH Prince Phillip
His Royal Highness
Buckingham Palace
London SW1A 1AA, England
Royalty V: 03/11/96

HRH Princess Caroline
Palais de Monaco
98015 Monte Carlo, 518
Royalty V: 03/12/96

HRH Princess Diana
Wilton Crescent 19
London-Belgravia, England
Royalty *V: 03/11/96*

HRH Princess Sarah
Buckingham Palace
London, SW1A 1AA England
Royalty *V: 03/11/96*

HRH Princess Stephanie
Palais de Monaco
98015 Monte Carlo, 518
Royalty *V: 03/12/96*

Maison Clos St-Matin
St Remy de Provence, France
Alternate *V: 09/13/96*

HRH Priness Caroline
La Maisin de la Source
St Remy de Provance, France
Royalty *V: 09/01/96*

HRH Queen Elizabeth
Buckingham Palace
London, SW1A 1AA England
Royalty *V: 03/11/96*

HUDSON STREET
Tri-Star TV
10202 W Washington Bl
Culver City, CA 90232
Production Office *V: 01/14/96*

HUMAN FACTOR
Universal TV
70 Universal City Plaza
Universal City, CA 91608
Production Office *V: 01/20/96*

HWA Talent
1964 Westwood Bl #400
Los Angeles, CA 90025
Talent Agency *V: 11/11/96*

Hack, Shelley
209 12th St
Santa Monica, CA 90402
Actress *V: 05/02/96*

Hackett, Buddy
800 N Whittier Dr
Beverly Hills, CA 90210
Actor *V: 01/18/96*

485 Fifth Ave #1000
New York, NY 10019
Alternate *V: 03/17/96*

Hackett, Jeff
1325 Ridsan Pl
London, Ont, Canada N5X 1X6
Hockey Star *V: 01/20/96*

Hackman, Gene
c/o Guttman
118 S Beverly Dr #201
Beverly Hills, CA 90212-3003
Actor *V: 01/21/96*

9696 Culver Bl #203
Culver City, CA 90232
Alternate *V: 02/11/96*

Hadfield, Chris A
NASA/LBJ Space Center
Houston, TX 77058
Astronaut *V: 02/02/96*

Haeggstrom Office
6404 Wilshire Bl #1100
Los Angeles, CA 90048
Talent Agency *V: 11/11/96*

Hagar, Sammy
Steady State
PO Box 5395
Novato, CA 94948
Singer *V: 02/02/96*

Hagen, Nina
InterTalent Agency
131 S Rodeo Dr #300
Beverly Hills, CA 90212
Singer *V: 10/23/96*

Hagen, Uta
c/o Kroll
390 W End Ave
New York, NY 10024
Actress *V: 02/12/96*

Hagerty, Julie
Innovative Artists
1999 Ave of the Stars #2850
Los Angeles, CA 90067
Actress *V: 12/11/96*

c/o Buchwald
10 E 44th St #500
New York NY 10017
Alternate *V: 09/04/96*

Haggard, Merle
Fuzzy Owens
PO Box 842
Bakersfield, CA 93302
Singer *V: 02/02/96*

Haggard, Merle, Cont.
PO Box 536
Palo Cedro, CA 96073
Alternate V: 06/30/96

Haggerty, HB
First Artists
10000 Riverside Dr #6
Toluca Lake, CA 91602
Actor V: 02/02/96

Hagman, Larry
23730 Malibu Colony Rd
Malibu, CA 90265
Actor V: 03/30/96

c/o ICM
8942 Wilshire Bl
Beverly Hills, CA 90211
Alternate V: 05/14/96

Hahn, Jessica
6345 Balboa Bl #375
Encino, CA 91316-1517
Celebrity V: 03/14/96

Haig Jr, Alexander
6142 Farver Rd
McLean, VA 22101
Politician V: 03/02/96

1155 15th St NW #800
Washington, DC 20005
Alternate V: 08/08/96

Haim, Corey
3209 Taresco Dr
Los Angeles, CA 90068
Actor V: 06/02/96

233 S St Andrews Place
Los Angeles CA 90049
Forwarded V: 03/15/96

Haines, Connie
880 Mandalay Ave #G-109
Clearwater, FL 34630-1231
Actress V: 01/12/96

Haise Jr, Fred W
NASA/LBJ Space Center
Houston, TX 77058
Astronaut V: 03/03/96

Haje, Khrystyne
c/o Rosenberg
8428 Melrose Pl-Suite C
Los Angeles, CA 90069
Actress V: 02/12/96

Haje, Khrystyne, Cont.
PO Box 8750
Universal Ciry, CA 91608
Alternate V: 01/23/96

Hale, Barbara
Shapira & Associates
15301 Ventura Bl #345
Sherman Oaks, CA 91403
Actress V: 12/13/96

PO Box 1980
N Hollywood, CA 91614
Alternate V: 03/03/96

PO Box 60611-261
Sherman Oaks, CA 91413
Alternate V: 11/01/96

Hall, Anthony Michael
c/o Buchwald
9229 Sunset Bl #710
Los Angeles, CA 90069
Actor V: 02/01/96

574 W End Ave #4
New York, NY 10024
Alternate V: 01/03/97

Hall, Arsenio
ABC-TV
77 W 66th St
New York, NY 10023
Actor V: 01/10/97

10989 Bluffside Dr #3418
Studio City CA 91604
Alternate V: 09/09/96

Hall, Deirdre
Shapira & Associates
15301 Ventura Bl #345
Sherman Oaks, CA 91403
Actress V: 12/13/96

Hall, Fawn
1319 Bishop Ln
Alexandria, VA 22032
Celebrity V: 11/28/96

8339 Chapel Lake Ct
Annandale, VA 22003
Alternate V: 04/18/96

Hall, Huntz
12512 Chandler Bl #307
N Hollywood, CA 91607
Actor V: 03/23/96

Hall, Jerry
2 Munroe Terrace
London SW10 0DL England
Model V: 09/09/96

Hall, Lasaundra
c/o Waugh
4731 Laurel Canyon Bl #5
N Hollywood, CA 91607
Actress V: 02/11/96

Hall, Lois
Artists Mgmt
1368 Benedict Canyon Dr
Beverly Hills, 90210-2020
Actress V: 01/22/96

Hall, Monty
519 N Arden Dr
Beverly Hills, CA 90210
Entertainer V: 09/09/96

Hall, Rich
PO Box 2350
Los Angeles, CA 90078
Actor V: 01/03/97

Hall, Tom T
PO Box 1246
Franklin, TN 37065-1246
Actor V: 01/13/96

PO Box 121089
Nashville, TN 37212
Alternate V: 01/11/96

Hall & Oates
Champian Entertainment
130 W 57th St
New York, NY 10019
Singer V: 02/12/96

Hallahan, Charles
Gersh Agency
232 N Canon Dr
Beverly Hills, CA 90210
Actor V: 02/18/96

Halliday & Associates
8899 Beverly Bl #620
Los Angeles, CA 90048
Talent Agency V: 11/11/96

Halprin & Associates
12304 Santa Monica Bl #104
Los Angeles, CA 90025
Talent Agency V: 02/02/96

Halsell Jr, James D
NASA/LBJ Space Center
Houston, TX 77058
Astronaut V: 03/03/96

Ham, Jack
409 Broad St
Sewiddey, PA 15143
Football Star V: 05/07/96

Hamel, Veronica
Wm Morris Agency
151 El Camino Dr
Beverly Hills, CA 90212
Actress V: 02/11/96

129 N Woodburn Dr
Los Angeles, CA 90049
Forwarded V: 04/18/96

Hamill, Dorothy
79490 Fairway Dr
Indian Wells, CA 92210
Olympian V: 04/03/96

Hamill, Mark
PO Box 1051
Santa Monica, CA 90406
Actor V: 11/11/96

PO Box 55
Malibu, CA 90265
Alternate V: 01/03/96

20358 Big Rock Rd
Malibu, CA 90265
Alternate V: 01/12/96

c/o APA
9000 Sunset Bl
Los Angeles, CA 90069
Forwarded V: 01/12/96

PO Box 124
Malibu, CA 90264
Forwarded V: 03/15/96

Hamilton, Ashley
10230 Wilshire Bl #1705
Los Angeles, CA 90024
Actor V: 10/10/96

Hamilton, Bobby
Petty Enterprises
311 Branson Mill Rd
Randleman, NC 27317
NASCAR Driver V: 02/08/96

Hamilton, Bobby, Cont.
NASCAR
1811 Volusia Ave
Daytona Beach, FL 32015
Alternate V: 01/21/96

Hamilton, George
9255 Doheny Rd #2302
Los Angeles, CA 90069-3234
Actor V: 03/14/96

10430 Wilshire Bl #1705
Los Angeles, CA 90024-4655
Alternate V: 01/31/96

14542 Ventura Bl #214
Sherman Oaks, CA 91403-5512
Alternate V: 11/10/96

Hamilton, Linda
8942 Wilshire Bl
Beverly Hills, CA 90211
Actress V: 12/11/96

19900 Pacific Coast Hwy
Malibu, CA 90265
Alternate V: 02/02/96

Hamilton, Lisa Gay
ABC-Audience Services
77 W 52nd St
New York, NY 10019
Actress V: 01/12/97

Hamilton, Scott
1 Erieview Plaza #1000
Cleveland, OH 90038
Olympian V: 03/03/96

Hamilton, Wendy
Playboy Promotions
8560 Sunset Bl
Los Angeles, CA 90069
Playmate V: 03/11/96

Hamlin, Harry
Gersh Agency
232 N Canon Dr
Beverly Hills, CA 90210
Actor V: 12/09/96

612 N Sepulveda Bl #10
Los Angeles, CA 90049
Alternate V: 04/06/96

Hamlisch, Marvin
970 Park Ave-5th Fl #65
New York, NY 10028
Composer V: 02/19/96

Hammer
1750 N Vine St
Hollywood, CA 90212
Rapper V: 01/14/96

Hammond, Jeff
Darwal Inc
6780 Hudspeth Rd
Harrisburg, NC 28705
NASCAR Crew V: 03/02/96

Hammond Jr, L Blaine
NASA/LBJ Space Center
Hoston, TX 77058
Astronaut V: 01/31/96

Han, Maggie
9255 Sunset Bl #710
Los Angeles, CA 90069
Actress V: 03/04/96

Hancock, Herbie
1250 N Doheny Dr
Los Angeles, CA 90069
Composer V: 03/17/96

1680 N Vine St
Hollywood, CA 90028
Alternate V: 09/03/96

Haney, Anne T
Borinstein/Oreck & Bogart
8271 Melrose Ave #110
Los Angeles, CA 90046
Actress V: 12/06/96

Hanks, Tom
PO Box 1650
Pacific Palisades, CA 90272
Actor V: 04/21/96

23414 Malibu Colony Dr
Malibu, CA 90265
Alternate V: 01/15/97

9830 Wilshire Bl
Beverly Hills, CA 90212
Forwarded V: 01/12/96

Hanmer, Dan
711 Newton St
Monterey, CA 93940
Actor V: 01/21/96

Hanna, William D
Hanna-Barbera
3400 W Cahuenga Bl
Los Angeles CA 90068
Animator V: 03/03/96

Hannah, Daryl
8306 Wilshire Bl #535
Beverly Hills, CA 90211-2382
Actress V: 11/01/96

171 W 71st St
New York, NY 10023
Alternate V: 05/05/96

Creative Artist Agency
9830 Wilshire Bl
Beverly Hills, CA 90212
Forwarded V: 01/14/96

c/o ICM
8942 Wilshire Bl
Beverly Hills, CA 90211
Forwarded V: 01/14/96

Hansen, Gunner
9131 College Parkway
Suite 13-B, Box #101
Ft Meyers, FL 33919
Actor V: 11/20/96

Harbaugh, Gregory J
NASA/LBJ Space Center
Hoston, TX 77058
Astronaut V: 01/31/96

Hardin, Ty
Beakel & Jennings
427 N Canon Dr
Beverly Hills, CA 90212
Actor V: 05/05/96

Hardison, Kadeem
19743 Valleyview Dr
Topanga, CA 90290
Actor V: 02/05/96

324 N Brighton St
Burbank, CA 91506
Alternate V: 04/05/96

Hardy, Robert
Upper Bolney House
Henley-on-Thames
Oxon RG9 4AQ, England
Actor V: 03/17/96

Harewood, Dorian
810 Prospect Bl
Pasadena, CA 91103-3242
Actor V: 08/28/96

1865 Hill Dr
Los Angeles, CA 90041
Forwarded V: 04/06/96

Hargitay, Mariska
Writers & Artists
924 Westwood Bl #900
Los Angeles, CA 90024
Actress V: 12/15/96

c/o TMCE
270 N Canon Dr #1064
Beverly Hills, CA 90210
Forwarded V: 01/11/96

Harlem Globetrotters
1000 S Fremont Ave
Alhambra, CA 91803-1345
Team Office V: 01/11/96

15301 Ventura B-Suite 430
Sherman Oaks, CA 91403
Alternate V: 04/10/96

Harmon, Deborah
Metro Talent Agency
4526 Wilshire Bl
Los Angeles, CA 90010
Actress V: 12/11/96

Harmon, Kelly
13224 Old Oak Lane
Los Angeles, CA 90049
Actress V: 12/01/96

Harmon, Mark
Paradigm Agency
10100 Santa Monica Bl-25th Fl
Los Angeles, CA 90067
Actor V: 12/13/96

2236 Encinitas Bl #A
Encinitas, CA 92024-4353
Alternate V: 07/14/96

Harper, Heck
13647 Gaffney #17
Oregon City, OR 97045
Celebrity V: 01/13/96

Harper, Jessica
3454 Gloretta Pl
Sherman Oaks, CA 91423
Actress V: 03/28/96

Camden ITG
822 S Robertson Bl #200
Los Angeles, CA 90035
Alternate V: 02/11/96

9229 Sunset Bl #710
Los Angeles, CA 90069
Forwarded V: 03/15/96

Harper, Ron
Los Angeles Clippers
3939 Figueroa
Los Angeles, CA 90037
Basketball Star V: 11/01/96

Harper, Tess
Wm Morris Agency
151 El Camino Dr
Beverly Hills, CA 90212
Actress V: 02/11/96

Buchwald & Associates
9229 Sunset Bl #710
Los Angeles, CA 90069
Alternate V: 12/06/96

Harper, Valerie
14 E 4th St
New York, NY 10012-1155
Actress V: 01/12/96

616 N Maple Dr
Beverly Hills, CA 90210
Alternate V: 06/16/96

Harrelson, Woody
Creative Artists Agency
9830 Wilshire Bl
Beverly Hills, CA 90212
Actor V: 12/07/96

Harring, Laura
12335 Santa Monica Bl #302
Los Angeles, CA 90025
Former Miss USA V: 01/13/96

Harrington, Robert
2609 Woodsdade Ave
Kannapolic, NC 28127
NASCAR Driver V: 11/11/96

Harris, Barbara
823 W Montrose-1st Fl
Chicago, IL 60613-1431
Actress V: 03/13/96

Harris, Bill
In Hollywood
6662 Whitley Terrace
Los Angles, CA 90068
Cable Host V: 03/03/96

c/o Showtime
10900 Wilshire Bl
Los Angeles, CA 90024
Alternate V: 02/12/96

Harris, Danielle
c/o APA
9000 Sunset Bl #1200
Los Angeles, CA 90069
Actress V: 02/11/96

Harris, Ed
Creative Artists Agency
9830 Wilshire Bl
Beverly Hills, CA 90212
Actor V: 12/07/96

Harris, Emmylou
PO Box 158568
Nashville, TN 37215
Singer V: 04/03/96

Harris, Franco
400 W North Ave
Pittsburgh, PA 15212
Football Star V: 03/25/96

Complex-D
800 Vinial St
Pittsburgh, PA 15212
Alternate V: 12/10/96

Harris, Jay
King Features
235 E 45th St
New York, NY 10017
Cartoonist V: 03/12/96

Harris, Jonathan
Sutton/Barth & Vennari
145 S Fairfax Ave #310
Los Angeles, CA 90036
Actor V: 12/15/96

16830 Marmaduke Pl
Encino, CA 91316
Alternate V: 05/14/96

Harris, Jonathan, Cont.
20th Century Artists
9744 Wilshire Bl #308
Beverly Hills, CA 90212
Forwarded V: 01/02/96

Harris, Julie
PO Box 1287
W Chatham, MA 02669
Actress V: 09/13/96

132 Barn Hill Rd
W Chatham, MA 02669
Alternate V: 03/01/96

Harris, Neal Patrick
c/o ICM
8942 Wilshire Bl
Beverly Hills, CA 90211
Actor V: 02/27/96

c/o Booh Schut
13351 Riverside Dr #D-450
Sherman Oaks, CA 91423
Alternate V: 03/26/96

Harris, Richard
Wm Morris Agency
151 El Camino Dr
Beverly Hills, CA 90212
Actor V: 06/13/96

Harris Jr, Bernard A
NASA/LBJ Space Center
Houston, TX 77058
Astronaut V: 02/02/96

Harrison, Dillard
9770 Avenida Monterey
Cypress, CA 90630
Olympian V: 10/23/96

Harrison, Gregory
Wm Morris Agency
151 El Camino
Beverly Hills, CA 90212
Actor V: 12/12/96

11570 Moorpark H
Studio City, CA 91604
Alternate V: 01/15/96

Harrison, Jenilee
20th Century Artists
15315 Magnolia Bl #429
Sherman Oaks, CA 91403
Actress V: 01/31/96

c\o Harry Weiss
7100 Hayvenhurst Ave #322
Van Nuys, CA 91406-3804
Forwarded V: 03/20/96

Harrison, Kathleen
91 Regent St
London W1, England
Actress V: 03/01/96

Harrison, Noel
5-11 Mortimer St
London W1, England
Actor V: 02/03/96

Harrold, Kathryn
Wm Morris Agency
151 El Camino
Beverly Hills, CA 90212
Actress V: 12/12/96

241 Central Park S #2-H
New York, NY 10019
Alternate V: 08/28/96

Harry, Debbie
c/o WMA
1325 Ave of the Americas
New York, NY 10019
Singer V: 11/01/96

1775 Broadway #701
New York, NY 10019
Forwarded V: 07/23/96

Harry, Jackee
Metro Talent Agency
4526 Wilshire Bl
Los Angeles, CA 90010
Actress V: 12/11/96

Hart, Johnny
King Features
235 E 45th St
New York, NY 10017
Cartoonist V: 03/10/96

1703 Kaiser St
Irvine, CA 92714
Alternate V: 03/02/96

Hart, Mary
Entertainment Tonight
5555 Melrose Ave
Hollywood, CA 90038
Celebrity V: 04/10/96

Hart, Mickey
Grateful Dead
PO Box 1073
San Rafael, CA 94915
Musician V: 12/01/96

Hart, Terry J
NASA/LBJ Space Center
Hoston, TX 77058
Astronaut V: 03/03/96

Hart Agency
8899 Beverly Bl #815
Los Angeles, CA 90048
Talent Agency V: 03/26/96

Hartford Whalers
Civic Center Coliseum
242 Trumbull St
Hartford, CT 06103
Production Office V: 01/31/96

Hartley, Mariette
Buckwald & Associates
9229 Sunset Bl #710
Los Angeles, CA 90069
Actress V: 12/06/96

10110 Empryian Way #304
Los Angeles, CA 90067
Alternate V: 02/03/96

Hartman, Lisa
Shapira & Associates
15301 Ventura Bl #345
Sherman Oaks, CA 91403
Actress V: 12/13/96

8489 West Third St #200
Los Angeles, CA 90048
Alternate V: 10/23/96

8606 Allenwood Rd
Los Angeles, CA 90046
Forwarded V: 01/10/96

12424 Wilshire Bl #840
Los Angeles, CA 90025
Forwarded V: 11/01/96

Hartman, Phil
Wm Morris Agency
151 El Camino
Beverly Hills, CA 90212
Actor V: 12/12/96

8008 Briar Summit Dr
Los Angeles, CA 90046
Alternate V: 01/03/97

Hartsfield Jr, Henry W
NASA/LBJ Space Center
Hoston, TX 77058
Astronaut V: 01/19/96

Harvey, Paul
Paulynne/Garcia
1035 Park Ave
River Forrest, IL 60305
Radio Star V: 03/13/96

Haskell, Peter
19924 Acre St
Northridge, CA 91324
Actor V: 06/16/96

Haskett, Gene
MI Int'l Speedway
12626 US 12
Brooklyn, MI 49230
NASCAR Official V: 03/02/96

Hass, Katie
Wildhorse Saloon
PO Box 148400
Nashville, TN 37214
Celebrity V: 01/11/96

Hasselhoff, David
ISO Mgmt
11342 Dona Lisa Dr
Studio City, CA 91604
Actor V: 01/14/96

4310 Sutton Pl
Van Nuys, CA 91403
Alternate V: 03/17/96

14431 Ventura Bl #415
Sherman Oaks, CA 91423
Alternate V: 10/23/96

c/o APA
9000 Sunset Bl #1200
Los Angeles, CA 90069
Forwarded V: 02/05/96

Fritz Dorazil
Schmidgasse 9/1/13
A-2320 Schwechat, Austria
Forwarded V: 03/17/96

Hatch, Richard
Gerler Agency
3349 Cahuenga Bl West #1
Los Angeles, CA 90068
Actor V: 12/08/96

Hatcher, Teri
Wm Morris Agency
151 El Camino
Beverly Hills, CA 90212
Actress V: 12/12/96

PO Box 1101
Sunland, CA 91041-1101
Alternate V: 03/14/96

Hatfield, Hurd
Ballinterry House
Rathcormac
County Cork, Ireland
Actor V: 03/12/96

Hauer, Rutger
Verenigde Nederland Film
Singel 440-1017 Av
Amsterdam, Holland
Actor V: 02/08/96

1AE Films
5 New Road, W Molesy
Surry KT18 1PT, England
Alternate V: 02/09/96

Wm Morris Agency
151 El Camino Dr
Beverly Hills, CA 90212
Forwarded V: 07/13/96

Hauk, Frederick H
NASA/LBJ Space Center
Houston, TX 77058
Astronaut V: 03/03/96

Hauser, Wings
261 S Figueroa St #395
Los Angeles, CA 90012-2503
Actor V: 08/28/96

Artists Group
10100 Santa Monica Bl #2490
Los Angeles, CA 90067
Alternate V: 12/04/96

14126 Marquesas Way
Marina del Rey, CA 90292
Forwarded V: 01/24/96

Hausl, Regina
Jettenburg 49
8230 Schneizlreuth, Germany
Skier V: 02/01/96

Haussmann, Ezard
Agentur Mattes
Mertzstrasse 14
8000 Munchen 80, Germany
Actor V: 02/23/96

Havens, Richie
c/o Wolfson
123 W 44th St #11F
New York, NY 10036
Singer V: 11/28/96

Haver, June
485 Halvern Dr
Los Angeles, CA 90049
Actress V: 04/01/96

Havers, Nigel
c/o Whitehall
125 Gloucester Rd
London SW7 4TE, England
Actor V: 03/17/96

c/o BBC TV Center
Woodlane
London W12 7RJ, England
Alternate V: 03/01/96

Havoc, June
Craig Agency
8485 Melrose Place-Suite E
Los Angeles, CA 90069
Actress V: 12/08/96

405 Old Long Rd
Stamford, CT 06903
Alternate V: 10/08/96

Hawke, Ethan
Creative Artists Agency
9830 Wilshire Bl
Beverly Hills, CA 90212
Actor V: 12/07/96

Hawking, Stephen W
U/C-Dept Applied Math
Silver St
Cambridge CB3 9EW, England
Scientist V: 11/01/96

Hawley, Steven A
NASA/LBJ Space Center
Houston, TX 77058
Astronaut V: 03/03/96

Hawn, Goldie
500 S Buena Vista St #1D6
Burbank, CA 91505-4808
Actress V: 01/12/96

Merchant Ivory Productions
250 W 57th St #1913-A
New York, NY 10019
Forwarded V: 03/14/96

Hawthorne, Nigel
c/o McReddie
91 Regent St
London W1R 7TB, England
Actor V: 03/17/96

Hayek, Julie
5645 Burning Tree Dr
La Canada, CA 91011
Actress V: 10/23/96

Hayek, Salma
Wm Morris Agency
151 El Camino Dr
Beverly Hills, CA 90212
Actress V: 12/12/96

Hayes, Isaac
Stone Manners Talent
8091 Selma Ave
Los Angeles, CA 90068
Actor V: 12/15/96

504 W 168th St
New York, NY 10032
Alternate V: 01/15/96

Hayes, Julia
7227 Winchester #266
Memphis, TN 38125
Model V: 01/02/97

Hayes, Peter Lind
3538 Pueblo Way
Las Vegas, NV 89109
Actor V: 11/10/96

Hayes, Wade
PO Box 128546
Nashville, TN 37212-8546
Singer V: 01/10/97

Hays, Robert
Paradigm Agency
10100 Santa Monica Bl-25th Fl
Los Angeles, CA 90067
Actor V: 12/13/96

Hazelwood, Doug
502 Dover
Victoria, TX 77901
Cartoonist V: 01/21/96

Head, Anthony Stewart
Smith & Associates
121 San Vicente Bl
Beverly Hills, CA 90211
Actor V: 01/15/97

Healy, Mary
3538 Pueblo Way
Las Vegas, NV 89109
Actress V: 03/09/96

Heard, John
c/o ICM
8942 Wilshire Bl
Beverly Hills, CA 90211
Actor V: 02/22/96

Heard, John, Cont.
347 W 84th St #5
New York, NY 10004
Alternate V: 12/14/96

Hearns, Tommy
19260 Britton Dr
Detroit, MI 48223
Boxing Star V: 12/11/96

Heart
1202 E Pike St #767
Seattle, WA 98122
Musical Group V: 12/12/96

PO Box 77505
San Francisco, CA 94107-0505
Alternate V: 01/15/96

Hecht Agency
12001 Ventura Place #320
Studio City, CA 91604
Talent Agency V: 11/11/96

Hect, Gina
Epstein/Wyckoff
280 S Beverly Bl #400
Beverly Hills, CA 90212
Actress V: 02/11/96

Hedison, David
Ambrosio & Mortimer
9150 Wilshire Bl #175
Beverly Hills, CA 90212
Actor V: 12/01/96

2940 Trudy Dr
Beverly Hills, CA 90210
Alternate V: 03/26/96

9454 Wilshire Bl #405
Beverly Hills, CA 90212
Forwarded V: 03/15/96

Hedison, Teri
605 Templeton Ct
Sunnyvale, CA 94087
Actress V: 03/15/96

Hedren, Tippi
Artists Group
10100 Santa Monica Bl #2490
Los Angeles, CA 90067
Actress V: 02/11/96

6867 Soledad Canyon Rd
Acton, CA 93510
Forwarded V: 02/02/96

Hedrick, Larry
PO Box 749
Statesville, NC 28677
Race Driver V: 05/01/94

Heesters, Nicole
ZBF Agentur
Leopoldstrasse 19
8000 Munchen 40, Germany
Actress V: 02/11/96

Hefner, Hugh
10236 Charing Cross Rd
Los Angeles, CA 90024
Publisher V: 05/05/96

Hegyes, Robert
12206 Tweed Ln
Los Angeles, CA 90049-4036
Actor V: 01/12/96

10323 Ilona Ave
Los Angeles, CA 90064-2503
Alternate V: 01/31/96

Heigl, Katherine
c/o Wilhemina
300 Park Ave
New York, NY 10010
Model V: 09/13/96

Helgenberger, Marg
c/o ICM
8942 Wilshire Bl
Beverly Hills, CA 90211
Actress V: 02/11/96

Heller, Joseph
NHP Inc
1225 1st St NW
Washington, DC 20005
Writer V: 10/23/96

Helm, Susan J
NASA/LBJ Space Center
Houston, TX 77058
Astronaut V: 03/03/96

Helmond, Katherine
Wm Morris Agency
151 El Camino
Beverly Hills, CA 90212
Actress V: 12/12/96

PO Box 10029
Beverly Hills, CA 90213
Forwarded V: 03/04/96

Helmond, Katherine, Cont.
2035 Davies Way
Los Angeles, CA 90046
Forwarded V: 03/26/96

Helmsley, Leona
36 Central Park Lane South
New York, NY 10019
Celebrity V: 03/03/96

Helton, Mike
Tallapega Speedway
PO Box 777
Tallapega, AL 35160
NASCAR Official V: 03/02/96

Hemingway, Mariel
c/o ICM
8942 Wilshire Bl
Beverly Hills, CA 90211
Actress V: 12/11/96

PO Box 2249
Ketchum, ID 83340
Alternate V: 01/05/96

Hemmings, David
60 Saint James St
London SW1, England
Director V: 03/01/96

Michael Whitehall
135 Gloucester Rd
London SW7, England
Alternate V: 02/28/96

Hemsley, Sherman
c/o Johnston
15043 Valley Heart Dr
Sherman Oaks, CA 91403
Actor V: 12/01/96

Henderson, Don
c/o AIM
5 Denmark St
London WC2H 8LP, England
Actor V: 03/17/96

Henderson, Florence
FHB Productions
PO Box 11295
Marina Del Rey, CA 90292
Actress V: 07/23/96

Artists Agency
10000 Santa Monica Bl #305
Los Angeles, CA 90067
Alternate V: 12/02/96

Henderson, Florence, Cont.
Artists Group
10100 Santa Monica Bl #2490
Los Angeles, CA 90067
 Forwarded V: 02/11/96

Henderson, Kelo
Rimrock Video
PO Box 5003
Apache Junction, AZ 85278
 Actor V: 12/12/96

Henderson/Hogan Agency
247 S Beverly Dr #102
Beverly Hills, CA 90210
 Talent Agency V: 02/23/96

Henley, Don
HK Mgmt
8900 Wilshire Bl #300
Beverly Hills, CA 90211-1906
 Singer V: 02/25/96

Henn, Mark
Disney Animation
PO Box 10200
Lake Buena Vista, FL 32830
 Cartoonist V: 12/01/96

Henner, Marilu
Wm Morris Agency
151 El Camino
Beverly Hills, CA 90212
 Actress V: 12/12/96

Henning, Linda Kaye
843 N Sycamore Ave
Los Angeles, CA 90038
 Actress V: 10/23/96

Henricks, Terence T
NASA/LBJ Space Center
Hoston, TX 77058
 Astronaut V: 01/31/96

Henriksen, Lance
c/o APA
9000 Sunset Bl #1200
Los Angeles, CA 90069
 Actor V: 02/11/96

9540 Dale Ave
Sunland, CA 91040
 Alternate V: 03/26/96

Henry, Gloria
11846 Ventura Bl #100
Studio City, CA 91604
 Actress V: 01/21/96

Hensley, Jimmy
Yarborough Racing
9617 Dixie River Rd
Charlotte, NC 28270
 NASCAR Driver V: 05/12/96

Hensley, Pamela
9526 Dalegrove Dr
Beverly Hills, CA 90210
 Actress V: 03/13/96

Henson & Associates
Tower Bldg-28th Fl
3900 Alameda
Burbank, CA 91595
 Production Office V: 06/15/96

Henstridge, Natasha
HWA Talent
1964 Westwood Bl #400
Los Angeles, CA 90025
 Actress V: 12/15/96

Hepburn, Katherine
244 E 49th St
New York, NY 10017
 Actress V: 07/01/96

Wm Morris Agency
151 El Camino Dr
Beverly Hills, CA 90212
 Alternate V: 01/14/96

Herlihy, Ed
16 Sutton Pl
New York, NY 10022
 Radio Star V: 03/11/96

Herman, Edward
Innovative Artists
1999 Ave of the Stars #2850
Los Angeles, CA 90067
 Actor V: 12/11/96

Herndon, Ty
Image Management
27 Music Square E
Nashville, TN 37203
 Singer V: 11/01/96

Herring, Rufus G
PO Box 128
Roseboro, NC 28382
 War Hero V: 02/04/96

Herrman, Edward
151 El Camino Dr
Beverly Hills, CA 90212
 Actor V: 01/21/96

Hershey, Barbara
c/o CAA
9830 Wilshire Bl
Beverly Hills, CA 90212
Actress V: 03/30/96

Hershiser, Orel
251 Chelton Cirle
Winter Park, FL 32789-6004
Baseball Star V: 01/12/96

Hervey/Grimes Agency
12444 Ventura Bl #103
Studio City, CA 91604
Talent Agency V: 02/07/96

Hesseman, Howard
Innovative Artists
1999 Ave of the Stars #2850
Los Angeles, CA 90067
Actor V: 12/11/96

7146 La Presa Dr
Hollywood, CA 90068
Alternate V: 02/13/96

Heston, Charlton
2859 Coldwater Canyon Dr
Beverly Hills, CA 90068
Actor V: 03/03/96

Hetrick, Jennifer
2510 Canyon Dr
Los Angeles, CA 90068
Actress V: 01/13/96

Heyerdahl, Thor
Guimar, Tenerife
Canary Islands, Spain
Explorer V: 12/01/96

Heywood, Anne
9966 Liebe Dr
Beverly Hills, CA 90210
Actress V: 02/19/96

Hickman, Dwayne
c/o DGIFC
PO Box 3352
Santa Monica, CA 90403
Actor V: 12/15/96

J Roberts Hickman
812 16th St #1
Santa Monica, CA 90403
Alternate V: 01/04/96

Hicks, Catherine
Smith & Associates
121 N San Vicente Bl
Beverly Hills, CA 90211
Actress V: 02/11/96

Hicks, Dan
PO Box 5481
Mill Valley, CA 94942
Musician V: 03/07/96

Hieb, Richard J
NASA/LBJ Space Center
Hoston, TX 77058
Astronaut V: 01/31/96

Higgins, Joel
24 Old Hill Rd
Westport, CT 06880
Actor V: 03/02/96

Hildegarde
230 E 48th St
New York, NY 10017
Singer V: 04/27/96

Hill, Carl
NASCAR
1811 Volusia Ave
Daytona Beach, FL 32015
NASCAR Official V: 03/14/96

Hill, Faith
7021 Mayflower Circle
Brentwood, TN 37027-6908
Actress V: 03/14/96

2502 Belmont Bl #B
Nashville, TN 37212
Alternate V: 07/29/96

PO Box 24266
Nashville, TN 37202
Forwarded V: 01/21/96

Hill, Steven
18 Jill Lane
Monsey, NY 10952
Actor V: 12/14/96

Hill, Terence
PO Box 818
Stockbridge, MA 01262
Actor V: 03/10/96

Hill Productions
1 Fifth Ave
New York, NY 10003
Alternate V: 04/11/96

Hill, Terence, Cont.
c/o Rialto
Bismarkstr 108
Berlin 1000-12, Germany
Forwarded V: 02/09/96

Hillary, Edmond
NZ High Commissioner
25 Golf Links
New Delhi, 110003 India
Explorer V: 03/01/96

NZ High Commissioner
228A Remuera Rd
Auckland, SE2 New Zealand
Alternate V: 01/11/96

Hillerman, John
7102 La Presa Dr
Los Angeles, CA 90068
Actor V: 03/26/96

Hillin, Bobby
Donlavey Racing
5011 Midlothian Turnpike
Richmond, VA 23224
NASCAR Driver V: 02/27/96

Hilmers, David C
NASA/LBJ Space Center
Hoston, TX 77058
Astronaut V: 01/31/96

Hines, Gregory
c/o UTA
15315 Magnolia Bl #429
Sherman Oaks, CA 91403
Actor V: 12/15/96

377 W 11th St #PH
New York, NY 10014
Alternate V: 03/12/96

Hingle, Pat
PO Box 2228
Carolina Beach, NC 28428
Actor V: 06/16/96

Blake Agency
415 N Camden Dr #121
Beverly Hills, CA 90210
Actor V: 12/06/96

Hinterseer, Ernst
Hahnenkammstrasse
6370 Kitzbuhel, Austria
Skier V: 01/19/96

Hirsch, Elroy
1440 Monroe St
Madison, WI 53711
Football Star V: 03/17/96

Hirsch, Judd
Agency For Performing Arts
9000 Sunset Bl #1200
Los Angeles, CA 90069
Actor V: 12/02/96

11 E 44th St
New York, NY 10017
Alternate V: 01/13/97

Hitch, David M
King Features
216 E 45th St
New York, NY 10017
Cartoonist V: 03/11/96

Ho, Don
277 Lewers St
Honolulu, HI 98615
Singer V: 01/31/96

Hobart, Rose
23388 Mulholland Dr
Woodland Hills, CA 91364
Actress V: 03/13/96

Hodder, Kane
3701 Senda Calma
Calabasas, CA 91302
Actor V: 01/11/97

Hodges, Craig
Chicago Bulls
980 Michigan Ave
Chicago, IL 60611
Basketball Star V: 04/05/96

Hodges, Joy
PO Box 254
Katonah, NY, 10536
Actress V: 03/13/96

PO Box 1262
Cathedral City, CA 92235
Alternate V: 01/13/96

Hodgins, Dick
King Features
235 E 45th St
New York, NY 10017
Cartoonist V: 02/14/96

Hoest, Bill
34 Sylvia Rd
Plainview, NY 11803
Cartoonist V: 01/21/96

Hoffman, Alice
3 Hurlbut St
Cambridge, MA 02138-1603
Author V: 11/11/96

Hoffman, Dustin
540 Madison Ave #2700
New York, NY 10022
Actor V: 03/01/96

9830 Wilshire Bl
Beverly Hills, CA 90212
Alternate V: 03/11/96

315 E 65th St
New York, NY 10021
Forwarded V: 03/12/96

111 W 40th St #20
New York, NY 10018
Forwarded V: 01/15/96

Hoffman, Jeffrey A
NASA/LBJ Space Center
Houston, TX 77058
Astronaut V: 03/03/96

Hoffs, Susanna
c/o GRF
1880 Century Park E #900
Los Angeles, CA 90067
Actress V: 02/11/96

9720 Wilshire Bl #400
Beverly Hills, CA 90212
Alternate V: 02/03/96

Hofmann, Peter
Schonrueth
8584 Kemnath, Germany
Singer V: 02/11/96

Hubschstrasse 8
8580 Bayreuth, Germany
Alternate V: 02/11/96

Hogan, Ben
6000 Western Pl #111
Ft Worth, TX 76107
Golfer V: 11/01/96

PO Box 11276
Ft Worth, TX 76110
Forwarded V: 09/18/96

Hogan, Hulk
4505 Morella Ave
N Hollywood, CA 91607
Wrestler V: 01/20/96

Hogan, Paul
JP Productions
7 Parr Ave-North Curl
NSW 2099, Australia
Actor V: 02/15/96

Hogarth, Burne
6026 W Lindenhurst Ave
Los Angles, CA 90036
Cartoonist V: 10/23/96

Hogestyn, Drake
Gage Group
9255 Sunset Bl #515
Los Angeles, CA 90069
Actor V: 03/20/96

Holbrook, Bill
King Features
235 E 45th St
New York, NY 10017
Cartoonist V: 06/18/96

1321 Weatherstone Way
Atlanta, GA 30324
Alternate V: 04/12/96

Holbrook, Hal
618 S Lucerne Bl
Los Angeles, CA 90005-3704
Actor V: 01/11/96

c/o APA
9000 Sunset Bl #1200
Los Angeles, CA 90069
Alternate V: 12/02/96

9100 Hazen Dr
Beverly Hills, CA 90210-1843
Forwarded V: 08/28/96

Holden, Rebecca
1010 16th Ave S
Nashville, TN 37212
Singer V: 03/21/96

Hollander Talent
3518 Cahuenga Bl West #316
Los Angeles, CA 90068
Talent Agency V: 11/11/96

Holley, Lee
King Features
235 E 45th St
New York, NY 10017
Cartoonist V: 04/21/96

Holliday, Polly
Blake Agency
415 N Camden Dr #121
Beverly Hills, CA 90210
Actress V: 12/06/96

Holliman, Earl
Buckwald & Associates
9229 Sunset Bl #710
Los Angeles, CA 90069
Actor V: 12/06/96

PO Box 1969
Studio City, CA 91604
Alternate V: 02/02/96

4249 Bellingham Ave
Studio City, CA 91604
Forwarded V: 01/21/96

Holly, Lauren
13601 Ventura Bl #99
Sherman Oaks, CA 91423
Actress V: 10/23/96

c/o UTA
9560 Wilshire Bl #500
Beverly Hills, CA 90212
Alternate V: 01/14/96

Hollywood CNTV Talent
1680 N Vine St #1105
Hollywood, CA 90028
Talent Agency V: 11/11/96

Hollywood Chamber
6255 Sunset Bl #911
Hollywood, CA 90028
Business Group V: 03/17/96

Hollywood Foreign Press
292 S La Cienega Bl #316
Beverly Hills, CA 90211
Press V: 03/17/96

Hollywood Radio/TV Society
5315 Laurel Canyon Bl #202
N Hollywood, CA 91607
Production Office V: 03/17/96

Hollywood Reporter
PO Box 1431
Hollywood, CA 90099-4927
Publisher V: 03/10/96

Hollywood Stuntman's Assn
1043 Rafael Dr
Arcadia, CA 91006
Offices V: 03/17/96

Holm, Celeste
88 Central Park W
New York, NY 10023
Actress V: 02/02/96

Holmes, Larry
896 Sheridan Dr
Easton, PA 18042
Boxing Star V: 09/14/96

413 Northampton St
Easton, PA 18042
Alternate V: 07/14/96

Holmquest, Donald L
NASA/LBJ Space Center
Houston, TX 77058
Astronaut V: 03/03/96

Holt, Hans
Weyrgstrasse #5
1030 Wien, Austria
Actor V: 01/19/96

Holt, Jennifer
Apartado Postal 170
Cuernavaca, Moreles 62000
Mexico
Actress V: 01/31/96

Holtz, Jurgen
Bornemannstrasse 18
6000 Frankfurt/Main, Germany
Actor V: 02/01/96

Home & Garden Television
9701 Madison Ave
Knoxville, TN 37932
Production Office V: 12/15/96

Home Box Office (HBO)
2049 Century Park E #1400
Los Angeles, CA 90067
Production Office V: 03/17/96

Home Shopping Network
1529 US Route 19 South
Clearwater, FL 33546
Production Office V: 12/15/96

Hong, James
c/o Lee
4150 Riverside Dr #212
Burbank, CA 91505
Actor V: 03/12/96

Hooker, John Lee
c/o Rosebud Agency
PO Box 170429
San Francisco, CA 94117
Singer V: 11/01/96

Hooks, Jan
Wm Morris Agency
151 El Camino Dr
Beverly Hills, CA 90212
Actress V: 12/01/96

Hooper, Brandon
3003 3rd St-Unit 4
Santa Monica, CA 90405-5488
Actor V: 01/31/96

Hope, Bob
10346 Moorpark St
N Hollywood, CA 91602-2499
Actor V: 11/01/96

Hopkins, Anthony
7 High Park Rd
Kew, Richmond
Surry TW9 3BL, England
Actor V: 06/18/96

c/o ICM
8942 Wilshire Blvd
Beverly Hills, CA 90211
Alternate V: 05/14/96

c/o Conway
18-21 Jermyn St
London SW1Y 6HB, England
Forwarded V: 03/14/96

Hopkins, Bo
6628 Ethel Ave
N Hollywood, CA 91606
Actor V: 01/12/96

Hopkins, Kate Lynn
1548 N Orange Grove Ave
Los Angeles, CA 90046-2618
Actress V: 01/12/96

Hopkins, Thelma
8967 Sunset Bl
Los Angeles, CA 90069
Singer V: 10/23/96

Hopper, Dennis
9830 Wilshire Bl
Beverly Hills, CA 90212
Actor V: 12/07/96

330 Indiana Ave
Venice, CA 90291
Alternate V: 07/14/96

Horkheimer, Dr Jack
3280 South Miami Ave
Miami, FL 33129
Scientist V: 03/25/96

Horn, Paul
Global Records
180 E Napa St
Sonoma, CA 96476
Musician V: 02/01/96

Hornaday, Linda
36554 Sierra Hwy
Palmdale, CA 93550
Race Driver V: 03/12/96

Hornaday, Ron
36554 Sierra Hwy
Palmdale, CA 93550
Race Driver V: 03/12/96

Horne, Lena
Volney Apartments
23 E 74th St
New York, NY 10021
Singer V: 05/15/96

5950 Canoga Ave #200
Woodland Hills, CA 91367
Alternate V: 01/19/96

2005 Massachusetts Ave NW
Lower Level
Washington, DC 20036
Forwarded V: 03/03/96

Horowitz, Scott J
NASA/LBJ Space Center
Houston, TX 77058
Astronaut V: 02/02/96

Horse, Michael
Bauman & Hiller
5750 Wilshire Bl #512
Los Angeles, CA 90036
Actor V: 12/05/96

5750 Wilshire Bl #512
Los Angeles, CA 90036
Alternate V: 03/15/96

Horsey, David
King Features
216 E 45th St
New York, NY 10017
Cartoonist V: 03/11/96

Horsley, Lee
Wm Morris Agency
151 El Camino
Beverly Hills, CA 90212
Actor V: 12/12/96

PO Box 456
Gypsum, CO 81637
Alternate V: 02/12/96

15054 E Dartmouth
Aurora, CO 80014
Forwarded V: 10/23/96

Horton, Jimmy
NASCAR
1811 Volusia Ave
Daytona Beach, FL 32015
NASCAR Driver V: 03/02/96

Horton, Peter
409 Santa Minica Bl #PH
Santa Monica, CA 90401
Actor V: 02/13/96

c/o Bauer
PO Box 5514
Beverly Hills, CA 90209
Alternate V: 01/11/96

c/o UTA
9560 Wilshire Bl #500
Beverly Hills, CA 90212
Forwarded V: 02/21/96

Horton, Robert
Century Artists
9744 Wilshire Bl #308
Beverly Hills, CA 90212
Actor V: 02/12/96

5317 Andasol Ave
Encino, CA 91316
Alternate V: 10/23/96

Horwitz, Dominique
ZBF Agentur
Jenfelder Allee 80
2000 Hamburg 70, Germany
Actress V: 02/01/96

Hoskins, Bob
Creative Artists Agency
9830 Wilshire Bl
Beverly Hills, CA 90212
Actor V: 12/07/96

30 Steel Rd
London NW3 4RE, England
Alternate V: 04/07/96

c/o Hutton Management
200 Fulham Rd
London SW10 9PN, England
Forwarded V: 01/17/96

Hottelet, Richard
120 Chestnut Hill Rd
Wilton, CT 06897
Radio Star V: 03/11/96

House, Tom
12794 Via Felino
Del Mar, CA 92014
Baseball Star V: 01/20/96

House of Representatives
9911 Pico Bl #1060
Los Angeles, CA 90035
Talent Agency V: 02/07/96

Housley, Phil
Winnipeg Jets
15-1430 Maroons Rd
Winnipeg, Manitoba, R3G 0L5
Hockey Star V: 11/09/96

Houston, Cissy
2160 N Central Rd
Ft Lee, NJ 07024-7547
Singer V: 02/03/96

Houston, Thelma
4296 Mt Vernon Dr
Los Angeles, CA 90008
Singer V: 06/16/96

Houston, Tommy
NASCAR
1811 Volusia Ave
Daytona Beach, FL 32015
NASCAR Driver V: 03/02/96

Houston, Whitney
2160 N Central Rd
Ft Lee, NJ 07024-7547
Singer V: 03/03/96

Wm Morris Agency
151 El Camino Dr
Beverly Hills, CA 90212
Alternate V: 12/17/96

c/o WHFC
Box 885288
San Francisco, CA 94188
Forwarded V: 11/01/96

Houston Astros
PO Box 288
The Astrodome
Houston, TX 77001-0288
Team Office V: 02/15/96

Houston Oilers
6910 Fannin St
Houston, TX 77030
Team Office V: 05/15/96

Houston Rockets
PO Box 272349
Houston, TX 77277
Team Office V: 02/15/96

The Summit
Ten Greenway Plaza
Houston, TX 77046
Alternate V: 11/11/96

Howard, Clint
Gold/Marshak & Associates
3500 W Olive Ave #1400
Burbank, CA 91505
Actor V: 12/10/96

Howard, Greg
King Features
235 E 45th St
New York, NY 10017
Cartoonist V: 03/12/96

Howard, Ken
59 E 54th St #22
New York, NY 10022
Actor V: 06/16/96

Howard, Ron
Imagine Inc
1925 Century Park E #2300
Los Angeles, CA 90067
Director V: 03/14/96

Howard, Susan
Kohner Agency
9300 Wilshire Bl #555
Beverly Hills, CA 90212-3211
Actress V: 11/26/96

Howard Talent West
11712 Moorpark St #205B
Studio City, CA 91604
Talent Agency V: 02/02/96

Howell, C Thomas
4522 Grand Ave
Ojai, CA 93023-9399
Actor V: 03/15/96

Howland, Beth
255 Amalfi Dr
Santa Monica, CA 90402
Actress V: 01/13/96

Hubbard, Freddie
c/o Merlin
17609 Ventura Bl #212
Encino, CA 91316
Musician V: 12/01/96

c/o Tooper
211 Thompson St
New York, NY 10012
Alternate V: 02/01/96

Hubert (Whitten), Janet
10061 Riverside Dr #204
Toluca Lake, CA 91602-2515
Actress V: 01/12/96

Hubley, Season
Buckwald & Associates
9229 Sunset Bl #710
Los Angeles, CA 90069
Actress V: 12/06/96

Hudner Jr, Thomas J
31 Allen Farm Ln #100
Concord, MA 01742
War Hero V: 02/09/96

Hughes, Barnard
1244 11th St #A
Santa Monica, CA 90401
Actor V: 01/02/96

Bloom Agency
9200 Sunset Bl #710
Los Angeles, CA 90069
Alternate V: 01/02/96

Hughes, Finola
4234 S Bel Air Dr
La Canada, CA 91001
Actress V: 10/10/96

Hughs, Finola, Cont.
Metro Talent Agency
4526 Wilshire Bl
Los Angeles, CA 90010
Alternate V: 12/11/96

c/o TMCE
270 N Canyon Dr #164
Beverly Hills, CA 90210
Forwarded V: 01/31/96

Gersh Agency
232 N Canon Dr
Los Angeles, CA 90210
Forwarded V: 02/25/96

Hughes, Kathleen
Atkins & Associates
303 S Crescent Hts Bl
Los Angeles, CA 90048
Actress V: 03/08/96

8818 Rising Glen Pl
Los Angeles, CA 90069
Alternate V: 03/26/96

Hunnicut, Gayle
174 Regents Park Rd
London NW1, England
Actress V: 02/21/96

Hunt, Bonnie
17715 Magnolia Bl
Encino, CA 91316
Actress V: 09/14/96

Hunt, Gareth
c/o Agency
388-396 Oxford St
London W1 9HE, England
Actor V: 07/03/96

Hunt, Helen
Creative Artists Agency
9830 Wilshire Bl
Beverly Hills, CA 90212
Actress V: 12/07/96

Hunt, Linda
Michael Bloom
233 Park Ave South-10th Fl
New York, NY 10003
Actress V: 11/01/96

Hunt, Marsha
13131 Magnolia Bl
Van Nuys, CA 91403
Actress V: 06/23/96

Hunter, Amy
Artists Group
10100 Santa Monica Bl #2490
Los Angeles, CA 90067
Actress V: 12/04/96

Hunter, Evan
Ed McBain
324 Main Ave-Box 339
Norwalk, CT 06851
Author V: 03/14/96

Hunter, Holly
c/o ICM
8942 Wilshire Bl
Beverly Hills, CA 90211
Actress V: 01/14/96

1223 Wilshire Bl #668
Santa Monica, CA 90403
Alternate V: 02/01/96

19528 Ventura Bl #343
Tarzana, CA 91356-2917
Forwarded V: 01/15/96

Hunter, Kim
SDB Partners
1801 Ave of the Stars #902
Los Angeles, CA 90067
Actress V: 12/13/96

42 Commerce St
New York, NY 10014
Alternate V: 01/31/96

Hunter, Rachel
23 Beverly Park
Beverly Hills, CA 90210-1500
Model V: 11/01/96

Ford Agency
344 E 59th St
New York, NY 10022
Alternate V: 04/04/96

1435 S Ocean Bl
Palm Beach, FL 33400
Forwarded V: 02/28/96

Hunter, Tab
223 N Guadalupe St #292
Santa Fe, NM 87501-1850
Actor V: 03/14/96

PO Box 1084
La Tierra Nueva
Santa Fe, NM 87501
Forwarded V: 03/15/96

Hunter, Tylo
Innovative Artists
1999 Ave of the Stars #2850
Los Angeles, CA 90067
Actress V: 12/11/96

Huppert, Isabelle
Le Studio Canal
17 rue Dumont Durville
Paris 75116, France
Actress V: 11/11/96

c/o Artmedia
40 Rue Francois
Paris 75008, France
Alternate V: 02/28/96

Hurley, Elizabeth
Oxford House-76 Oxford St
London WIN OAX, England
Model V: 11/01/96

c/o CAA
9830 Wilshire Bl
Beverly Hills, CA 90212
Alternate V: 01/14/96

Hurt, John
Ascott-Under Wy'Wd
Oxfordshire, England
Actor V: 01/12/96

c/o Belfrage
46 Abermarle St
London W1X 4PP England
Alternate V: 09/09/96

46 Albermarle St
London W1x 4PP, England
Alternate V: 10/23/96

Hurt, Mary Beth
1619 Broadway #900
New York, NY 10019
Actress V: 03/26/96

Hurt, William
370 Lexington Ave #808
New York, NY 10017
Actor V: 10/23/96

8942 Wilshire Bl
Beverly Hills, CA 90211
Forwarded V: 07/26/96

Hurwitz Associates
427 N Canon Dr #215
Beverly Hills, CA 90210
Talent Agency V: 03/29/96

Hussey, Olivia
Frozen Flame Enterprises
PO Box 2507
Canyon County, CA 91386-2507
Actress V: 01/02/97

CNA & Associates
1801 Ave of the Stars #1250
Los Angeles, CA 90067
Alternate V: 12/08/96

21334 Colina Dr
Topanga Canyon, CA 90290
Alternate V: 02/17/96

14 Glebe House
Fitzroy Mews
London WIP 5DP, England
Forwarded V: 11/01/96

Hussey, Ruth
3361 Don Pablo Dr
Carlsbad, CA 92008
Actress V: 02/01/96

Huston, Anjelica
57 Windward Ave
Venice, CA 90291
Actress V: 10/23/96

74 Market St
Venice, CA 90291
Alternate V: 03/26/96

Hutchins, Will
3461 Waverly Dr #108
Los Angeles, CA 90027
Actor V: 03/03/96

Hutton, Betty
1350 N Highland
Newport, RI 02840
Actress V: 01/31/96

Hutton, Lauren
54 Bond St
New York, NY 10012
Actress V: 02/11/96

382 Lafayette St #6
New York, NY 10003
Alternate V: 10/23/96

c/o CAA
9830 Wilshire Bl
Beverly Hills, CA 90212
Alternate V: 02/21/96

Hutton, Lauren, Cont.
c/o IMG
170 Fifth Ave
New York, NY 10010
Alternate V: 11/01/96

Hutton, Timothy
c/o UTA
9560 Wilshire Bl #500
Beverly Hills, CA 90212
Actor V: 01/11/96

RR2-Box 3318, Cushman Rd
Patterson, NY 12563
Alternate V: 02/13/96

52 W 82nd St
New York, NY 10020
Forwarded V: 05/15/96

Hyatt, Missy
WCW/Turner
One CNN Center-Box 105366
Atlanta, GA 30348-5366
Celebrity V: 03/26/96

Hyde, Harry
PO Box 291
Harrisburg, NC 28075
NASCAR Driver V: 11/11/96

Hyde-White, Alex
8271 Melrose Ave #110
Los Angeles, Ca 90046
Actor V: 06/02/96

Hyer, Martha
1216 La Rambla
Santa Fe, NM 87501
Actress V: 06/23/96

Hylands, Scott
12831 Mulholland Dr
Beverly Hills, CA 90210
Actor V: 07/21/96

Hylton, James
13200 Asheville Hwy
Inman, SC 29349
NASCAR Driver V: 03/14/96

Hynde, Chrissie
3 E 54th St #1400
New York, NY 10022
Singer V: 09/20/96

IF NOT FOR YOU
Touchstone-TV/Admin Bldg
4024 Radford Ave-#137
Burbank, CA 91505
Production Office V: 10/23/96

IFA Talent
8730 Sunset Bl #490
Los Angeles, CA 90069
Talent Agency V: 11/11/96

IN CONCERT
157 Columbus Ave-2nd Fl
New York, NY 10023
Production Office V: 01/20/96

IN THE DARK
WB-TV
1438 N Gower
Hollywood, CA 90028
Audience Services V: 01/13/97

IN THE HOUSE
Walt Disney TV
500 S Buena Vista Bldg 21
Burbank, CA 91521
Production Office V: 10/23/96

c/o UPN-TV
5555 Melrose Ave-Marathon 1200
Los Angeles, CA 90038
Alternate V: 12/15/96

INK
CBS-TV
51 W 52nd St
New York, NY 10019
Viewer Services V: 11/11/96

DreamWorks SKG
4024 Radford Ave
Norvert Bldg-Suite 302
Studio City, CA 91604
Alternate V: 12/15/96

INSIDE EDITION
12400 Wilshire Bl #1160
Los Angeles, CA 90025
Production Office V: 02/10/96

30 Rockefeller Plaza
New York, NY 10112
Alternate V: 11/20/96

c/o King World
402 E 76th St
New York, NY 10021
Alternate V: 02/10/96

Ice T
Wm Morris Agency
151 El Camino Dr
Beverly Hills, CA 90212
Singer V: 01/14/96

Idol, Billy
8209 Melrose Ave
Los Angeles, CA 90046-6832
Singer V: 10/10/96

c/o AuCoin
645 Madison Ave
New York, NY 10022
Forwarded V: 03/24/96

Iglesias, Julio
5 Indian Creek Dr
Miami, FL 33154
Singer V: 07/19/96

1177 Kane Concourse
Miami, FL 33154
Alternate V: 03/30/96

Iman
Wm Morris Agency
151 El Camino
Beverly Hills, CA 90212
Actress V: 12/12/96

639 N Larchmont Bl #207
Los Angeles, CA 90004
Alternate V: 08/08/96

In Style Magazine
1271 Ave of the Americas
New York, NY 10021
Publisher V: 02/10/96

Indiana Pacers
300 E Market St
Indianapolis, IN 46204
Team Office V: 02/15/96

Indianapolis Colts
PO Box 24100
Indianapolis, IN 4624-0100
Team Office V: 03/03/96

Indy Cars
390 Enterprise Court
Bloomfield Hills, MI 84302
Business Group V: 01/31/96

Ingram, James
867 Muirfield Rd
Los Angeles, CA 90005
Singer V: 02/02/96

Inman, John
Thomas Artists
11-13 Broad Court
London WC2B 5QN, England
Actor V: 03/21/96

Innovative Artists
1999 Ave of the Stars #2850
Los Angeles, CA 90067
Talent Agency V: 02/02/96

Int'l Creative Mgmt
8942 Wilshire Bl
Beverly Hills, CA 90211
Talent Agency V: 03/29/96

40 W 57th St
New York, NY 10019
Alternate V: 03/30/96

388/396 Oxford St
London W1, England
Alternate V: 01/20/96

Int'l Hockey League
3850 Priority Way #100
Indianapolis, IN 46240
League Office V: 02/10/96

Int'l Museum of Photography
George Eastman House
900 East Ave
Rochester, NY 14607
Archive V: 03/20/96

Int'l Press Assn
PO Box 8560
Universal City, 91608
Production Office V: 03/17/96

Int'l Stunt Assn
3518 Cahuenga Bl W #300
Hollywood, CA 90068
Production Office V: 03/17/96

Ireland, Kathy
Sterling Winters
1900 Avenue of the Stars #739
Los Angeles, CA 90067
Model V: 10/23/96

111 E 22nd St
New York, NY 10010
Alternate V: 03/01/96

Ireland, Kathy, Inc.
9000 Sunset Bl #1200
Los Angeles, CA 90069
Forwarded V: 12/02/96

Irons, Jeremy
194 Old Brompton St
London, SW5 England
Actor V: 03/03/96

c/o CAA
9830 Wilshire Bl
Beverly Hills, CA 90210
Forwarded V: 01/12/96

Ironside, Michael
Gold & Marshak
3500 W Olive Ave # 1400
Burbank, CA 91505
Actor V: 09/14/96

Irvan, Ernie
1027 Central Dr
Concord, NC 28027
Race Driver V: 11/11/96

McClure Racing
Rt 10, Box 780
Abington, VA 24210
Alternate V: 06/29/96

Irving, Amy
c/o ICM
8942 Wilshire Bl
Beverly Hills, CA 90211
Actress V: 12/11/96

11693 San Vicente Bl #335
Los Angeles, CA 90049
Forwarded V: 04/06/96

Islam, Yusef
Cat Stevens
3 Furlong Rd
London N7 8LA, England
Islamic Teacher V: 09/10/96

Issak, Chris
IFA Talent
8730 Sunset Bl #490
Los Angeles, CA 90069
Actor V: 12/11/96

It Model Mgmt
526 N Larchmont Bl
Los Angeles, CA 90004
Talent Agency V: 02/07/96

Ito, Robert
Chateau/Billings
5657 Wilshire Bl
Los Angeles, CA 90036
Actor V: 03/19/96

Ivins, Marsha
NASA/LBJ Space Center
Hoston, TX 77058
Astronaut V: 03/03/96

J

JAG
Paramount TV
5555 Melrose Ave
Clara Bow Bldg-Room 204
Hollywood, CA 90038
Production Office V: 12/15/96

JAMIE FOXX SHOW
Warner TV
1438 N Gower
Hollywood, CA 90028
Viewer Services V: 11/11/96

JEFF FOXWORTHY SHOW
Brillstein Grey
9150 Wilshire Bl #350
Beverly Hills, CA 90212
Production Office V: 01/14/96

Studio Center
4024 Radford Ave
Studio City, CA 91604
Alternate V: 12/15/96

JENNY JONES SHOW
NBC Tower/4th Fl
454 N Columbus Dr
Chicago, IL 60611
Production Office V: 02/25/96

JEOPARDY
Sony Studios
10202 Washington Bl
CulverCity, CA 90232
Production Office V: 01/20/96

JERRY SPRINGER SHOW
Jerry Springer
454 N Columbus Dr-2nd Fl
Chicago, IL 60611-5502
Production Office V: 06/22/96

JOHN LARROQUETTE SHOW
Sunset-Gower Studios
1438 N Gower
Los Angeles, CA 90028
Production Office V: 11/20/96

c/o NBC-TV
30 Rockefeller Plaza
New York, NY 10112
Alternate V: 12/15/96

JS Represents
509 N Fairfax Ave #216
Los Angeles, CA 90036
Talent Agency V: 11/11/96

JUST SHOOT ME
NBC-TV
30 Rockefeller Plaza
New York, NY 10112
Audience Services V: 01/13/97

Jackee
8649 Metz Pl
Los Angeles, CA 90069
Actress V: 03/26/96

Jackman & Taussig
1815 Butler Ave-#120
Los Angeles, CA 90025
Talent Agency V: 02/02/96

Jackson, Alan
PO Box 121945
Nashville, TN 37212-1945
Singer V: 11/01/96

Jackson, Anne
90 Riverside Dr
New York, NY 10024
Actress V: 04/15/96

Jackson, Glenda
51 Harvey Rd
Blackheath
London SE3, England
Actress V: 03/03/96

Crouch Association
59 Firth St
London W1, England
Alternate V: 01/19/96

Jackson, Janet
HK Mgmt
8900 Wilshire Bl #300
Beverly Hills, CA 90211
Singer V: 12/01/96

Jackson, Janet, Cont.
c/o JJFC
PO Box 884988
San Francisco, CA 94188
Alternate V: 11/01/96

Jackson, Jeremy
c/o MGA
4444 Lankershim Bl #207
N Hollywood, CA 91602
Actor V: 11/01/96

Jackson, Jesse
930 E 50th St
Chicago, IL 60615
Politician V: 07/03/96

Jackson, Kate
151 El Camino Dr
Beverly Hills, CA 90212
Actress V: 01/15/96

1628 Marlay Dr
Los Angeles, CA 90069
Alternate V: 03/26/96

c/o ICM
8942 Wilshire Bl
Beverly Hills, CA 90211
Alternate V: 02/21/96

Jackson, LaToya
301 Park Ave #1970
New York, NY 10022
Singer V: 03/23/96

Jackson, Michael
Sycamore Valley Ranch
Zacca Landeras
Santa Ynez, CA 93460
Singer V: 07/01/96

c/o MJJ
9255 W Sunset Bl #1100
Los Angeles, CA 90069-3309
Alternate V: 01/12/96

c/o CAA
9830 Wilshire Bl
Beverly Hills, CA 90212
Forwarded V: 01/14/96

c/o MJJ
2100 Colorado Ave
Santa Monica, CA 90404
Forwarded V: 11/01/96

Jackson, Reggie
325 Elder Ave
Seaside, CA 93955-3506
Baseball Star V: 01/11/96

Jackson, Samuel L
8942 Wilshire Bl
Beverly Hills, CA 90211
Actor V: 01/14/96

Jackson, Sherry
1163 Cherokee
Topanga, CA 90290-9726
Actress V: 01/31/96

Jackson, Tito
23726 Long Valley Rd
Hidden Hills, CA 91302-2408
Singer V: 01/12/96

Jackson, Victoria
Kohner Agency
9300 Wilshire Bl #555
Beverly Hills, CA 90212
Actress V: 12/11/96

Wm Morris Agency
1325 Ave of America's
New York, NY 10019
Alternate V: 01/10/96

8330 Lookout Mountain Dr
Los Angeles, CA 90046
Forwarded V: 01/03/97

Jackson, Wanda
PO Box 891498
Oklahoma City, OK 73189-1498
Singer V: 08/28/96

Jacobi, Derek
76 Oxford St
London W1N 0AX England
Actor V: 09/09/96

Jacobi, Lou
240 Central Park South
New York, NY 10019
Actor V: 03/14/96

Jaekel, Richard
23388 Mulholland Dr
Woodland Hills, CA 91364-2733
Actor V: 03/14/96

Jagger, Bianca
Media Artists
8383 Wilshire Bl #954
Beverly Hills, CA 90211
Model V: 02/21/96

530 Park Ave #18D
New York, NY 10021
Alternate V: 01/19/96

Jagger, Mick
Cheyenne Walk, Chelsea
London SW3, England
Singer V: 03/16/96

The Rolling Stones
1776 Broadway #507
New York, NY 10019
Alternate V: 01/14/96

James, Anthony
c/o CNA
1801 Ave of the Stars #1250
Los Angeles, CA 90067
Actor V: 02/23/96

James, Brion
9000 Sunset Bl #1200
Los Angeles, CA 90069
Actor V: 02/26/96

James, Clifton
c/o Gage
9255 Sunset Bl #515
Los Angeles, CA 90069
Actor V: 01/03/96

James, Clive
Peters Company
Chambers #500-Chelsea Harbour
London SW10 0XF, England
Journalist V: 02/05/96

James, Kate
Men/Women Agency
20 W 20th St #600
New York, NY 10011
Model V: 11/01/96

James, Kevin
431 Wright St
Jonesville, MI 49250
Magician V: 06/27/96

James, Richard
ST-Voyager
5555 Melrose Ave
Hollywood, CA 90036
Designer V: 02/15/96

James, Sonny
PO Box 158433
Nashville, TN 37215
Singer V: 01/18/96

c/o McFadden
818 18th Ave South
Nashville, TN 37203
Alternate V: 02/02/96

Jameson, Jenna
9800 D Topanga Canyon #343
Chatswortho, CA 91311
Actress V: 10/23/96

Jameson, Louise
Jeremy Conway
8 Cavendish Place
London, W1M 9DJ England
Actress V: 03/12/94

Jan & Dean
18932 Gregory Ln
Huntington Beach, CA 92646-1917
Musical Group V: 01/21/96

Janis, Conrad
300 N Swall Dr #251
Beverly Hills, CA 90210
Actor V: 06/16/94

Janssen, Famke
Wm Morris Agency
151 S El Camino Dr
Beverly Hills, CA 90212
Actress V: 09/13/96

1325 Ave of the Americas
New York, NY 10019
Alternate V: 09/13/96

Jarre, Maurice
27011 Sea Vista Dr
Malibu, CA 90265
Composer V: 03/15/96

Jarrett, Dale
Yates Racing
115 DeWelle St
Charlotte, NC 28208
NASCAR Driver V: 02/08/96

Jarrett, Ned
NASCAR
1811 Volusia Ave
Daytona Beach, FL 32015
NASCAR Driver V: 03/02/96

Jay Talent Agency
6269 Selma Ave #15
Hollywood, CA 90028
Talent Agency V: 03/16/96

Jean, Gloria
6625 Variel Ave
Canoga Park, CA 91306
Actress V: 08/15/96

20309 Leadwell St
Canoga Park, CA 91303
Alternate V: 05/22/96

Jeavons, Colin
c/o Stone
25 Whitehall
London SW1A 2BS, England
Actor V: 03/17/96

Jeffreys, Anne
121 S Bentley Ave
Los Angeles, CA 90049
Actress V: 02/02/96

c/o Artists Group
10100 Santa Monica Bl #2490
Los Angeles, CA 90067
Alternate V: 02/21/96

Jeffries, Lionel
c/o Agency
76 Oxford St
London W1N 0AX, England
Actor V: 03/03/96

Jemison, Mae C
NASA/LBJ Space Center
Hoston, TX 77058
Astronaut V: 03/03/96

Jeni, Richard
Paradigm Agency
10100 Santa Monica Bl-25th Fl
Los Angeles, CA 90067
Actor V: 12/13/96

Jenkins, Daniel
Bloom Agency
9255 Sunset Bl #710
Los Angeles, CA 90069
Actor V: 03/20/96

Jenner, Bruce
PO Box 11137
Beverly Hills, CA 90213-4137
Olympian V: 01/31/96

Jenner, Bruce, Cont.
3133 Abington Dr
Beverly Hills, CA 90210
Alternate V: 11/28/96

PO Box 665
Malibu, CA 90265
Forwarded V: 07/01/96

Jennings, Doug
7807 Evening Star Lane
Tallahasse, FL 32312
Baseball Star V: 12/10/96

Jennings, Peter
ABC-TV
77 W 66th St
New York, NY 10023
News Anchor V: 01/14/96

Jennings, Waylon
1117 17th Ave S
Nashville, TN 37212
Singer V: 01/18/96

Waylons Pony Express
PO Box 121556
Nashville, TN 37212
Alternate V: 02/19/96

824 Old Hickory Bl
Brentwood, TN 37027
Forwarded V: 01/09/97

Jennings & Associates
28035 Dorothy Dr #210A
Agoura, CA 91301
Talent Agency V: 03/29/96

Jens, Salome
9400 Readcrest Dr
Beverly Hills, CA 90210
Actress V: 04/19/96

Bauman & Hiller
5750 Wilshire Bl #512
Los Angeles, CA 90036
Alternate V: 12/05/96

Jergens, Adele
c/o Langan
32108 Village #32
Camarillo, CA 93010
Actress V: 05/22/96

Jernigan, Tamara E
NASA/LBJ Space Center
Hoston, TX 77058
Astronaut V: 01/19/96

Jet Magazine
Johnson Publications
820 S Michigan Ave
Chicago, IL 60605
Publisher V: 02/10/96

Jett, Brent W
NASA/LBJ Space Center
Houston, TX 77058
Astronaut V: 02/02/96

Jett, Joan
QBQ Entertainment
341 Madison Ave-14th Fl
New York, NY 10017-3705
Singer V: 09/09/96

Jillian, Ann
4241 Woodcliff Rd
Sherman Oaks, CA 91403
Actress V: 01/12/96

Wm Morris Agency
151 El Camino
Beverly Hills, CA 90212
Alternate V: 12/12/96

Jobe, Emmett
Phoenix Int'l Raceway
PO Box 13088
Phoenix, AZ 85002
NASCAR Official V: 03/02/96

Joel, Billy
c/o QBC
341 Madison Ave-14th Fl
New York, NY 10017
Singer V: 01/14/96

128 Central Park South
New York, NY 10019
Alternate V: 03/18/96

280 Elm St
Southampton, NY 11968-3464
Alternate V: 08/28/96

Maritime Music
200 W 57th St #308
New York, NY 10019
Forwarded V: 03/14/96

John, Elton
125 Kensington\High St
London W8 55N, England
Singer V: 01/03/96

John, Elton, Cont.
Reid/Singes House
32 Galena Rd
London W6 0LT, England
Alternate V: 02/03/96

Rocket Records/Worldwide Plaza
825 Eighth Ave
New York, NY 10019
Forwarded V: 01/10/97

3660 Peachtree St NW
Altanta, GA 30305
Forwarded V: 01/15/96

Johncock, Gordon
1042 Becker Rd
Hastings, MI 49053
Race Driver V: 02/18/96

2239 W Windrose Dr
Phoenix, AZ 85029
Alternate V: 03/01/96

Johns, Glynis
Smith & Associates
121 N San Vicente Bl
Beverly Hills, CA 90211
Actress V: 12/15/96

555 Fifth Ave
New York, NY 10017
Alternate V: 03/01/96

Johnson, Addison
King Features
235 E 45th St
New York, NY 10017
Cartoonist V: 02/28/96

Johnson, Anne-Marie
Gold/Marshak & Associates
3500 W Olive Ave #1400
Burbank, CA 91505
Actress V: 12/10/96

Johnson, Arte
2725 Bottlebrush Dr
Los Angeles, CA 90026
Actor V: 01/11/96

Johnson, Beverly
c/o Chasin
190 N Canon Dr #201
Beverly Hills, CA 90212
Actress V: 02/21/96

Johnson, Don
c/o ICM
8942 Wilshire Bl
Beverly Hills, CA 90211
Actor V: 01/14/96

Johnson, Earvin 'Magic'
9100 Wilshire Bl
Suite 1060, West Tower
Beverly Hills, CA 90212
Basketball Star V: 02/28/96

Beverly Estates
13100 Mulholland Dr
Beverly Hills, CA 90210
Alternate V: 02/11/96

Johnson, Frank
King Features
235 E 45th St
New York, NY 10017
Cartoonist V: 01/19/96

Johnson, Junior
Johnson & Associates
Rt 2, Box 161A & 162
Rhonda, NC 28670
NASCAR Owner V: 02/12/96

Johnson, Lynn-Holly
Cavaleri & Associates
405 Riverside Dr #200
Burbanks, CA 91506
Actress V: 12/07/96

6605 Hollywood Bl #220
Los Angeles, CA 90028
Alternate V: 01/10/96

Johnson, Michelle
6430 Sunset Bl #701
Los Angles, CA 90069
Model V: 11/01/96

10351 Santa Monica Bl #211
Los Angeles, CA 90025
Alternate V: 01/31/96

Johnson, Russell
Amstel-Eisenstadt-Frasier
6310 San Vicente Bl #401
Los Angeles, CA 90048
Actor V: 12/01/96

Jones, Chuck
PO Box Box 2319
Costa Mesa, CA 92628-2319
Cartoonist V: 04/02/96

Jones, Davy
PO Box 400
Beavertown, PA 17813
Actor V: 02/03/96

Jones, Davy
Radius Motorsports
PO Box 950
Denver, NC 28037
NASCAR Driver V: 02/08/96

Jones, Dean
Blake Agency
415 N Camden Dr #121
Beverly Hills, CA 90210
Actor V: 12/06/96

Jones, George
11 Music Circle South
Nashville, TN 37203
Singer V: 11/01/96

Jones, Grace
PO Box 82
Great Neck, NY 11021
Actress V: 03/14/96

166 Bank St
New York, NY 10014
Alternate V: 03/26/96

Jones, Jack
78-825 Osage Trail
Indian Wells, CA 92210
Singer V: 03/01/96

3965 Deervale
Sherman Oaks, CA 91403
Alternate V: 03/05/96

Jones, James Earl
Bauman & Hiller
5750 Wilshire Bl #512
Los Angeles, CA 90036
Actor V: 12/05/96

390 West End Ave
New York, NY 10024
Alternate V: 10/10/96

Dale Olson/Carthay Circle
6310 San Vicente Bl #340
Los Angeles, CA 90048
Alternate V: 11/01/96

Jones, Janet
9100 Wilshire Bl #1000W
Beverly Hills, CA 90212-3413
Actress V: 06/22/96

Jones, Jeffrey
Bloom Agency
9200 Sunset Bl #710
Los Angeles, CA 90069
Actor V: 02/18/96

Jones, Jennifer
264 N Glenroy Ave
Los Angeles, CA 90077
Actress V: 01/05/96

Jones, Jenny
454 N Columbus Dr
Chicago, IL 60611
TV Host V: 07/06/96

Jones, John Marshall
1930 Century Park W #403
Los Angeles, CA 90067
Actor V: 01/11/97

Jones, KC
6734 Cortez Pl NW
Bremerton, WA 98311-8911
Basketball Star V: 11/01/96

Jones, LQ
Gerler Agency
3349 Cahuenga Bl West #1
Los Angeles, CA 90068
Actor V: 12/08/96

2144 1/2 N Cahuenga Bl
Hollywood, CA 90068
Alternate V: 03/21/96

Jones, Marcia Mae
4541 Hazeltine Ave #4
Sherman Oaks, CA 91423
Actress V: 10/23/96

Jones, Mickey
c/o Lichtman
4439 Worster Ave
Studio City, CA 91604
Actor V: 02/01/96

Jones, Parnelli
20555 Earl St
Torrance, CA 90503
Race Driver V: 02/02/96

PO Box W
Torrence, CA 90508
Alternate V: 03/11/96

Jones, Quincy
Wm Morris Agency
151 El Camino Dr
Beverly Hills, CA 90212
Musician V: 01/14/96

Jones, Renee
Kohner Agency
9300 Wilshire Bl #555
Beverly Hills, CA 90212
Actress V: 02/21/96

Jones, Sam
Artists Agency
10000 Santa Monica Bl #305
Los Angeles, CA 90067
Actor V: 12/03/96

15417 Tierra Dr
Wheaton, MD 20906
Alternate V: 05/10/96

12700 Ventura Bl #340
Studio City, CA 91604
Forwarded V: 03/15/96

Jones, Shirley
Cosden Agency
3518 Cahuenga Bl West #216
Los Angeles, CA 90068
Actress V: 12/08/96

701 N Oakhurst Dr
Beverly Hills, CA 90210
Alternate V: 02/02/96

Jones, Thomas D
NASA/LBJ Space Center
Houston, TX 77058
Astronaut V: 03/03/96

Jones, Tom
10100 Santa Monica Bl #205
Los Angeles, CA 90067
Singer V: 02/25/96

Jones, Tommy Lee
PO Box 966
San Saba, TX 76877
Actor V: 05/10/96

8942 Wilshire Bl
Beverly Hills, CA 90211
Alternate V: 01/14/96

Jordan, Lee Roy
2425 Burbank
Dallas, TX 75235
Football Star V: 05/14/96

Jordan, Michael
c/o Chicago Bulls
980 N Michigan Ave #1600
Chicago, IL 60611
Basketball Star V: 01/12/96

Jordan, William
10806 Lindbrook Ave #4
Los Angeles, CA 90024
Actor V: 07/21/96

Josephson, Erland
TAG/Traum Film
Weyerstrasse 88
5000 Cologne 1, Germany
Actor V: 02/08/96

Jourdan, Louis
1139 Maybrook Dr
Beverly Hills, CA 90210
Actor V: 04/02/96

Jovi, Bon
Bon Jovi Mgmt
250 W 57th St #603
New York, NY 10107
Singer V: 11/01/96

Joyce, Elaine
20th Century Artists
15315 Magnolia Bl #429
Sherman Oaks, CA 91403
Actress V: 12/15/96

724 N Roxbury Dr
Beverly Hills, CA 90210
Alternate V: 03/14/96

Judd, Ashley
Wm Morris Agency
151 El Camino Dr
Beverly Hills, CA 90212
Actress V: 01/03/96

PO Box 2504
Malibu, CA 90265
Alternate V: 03/14/96

Judd, Naomi
1321 Murfreesboro Rd #100
Nashville, TN 37217
Singer V: 02/04/96

Judd, Wynonna
PO Box 682068
Franklin, TN 37068
Singer V: 02/02/96

Judd, Wynonna, Cont.
3907 Alameda Ave-2nd Fl
Burbank, CA 91505
Alternate V: 01/14/96

c/o Pro-Tours
209 10th Ave S #347
Nashville, TN 37203-4159
Forwarded V: 03/14/96

Jump, Gordon
1631 Hillcrest Ave
Glendale, CA 91202
Actor V: 06/16/96

Jurasik, Peter
Innovative Artists
1999 Ave of the Stars #2850
Los Angeles, CA 90067
Actor V: 02/23/96

969 1/2 Manzanita St
Los Angeles, CA 90029
Forwarded V: 03/27/96

Jurgensen, Sonny
PO Box 53
Mt Vernon, VA 22121
Football Star V: 12/11/96

Just For Laughs
22 Miller Ave
Mill Valley, CA 94941
Publisher V: 03/26/96

Justman, Robert
PO Box 491008
Los Angeles, CA 90049-9008
Producer V: 02/26/96

K

KING OF THE HILL
FOX-TV
PO Box 900
Beverly Hills, CA 90213
Audience Services V: 01/13/97

KIRK
c/o WB-TV
1438 N Gower
Hollywood, CA 90028
Production Office V: 12/15/96

Kaake, Jeff
22742 Berdon St
Woodland Hills, CA 91367
Actor V: 01/11/97

Kaczmarek, Jane
Innovative Artists
1999 Ave of the Stars #2850
Los Angeles, CA 90067
Actress V: 12/11/96

Kaelin, Brian 'Kato'
Media Artists
8383 Wilshire Bl #954
Beverly Hills, CA 90211
Personality V: 12/11/96

Kahana's Stunt School
21828 Lassen #E
Chatsworth, CA 91311
Stunt School V: 02/02/96

Kahn, Madeline
975 Park Ave #9-A
New York, NY 10028
Actress V: 05/02/96

Kalitta, Connie
American Int'l Airways
804 Willow Run Airport
Ypsilanti, MI 48198
Drag Racer V: 10/23/96

Kamakona, Danny
c/o Cavaleri
849 S Broadway #750
Los Angeles, CA 90014
Actor V: 03/14/96

Kamel, Stanley
9300 Wilshire Bl #410
Beverly Hills, CA 90212
Actor V: 01/11/97

Kane, Bob
8455 Fountain Ave #725
Los Angeles, CA 90069
Cartoonist V: 04/20/96

Kane, Carol
Innovative Artists
1999 Ave of the Stars #2850
Los Angeles, CA 90067
Actress V: 12/11/96

1416 N Havenhurst Dr #1C
Los Angeles, CA 90046
Alternate V: 02/03/96

Kansas City Chiefs
One Arrowhead Dr
Kansas City, MO 64129
Team Office V: 05/15/96

Kansas City Royals
PO Box 419969
Royals Stadium
Kansas City, MO 64141
Team Office V: 02/15/96

Kaplan, Gabe
9551 Hidden Valley Rd
Beverly Hills, CA 90210
Actor V: 06/16/96

Shapira & Associates
15301 Ventura Bl #345
Sherman Oaks, CA 91403
Alternate V: 12/14/96

Kaplan-Stahler Agency
8383 Wilshire Bl #923
Beverly Hills, CA 90211
Talent Agency V: 03/29/96

Kaplin, Marvin
1418 N Highland Ave #102
Los Angeles, CA 90028
Actor V: 02/18/96

Kapture, Mitzi
8281 Melrose Ave #200
Los Angeles, CA 90046
Actress V: 10/23/96

11866 Tiara St
N Hollywood, CA 91607-1334
Alternate V: 01/21/96

4705 Ruffin Rd
San Diego, CA 92123
Forwarded V: 11/01/96

Karen, James
Ambrosio & Mortimer
9150 Wilshire Bl #175
Beverly Hills, CA 90212
Actor V: 12/01/96

Karg/Weissenbach Agency
329 N Wetherly Dr #101
Beverly Hills, CA 90211
Talent Agency V: 03/29/96

Karras, Alex
7943 Woodrow Wilson Dr
Los Angeles, CA 90046
Actor V: 07/04/96

Kasdan, Lawrence
c/o UTA
9560 Wilshire Bl-5th Fl
Beverly Hills, CA 90212
Author V: 03/01/96

Kasem, Casey
c/o Stern
11755 Wilshire Bl #2320
Los Angeles, CA 90025
Radio Star V: 02/10/96

9540 Washington Bl
Culver, CA 90232
Alternate V: 01/12/97

Kasem, Jean
138 N Mapleton Dr
Los Angeles, CA 90077
Actress V: 05/10/96

Katsulas, Andreas
Innovative Artists
1999 Ave of the Stars #2850
Los Angeles, CA 90067
Actor V: 02/23/94

Katt, William
26608 Sunflower Ct
Calabasas, CA 91302-2948
Actor V: 03/14/96

Artists Agency
10000 Santa Monica Bl #305
Los Angeles, CA 90067
Alternate V: 01/22/96

25218 Malibu Rd
Malibu, CA 90265
Alternate V: 01/15/96

13946 La Maida St
Sherman Oaks, CA 91423
Forwarded V: 10/23/96

Katzenberg, Jeffrey
c/o DreamWorks SKG
100 Universal City Plaza
Universal City, CA 91608
Producer V: 01/14/96

Kaufman, Deb
c/o ESPN-TV
935 Middle St
Bristol, CT 06010
Commentator V: 01/20/96

Kavandi, Janet L
Nasa/Johnson Space Center
Houston, TX 77058-3696
Astronaut V: 11/01/96

Kavner, Julie
25154 Malibu Rd #2
Malibu, CA 90265
Actress V: 02/03/96

8942 Ventura Bl
Beverly Hills, CA 90211
Alternate V: 02/22/96

Kawato, Masajiro
4850 156th Ave NE #25
Redmond, WA 98052
War Hero V: 01/31/96

Kay, Dianne
1559 Palisades Dr
Pacific Palisades, CA 90077
Actress V: 05/22/96

Kaye, Darwood
11129 Western Hills Dr
Riverside, CA 92505
Actor V: 01/09/97

Kazan, Elia
174 E 95th St
New York, NY 10128-2511
Director V: 05/22/96

Kazan, Lainie
9903 Santa Monica Bl #283
Beverly Hills, CA 90212
Actress V: 10/23/96

Bresler/Kelly/Kipperman
15760 Ventura Bl #1730
Encino, CA 91436
Forwarded V: 02/22/96

Kazarian/Spencer Agency
11365 Ventura Bl #100
Studio City, CA 91604
Talent Agency V: 11/11/96

Keach Jr, Stacy
Wm Morris Agency
151 El Camino Dr
Beverly Hills, CA 90212
Actor V: 09/09/96

27425 Winding Way
Malibu, CA 90265
Alternate V: 03/03/96

Keach Sr, Stacy
3969 Longridge Ave
Sherman Oaks, CA 91423
Actor V: 03/26/96

Kean, Jane
28128 W Pacific Coast Hwy
Malibu, CA 90265
Actress V: 11/20/96

Keane, Bill
King Features
235 E 45th St
New York, NY 10017
Cartoonist V: 03/04/96

Keating, Charles
c/o Buchwald
10 E 44th St
New York, NY 10017
Actor V: 12/01/96

Keaton, Diane
Wm Morris Agency
1325 Ave of the Americas
New York, NY 10019
Actress V: 06/09/96

2255 Verde Oak Dr
Los Angeles, CA 90068
Alternate V: 12/01/96

Keaton, Michael
11901 Santa Monica Bl #547
Los Angeles, CA 90025
Actor V: 11/01/96

9830 Wilshire Bl
Beverly Hills, CA 90212
Alternate V: 12/01/96

Keeshan, Bob
Captain Kangaroo
40 W 57th St
New York, NY 10019
Celebrity V: 03/01/96

Keil, Richard
Stevens Talent
3518 W Cahuenga Bl #301
Los Angeles, CA 90068
Actor V: 12/15/96

Keitel, Harvey
151 El Camino Dr
Beverly Hills, CA 90212
Actor V: 01/14/96

Keitel, Harvey, Cont.
110 Hudson St #9A
New York, NY 10013-2352
Alternate V: 11/01/96

Keith, Brian
Blake Agency
415 N Camden Dr #121
Beverly Hills, CA 90210
Actor V: 12/06/96

23449 Malibu Canyon Rd
Malibu, CA 90265
Alternate V: 03/01/96

Keith, David
Wm Morris Agency
151 El Camino
Beverly Hills, CA 90212
Actor V: 12/12/96

304 Stone Rd
Knoxville, TN 37920
Alternate V: 02/14/96

Keith, Penelope
London Mgmt
235-241 Regent St
London W1A 2JT, England
Actress V: 03/17/96

Keller, Jason
112 Sulphur Springs Rd
Greenville, SC 29609
NASCAR Driver V: 01/20/96

Keller, Marthe
Lamonstrasse 9
8 Munich, 80 Germany
Actress V: 03/15/96

Keller, Mary Page
Wm Morris Agency
151 El Camino Dr
Beverly Hills, CA 90212
Actress V: 02/22/96

Kellerman, Sally
Innovative Artists
1999 Ave of the Stars #2850
Los Angeles, CA 90067
Actress V: 12/11/96

7944 Woodrow Wilson
Los Angeles, CA 90046
Alternate V: 02/12/96

Kelley, DeForest
Lincoln Enterprises
14710 Arminta St
Van Nuys, CA 91403
Actor V: 03/01/96

Blake Agency
415 N Camden Dr #121
Beverly Hills, CA 90210
Forwarded V: 01/27/96

Kelly, Moira
Gersh Agency
232 N Canon Dr
Beverly Hills, CA 90210
Actress V: 12/09/96

Kelman/Arletta Agency
7813 Sunset Bl
Los Angeles, CA 90046
Talent Agency V: 03/15/96

Kelsey, Linda
Kohner Agency
9300 Wilshire Bl #555
Beverly Hills, CA 90212
Actress V: 12/11/96

9200 Sunset Bl #625
Los Angles, CA 90069
Alternate V: 10/23/96

Kelso, Susan
King Features
216 E 45th St
New York, NY 10017
Cartoonist V: 05/11/96

Kemp, Jeromy
Marina Martin
6A Danbury St
London N1 8JJ, England
Actor V: 02/28/96

Kemp Talent
9812 Vidor Dr #101
Los Angeles, CA 90035
Talent Agency V: 11/11/96

Kendall, Felicity
Chatto/Prince of Wales Theatre
Coventry St
London W1V 7FE, England
Actress V: 03/06/96

The Globe Theatre
Shaftsbury Ave
London W1, England
Alternate V: 03/14/96

Kennedy, Edward M
US Senate
2400 JFK Bldg-Gov't Center
Boston, MA 02203
Politician V: 03/09/96

636 Chain Bridge Rd
McClean, VA 22101
Alternate V: 01/13/97

Kennedy, George
Paradigm Agency
10100 Santa Monica Bl-25th Fl
Los Angeles, CA 90067
Actor V: 02/01/96

Bauman & Hiller
5750 Wilshire Bl #512
Los Angeles, CA 90036
Alternate V: 12/05/96

Kennedy, Jayne
Wm Morris Agency
151 El Camino Dr
Beverly Hills, CA 90212
Actress V: 02/02/96

Kennedy, Leon Isaac
20550 Wyandotte St
Canoga Park, CA 91306-2833
Actor V: 01/31/96

Kennedy, Ted
US Senate Bldg
Washington, DC 20510
Politician V: 03/10/96

Kennedy Jr, John F
c/o George
1633 Broadway-41st Fl
New York, NY 10019
Publisher V: 01/14/96

1040 5th Ave
New York, NY 10028
Alternate V: 03/14/96

20 N Moore St
New York, NY 10013-2435
Forwarded V: 03/14/96

Kennedy Jr, Robert
78 N Broadway
White Plains, NY 10603
Politician V: 02/17/96

Kensit, Patsy
50 Lissom St-Unit 1B
London NW1 5DF, England
Actress V: 02/03/96

Gersh Agency
232 N Canon Dr
Beverly Hills, CA 90210
Forwarded V: 12/09/96

Kent, Jean
London Mgmt
235 Regent St
London W1, England
Actress V: 03/12/96

Kentucky Headhunters
Gangwisch & Associates
1706 Grand Ave
Nashville, TN 37212
Musical Group V: 03/14/96

Kercheval, Ken
PO Box 1350
Los Angeles, CA 90078
Actor V: 12/19/96

Kerns, Joanna
Creative Artists Agency
9830 Wilshire Bl
Beverly Hills, CA 90212
Actress V: 12/07/96

PO Box 49216
Los Angeles, CA 90049
Alternate V: 01/08/96

Kerr, Deborah
7250 Klosters
Grisons, Switzerland
Actress V: 03/03/96

Viertel, Los Montaros
E-29600 Marbella
Malaga, Spain
Alternate V: 03/02/96

Kerrigan, Nancy
7 Cedar Ave
Stoneham, MA 02180
Olympiam V: 03/14/96

c/o ProServ
1101 Wilson Bl
Arlington, VA 22209
Alternate V: 01/31/96

Kerwin, Joseph P
NASA/LBJ Space Center
Houston, TX 77058
Astronaut V: 03/03/96

Kerwin Agency
1605 N Cahuenga Bl #202
Los Angeles, CA 90028
Talent Agency V: 03/29/96

Ketcham, Hank
512 Pierce St
Monterey, CA 93953
Cartoonist V: 06/17/96

78 Rue du Rhone
1204 Geneva
Switzerland
Alternate V: 05/10/96

King Features
235 E 45th St
New York, NY 10017
Forwarded V: 02/21/96

Kettle, Roger
King Features
216 E 45th St
New York, NY 10017
Cartoonist V: 03/11/96

Key, Ted
King Features
235 E 45th St
New York, NY 10017
Cartoonist V: 03/13/96

1694 Glenhardie Rd
Wayne, PA 19087
Alternate V: 07/09/96

Key/Fox Pictures
PO Box 900
Beverly Hills, CA 90213
Production Office V: 12/15/96

Keyes, Evelyn
c/o Shaw
999 N Doheny Dr #506
Los Angeles, CA 90069
Actress V: 05/22/96

Khambatta, Persis
PO Box 46539
Los Angeles, CA 90046
Actress V: 02/15/96

Khambatta, Persis, Cont.
c/o Triton
1964 Westwood Bl #400
Los Angeles, CA 90025
Alternate V: 01/13/96

Khan, Ali Akbar
Ali Akbar Music College
215 West End Ave
San Rafael, CA 94901
Composer V: 10/23/96

Kidder, Margot
PO Box 829
Los Angeles, CA 90078-0829
Actress V: 02/10/96

Kidman, Nicole
c/o CAA
9830 Wilshire Bl
Beverly Hills, CA 90212
Actress V: 01/14/96

Odin Productions
4400 Coldwater Canyon Ave #220
Studio City, CA 91604
Alternate V: 07/13/96

Kiel, Richard
40356 Oak Park Way #T
Oakhurst, CA 93644
Actor V: 02/17/96

Kilby, Jack
6600 LBJ Freeway #4155
Dallas, TX 75240-6507
Inventor V: 02/01/96

7723 Midbury
Dallas, TX 75230
Forwarded V: 02/10/96

Kiley, Richard
Ryerson Rd
Warwick, NY 10990
Actor V: 10/10/96

Killebrew, Harmon
PO Box 14550
Scottsdale, AZ 85267
Baseball Star V: 11/26/96

Kilmer, Val
PO Box 362
Tesuque, NM 87574
Actor V: 03/26/96

Kilmer, Val, Cont.
Rt4 Box 23
Santa Fe, NM 87501
Alternate V: 02/02/96

c/o CAA
9830 Wilshire Bl
Beverly Hills, CA 90210
Forwarded V: 11/16/96

Kimball, Ward
8910 Ardendale Ave
San Gabriel, CA 91775
Cartoonist V: 03/20/96

Kincaid, Aron
12307 Ventura-Suite C
N Hollywood, CA 91604
Actor V: 01/02/96

Kind, Roslyn
Epstein/Wyckoff
280 S Beverly Dr #400
Beverly Hills, CA 90212
Actress V: 02/22/96

King, Alan
888 7th Ave #3800
New York, NY 10106
Actor V: 01/05/96

King, Ben E
Smiling Clown Music
PO Box 1097
Teaneck, NJ 07666
Singer V: 02/03/96

King, Billy Jean
World Team Tennis
445 N Wells #404
Chicago, IL 60610
Tennis Star V: 01/05/96

King, Cammie
511 Cypress St
Ft Bragg, CA 95437-5417
Actress V: 11/11/96

King, Carole
Robinson Bar Ranch
Stanley, ID 83278
Singer V: 02/01/96

c/o APA
9000 Sunset Bl #1200
Los Angeles, CA 90069
Forwarded V: 02/22/96

King, Don
Don King
32 E 69th St
New York, NY 10021
Sports Promoter V: 01/14/96

968 Pinehurst Dr
Las Vegas, NV 89109
Alternate V: 11/28/96

King, Larry
CNN-Larry King Live
820 1st St NE
Washington, DC 20002
TV Host V: 01/14/96

Mutual Broadcasting
1755 S Jefferson Davis Hwy
Arlington, VA 22202
Alternate V: 02/10/96

10801 Lockwood Dr #230
Silver Spring, MD 20901-1563
Alternate V: 08/28/96

King, Perry
3647 Wrightwood Dr
Studio City, CA 91604
Actor V: 02/03/96

King, Stephen
PO Box 1186
Bangor, ME 04401
Author V: 02/12/96

c/o CAA
9830 Wilshire Bl
Beverly Hills, CA 90212
Alternate V: 01/14/96

49 Florida Ave
Bangor, ME 04401-3005
Alternate V: 01/05/96

King, Tony
1333 N Sweetzer #2G
Los Angeles, CA 90046
Actor V: 06/16/96

King Features Syndicate
235 E 45th St
New York, NY 10017
Publisher V: 11/19/96

King World Entertainment
12400 Wilshire Bl #1200
Los Angeles, CA 90025
Production Office V: 03/17/96

Kings X Band
PO Box 968
Katy, TX 77491
Musical Group V: 01/22/96

Kingsley, Ben
c/o Agency
388-396 Oxford St
London W1, England
Actor V: 04/01/96

New Penworth House
Stratford Upon Avon
Warwickshire OV3 7QX, England
Alternate V: 03/17/96

Kingston, Kenny
11561 Dona Dorotea Dr
Studio City, CA 91604
Astrologer V: 02/28/96

Kinmont, Kathleen
House of Representatives
9911 Pico Bl #1060
Los Angeles, CA 90035
Actress V: 12/10/96

5261 Cleon Ave
N Hollywood, CA 91601
Alternate V: 10/23/96

Kinnear, Greg
Wm Morris Agency
151 El Camino Dr
Beverly Hills, CA 90212
Actor V: 01/14/96

Kinser, Steve
King Racing
103 Center Ln
Huntsville, NC 28078
NASCAR Driver V: 02/08/96

Kinskey, Leonid
15009 Tamarack Lane
Fountain Hill, AZ 85268
Actor V: 06/15/96

Kinski, Nastassja
Wm Morris Agency
151 El Camino
Beverly Hills, CA 90212
Actress V: 12/12/96

11 W 81st St
New York, NY 10024
Alternate V: 01/31/96

Kinski, Nastassja, Cont.
c/o TFI
305 Ave le Jour Se Leve
Boulogne 92100, France
Alternate V: 11/11/96

c/o Interscope
10900 Wilshire Bl #1400
Los Angeles, CA 90024
Forwarded V: 03/14/96

Kirby, Bruno
c/o MTA
4526 Wilshire Bl
Los Angeles, CA 90010
Actor V: 02/07/96

Kirby, Durwood
Rt7-Box 374
Sherman, CT 06784
Actor V: 06/09/96

Kirk, Tommy
422 Second St-Suite Y
Paintsville, KY 41240
Actor V: 06/16/96

Kirkland, Sally
Buchwald Agency
9229 Sunset Bl #710
Los Angeles, CA 90069
Actress V: 12/22/96

Kirkpatrick, Jeane
6812 Granby St
Bethesda, MD 20817
Politician V: 04/20/96

Kiser, Terry
House of Representatives
9911 Pico Bl #1060
Los Angeles, CA 90035
Actor V: 12/10/96

5750 Wilshire Bl #512
Los Angeles, CA 90036
Alternate V: 10/23/96

Kissinger, Henry
River House
435 E 52nd St
New York, NY 10022
Politician V: 07/16/96

c/o Kissinger Associates
350 Park Ave
New York, NY 10022-6022
Alternate V: 04/01/96

Kissinger, Henry, Cont.
Strategic Study
1800 K St NW #1021
Washington, DC 20006
Forwarded V: 03/02/96

Kitaen, Tawny
PO Box 16693
Beverly Hills, CA 90209
Actress V: 02/10/96

1880 Century Park E #900
Los Angeles, CA 90067
Forwarded V: 08/08/96

Kitaro
Geffen Records
9100 Sunset Bl
Los Angeles, CA 90069
Musician V: 11/27/96

Kitt, Eartha
125 Boulder Ridge Rd
Scarsdale, NY 10583
Actress V: 01/03/96

1524 LaBaig Ave
Los Angeles, CA 90028
Alternate V: 11/27/96

The Agency
40 W 57th St
New York, NY 10019
Forwarded V: 11/11/96

Kjar Agency
10643 Riverside Dr
Toluca Lake, CA 91602
Talent Agency V: 03/05/96

Klasky/Csupo
1258 N Highland Ave
Hollywood, CA 90038
Cartoonist V: 02/04/96

Klass Associates
144 S Beverly Dr #405
Beverly Hills, CA 90212
Talent Agency V: 02/07/96

Klein, Calvin
205 W 39th St
New York, NY 10018
Designer V: 01/16/96

Klein, Robert
Conversation Company
Edgehill Sleepy Hollow Rd
Briarcliff Manor, NY 10510
Actor V: 04/02/96

Conversation Company
697 Middleneck Rd
Great Neck, NY 11023
Alternate V: 07/02/96

Klemperer, Werner
44 W 62nd St-10th Fl
New York, NY 10023
Actor V: 03/27/96

1229 Horn Ave
Los Angeles, CA 90069
Alternate V: 03/21/96

Kline, Kevin
45 W 67th St #27-B
New York, NY 10023
Actor V: 04/01/96

1636 3rd Ave #309
New York, NY 10128-3622
Alternate V: 01/15/96

Klous, Pat
18096 Karen Dr
Encino, CA 91316
Actress V: 04/27/96

Klugman, Jack
22548 Pacific Coast Hwy #110
Malibu, CA 90265
Actor V: 03/03/96

Knef, Hildegard
Agentur Lentz
Holbeinstrasse 4
8000 Munchen 80, Germany
Singer V: 01/17/96

Maria-Theresiastrasse
800 Munchen-Bogenhausen
Germany
Alternate V: 04/27/96

Knight, Christopher
7738 Chandelee Pl
Los Angeles, CA 90046
Actor V: 06/09/96

Knight, Edmond
52 Cranmere Ct
London SW3, England
Actor V: 03/01/96

c/o Agent
9 Cork St
London W1X 1PD, England
Alternate V: 02/01/96

Knight, Gladys
21201 Tulsa St
Chatsworth, CA 91311
Singer V: 10/23/96

Knight-Pulliam, Keisha
PO Box 866
Teaneck, NJ 07666
Actress V: 02/03/96

Knittel, Luise Rainer
Vico-Morcotte 6911
Switzerland
Actress V: 01/19/96

Knokem, Heinz
Ahornweg 7
D-4505 Bad Ibure, Germany
War Hero V: 03/17/96

Knotts, Don
c/o Freed
2029 Century Park E #600
Los Angeles, CA 90067
Actor V: 02/02/96

Knox, Elyse
c/o Harmon
320 N Gunston
Los Angeles, CA 90049
Actress V: 04/27/96

Kober, Jeff
308 N Arden Bl
Los Angeles, CA 90004
Actor V: 01/04/96

Ambrosio & Mortimer
9150 Wilshire Bl #175
Beverly Hills, CA 90212
Alternate V: 12/01/96

Koch, Howard
5555 Melrose Ave #3000
Los Angeles, CA 90038-3197
Producer V: 01/20/96

Koenig, Walter
Moss & Associates
733 N Seward St-Penthouse
Los Angeles, CA 90038
Actor V: 12/12/96

PO Box 4395
N Hollywood, CA 91607
Alternate V: 02/02/96

Kohner Agency
9300 Wilshire Bl #555
Beverly Hills, CA 90212
Talent Agency V: 11/20/96

Kohner, Susan
710 Park Ave #14-E
New York, NY 10021
Actress V: 10/23/96

Kollner, Eberhard
An Der Trainierbahn 7
115366 Neuenhagenn, Germany
Cosmonaut V: 10/23/96

Koontz, Dean
PO Box 9529
Newport Beach, CA 92658
Author V: 10/23/96

PO Box 5686
Orange, CA 92613-5686
Alternate V: 03/02/96

Koop, C Everett
6707 Democracy Bl #107
Bethesda, MD 20817
Physician V: 10/23/96

Kopell, Bernie
19413 Olivos Dr
Tarzana, CA 91356
Actor V: 06/16/96

Koppel, Ted
ABC-TV/Nightline
1717 DeSales St NW
Washington, DC 20036
Commentator V: 03/19/96

ABC-TV
77 W 66th St
New York, NY 10023
Alternate V: 01/14/96

Korman, Harvey
1136 Stradella Rd
Los Angeles, CA 90049
Actor V: 06/16/96

Koshiroe, Matsumoto
Kabukiza Theatre
12 15-4 Ginza
Chuoku, Tokyo 104 Japan
Actor V: 03/20/96

Koslo, Paul
Artists Agency
10000 Santa Monica Bl #305
Los Angeles, CA 90067
Actor V: 12/03/96

Kotke, Leo
PO Box 7308
Carmel, CA 93921
Musician V: 12/01/96

Kotzky, Alex
King Features
235 E 45th St
New York, NY 10017
Cartoonist V: 02/16/96

Koury, Rex
5370 Happy Pines Dr
Foresthill, CA 95631
Composer V: 09/18/96

Kovalenok, Vladimir S
3 Ap 22-Hovanskaya St
129 515 Moscow, Russia
Cosmonaut V: 10/23/96

Kove, Martin
Stone Manners
8091 Selma Ave
Los Angeles, CA 90046
Actor V: 03/17/96

19155 Rosita St
Tarzana, CA 91356
Alternate V: 04/06/96

Koz, Dave
PO Box 48425
Los Angeles, CA 90048
Musician V: 01/31/96

Kozak, Harley Jane
c/o UTA
9560 Wilshire Bl-5th Fl
Beverly Hills, CA 90212
Actress V: 02/22/96

Kozlowski, Linda
Wm Morris Agency
151 El Camino
Beverly Hills, CA 90212
Actress V: 12/12/96

Kozlowski, Linda, Cont.
PO Box 5617
Beverly Hills, CA 90210
Alternate V: 10/23/96

Kramer, Stepfanie
Kohner Agency
9300 Wilshire Bl #555
Beverly Hills, CA 90212
Actress V: 02/22/96

8455 Beverly Bl #505
Los Angeles, CA 90048-3416
Alternate V: 04/27/96

Krauss, Alison
1017 16th Ave South
Nashville, TN 37212-2302
Singer V: 08/28/96

Krebbs, John
Diamond Ridge
3232 Amoruso Way
Amoruso, CA 95747
Race Driver V: 03/12/96

Krebs, Art
NASCAR
1811 Volusia Ave
Daytona Beach, FL 32015
NASCAR Official V: 03/14/96

Kregel, Kevin R
NASA/LBJ Space Center
Houston, TX 77058
Astronaut V: 02/02/96

Kreskin
PO Box 1383
W Caldwell, NJ 07006
Mentalist V: 01/09/97

Krige, Alice
Paradigm Talent
10100 Santa Monica Bl-25th Fl
Los Angeles, CA 90067
Actress V: 12/15/96

Krikalev, Sergei
NASA/LBJ Space Center
Houston, TX 77058
Astronaut V: 02/02/96

Kristel, Sylvia
Edrick/Rich Mgmt
2400 Whitman Place
Los Angeles, CA 90068
Actress V: 11/01/96

Kristofferson, Kris
Rothbaum/Gardner
38 Music Square W #218
Nashville, TN 37203
Actor V: 02/02/96

Krofft, Sid & Marty
Krofft Entertainment
419 Larchmont Bl #11
Los Angeles, CA 90004
Puppeteers V: 02/02/96

Kruger, Hardy
Albert-Beit-Weg
20149 Hamburg, Germany
Actor V: 03/15/96

Kruger, Pit
Geleitstrasse 10
6000 Frankfurter/Main
70 Germany
Actor V: 01/17/96

Kruglov & Associates
7060 Hollywood Bl #1220
Los Angeles, CA 90028
Talent Agency V: 03/17/96

Kruse, Christina
c/o Gasthof
Alte Dorfstrasse 190069
D-21272 Egestorf, Germany
Model V: 11/01/96

Kubek, Tony
3311 N McDonald
Appleton, WI 54911
Baseball Star V: 01/20/96

Kubrick, Stanley
PO Box 123
Borehamwood, Herts, England
Director V: 03/20/96

Kudrow, Lisa
Creative Artists Agency
9830 Wilshire Bl
Beverly Hills, CA 90212
Actress V: 12/07/96

Howard Entertainment
10850 Wilshire Bl-4th Fl
Los Angeles, CA 90024-4305
Alternate V: 08/28/96

Warner Studios
4000 Warner Bl417
Burbank, CA 91505
Alternate V: 11/11/96

Kuhaulua, Jessie
Azumazeki Stable
4-6-4 Higashi Komagata
Ryogoku, Tokyo, Japan
Sumo V: 01/04/96

Kupcinet, Kari
1730 N Clark St #3311
Chicago, IL 60614-5862
Actress V: 01/12/96

Kurosawa, Akira
Seijo 2-21-6, Setagaja-ku
Tokyo 157, Japan
Director V: 03/17/96

Kurtz, Swoosie
c/o APA
9000 Sunset Bl #1200
Los Angeles, CA 90069
Actress V: 12/02/96

Wm Morris Agency
151 El Camino Dr
Beverly Hills, CA 90212
Forwarded V: 02/22/96

Kusatsu, Clyde
Paradigm Agency
10100 Santa Monica Bl-25th Fl
Los Angeles, CA 90067
Actor V: 12/13/96

Kwan, Nancy
4154 Woodman Ave
Sherman Oaks, CA 91403
Actress V: 12/07/96

c/o CAA
1427 3rd St Prominade #205
Santa Monica, CA 90401
Alternate V: 04/27/96

Kwouk, Burt
London Mgmt
235-241 Regent St
London W1A 2JT, England
Actor V: 03/17/96

Kyle, Rote
1175 York Ave
New York, NY 10021
Football Star V: 05/14/96

Kyo, Machiko
Olimpia, Copu 6-35
Jingumae, Shibuyaku
Tokyo, Japan
Actress V: 11/28/96

L

LA Artists
2566 Overland Ave #550
Los Angeles, CA 90064
Talent Agency V: 02/03/96

LA Press Club
480 Riverside Dr
Burbank, CA 91506
Production Office V: 03/03/96

LA Talent
8335 Sunset Bl
Los Angeles, CA 90069
Talent Agency V: 03/29/96

LAPD/LIFE ON THE BEAT
WB-TVx 900
Beverly Hills, CA 90213
Audience Services V: 04/12/96

LARRY KING LIVE
c/o CNN
820 1st NE
Washington, DC 20002
Production Office V: 01/14/96

Late Late Show w/Tom Snyder
CBS-TV City
7800 Beverly Bl
Los Angeles, CA 90036
Production Office V: 03/12/96

Late Night w/Conan O'Brien
NBC-TV
30 Rockefeller Pl
New York, NY 10011
Production Office V: 01/02/96

Late Show w/David Letterman
Ed Sullivan Theatre
1697 Broadway
New York, NY 10019
Production Office V: 01/01/96

Later With Greg Kinnear
NBC Productions
3000 W Alameda Ave #2908
Burbank, CA 91523
Production Office V: 03/26/96

LAW & ORDER
Wolf Films-Universal
W 23rd St-Hudson River Pier 62
New York, NY 10011
Production Office V: 01/12/96

NBC-TV
30 Rockefeller Plaza
New York, NY 10112
Alternate V: 12/15/96

Universal TV
70 Universal City Plaza
Universal City, CA 91608
Forwarded V: 01/20/96

LAWLESS
FOX-TV
PO Box 900
Beverly Hills, CA 90213
Audience Services V: 01/13/97

LE FEMME NIKITA
USA-TV Network
1900 Ave of the Stars #1290
Los Angeles, CA 90067
Production Office V: 01/11/97

LEEZA
Paramount Studios
5555 Melrose Ave
Los Angeles, CA 90038
Production Office V: 01/20/96

PO Box 4321
Hollywood, CA 90068
Alternate V: 01/11/96

LIFE WITH ROGER
Warner TV
1438 N Gower
Hollywood, CA 90028
Viewer Services V: 11/11/96

LIFE'S WORK
Touchstone/Disney Studios
500 S Buena Vista Bl
Burbank, CA 91521-0668
Production Office V: 11/11/96

ABC-TV
77 W 66th St
New York, NY 10023
Alternate V: 11/11/96

LIFE...AND STUFF
Columbia TriStar TV
10202 W Washington Bl
Culver City, CA 90232
Production Office *V: 12/15/96*

CBS-TV
51 W 52nd St
New York, NY 10019
Alternate *V: 01/13/97*

LIVE W/REGIS & KATHIE LEE
30 Rockefeller Plaza
New York, NY 10112
Production Office *V: 01/20/96*

LIVING SINGLE
Fox-TV
PO Box 900
Beverly Hills, CA 90213
Production Office *V: 12/15/96*

LOCAL HEROES
Paramount
5555 Melrose Ave
Bow Building, Room 115
Los Angeles, CA 90038
Production Office *V: 03/23/96*

LOIS & CLARK
300 Television Plz
Bldg 136-RM 139
Burbank, CA 91505
Production Office *V: 01/16/96*

ABC-TV
77 W 66th St
New York, NY 10023
Alternate *V: 12/15/96*

LOUIE
CBS/MTM Studios
4024 Radford, 2nd Fl Admit
Studio City, CA 91604
Production Office *V: 10/23/96*

LOVE AND MARRIAGE
Fox-TV
PO Box 900
Beverly Hills, CA 90213
Viewer Services *V: 11/11/96*

LOVE AND WAR
Shukovsky/English
4024 Radford Ave
Admit Bldg, Suite 330
Studio City, CA 91604
Production Office *V: 03/14/96*

LOVE CONNECTION
8601 Beverly Bl
Los Angeles, CA 90048
Production Office *V: 01/09/97*

LOVING
ABC-TV
320 W 66th St
New York, NY 10023
Production Office *V: 03/19/96*

LUSH LIFE
FOX-TV
PO Box 900
Beverly Hills, CA 90213
Viewer Services *V: 11/11/96*

LW 1 Inc
8383 Wilshire Bl #649
Beverly Hills, CA 90211
Talent Agency *V: 03/19/96*

LaBelle, Patty
Paz Entertainment
2041 Locust St
Philadelphia, PA 19103
Singer *V: 01/21/96*

LaLanne, Jack
Befit Entertainment
PO Box 1023
San Louis Obispo, CA 93406
Fitness Expert *V: 05/10/96*

LaPlaca, Alison
8380 Melrose Ave #207
Los Angeles, CA 90069
Actress *V: 10/23/96*

LaRosa, Julius
67 Sycamore Ln
Irvington, NY 10028
Radio Star *V: 03/11/96*

LaRue, Florence
4300 Louise Ave
Encino, CA 91316
Actress *V: 04/27/96*

Labonte, Bobby
9900 Twin Lakes Pkway
Charlotte, NC 28269
NASCAR Driver *V: 10/23/96*

Labonte, Terry
Davis Racing
11 N Robbins St
Thomasville, NC 27360
NASCAR Driver *V: 03/02/96*

Lacey, Deborah
House of Representatives
9911 Pico Bl #1060
Los Angeles, CA 90035
Actress V: 12/10/96

Ladd, Cheryl
PO Box 1329
Santa Ynez, CA 93460-1329
Actress V: 10/23/96

c/o ICM
8942 Wilshire Bl
Beverly Hills, CA 90211
Alternate V: 12/11/96

PO Box 17111
Beverly Hills, CA 90209
Alternate V: 05/10/96

Lafontaine, Pat
Buffalo Sabres
Memorial Auditorium
Buffalo, NY 14202
Hockey Star V: 11/20/96

Lagenkamp, Heather
c/o Badgley Connor
9229 Sunset Bl #311
Los Angeles, CA 90069
Actress V: 12/04/96

Lagerfeld, Karl
3 W 57th
New York, NY 10023
Designer V: 01/14/96

Lahti, Christine
500 25th St
Santa Monica, CA 90402-3140
Actress V: 01/12/96

927 Berkeley St
Santa Monica, CA 90403-2307
Alternate V: 05/04/96

c/o CAA
9830 Wilshire Bl
Beverly Hills, CA 90212
Alternate V: 02/22/96

Laine, Cleo
International Artistes
235 Regent St-Mezz Fl
London W1R 8AX, England
Singer V: 03/20/96

Laine, Cleo, Cont.
Old Rectory
Wavendon
Milton Keys MK17 8LT, England
Alternate V: 03/02/96

Laine, Frankie
352 San Gorgonio St
San Diego, CA 92106
Singer V: 03/02/96

14322 Califa
Van Nuys, CA 91401
Alternate V: 06/06/96

Lake, Rickie
The Rickie Lake Show
401 5th Ave-7th Fl
New York, NY 10016-3317
Actress V: 01/12/96

151 El Camino Dr
Beverly Hills, CA 90212
Alternate V: 02/22/96

Lamarr, Hedy
568 Orange Dr #47
Altamonte Springs, FL 32701
Actress V: 02/02/96

Lamas, Lorenzo
PO Box 500907
San Diego, CA 92150-0907
Actor V: 03/14/96

c/o Shapira
15301 Ventura Bl #345
Sherman Oaks, CA 91403
Alternate V: 02/04/96

Lamb, Debra
16633 Ventura Bl #1240
Encino, CA 91436
Actress V: 11/20/96

Lambert, Christopher
9560 Wilshire Bl #500
Beverly Hills, CA 90212
Actor V: 02/01/96

9 Ave Tremply-C/Lui
1209 Geneva, Switzerland
Alternate V: 02/09/96

Lamm, Becky
Craig Agency
8485 Melrose Place #E
Los Angeles, CA 90069
Actress V: 02/22/96

Lamparski, Richard
924-D Garden St
Santa Barbara, CA 93101
Author V: 03/27/96

Lampert, Zohra
Buckwald & Associates
9229 Sunset Bl #710
Los Angeles, CA 90069
Actress V: 12/06/96

Lampton, Dr Michael
Space Science Lab/UC Berkley
Berkley, CA 94720
Astronaut V: 04/16/96

NASA/LBJ Space Center
Hoston, TX 77058
Alternate V: 01/19/96

Landau, Martin
1501 Skylark Lane
Los Angeles, CA 90069
Actor V: 03/19/96

7455 Palo Vista Dr
Los Angeles, CA 90046
Alternate V: 01/15/96

Landers, Ann
435 N Michigan Ave
Chicago, IL 60611
Columnist V: 01/14/96

401 Wabash Ave
Chicago, IL 60611
Forwarded V: 01/23/96

Landers, Audrey
3112 Nicada Dr
Bel Air, CA 90077
Actress V: 03/02/96

Capitol Artists
8383 Wilshire Bl #954
Beverly Hills, CA 900211
Alternate V: 02/22/96

Landers, Judy
1913 N Beverly Dr
Beverly Hills, CA 90210
Actress V: 01/03/96

Landesberg, Steve
c/o APA
9000 Sunset Bl #1200
Los Angeles, CA 90069
Actor V: 12/02/96

Landis, John
7920 Sunset Bl-6th Fl
Los Angeles, CA 90046
Director V: 03/01/96

Landry, Tom
8411 Preston Rd #720
Dallas, TX 75225
Football Star V: 11/04/96

Landsburg, Valerie
22745 Chamera Lane
Los Angeles, CA 90290
Actress V: 04/27/96

Lane, Abbe
c/o Leff
444 N Faring Rd
Los Angeles, CA 90077
Singer V: 04/27/96

Lane, Diane
2220 Ave of the Stars #1004
Los Angeles, CA 90067
Actress V: 11/01/96

111 W 40th St #2000
New York, NY 10018
Alternate V: 02/10/96

Lane, Dick
18100 Meyers
Detroit, MI 48235
Football Star V: 01/09/96

Lane Talent Agency
13455 Ventura Bl #240
Sherman Oaks, CA 91423
Talent Agency V: 03/04/96

Lang, Katherine Kelly
c/o APA
9000 Sunset Bl #1200
Los Angeles, CA 90069
Actress V: 02/22/96

317 S Carmelina Ave
Los Angeles, CA 90049
Alternate V: 05/01/96

Langdon, Sue Ane
24115 Long Valley Rd
Hidden Hills, CA 91302
Actress V: 02/01/96

Lange, Hope
1801 Ave of the Stars #902
Los Angeles, CA 90067
Actress V: 02/22/96

Lange, Hope, Cont.
c/o Hollerith
803 Bramble Way
Los Angeles, CA 90049
Alternate V: 04/05/96

Lange, Jessica
c/o CAA
9830 Wilshire Bl
Beverly Hills, CA 90212
Actress V: 05/12/96

1720 Kaweah Dr
Pasadena, CA 91105
Alternate V: 03/15/96

Lange, KD
2001 Pinehurst
Los Angeles, CA 90068
Singer V: 01/31/96

Lange, Ted
20th Century Artists
15315 Magnolia Bl #429
Sherman Oaks, CA 91403
Actor V: 12/15/96

Langella, Frank
21114 Lighthill Dr
Topanga, CA 90290
Actor V: 03/15/96

Innovative Artists
1999 Ave of the Stars #2850
Los Angeles, CA 90067
Alternate V: 10/10/96

2121 Avenue of the Stars #950
Los Angeles, CA 90067
Forwarded V: 10/23/96

Langford, Frances
PO Box 96
Jensen Beach, FL 33457
Actress V: 01/31/96

Langley, Elmo
NASCAR
1811 Volusia Ave
Daytona Beach, FL 32015
Race Driver V: 03/12/96

Langlois, Lisa
House of Representatives
9911 Pico Bl #1060
Los Angeles, CA 90035
Actress V: 12/10/96

Langlois, Lisa, Cont.
9105 Carmilita Ave #1
Beverly Hills, CA 90210
Alternate V: 03/15/96

Lansbury, Angela
Wm Morris Agency
151 El Camino Dr
Beverly Hills, CA 90212
Actress V: 02/22/96

635 N Bonhill Rd
Los Angeles, CA 90049-2301
Alternate V: 03/15/96

Larroquette, John
5874 Deerhead Rd
Malibu, CA 90265
Actor V: 10/23/96

c/o CAA
9830 Wilshire Bl
Beverly Hills, CA 90212
Alternate V: 01/14/96

PO Box 6010
Malibu, CA 90265
Forwarded V: 04/02/96

Larsen, Don
PO Box 3863
Hayden Lake, ID 83835-2863
Baseball Star V: 01/31/96

17090 Copper Hill
Morgan Hill, CA 95037
Alternate V: 03/12/96

Larson, Jack
449 Skyewiay Rd N
Los Angeles, CA 90049
Actor V: 02/22/96

Skyewiay Productions
9336 W Washington Bl
Culver City, CA 90230
Alternate V: 01/21/96

Larson, Wolf
10600 Holmann Ave #1
Los Angeles, CA 90024
Actor V: 09/14/96

Lasorda, Tommy
1000 Elysian Park Ave
Los Angeles, CA 90012
Baseball Star V: 02/21/96

Lasser, Louise
200 E 71st St #20C
New York, NY 10021
Actress V: 05/20/96

Lasswell, Fred
King Features
235 E 45th St
New York, NY 10017
Cartoonist V: 04/23/96

Latham, Louise
Badgley Connor
9229 Sunset Bl #311
Los Angeles, CA 90069
Actress V: 12/04/96

Lauder, Estee
767 5th Ave
New York, NY 10153
Executive V: 03/01/96

Lauer, Andrew
Gersch Agency
232 N Canon Dr
Beverly Hills, CA 90210
Actor V: 11/26/96

Laughlin, Tom
PO Box 25355
Los Angeles, CA 90025
Actor V: 02/03/96

Lauper, Cyndi
3575 Cahuenga Bl W #450
Los Angeles, CA 90068
Singer V: 01/31/96

853 7th Ave #9-D
New York, NY 10019
Alternate V: 03/01/96

Lauren, Dyanna
2264 Ventura Bl #257
Woodland Hills, CA 91364
Actress V: 01/21/96

Lauria, Dan
601 N Cherokee Ave
Los Angeles, CA 90004
Actor V: 07/14/96

Laurie, Piper
2210 Wilshire Bl #931
Santa Monica, CA 90403
Actress V: 01/21/96

Laurie, Piper, Cont.
907 12th St #4
Santa Monica, CA 90403
Alternate V: 02/02/96

Wm Morris Agency
151 El Camino Dr
Beverly Hills, CA 90212
Forwarded V: 02/22/96

Lauter, Ed
Artists Agency
10000 Santa Monica Bl #305
Los Angeles, CA 90067
Actor V: 12/03/96

Lavin, Linda
20781 Big Rock Rd
Malibu, CA 90265
Actress V: 06/20/96

Law, John Phillip
Artists Group
10100 Santa Monica Bl #2490
Los Angeles, CA 90067
Actor V: 12/04/96

1339 Miller Dr
Los Angeles, CA 90069
Alternate V: 03/02/96

Lawless, Lucy
PO Box 49859
Los Angeles, CA 90049
Actress V: 12/15/96

WB-Audience Services
1438 N Gower
Hollywood, CA 90028
Alternate V: 01/12/97

Lawless, Paul
6 Whynwood Rd
Simsbury, CT 06070
Hockey Star V: 01/12/97

Lawley Jr, William R
3547 Dalraida Ct
Montgomery, AL 36109
War Hero V: 02/01/96

Lawrence, Carol
151 El Camino
Beverly Hills, CA 90212
Actress V: 12/12/96

12337 Ridge Circle
Los Angeles, CA 90049
Alternate V: 11/30/96

Lawrence, Danny
c/o Childress
PO Box 1189-Industrial Dr
Welcome, NC 27374
NASCAR Crew V: 03/12/96

Lawrence, Joey
Bloom Agency
9255 Sunset Bl #710
Los Angeles, CA 90069
Actor V: 12/06/96

846 N Cahuenga Bl
Los Angeles, CA 90038
Alternate V: 11/10/96

Lawrence, Martin
c/o UTA
9560 Wilshire Bl #500
Beverly Hills, CA 90212
Actor V: 02/01/96

Lawrence, Sharon
PO Box 46208
Los Angeles, CA 90046
Actress V: 10/23/96

2144 Beach Knoll Dr
W Hollywood, CA 90046
Alternate V: 01/15/97

Lawrence, Steve
820 Greenway Dr
Beverly Hills, CA 90210
Singer V: 03/07/96

Lawrence, Tracy
1100 17th Avenue South
Nashville, TN 37212
Singer V: 11/01/96

Lawrence, Vicki
6000 Lido Ln
Long Beach, CA 90803
Actress V: 01/10/97

Lawrence, Wendy B
NASA/LBJ Space Center
Houston, TX 77058
Astronaut V: 02/02/96

Lawrence Agency
3575 Cahuenga Bl West #125
Los Angeles, CA 90068
Talent Agency V: 01/15/96

Lawson, Twiggy
Neville Shulman
4 George's House
15 Hanover Square
London W1R, England
Actress V: 11/01/96

Rosenberg Office
8428 Melrose Pl-Suite C
Los Angeles, CA 90069
Alternate V: 12/13/96

4 St George's Houses
15 Hannover Square #1
London, W1R 9AJ England
Forwarded V: 01/12/96

Laye, Evelyn
109 Jermyn St
London SW1, England
Actress V: 03/01/96

Lazenby, George
Sutton/Barth & Vennari
145 S Fairfax Ave #310
Los Angeles, CA 90036
Actor V: 12/15/96

1127 21st St #2
Santa Monica, CA 90403
Alternate V: 03/03/96

509 S Gretna Green Way
Los Angeles, CA 90094
Forwarded V: 09/14/96

Le Beauf, Sabrina
822 S Robertson Bl
Los Angeles, CA 90069
Actress V: 10/23/96

c/o APA
9000 Sunset Bl
Los Angeles, CA 90069
Alternate V: 01/20/96

LeBlanc, Matt
Brillstein/Grey
9150 Wilshire Bl #350
Beverly Hills, CA 90212-3427
Actor V: 03/14/96

c/o UTA
9560 Wishire Bl #500
Beverly Hills, CA 90212
Alternate V: 10/10/96

LeBrock, Kelly
PO Box 57593
Sherman Oaks, CA 91403
Actress V: 11/01/96

PO Box 727
Los Olivos, CA 93441-0727
Alternate V: 02/21/96

LeDoux, Harold
King Features
235 E 45th St
New York, NY 10017
Cartoonist V: 04/19/96

LeGuin, Ursula K
Virginia Kidd
Box 278
Milford, PA 18337
Author V: 03/20/96

LeHane, Denis
Whitaker Agency
12725 Ventura Bl #F
Studio City, CA 91604
Actor V: 02/01/96

Totten Productions
19548 Vose St
Reseda, CA 91335
Forwarded V: 01/02/96

LeMat, Paul
Artists Agency
10000 Santa Monica Bl #305
Los Angeles, CA 90067
Actor V: 12/03/96

1100 N Alta Loma #805
Los Angeles, CA 90069
Alternate V: 01/06/96

LeRoy, Gloria
Gold/Marshak
3500 W Olive Ave #1400
Burbank, CA 91505
Actress V: 12/10/96

Leach, Robin
875 3rd Ave #1800
New York, NY 10022
Celebrity V: 03/02/96

Leachman, Cloris
c/o MTA
4526 Wilshire Bl
Los Angeles, CA 90010
Actress V: 09/14/96

Leachman, Cloris, Cont.
13127 Boca de Canon Lane
Los Angeles, CA 90049
Alternate V: 10/23/96

77 Ave Rd 416
Toronto Ont Canada M3R 5R8
Alternate V: 06/22/96

2045 Mandeville Canyon
Los Angeles, CA 90049
Forwarded V: 01/15/96

Lear, Norman
Act III Productions
5555 Melrose Ave
Hollywood, CA 90038
Producer V: 01/11/96

1999 Ave of the Stars #500
Los Angeles, CA 90067
Alternate V: 03/01/94

Learned, Michael
1600 N Beverly Dr
Beverly Hills, CA 90210
Actress V: 01/03/96

Henderson & Hogan Agency
247 S Beverly Dr #102
Beverly Hills, CA 90210
Alternate V: 12/10/96

Leary, Dennis
Wm Morris Agency
151 S El Camino Dr
Beverly Hills, CA 90212
Actor V: 10/10/96

Lederer, Francis
PO Box 32
Canoga Park, CA 91305
Actor V: 04/06/94

23134 Sherman Way
Canoga Park, CA 91307
Alternate V: 06/16/94

Lee, Anna
c/o TMCE
270 N Canon Dr-Suite 1064
Beverly Hills, CA 90210
Actress V: 12/02/96

ABC-TV
4151 Prospect Ave
Hollywood, CA 90027
Alternate V: 12/27/96

Lee, Brenda
2174 Carson St
PO Box 101188
Nashville, TN 37210-1188
Singer V: 11/01/96

Lee, Christopher
Shapira & Associates
15301 Ventura Bl #345
Sherman Oaks, CA 91403
Actor V: 12/14/96

5 Sandown House
Wheat Field Terrace
London W4, England
Alternate V: 03/14/96

Buchwald Agency
9229 Sunset Bl #710
Los Angeles, CA 90069
Alternate V: 01/30/96

Lee, Gordon Porky
7110 Highway 2 #22
Commerce City, CO 80022
Actor V: 09/11/96

Lee, Hyapatia
PO Box 1924
Indianapolis, IN 46206
Actress V: 02/13/94

Lee, Jason Scott
9560 Wishire Bl #500
Beverly Hills, CA 90212
Actor V: 10/10/96

PO Box 1083
Pearl City, HI 96782
Alternate V: 01/13/97

Lee, Mark C
NASA/LBJ Space Center
Hoston, TX 77058
Astronaut V: 01/31/96

Lee, Michele
4526 Wilshire Bl
Los Angeles, CA 90010
Actress V: 02/22/96

Lee, Pamela
8730 Sunset Bl #220
Los Angeles, CA 90069
Actress V: 01/14/96

5433 Beethoven St
Los Angeles, CA 90068
Alternate V: 01/13/97

Lee, Peggy
11404 Bellagio Rd
Los Angeles, CA 90049
Singer V: 01/31/96

Lee, Ruta
Craig Agency
8485 Melrose Place-Suite E
Los Angeles, CA 90069
Actress V: 12/08/96

2623 Laurel Canyon Rd
Los Angeles, CA 90046
Alternate V: 10/11/94

Lee, Spike
Forty Acres & A Mule
124 DeKalb Ave
Brooklyn, NY 11217
Director V: 02/13/94

c/o ICM
8942 Wilshire Bl
Beverly Hills, CA 90211
Alternate V: 01/14/96

Lee, Stan
King Features
235 E 45th St
New York, NY 10017
Cartoonist V: 03/10/96

Marvel Comics
387 Park Ave South
New York, NY 10016
Alternate V: 02/12/96

Lee, Tommy
4970 Summit View Dr
Westlake Village, CA 91362
Actor V: 04/06/94

Lee & Associates
8961 Sunset Bl-Suite V
Los Angeles, CA 90069
Talent Agency V: 02/02/96

Leeds, Phil
c/o Sanders
8831 Sunset Bl #304
Los Angeles, CA 90064
Actor V: 03/30/96

Leestma, David C
NASA/LBJ Space Center
Hoston, TX 77058
Astronaut V: 01/31/96

Legrand, Michel
F-Sharp Productions
157 W 57th St
New Your, NY 10019
Composer V: 09/09/96

Lehrer, Jim
c/o The News Hour
2700 S Quincy St #250
Arlington VA 22206
Correspondant V: 01/14/96

Leibman, Ron
c/o Hurwitz
427 N Canon Dr #215
Bevrly Hills, CA 90210
Actor V: 02/27/96

Leigh, Barbara
PO Box 246
Los Angeles, CA 90028-0246
Actress V: 10/23/96

Leigh, Janet
Amstel-Eisenstadt-Frasier
6310 San Vicente Bl #401
Los Angeles, CA 90048
Actress V: 12/01/96

1625 Summit Ridge Dr
Beverly Hills, CA 90210
Alternate V: 03/03/96

Leigh, Jennifer Jason
c/o ICM
8942 Wilshire Bl
Beverly Hills, CA 90211
Actress V: 12/11/96

2400 Whitman Place
Los Angeles, CA 90068
Alternate V: 01/21/96

Leighton, Laura
924 Westwood Bl-9th Fl
Los Angeles, CA 90024
Actress V: 01/14/96

8033 Sunset Bl #4048
Los Angeles, CA 90046
Alternate V: 01/11/97

Lein, Jennifer
ST-Voyager
5555 Melrose Ave
Hollywood, CA 90036
Actress V: 02/15/96

Leisure, David
c/o APA
9000 Sunset Bl #1200
Los Angeles, CA 90069
Actor V: 12/02/96

Leman, Catherine G
NASA/LBJ Space Center
Houston, TX 77058
Astronaut V: 02/02/96

Lembeck, Michael
9171 Wilshire Bl #436
Bevelry Hills, CA 90210
Actor V: 10/23/96

Lemke, Cheryl
Weather Channel
2600 Cumberland Pkwy
Atlanta, GA 30339
Commentator V: 01/20/96

Lemmon, Chris
Artists Agency
10000 Santa Monica Bl #305
Los Angeles, CA 90067
Actor V: 12/03/96

80 Murray St
South Gastonbury, CT 06073
Alternate V: 10/23/96

Lemmon, Jack
141 S El Camino Dr #201
Beverly Hills, CA 90212
Actor V: 11/01/96

c/o CAA
9830 Wilshire Bl
Beverly Hills, CA 90210
Alternate V: 02/12/96

Lemon, Meadowlark
Blue Ox Talent
4130 N Goldwater Bl #121
Scottsdale, AZ 85251
Basketball Star V: 01/21/96

Lenhoff/Robinson Talent
1728 S La Cienega Bl
Los Angeles, CA 90035
Talent Agency V: 11/11/96

Lennie, Angus
Jean Drysdale
15 Pembroke Gardens
London W8, England
Actor V: 02/17/96

Lennon Sisters
PO Box 1492
Birmingham, NY 13902
Singers V: 03/02/96

1984 State Hwy 165
Branson, MO 65616-8936
Alternate V: 01/11/96

3230 Corinth Ave
Los Angeles, CA 90006
Forwarded V: 03/02/96

Lennox, Annie
28 Alexander St
London W2, England
Singer V: 05/16/96

Leno, Jay
1151 Tower Dr
Beverly Hills, CA 90210
TV Host V: 05/15/96

c/o ICM
8942 Wilshire Bl
Beverly Hills, CA 90211
Alternate V: 01/14/96

General Mgmt Grp
9000 Sunset Bl #400
Los Angeles, CA 90069
Alternate V: 08/28/96

NBC Productions
The Tonight Show
3000 W Alameda Ave
Burbank, CA 91523
Forwarded V: 11/10/96

PO Box 7885
Burbank, CA 91510-7885
Forwarded V: 01/13/97

Lenoir, William
NASA/LBJ Space Center
Hoston, TX 77058
Astronaut V: 01/19/96

Lenz, Kay
Gage Group
9255 Sunset Bl #515
Los Angeles, CA 90069
Actress V: 02/22/96

5930 Manola Way
Los Angeles, CA 90068
Alternate V: 04/21/96

Leonard, Sugar Ray
13916 King George Way
Upper Marlboro, MD 20772-5950
Boxing Star V: 03/30/96

4922 Fairmont Ave #200
Bethesda, MD 20814
Alternate V: 01/13/97

Leong, Al
c/o Tannen
1800 N Vine St #120
Los Angeles, CA 90028
Actor V: 01/29/96

Leoni, Tea
811 Hampton Ave
Venice, CA 90291
Actress V: 10/23/96

Robinson Mgmt
10683 Santa Monica Bl
Los Angeles, CA 90025
Alternate V: 06/09/96

Leslie, Joan
c/o Caldwell
2228 N Catalina St
Los Angeles, CA 90027
Actress V: 04/21/96

Leto, Jared
Innovative Artists
1999 Ave of the Stars #2850
Los Angeles, CA 90067
Actor V: 12/15/96

Letterman, David
Lee Gabler
9830 Wilshire Bl
Beverly Hills, CA 90212
TV Host V: 01/11/96

Ed Sullivan Theatre
1697 Broadway
New York, NY 10019
Alternate V: 03/19/96

CBS-TV
7800 Beverly Bl
Los Angeles, CA 90036
Forwarded V: 11/26/96

Lettermen
PO Box 570727
Tarzana, CA 91357-0727
Musical Group V: 11/01/96

Levin, Ira
c/o HOA
40 E 49th St
New York, NY 10017
Author V: 02/18/96

Levin Agency
8484 Wilshire Bl #1200
Beverly Hills, CA 90211
Talent Agency V: 03/17/96

Levison, Barry
9830 Wilshire Bl
Beverly Hills, CA 90210
Director V: 01/15/96

Levy & Associates
9701 Wilshire Bl #1200
Beverly Hills, CA 90212
Talent Agency V: 11/11/96

Lewis, Al
PO Box 277
New York, NY 10044-0205
Actor V: 01/31/96

Abrams Artists
9200 Sunset Bl #625
Los Angeles, CA 90069
Alternate V: 03/01/96

Lewis, Carl
PO Box 57-1990
Houston, TX 77257-1990
Track Star V: 10/23/96

Lewis, Charlotte
c/o MTA
4526 Wilshire Bl
Los Angeles, CA 90010
Actress V: 10/10/96

Lewis, Gary
PO Box 53664
Indianapolis, IN 46253
Musician V: 03/05/96

Lewis, Geoffrey
Wm Morris Agency
151 El Camino Dr
Beverly Hills, CA 90212
Actor V: 11/27/96

Lewis, Huey
PO Box 819
Mill Valley, CA 94942
Singer V: 05/31/96

Lewis, Jerry
1701 Waldman Ave
Las Vegas, NV 89102
Actor V: 12/02/96

Lewis, Jerry Lee
JKL Enterprises
Box 384
Nesbit, MS 38651
Singer V: 11/01/96

Embry Int'l
PO Box 23162
Nashville, TN 37202
Alternate V: 02/02/96

Kerrie's Enterprise
4966 Quince Rd
Memphis, TN 38117
Alternate V: 02/28/96

PO Box 3864
Memphis, TN 38103
Forwarded V: 02/13/96

Lewis, Joe
Precision Products
Hwy 16-PO Box 569
Denver, NC 28037
NASCAR Crew V: 03/12/96

Lewis, Juliette
Wm Morris Agency
151 El Camino
Beverly Hills, CA 90212
Actress V: 12/12/96

Lewis, Monica
c/o Lang
606 Mountain Rd
Beverly Hills, CA 90210
Singer V: 05/13/96

Lewis, Richard
Innovative Artists
1999 Ave of the Stars #2850
Los Angeles, CA 90067
Actor V: 12/11/96

8170 Beverly Bl #305
Los Angeles, CA 90048
Alternate V: 10/23/96

Lewis, Shari
603 N Alta Dr
Beverly Hills, CA 90210
Actress V: 02/04/96

Li, Gong
Xi'an Films
Xi'an City, Shaanxi Provence
China
Actress V: 12/01/96

Library of Congress
M/B/RS Division
Room 338
Washington, DC 20540
Archive V: 03/20/96

Licht, Jeremy
c/o Freed
2029 Century Park E #600
Los Angeles, CA 90067
Actor V: 09/09/96

Lichtman Company
4439 Worster Ave
Studio City, CA 91604
Talent Agency V: 02/02/96

Liddy, G Gordon
9909 E Joshua Tree Lane #E
Scottsdale, AZ 85253
Celebrity V: 05/06/96

Liefeld, Rob
Image Comics
PO Box 25468
Anaheim, CA 92825
Cartoonist V: 12/01/96

Life In Hell Cartoon
2219 Main St #E
Santa Monica, CA 90405
Cartoonist V: 01/13/96

Life Magazine
41 W 25th St
New York, NY 10010
Publisher V: 02/10/96

Lifetime Network
309 W 49th St
New York, NY 10019
Production Office V: 12/15/96

36-12 35th Ave
Astoria, NY 11106
Alternate HQ V: 03/01/96

10880 Wilshire Bl #2010
Los Angeles, CA 90024
Alternate V: 03/17/96

Lifford, Tina
Ambrosio/Mortimer
9150 Wilshire Bl #175
Beverly Hills, CA 90212
Actress V: 01/15/97

Light, Judith
8942 Wilshire Bl
Beverly Hills, CA 90211
Actress V: 12/11/96

2930 Beverly Glen Circle #30
Los Angeles, CA 90077
Forwarded V: 01/27/96

Light Agency
6404 Wilshire Bl #900
Los Angeles, CA 90048
Talent Agency V: 02/12/96

Lightfoot, Gordon
1365 Yonge St #207
Toronto, Ontario, Canada
Singer V: 01/28/96

Lim, Pik-Sen
c/o OCA
34 Grafton Terrace
London NW5 4HY, England
Actress V: 03/01/96

Limbaugh, Rush
124 W 60th St #47H
New York, NY 10023
Commentator V: 03/12/96

924 Westwood Bl-9th Fl
Los Angeles, CA 90024
Alternate V: 01/14/96

366 Madison Ave #700
New York, NY 10017
Forwarded V: 01/11/97

Lincoln, Lar Park
Premiere Artists Agency
8899 Beverly Bl #510
Los Angeles, CA 90048
Actress V: 12/13/96

Lind, DeDe
PO Box 1712
Boca Raton, FL 33429
Playmate V: 01/13/97

Lind, Don L
NASA/LBJ Space Center
Houston, TX 77058
Astronaut V: 03/03/96

Linden, Hal
Wm Morris Agency
151 El Camino
Beverly Hills, CA 90212
Actor V: 12/12/96

416 N Bristol Ave
Los Angeles, CA 90049
Alternate V: 12/01/96

8730 Sunset Bl #4705
Los Angeles, CA 90069
Forwarded V: 10/23/96

Linder, Kate
Stone Manners Talent
8091 Selma Ave
Los Angeles, CA 90046
Actress V: 02/22/96

Linder & Associates
2049 Century Park E #2750
Los Angeles, CA 90067
Talent Agency V: 02/02/96

Lindley, Audra
House of Representatives
9911 Pico Bl #1060
Los Angeles, CA 90035
Actress V: 12/10/96

Lindsay, George
10000 Santa Monica Bl #305
Los Angeles, CA 90067
Actor V: 01/09/97

Lindsay, Shona
c/o Glass
28 Berkeley Square
London W1X 6HD, England
Actress V: 03/06/96

Lineger, Jerry M
NASA/LBJ Space Center
Houston, TX 77058
Astronaut V: 02/02/96

Linkletter, Art
1100 Belair Rd
Los Angeles, CA 90077
Celebrity V: 03/02/96

Linn, Teri Ann
4267 Marina City Dr #312
Marina del Rey, CA 90292
Actress V: 01/15/96

Linn-Baker, Mark
2700 Neison Way #1624
Santa Monica, CA 90405
Actor V: 12/01/96

Linnehan, Richard M
NASA/LBJ Space Center
Houston, TX 77058
Astronaut V: 02/02/96

Linville, Joanne
3148 Fryman Rd
Studio City, CA 91604
Actress V: 02/04/96

Linville, Larry
c/o Cosden
3518 Cahuenga Bl W #216
Los Angeles, CA 90068
Actor V: 03/12/96

18261 San Fernando Mission Bl
Northridge, CA 91326
Alternate V: 07/14/96

Liotta, Ray
c/o CAA
9830 Wilshire Bl
Beverly Hills, CA 90212
Actor V: 01/22/96

Rogers & Cowan Agency
1888 Century Park E #500
Los Angeles, CA 90068
Alternate V: 03/10/96

Lipton, Peggy
Innovative Artists
1999 Ave of the Stars #2850
Los Angeles, CA 90067
Actress V: 02/22/96

2576 Benedict Canyon Rd
Beverly Hills, CA 90210
Alternate V: 02/22/96

Lister, Moira
Richard Stone
18 York Bld
London WC2N 6JU, England
Actress V: 01/23/96

Lister, Tiny
Gersh Agency
232 N Canon Dr
Beverly Hills, CA 90210
Actor V: 12/09/96

Lithgow, John
9830 Wilshire Bl
Beverly Hills, CA 90212
Actor V: 12/07/96

1319 Warnall Ave
Los Angeles, CA 90024
Alternate V: 01/21/96

Little, Chad
Diamond Ridge Motorsports
5901 Orr Road
Charlotte, NC 28213
NASCAR Driver V: 10/23/96

W 1311 Sprague Ave
Spokane, WA 99204
Alternate V: 03/14/96

Little, Rich
8916 Canyon Spring Rd
Las Vegas, NV 89117
Commedian V: 10/23/96

24800 Pacific Coast Hwy
Malibu, CA 90265
Actor V: 03/15/96

Little, Tawny
17941 Sky Park Circle #F
Irvine, CA 92714
Actress V: 04/13/96

Little Richard
c/o Penniman
Hyatt Sunset Hotel
8401 W Sunset Bl
Los Angeles, CA 90069
Singer V: 01/22/96

Littler, Gene
PO Box 1949
Rancho Santa Fe, CA 92067
Golfer V: 01/14/96

Lively, Robyn
9200 Sunset Bl #625
Los Angeles, CA 90069
Actress V: 02/04/96

Livingston, Barry
11310 Blix St
N Hollywood, CA 91602
Actor V: 09/09/96

Livingston, Stanley
PO Box 1782
Studio City, CA 91604
Actor V: 09/09/96

Lizer, Kari
4249 Costello Ave
Sherman Oaks, CA 91423
Actress V: 05/03/96

Llewellyn, Desmond
Linkwell, Old Town
Bexhill On Sea
E Sussex TN40 2HA, England
Actor V: 10/11/96

Llewellyn, John A
NASA/LBJ Space Center
Houston, TX 77058
Astronaut V: 03/03/96

Lloyd, Christopher
c/o Managemint
PO Box 491246
Los Angeles, CA 90049
Actor V: 12/04/96

Gersh Agency
232 N Canon Dr
Beverly Hills, CA 90210
Alternate V: 12/09/96

Lloyd, Norman
1813 Old Ranch Rd
Los Angeles, CA 90049
Actor V: 01/18/96

Lo Bianco, Tony
Shapira & Associates
15301 Ventura Bl #345
Sherman Oaks, CA 91403
Actor V: 12/14/96

Locane, Amy
8942 Wilshire Bl
Beverly Hills, CA 90211
Actress V: 01/11/97

Location Update
6922 Hollywood Bl #612
Hollywood, CA 90028
Publication V: 03/03/96

Locke, Sondra
PO Box 69865
Los Angeles, CA 90069
Actress V: 04/18/96

Lockhart, Anne
Henderson & Hogan Agency
247 S Beverly Dr #102
Bevery Hills, CA 90210
Actress V: 12/10/96

Lockhart, Anne, Cont.
191 Upper Lake Rd
Thousand Oaks, CA 91361-5137
Alternate V: 08/28/96

Lockhart, June
9000 Sunset Bl #1200
Los Angeles, CA 90069
Actress V: 12/02/96

404 San Vicente Bl #208
Santa Monica, CA 90402
Alternate V: 12/07/96

PO Box 260207
Encino, CA 91426
Forwarded V: 02/22/96

Lockhart, Keith
301 Massachusetts Ave
Boston, MA 02115
Conductor V: 01/13/96

Locklear, Heather
Creative Artists Agency
9830 Wilshire Bl
Beverly Hills, CA 90212
Actress V: 12/07/96

4970 Summit View Dr
Westlake Village, CA 91362
Alternate V: 02/19/96

Lofton, Cirroc
Star Trek-DS9
5555 Melrose Ave
Hollywood, CA 90036
Actor V: 02/23/96

Loggia, Robert
Creative Artists Agency
9830 Wilshire Bl
Beverly Hills, CA 90212
Actor V: 12/07/96

Loggia, Robert
12659 Promontory Rd
Los Angeles, CA 90049
Actor V: 02/01/96

Loggins, Kenny
670 Oak Springs Lane
Santa Barbara, CA 93108-1101
Singer V: 01/12/96

Lollobrigida, Gina
Via Appia Antica 223
Roma I-00179, Italy
Actress V: 11/01/96

Lom, Hebert
Wm Morris Agency
147 Wardour St
London W1V 3DF, England
Actor V: 03/12/96

Lombard, Karina
Wm Morris Agency
151 El Camino Dr
Bevrly Hills, CA 90212
Model V: 12/01/96

London, Bobby
King Features
235 East 45th St
New York, NY 10017
Cartoonist V: 02/16/96

London, Julie
16074 Royal Oak Rd
Encino, CA 91316
Actress V: 02/04/96

London, Lisa
1680 N Vine St #203
Hollywood, CA 90028
Actress V: 03/26/96

Lone, John
Levine/Thall/Plotkin
1740 Broadway
New York, NY 10019
Actor V: 02/02/96

1341 Ocean Ave #104
Santa Monica, CA 90401
Alternate V: 03/27/96

Long, Glen
Sears Point Int'l Raceway
Hwys 37 & 121
Sonoma, CA 95476
NASCAR Official V: 03/02/96

Long, John
King Features
235 E 45th St
New York, NY 10017
Cartoonist V: 06/02/96

Long, Shelley
9830 Wilshire Bl
Beverly Hills, CA 90212
Actress V: 12/07/96

Lopat, Ed
99 Oak Trail Rd
Hillsdale, NJ 07205
Baseball Star V: 05/14/96

Lopez, Dan
77 N Ellsworth Ave
San Mateo, CA 94401
Cartoonist V: 03/12/96

Lopez, Trini
1139 Abrigo Rd
Palm Springs, CA 92262
Singer V: 01/16/96

Sterling & Talman
PO Box 5333
Beverly Hills, CA 90210
Alternate V: 01/11/96

Lopez-Alegria, Michael E
NASA/LBJ Space Center
Houston, TX 77058
Astronaut V: 02/02/96

Lord, Jack
4999 Kahala Ave
Honolulu, HI 96816
Actor V: 08/23/96

Lord, Marjorie
1110 Maytor Pl
Beverly Hills, CA 90210
Actress V: 05/13/96

Lords, Traci
Ambrosio & Mortimer
9150 Wilshire Bl #175
Beverly Hills, CA 90212
Actress V: 12/01/96

Loren, Sophia
6 Rue Charles Bonnet
Geneva, Switzerland
Actress V: 04/11/96

La Concordia Ranch
1151 Hidden Valley Rd
Thousand Oaks, CA 91361
Alternate V: 03/10/96

Camden ITG
822 S Robertson Bl #200
Los Angeles, CA 90035
Forwarded V: 02/22/96

Via di Villa Ada 10
I-00199 Rome, Italy
Forwarded V: 01/17/96

c/o Cineart
36 rue de Ponthieu
Paris F-75008, France
Forwarded V: 11/01/96

Lorenzan, Fred
c/o ReMax
575-2 W St Charles Rd
Elmhurst, IL 60126
NASCAR Driver V: 03/02/96

Lorimar Telepictures
10202 W Washington Bl
Culver City, CA 90232
Production Office V: 03/17/96

300 S Lorimar Plaza
Burbank, CA 91505
Alternate V: 03/19/96

Loring, Gloria
14755 Ventura #744
Sherman Oaks, CA 91423
Actress V: 01/02/96

c/o Craig
8485 Melrose Place-Suite E
Los Angeles, CA 90069
Alternate V: 02/22/96

Loring, Lisa
c/o MME
11130 Huston St #6
Hollywood, CA 91601
Actress V: 11/11/96

Loring, Lynn
506 N Camden Dr
Beverly Hills, CA 90210
Actress V: 04/27/96

Los Angeles Clippers
LA Sports Arena
3939 S Figueroa
Los Angeles, CA 90037
Team Office V: 02/15/96

Los Angeles Dodgers
100 Elysian Park Ave
Dodger Stadium
Los Angeles, CA 90012
Team Office V: 02/15/96

Los Angeles Kings
Great Western Forum
3900 W Manchester Bl
Box 17013
Inglewood, CA 90306
Team Office V: 01/31/96

Los Angeles Lakers
PO Box 10
Inglewood, CA 90306
Team Office V: 02/15/96

Los Angeles Rams
2327 W Lincoln Ave
Anaheim, CA 92801
Team Office V: 05/15/96

Los Lobos
PO Box 1304
Burbank, CA 91507
Musical Group V: 02/01/96

Loudon, Dorothy
101 Central Park W
New York, NY 10023
Actress V: 04/27/96

Louganis, Greg
PO Box 4068
Malibu, CA 90265
Olympic Diver V: 02/24/96

Loughlin, Lori
Wm Morris Agency
151 El Camino
Beverly Hills, CA 90212
Actress V: 12/12/96

Louis-Dreyfus, Julia
c/o UTA
9560 Wilshire Bl-5th Fl
Beverly Hills, CA 90212
Actress V: 02/22/96

131 Rodeo Dr #300
Beverly Hills, CA 90212
Alternate V: 01/31/96

9911 W Pico Bl-PH1
Los Angeles, CA 90035-2718
Forwarded V: 01/03/97

Louise, Tina
310 East 46th St #18T
New York, NY 10017
Actress V: 05/16/96

9565 Lime Orchard Rd
Beverly Hills, CA 90210
Alternate V: 07/27/96

Lounge, John M
NASA/LBJ Space Center
Houston, TX 77058
Astronaut V: 01/31/96

Lousma, Jack R
NASA/LBJ Space Center
Houston, TX 77058
Astronaut V: 03/03/96

Love, Courtney
Wm Morris Agency
151 El Camino Dr
Beverly Hills, CA 90212
Singer V: 01/14/96

33401 NE 78th St
Carnation, WA 98014
Alternate V: 01/13/97

Gold Mtn Mgmt
3575 Cahuenga Bl W #450
Los Angeles, CA 90068
Alternate V: 06/09/96

Loveless, Patty
Fitzgerald Hartley
1908 Wedgewood Ave
Nashville, TN 37212
Singer V: 11/01/96

60 Music Square East
Nashville, TN 37203
Alternate V: 03/05/96

Lovell & Associates
7095 Hollywood Bl #1006
Los Angeles, CA 90028
Talent Agency V: 03/13/96

Lovell Jr, James A
NASA/LBJ Space Center
Houston, TX 77058
Astronaut V: 03/03/96

Lovett, Lyle
8942 Wilshire Bl
Beverly Hills, CA 90211
Singer V: 01/14/96

Lovitz, Jon
Creative Artists Agency
9830 Wilshire Bl
Beverly Hills, CA 90212
Actor V: 12/07/96

4735 Viviana Dr
Tarzana, CA 91356
Alternate V: 01/03/97

Low, G David
NASA/LBJ Space Center
Hoston, TX 77058
Astronaut V: 01/31/96

Lowe, Chad
7020 Sunset Bl-4th Fl
Los Angeles, CA 90046
Actor V: 12/15/96

Lowe, Rob
Wm Morris Agency
151 El Camino Dr
Beverly Hills, CA 90212
Actor V: 01/14/96

270 N Canon Dr #1072
Beverly Hills, CA 90210-5323
Forwarded V: 03/15/96

Lowell, Carey
c/o ICM
8942 Wilshire Bl
Beverly Hills, CA 90211
Actress V: 12/15/96

c/o NBC
30 Rockefeller Plaza
New York, NY 10112
Alternate V: 11/11/96

LuPone, Patti
Lantz Office
888 7th Ave #2500
New York, NY 10106
Singer V: 10/23/96

8942 Wilshire Bl
Beverly Hills, CA 90211
Forwarded V: 08/22/96

Lucas, George
PO Box 2009
San Rafael, CA 94912
Producer V: 01/11/96

Lucci, Susan
505 S Beverly Dr #683
Beverly Hills, CA 90212
Actress V: 01/31/96

PO Box 621
Quogue, NY 11959
Alternate V: 10/23/96

16 Carteret Pl
Garden City, NJ 11530
Alternate V: 03/16/96

c/o ICM
8942 Wilshire Bl
Beverly Hills, CA 90211
Forwarded V: 03/30/96

Lucid, Shannon W
NASA/LBJ Space Center
Houston, TX 77058
Astronaut V: 03/03/96

Luckinbill, Lawrence
RR 3-Flintlock Ridge Rd
Katonah, NY 10536-9803
Actor V: 03/06/96

560 Tigertail Rd
Los Angeles, CA 90049
Alternate V: 12/05/96

Lucking, William
9229 Sunset Bl #607
Los Angeles, CA 90069
Actor V: 02/04/96

Ludlum, Robert
Heinz Zwack
Harthausenerstrasse 28
8011 Grafbrunnn, Germany
Author V: 03/17/96

Henry Morrison
PO Box 235
Bedford Hills, NY 10507
Alternate V: 01/13/97

Luft, Lorna
Golden/Goldberg
9100 Wishire Bl #455
Beverly Hills, CA 90212-3415
Actress V: 07/14/96

5757 Wilshire Bl #240
Los Angeles, CA 90036-3682
Alternate V: 02/01/96

Lujack, Johnny
3700 Harrison St
Davenport, IA 52806
Football Star V: 03/08/96

Lulu
c/o Elson
1 Richmond Mews
London W1V 5AG, England
Actress V: 03/06/96

Lumet, Sydney
1 W 81st St #40B
New York, NY 10024-6048
Director V: 02/01/96

Lumley, Joanna
Paradigm Agency
10100 Santa Monica Bl-25th Fl
Los Angeles, CA 90067
Actress V: 12/13/96

Lumley, Joanna, Cont.
c/o MLR
200 Fulham Rd
London SW10 9PN, England
Alternate V: 03/06/96

Luna, Barbara
c/o Moss
733 N Seward St #PH
Los Angeles, CA 90038
Actress V: 02/22/96

Lunceford, Terry
7200 Saranac St #40
La Mesa, CA 91394
Magician V: 06/27/96

Lund, Deanna
545 Howard St
Salem, VA 24153
Actress V: 03/03/96

Lunden, Joan
1965 Broadway #500
New York, NY 10023
TV Host V: 04/27/96

Good Morning America
77 W 66th St
New York, NY 10023
Alternate V: 01/14/96

Lundgren, Dolph
29055 Cliffside Dr
Malibu, CA 90265
Actor V: 04/10/96

1875 Century Park East
Los Angeles, CA 90067-2598
Alternate V: 12/08/96

Lupus, Peter
11375 Dona Lisa Dr
Studio City, CA 91604
Actor V: 02/01/96

6442 Coldwater Canyon #211
N Hollywood, CA 91606
Alternate V: 06/18/96

Luzinski, Greg
320 Jackson Rd
Medford, NJ 08055
Baseball Star V: 01/20/96

Lyden, Pierce
291 N Olive St
Orange, CA 92666
Actor V: 02/02/96

Lynch, Kelly
Wm Morris Agency
151 El Camino Dr
Beverly Hills, CA 90212
Actress V: 02/22/96

1970 Mandeville Canyon Rd
Los Angeles, CA 90049
Alternate V: 07/14/96

Lynch, Richard
c/o Sindell
8271 Melrose Ave #202
Los Angeles, CA 90046
Actor V: 03/27/96

Lynley, Carol
Gerler Agency
3349 Cahuenga Bl West #1
Los Angeles, CA 90068
Actress V: 12/08/96

PO Box 2190
Malibu, CA 90265
Alternate V: 06/03/96

Lynn, Amber
12400 Ventura Bl #329
Studio City, 91604-2406
Actress V: 03/14/96

Lynn, Betty
10424 Tennessee Ave
Los Angeles, CA 90064
Actress V: 07/26/96

Lynn, Kate
c/o Hopkins
1548 N Orange Grove Ave
Los Angeles, CA 90046-2618
Actress V: 06/22/96

Lynn, Loretta
PO Box 40325
Nashville, TN 37204-0325
Singer V: 01/21/96

PO Box 120369
Nashville, TN 37212-0369
Alternate V: 03/04/96

Lynne & Reilly Agency
Toluka Plaza Building
6735 Forest Lawn Dr #313
Hollywood, CA 90068
Talent Agency V: 11/11/96

M

MAD ABOUT YOU
Culver Studios
9336 Washington Bl
Culver City, CA 90232
Production Office V: 01/20/96

c/o NBC-TV
30 Rockefeller Plaza
New York, NY 10112
Alternate V: 12/15/96

MALCOLM & EDDIE
Sony/ Gable Bldg
10202 W Washington Bl
Culver City, CA 90232
Production Office V: 10/23/96

UPN-TV
5555 Melrose Ave-Marathon 1200
Los Angeles, CA 90038
Alternate V: 11/11/96

MALONEY
CBS-TV
51 W 52nd St
New York, NY 10019
Viewer Services V: 11/11/96

La Mesa Productions
8120 Webb Ave
N Hollywood, CA 91605
Alternate V: 12/15/96

MANN AND MACHINE
Universal TV
70 Universal City Plaza
Universal City, CA 91608
Production Office V: 01/20/96

MARRIED WITH CHILDREN
Sony Studios
10202 Washington Bl
Culver City, CA 90232
Production Office V: 01/20/96

Fox-TV
PO Box 900
Beverly Hills, CA 90213
Alternate V: 12/15/96

MARTIN
Fox-TV
PO Box 900
Beverly Hills, CA 90213
Production Office V: 12/15/96

MATLOCK
Viacom/Audience Services
10 Universal City Plz
Universal City, CA 91608
Production Office V: 01/21/96

MATT WATERS
TriStar Television
4063 Radford-2nd Fl Admit
Studio City, CA 91604
Production Office V: 10/23/96

MAYBE THIS TIME
Jacobs Prods/Anim Bldg 2A-7
500 South Buena Vista
Burbank, CA 91521-1701
Production Office V: 10/23/96

MCA-TV
100 Universal City Plaza
Universal City, CA 91608
Production Office V: 03/17/96

MCKENNA
ABC-TV
2020 Ave of the Stars
Los Angeles, CA 90067
Production Office V: 01/21/96

ME AND THE BOYS
ABC-TV
2020 Ave of the Stars
Los Angeles, CA 90067
Production Office V: 01/21/96

MELROSE PLACE
Fox-TV
PO Box 900
Beverly Hills, CA 90213
Production Office V: 12/15/96

MEN BEHAVING BADLY
NBC-TV
30 Rockefeller Plaza
New York, NY 10112
Viewer Services V: 11/11/96

MGA
4444 Lankershim Bl #207
N Hollywood, CA 91602
Talent Agency V: 02/02/96

MGF Magazine
3 W 18th St
New York, NY 10011
Publisher V: 03/03/96

MGM/Warner Brothers
4000 Warner Blvd
Burbank, CA 91522
Production Office V: 12/15/96

MILLENNIUM
Fox-TV
PO Box 900
Beverly Hills, CA 90213
Viewer Services V: 11/11/96

MISS AMERICA PAGEANT
Pageant HQ
1325 Broadwalk
Atlantic City, NJ 08401
Production Office V: 01/07/96

MISS TEEN USA
6420 Wishire Bl
Los Angeles, CA 90048
Production Office V: 01/14/96

MISTER ROGERS
4802 Fifth Ave
Pittsburgh, PA 15213
Production Office V: 01/13/96

MOESHA
Sunset Gower Studios
1438 N Gower St-Box 37
Hollywood, CA 90028
Production Office V: 10/23/96

UPN-TV
5555 Melrose Ave-Marathon 1200
Los Angeles, CA 90038
Alternate V: 12/15/96

MONROES
Warner Brothers
4000 Warner Bl
Burbank, CA 91522
Production Office V: 01/14/96

MR & MRS SMITH
CBS-TV
51 W 52nd St
New York, NY 10019
Viewer Services V: 11/11/96

Warner Brothers TV
6767 Forest Lawn Dr-#100
Los Angeles, CA 90068
Alternate V: 12/15/96

MR RHODES
NBC-TV
30 Rockefeller Plaza
New York, NY 10112
Viewer Services V: 11/11/96

MSNBC
2200 Fletcher Ave
Ft Lee, NJ 07024
Production Office V: 12/15/96

MTV/Nichelodeon
1515 Broadway
New York, NY 10036
Production Office V: 11/11/96

MUDDLING THROUGH
Sony Studios
10202 Washington Bl
Culver City, CA 90232
Production Office V: 01/20/96

MURDER ONE
Bochco Prod/Fox TV
10201 W Pico Bl
Los Angeles, CA 90035
Production Office V: 10/23/96

ABC-TV
77 W 66th St
New York, NY 10023
Alternate V: 12/15/96

MURDER, SHE WROTE
Universal Television
100 Universal City Plz, Bl507
Universal Ctiy, CA 91608
Production Office V: 10/23/96

Universal TV
70 Universal City Plaza
Universal City, CA 91608
Alternate V: 01/20/96

MURPHY BROWN
Warner Bros-TV
4000 Warner Bl-Bldg5 Rm21
Universal City, CA 91608
Production Office V: 10/23/96

CBS-TV
51 W 52nd St
New York, NY 10019
Alternate V: 12/15/96

MY GUYS
Witt/Thomas
1438 N Gower St-Bldg 35-4th Fl
Hollywood, CA 90028
Production Office V: 10/23/96

MY SO CALLED LIFE
ABC-TV
2020 Ave of the Stars
Los Angeles, CA 90067
Production Office V: 01/21/96

Mystery Science Theatre 3000
Satellite News/Best Brains
PO Box 5325
Hopkins, MN 55343
Production Office V: 03/11/96

MacCorkindale, Simon
1900 Ave of the Stars
Suite 2270
Los Angeles, CA 90067
Actor V: 02/02/96

MacCready, Dr Paul
AeroVironment
222 E Huntington Dr
Monrovia, CA 91016-3424
Scientist V: 02/09/96

MacDowell, Andie
c/o ICM
8942 Wilshire Bl
Beverly Hills, CA 90211
Actress V: 01/14/96

MacGraw, Ali
Artists Group
10100 Santa Monica Bl #2490
Los Angeles, CA 90067
Actress V: 12/04/96

10345 W Olymlic Bl #200
Los Angeles, CA 90064
Alternate V: 02/22/96

27040 Malibu Cove Colony Dr
Malibu, CA 90265
Alternate V: 04/04/96

Bauman & Hiller
5750 Wilshire Bl #512
Los Angeles, CA 90036
Forwarded V: 03/19/96

MacIntosh, Craig
King Features
216 E 45th St
New York, NY 10017
Cartoonist V: 02/07/96

MacKenzie, Gisele
Kjar Agency
10643 Riverside Dr
Toluca, CA 91602
Actress V: 12/11/96

11014 Blix Ave
N Hollywood, CA 91602
Alternate V: 04/27/96

MacLachlan, Janet
20th Century Artists
15315 Magnolia Bl #429
Sherman Oaks, CA 91403
Actress V: 12/15/96

1919 N Taft Ave
Los Angeles, CA 90068
Alternate V: 05/14/96

MacLachlan, Kyle
c/o UTA
9560 Wilshire Bl #500
Beverly Hills, CA 90212
Actor V: 01/14/96

828 Venezia Ave
Venice, CA 90291
Alternate V: 07/12/96

MacLaine, Shirley
c/o ICM
8942 Wilshire Bl
Beverly Hills, CA 90211
Actress V: 01/14/96

MacLaine Entertainment
25200 Old Malibu Rd
Malibu, CA 90262
Alternate V: 03/01/96

MacLeod, Gavin
Gage Group
9255 Sunset Bl #515
Los Angeles, CA 90069
Actor V: 02/09/96

1025 Fifth Ave
New York, NY 10028
Alternate V: 01/03/97

MacRae, Meredith
c/o Zadeh
11759 Iowa Ave
Los Angeles, CA 90025
Actress V: 02/22/96

518 Pacific Ave
Manhattan Beach, CA 90266
Alternate V: 02/21/96

MacRae, Sheila
Ambrosio & Mortimer
9150 Wilshire Bl #175
Beverly Hills, CA 90212
Actress V: 12/01/96

Macnee, Patrick
c/o Schechter
9300 Wilshire Bl #410
Beverly Hills, CA 90212
Actor V: 03/01/96

PO Box 1685
Palm Springs, CA 92263
Forwarded V: 07/12/96

Macpherson, Elle
Women Inc
107 Green St
New York, NY 10012
Model V: 01/07/96

c/o ICM
8942 Wilshire Bl
Beverly Hills, CA 90211
Alternate V: 01/14/96

Macy, Bill
10130 Angelo Circle
Beverly Hills, CA 90210
Actor V: 02/28/96

Madden, Dave
1800 N Vine St #120
Los Angeles, CA 90028
Actor V: 03/01/96

Madden, John
c/o Fox-TV
10201 W Pico Bl
Los Angeles, CA 90035
TV Host V: 01/14/96

Int'l Mgmt Grp
22 E 71st St
New York, NY 10021
Alternate V: 01/05/96

Madden, John, Cont.
c/o CBS Sports
51 W 52nd St
New York, NY 10019
Forwarded V: 04/23/96

Mademoiselle Talent
8693 Wilshire Bl #200
Beverly Hills, CA 90211
Talent Agency V: 02/02/96

Madison Square Gardens
Business Offices
4 Pennsylvania Plaza
New York, NY 10001
Business Group V: 02/01/96

Madonna
c/o ICM
8942 Wilshire Bl
Beverly Hills, CA 90211
Singer V: 03/30/96

Fred De Mann Mgmt
8000 Beverly Bl
Los Angeles, CA 90048
Alternate V: 11/01/96

Madsen, Virginia
9354 Claircrest Dr
Beverly Hills, CA 90210
Actress V: 10/23/96

Creative Artists Agency
9830 Wilshire Bl
Beverly Hills, CA 90212
Alternate V: 12/07/96

Mahaffey, John
3100 Richmond Ave #500
Houston, TX 77098
Golfer V: 01/17/96

Maharis, George
13150 Mulholland Dr
Beverly Hills, CA 90210
Actor V: 03/27/96

Mailer, Norman
142 Columbia Heights Pl
Brooklyn, NY 11201
Author V: 05/15/96

Major, John
10 Downing Street
London SW1A 2AA, England
Politician V: 11/01/96

Major Clients Agency
345 N Maple Dr #395
Beverly Hills, CA 90210
Talent Agency V: 11/11/96

Majors, Lee
Shapira & Associates
15301 Ventura Bl #345
Sherman Oaks, CA 91403
Actor V: 12/14/96

625 San Marco Dr
Fort Lauderdale, FL 33301
Alternate V: 10/23/96

411 Isle of Capri Dr
Ft Lauderdale, FL 33301
Forwarded V: 02/03/96

Mako
Amstel-Eisenstadt-Frasier
6310 San Vicente Bl #401
Los Angeles, CA 90048
Actor V: 12/01/96

East West Players
4424 Santa Monica Bl
Los Angeles, CA 90029
Forwarded V: 01/22/96

Malandro, Kristina
2518 Cardigan Ct
Los Angeles, CA 90077-1337
Actress V: 02/23/96

10647 Wilkins Ave #307
Los Angeles, CA 90024
Alternate V: 03/27/96

Malden, Karl
Gersh Agency
232 N Canon Dr
Beverly Hills, CA 90210
Actor V: 12/09/96

1845 Mandeville Canyon Rd
Los Angeles, CA 90049
Alternate V: 04/28/96

Malick, Wendy
Innovative Artists
1999 Ave of the Stars #2850
Los Angeles, CA 90067
Actress V: 01/15/97

Malkovich, John
8942 Wilshire Bl
Beverly Hills, CA 90211
Actor V: 01/14/96

Malkovich, John, Cont.
1322 S Genesee Ave
Los Angeles, CA 90019
Alternate V: 02/20/96

335 Maple Dr #135
Beverly Hills, CA 90210-3858
Forwarded V: 11/01/96

Malloy, Larkin
c/o Douglas
1501 Broadway #703
New York, NY 10036
Actor V: 03/20/96

Malone, Dorothy
Shapiro Mgmt
2147 Beachwood Dr
Los Angeles, CA 90068
Actress V: 03/21/96

PO Box 7287
Dallas, TX 75209
Alternate V: 10/23/96

Malone, Nancy
11624 Sunshine Terrace
Studio City, CA 91604
Actress V: 06/09/96

Malot, Pierre
Artmedia
10 Ave George-V
F-75008 Paris, France
Actor V: 02/11/96

Mamet, David
PO Box 381589
Cambridge, MA 02238
Writer V: 01/14/96

Management Jovanovic
Kathi-KobusStrasse 24
8000 Munchen 40 Germany
Talent Agency V: 03/15/96

Mancini, Ray 'Boom-Boom'
2611 25th St
Santa Monica, CA 90405-2817
Boxing Star V: 02/01/96

807 Cambridge Ave
Youngstown, OH 44502
Alternate V: 02/02/96

750 Bundy Dr #108
Los Angeles, CA
Forwarded V: 05/12/96

Mancuso, Frank G
MGM-UA
1350 Ave of the America's
New York, NY 10019
Producer V: 12/01/96

Mancuso, Nick
c/o Camden ITG
822 S Roberson Bl #200
Los Angles, CA 90035
Actor V: 10/23/96

7160 Grasswood Ave
Malibu, CA 90265
Alternate V: 03/27/96

Gold & Marshak
3500 W Olive Ave #1400
Burbank, CA 91505
Forwarded V: 09/11/96

8942 Wilshire Bl
Beverly Hills, CA 90211
Forwarded V: 10/10/96

Mandela, Nelson
51 Plain St
Johannesburg 2001, RSA
Politican V: 11/01/96

Mandrell, Barbara
PO Box 620
Hendersonville, TN 37077-06200
Singer V: 10/23/96

Mandrell Mgmt
PO Box 800
Hendersonville, TN 37077
Alternate V: 02/02/96

128 River Rd
Hendersonville, TN 37075
Forwarded V: 04/27/96

Mandrell, Erlene
Mandrell Mgmt
PO Box 800
Hendersonville, TN 37077
Singer V: 02/02/96

Mandrell, Louise
Mandrell Mgmt
PO Box 800
Hendersonville, TN 37077-0800
Singer V: 11/23/96

1522 Demonbreun St
Nashville, TN 37203
Forwarded V: 01/07/96

Manetti, Larry
Epstein/Wyckoff
280 S Beverly Dr #400
Beverly Hills, CA 90212
Actor V: 03/17/96

Manhoff, Dinah
Innovative Artists
1999 Ave of the Stars #2850
Los Angeles, CA 90067
Actress V: 12/11/96

Manilow, Barry
Wm Morris Agency
151 El Camino Dr
Beverly Hills, CA 90212
Singer V: 01/14/96

c/o Stiletto Ent
5443 Beethoven St
Los Angeles, CA 90066
Alternate V: 03/01/96

Mann, Carol
6 Cape Chestnut
The Woodlands, TX 76110
Golfer V: 02/04/96

Mann, Herbie
Kokopelli Music
PO Box 8200
Santa Fe, NM 87504
Musician V: 10/23/96

Manners, Daniel
717 Santecito Dr
Santa Barbara, CA 93108-1933
Actor V: 01/13/96

Manoff, Dinah
Innovative Artists
1999 Ave of the Stars #2850
Los Angeles, CA 90067
Actress V: 02/22/96

Mantley, John
4121 Longridge Ave
Sherman Oaks, CA 91423
Author V: 01/04/96

13535 Ventura Bl #205
Sherman Oaks, CA 91423
Alternate V: 02/01/96

Mantooth, Randolph
Stone Manners Talent
8091 Selma Ave
Los Angeles, CA 90068
Actor V: 12/15/96

Mantooth, Randolph, Cont.
PO Box 280
Agoura, CA 91376
Alternate V: 11/10/96

2908 1/2 Griffith Park Bl
Los Angeles, CA 90027-3315
Forwarded V: 02/01/96

Maples Trump, Maria
721 5th Ave
New York, NY 10022
Model V: 10/23/96

Marais, Jean
Les Films 13
15 Ave Hoche
Paris 75008, France
Actor V: 02/09/96

Agence Cineart
34 ave Champs-Elysees
Paris 75008, France
Alternate V: 01/17/96

Marceau, Marcel
Compagne De Mime
21 Rue Jean-Mermoz
Paris 75008, France
Mime V: 03/10/96

Theatre De Champs Elysees
15 Ave Montaigne
Paris 75008, France
Alternate V: 02/18/96

Marceau, Sophie
30 ave Charles-de-Gaulle
Nuilly-sur-Seine 92200, France
Actress V: 01/17/96

13 rue Madeleine Michelle
Nuilly-sur-Seine 92200, France
Alternate V: 10/10/96

March, Jane
Storm Mgmt
5 Jubilee Place #100
London SW3 3TD, England
Actress V: 06/18/96

Marchand, Nancy
151 El Camino
Beverly Hills, CA 90212
Actress V: 12/12/96

205 W 89th St-Suite 6S
New York, NY 10024
Alternate V: 04/27/96

Marcis, Dave
Marcis Racing
PO Box 645
Skyland, NC 28776
NASCAR Driver V: 03/02/96

Marcovicci, Andrea
8273 W Norton Ave
Los Angeles, CA 90046
Actress V: 03/25/96

Marcus, Jerry
King Features
235 E 45th St
New York, NY 10017
Cartoonist V: 05/01/96

Maren, Elizabeth
3126 Oakcrest Dr
Los Angeles, CA 90068
Actress V: 01/11/96

Maren, Jerry
3126 Oakcrest Dr
Los Angeles, CA 90068
Actor V: 11/20/96

Margaret, Ann
5644 Cahuenga Bl #336
N Hollywood, CA 91601
Actress V: 10/23/96

Margulies, Jimmy
King Features
216 E 45th St
New York, NY 10017
Cartoonist V: 03/11/96

Marin, Richard 'Cheech'
c/o CAA
9830 Wilshire Bl
Beverly Hills, CA 90212
Actor V: 03/01/96

Marinaro, Ed
Innovative Artists
1999 Ave of the Stars #2850
Los Angeles, CA 90067
Actor V: 12/11/96

1466 N Doheny Dr
Los Angeles, CA 90069
Alternate V: 06/17/96

Marino, Dan
7500 SW 30th St
Davie, FL 33329
Football Star V: 10/23/96

Marino, Dan, Cont.
3415 Stallion Lane
Weston, FL 33331
Alternate V: 01/10/97

Mark, Marky
Hogland Entertainment
888-7th Ave #2900
New York, NY 10019
Singer V: 06/18/96

Markham, Monte
Shapira & Associates
15301 Ventura Bl #345
Sherman Oaks, CA 91403
Actor V: 12/14/96

PO Box 607
Malibu, CA 90265
Alternate V: 12/01/96

26328 Ingleside
Malibu, CA 90265
Forwarded V: 03/21/96

Marlin, Sterling
McClure Racing
Rt 10-Box 780
Abingdon, VA 24210
NASCAR Driver V: 02/08/96

Stavola Racing
PO Box 339
Harrisburg, NC 28075
Alternate V: 03/02/96

RR 2-Box 162
Ronda, NC 28670
Alternate V: 03/02/96

Marsalis, Wynton
70 Lincoln Center Plaza
New York, NY 10023-6583
Musician V: 10/23/96

9000 Sunset Bl #1200
Los Angeles, CA 90069
Alternate V: 01/14/96

Marshall, EG
Paradigm Agency
10100 Santa Monica Bl-25th Fl
Los Angeles, CA 90067
Actor V: 12/13/96

Bryan Lake Rd/FRD #2
Mt Kisco, NY 10549
Alternate V: 02/02/96

Marshall, Garry
c/o ICM
8942 Wilshire Bl
Beverly Hills, CA 90211
Producer V: 12/11/96

Marshall, James
c/o ICM
8942 Wilshire Bl
Beverly Hills, CA 90211
Actor V: 01/27/96

Marshall, Paula
Innovative Artists
1999 Ave of the Stars #2850
Los Angeles, CA 90067
Actress V: 01/15/97

Marshall, Penny
Creative Artists Agency
9830 Wilshire Bl
Beverly Hills, CA 90212
Actress V: 12/07/96

7150 La Presa Dr
Los Angeles, CA 90068
Alternate V: 05/16/96

1849 Sawtelle Bl #500
Los Angeles, CA 90025
Forwarded V: 02/01/96

Marshall, Peter
16714 Oakview Dr
Encino, CA 91316
Celebrity V: 06/16/96

Marshall Agency
23900 Hawthorne Bl #100
Torrence, CA 90505
Talent Agency V: 02/02/96

Marshall Tucker Band
Cabin Fever
100 W Putnam
Greenwich, CT 06830
Musical Group V: 02/02/96

Martel Agency
1680 N Vine St #203
Hollywood, CA 90028
Talent Agency V: 02/19/96

Martens, Wilford
Wetstraat 16
Brussel 1000, Belgium
Politician V: 03/01/96

Marth, Frank
8538 Eastwood Rd
Los Angeles, CA 90046
Actor V: 03/20/96

Martika
8995 Elevado Ave
Los Angeles, CA 90069
Actress V: 01/21/96

Martin, Andrea
Gilla Roos
9744 Wilshire Bl #203
Beverly Hills, CA 90212
Actress V: 02/22/96

Wm Morris Agency
151 El Camino Dr
Beverly Hills, CA 90212
Alternate V: 02/22/96

Martin, Helen
1440 N Fairfax #109
Los Angles, CA 90046-3939
Actress V: 04/27/96

Martin, Jared
Kohner Agency
9300 Wilshire Bl #555
Beverly Hills, CA 90212
Actor V: 05/06/96

Martin, Joe
King Features
235 E 45th St
New York, NY 10017
Cartoonist V: 04/23/96

Martin, Kellie
Gersh Agency
232 N Canon Dr
Beverly Hills, CA 90210
Actress V: 02/22/96

Martin, Mark
Roush Racing
PO Box 1089
Liberty, NC 27298
NASCAR Driver V: 03/02/96

Martin, Pamela Sue
4108 Farmdale Ave
N Hollywood, CA 91604
Actress V: 10/23/96

Martin, Steve
PO Box 929
Beverly Hills, CA 90213
Actor V: 11/20/96

Martin, Steve, Cont.
c/o ICM
8942 Wilshire Bl
Beverly Hills, CA 90211
Alternate V: 01/14/96

Martinelli, Elsa
Consul Cinemat
Viale Parioli 5994
Roma I-00197 Italy
Actress V: 11/01/96

Martinez, A
6835 Wildlife Rd
Malibu, CA 90265
Actor V: 01/16/96

Martini, Steven
c/o HWA
1964 Westwood Bl #400
Los Angeles, CA 90025
Actor V: 01/15/97

Mason, Marsha
c/o ICM
8942 Wilshire Bl
Beverly Hills, CA 90211
Actress V: 12/11/96

Massey, Daniel
Leading Artists
68 Saint James St
London SW1, England
Actor V: 02/16/96

c/o Agency
388 Oxford St
London W1, England
Alternate V: 02/28/96

Mast, Rick
Precision Racing
PO Box 569
Denver, NC 28037
NASCAR Driver V: 03/02/96

Masterson, Mary Stuart
PO Box 1249
White River Jct, VT 05001
Actress V: 03/02/96

c/o ICM
40 W 57th St
New York, NY 10019
Forwarded V: 03/02/96

Mastrantonio, Mary Elizabeth
8942 Wilshire Bl
Beverly Hills, CA 90211
Actress V: 12/01/96

Masur, Richard
Smith & Associates
121 N San Vicente Bl
Beverly Hills, CA 90211
Actor V: 12/15/96

Matera, Fran
King Features
235 E 45th St
New York, NY 10017
Cartoonist V: 02/14/96

Matheson, Tim
Creative Artists Agency
9830 Wilshire Bl
Beverly Hills, CA 90212
Actor V: 12/07/96

Mathews, Banjo
PO Box 426
Arden, NC 28704
NASCAR Driver V: 03/02/96

Mathias, Bob
7469 E Pine Ave
Fresno, CA 93727
Track Star V: 02/01/96

Mathis, Johnny
PO Box 69278
Los Angeles, CA 90069-0278
Singer V: 03/03/96

3500 W Olive Ave #750
Burbank, CA 91505
Alternate V: 11/01/96

1469 Stebbins Terrace
Los Angeles, CA 90069
Alternate V: 01/05/96

Mathis, Samantha
Wm Morris Agency
151 S El Camino Dr
Beverly Hills, CA 90212
Actress V: 10/10/96

PO Box 480137
Los Angeles, CA 90048
Alternate V: 01/13/97

Matlin, Marlee
12304 Santa Monica Bl #119
Los Angeles, CA 90025
Actress V: 03/21/96

Mattea, Kathy
706 18th Ave South
Nashville, TN 37203
Singer V: 01/21/96

Matthau, Walter
1999 Ave of the Stars #2100
Los Angeles, CA 90067
Actor V: 10/23/96

278 Toyopa Dr
Pacific Palisades, CA 90272
Alternate V: 04/01/96

Mattingly, Thomas K
NASA/LBJ Space Center
Houston, TX 77058
Astronaut V: 03/03/96

Mattioli, Dr Joseph
Pocono Int'l Raceway
PO Box 500
Long Pond, PA 18334
NASCAR Official V: 03/02/96

Mature, Victor
PO Box 706
Rancho Santa Fe, CA 92067
Actor V: 02/27/96

Mauldin, Bill
North American Syndicate
2821 Europa Dr
Costa Mesa, CA 92626-3525
Cartoonist V: 01/02/96

Maven, Max
1746 N Orange Dr #1106
Los Angeles, CA 90028
Magician V: 03/09/96

Max, Peter
118 Riverside Dr
New York, NY 10024
Artist V: 04/16/96

Maxwell-Reid, Daphne
Wm Morris Agency
151 El Camino Dr
Beverly Hills, CA 90212
Actress V: 02/22/96

May, Robert Alden
Cine-F/X Studios
190 Main St
Big Pine, CA 93513
FX Master V: 04/01/96

Mayall, John
c/o AFTG
816 W Evergreen
Chicago, IL 60622
Musician V: 06/18/96

Mayfield, Jeremy
Yarborough Racing
9617 Dixie River Rd
Charlotte, NC 28270
NASCAR Driver V: 02/08/96

Kranefuss-Haas Racing
163 Rolling Hills Rd
Mooresville, NC 28115
Alternate V: 10/23/96

Maynard, Don
6545 Butterfield Dr
El Paso, TX 79932
Football Star V: 02/13/96

Mayo, Virginia
109 E Avenida de las Arboles
Thousand Oaks, CA 91360
Actress V: 05/12/96

c/o Webb
7500 Devista Dr
Los Angeles, CA 90046
Alternate V: 02/22/96

Mayo, Whitman
Paradigm Agency
10100 Santa Monica Bl-25th Fl
Los Angeles, CA 90067
Actor V: 12/13/96

Mayron, Melanie
Gersh Agency
232 N Canon Dr
Beverly Hills, CA 90210
Actress V: 12/09/96

7510 W Sunset Bl
Los Angeles, CA 90046
Alternate V: 10/23/96

1418 N Ogden Drive
Los Angeles, CA 90046
Forwarded V: 02/03/96

210 W 70th St #1503
New York, NY 10023
Forwarded V: 03/21/96

Mays, Willie
PO Box 2410
Menlo Park, CA 94026
Baseball Star V: 01/12/96

Mazar, Debbi
Flick East-West
9057 Nemo St #A
W Hollywood, CA 90046
Actress V: 02/22/96

Mazza, Valeria
344 E 59th St
New York, NY 10012-1155
Model V: 11/11/96

Mazzucchelli
326 Washington
Hoboken, NJ 07030
Artist V: 02/21/96

McArdle, Andrea
713 Disston St
Philadelphia, PA 19111
Actress V: 03/23/96

McArthur, Alex
10435 Wheatland Ave
Sunland, CA 91040
Actor V: 03/12/96

McArthur Jr, William S
NASA/LBJ Space Center
Houston, TX 77058
Astronaut V: 03/03/96

McBain, Diane
c/o Walker
156 Keats Circle
Ventura, CA 93003-5513
Actress V: 05/06/96

McBain, Ed
Evan Hunter
Box 339-324 Main Ave
Norwalk, CT 06851
Author V: 03/14/96

McBride, Jeff
305 W 52nd St
New York, NY 10013
Magician V: 03/09/96

McBride, Jon A
NASA/LBJ Space Center
Houston, TX 77058
Astronaut V: 03/03/96

McBroom, Amanda
Ambrosio/Mortimer
9150 Wilshire Bl #175
Beverly Hills, CA 90212
Actress V: 02/22/96

McCall, Mitzi
Epstein/Wyckoff & Associates
280 S Beverly Dr #400
Beverly Hills, CA 90212
Actress V: 12/08/96

3635 Wrightwood Dr
Studio City, PA 91604
Alternate V: 03/23/96

McCalla, Irish
c/o McIntyres
920 Oak Terrace
Prescott, AZ 86301
Actress V: 02/01/96

McCallister, Lon
PO Box 6040
Stateline, NV 89449
Actor V: 06/15/96

McCallum, David
Buckwald & Associates
9229 Sunset Bl #710
Los Angeles, CA 90069
Actor V: 12/06/96

40 W 62nd St-#9 West
New York, NY 10021
Alternate V: 01/12/96

McCambridge, Mercedes
Hartig Agency
114 E 28th St
New York, Ny 10016
Actress V: 04/08/96

2500 Torrey Pines Rd #1203
La Jolla, CA 92037
Alternate V: 02/03/96

McCandless, Bruce
NASA/LBJ Space Center
Houston, TX 77058
Astronaut V: 03/03/96

McCarthy, Andrew
4708 Vesper Ave
Sherman Oaks, CA 91403
Actor V: 02/03/96

McCarthy, Jenny
2112 Broadway
Santa Monica, CA 90404-2912
Actress V: 01/11/97

McCarthy, Joseph J
2305 Lawson Rd-Apt D
Delray Beach, FL 33445
War Hero V: 03/17/96

McCarthy, Kevin
Innovative Artists
1999 Ave of the Stars #2850
Los Angeles, CA 90067
Actor V: 12/11/96

McCarthy, Nobu
c/o Cuthbert
372 N Encinitas
Monrovia, CA 91016
Actress V: 03/23/96

McCashin, Constance
c/o MTA
4526 Wilshire Bl
Los Angeles, CA 90010
Actress V: 02/22/96

McCay, Peggy
Special Artists
335 N Maple Dr #360
Beverly Hills, CA 90210
Actress V: 02/22/96

McClanahan, Rue
9454 Wilshire Bl #405
Beverly Hills, CA 90212-2907
Actress V: 11/01/96

c/o APA
9000 Sunset Bl #1200
Los Angeles, CA 90069
Alternate V: 12/02/96

1660 Woodvale Rd
Encino, CA 91436
Forwarded V: 01/03/97

McClory, Sean
6612 Whitley Terrace
Los Angeles, CA 90069
Actor V: 06/14/96

McClure, Morgan
McClure Racing
Rt 10-Box 780
Abington, VA 24210
NASCAR Owner V: 03/02/96

McConaughey, Matthew
PO Box 1202
Malibu, CA 90265-1202
Actor V: 01/10/97

McConnell, Judith
3300 Bennett Dr
Los Angeles, CA 90068
Actress V: 01/19/96

McCoo, Marilyn
Wm Morris Agency
151 El Camino Dr
Beverly Hills, CA 90212
Singer V: 02/22/96

PO Box 7905
Beverly Hills, CA 90212
Alternate V: 01/12/96

McCord, Kent
Sindell & Associates
8271 Melrose Ave #202
Los Angeles, CA 90069
Actor V: 12/14/96

1738 N Orange Grove
Los Angeles, CA 90046
Alternate V: 03/15/96

McCormick, Maureen
Artists Group
10100 Santa Monica Bl #2490
Los Angeles, CA 90067
Actress V: 02/22/96

McCoy, Neal
PO Box 9610
Longview, TX 75608-9610
Singer V: 11/01/96

McCoy, Sylvester
BBC-TV Center
Wood Lane
London, W12 8QT England
Actor V: 03/01/96

McCulley, Michael J
NASA/LBJ Space Center
Hoston, TX 77058
Astronaut V: 01/31/96

McDermott, Dylan
ABC-TV
77 W 66th St
New York, NY 10023
Actor V: 01/10/97

McDermott, Dylan, Cont.
2700 Neilson Way #1133
Santa Monica, CA 90405
Alternate V: 01/15/97

McDivitt, James A
PO Box 3501
Anaheim, CA 92803
Astronaut V: 01/14/97

Rockwell Int'l
1745 Jeff Davis Hwy #1200
Arlington, VA 22202
Alternate V: 03/30/96

NASA/LBJ Space Center
Houston, TX 77058
Forwarded V: 03/03/96

McDonald, Country Joe
PO Box 7158
Berkeley, CA 94707-0158
Singer V: 03/15/96

McDowall, Roddy
3110 Brookdale Rd
Studio City, CA 91604
Actor V: 03/03/96

Innovative Artists
1999 Ave of the Stars #2850
Los Angeles, CA 90067
Alternate V: 12/11/96

McDowell, Malcolm
10100 Santa Monica Bl-25th Fl
Los Angeles, CA 90067
Actor V: 12/13/96

Markham/Frogget Agency
4 Windmill St
London W1P 1HF, England
Alternate V: 02/18/96

McEnery, Peter
Peters Ltd
10 Buckingham St
London W1, England
Actor V: 01/12/96

Norman Boyack
9 Cork St
London W1, England
Alternate V: 02/28/96

McEnroe, John
23712 Malibu Colony Dr
Malibu, CA 90265
Tennis Star V: 03/02/96

McEntire, Reba
Starstruck Talent
PO Box 121996
Nashville, TN 37212-1996
Singer V: 02/02/96

Wm Morris Agency
151 El Camino Dr
Beverly Hills, CA 90212
Alternate V: 02/22/96

McFadden, Gates
Innovative Artists
1999 Ave of the Stars #2850
Los Angeles, CA 90067
Actress V: 12/11/96

2332 E Allview Terrace
Los Angeles, CA 90068-3021
Alternate V: 02/04/96

2510 Canyon Dr
Los Angeles, CA 90068
Forwarded V: 02/01/96

Star Trek-TNG/Paramount
5555 Melrose Ave
Hollywood, CA 90038
Forwarded V: 03/04/96

McFerrin, Bobby
Original Artists
853 Broadway #1901
New York, NY 10003
Singer V: 12/01/96

McGavin, Darren
Gersh Agency
232 N Canon Dr
Beverly Hills, CA 90210
Actor V: 12/09/96

8643 Holloway Plaza
Los Angeles, CA 90069
Alternate V: 03/02/96

PO Box 2939
Beverly Hills, CA 90213
Forwarded V: 03/17/96

McGee, Henry
c/o CDA
47 Courtfield Rd Apt-20
London SW7 4DB, England
Actor V: 03/17/96

McGillis, Kelly
13428 Maxella Ave #513
Marina del Rey, CA 90292
Actress V: 05/18/96

303 Whitehead St
Key West, FL 33040
Alternate V: 12/01/96

2699 S Bayshore Dr #400
Miami, FL 33133-5408
Forwarded V: 03/30/96

The Agency
40 W 57th St
New York, NY 10019
Forwarded V: 03/17/96

McGinley, John
Innovative Artists
1999 Ave of the Stars #2850
Los Angeles, CA 90067
Actor V: 12/11/96

McGinnis, Doug
5341 Silverlode Dr
Placerville, CA 95667
Stuntman V: 11/11/96

McGlynn, Dennis
Dover Downs Speedway
PO Box 843
Dover, DE 19903
NASCAR Official V: 03/02/96

McGoohan, Patrick
Innovative Artists
1999 Ave of the Stars #2850
Los Angeles, CA 90067
Actor V: 12/11/96

16808 Bollinger Dr
Pacific Palisades, CA 90272
Alternate V: 02/03/96

McGovern, Elizabeth
9161 Hazen Dr
Beverly Hills, CA 90210
Actress V: 03/21/96

McGovern, George S
Friendship Station
Box 5591
Washington, DC 20016
Politician V: 03/20/96

McGovern, Maureen
163 Amsterdam Ave #174
New York, NY 10023-5001
Actress V: 10/23/96

529 W 42nd St #7F
New York, NY 10036
Forwarded V: 03/23/96

McGraw, Tug
PO Box 7575
Philadelphia, PA 19101
Baseball Star V: 01/12/96

Coleshill Rose Valley Rd
Media, PA 19063
Alternate V: 01/20/96

1 Dale Lane
Wallingford, PA 19086
Forwarded V: 12/10/96

McGuinn, Roger
c/o Rush
1600 Varick St
New York, NY 10013
Singer V: 01/05/96

McGuire, Dorothy
10351 Santa Monica Bl #300
Los Angeles, CA 90025
Actress V: 05/16/96

121 Copley Pl
Beverly Hills, CA 90210
Forwarded V: 03/22/96

McHattie, Stephen
c/o Buchwald
9229 Sunset Bl #710
Los Angeles, CA 90069
Actor V: 03/11/96

McKay, Gardner
445 Kawailoa Rd #10
Kailua, HI 96734-3167
Actor V: 02/12/96

McKay, Jan
252 Lumahai Pl
Honolulu, HI 96825-2120
Actor V: 02/02/96

McKay, Woody
Darlington Raceway
PO Box 500
Darlington, SC 29532
NASCAR Official V: 03/02/96

McKean, Michael
275 Bell Canyon Rd
Canoga Park, CA 91307
Actor V: 09/11/96

833 Thornhill Rd
Calabasas, CA 91302-2161
Alternate V: 01/03/97

McKearn, Leo
Hatton & Baker
18 Jermyn St
London SW1Y 6HN, England
Actor V: 02/28/96

McKellar, Danica
c/o APA
9000 Sunset Bl #1200
Los Angeles, CA 90069
Actress V: 02/22/96

McKenna, Virginia
Cherry Tree Cottage
Cold Harbour, Dorking
Surry RH5 6HA, England
Actress V: 02/17/96

McKeon, Nancy
PO Box 1873
Studio City, CA 91614
Actress V: 06/17/96

McKern, Leo
c/o Richard Hatton
29 Roehampton Lane
London SW15 5JR, England
Actor V: 12/01/96

c/o Agency
388-396 Oxford St
London W1 9HE, England
Forwarded V: 03/17/96

McKinnon, Mona
4756 Aynsley Circle
Memphis, TN 38117-4002
Personality V: 02/01/96

McKuen, Rod
1155 Angelo Dr
Beverly Hills, CA 90210
Singer V: 01/18/96

McLachlan, Sarah
1717 W 4th Ave
Vancover, BC, V6J 1M2, Canada
Singer V: 03/02/96

McLaughlin, Lise-Ann
c/o Stone
9 Newburgh St
London W1V 1LH, England
Actress V: 03/06/96

McLerie, Allyn Ann
3344 Campanil Dr
Santa Barbara, CA 93109
Actress V: 03/23/96

McMahon, Ed
McMahon Communications
12000 Crest Court
Beverly Hills, CA 90210
Host V: 02/02/96

1050 Summit Dr
Beverly Hills, CA 90210-2832
Alternate V: 04/07/96

McMahon, Jim
Zucker Sports Mgmt
5 Revere Dr #201
Northbrook, IL 60062
Football Star V: 07/14/96

Arizona Cardinals
8701 S Hardy
Tempe, AZ 85284
Forwarded V: 12/01/96

McMonagle, Donald R
NASA/LBJ Space Center
Hoston, TX 77058
Astronaut V: 01/31/96

McNamara, Robert S
1455 Pennslyvania Ave NW
Suite 515
Washington, DC 20004
Politician V: 04/14/96

2412 Tracy Place
Washington, DC 20008
Alternate V: 02/14/96

McNeil, Kate
Buchwald Agency
9229 Sunset Bl #710
Los Angeles, CA 90069
Actress V: 02/22/96

McNeill, Robert Duncan
Smith & Associates
121 N San Vicente Bl
Beverly Hills, CA 90211
Actor V: 11/01/96

McNeil, Don
110 Dewindt Rd
Winnetka, IL 60093
Radio Star V: 01/20/96

McNichol, Jimmy
PO Box 5813
Sherman Oaks, CA 91413-5813
Actor V: 04/12/96

McNichol, Kristy
15060 Ventura Bl #350
Sherman Oaks, CA 91403
Actress V: 04/01/96

PO Box 5813
Sherman Oaks, CA 91413-5813
Alternate V: 01/22/96

14355 Millbrook Dr
Sherman Oaks, CA 91423
Forwarded V: 04/12/96

McQuagg, Sam
8886 Hamilton Rd
Midland, GA 31820
NASCAR Driver V: 03/02/96

McRaney, Gerald
329 N Wetherly Dr #101
Beverly Hills, CA 90211
Actor V: 03/27/96

McRoberts, Briony
c/o Green
2 Conduit St
London W1R 9TG, England
Actress V: 03/06/96

McShane, Ian
c/o Agency
388 Oxford St
London W1, England
Actor V: 03/14/96

c/o ICM
8942 Wilshire Bl
Beverly Hills, CA 90211
Alternate V: 12/11/96

76 Oxford St
London W1N 0AX, England
Alternate V: 03/27/96

c/o Humiston
11620 Wilshire Bl #700
Los Angeles, CA 90025-1781
Forwarded V: 11/10/96

McVey, Tyler
4717 Laurel Canyon Bl #206
N Hollywood, CA 91607
Actor V: 07/03/96

McVie, Christine
9744 Lloydcrest Dr
Beverly Hills, CA 90210
Singer V: 06/17/96

McWilliams, Caroline
2195 Mandeville Canyon Rd
Los Angeles, CA 90049
Actress V: 03/23/96

Premiere Artists Agency
8899 Beverly Bl #510
Los Angeles, CA 90048
Alternate V: 12/13/96

Meade, Carl J
NASA/LBJ Space Center
Hoston, TX 77058
Astronaut V: 01/31/96

Meadowlands Arena
Byrne Meadowlands Arena
PO Box 504
E Rutherford, NJ 07073
Business Group V: 02/01/96

Meadows, Jayne
Artists Group
10100 Santa Monica Bl #2490
Los Angeles, CA 90067
Actress V: 12/04/96

16185 Woodvale Rd
Encino, CA 91436
Alternate V: 03/23/96

Meaney, Colm
11921 Laurel Hills Rd
Studio City, CA 91604
Actor V: 11/01/96

Gage Group
9255 Sunset Bl #515
Los Angeles, CA 90069
Alternate V: 12/08/96

Star Trek-DS9
5555 Melrose Ave
Hollywood, CA 90036
Alternate V: 02/23/96

Meaney, Kevin
Gersh Agency
232 N Canon Dr
Beverly Hills, CA 90210
Actor V: 01/15/96

Means, Jimmy
Means Racing
102 Greenbriar Dr
Forest City, NC 28043
NASCAR Driver V: 03/02/96

Meara, Anne
Innovative Artists
1999 Ave of the Stars #2850
Los Angeles, CA 90067
Actress V: 02/22/96

1776 Broadway #1800
New York, NY 10019
Alternate V: 01/05/96

Meat Loaf
Marvin Aday/Left Bank Mgmt
6255 Sunset Bl #2100
Los Angeles, CA 90028
Singer V: 01/05/96

Mechsner, Susan
Jamison Green
1408 S Palm Ave
San Gabriel, CA 91776
Actress V: 04/23/96

Medal of Honor Society
1317 E Hale St
Mesa, Az 85203
Society V: 03/15/96

Media Artist Group
8383 Wilshire Bl #954
Beverly Hills, CA 90211
Talent Agency V: 02/02/96

Media/Fox Pictures
PO Box 900
Beverly Hills, CA 90213
Production Office V: 12/15/96

Medina, Patricia
Thornton & Associates
12001 Ventura Place #201
Studio City, CA 91604
Actress V: 12/15/96

Medley, Bill
9841 Hot Springs Dr
Hunting Beach CA 92646
Singer V: 02/14/96

Melanie
131 Garden Ave #101
Clearwater, FL 34615
Singer V: 01/04/96

Melini, Angela
Playmate Promotions
8560 Sunset Bl
Los Angeles, CA 90069
Playmate V: 03/12/96

Mellencamp, John
Rt1 Box 361
Nashville, TN 47448
Singer V: 02/12/96

Belmont Mall Studio
Belmont, IN 47401
Alternate V: 02/11/96

Melling, Harry
PO Box 665
Dawsonville, GA 28677
Race Driver V: 03/12/96

Melnick, Bruce E
NASA/LBJ Space Center
Hoston, TX 77058
Astronaut V: 01/31/96

Melton, Sid
Commercials Unlimited
9601 Wilshire Bl #620
Beverly Hills, CA 90210
Actor V: 02/04/96

Melvin, Allan
271 N Bowling Green Way
Los Angeles, CA 90049
Actor V: 09/16/96

Melvin, Murry
Joy Jameson Ltd
7 West Eaton Place Mews
London, SW1 1X8LY England
Actor V: 03/16/96

Menot, Roya
House of Reps
9911 Pico Bl #1060
Los Angeles, CA 90035
Actress V: 02/23/96

Menzel, Jerry
c/o MK2
55 rue Traversiere
Paris 75012, France
Actor V: 02/09/96

Menzies, Heather
PO Box 5973-1006
Sheman Oaks, CA 91403
Actress V: 04/02/96

Mercer, Marian
The Agency
1800 Ave of the Stars #400
Los Angeles, CA 90067
Actress V: 02/23/96

Meredith, Burgess
25 Malibu Colony Rd-Box 757
Malibu, CA 90265
Actor V: 11/04/96

23736 Malibu Colony Dr
Malibu, CA 90265
Forwarded V: 03/21/96

Meredith, Don
PO Box 597
Santa Fe, NM 87504
Actor V: 04/21/96

Meriwether, Lee
Webb Enterprises
13834 Magnolia Bl
Sherman Oaks, CA 91423
Actress V: 12/15/96

12139 Jeanette Place
Granada Hills, CA 91344
Alternate V: 02/23/96

PO Box 260402
Encino, CA 91426
Forwarded V: 12/04/96

Merkle, Angela
Schonhauser Allee 104
1071 Berlin, Germany
Politician V: 02/01/96

Merli, Gino
605 Gino Merli Dr
Peckville, PA 18452
War Hero V: 02/09/96

Merrill, Dina
Gersh Agency
232 N Canon Dr
Beverly Hills, CA 90210
Actress V: 12/09/96

Metal Edge Magazine
233 Park Ave South
New York, NY 10003
Publisher V: 02/10/96

Metcalf, Eric
14800 Winding Way Dr
N Royalton, OH 44133
Actor V: 09/11/96

Metcalf, Laurie
11845 Kling St
N Hollywood, CA 91607-4009
Actress V: 12/07/96

Metcalf, Mark
Hagan Racing
PO Box 2010
Thomasville, NC 27360
NASCAR Crew V: 02/27/96

Metro-Goldwyn-Meyer
10000 W Washington Bl
Culver City, CA 90232
Production Office V: 03/17/96

Metropolitan Talent
4526 Wilshire Bl
Los Angeles, CA 90010
Talent Agency V: 02/02/96

Meyer, Russ
PO Box 3748
Hollywood, CA 90078
Director V: 11/01/96

Meyers, David
10 Summit Ave
Mill Valley, CA 94941
Producer V: 03/25/96

Meyers, Mike
c/o NBC
30 Rockefeller Plaza
New York, NY 10112
Actor V: 02/27/96

Meyers, Russell
770 N Orange Ave
Orlando, FL 32801
Cartoonist V: 02/14/96

Tribune Media
64 E Concord St
Orlando, FL 32800
Alternate V: 01/12/96

Miami Dolphins
Joe Robbie Stadium
2269 NW 199th St
Miami, FL 33056
Team Office V: 05/15/96

Miami Heat
Miami Arena
Miami, FL 33136-4102
Team Office V: 02/15/96

Miami Sound Machine
1575 NW 27th Ave
Miami, FL 33125
Musical Group V: 01/03/96

8730 Sunset Bl #600
Los Angeles, CA
Alternate V: 01/09/96

8390 SW 4 St
Miami, FL 33144
Forwarded V: 03/15/96

Michael, Gene
49 Union Ave
Upper Saddle River, NJ 07458
Baseball Star V: 11/01/96

Michael, George
2 Eden Place
London W8, England
Singer V: 02/01/96

2222 Mount Calvary Rd
Santa Barbara, CA 93105
Alternate V: 03/01/96

Michaels, Julie
PO Box 7304
N Hollywood, CA 91603
Actress V: 03/26/96

Michaels, Lorne
Broadway Video
1619 Broadway-9th Fl
New York, NY 10019
Producer V: 01/14/96

Michel, F Curtis
NASA/LBJ Space Center
Houston, TX 77058
Astronaut V: 03/03/96

Midkiff, Dale
4640 Mary Ellen Ave
Sherman Oaks, CA 91423-3322
Actor V: 03/14/96

Midler, Bette
820 N San Vicente Bl #69-D
Los Angeles, CA 90069
Actress V: 01/16/96

Mifune, Toshiro
9-30-7/Seijyo-Machi/Setagayaku
Tokyo 157, Japan
Actor V: 03/12/96

Milano, Alyssa
Wm Morris Agency
151 El Camino Dr
Beverly Hills, CA 90212
Actress V: 02/23/96

Miles, Joanna
2064 N Vine St
Los Angeles, CA 90068
Actress V: 02/26/96

Miles, Sarah
GRF International
82 Brook St
London W1Y 1YG, England
Actress V: 03/23/96

Marina Martin
6A Danbury St
London N1 8JJ, England
Alternate V: 02/28/96

Miles, Sylvia
240 Central Park South
New York City, NY 10019
Actress V: 03/01/96

Miles, Vera
PO Box 1704
Big Bear Lake, CA 92315-1704
Actress V: 02/04/96

Miller, Ann
Artists Group
10100 Santa Monica Bl #2490
Los Angeles, CA 90067
Actress V: 12/04/96

618 N Alta Dr
Beverly Hills, CA 90210
Alternate V: 11/28/96

Miller, Arthur
RR 1, Box 320
Tophet Road
Roxbury, CT 06783
Author V: 09/22/96

Miller, Butch
Miller Fan Club
2750 Pineridge Dr-Suite D
Grand Rapids, MI 49504
Race Driver V: 02/27/96

Miller, Cheryl
Tishman Agency
6767 Forest Lawn Dr
Los Angeles, CA 90068
Actress V: 01/12/96

Miller, David Wiley
King Features
235 E 45th St
New York, NY 10017
Cartoonist V: 07/30/96

Miller, Dennis
814 N Mansfield Ave
Los Angeles, CA 90038-3408
Actor V: 11/10/96

9560 Wilshire Bl #516
Beverly Hills, CA 90212
Alternate V: 01/13/97

Miller, Denny
323 E Matilija St #112
Ojai, CA 93023-2775
Actor V: 01/21/96

Miller, Dick
Gizmo Productions
8852 Wonderland Ave
Los Angeles, CA 90046
Actor V: 10/23/96

Miller, Johnny
PO Box 2260
Napa, CA 94558-2260
Golfer V: 02/18/96

Miller, Mitch
345 W 58th St
New York, NY 10019
Composer V: 02/04/96

Miller, Sharron
15301 Ventura Bl #345
Sherman Oaks, CA 91403
Director V: 03/01/96

Miller, Ty
450 1/2 Entrada Dr
Santa Monica, CA 90402-1304
Actor V: 01/12/96

Mills, Ally
c/o Schoen
606 Larchmont Bl #309
Los Angeles, CA 90004
Actress V: 02/22/96

Mills, Billy
124 Pecos
Raton, NM 87740
Olympian V: 07/01/96

Mills, Donna
Wm Morris Agency
151 El Camino
Beverly Hills, CA 90212
Actress V: 12/12/96

2660 Benedict Canyon
Beverly Hills, CA 90210
Alternate V: 10/23/96

3970 Overland Ave
Culver City, CA 90230
Forwarded V: 01/12/96

Mills, Hayley
Smith & Associates
121 N San Vicente Bl
Beverly Hills, CA 90211
Actress V: 12/15/96

81 High St
Hampton, Middlesex, England
Alternate V: 02/01/96

c/o Agency
388 Oxford St
London W1, England
Forwarded V: 03/11/96

Mills, John
Thames TV Ltd
306-316 Euston Rd
London NW1 3BB, England
Actor V: 03/22/96

Denham Village
Hill House
Buckinghamshire, England
Forwarded V: 12/17/96

Mills, Juliet
c/o Caulfied
4770 9th St #B
Carpenteria, CA 93013-1804
Actress V: 03/14/96

2890 Hidden Valley Lane
Santa Barbara, CA 93108
Alternate V: 01/05/96

4036 Foothill Rd
Carpinteria, CA 90313
Forwarded V: 02/12/96

Milmoe, Caroline
Martin-Smith
Half Moon Chamber
Chapel Walks
Manchester M2 1HN, England
Actress V: 06/03/96

Milner, Martin
1930 Century Park W #403
Los Angeles, CA 90067
Actor V: 10/23/96

Artists Group
10100 Santa Monica Bl #2490
Los Angeles, CA 90067
Alternate V: 01/28/96

Milsap, Ronnie
Denise Gentry
PO Box 121831
Nashville, TN 37212-1831
Singer V: 07/14/96

PO Box 40325
Nashville, TN 37204-0325
Alternate V: 01/21/96

Plan A
1900 Church St #102
Nashville, TN 37203
Alternate V: 02/02/96

PO Box 23109
Nashville, TN 37203
Forwarded V: 01/21/96

Milwaukee Brewers
Milwaukie County Stadium
Milwaukie, WI 53214
Team Office V: 02/15/96

Milwaukee Bucks
1001 N 4th St
Milwaukie, WI 53203-1312
Team Office V: 02/15/96

Mimieux, Yvette
500 Perugia Way
Los Angeles, CA 90077
Actress V: 11/28/96

Miner, Jan
PO Box 293
Southbury, CT 06488
Actress V: 03/23/96

Minnelli, Liza
LM Concerts
PO Box 790039
Middle Village, NY 11379-0039
Singer V: 11/01/96

LM Concerts
200 W 57th St #908
New York, NY 10019
Alternate V: 01/21/96

150 E 69th St #21G
New York, NY 10021
Forwarded V: 12/01/96

Minnesota Timberwolves
600 First Ave
N Minneapolis, MN 55403
Team Office V: 02/15/96

Minnesota Twins
501 Chicago Ave South
HH Humphrey Metrodome
Minneapolis, MN 55415
Team Office V: 02/15/96

Minnesota Vikings
9520 Viking Dr
Eden Prairie, MN 55344
Team Office V: 02/15/96

Miramar Agency
9157 Sunset Bl #300
Los Angeles, CA 90069
Talent Agency V: 03/19/96

Mirren, Helen
Al Parker
55 Park Lane
London W1, England
Actress V: 02/28/96

Miss America Paget
PO Box 119
Atlantic City, NJ 08404
Production Office V: 01/13/97

Mitchell, Edgar D
NASA/LBJ Space Center
Houston, TX 77058
Astronaut V: 11/11/96

Mitchell, George
US Senate
Washington, DC 20510-1902
Politician V: 04/04/96

Mitchell, Kevin
45110 Logan Ave
San Diego, CA 92113
Baseball Star V: 01/11/96

Mitchell, Sasha
9057 Nemo St-Suite A
W Hollywood, CA 90069
Actress V: 03/23/96

Mitchell Agency
4605 Lankershim Bl #201
N Hollywood, CA 91602
Talent Agency V: 03/17/96

Mitchner, James A
2706 Mountain Laurel Ln
Austin, TX 78703-1143
Author V: 01/16/96

Mitchum, John
15612 Liberty Circle
Neveda City, CA 95959
Actor V: 01/03/96

c/o Mitchum/Callow Prod
808 N Vine St
Falbrook, CA 92028
Alternate V: 01/02/96

Wild West Film Fest
87 Snell St
Sonora, CA 95370
Forwarded V: 02/10/96

Mitchum, Robert
PO Box 52516
Montecito, CA 93108
Actor V: 09/04/96

860 San Ysidro Rd
Santa Barbara, CA 93108
Alternate V: 04/10/96

Miyamura, Hiroshi H
1905 Mossman
Gallup, NM 87301
War Hero V: 02/04/96

Miyori, Kim
Smith & Associates
121 N San Vicente Bl
Beverly Hills, CA 90211
Actress V: 12/15/96

Mobley, Mary Ann
2751 Hutton Dr
Beverly Hills, CA 90210
Actress V: 03/13/96

Mobley, Mary Ann, Cont.
Wm Morris Agency
151 El Camino Dr
Beverly Hills, CA 90212
Alternate V: 02/01/96

Modine, Matthew
9696 Culver Bl #203
Culver City, CA 90232
Actor V: 06/07/96

Modrzejewski, Robert J
4725 Oporto Dr
San Diego, CA 92124
War Hero V: 01/16/96

Moe, Tommy
PO Box 100
Girdwood, AL 99587
Olympian V: 10/23/96

Moffet, Randy
110 Lakeover Dr
Athens, GA 30606
Baseball Star V: 12/10/96

Moise, Patty
NASCAR
1811 Volusia Ave
Daytona Beach, FL 32015
NASCAR Driver V: 03/02/96

Molinaro, Al
PO Box 9218
Glendale, CA 91226
Actor V: 01/14/96

Moll, Richard
Gold/Marshak
3500 W Olive Ave #1400
Burbank, CA 91505
Actor V: 12/10/96

Moller, Ralph
555 S Barrington Ave #325
Los Angeles, CA 90049
Fitness Expert V: 01/17/96

Mondale, Walter
2200 First Bank Place E
Minneapolis, MN 55411
Former VP USA V: 07/03/96

Mondale, Walter
Unit 45005, Box 258
APO-AP Tokyo, 96337-0001
Alternate V: 01/13/97

Money, Eddie
PO Box 1994
San Francisco, CA 94101
Singer V: 09/09/96

Monoson, Lawrence
CBS-Audience Services
51 W 52nd St
New York, NY 10019
Actor V: 12/12/96

Monroe, Caroline
c/o ICM
8942 Wilshire Bl
Beverly Hills, CA 90211
Actress V: 10/10/96

Montalban, Ricardo
1423 Oriole Dr
Los Angeles, CA 90069
Actor V: 08/24/96

Montana, Joe
326 Castilian Way
San Mateo, CA 94402
Football Star V: 11/01/96

PO Box 7342
Menlo Park, CA 94026
Alternate V: 01/16/96

KC Chiefs
1 Arrowhead Dr
Kansas City, MO 64129
Forwarded V: 02/01/96

Montana, Monte
10234 Escondito Canyon
Aqua Dulce, CA 91350
Actor V: 03/02/96

10326 Montana Lane
Aqua Dulce, CA 91350
Alternate V: 02/03/96

520 Murray Canyon
Palm Springs, CA 92264
Forwarded V: 05/22/96

Montgomery, Belinda
20th Century Artists
15315 Magnolia Bl #429
Sherman Oaks, CA 91403
Actress V: 12/15/96

Montgomery, George
PO Box 2187
Rancho Mirage, CA 92270
Actor V: 03/02/96

Montgomery, John Michael
PO Box 639
Danville, KY 40423-0639
Singer V: 11/01/96

Montgomery, Julia
8380 Melrose Ave #207
Los Angeles, CA 90069
Actress V: 10/23/96

Montiel, H Pierre
103 W 73rd St
New York, NY 10023
Artist V: 01/09/96

Montreal Canadians
Montreal Forum
2313 St Catherine West
Montreal, Quebec, Canada H3H 1N2
Team Office V: 02/01/96

Montreal Expos
PO Box 500, Station M
Olympic Stadium
Montreal Quebec
Canada H1V 3P2
Team Office V: 02/15/96

Moody, Bobby
c/o Childress
PO Box 1189-Industrial Dr
Welcome, NC 27374
Race Driver V: 03/12/96

Moody, Ron
28 Berkeley Square
London WIX 6HD, England
Actor V: 01/08/96

Moore, Alvy
487 Desert Falls Dr N
Palm Desert, CA 92211
Actor V: 11/20/96

Moore, Archie
3517 East St
San Diego, CA 92101
Boxing Star V: 01/11/96

Moore, Bud
4 Duck Lane
Isle of Pines, SC 29451
NASCAR Driver V: 03/02/96

c/o Moore Motorsports
400 N Fairview Ave
Spartanburg, SC 29304
Alternate V: 03/02/96

Moore, Clayton
4720 Park Olivo
Calabasas, CA 91302
Actor V: 02/04/96

Moore, Constance
10450 Wilshire Bl #1-B
Los Angeles, CA 90024
Actress V: 03/02/96

Moore, Debbi
Stone Manners
8091 Selma Ave
Los Angeles, CA 90046
Actress V: 03/11/96

Moore, Demi
c/o CAA
9830 Wilshire Bl
Beverly Hills, CA 90212
Actress V: 01/16/96

Moore, Dudley
73 Market St
Venice, CA 90291
Actor V: 01/08/96

5505 Ocean Front Walk
Marina Del Rey, CA 90292
Alternate V: 02/05/96

Moore, John Travers
827 N Justice
Hendersonville, NC 28739
Author V: 01/11/96

Moore, Juanita
3802-L Dunsford Lane
Inglewood, CA 90305
Actress V: 02/18/96

Moore, Mary Tyler
927 Fifth Ave
New York, NY 10021
Actress V: 11/01/96

510 E 86th St #21A
New York, NY 10010
Alternate V: 02/01/96

MTM Enterprises
4024 Radford Ave
Studio City, CA 91604
Alternate V: 07/03/96

Moore, Melba
7004 Kennedy Bl East #325D
Guttenberg, NJ 07093-5029
Singer V: 01/12/96

Moore, Melissa Anne
PO Box 802
Stillwater, MN 55082
Actress V: 10/23/96

11288 Ventura Bl #B-732
Studio City, CA 91604
Alternate V: 01/21/96

Moore, Roger
Chalet Fenil, Grund Bei
Staad, Switzerland
Actor V: 03/10/96

c/o Agency
388-396 Oxford St
London W1 9HE, England
Forwarded V: 03/17/96

Moore Artists
1551 S Robertson Bl
Los Angeles, CA 90035
Talent Agency V: 02/02/96

Moreau, Jeanne
George Beaume
3 Quia Malquais
Paris 75006, France
Actress V: 03/02/96

193 rue de l'Universite
75 007 Paris France
Alternate V: 06/17/96

c/o UFA
Kleiststrasse 13-26-1000
Berlin 30, Germany
Forwarded V: 02/09/96

Moreno, Rita
c/o APA
9000 Sunset Bl
Los Angeles, CA 90069
Actress V: 10/23/96

1620 Amalfi Dr
Pacific Palisades, CA 90272
Alternate V: 05/12/96

Moret, Angelique
2151 El Camino #1115
Beverly Hills, CA 90210
Actress V: 02/21/96

Morey, Bill
6310 San Vicente Bl
Beverly Hills, CA 90211
Actor V: 01/16/94

Morgan, Debbi
Stone Manners Talent
8091 Selma Ave
Los Angeles, CA 90068
Actress V: 12/15/96

Morgan, Harry
13172 Boca de Canon Ln
Los Angeles, CA 9049
Actor V: 02/01/96

Artists Group
10100 Santa Monica Bl #2490
Los Angeles, CA 90067
Alternate V: 01/15/96

Morgan, Jaye P
1185 La Grange Ave
Newbury Park, CA 91320-5316
Singer V: 08/28/96

Morgan, Lorrie
Susan Nadler Mgmt
1313 16th Ave South
Nashville, TN 37212
Singer V: 11/01/96

Morgan, Shelley Taylor
Pakula & King Agency
9229 Sunset Bl #315
Los Angeles, CA 90069
Actress V: 12/12/96

Morganna
PO Box 20281
Columbus, Ohio 43220
Celebrity V: 11/01/96

Moriarity, Cathy
8942 Wilshire Bl
Beverly Hills, CA 90211
Actress V: 12/11/96

Moriarty, Michael
Gage Group
9255 Sunset Bl #515
Los Angeles, CA 90069
Actor V: 03/11/96

MM Fan Club
PO Box 68
Soddy Daisy, TN 37379
Alternate V: 01/12/96

Morissette, Alanis
Maverick Entertainment
75 Rockefeller Plz #2100
New York, NY 10019
Singer V: 10/10/96

Morita, Pat
4007 Sunswept Dr
Studio City, CA 91604
Actor V: 02/28/96

Morris, Garret
3740 Barham Bl #E1167
Los Angeles, CA 90068
Actor V: 01/03/97

Morris, Gary
19905 S Bundy Dr-PH
Los Angeles, CA 90025
Singer V: 03/05/96

Gurley Company
3322 W End Ave #11
Nashville, TN 37203
Alternate V: 10/23/96

Morris, Howard
2723 Carmar Dr
Los Angeles, CA 90046-1008
Actor V: 02/01/96

Amsel/Eisenstadt
6310 San Vicente Bl #407
Los Angeles, CA 90048
Alternate V: 02/26/96

Morrison, Patricia
400 S Hauser Bl #9-L
Los Angeles, CA 90036
Actress V: 04/16/96

Morrison, Tommy
PO Box 701107
Tulsa, OK 74170-1107
Boxing Star V: 01/10/97

Morrison, Toni
c/o ICM
8942 Wilshire Bl
Beverly Hills, CA 90211
Author V: 01/14/96

Morrow, Rob
Wm Morris Agency
151 El Camino Dr
Beverly Hills, CA 90212
Actor V: 01/14/96

Morse, Barry
PO Box 1572
Jasper, Alberta, Canada
Actor V: 04/23/96

Morse, David
Wm Morris Agency
151 El Camino Dr
Beverly Hills, CA 90212
Actor V: 09/13/96

c/o Bikoff Agency
8721 Santa Monica Bl #21
W Hollywood, CA 90069
Alternate V: 03/17/96

Morse, Helen
147A King St
Sydney, NSW 2000, Australia
Actress V: 03/02/96

Morse, Robert
13830 Davana Terrace
Sherman Oaks, CA 91403
Actor V: 11/20/96

Baumen/Hiller
5750 Wilshire Bl #512
Los Angeles, CA 90036
Alternate V: 02/28/96

Morton, Joe
Schoen Agency
606 N Larchmont Bl #309
Los Angeles, CA 90004
Actor V: 12/13/96

Mosley, Bryan
Granada TV
36 Golden Square
London W1R 4AH, England
Actor V: 03/17/96

Moss, Kate
Elite Model Mgmt
111 E 22nd St #200
New York, NY 10010
Model V: 11/01/96

Women Inc
107 Green St
New York, NY 10012
Alternate V: 01/07/96

Calvin Klein
205 W 39th St
New York, NY 10018
Alternate V: 01/13/96

Moss & Associate
733 N Seward St-#PH
Los Angeles, CA 90038
Talent Agency V: 03/21/96

Most, Don
Epstein/Wyckoff
280 S Beverly Dr #400
Beverly Hills, CA 90212
Actor V: 12/08/96

Motion Picture Assn
14144 Ventura Bl
Sherman Oaks, CA 91423
Production Office V: 03/17/96

Motley Crue
Top Rock
9229 Sunet Bl #607
Los Angeles, CA 90069
Musical Group V: 03/14/96

Motown Records
Fan Mail
5750 Wilshire Bl #300
Los Angeles, CA 90036-3697
Musical Group V: 08/29/96

Movie Channel
1633 Broadway
New York, NY 10019
Network HQ V: 03/01/96

100 Universal City Plz-31st Fl
Unversal City, CA 91608
Alternate V: 03/17/96

Movie Club
12 Moray Ct
Baltimore, MD 21236
Publication V: 01/12/96

Movie Screen Magazine
Readers Services
35 Wilbur St
Lynbrook, NY 11563
Publisher V: 02/10/96

Moviecorp VII
3131 Lakeshore Bl W
Toronto, M8V 1K9 Ontario
Canada
Production Office V: 03/01/96

92 Isabella St
Toronto, M4Y 1N4 Ontario
Canada
Alternate V: 03/01/96

Movieline
1141 S Beverly Drive
Los Angeles, CA 90099-2024
Publisher V: 03/21/96

Movies From Fox
PO Box 900
Beverly Hills, CA 90213-0900
Production Office V: 12/15/96

Movita
2766 Motor Ave
Los Angeles, CA 90064
Actress V: 02/18/96

Mudd, Roger
7167 Old Dominion Dr
McLean, VA 22101
Commentator V: 03/01/96

3620 27th St South
Arlington, VA 22206
Alternate V: 02/16/96

Mueller-Stahl, Armin
Gartnweg 31
2430 Sirksdprf, Germany
Actor V: 01/17/96

Muir, Esther
587 Heritage Hills Dr #D
Somers, NY 10589-1908
Actress V: 02/18/96

Muldaur, Diana
Artists Group
10100 Santa Monica Bl #2490
Los Angeles, CA 90067
Actress V: 12/04/96

259 Quadro Vecchio Dr
Pacific Palisades, CA 90272
Alternate V: 04/18/96

Muldaur, Maria
PO Box 5535
Mill Valley, CA 94942-5525
Singer V: 02/27/96

Mulder, Karen
Elite Model Mgmt
8 bis, rue Le Cuirot
Paris F-75014 France
Model V: 11/01/96

Mulgrew, Kate
c/o MTA
4526 Wilshire Bl
Los Angeles, CA 90010
Actress V: 03/27/96

Mulhare, Edward
Henderson/Hogan
247 S Beverly Dr #102
Beverly Hills, CA 90210
Actor V: 02/16/96

Mulhern, Matt
9171 Wilshire Bl #436
Beverly Hills, CA 90210
Actor V: 01/16/96

Mull, Martin
338 Chadbourne Ave
Los Angeles, CA 90049
Actor V: 01/22/96

Mullane, Richard
NASA/LBJ Space Center
Houston, TX 77058
Astronaut V: 03/03/96

Mullard, Arthur
Essannay Ltd
75 Hammersmith Rd
London W14, England
Actor V: 02/27/96

Mullavey, Greg
606 N Larchmont #309
Los Angeles, CA 90004
Actor V: 11/11/96

Muller, Lillian
3435 Ocean Park Bl #112-C
Santa Monica, CA 90405
Playmate V: 01/13/97

Muller, Marius
ZBF Agentur
Leopoldstrasse 19
8000 Munchen 40, Germany
Actor V: 01/17/96

Mulligan, Richard
419 Larchmont Bl #129
Los Angeles, CA 90004
Actor V: 03/24/96

Mulloy, John
Childress Racing
PO Box 1189-Industrial Dr
Welcome, NC 27374
NASCAR Crew V: 03/12/96

MultiMedia Films
10401 W Jefferson Bl
Culver City, CA 90232
Production Office V: 03/17/96

Mumy, Bill
2419 Laurel Pass Ave
Los Angeles, CA 90046
Actor V: 02/04/96

8383 Wilshire Bl #954
Beverly Hills, CA 90211
Forwarded V: 03/15/96

Babylon Productions
8615 Tamarack Ave
Sun Valley, CA 91352
Forwarded V: 01/14/96

Sindell & Associates
8271 Melrose Ave #202
Los Angeles, CA 90069
Forwarded V: 12/14/96

Munro, Caroline
c/o ICM
76 Oxford St
London W1N OAX, England
Actress V: 10/23/96

22 Grafton St
London W1, England
Forwarded V: 01/17/96

Murphy, Ben
Artists Agency
10000 Santa Monica Bl #305
Los Angeles, CA 90067
Actor V: 12/03/96

3601 Vista Pacifica #17
Malibu, CA 90265
Alternate V: 06/17/96

Murphy, Eddie
c/o ICM
8942 Wilshire Bl
Beverly Hills, CA 90211
Actor V: 01/14/96

152 W 57th St #4700
New York, NY 10019
Alternate V: 01/20/96

Murphy, John Cullen
King Features
235 E 45th St
New York, NY 10017
Cartoonist V: 05/01/96

Murphy, Michael Martin
207K Paseo del Pueblo Sur
Taos, NM 87571
Singer V: 02/02/96

Murphy, Terry
Hard Copy/Paramount
5555 Melrose Ave
Hollywood, CA 90038-3197
Commentator V: 01/31/96

Murphy Agency
6014 Greenbush Ave
Van Nuys, CA 91401
Talent Agency V: 02/19/96

Murray, Barbara
Rank Organization
6 Connaught Pl
London W2 2EZ, England
Actress V: 01/17/96

Murray, Bill
c/o CAA
9830 Wilshire Bl
Beverly Hills, CA 90212
Actor V: 01/14/96

RD 1-PO Box 573
Washingtin Springs Rd
Palisades, NY 10964
Alternate V: 03/27/96

Murray, Don
Blake Agency
415 N Camden Dr #121
Beverly Hills, CA 90210
Actor V: 12/06/96

1201 La Patera Canyon Rd
Goleta, CA 93117
Alternate V: 02/05/96

Murray, Jan
1157 Calle Vista Dr
Beverly Hills, CA 90210
Actor V: 09/09/96

Murtagh, Kate
15146 Moorpark St
Sherman Oaks, CA 91403
Actress V: 06/17/96

Musante, Tony
20th Century Artists
15315 Magnolia Bl #429
Sherman Oaks, CA 91403
Actor V: 12/15/96

38 Bedford St
New York, NY 10014
Alternate V: 06/18/96

Museum of Modern Art
Department of Film
11 W 53rd St
New York, NY 10019
Archive V: 03/20/96

Museum of TV & Radio
25 W 52nd St
New York, NY 10014
Archive V: 01/30/96

Musgrave, F Story
NASA/LBJ Space Center
Houston, TX 77058
Astronaut V: 03/03/96

Musgrave, Ted
Radius Motorsports
PO Box 950
Denver, NC 28037
NASCAR Driver V: 03/02/96

Musial, Stan
1655 Des Perez Rd #125
St Louis, MO 63131
Baseball Star V: 12/01/96

Mussolini, Alessandra
Camera di Deputati
Gruppo del MSI-DN
I-00100 Rome, Italy
Politician V: 12/19/96

Muti, Ornella
17a Via N Martelli 3
Rome, Italy
Actress V: 01/17/96

Myers, Cynthia
PO Box 5000-82
Palmdale, CA 93535
Model V: 10/23/96

PO Box 901358
Palmdale, CA 93590-1358
Alternate V: 10/23/96

Myers, Danny
Childress Racing
PO Box 1189-Industrial Dr
Welcome, NC 27374
NASCAR Crew V: 03/12/96

Myers, Mike
9150 Wilshire Bl #350
everly Hills, CA 90212
Actor V: 01/03/96

N

NASA
NASA/LBJ Space Center
Houston, TX 77058
Test Center V: 12/15/96

NASA Magazine
Internal ComBranch
Code P-2 NASA HQ
Washington, DC 20402
Publisher V: 03/03/96

NASCAR Fan Membership
PO Box 2875
Daytona Beach, FL 32015-2875
Fan Service V: 03/14/96

NASCAR Organization
1811 Volusia Ave
Daytona Beach, FL 32015
Production Office V: 03/14/96

NASH BRIDGES
DJ Company/Rysher
PO Box 6909
Burbank, CA 91505
Production Office V: 12/15/96

CBS-TV
51 W 52nd St
New York, NY 10019
Alternate V: 12/15/96

NBC-TV
30 Rockefeller Plaza
New York, NY 10112
Network HQ V: 03/01/96

3000 W Alemeda
Burbank, CA 91523
Alternate V: 03/01/96

NED AND STACEY
Fox-TV
PO Box 900
Beverly Hills, CA 90213
Production Office V: 12/15/96

New Adventures Of Robin Hood
c/o TNT
One CNN Center
PO Box 105366
Atlanta, GA 30348
Audience Services V: 12/12/96

NEW YORK NEWS
WB-TV
460 West 16th ST-6th Fl
New York, NY 10011
Production Office V: 10/23/96

NEW YORK UNDERCOVER
Fox-TV
PO Box 900
Beverly Hills, CA 90213
Production Office V: 12/15/96

NEWS HOUR
Jim Lehrer
2700 S Quincy St #250
Arlington, VA 22206
Production Office V: 01/14/96

NEWSRADIO
NBC-TV
30 Rockefeller Plaza
New York, NY 10112
Production Office V: 12/15/96

NICK FRENO:LICENSED TEACHEI
WB-TV
1438 N Gower
Hollywood, CA 90028
Viewer Services V: 11/11/96

NIGHTLINE
ABC-TV
1717 De Sales St NW
Washington, DC 20036
Production Office V: 03/19/96

NURSES
Witt/Thomas Production
846 N Cahuenga Bl
Hollywood, CA 90038
Production Office V: 01/20/96

NYPD BLUE
ABC-TV
77 W 66th St
New York, NY 10023
Production Office V: 12/15/96

Bochco Prod/Fox TV
10201 W Pico Bl
Los Angeles, CA 90035
Alternate V: 01/16/96

Bochco Prods/Fox TV
5555 Melrose Ave
Culver City, CA 90232
Forwarded V: 10/23/96

Nabor, John
PO Box 50107
Pasadena, CA 91115
Olympian V: 01/21/96

Nabors, Jim
151 El Camino Dr
Beverly Hills, CA 90212
Actor V: 01/21/96

215 Kulamanu
Honolulu, HI 96816
Alternate V: 04/01/96

Nader, George
893 Camino del Sur
Palm Springs, CA 92262
Actor V: 01/14/96

Nader, Ralph
PO Box 19367
Washington, DC 20036
Consumer Advocate V: 09/02/96

Nagel, Steven R
NASA LBJ Space Center
Houston, TX 77058
Astronaut V: 03/03/96

Najimy, Kathy
Creative Artists Agency
9830 Wilshire Bl
Beverly Hills, CA 90212
Actress V: 12/07/96

120 W 45th St #3601
New York, NY 10036-4041
Alternate V: 02/01/96

Namath, Joe
300 E 51st St #11A
New York, NY 10022
Football Star V: 12/10/96

Napier, Charles
Star Route Box 60H
Caliente, CA 93518
Actor V: 02/12/96

c/o Triton
1964 Westwood Bl #900
Los Angeles, CA 90024
Alternate V: 01/16/96

Naples, Toni
Wilder Agency
8306 Wilshire Bl #724
Beverly Hills, CA 90211-2382
Actress V: 03/14/96

Nash, Graham
14930 Ventura Bl #205
Sherman Oaks, CA 91403-3489
Singer V: 08/28/96

Nashville Network
2806 Opryland Dr
Nashville, Tn 37214
Network HQ V: 03/01/96

Nat'l Archives
Motion Picture/Sound/Video
Pennsylvania Ave & 8th St NW
Washington, DC 20408
Archive V: 01/30/96

Nat'l Assn of Fan Clubs
Ms Linda Kay
PO Box 7487
Burbank, CA 91510
Fan Service V: 02/12/96

Nat'l Center Film & Video
American Film Institute
PO Box 27999
2021 N Western Ave
Los Angeles, CA 90027
Archive V: 03/20/96

Nat'l Endowment of Arts
1100 Pennsylvania Ave NW
Washington, DC 20506
Offices V: 01/27/96

Nat'l Enquirer
600 South East Coast Ave
Lantana, FL 33462
Publisher V: 02/10/96

Nat'l Examiner
5401 NW Broken Sound Bl
Boca Raton, FL 33487
Publisher V: 02/10/96

Nat'l Football League
410 Park Ave
New York, NY 10022
League HQ V: 02/10/96

Nat'l League HQ
350 Park Ave
New York, NY 10022
Team Office V: 02/15/96

Nathe & Associates
8281 Melrose Ave #200
Los Angeles, CA 90046
Talent Agency V: 02/19/96

Neal, Patricia
45 East End Ave #4C
New York, NY 10028
Actress V: 11/20/96

Paradigm Agency
10100 Santa Monica Bl-25th Fl
Los Angeles, CA 90067
Alternate V: 12/13/96

Nealon, Kevin
5039 1/2 Rosewood Ave
Los Angeles, CA 90004
Actor V: 01/03/97

Needham, Connie
20th Century Artists
15315 Magnolia Bl #429
Sherman Oaks, 91403
Actress V: 02/01/96

Needham, Tracey
Badgley Conner
9229 Sunset Bl #311
Los Angeles, CA 90069
Actress V: 01/15/97

Neeson, Liam
Susan Culley Associates
150 S Rodeo Dr-Suite 220
Beverly Hills, CA 90212
Actor V: 01/10/97

180 W 59th St
New York, NY 10019
Forwarded V: 03/15/96

Neill, Noei
331 Sage Lane
Santa Monica, CA 90402
Actress V: 03/02/96

Nelson, Byron
Rt2-Fairway Ranch/Litsey Rd
Roanoake, TX 76262
Golfer V: 02/04/96

Nelson, Craig T
c/o ICM
8942 Wilshire Bl
Beverly Hills, CA 90211
Actor V: 01/12/96

9171 Wilshire Bl #436
Beverly Hills, CA 90212
Forwarded V: 03/15/96

Nelson, Gary
NASCAR
1811 Volusia Ave
Daytona Beach, FL 32015
NASCAR Inspector V: 03/02/96

Nelson, George D
NASA/LBJ Space Center
Houston, TX 77058
Astronaut V: 03/03/96

Nelson, Judd
Gersh Agency
232 N Canon Dr
Beverly Hills, CA 90210
Actor V: 01/15/96

Nelson, Ray Faraday
333 Ramona Ave
El Cerrito, CA 94530
Author V: 03/01/96

Nelson, Tracy
Gersh Agency
232 N Canon Dr
Beverly Hills, CA 90210
Actress V: 12/09/96

Bresler/Kelly/Kipperman
15760 Ventura Bl #1730
Encino, CA 91436
Alternate V: 02/23/96

405/407 Sycamore Rd
Santa Monica, CA 90402
Forwarded V: 08/15/96

13263 Ventura Bl #10
Studio City, CA 91604
Forwarded V: 11/11/96

Nelson, Willie
PO Box 2789
Danbury, CT 06813
Singer V: 02/02/96

PO Box 3280
Austin, TX 78764-0260
Alternate V: 10/23/96

Rt1-Briarcliff TT
Spicewood, TX 78669
Forwarded V: 07/07/96

Nemec, Corin 'Corky'
Wilkinson & Lipsman
8170 Beverly Bl #205
Los Angeles, CA 90048-4513
Actor V: 11/10/96

Nemechek, Joe
PO Box 177
Mooresville, NC 28115
NASCAR Driver V: 01/20/96

McClure Motorsports
Rt 10-Box 780-Hwy 11
Abingdon, VA 24210
Alternate V: 03/14/96

McClure Motorsports
PO Box 1131
Mooresville, NC 28115
Forwarded V: 03/14/96

Nero, Franco
Gersh Agency
232 N Canon Dr
Beverly Hills, CA 90210
Actor V: 12/09/96

Via di Monte del Gallo 26
I-00165 Rome, Italy
Alternate V: 01/17/96

P Petri/M Diberty
Via Margutta 1-A
00187 Rome, Italy
Forwarded V: 01/11/96

Nero, Peter
11806 N 56th St #B
Tampa, FL 33617
Pianist V: 01/13/97

Nesmith, Michael
11858 La Grange Ave
Los Angeles, CA 90025
Singer V: 11/01/96

Nettles, John
Saraband Associates
265 Liverpool Rd
London N1 1LX, England
Actor V: 03/17/96

Nettleton, Lois
Artists Group
10100 Santa Monica Bl #2490
Los Angeles, CA 90067
Actress V: 12/04/96

Neuwirth, Bebe
212 1/2 S Poinsettia Pl
Los Angeles, CA 90036
Actress V: 10/10/96

Neville, Aaron
Wm Morris Agency
151 El Camino Dr
Beverly Hills, CA 90212
Singer V: 01/14/96

Nevins, Claudette
Gold/Marshak & Associates
3500 W Olive Ave #1400
Burbank, CA 91505
Actress V: 12/10/96

New England Patriots
Sullivan Stadium-Route 1
Foxboro, MA 02035
Team Office V: 02/15/96

New Horizon Pictures
11600 San Vincente Bl
Los Angeles, CA 90049
Production Office V: 03/17/96

New Jersey Devils
Byrne Meadowlands Arena
PO Box 504
E Rutherford, NJ 07073
Team Office V: 02/01/96

New Jersey Nets
Brendan Byrne Arena
E Rutherford, NJ 07073
Team Office V: 02/15/96

New Orleans Saints
6928 Saints Ave
Metairie, LA 70003
Team Office V: 02/15/96

New Vision Entertainment
5757 Wilshire Bl #600
Los Angeles, CA 90036
Production Office V: 03/17/96

New World Entertainment
1440 S Sepulveda Bl
Los Angeles, CA 90025
Production Office V: 03/17/96

New York Giants
Giants Stadium
East Rutherford, NJ 07073
Team Office V: 02/15/96

New York Islanders
Nassau Vets Memorial Coliseum
Unionldale, NY 11553
Team Office V: 02/01/96

New York Jets
1000 Fulton Ave
Hempstead, NY 11550
Team Office V: 02/15/96

New York Mets
Shea Stadium
Flushing, NY 11368
Team Office V: 02/15/96

New York Nicks
2 Pennsylvania Plaza
New York, NY 10001
Team Office V: 02/15/96

New York Public Library
Performing Arts Reserch Center
Dance Collection
111 Amsterdam Ave
New York, NY 10009
Archive V: 03/20/96

New York Rangers
Madison Square Gardens
4 Pennsylvania Plaza
New York, NY 10001
Team Office V: 02/01/96

New York Times
229 W 43rd
New York, NY 10036
Publisher V: 02/01/96

New York Yankees
Yankee Stadium
Bronx, NY 10451
Team Office V: 02/15/96

New Yorker Magazine
20 W 43rd St
New York, NY 10036
Publisher V: 02/10/96

Newcombe, Don
Marianne Ocampo
4042 W 226th St
Torrance, CA 90505
Baseball Star V: 01/12/96

Newhart, Bob
Wm Morris Agency
151 El Camino
Beverly Hills, CA 90212
Actor V: 12/12/96

420 Amapola Lane
Los Angeles, CA 90077
Alternate V: 04/21/96

Newly, Anthony
c/o APA
9000 Sunset Bl #1200
Los Angeles, CA 90069
Singer V: 01/11/96

Newman, James H
NASA/LBJ Space Center
Houston, TX 77058
Astronaut V: 03/03/96

Newman, Laraine
Gold/Marshak
3500 W Olive Ave #1400
Burbank, CA 91505
Actress V: 12/10/96

10480 Ashton Ave
Los Angeles, CA 90024
Alternate V: 01/03/97

Newman, Paul
c/o CAA
9830 Wilshire Bl
Beverly Hills, CA 90212
Actor V: 01/14/96

477 Madison Ave
New York, NY 10022-5802
Alternate V: 11/01/96

1120 5th Ave #1C
New York, NY 10128
Forwarded V: 11/01/96

Newman, Phyllis
Gage Group
9255 Sunset Bl #515
Los Angeles, CA 90069
Actress V: 12/08/96

Newmar, Julie
204 S Carmelina Ave
Los Angeles, CA 90049
Actress V: 10/10/96

c/o Sindell
8271 Melrose Ave #202
Los Angeles, CA 90046
Forwarded V: 03/06/96

Newton, Juice
c/o Agent
PO Box 293323
Lewisville, TX 75029-3323
Singer V: 02/02/96

Newton, Wayne
Wm Morris Agency
151 El Camino
Beverly Hills, CA 90212
Actor V: 12/12/96

Flying Eagle
3422 Happy Lane
Las Vegas, NV 89120
Alternate V: 02/02/96

6629 S Pecos
Las Vegas, NV 89120
Forwarded V: 01/03/97

Newton-John, Olivia
PO Box 2710
Malibu, CA 90265
Singer V: 10/23/96

Nguyen, Dustin
Hurwitz Associates
427 N Canon Dr #215
Beverly Hills, CA 90210
Actor V: 12/10/96

218 1/4 S Poinsettia Pl
Los Angeles, CA 90036-2850
Forwarded V: 02/01/96

Nicholas, Denise
Kohner Agency
9300 Wilshire Bl #555
Beverly Hills, CA 90212
Actress V: 12/11/96

Nichols, Bobby
8681 Glenlyon Ct
Ft Meyers, FL 33912
Golfer V: 02/04/96

Nichols, Mike
35 E 76th St
New York, NY 10021
Director V: 02/03/96

Nichols, Nichelle
Artists Group
1930 Century Park W #403
Los Angeles, CA 90067
Actress V: 02/04/96

23281 Leonora Dr
Woodland Hills, CA 91367
Alternate V: 03/30/96

Nicholson, Jack
c/o BKK
15760 Ventura Bl #1730
Encino, CA 91436
Actor V: 11/01/96

9544 Lime Orchard Rd
Beverly Hills, CA 90210
Alternate V: 01/15/96

Nickelodeon/MTV
1515 Broadway
New York, NY 10036
Network HQ V: 11/11/96

Nicklaus, Jack
11780 US HWY 1
Palm Beach, FL 33408
Golfer V: 11/11/96

11397 Old Harbor Rd
N Palm Beach, FL 33408
Alternate V: 11/11/96

1208 US HWY 1
N Palm Beach, FL 33408
Forwarded V: 01/02/96

Nickson, Julia
c/o MTA
4526 Wilshire Bl
Los Angeles, CA 90010
Actress V: 02/23/96

Nicollier, Claude
NASA/LBJ Space Center
Houston, TX 77058
Astronaut V: 02/02/96

Niekro, Joe
39 Shadow Ln
Lakeland, FL 33813
Baseball Star V: 12/10/96

Nielsen, Brigitte
c/o Bartels
PO Box 57593
Sherman Oaks, CA 91413
Actress V: 02/23/96

Nielsen, Leslie
1622 Viewmont Dr
Los Angeles, CA 90069
Actor V: 03/09/96

Bresler/Kelly
15760 Ventura Bl #1730
Encino, CA 91436
Alternate V: 12/06/96

Nielsen, Norm
PO Box 34300
Las Vegas, NV 89133-4300
Magician V: 07/03/96

Niemi, Lisa
10960 Dickens St #302
Sherman Oaks, CA 91423
Actress V: 01/16/96

Nilsson, Harry
23960 Long Valley Rd
Hidden Hills, CA 91302
Singer V: 02/03/96

Nimmo, Derek
Grafton House, #42-43
2-3 Golden Square
London W1R 3AD, England
Actor V: 03/17/96

Nimoy, Leonard
Gersh Agency
232 N Canon Dr
Beverly Hills, CA 90210
Actor V: 12/09/96

17 Gateway Dr
Batavia, NY 14020
Alternate V: 11/11/96

PO Box 5617
Beverly Hills, CA 90210
Forwarded V: 06/11/96

Nine Inch Nails
2337 W 11th St #7
Cleveland, OH 44113
Musical Group V: 01/02/97

Nitty Gritty Dirt Band
c/o HCF
4155 E Jewell Ave #412
Denver, CO 80222
Musical Group V: 02/02/96

Niven, Larry
136 El Camino Dr
Beverly Hills, CA 90212
Writer V: 10/23/96

Noble, James
Paradigm Agency
10100 Santa Monica Bl-25th Fl
Los Angeles, CA 90067
Actor V: 12/13/96

Nodel, Mart
117 Lake Irene Dr
W Palm Beach, FL 33411
Cartoonist V: 09/11/96

Noiret, Philippe
Le Studio Canal
17 rue Dumont Durville
Paris 75116, France
Actor V: 11/11/96

Gori Group
Via Barnaba Oriani 19
Rome 00197, Italy
Forwarded V: 02/09/96

Nolan, Jeanette
RR #1
Troy, MT 59935
Actress V: 10/23/96

1417 Samona Way
Laguna Beach, CA 92651
Alternate V: 03/01/96

Nolan, Kathleen
House of Representatives
9911 Pico Bl #1060
Los Angeles, CA 90035
Actress V: 12/10/96

360 E 55th St #PH
New York, NY 10022
Alternate V: 02/03/96

Nolin, Gena Lee
Wm Morris Agency
151 El Camino
Beverly Hills, CA 90212
Actress V: 10/23/96

c/o Baywatch
5433 Beethoven St
Los Angeles, CA 90066
Forwarded V: 09/15/96

Nolte, Nick
Kingsgate Films
6153 Bonsall Dr
Malibu, CA 90265
Actor V: 11/01/96

c/o ICM
8942 Wilshire Bl
Beverly Hills, CA 90211
Alternate V: 12/11/96

Norman, Greg
1 Erieview Plaza
Cleveland, OH 44114-1782
Golfer V: 02/04/96

Norris, Christopher
Sutton/Barth & Vennari
145 S Fairfax Ave #310
Los Angeles, CA 90036
Actress V: 12/15/96

Norris, Chuck
PO Box 872
Navasota, TX 77868
Actor V: 11/20/96

North, Jay
290 NE 1st Ave
Lake Butler, FL 32054-1202
Actor V: 08/28/96

North, Oliver
RR1-Box 560
Bluemont, VA 22012-9414
Celebrity V: 11/11/96

North, Sheree
Writers & Artists
924 Westwood Bl #900
Los Angeles, CA 90024
Actress V: 12/15/96

1467 Palisades Dr
Pacific Palisades, CA 90272
Alternate V: 06/18/96

Northrup, Jim
Freeman-Bocci
4320 Delemere
Royal Oak, MI 48073
Baseball Star V: 10/23/96

Norton, Ken
4 Cantilena
San Clemente, CA 92673-2738
Boxing Star V: 01/12/96

16 S Peek Dr
Laguna Niguel, CA 92677
Forwarded V: 02/01/96

Norton-Taylor, Judy
6767 Forest Lawn Dr #115
Los Angeles, CA 90068
Actress V: 02/03/96

Noth, Christopher
c/o UTA
9560 Wishire Bl #500
Beverly Hills, CA 90212
Actor V: 10/10/96

Notre Dame Football
Players Coach
PO Box 518
Notre Dame, IN 46556
Team Office V: 02/01/96

Nouri, Michael
Paradigm Agency
10100 Santa Monica Bl-25th Fl
Los Angeles, CA 90067
Actor V: 12/13/96

Novello, Don
PO Box 245
Fairfax, CA 94930
Actor V: 08/08/96

Nugent, Ted
Madhouse Mgmt
PO Box 15101
Ann Arbor, MI 48106
Singer V: 01/11/96

Nuyen, France
Gage Group
9255 Sunset Bl #515
Los Angeles, CA 90069
Actress V: 12/08/96

O'Bannon, Ed
New Jersey Mets
Meadowlands Arena
East Rutherford, NJ 07073
Basketball Star V: 10/23/96

O

O'Brian, Hugh
3195 Benedict Canyon Rd
Beverly Hills, CA 90210
Actor V: 02/01/96

10826 Ayres Ave
Los Angeles, CA 90064
Alternate V: 03/16/96

c/o Foundation
10880 Wilshire Bl #900
Los Angeles, CA 90024
Forwarded V: 01/11/96

O'Brien, Margaret
1250 La Preresa Dr
Thousand Oaks, CA 91362
Actress V: 02/12/96

O'Connor, Bryan D
NASA/LBJ Space Center
Hoston, TX 77058
Astronaut V: 01/31/96

O'Connor, Carroll
30826 Broad Beach Rd
Malibu, CA 90265
Actor V: 02/01/96

c/o Larner
130 W 57th St #10A
New York, NY 10019
Forwarded V: 01/17/96

O'Connor, Donald
PO Box 20204
Sedona, AZ 86341
Actor V: 06/01/96

O'Day, Molly
PO Box 2123
Avila Beach, CA 93424
Actress V: 07/03/96

O'Donnell, Chris
Creative Artists Agency
9830 Wilshire Bl
Beverly Hills, CA 90212
Actor V: 12/07/96

1724 N Vista St
Los Angeles, CA 90046
Alternate V: 01/15/96

O'Donnell, Rosie
Creative Artists Agency
9830 Wilshire Bl
Beverly Hills, CA 90212
Actress V: 01/14/96

Bernie Young
9800 Topanga Canyon Bl #D
Chatsworth, CA 91311
Alternate V: 12/01/96

O'Driscoll, Martha
c/o Appleton
22 Indian Circle Dr
Miami Beach, FL 33154
Actress V: 05/01/96

O'Hara, Catherine
c/o ICM
8942 Wilshire Bl
Beverly Hills, CA 90211
Actress V: 02/23/96

O'Hara, Maureen
Lugdine Park Glengariff
County Cork, Ireland
Actress V: 03/12/96

PO Box 1400
Christiansted, St Croix
Virgin Islands 00821
Alternate V: 07/05/96

O'Hare, Michael
Friends of MO
PO Box 6541
Edgemere, MD 21219
Fan Service V: 01/12/96

O'Keefe, Michael
Paradigm Agency
10100 Santa Monica Bl 25th Fl
Los Angeles, CA 90067
Actor V: 01/21/96

O'Keefe, Miles
PO Box 216
Malibu, CA 90265
Actor V: 02/03/96

O'Leary, Brian T
NASA/LBJ Space Center
Houston, TX 77058
Astronaut V: 03/03/96

O'Neal, Griffin
14209 Riverside Dr
Van Nuys, CA 91402
Actor V: 02/07/96

O'Neal, Ron
Paradigm Agency
10100 Santa Monica Bl-25th Fl
Los Angeles, CA 90067
Actor V: 12/13/96

O'Neal, Ryan
21368 Pacific Coast Hwy
Malibu, CA 90265
Actor V: 03/12/96

328 S Beverly Dr #A
Beverly Hills, CA 90212
Alternate V: 01/11/96

O'Neal, Shaquille
c/o Orlando Magic
One Magic Pl
Orlando, FL 32801
Basketball Star V: 01/14/96

PO Box 951840
Lake Mary, FL 32795-1840
Alternate V: 01/10/97

501 John St
Manhattan Beach, CA 90266-5834
Forwarded V: 01/10/97

O'Neal, Tatum
Innovative Artists
1999 Ave of the Stars #2850
Los Angeles, CA 90067
Actress V: 12/11/96

200 East End Ave, #16H
New York, NY 10128-7833
Alternate V: 05/12/96

O'Neill, Dick
Borinstein/Oreck
8271 Melrose Ave #110
Los Angeles, CA 90046
Actor V: 01/12/96

O'Neill, Ed
2607 Grand Canal
Venice, CA 90291
Actor V: 03/27/96

O'Neill, Jennifer
Shapira & Associates
15301 Ventura Bl #345
Sherman Oaks, CA 91403
Actress V: 12/13/96

32356 Mulholland Hwy
Malibu, CA 90265
Alternate V: 12/01/96

O'Sullivan, Maureen
1839 Union St
Schenectady, NY 12309
Actress V: 11/05/96

O'Toole, Annette
360 Morton St
Ashland, OR 97520-3065
Actress V: 04/04/96

Wm Morris Agency
151 El Camino
Beverly Hills, CA 90212
Alternate V: 02/23/96

O'Toole, Peter
Veerline Ltd
8 Baker St
London W1A 1DA, England
Actor V: 11/01/96

98 Heath St
London, NW3 England
Alternate V: 03/15/96

ON OUR OWN
WB-TV
4000 Warner Bl
Burbank, CA 91522
Production Office V: 01/20/96

ONE LIFE TO LIVE
ABC-TV
56 W 66th St
New York, NY 10023
Production Office V: 01/21/96

OPRAH WINFREY SHOW
30 Rockefeller Plaza
New York, NY 10112
Production Office V: 11/20/96

Harpo Inc
PO Box 909715
Chicago, IL 60690
Alternate V: 01/12/96

ORLEANS
Paramount TV
5555 Melrose Ave
Hollywood, CA 90038
Production Office V: 12/15/96

CBS-TV
51 W 52nd St
New York, NY 10019
Alternate V: 01/13/97

Oak Ridge Boys
Sterban/Allen/Bonsall
329 Rockland Rd
Hendersonville, TN 37075
Musical Group V: 02/02/96

Oakland A's
Oakland-Alameda County Stadium
Oakland, CA 94621
Team Office V: 02/15/96

Phoenix Municipal Stadium
5999 E Van Buren
Phoenix, AZ 85008
Alternate V: 01/20/96

Oakland Raiders
Oakland-Alameda County Stadium
Oakland, CA 94621
Team Office V: 01/12/96

Oates, John
Horizon Entertainment
130 W 57th St #12-B
New York, NY 100193
Architect V: 10/23/96

Ocasek, Ric
Rascoff/Zysblat
110 W 57th St #PH
New York, NY 10019
Singer V: 09/15/96

Ochoa, Ellen
NASA/LBJ Space Center
Houston, TX 77058
Astronaut V: 03/03/96

Oerter, Al
5485 Avenieda Pescadera
Ft Meyers, FL 33931-4209
Olympian V: 01/11/96

Ogilvy, Ian
Gage Group
9255 Sunset Bl #515
Los Angeles, CA 90069
Actor V: 12/08/96

c/o Whitehall
125 Gloucester Rd
London SW7 4TE, England
Forwarded V: 03/17/96

Oh, Soon-Teck
Lee & Associates
8961 Sunset Bl-Suite V
Los Angeles, CA 90069
Actor V: 12/11/96

Olandt, Ken
Gold & Marshak
3500 W Olive Ave #1400
Burbank, CA 91505
Actor V: 09/15/96

Oldman, Gary
c/o ICM
76 Oxford St
London W1N 0AX, England
Actor V: 02/03/96

Oliver, Pam
c/o ESPN
935 Middle St
Bristol, CT 06010
Commentator V: 02/01/96

Olmos, Edward James
Artists Agency
10000 Santa Monica Bl #305
Los Angeles, CA 90067
Actor V: 12/03/96

2020 Ave of the Stars #500
Century City, CA 90067
Alternate V: 11/01/96

Olsen, Ashley
WB-TV
4000 Warner Bl
Burbank, CA 91522
Actress V: 01/14/96

Olsen, Mary Kate
WB-TV
4000 Warner Bl
Burbank, CA 91522
Actress V: 01/14/96

Olsen, Susan
3580 Wilshire Bl
Los Angeles, CA 90010
Actress V: 09/15/96

Omnipop
10700 Ventura Bl-2nd Fl
Studio City, CA 91604
Talent Agency V: 01/20/96

Ono, Yoko
c/o Starpeace
1 W 72nd St
New York, NY 10023
Singer V: 03/15/96

Onorati, Peter
4191 Stanbury St
Sherman Oaks, CA 91403
Actor V: 01/12/96

Ontkean, Michael
7120 Grasswood Ave
Malibu, CA 90265
Actor V: 02/03/96

Innovative Artists
1999 Ave of the Stars #2850
Los Angeles, CA 90067
Alternate V: 12/11/96

Orange Grove Group
12178 Ventura Bl #205
Studio City, CA 91614
Talent Agency V: 02/02/96

Oravetz, Ernie
4417 W Paul Ave
Tampa, FL 33611
Baseball Star V: 01/06/96

Orbach, Jerry
1930 Century Park W #430
Los Angeles, CA 90067
Actor V: 10/23/96

Orbach, John Phillip
Artists Group
10100 Santa Monica Bl #2490
Los Angeles, CA 90067
Actor V: 12/04/96

Orion Pictures/TV
1888 Century Park E 6th Fl
Los Angeles, CA 90067
Production Office V: 03/17/96

Orlando Magic
PO Box 76
Orlando, FL 32802
Team Office V: 02/15/96

One Magic Place
Orlando Arena
Orlando, FL 32801-1114
Alternate V: 11/11/96

Ormond, Julia
c/o CAA
9830 Wilshire Bl
Beverly Hills, CA 90212
Actress V: 01/14/96

Marmont Mgmt/Langham House
302/308 Regent St
London W1R 5AL, England
Alternate V: 10/23/96

Osborne, John
c/o Agent
91 Regent St
London W1, England
Author V: 03/15/96

Osbrink Talent
4605 Lankershim Bl #401
N Hollywood, CA 91602
Talent Agency V: 02/02/96

Oslin, KT
Moress/Nanas/Shea
1209 16th Ave South
Nashville, TN 37212
Singer V: 02/02/96

Osmond, Cliff
630 Benvenida
Pacific Palisades, CA 90272
Actor V: 06/18/96

c/o Sanders
8831 Sunset Bl #304
Los Angeles, CA 90069
Alternate V: 02/16/96

Osmond, Donny
Entertainment Corporation
1560 Brookhollow Dr #114
Santa Ana, CA 92705
Singer V: 03/02/96

Osmond, Marie
United Mgmt
3325 N University Ave
Provo, UT 84604
Actress V: 02/02/96

PO Box 6000
Provo, UT 84603
Alternate V: 06/25/96

Wm Morris Agency
151 El Camino Dr
Beverly Hills, CA 90210
Forwarded V: 11/01/96

Osterhage, Jeff
210 N Cordova #D
Burbank, CA 91505
Actor V: 03/22/96

Oswald, Steven S
NASA/LBJ Space Center
Hoston, TX 77058
Astronaut V: 01/31/96

Otis, Carre
166 Geary St
San Francisco, CA 94108
Actress V: 11/01/96

1900 Ave of the Stars #1040
Los Angels, CA 90067
Alternate V: 01/10/97

Otis & Associates
373 S Robertson Bl
Beverly Hills, CA 90211
Talent Agency V: 02/02/96

Ottawa Senators
301 Moodie Dr #200
Nepean, Ontario, Canada K2H 9C4
Team Office V: 02/01/96

Overall, Park
Gersh Agency
232 N Canon Dr
Beverly Hills, CA 90210
Actress V: 12/09/96

20 Ironside St #18
Marina del Rey, CA 90292
Alternate V: 09/15/96

4904 Sancola Ave
N Hollywood, CA 91602
Forwarded V: 02/03/96

Overmeyer, Robert F
NASA/LBJ Space Center
Houston, TX 77058
Astronaut V: 03/03/96

Ovitz, Michael
Walt Disney Studios
500 S Buena Vista St
Burbank, CA 91521
Studio Executive V: 01/14/96

Owens, Cotton
7605 White Ave
Spartanburg, SC 29303
NASCAR Driver V: 03/02/96

Oxenberg, Catherine
Shapira & Associates
15301 Ventura Bl #345
Sherman Oaks, CA 91403
Actress V: 12/13/96

1526 N Beverly Dr
Beverly Hills, CA 90210
Alternate V: 11/01/96

Oz, Frank
PO Box 20750
New York, NY 10023
Actor V: 01/13/97

Ozbourne, Ozzy
151 El Camino Dr
Beverly Hills, CA 90212
Singer V: 01/14/96

P

PARTY GIRL
FOX-TV
PO Box 900
Beverly Hills, CA 90213
Viewer Services V: 11/11/96

PARTY OF FIVE
Fox-TV
PO Box 900
Beverly Hills, CA 90213
Production Office V: 12/15/96

PAULY
Fox-TV
PO Box 900
Beverly Hills, CA 90213
Audience Services V: 01/13/97

PBS-TV
1320 Braddock Place
Alexandria, VA 22314
Production Office V: 02/01/96

PEARL
Witt-Thomas Prod
5842 Sunset Bl, Bldg 11-2nd Fl
Hollywood, CA 90028
Production Office V: 12/15/96

CBS-TV
51 W 52nd ST
New York, NY 10019
Alternate V: 11/11/96

PICKET FENCES
20th Century Fox
PO Box 900-Trailer 757
Beverly Hills, CA 90213
Production Office V: 10/23/96

POLTERGEIST: THE LEGACY
WB-TV
1438 N Gower
Hollywood, CA 90028
Audience Services V: 04/12/96

PRICE IS RIGHT
Goodson Productions
5750 Wilshire Bl #475 W
Los Angeles, CA 90036-3697
Production Office V: 11/01/96

PRIME TIME LIVE
147 Columbus Ave
New York, NY 10023
Production Office V: 01/21/96

PRINCE STREET
NBC-TV
30 Rockefeller Plaza
New York, NY 10112
Audience Services V: 01/13/97

PROFILER
NBC-TV
30 Rockefeller Plaza
New York, NY 10112
Viewer Services V: 11/11/96

PROMISED LAND
Bochco Prod/Bungalow 4
4024 Radford Ave
Studio City, CA 91604
Production Office V: 12/15/96

CBS-TV
51 W 52nd St
New York, NY 10019
Alternate V: 11/11/96

PUBLIC MORALS
CBS-TV
51 W 52nd St
New York, NY 10019
Viewer Services V: 11/11/96

Paar, Jack
9 Chateau Ridge Dr
Greenwich, CT 06830
Celebrity V: 03/04/96

Pace, Judy
4139 Cloverdale
Los Angeles, CA 90008
Actress V: 06/17/96

Pacific Film Archive
University Art Museum
University of California
2625 Durant Ave
Berkeley, CA 94720
Archive V: 03/20/96

Pacino, Al
9830 Wilshire Bl
Beverly Hills, CA 90212
Actor V: 01/14/96

350 Park Ave #900
Ne York, NY 10022
Alternate V: 11/01/96

Chal Productions
301 W 57th St #16-C
New York, NY 10019
Forwarded V: 12/15/96

Page, Anita
929 Rutland Ave
Los Angeles, CA 90042
Actress V: 01/13/96

Page, Betty
Gersh Agency
232 N Canon Dr
Beverly Hills, CA 90210
Model V: 11/01/96

Page, LaWanda
c/o Starwil
6253 Hollywood Bl #730
Los Angeles, CA 90028
Actress V: 12/15/96

1056 W 84th St
Los Angeles, CA 90044
Alternate V: 01/12/96

Page, Patti
1412 San Lucas Ct
Salana Beach, CA 92075
Actress V: 12/11/96

314 Huntley Dr
Beverly Hills, CA 90211
Alternate V: 01/06/96

Paget, Debra
737 Kuhlman Rd
Houston, TX 77024
Actress V: 12/01/96

Paige, Janis
Artists Group
10100 Santa Monica Bl #2490
Los Angeles, CA 90067
Actress V: 12/04/96

1700 Rising Glen Rd
Los Angeles, CA 90069
Alternate V: 04/21/96

Pakula & King
9229 Sunset Bl #315
Los Angles, CA 90069
Talent Agency V: 11/11/96

Palance, Jack
Hurwitz Associates
427 N Canon Dr #215
Beverly Hills, CA 90210
Actor V: 12/10/96

Star Rt 1-Box 805
Tehachapi, CA 93561
Alternate V: 02/03/96

Palance, Jack, Cont.
PO Box 6201
Tehatchapi, CA 93561
Forwarded V: 01/13/96

Palin, Michael
BBC-TV Center
London W12, England
Actor V: 02/23/96

Gumby Corporation
68A Delancy St
London NW7 7RY, England
Alternate V: 07/30/96

Pall, Gloria
12828 Victory Bl #163
N Hollywood, CA 91606
Actress V: 02/02/96

Palmer, Arnold
PO Box 52
Youngstown, PA 15696
Golfer V: 05/02/96

Palmer, Betsy
4040 Farmdale Ave
Studio City, CA 91604
Actress V: 03/11/96

c/o Lemack
215 S La Cienega Bl #203
Beverly Hills, CA 90211
Alternate V: 01/13/96

630 Benvenida
Pacific Palisades, CA 90272
Forwarded V: 06/18/96

Palmer, Robert
2-A Chelsea Manor
Blood St
London SW3, England
Singer V: 01/11/96

Palminteri, Chazz
Creative Artists Agency
9830 Wilshire Bl
Beverly Hills, CA 90212
Actor V: 12/07/96

Paltrow, Gwyneth
c/o ICM
8942 Wilshire Bl
Beverly Hills, CA 90211
Actress V: 12/15/96

Paquin, Anna
c/o Double Happy
PO Box 9585
Wellington, New Zealand
Actress V: 12/01/96

Paradigm Talent
10100 Santa Monica Bl-25th Fl
Los Angeles, CA 90067
Talent Agency V: 02/02/96

Paradis, Vanessa
c/o Artmedia
10 Ave George-V
F-75008 Paris, France
Actress V: 02/11/96

Paragon Talent
8439 Sunset Bl #301
Los Angeles, CA 90069
Talent Agency V: 03/17/96

Paramount Motion Pictures
15260 Ventura Bl #1140
Sherman Oaks, CA 91403
Production Office V: 03/17/96

Paramount Studios
5555 Melrose Ave
Hollywood, CA 90038
Production Office V: 04/02/96

Parazynski, Scott E
NASA/LBJ Space Center
Houston, TX 77058
Astronaut V: 02/02/96

Pare, Michael
Wm Morris Agency
151 El Camino
Beverly Hills, CA 90212
Actor V: 12/12/96

2804 Pacific Ave
Venice, CA 90291
Alternate V: 05/07/96

Aurora Productions
9606 Santa Monica Bl
Beverly Hills, CA 90211
Forwarded V: 10/23/96

Parker, Brant
King Features
235 E 45th St
New York, NY 10017
Cartoonist V: 02/15/96

Parker, Eleanor
2195 La Paz Way
Palm Springs, CA 92262
Actress V: 03/02/96

Parker, Fess
633 E Cabrillo Bl
Santa Barbara, CA 93103
Actor V: 01/20/96

Parker, James
5448 Wingbourne Ct
Columbia, MD 21045
Football Star V: 05/14/96

Parker, Jameson
Stone Manners Talent
8091 Selma Ave
Los Angeles, CA 90046
Actor V: 12/15/96

4345 Laurel Canyon Bl
Studio City, CA 91604
Alternate V: 03/17/96

Parker, Jean
617 Columbus E
Glendale, CA 91205
Actress V: 01/13/97

Parker, Lu
8 Yeamans Rd
Charleston, SC 29407
Miss USA V: 01/13/97

Parker, Robert A
NASA/LBJ Space Center
Houston, TX 77058
Astronaut V: 03/03/96

Parkinson, Dian
Purrfect Productions
PO Box 430
Newbury Park, CA 91320
Actress V: 01/13/96

4655 Natick Ave #1
Sherman Oaks, CA 91403
Alternate V: 02/18/96

Parks, Rosa
231 W Layfayette St
Dearborn, MI 48226
Activist V: 06/17/96

Parrish, Julie
PO Box 247
Santa Monica, CA 90406-0247
Actress V: 11/01/96

Parsons, Benny
NASCAR
1811 Volusia Ave
Daytona Beach, FL 32015
NASCAR Driver V: 03/02/96

Parsons, Estelle
505 West End Ave
New York, NY 10024
Actress V: 10/23/96

Parsons, Phil
NASCAR
1811 Volusia Ave
Daytona Beach, FL 32015
NASCAR Driver V: 03/02/96

Partch, Virgil
King Features
235 E 45th St
New York, NY 10017
Cartoonist V: 02/01/96

Parton, Dolly
Rt 1-Crockett Rd
Brentwood, TN 37027
Actress V: 02/04/96

700 Dollywood Ln
Pigeon Forge, TN 37863-4101
Alternate V: 04/01/96

c/o ICM
8942 Wilshire Bl
Beverly Hills, CA 90211
Forwarded V: 01/14/96

PO Box 150307
Nashville, TN 37215
Forwarded V: 10/23/96

Paschall, Jim
Rt 2-Box 450
Denton, NC 27238
NASCAR Driver V: 03/02/96

Pastorelli, Robert
Gage Group
9255 Sunset Bl #515
Los Angeles, CA 90069
Actor V: 12/08/96

Patinkin, Mandy
200 W 90th St
New York, NY 10024
Actor V: 03/17/96

Patitz, Sophie
Elite Model Mgmt
8 bis-rue Le Cuirot
Paris F-75014, France
Model V: 11/01/96

111 E 22nd St
New York, NY 10010
Alternate V: 10/23/96

Patitz, Tatjana
Elite Model Mgmt
8 bis-rue Le Cuirot
Paris F-75014, France
Model V: 11/01/96

Patric, Jason
814 N Stanley
Los Angeles, CA 90046
Actor V: 10/23/96

Patrick, Dennis
Bauman & Hiller
5750 Wilshire Bl #512
Los Angeles, CA 90036
Actor V: 12/05/96

Patrick, Jason
10683 Santa Monica Bl
Los Angeles, CA 90025-4807
Actor V: 01/15/96

Patrick, Robert
c/o UTA
15315 Magnolia Bl #429
Sherman Oaks, CA 91403
Actor V: 12/15/96

Patterson, Floyd
Box 336-Springtown Rd
New Paltz, NY 12561
Boxing Star V: 11/01/96

Patterson, Lorna
c/o Paradigm
10100 Santa Monica Bl 25th Fl
Los Angeles, CA 90067
Actress V: 02/01/96

Paulson, Pat
PO Box 5734
Santa Rosa, CA 95402
Actor V: 01/09/97

Pavarotti, Luciano
941 Via Giardini
41040 Saliceta S Guiliano
Modena, Italy
Opera Tenor V: 01/02/96

Paxton, Bill
9830 Wilshire Bl
Beverly Hills, CA 90212
Actor V: 12/07/96

Paycheck, Johnny
Bo Shar
1321 Murfreesboro Rd #600
Nashville, TN 37217
Singer V: 02/02/96

Payne, Roy
502-C Performance Rd
Mooresville, NC 28115
NASCAR Driver V: 01/21/96

Pays, Amanda
3541 N Knoll Dr
Los Angeles, CA 90068-1524
Actress V: 03/14/96

9030 Calle Juela Dr
Beverly Hills, CA 90210
Alternate V: 02/26/96

Wm Morris Agency
151 El Camino Dr
Beverly Hills, CA 90212
Forwarded V: 02/23/96

Payton, Walter
300 N Martingale Rd #340
Schaumburg, IL 60173-2087
Football Star V: 08/28/96

Pearson, David
PO Box 8099
Spartanburg, SC 29305
NASCAR Driver V: 03/02/96

Pearson, Larry
NASCAR
1811 Volusia Ave
Daytona Beach, FL 32015
NASCAR Driver V: 03/02/96

Peck, Gregory
PO Box 837
Beverly Hills, CA 90213-0837
Actor V: 05/07/96

375 N Carolwood Dr
Los Angeles, CA 90024
Alternate V: 11/12/96

Peck, Tom
PO Box 249
McConnellsburg, PA 17233
Race Driver V: 03/12/96

Peeples, Nia
Gersh Agency
232 N Canon Dr
Beverly Hills, CA 90212
Actress V: 02/23/96

PO Box 218033
Waco, TX 76702
Alternate V: 01/13/97

Pelikan, Lisa
PO Box 57333
Sherman Oaks, CA 91403
Actress V: 02/28/96

Pellegrini, Margaret
5018 N 61st Ave
Glendale, AZ 85301
Actress V: 01/15/96

Peluso, Lisa
Buckwald & Associates
9229 Sunset Bl #710
Los Angeles, CA 90069
Actress V: 01/17/96

Pemberton, Robin
Penske Racing
6 Knob Hill Dr
Mooresville, NC 28115
NASCAR Crew V: 02/08/96

Pemberton, Ryan
Yates Racing
115 Dwelle St
Charlotte, NC 27374
NASCAR Crew V: 02/27/96

Pena, Elizabeth
Paradigm Agency
10100 Santa Monica Bl #2500
Los Angeles, CA 90067
Actress V: 12/13/96

Penn, Sean
Clyde Is Hungry Prod
22333 Pacific Coast Hwy
Malibu, CA 90265-2630
Director V: 04/13/96

c/o PMK
955 S Carillo Dr #200
Los Angeles, CA 90048
Forwarded V: 04/15/96

Kaufman/Bernstein
2049 Century Park E #2500
Los Angeles, CA 90067-3127
Forwarded V: 03/14/96

Penn & Teller
c/o ICM
8942 Wilshire Bl
Beverly Hills, CA 90211
Comedy Team V: 02/08/96

1325 Ave of the America's
New York, NY 10019
Alternate V: 04/21/96

Penny, Joe
10453 Sarah St
N Hollywood, CA 91602
Actor V: 03/17/96

Penske, Roger
Penske Racing
6 Knob Hill Rd
Mooreville, NC 28115
NASCAR Owner V: 03/02/96

People Weekly
Time & Life Bldg
Rockefeller Plaza
New York, NY 10020-1393
Publisher V: 03/01/96

Pep, Willie
166 Bunce Rd
Wethersfield, CT 06109-3213
Boxing Star V: 03/30/96

Perez, Rosie
c/o CAA
9830 Wilshire Bl
Beverly Hills, CA 90212
Actress V: 01/14/96

c/o Robinson
10683 Santa Monica Bl
Los Angeles, CA 90025-4807
Forwarded V: 03/14/96

Perkins, Barbara
1930 Century Park W #403
Los Angeles, CA 90067
Actress V: 10/23/96

Artists Group
10100 Santa Monica Bl #2490
Los Angeles, CA 90067
Forwarded V: 12/04/96

Perkins, Elizabeth
c/o CAA
9830 Wilshire Bl
Beverly Hills, CA 90212
Actress V: 02/23/96

Perkins, Millie
2511 Canyon Dr
Los Angeles, CA 90068
Actress V: 02/19/96

Perlman, Rhea
Creative Artists Agency
9830 Wilshire Bl
Beverly Hills, CA 90212
Actress V: 12/07/96

31020 Broad Beach
Malibu, CA 90285
Alternate V: 03/17/96

Perlman, Ron
Gersh Agency
232 N Canon Dr
Beverly Hills, CA 90210
Actor V: 12/09/96

Perot, H Ross
Perot Systems
12377 Merit Dr #1700
Dallas, TX 75251
Politician V: 11/16/96

Perrine, Valerie
SDB Partners
1801 Ave of the Stars #902
Los Angeles, CA 90067
Actress V: 12/13/96

c/o SDB
14411 Riverside Dr
Sherman Oaks, CA 91423
Alternate V: 02/23/96

9744 Wilshire Bl #308
Beverly Hills, CA 90212
Alternate V: 10/23/96

Perry, Gaylord
PO Box 1958
Kill Devil Hills, NC 27948-1958
Baseball Star V: 08/28/96

Perry, Luke
Wm Morris Agency
151 El Camino
Beverly Hills, CA 90212
Actor V: 12/12/96

19528 Ventura Bl #533
Tarzana, CA 91356
Alternate V: 01/21/96

Perry, Matthew
Wm Morris Agency
151 El Camino
Beverly Hills, CA 90212
Actor V: 12/12/96

Perry, Steve
PO Box 97
Larkspur, CA 94939
Actor V: 03/27/96

1401 Pathfinder Ave
Westlake Village, CA 91362
Alternate V: 03/27/96

Persoff, Nehemiah
Bauman & Hiller
5750 Wilshire Bl #512
Los Angeles, CA 90036
Actor V: 12/05/96

Pesci, Joe
Creative Artists Agency
9830 Wilshire Bl
Beverly Hills, CA 90212
Actor V: 12/07/96

Fallu Productions
PO Box 6
Lavallette, NJ 08735
Alternate V: 10/23/96

Pescow, Donna
Kohner Agency
9300 Wilshire Bl #555
Beverly Hills, CA 90212
Actress V: 12/11/96

2179 W 21st St
Los Angeles, CA 90018
Alternate V: 01/09/96

Peter Paul & Mary
648 N Robertson Bl
Los Angeles, CA 90069
Musical Group V: 11/01/96

27 W 67th St
New York, NY 10023
Alternate V: 03/10/96

PO Box 135
Bearsville, NY 12409
Forwarded V: 04/22/96

Peters, Bernadette
Wm Morris Agency
151 El Camino Dr
Beverly Hills, CA 90212
Actress V: 02/23/96

323 W 80th St
New York, NY 10024
Forwarded V: 04/07/96

Peters, Brock
Paradigm Agency
10100 Santa Monica Bl-25th Fl
Los Angeles, CA 90067
Actor V: 12/13/96

Peters, Jean
507 N Palm Dr
Beverly Hills, CA 90210
Actress V: 01/14/96

Peters, Jon
9 Beverly Park
Beverly Hills, CA 90210
Producer V: 01/11/96

Petersen, Wolfgang
Chasin Agency
190 N Canon Dr #201
Beverly Hills, CA 90210
Director V: 01/17/96

Peterson, Cassandra
Queen B Productions
14755 Ventura Bl #1-710
Sherman Oaks, CA 91403
Actress V: 01/21/96

Panacea Entertainment
2705 Glendower Ave
Los Angeles, CA 90027
Alternate V: 11/10/96

c/o CAA
9830 Wilshire Bl
Beverly Hills, CA 90212
Forwarded V: 02/26/96

Peterson, Donald H
NASA/LBJ Space Center
Houston, TX 77058
Astronaut V: 03/03/96

Peterson, Paul
14530 Denker Ave
Gardena, CA 90247
Actor V: 01/31/96

Peterson, Paul, Cont.
Sutton/Barth & Vennari
145 S Fairfax Ave #310
Los Angeles, CA 90036
Alternate V: 12/15/96

Petrenko, Nina Zmievskaya
Int'l Skating Center
1375 Hopmeadow St
Simsbury, CT 06070
Ice Skating Coach V: 01/09/96

Petrenko, Viktor
Int'l Skating Center
1375 Hopmeadow St
Simsbury, CT 06070
Olympian V: 01/09/96

Petrenko, Vladimir
Int'l Skating Center
1375 Hopmeadow St
Simsbury, CT 06070
Olympian V: 01/09/96

Pett, Joel
King Features
216 E 45th St
New York, NY 10017
Cartoonist V: 03/11/96

Pettit, Bob
7 Garden Lane
New Orleans, LA 70124
Basketball Star V: 11/01/96

Petty, Kyle
830 W Lexington
High Point, NC 27262
NASCAR Driver V: 02/17/96

1811 Volusia Ave
Daytona Beach, FL 32015
Alternate V: 01/21/96

Sabco Racing
PO Box 560579
Charlotte, NC 28256
Alternate V: 11/20/96

Petty, Lee
Petty Enterprises
Rt 4-Box 86
Randleman, NC 27317
NASCAR Driver V: 03/02/96

Petty, Lori
Creative Artists Agency
9830 Wilshire Bl
Beverly Hills, CA 90212
Actress V: 12/07/96

Petty, Lori, Cont.
12301 Wilshire Bl #200
Los Angeles, CA 90025-1007
Forwarded V: 03/15/96

Petty, Lynda
Petty Enterprises
Rt 4-Box 86
Randleman, NC 27317
NASCAR Driver V: 03/02/96

Petty, Maurice
Petty Enterprises
Rt 4-Box 86
Randleman, NC 27317
NASCAR Driver V: 03/02/96

Petty, Richard
Rt 3-Box 631
Randleman, NC 27317
NASCAR Driver V: 07/02/96

Pfeiffer, Michelle
c/o ICM
8942 Wilshire Bl
Beverly Hills, CA 90211
Actress V: 03/11/96

721 N Fairview St
Burbank, CA 91505-3002
Alternate V: 11/01/96

2210 Wilshire Bl #998
Santa Monica, CA 90403
Forwarded V: 03/15/96

Phair, Liz
c/o ICM
8942 Wilshire Bl
Beverly Hills, CA 90211
Singer V: 01/14/96

Pham, Tuan
4C-1000-Soc Son
Hanoi, Vietnam
Cosmonaut V: 10/23/96

Phelps, Peter
Barbara Lean
261 Miller St
N Sydney, NSW, Australia
Actor V: 01/03/96

Philadelphia 76ers
Veterans Stadium
PO Box 25040
Phildelphia, PA 19147
Team Office V: 02/15/96

Philadelphia Eagles
Broad St & Pattison Ave
Philadelphia, PA 19148
Team Office V: 02/15/96

Philadelphia Flyers
The Spectrum
Philadelphia, PA 19148
Team Office V: 02/01/96

Philadelphia Phillies
PO Box 7575
Veterans Stadium
Philadelphia, PA 19101
Team Office V: 02/15/96

Philbin, Regis
c/o 'Live'
7 Lincoln Square-5th Fl
New York, Ny 10023
TV Host V: 03/30/96

Phillips, Chynna
938 2nd St #302
Santa Monica, CA 90403
Actress V: 02/01/96

Phillips, Ethan
Writers & Artists
924 Westwood Bl #900
Los Angeles, CA 90024
Actor V: 12/15/96

ST-Voyager
5555 Melrose Ave
Hollywood, CA 90036
Alternate V: 02/15/96

Phillips, Julianne
Innovative Artists
1999 Ave of the Stars #2850
Los Angeles, CA 90067
Actress V: 12/11/96

2227 Mandeville Canyon Rd
Los Angeles, CA 90049
Alternate V: 01/21/96

Phillips, Lou Diamond
Innovative Artists
1999 Ave of the Stars #2850
Los Angeles, CA 90067
Actor V: 12/11/96

Phillips, Mackenzie
c/o Bauman/Hiller
5750 Wilshire Bl #512
Los Angeles, CA 90036
Actress V: 02/23/96

Phillips, Michele
Ambrosio & Mortimer
9150 Wilshire Bl #175
Beverly Hills, CA 90212
Actress V: 12/01/96

Phoenix Cardinals
PO Box 888
Phoenix, AZ 85001
Team Office V: 01/02/97

Phoenix Firebirds
PO Box 8303
Scottsdale, AZ 85252-8303
Team Office V: 01/21/97

Phoenix Suns
PO Box 1361
Phoenix, AZ 85001
Team Office V: 01/02/97

Piazza, Mike
1000 Elysian Park Ave
Los Angeles, CA 90012
Baseball Star V: 01/20/96

Picardo, Robert
Gersh Agency
232 N Canon Dr
Beverly Hills, CA 90210
Actor V: 12/09/96

Picasso, Paloma
Lopez/Cambil Ltd
37 W 57th St
New York, NY 10019
Celebrity V: 11/01/96

Quintana Roo Ltd
291A Brompton Rd
London SW3 2DY, England
Alternate V: 11/01/96

1021 Park Ave
New York, NY 10021
Forwarded V: 05/15/96

Pickett, Cindy
c/o Innovative Atrists
1999 Ave of the Stars #2850
Los Angeles, CA 90067
Actress V: 02/23/96

Pierce, David Hyde
Silver/Massetti & Associates
8730 Sunset Bl #480
Los Angeles, CA 90069
Actor V: 12/14/96

Pierce, David Hyde, Cont.
9255 Sunset Bl #710
Los Angeles, CA 90069
Alternate V: 10/23/96

Bloom Agency
9200 Sunset Bl #710
Los Angeles, CA 90069
Forwarded V: 10/23/96

Pierce, Stack
Haeggstrom Office
6404 Wilshire Bl #1100
Los Angeles, CA 90048
Actor V: 12/10/96

Pierpoint, Eric
Buckwald & Associates
9229 Sunset Bl #710
Los Angeles, CA 90069
Actor V: 12/06/96

Pignatano, Joe
150 78th St
Brooklyn, NY 11209
Baseball Star V: 02/08/96

Pilcher, Andrew
King Features
216 E 45th St
New York, NY 10017
Cartoonist V: 03/11/96

Pine, Robert
House of Representatives
9911 Pico Bl #1060
Los Angeles, CA 90035
Actor V: 12/10/96

Pinewood Studios
Iver Heath
Buckinghamshire SL0 0NH
England
Production Office V: 01/13/96

Piscopo, Joe
Wm Morris Agency
1350 Sixth Ave
New York, NY 10019
Actor V: 03/20/96

8665 Burton Way #5
Los Angeles, CA 90048
Alternate V: 01/03/97

Pistone, Tom
7858 Old Concord Rd
Charlotte, NC 28213
NASCAR Driver V: 03/02/96

Pitney, Gene
8901-6 Miles Rd
Caledonia, WS 53108
Singer V: 03/02/96

Pitt, Brad
9150 Wilshire Bl #350
Beverly Hills, CA 90212-3427
Actor V: 03/14/96

c/o CAA
9830 Wilshire Bl
Beverly Hills, CA 90212
Alternate V: 01/27/96

Pitt, Ingrid
c/o Agent
4 Waterloo Pl
London SW1Y 4AW, England
Actress V: 03/06/96

4 Court Lodg-48 Sloane Sq
London SW1, England
Alternate V: 11/22/96

Chiller Theatre
PO Box 23
Rutherford, NJ 07070
Forwarded V: 01/12/96

Pittsburgh Pinguins
Civic Arena
Pittsburgh, PA 15219
Team Office V: 01/02/97

Pittsburgh Pirates
PO Box 7000
Three Rivers Stadium
Pittsburgh, PA 15212
Team Office V: 01/02/97

Pittsburgh Steelers
Three Rivers Stadium
300 Stadium Circle
Pittsburgh, PA 15212
Team Office V: 01/02/97

Place, Mary Kay
Gersh Agency
232 N Canon Dr
Beverly Hills, CA 90210
Actress V: 12/09/96

Plakson, Suzie
Innovative Artists
1999 Ave of the Stars #2850
Los Angeles, CA 90067
Actress V: 12/11/96

Playboy Enterprises
Playmate Fanmail
2112 Broadway St
Santa Monica, CA 90404-2912
Fan Services V: 03/14/96

Playboy Magazine
680 N Lake Shore Drive
Chicago, IL 60611
Production Office V: 02/16/96

919 N Michigan Ave
Chicago, IL 60611
Alternate V: 03/01/96

Playboy Products
PO Box 1554
Elk Grove Village, IL 60007
Production Office V: 03/10/96

Player, Gary
Int'l Mgmt Grp
1 Erieview Plaza
Cleveland, OH 44114
Golfer V: 01/16/96

PO Box 785629
Sandton 2146, South Africa
Alternate V: 02/04/96

Players Talent
8770 Shoreham Dr #2
W Hollywood, CA 90069
Talent Agency V: 02/02/96

Playmate Fan Mail
500 N Michigan Ave #1920
Chicago, IL 60611
Production Office V: 02/12/96

Pleshette, Suzanne
PO Box 1492
Beverly Hills, CA 90213
Actress V: 10/23/96

Plimpton, Martha
502 Park Ave #15-G
New York, NY 10022
Actress V: 10/23/96

Plumb, Eve
c/o Cosden
3518 Cahuenga Bl W #216
Los Angeles, CA 90068
Actress V: 02/23/96

Plummer, Amanda
Innovative Artists
1999 Ave of the Stars #2850
Los Angeles, CA 90067
Actress V: 12/11/96

Plummer, Christopher
49 Wampum Hill Rd
Weston, CT 06883
Actor V: 03/24/96

Podewell, Cathy
9200 Sunset Bl #1232
Los Angeles, CA 90069
Actress V: 11/01/96

Shapira Associates
15301 Ventura Bl #345
Sherman Oaks, CA 91403
Forwarded V: 01/09/96

Pogue, William R
NASA/LBJ Space Center
Houston, TX 77058
Astronaut V: 03/03/96

Pohl, Dan
11609 S Tusaye Ct
Phoenix, AZ 85044
Golfer V: 02/04/96

Poitier, Sidney
9255 Doheny Rd
W Hollywood, CA 90069-3201
Actor V: 01/12/96

1221 Stone Canyon Rd
Los Angeles, CA 90077-2919
Alternate V: 10/23/96

Polanski, Roman
Beaume Agency
201 rue Faubourg St Honore
Paris 75008, France
Director V: 09/15/96

37 Bis Rue de Ponthien
Paris 75008, France
Alternate V: 10/23/96

Penta Int'l
8 Queen St
London W1X 7PH, England
Forwarded V: 02/09/96

Pollack, Cheryl
1999 Ave of the Stars #2850
Los Angeles, CA 90067
Actress V: 01/11/97

Pollack, Sydney
13525 Lucca Dr
Pacific Palisades, CA 90272
Directory V: 01/15/96

Pollard, Larry
NASCAR
1811 Volusia Ave
Daytona Beach, FL 32015
NASCAR Driver V: 03/02/96

Pollard, Michael J
29652 Cuthbert Rd
Malibu, CA 90265
Actor V: 05/04/96

c/o Bikoff
621 N Orlando #8
W Hollywood, CA 90048
Alternate V: 03/16/96

Ponti, Carlo
Chalet Daniel
Burgenstock
Nidwalden, Switzerland
Producer V: 09/27/96

Ponty, Jean-Luc
c/o ICM
8942 Wilshire Bl
Beverly Hills, CA 90211
Musician V: 11/28/96

Pope John Paul II
Palazzo Apostolico
Vatican City, Italy
Religious Leader V: 01/30/97

Porizkova, Paulina
Creative Artists Agency
9830 Wilshire Bl
Beverly Hills, CA 90212
Actress V: 12/07/96

331 Newbury St
Boston, MA 02115
Alternate V: 03/02/96

Porretta, Matthew
Artists Agency
10000 Santa Monica Bl #305
Los Angeles, CA 90067
Actor V: 01/15/97

Porter, Don
2049 Century Park E #2500
Los Angeles, CA 90067
Actor V: 10/23/96

Portland Trailblazers
700 NE Multnomah St #600
Portland, OR 97232
Team Office V: 02/15/97

Portman, Natalie
c/o ICM
8942 Wilshire Bl
Beverly Hills, CA 90211
Actress V: 12/15/96

Posey, Parker
Wm Morris Agency
151 El Camino
Beverly Hills, CA 90212
Actress V: 01/15/97

Post, Markie
Creative Artists Agency
9830 Wilshire Bl
Beverly Hills, CA 90212
Actress V: 12/07/96

10153 1/2 Riverside Dr #333
Toluca Lake, CA 91602
Alternate V: 11/20/96

Poston, Tom
2930 Deep Canyon Dr
Beverly Hills, CA 90210-1010
Actor V: 07/13/96

1 N Venice Bl #106
Venice, CA 90291
Forwarded V: 02/02/96

Potomac Productions
PO Box 5973-215
Sherman Oaks, CA 91413
Alternate V: 12/10/96

Potts, Annie
Wm Morris Agency
151 El Camino
Beverly Hills, CA 90212
Actress V: 12/12/96

7920 Sunset Bl #350
Los Angeles, CA 90046
Alternate V: 03/20/96

Pounder, CCH
Smith & Associates
121 N San Vicente Bl
Beverly Hills, CA 90211
Actress V: 12/15/96

Povich, Maury
250 W 57th St #26W
New York, NY 10019
TV Host V: 02/10/96

Powell, Colin
310 S Henry St
Alexandria, VA 22314
War Hero V: 02/01/96

Powell, Jane
150 W End Ave #26C
New York, NY 10023-5743
Actress V: 03/03/96

Artists Group
10100 Santa Monica Bl #2490
Los Angeles, CA 90067
Alternate V: 12/04/96

Powell, Robert
388 Oxford St
London W1, England
Actor V: 02/24/96

Powers, Mala
10543 Valley Spring Ln
Toluca Lake, CA 91602
Actress V: 03/17/96

151 El Camino Dr
Beverly Hills, CA 90212
Forwarded V: 01/16/96

Powers, Stefanie
PO Box 67951
Los Angeles, CA 90067
Actress V: 06/25/96

Powter, Susan
RPR & Associates
5952 Royal Lane #264
Dallas, TX 75230
Fitness Expert V: 01/14/96

Prange, Laurie
1519 Sargent Pl
Los Angeles, CA 90026
Actress V: 05/15/96

Prather, Joan
31647 Sea Level Dr
Malibu, CA 90265
Actress V: 05/15/96

Precourt Jr, Charles J
NASA/LBJ Space Center
Houston, TX 77058
Astronaut V: 02/02/96

Premiere Artists Agency
8899 Beverly Bl #510
Los Angeles, CA 90048
Talent Agency V: 02/02/96

Premiere Magazine
2 Park Ave
New York, NY 10016
Publisher V: 03/21/96

Prentice, John
King Features
235 E 45th St
New York, NY 10017
Cartoonist V: 04/13/96

Prentiss, Paula
Gersh Agency
232 N Canon Dr
Beverly Hills, CA 90210
Actress V: 12/09/96

719 N Foothill Rd
Beverly Hills, CA 90210
Alternate V: 02/16/96

Presle, Micheline
6 rue Antoine Dubois
F-75006 Paris, France
Actress V: 05/15/96

Presley, Lisa-Marie
1167 Summit Dr
Beverly Hills, CA 90210
Celebrity V: 01/13/97

Presley, Priscilla
Wm Morris Agency
151 El Camino
Beverly Hills, CA 90212
Actress V: 12/12/96

Siegel & Feldstein
1990 Bundy Dr #200
Los Angles, CA 90025
Alternate V: 01/21/96

1167 Summit Dr
Beverly Hills, CA 90210
Alternate V: 03/02/96

Graceland
PO Box 16508
Memphis, TN 38186-0508
Forwarded V: 09/21/96

Presley, Robert
Jackson Motorsports
PO Box 726-Airport Rd
Arden, NC 28704
NASCAR Driver V: 02/08/96

NASCAR
1811 Volusia Ave
Daytona Beach, FL 32015
Alternate V: 03/14/96

Pressman, Lawrence
15033 Encanto Dr
Sherman Oaks, CA 91403
Actor V: 03/12/96

Preston, Kelly
c/o ICM
8942 Wilshire Bl
Beverly Hills, CA 90211
Actress V: 12/11/96

12522 Moorpark St #109
Studio City, CA 91604
Alternate V: 11/28/96

Previn, Andre
135 N Grand Ave
Los Angeles, CA 90067
Composer V: 02/01/96

Price, Ray
c/o Faragher
123 Taggert
Nashville, TN 37205
Singer V: 02/02/96

Prickett, Carl
c/o Bergon
336 E 17th St
Costa Mesa, CA 92627
Actor V: 01/21/96

Pride, Charlie
c/o Hexter
10620 Marquis Lane
Dallas, TX 75229
Singer V: 02/02/96

PO Box 670507
Dallas, TX 75367
Forwarded V: 01/01/96

Priest, Pat
PO Box 1298
Hatley, ID 83334
Actress V: 03/30/96

Priestly, Jason
1811 Whitely Ave
Los Angeles, CA 90028
Actor V: 06/21/96

Prima Model Mgmt
933 N La Brea Ave #200
Los Angeles, CA 90038
Talent Agency V: 02/02/96

Prince
9830 Wilshire Bl
Beverly Hills, CA 90212
Singer V: 01/14/96

9401 Kiowa Trail
Chanhassen, MN 5317
Alternate V: 03/17/96

Principal, Victoria
814 Cynthia St
Beverly Hills, CA 90210-3519
Actress V: 01/02/96

Prine, Andrew
3264 Longridge Ave
Beverly Hills, CA 90210
Actor V: 01/21/96

Prinze Jr, Freddie
Gersh Agency
232 N Canon Dr
Beverly Hills, CA 90210
Actor V: 12/15/96

Privilege Agency
8170 Beverly Bl #204
Los Angeles, CA 90048
Talent Agency V: 02/02/96

Pro Football HOF
2121 George Halas Dr NW
Canton, OH 44708
Museum V: 01/02/97

Pro-Sport & Entertainment
1990 S Bundy Dr #700
Los Angeles, CA 90025
Talent Agency V: 01/02/97

Prochnow, Jurgen
c/o Wm Morris
151 El Camino Dr
Beverly Hills, CA 90212
Actor V: 03/01/96

Lamonstrasse 98
Munich 81679, Germany
Alternate V: 01/21/96

Producers Guild
400 S Beverly Dr #211
Beverly Hills, CA 90212
Guild Office V: 01/02/97

Progressive Artists
400 S Beverly Dr #216
Beverly Hills, CA 90212
Talent Agency V: 01/02/97

Prosky, Robert
Gersh Agency
232 N Canon Dr
Beverly Hills, CA 90210
Actor V: 12/09/96

Provenza, Paul
Gersh Agency
232 N Canon Dr
Beverly Hills, CA 90210
Actor V: 12/09/96

Provost, Jon
c/o JPA
627 Montclair Dr
Santa Rosa, CA 95409
Actor V: 09/06/96

Prowse, Dave
7 Carlyle Rd
Croydon CR0 7HN, England
Actor V: 02/14/96

c/o Prowse Fitness Center
12 Marshalsea Rd
London SE1, England
Alternate V: 04/13/96

Pullman, Bill
2599 Glen Green
Los Angeles, CA 90068
Actor V: 10/23/96

Punch, Jerry
NASCAR
1811 Volusia Ave
Daytona Beach, FL 32015
NASCAR Announcer V: 03/02/96

Purcell, Lee
Artists Agency
10000 Santa Monica Bl #305
Los Angeles, CA 90067
Actress V: 12/02/96

1317 N San Fernando Rd #167
Burbank, CA 91504
Alternate V: 01/02/96

Purcell, Sarah
4735 Sepulveda Bl #413
Sherman Oaks, CA 91403
Actress V: 10/23/96

6525 Esplanade St
Playa del Rey, CA 90293
Alternate V: 10/10/96

Purl, Linda
Gersh Agency
232 N Canon Dr
Beverly Hills, CA 90210
Actress V: 12/09/96

Purvis, Jeff
NASCAR
1811 Volusia Ave
Daytona Beach, FL 32015
NASCAR Driver V: 03/26/96

Puzo, Mario
866 Manor Lane
Bay Shore, NY 11706
Author V: 01/13/97

Pyle, Denver
10614 Whipple St
N Hollywood, CA 91602
Actor V: 03/01/96

Q

QVC
1365 Enterprise Dr
West Chester, PA 19380
Production Office V: 01/02/97

Quaid, Dennis
c/o ICM
8942 Wilshire Bl
Beverly Hills, CA 90211
Actor V: 01/14/96

11718 Barrington Ct #508
Los Angeles, CA 90049
Alternate V: 03/04/96

9665 Wilshire Bl #200
Beverly Hills, CA 90212
Forwarded V: 10/23/96

Quaid, Randy
c/o TMCE
270 N Canon Dr #1064
Beverly Hills, CA 90210
Actor V: 01/11/96

Quaid, Randy, Cont.
PO Box 17372
Beverly Hills, CA 90209
Alternate V: 02/19/96

Quality Artists
5455 Wilshire Bl #1807
Los Angles, CA 90036
Talent Agency V: 01/02/97

Quayle, J Danforth
Campaign America
11711 N Pennsylvania St #100
Carmel, IN 46032
Former VP-USA V: 02/28/96

7 N Jefferson St
Huntington, IN 46750
Alternate V: 12/27/96

Quebec Nordiques
Colisee de Quebec
2205 Ave du Colisee
Quebec, Quebec, Canada G1L 4W7
Team Office V: 01/01/97

Quigley, Joan
1055 California St #14
San Francisco, CA 94108
Psychic V: 03/17/96

Quigley, Linnea
13659 Victory Bl #467
Van Nuys, CA 91401
Actress V: 03/20/96

Purrfect Productions
PO Box 430
Newbury Park, CA 91320
Forwarded V: 01/13/96

Quinlan, Kathleen
PO Box 2465
Malibu, CA 90265
Actress V: 01/19/96

Quinn, Aidan
9830 Wilshire Bl
Beverly Hills, CA 90212
Actor V: 12/07/96

Quinn, Anthony
60 East End Ave
New York, NY 10028
Actor V: 10/23/96

PO Box 479
Bristol, RI 02809-0479
Alternate V: 01/13/97

R

REAL TV
WB-TV
1438 N Gower
Hollywood, CA 90028
Audience Services V: 04/12/96

RELATIVITY
8660 Hayden Place
Culver City, CA 90232
Production Office V: 11/11/96

ABC-TV
77 W 66th St
New York, NY 10023
Alternate V: 11/11/96

RESCUE 911
Shapiro Productions
520 Broadway-Suite 220
Santa Monica, CA 90401
Production Office V: 10/23/96

RICKIE LAKE SHOW
c/o Rickie Lake
401 5th Ave
New York, NY 10016-3317
Production Office V: 01/12/96

ROLANDA SHOW
Rolanda Watts
325 E 75th St-4th Fl
New York, NY 10021
Production Office V: 01/16/96

ROOM FOR TWO
c/o Warner TV
4000 Warner Bl
Burbank, CA 91522
Production Office V: 01/20/96

ROSEANNE
c/o CBS-MTM Studios
4024 Radford Ave #3
Studio City, CA 91604
Production Office V: 01/20/96

c/o ABC-TV
77 W 66th St
New York, NY 10023
Alternate V: 12/15/96

Rabbitt, Eddie
c/o Moress
1209 16th Ave S
Nashville, TN 37212
Singer V: 10/18/96

Rachins, Alan
c/o APA
9000 Sunset Bl #1200
Los Angeles, CA 90069
Actor V: 03/17/96

Radatz, Dick
PO Box 348
Braintree, MA 02184
Baseball Star V: 11/01/96

Rae, Charlotte
10790 Wilshire Bl #903
Los Angeles, CA 90024-4448
Actress V: 01/12/96

PO Box 49991
Los Angeles, CA 90067
Alternate V: 01/13/97

Rael Company
9255 Sunset Bl #425
Los Angeles, CA 90069
Talent Agency V: 02/02/96

Raffin, Deborah
Shapira & Associates
15301 Ventura Bl #345
Sherman Oaks, CA 91403
Actress V: 12/13/96

2630 Eden Place
Beverly Hills, CA 90210
Alternate V: 12/10/96

Ragar, Ken
NASCAR
1811 Volusia Ave
Daytona Beach, FL 32015
NASCAR Driver V: 03/02/96

Rahal, Bobby
934 Crescent Bl
Glenellyn, IL 60137
Race Driver V: 03/01/96

Railsback, Steve
PO Box 1308
Hollywood, CA 90078
Actor V: 04/06/96

Rainer, Luise
Vico Morcote
Lake Lugano
Switzerland CH-6911
Actress V: 03/01/**96**

Raines, Christina
Bauman & Hiller
5750 Wilshire Bl #512
Los Angeles, CA 90036
Actress V: 12/05/96

Rainey, Ford
F Amsel
6310 San Vincente Bl #407
Los Angles, CA 90048
Actor V: 01/21/96

Rainwater, Gregg
PO Box 291836
Los Angeles, CA 90078
Actor V: 04/01/96

Raitt, Bonnie
1344 Spalding Ave
Los Angeles, CA 90046
Singer V: 12/01/96

PO Box 626
Los Angeles, CA 90078
Alternate V: 01/14/96

c/o Gold Mountain
120 W 44th St #704
New York, NY 10036
Alternate V: 01/12/96

c/o Gold Mountain
1111 16th Ave S #PH
Nashville, TN 37212
Forwarded V: 01/12/96

Ralston, Vera
4121 Cresciente Dr
Santa Barbara, CA 93110
Actress V: 01/30/96

Ramis, Harold
12921 Evanston St
Los Angeles, CA 90049-3714
Actor V: 11/01/96

14198 Alisal Ln
Santa Monica, CA 90402
Alternate V: 03/27/96

Rampal, Jean-Pierre
Colbert Artists
111 W 57th St
New York, NY 10019
Musician V: 02/09/96

Rampling, Charlotte
1 Ave Emile Augier
78290 Croissy-sur-Seine, France
Actress V: 03/01/96

London Mgmt
235 Regent St
London W1, England
Alternate V: 02/28/96

Randall, Tony
The Beresford
1 W 81st St #6D
New York, NY 10024
Actor V: 03/03/96

Randolph, John
1850 N Whitley Pl
Los Angeles, CA 90028
Actor V: 03/27/96

Randolph, Joyce
295 Central Park W #18A
New York, NY 10024
Actress V: 11/20/96

Rapaport, Michael
c/o IAA
1999 Ave of the Stars #2850
Los Angeles, CA 90067
Actor V: 09/15/96

Raphael, Sally Jesse
Creative Artists Agency
9830 Wilshire Bl
Beverly Hills, CA 90212
TV Host V: 12/07/96

510 W 57th St #200
New York, NY 10019
Alternate V: 03/17/96

Rasche, David
Gersh Agency
232 N Canon Dr
Beverly Hills, CA 90210
Actor V: 12/09/96

687 Grove Ln
Santa Barbara, CA 93105-2449
Alternate V: 11/01/96

Rashad, Phylicia
Rothschild Productions
330 E 48th St
New York, NY 10017
Actress V: 10/23/96

c/o APA
9000 Sunset Bl #1200
Los Angeles, CA 90069
Alternate V: 12/02/96

130 W 42nd St #2400
New York, NY 10036
Forwarded V: 02/02/96

Rather, Dan
CBS-TV
51 W 52nd St
New York, NY 10019
Correspondant V: 01/14/96

Rawls, Lou
109 Fremont Place
Los Angeles, CA 90005
Singer V: 09/12/96

Readdy, William F
NASA/LBJ Space Center
Hoston, TX 77058
Astronaut V: 01/31/96

Reagan, Michael
10880 Wilshire Bl-7th Fl
Los Angeles, CA 90024
Celebrity V: 02/02/96

4740 Allott Ave
Sherman Oaks, CA 91403
Alternate V: 01/13/97

Reagan, Nancy
668 St Cloud Rd
Bel Air, CA 90077
Former 1st Lady V: 11/07/96

Reagan, Ronald
11000 Wilshire Bl
Los Angeles, CA 90024
Former President V: 11/07/96

Rancho del Cielo
Santa Barbara, CA 93108
Alternate V: 03/18/96

2121 Ave of the Stars
Los Angeles, CA 90067
Forwarded V: 01/12/96

Reagan Jr, Ronald
2612 28th Ave W
Seattle, WA 98199-3320
Celebrity V: 01/12/96

Reason, Rex
20105 Rhapsody Rd
Walnut Creek, CA 91789
Actor V: 02/03/96

Rector, Jeff
JR Fan Club
10748 Aqua Vista St
N Hollywood, CA 91602
Fan Service V: 01/10/96

Reddy, Helen
820 Stanford St
Santa Monica, CA 90403
Singer V: 11/01/96

Redford, Robert
c/o CAA
9830 Wilshire Bl
Beverly Hills, CA 90212
Actor V: 01/14/96

RR3 Box 837
Provo, Utah 84604
Alternate V: 05/02/96

1101-E Montana Ave
Santa Monica, CA 90403
Forwarded V: 10/23/96

1223 Wilshire Bl #412
Santa Monica, CA 90403
Forwarded V: 11/01/96

Redgrave, Lynn
21342 Colina Dr
Topanga, CA 90290
Actress V: 06/17/96

PO Box 1207
Topanga, CA 90290
Alternate V: 01/03/97

Redgrave, Vanessa
c/o Agency
15 Golden Square
London W1R 3AG, England
Actress V: 02/28/96

1 Ravenscourt Rd
London W6, England
Alternate V: 06/17/96

Reece, Gabrielle
Elle Magazine
1633 Broadway
New York, NY 10019
Model V: 11/01/96

Reed, Oliver
Houmit Lane, Houmit Vale
Guernsey, Channel Islands
England
Actor V: 12/11/96

Reed, Pamela
1875 Century Park E #1300
Los Angeles, CA 90067
Actress V: 11/27/96

Reed, Shanna
Shapira Agency
15301 Ventura Bl #345
Sherman Oaks, CA 91403
Actress V: 02/24/96

Reed Hall, Alaina
Chasin Agency
190 N Canon Dr #201
Beverly Hills, CA 90210
Actress V: 02/24/96

Reese, Della
1910 Bel Air Rd
Los Angeles, CA 90077
Actress V: 06/17/96

Reeve, Christopher
121 Treadwell Hollow Rd
Williamstown, MA 01267
Actor V: 06/06/96

PO Box 26
Springfield, NJ 07081
Alternate V: 09/15/96

Reeves, Del
Grand Ole Opry
2804 Opryland Dr
Nashville, TN 37214
Singer V: 02/02/96

Reeves, Keanu
9460 Wilshire Bl-7th Fl
Beverly Hills, CA 90121-2732
Actor V: 08/28/96

c/o CAA
9830 Wilshire Bl
Beverly Hills, CA 90210
Forwarded V: 01/10/96

Reeves, Martha
PO Box 1987
Paramount, CA 90723-1987
Singer V: 05/04/96

Reeves, Steve
Classic Images
PO Box 807
Valley Center, CA 92082
Actor V: 03/12/96

Regalbuto, Joe
Schoen Agency
606 N Larchmont Bl #309
Los Angeles, CA 90004
Actor V: 12/13/96

724 24th St
Santa Monica, CA 90405
Alternate V: 04/06/96

Regher, Duncan
Artists Agency
10000 Santa Monica Bl #305
Los Angeles, CA 90067
Actor V: 03/17/96

Reid, Daphne Maxwell
Wm Morris Agency
151 El Camino
Beverly Hills, CA 90212
Actress V: 12/12/96

Reid, Tim
c/o MTA
4526 Wilshire Bl
Los Angeles, CA 90010
Actor V: 01/10/96

11342 Dona Lisa
Studio City, CA 91604
Forwarded V: 03/02/96

Reightler Jr, Kenneth S
NASA/LBJ Space Center
Hoston, TX 77058
Astronaut V: 01/31/96

Reilly, Charles Nelson
2341 Gloaming Way
Beverly Hills, CA 90210
Actor V: 06/17/96

Reiner, Carl
Creative Artists Agency
9830 Wilshire Bl
Beverly Hills, CA 90212
Actor V: 12/07/96

Reiner, Carl, Cont.
714 N Rodeo Dr
Santa Monica, CA 90403
Alternate V: 11/01/96

Reiner, Rob
255 S Chadbourne Ave
Los Angeles, CA 90049
Producer V: 05/16/96

Reinhold, Judge
Innovative Artists
1999 Ave of the Stars #2850
Los Angeles, CA 90067
Actor V: 12/11/96

Reiser, Paul
4243 Colfax Ave #C
Studio City, CA 91604
Actor V: 03/12/96

Remini, Leah
Rick Seigel Mgmt
1940 Westwood Bl #169
Los Angeles, CA 90025
Actress V: 01/09/96

Culver Studios
9336 W Washington Bl
Culver City, CA 99232
Alternate V: 01/13/96

Remsen, Bert
Stone Manners Talent
8091 Selma Ave
Los Angeles, CA 90068
Actor V: 12/15/96

Renee, Kim
7790 Royal Oaks Rd
Laas Vegas, NV 89123
Stunt Person V: 03/17/96

Renfro, Brad
322 Foxboro Drive
Walnut, CA 91789
Actor V: 01/12/96

Renna, Doris Day
16222 Monterey Lane 279
Huntington Beach, CA 92649
Actress V: 01/12/96

Reno, Hunter
Elite Agency
111 E 22nd St #200
New York, NY 10010
Model V: 09/14/96

Republic Pictures
12636 Beatrice St
PO Box 66930
Los Angeles, CA 90066
Production Office V: 03/17/96

Request I & II
685 Third Ave
New York, NY 10017-4085
Production Office V: 01/12/96

Retton, Mary Lou
322 Vista Del Mar
Redondo Beach, CA 90277
Olympian V: 10/23/96

1815 Via del Prado #209
Redondo Beach, CA 90277
Alternate V: 02/01/96

Revill, Clive
15029 Encanto Dr
Sherman Oaks, CA 91403
Actor V: 01/21/96

Reynolds, Burt
16133 Jupiter Farms Rd
Jupiter, FL 33478
Actor V: 11/13/96

1061 Indian Town Rd
Jupiter, FL 33458
Alternate V: 03/26/96

Wm Morris
151 El Camino Dr
Beverly Hills, CA 90212
Forwarded V: 01/14/96

Reynolds, Debbie
305 Convention Center Dr
Las Vegas, NV 89109
Actress V: 03/01/96

Rhys-Davies, John
Buckwald & Associates
9229 Sunset Bl #710
Los Angeles, CA 90069
Actor V: 12/06/96

8033 Sunset Bl #9
Los Angeles, CA 90046
Alternate V: 01/16/96

2036 Stanley Hills Dr
Los Angeles, CA 90046-7753
Forwarded V: 11/10/96

Ricci, Christina
PO Box 866
Teaneck, NJ 07666
Actress V: 01/02/97

8942 Wilshire Bl
Beverly Hills, CA 90211
Alternate V: 10/23/96

Rice, Donna
c/o Jennings
28035 Dorothy Dr #210A
Agoura, CA 91301
Actress V: 02/24/96

Richard, Cliff
St George's Hill
Weybridge, England
Actor V: 08/16/96

Richards, Ann W
PO Box 684746
Austin, TX 78768
Governor V: 10/23/96

Richards, Michael
c/o ICM
8942 Wilshire Bl
Beverly Hills, CA 90211
Actor V: 01/14/96

Richards, Richard N
NASA/LBJ Space Center
Hoston, TX 77058
Astronaut V: 01/31/96

Richards, Rusty
Box 100, Star Route
Modjeska, CA 92676-9801
Singer V: 11/11/96

Richardson, Ashley
L Danford
91-5th Ave #401
New York, NY 10003
Model V: 09/14/96

Richardson, Dot
USC Medical Center
1200 N State St #GH-3900
Los Angeles, CA 90033
Olympian V: 01/13/97

Richardson, Miranda
c/o Gardner
15 Kensington High St
London W8 5NP, England
Actress V: 10/23/96

Richardson, Miranda, Cont.
195 Devonshire Rd
London SE23 3NJ, England
Forwarded V: 01/02/96

Richardson, Natasha
c/o ICM
8942 Wilshire Bl
Beverly Hills, CA 90211
Actress V: 01/14/96

Richardson, Patricia
253 26th St #A-312
Santa Monica, CA 90402-2523
Actress V: 01/09/97

Richie, Lionel
c/o LRFC
PO Box 9055
Calabasas, CA 91372-9055
Singer V: 12/15/96

10794 Wilkens Ave #303
Los Angeles, CA 90024
Alternate V: 01/13/97

Richmond, Peter
Craig Agency
8485 Melrose Place-Suite E
Los Angeles, CA 90069
Actor V: 12/08/96

Rickles, Don
Bresler/Kelly
15760 Ventura Bl #1730
Encino, CA 91436
Actor V: 12/06/96

925 N Alpine Dr
Beverly Hills, CA 90210
Alternate V: 02/04/96

9056 Santa Monica Bl #100
Hollywood, CA 90069
Forwarded V: 01/12/96

Rickman, Alan
c/o ICM
76 Oxford St
London W1N 0AX, England
Actor V: 11/07/96

Ride, Sally K
NASA/LBJ Space Center
Hoston, TX 77058
Astronaut V: 01/19/9

Ride, Sally K, Cont.
c/o Rhoads
Washington Speakers Bureau
123 N Henry St
Alexandria, VA 22314
Alternate V: 03/17/96

Rider, Chuck
Bahari Racing
47 Rolling Hills Rd
Mooresville, NC 28115
NASCAR Owner V: 03/02/96

Rigby, Cathy
2695 Camino del Sol
Fullerton, CA 92663
Olympian V: 10/10/96

Rigg, Diana
2-4 Noel St
London W1V 3RB England
Actress V: 02/21/97

c/o Larner
130 W 57th St #10A
New York, NY 10019
Forwarded V: 02/15/96

c/o London Mgmt
235-241 Regent St
London W1A 2JT England
Forwarded V: 01/04/96

Rightous Brothers
Barry Riclera
9841 Hot Springs Dr
Huntington Beach, CA 92646
Singers V: 02/15/96

Frontier Hotel & Casino
Las Vegas, NV
Alternate V: 03/12/96

Riley, Jeannie C
PO Box 680454
Franklin, TN 37068-0454
Singer V: 01/09/97

Riley, Pat
PO Box 12819
Albany, NY 12212-2817
Basketball Coach V: 08/28/96

Ringwald, Molly
Wm Morris
151 El Camino
Beverly Hills, CA 90212
Actress V: 03/05/96

Rippy, Rodney A
3939 Veselich Ave #251
Los Angeles, CA 90039-1435
Actor V: 05/06/96

Ritenoure, Lee
11806 Dorothy St #108
Los Angeles, CA 9049-5469
Singer V: 01/13/97

Ritter, John
Wm Morris
151 El Camino
Beverly Hills, CA 90212
Actor V: 01/02/96

9545 Dalegrove Dr
Beverly Hills, CA 90210
Alternate V: 11/01/96

15030 Ventura Bl #806
Sherman Oaks, CA 91403
Forwarded V: 10/23/96

Rivera, Geraldo
555 W 57th St #1100
New York, NY 10019
TV Host V: 02/10/96

Rivers, Joan
Joan's World
113 Post Rd E
Westport, CT 06880
Entertainer V: 01/12/96

10 Bay St #156
Westport, CT 06880
Alternate V: 01/12/96

1 E 62nd St
New York, NY 10021
Alternate V: 11/01/96

Wm Morris Agency
151 El Camino
Beverly Hills, CA 90212
Forwarded V: 01/14/96

Robards, Jason
Paradigm Agency
10100 Santa Monica Bl-25th Fl
Los Angeles, CA 90067
Actor V: 12/13/96

10 E 44th St #500
New York, NY 10017
Alternate V: 01/13/97

Robards, Jason, Cont.
200 W 57th St #900
New York, NY 10019
Forwarded V: 01/15/96

10 E 57th St #900
New York, NY 10019
Forwarded V: 01/03/97

Robbins, Tim
c/o ICM
8942 Wilshire Bl
Beverly Hills, CA 90211
Actor V: 01/14/96

Roberts, Doris
c/o APA
9000 Sunset Bl 1200
Los Angeles, CA 90069
Actress V: 02/24/96

Roberts, Eric
UTA
9560 Wilshire Bl-5th Fl
Beverly Hills, CA 90212
Actor V: 02/15/96

2605 Ivanhoe Dr
Los Angeles, CA 90039
Alternate V: 01/16/96

Roberts, Julia
ICM-Goldsmith
8942 Wilshire Bl
Beverly Hills, CA 90211
Actress V: 01/16/96

6220 Del Valle Dr
Los Angeles, CA 90048-5306
Alternate V: 01/12/96

Roberts, Oral
777 Lewis St
Tulsa, OK 74130
Evangelist V: 10/23/96

Roberts, Tanya
Gold/Marshak
3500 W Olive Ave #1400
Burbank, CA 91505
Actress V: 12/10/96

7436 Del Zuro Dr
Los Angeles, CA 90046-1328
Alternate V: 11/10/96

Robertson, Cliff
c/o ICM
8942 Wilshire Bl
Beverly Hills, CA 90211
Actor V: 12/11/96

325 Dunemere Dr
La Jolla, CA 92037
Alternate V: 03/26/96

PO Box 940
Water Mill, NY 11976
Forwarded V: 03/14/96

Robertson, Dale
Shapira Agency
15301 Ventura Bl #345
Sherman Oaks, CA 91403
Actor V: 03/11/96

Robertson, T Wayne
NASCAR
1811 Volusia Ave
Daytona Beach, FL 32015
NASCAR Driver V: 03/14/96

Robie, Wendy
Gage Group
9255 Sunset Bl #515
Los Angeles, CA 90069
Actress V: 12/08/96

Robinson, Andrew
2671 Byron Pl
Los Angeles, CA 90046
Actor V: 10/23/96

Paradigm Agency
10100 Santa Monica Bl-25th Fl
Los Angeles, CA 90067
Alternate V: 03/11/96

Robinson, Ann
1359 Elysian Park Dr
Los Angeles, CA 90026
Actress V: 08/08/96

Robinson, Brooks
36 S Charles St #2000
Baltimore, MD 21201
Baseball Star V: 01/13/96

Robinson, Holly
Wm Morris Agency
151 El Camino
Beverly Hills, CA 90212
Actress V: 12/12/96

Robinson, Holly, Cont.
10683 Santa Monica Bl
Los Angeles, CA 90025-4807
Forwarded V: 03/16/96

Robinson, Pat
1000 Centeerville Tnpk
Virginia Beach, VA 23463
Religious Leader V: 12/12/96

Robinson, Shawna
1811 Volusia Ave
Daytona Beach, FL 32015
NASCAR Driver V: 10/23/96

Robinson, Smokey
613 N Oakhurst Dr
Beverly Hills, CA 90210
Singer V: 10/23/96

17085 Rancho St
Encino, CA 91316
Alternate V: 01/16/96

Roddenberry, Majel Barrett
20th Century Artists
15315 Magnolia Bl #429
Sherman Oaks, CA 91403
Actress V: 02/26/96

9147 Leander Pl
Beverly Hills, CA 90210
Alternate V: 05/04/96

10615 Bellagio Rd
Los Angeles, CA 90077
Alternate V: 10/09/96

Lincoln Enterprises
PO Box 691370
Los Angeles, CA 90069
Forwarded V: 06/10/96

Rodgers, Bill
353 Marketplace, Fanuil Hall
Boston, MA 02109
Olympian V: 10/23/96

Rodriguez, Johnny
c/o Woolsey
1000 18th Ave S
Nashville, TN 37203
Singer V: 02/02/96

Roe, Tommy
c/o DHM
PO Box 26037
Minneapolis, MN 55447
Singer V: 10/23/96

Roebuck, Dan
PO Box 950597
Mission Hills, CA 91395-0597
Actor V: 01/12/96

Rogers, Fred
c/o PBS
1329 Braddock Pl
Alexandria, VA 22314
Educator V: 02/01/96

Mr Rogers
4802 5th Ave
Pittsburgh, PA 15213
Alternate V: 11/20/96

Rogers, Kenny
PO Box 24240
Nashville, TN 37202-4240
Singer V: 12/12/96

Rogers, Mimi
Creative Artists Agency
9830 Wilshire Bl
Beverly Hills, CA 90212
Actress V: 12/07/96

Rogers, Wayne
Artists Agency
10000 Santa Monica Bl #305
Los Angeles, CA 90067
Actor V: 12/03/96

11828 La Grange Ave
Los Angeles, CA 90025
Alternate V: 03/26/96

Roker, Roxie
Gage Agency
9255 Sunset Bl #515
Los Angeles, 90069
Actress V: 02/02/96

Rolanda Show
325 E Fifth St-4th Fl
New York, NY 10021
Production Office V: 11/01/96

Rolling Stone Magazine
1290 Ave of the Americas
New York, NY 10104
Publisher V: 02/10/96

Roman, Phil
10635 Riverside Dr
Toluka Lake, CA 91602
Cartoonist V: 02/04/96

Roman, Phil, Cont.
PO Box 7706
N Hollywood, CA 91617-7706
Alternate V: 03/30/96

Roman, Ruth
1220 Cliff Dr
Laguna Beach, CA 92651
Actress V: 05/15/96

Romano Modeling
PO Box 1951
Palm Springs, CA 92263
Talent Agency V: 11/11/96

Romanus, Richard
Chasin Agency
8899 Beverly Bl 7th Fl
Los Angeles, CA 90048
Actor V: 12/07/96

Romeo, Chuck
NASCAR
1811 Volusia Ave
Daytona Beach, FL 32015
NASCAR Official V: 03/14/96

Rominger, Kent V
NASA/LBJ Space Center
Houston, TX 77058
Astronaut V: 02/02/96

Romjim, Rebecca
Next Model Mgmt
115 E 57th St #1540
New York, NY 10022
Model V: 11/01/96

Roney, Bruce
NASCAR
1811 Volusia Ave
Daytona Beach, FL 32015
NASCAR Official V: 03/14/96

Ronstadt, Linda
Asher Mgmt
644 N Doheny Dr
Los Angeles, CA 90049
Singer V: 02/02/96

Rooney, Andy
254 Rowayton Ave
Norwalk, CT 06853
Author V: 02/09/96

Rooney, Mickey
Artists Group
10100 Santa Monica Bl #2490
Los Angeles, CA 90067
Actor V: 12/04/96

Rooney, Mickey, Cont.
31351 Via Colinas
Westlake Village, CA 91362
Alternate V: 01/11/96

1400 Red Sail Circle
Westlake Village, CA 91361
Forwarded V: 10/23/96

Rosado, Eduardo
Calle 3 Av Cupules No. 112-A
Col Garcia Gineres
Merida, Yucatan, Mexico 97070
Opera Singer V: 11/01/96

Rosamund, John
4 Deans Yard
London SW1P, England
Actor V: 03/01/96

Rose, Axl
15250 Ventura Bl #900
Sherman Oaks, CA 91403-3221
Singer V: 05/22/96

Rose, Charlie
c/o NBC
30 Rockefeller Plaza
New York, NY 10112
Correspondant V: 01/14/96

Rose, David
King Features
216 E 45th St
New York, NY 10017
Cartoonist V: 03/11/96

Rose, Jamie
Gold/Marshak
3500 W Olive Ave #1400
Burbank, CA 91505
Actress V: 12/10/96

Rose, Pete
6248 NW 32nd Terrace
Boca Raton, FL 33496-3326
Baseball Star V: 11/10/96

Rose Marie (Mazetta)
Ambrosio & Mortimer
9150 Wilshire Bl #175
Beverly Hills, CA 90212
Actress V: 12/01/96

6916 Chisolm Ave
Van Nuys, CA 91406
Alternate V: 05/02/96

Roseanne
Wm Morris
151 El Camino
Beverly Hills, CA 90212
Actress V: 01/14/96

2029 Century Park E #3950
Los Angeles, CA 90067-3025
Forwarded V: 01/12/96

Rosenberg Office
Marion Rosenberg
8428 Melrose Pl-Suite C
Los Angeles, CA 90069
Talent Agency V: 02/23/96

Ross, Diana
RTC Mgmt
PO Box 1683
New York, NY 10185
Singer V: 01/11/96

Ross, Donald K
15871 Glenwood Rd SW
Port Orchard, WA 98366
War Hero V: 03/17/96

Ross, Jerry L
NASA/LBJ Space Center
Houston, TX 77058
Astronaut V: 03/03/96

Ross, Katherine
Artists Agency
10000 Santa Monica Bl #305
Los Angeles, CA 90067
Actress V: 12/02/96

33050 Pacific Coast Hwy
Malibu, CA 90265
Alternate V: 06/17/96

Ross, Marion
Artists Agency
10000 Santa Monica Bl #305
Los Angeles, CA 90067
Actress V: 12/02/96

Roth, Tim
c/o Markham
Julian House/4 Windmill St
London W1P 1HF, England
Actor V: 10/23/96

Roundtree, Richard
Stone Manners Talent
8091 Selma Ave
Los Angeles, CA 90068
Actor V: 12/15/96

Rourke, Mickey
1020 Benedict Canyon Rd
Beverly Hills, CA 90210
Actor V: 03/14/96

Roush, Jack
Roush Racing
PO Box 1089
Liberty, NC 27298
NASCAR Owner V: 03/02/96

Rowe, Misty
50 Pierrepont Dr
Ridgefield, CT 06877-2020
Actress V: 03/14/96

Rowlands, Gena
7917 Woodrow Wilson Dr
Los Angeles, CA 90046
Actress V: 04/21/96

Royal, Billy Joe
c/o Entertainmnet
48 Music Square E
Nashville, TN 37204
Singer V: 02/02/96

RuPaul
Wm Morris Agency
151 El Camino
Beverly Hills, CA 90212
Model V: 12/12/96

Rubinstein, Zelda
8730 Sunset Bl #220W
Los Angeles, CA 90069
Actress V: 02/26/96

Rucker, Darlus
L Danford
91-5th Ave #401
New York, NY 10003
Model V: 09/14/96

Rudd, Ricky
PO Box 7586
Richamond, VA 23231
NASCAR Driver V: 03/14/96

Hendrick Motor Sports
5315 Stowe Lane-PO Box 9
Harrisburg, NC 28075
Forwarded V: 03/02/96

Ruehl, Mercedes
129 MacDougal St
New York, NY 10012-1265
Actress V: 05/04/96

Ruehl, Mercedes, Cont.
Box 178-Old Chelsea Station
New York, NY 10011
Alternate V: 01/15/96

Smith & Associates
121 N San Vicente Bl
Beverly Hills, CA 90211
Forwarded V: 01/21/96

Runco Jr, Mario
NASA/LBJ Space Center
Hoston, TX 77058
Astronaut V: 01/31/96

Rush, Barbara
1708 Tropical Ave
Beverly Hills, CA 90210
Actress V: 03/01/96

Russ, Tim
c/o Insiders
PO Box 8248
Long Beach, CA 90808
Actor V: 01/14/96

Stone Manners
8091 Selma Ave
Los Angles, CA 90046
Alternate V: 11/01/96

ST-Voyager
5555 Melrose Ave
Hollywood, CA 90036
Forwarded V: 02/15/96

Russ, William
Bresler/Kelly
15760 Ventura Bl #1730
Encino, CA 91436
Actor V: 12/06/96

Russell, Betsy
Henderson & Hogan Agency
247 S Beverly Dr #102
Bevery Hills, CA 90210
Actress V: 12/10/96

111 Sweetzer Ave #3
Los Angeles, CA 90043
Forwarded V: 03/05/96

13926 Magnolia Bl
Sherman Oaks, CA 91423
Forwarded V: 04/22/96

Russell, Jane
2934 Lorita Rd
Santa Barbara, CA 93108-1632
Actress V: 02/01/96

c/o Webb
7500 Devista Dr
Los Angeles, CA 90046
Alternate V: 02/24/96

Russell, Ken
16 Salisbury Pl
London W1H 1FH, England
Director V: 10/23/96

Russell, Kurt
Creative Artists Agency
9830 Wilshire Bl
Beverly Hills, CA 90212
Actor V: 12/07/96

Russell, Theresa
Wm Morris Agency
151 El Camino
Beverly Hills, CA 90212
Actress V: 12/12/96

9454 Lloydcrest Dr
Beverly Hills, CA 90210
Alternate V: 01/02/96

Russo, Rene
Progressive Artists Agency
400 S Beverly Dr #216
Beverly Hills, CA 90212
Actress V: 12/13/96

Rutan, Dick
Voyager Aircraft
Hanger 77
Mojave, CA 93501
Test Pilot V: 02/02/96

Rutherford, Ann
826 Greenway Dr
Beverly Hills, CA 90210
Actress V: 03/30/96

Rutherford, Kelly
Wm Morris Agency
151 El Camino Dr
Beverly Hills, CA 90212
Actress V: 02/24/96

Ruttman, Joe
Moroso Racing
3 Knob Hill Rd
Mooresville, NC 28115
NASCAR Driver V: 03/02/96

Ryan, Meg
8942 Wilshire Bl
Beverly Hills, CA 90211
Actress V: 02/24/96

11718 Barrington Ct #508
Los Angeles, Ca 90049
Alternate V: 02/01/96

Rydell, Bobby
917 Bryn Mawr Ave
Narberth, PA 19072
Singer V: 03/04/96

Ryder, Winona
c/o 3 Arts
760 N La Cienga Bl #200
Beverly Hills, CA 90212-2732
Actress V: 11/01/96

240 Centre St
New York, NY 10013
Alternate V: 12/15/96

Ryerson, Ann
935 Gayley Ave
Los Angeles, CA 90024
Actress V: 12/15/96

S

SABRINA, THE TEENAGE WITCH
Viacom Prod/Bldg 506 #E
100 Universal City Plaza
Universal City, CA 91608
Production Office V: 11/11/96

SALLY JESSE RAPHAEL
30 Rockefeller Plaza
New York, NY 10112
Production Office V: 01/20/96

SANTA BARBARA
c/o NBC/Dobson
3000 W Alameda Ave
Burbank, CA 91523
Production Office V: 03/26/96

SATURDAY NIGHT LIVE
NBC Productions
30 Rockefeller Plaza
New York, NY 10112
Production Office V: 01/10/96

SATURDAY NIGHT LIVE, Cont.
NBC Productions
330 Bob Hope Dr
Burbank, CA 91523
Alternate V: 01/20/96

SAVANNAH
WB-TV
1438 N Gower
Hollywood, CA 90028
Audience Services V: 04/12/96

SDB Partners
1801 Ave of the Stars #902
Los Angeles, CA 90067
Talent Agency V: 11/11/96

SECOND NOAH
MT2 Services
9200 Sunset Bl-Suite 1103
Los Angeles, CA 90069
Production Office V: 11/11/96

ABC-TV
77 W 66th St
New York, NY 10023
Alternate V: 12/15/96

SECRET SERVICE GUY
FOX-TV
PO Box 900
Beverly Hills, CA 90213
Audience Services V: 01/13/97

SEINFELD
NBC-TV
30 Rockefeller Plaza
New York, NY 10112
Production Office V: 12/15/96

Castle Rock
4024 Radford Ave
Bldg 5-#204
Studio City, CA 91604
Alternate V: 11/20/96

Castle Rock
335 N Maple Dr #135
Beverly Hills, CA 90210
Alternate V: 03/26/96

SENTINEL
Pet Fly Productions
3100 Burbank Bl #201
Burbank, CA 91515
Production Office V: 10/23/96

SEVENTH HEAVEN
Warner TV
1438 N Gower
Hollywood, CA 90028
Viewer Services V: 11/11/96

SIMPSONS
Fox-TV
PO Box 900
Beverly Hills, CA 90213
Production Office V: 12/15/96

SISTER, SISTER
WB-TV
1438 N Gower
Hollywood, CA 90028
Production Office V: 12/15/96

60 MINUTES
CBS Broadcast Center
524 W 57th St
New York, NY 10019
Production Office V: 03/14/96

SLIDERS
Fox-TV
PO Box 900
Beverly Hills, CA 90213
Production Office V: 12/15/96

SMART GUY
WB-TV
1438 N Gower
Hollywood, CA 90028
Audience Services V: 01/13/97

SOCIAL STUDIES
UPN-TV
5555 Melrose Ave-Marathon 1200
Los Angeles, CA 90038
Audience Services V: 01/13/97

SOMETHING SO RIGHT
NBC-TV
30 Rockefeller Plaza
New York, NY 10112
Viewer Services V: 11/11/96

SOMETHINGS GOT GIVE
Culver Studios
9336 Washington Bl
Culver City, CA 90232
Production Office V: 01/20/96

SPARKS
Raleight Studios
5300 Melrose Ave-Flynn Trailer
Los Angeles, CA 90038
Production Office V: 10/23/96

SPARKS, Cont.
UPN-TV
5555 Melrose Ave-Marathon 1200
Los Angeles, CA 90038
Alternate V: 11/11/96

SPIN CITY
Dreamworks TV
10 Universal City Plaza
Universal City, CA 91608
Production Office V: 11/11/96

SPY GAME
ABC-TV
77 W 66th St
New York, NY 10023
Audience Services V: 01/13/97

STAND BY YOUR MAN
FOX TV
PO Box 900
Beverly Hills, CA 90213
Production Office V: 01/20/96

STAR TREK:CLASSIC
UPN-TV
5555 Melrose Ave-Marathon 1200
Los Angeles, CA 90038
Production Office V: 01/21/96

STAR TREK:DS9
UPN-TV
5555 Melrose Ave-Marathon 1200
Los Angeles, CA 90038
Production Office V: 01/21/96

STAR TREK:TNG
UPN-TV
5555 Melrose Ave-Marathon 1200
Los Angeles, CA 90038
Production Office V: 01/21/96

STAR TREK:VOYAGER
UPN-TV
5555 Melrose Ave-Marathon 1200
Los Angeles, CA 90038
Production Office V: 12/15/96

Raleigh Studios
5300 Melrose Ave-Flynn Trailer
Los Angeles, CA 90038
Alternate V: 10/23/96

STARZ Network
5445 DTC Parkway #600
Englewood, CO 80111
Production Office V: 12/15/96

STEP BY STEP
WB-TV
4000 Warner Bl
Burbank, CA 91522
Production Office V: 01/16/96

STEVE HARVEY SHOW
WB-TV
1438 N Gower
Hollywood, CA 90028
Viewer Services V: 11/11/96

STREET JUSTICE
Cannell Productions
7083 Hollywood Bl
Los Angeles, CA 90028
Production Office V: 01/20/96

STUDS
Fox-TV
5746 Sunset Bl
Los Angeles, CA 90069
Production Office V: 01/20/96

SUDDENLY SUSAN
NBC-TV
30 Rockefeller Plaza
New York, NY 10112
Viewer Services V: 11/11/96

SUPER BLOOPERS
Dick Clark Productions
3003 W Olive
Burbank, CA 91505
Production Office V: 01/07/96

SWEET JUSTICE
Columbia TV
10202 W Washington Bl
Gable Bldg-Rm 204
Culver City, CA 90232
Production Office V: 11/20/96

Sabates, Felix
Sabco Racing
PO Box 560579
Charlotte, NC 28256
NASCAR Owner V: 03/02/96

Sabatini, Gabriela
c/o Proserv
1101 Wilson Bl-# 1800
Arlington, VA 22209
Tennis Star V: 03/02/96

217 E Redwood St #1800
Baltimore, MD 21202
Alternate V: 01/01/96

Sabato Jr, Anthonio
Wm Morris Agency
151 El Camino
Beverly Hills, CA 90212
Actor V: 12/12/96

Sachs, Andrew
c/o Stone
25 Whitehall
London SW1A 2BS, England
Actor V: 03/17/96

Sacks, Greg
Sabco Racing
5901 Orr Rd
Charlotte, NC 28213
NASCAR Driver V: 02/08/96

Sacramento Kings
One Sports Pkwy
Sacramento, CA 95834
Team Office V: 02/15/96

Sagal, Katey
Progressive Artists Agency
400 S Beverly Dr #216
Beverly Hills, CA 90212
Actress V: 12/13/96

Sagendorf, Bud
King Features
235 E 45th St
New York, NY 10017
Cartoonist V: 02/04/96

Sager, Carole Bayer
658 Nimes Rd
Los Angeles, CA 90077
Composer V: 03/21/96

Saget, Bob
c/o ICM
8942 Wilshire Bl
Beverly Hills, CA 90211
Actor V: 12/11/96

Saint, Eva Marie
Metro Talent Agency
4526 Wilshire Bl
Los Angeles, CA 90010
Actress V: 12/11/96

The Westholme
10590 Wilshire Bl #408
Los Angeles, CA 90024
Forwarded V: 01/13/96

Saint James, Susan
c/o Marlene Fait
854 N Genesee Ave
Hollywood, CA 90046
Actress V: 02/15/96

Saint-Marie, Buffy
2729 Westshire Dr
Los Angeles, CA 90068
Singer V: 01/15/96

RR1-Box 368
Kapaa, Kauai, HI 96746
Alternate V: 12/02/96

Sajak, Pat
3400 Riverside Dr
Burbank, CA 91505
TV Host V: 01/16/96

1541 N Vine St
Hollywood, CA 90028
Alternate V: 03/16/96

Saldana, Theresa
Kohner Agency
9300 Wilshire Bl #555
Beverly Hills, CA 90212
Actress V: 12/11/96

Salinger, JD
Rural Route #3
Box 176
Cornish Flat, NH 03745
Author V: 03/02/96

Salome, Jens
c/o Badgley Conner
9229 Sunset Bl #3115
Los Angeles, CA 90069
Actress V: 11/01/96

Salt, Jennifer
9045 Elevado St
W Hollywood, CA 90069
Actress V: 01/19/96

Sammer, Mattias
Romantik Hotel Lennhof
Menglinghauserstrasse 20
4600 Dortmund 50, Germany
Actor V: 02/01/96

Samms, Emma
2934 1/2 N Beverly Glen Cir #417
Los Angles, CA 90077
Actress V: 10/13/96

Samuel Goldwyn Company
10203 Santa Monica Bl
Los Angeles, CA 90067
Production Office V: 01/02/97

San Antonio Spurs
600 E Market #102
San Antonio, TX 78205
Team Office V: 01/02/97

San Diego Chargers
SD-Jack Murphy Stadium
9449 Friars Rd
San Diego, CA 92120
Team Office V: 01/02/97

San Diego Padres
9449 Friars Rd
PO Box 2000
San Diego, CA 92120
Team Office V: 01/02/97

San Francisco 49ers
4949 Centennial Bl
Santa Clara, CA 95054-1229
Team Office V: 01/02/97

San Francisco Giants
3-Com Park
San Francisco, CA 94124
Team Office V: 01/02/97

San Giacomo, Laura
13035 Woodbridge St
Studio City, CA 91604
Actress V: 03/22/96

San Jose Sharks
San Jose Arena
525 W Santa Clara St
San Jose, CA 95113
Team Office V: 01/02/97

PO Box 1240
San Jose, CA 95113
Alternate V: 01/02/97

Sanda, Dominique
George Beaume
3 Quia Malquais
Paris 75006, France
Actress V: 03/02/96

Sanders Agency
8831 Sunset Bl #304
Los Angeles, CA 90069
Talent Agency V: 03/13/96

Sandler, Adam
c/o CAA
9830 Wilshire Bl
Beverly Hills, CA 90212
Actor V: 01/14/96

9000 Sunset Bl #1200
Los Angeles, CA 90069
Alternate V: 01/03/97

Sandrelli, Stefania
Italian Int'l
Via Degli Scialoja 18
Rome 00196, Italy
Actress V: 02/09/96

Sands, Tommy
c/o TSAM
4312 Troost Ave
N Hollywood, CA 91604
Actor V: 10/10/96

11833 Gilmore St #17
N Hollywood, CA 91606-2864
Alternate V: 08/28/96

Sansome, Chip
United Media
200 Madison Ave
New York, NY 10016
Cartoonist V: 01/13/96

Sara, Mia
Gersh Agency
232 N Canon Dr
Beverly Hills, CA 90210
Actress V: 01/15/97

Sarandon, Chris
107 Glasco Turnpike
Woodstock, NY 12498
Actor V: 01/21/96

Sarandon, Susan
c/o ICM
8942 Wilshire Bl
Beverly Hills, CA 90211
Actress V: 03/30/96

Sarducci, Fr Guido
c/o Don Novello
PO Box 245
Fairfax, CA 94930
Comedy Star V: 04/19/96

Satterfield, Paul
PO Box 6945
Beverly Hills, CA 90212
Actor V: 10/23/96

Satterfield, Paul, Cont.
757 N Kihhea Dr
Los Angeles, CA 90046
Alternate V: 01/11/96

Saunders, Jennifer
Peters/The Chambers
Chelsea Harbour-Lots Rd
London SW10 0XF, England
Actress V: 03/20/96

Saunders, John R
Watkins Glen Speedway
Box 500-T
Watkins Glen, NY 14891
NASCAR Official V: 03/02/96

Savage, Ann
1541 N Hayworth Ave #203
Los Angeles, CA 90046-3320
Actress V: 01/12/96

Savage, Fred
1450 Belfast Dr
Los Angeles, CA 90069
Actor V: 12/01/96

Savage, John
Artists Agency
10000 Santa Monica Bl #305
Los Angeles, CA 90067
Actor V: 12/03/96

Savage Agency
6212 Banner Ave
Los Angeles, CA 90038
Talent Agency V: 03/14/96

Savant, Doug
Bloom Agency
9255 Sunset Bl #710
Los Angeles, CA 90069
Actor V: 11/01/96

1015 E Angeleno Ave
Burbank, CA 91501-1420
Alternate V: 01/13/97

Sawer, Elton
Davis Racing
11 N Robbins St
Thomasville, NC 27360
NASCAR Driver V: 03/02/96

Sawyer, Diane
ABC-TV
77 West 66th St
New York, NY 10023
Correspondant V: 09/06/96

Sawyer, Paul
Richmond Int'l Raceway
PO Box 9257
Richmond, VA 23227
NASCAR Official V: 03/02/96

Sawyer Brown
Scholten/Miller
4219 Hillsboro Rd #318
Nashville, TN 37215
Musical Group V: 02/02/96

Saxon, John
2432 Banyon Dr
Los Angeles, CA 90049
Actor V: 02/24/96

Sayers, Gale
624 Buck Rd
Northbrook, IL 60062
Football Star V: 02/03/96

Scacchi, Greta
Smith & Associates
121 N San Vicente Bl
Beverly Hills, CA 90211
Actress V: 12/15/96

121 N San Vicente Bl
Beverly Hills, CA 90211
Alternate V: 02/24/96

Scaduto, Al
250 Birchwood Park Dr
Jericho, NY 11753
Cartoonist V: 01/13/96

Scaggs, Boz
Howard Rose Agency
8900 Wilshire Bl #320
Beverly Hills, CA 90211
Singer V: 10/23/96

Scagnetti Agency
5118 Vineland Ave #102
N Hollywood, CA 91601
Talent Agency V: 02/02/96

Scales, Prunella
c/o Conway
18/21 Jermyn St
London SW1Y 6HB, England
Actress V: 03/20/96

Scalia, Jack
Wm Morris Agency
151 El Camino Dr
Beverly Hills, CA 90212
Actor V: 02/12/96

Scarabelli, Michele
4720 Vineland Ave #216
N Hollywood, CA 91602
Actress V: 11/01/96

Scarwid, Diana
Gersh Agency
232 N Canon Dr
Beverly Hills, CA 90210
Actress V: 12/09/96

Schaal, Wendy
Gage Group
9255 Sunset Bl #515
Los Angeles, CA 90069
Actress V: 12/08/96

Schaeffer, Paul
Ed Sullivan Theatre
1697 Broadway
New York, NY 10019
Musician V: 03/19/96

Schallert, William
14920 Ramos Pl
Pacific Palisades, CA 90272
Actor V: 02/15/94

Schecter Company
9300 Wilshire Bl #410
Beverly Hills, CA 90212
Talent Agency V: 02/19/96

Scheider, Roy
PO Box 364
Sagaponack, NY 11962-0364
Actor V: 08/28/96

Schell, Maximilian
Innovative Artists
1999 Ave of the Stars #2850
Los Angeles, CA 90067
Actor V: 12/11/96

2869 Royston Pl
Beverly Hills, CA 90210
Alternate V: 01/15/96

Schelmerding, Kirk
Childress Racing
PO Box 1189-Industrial Dr
Welcome, NC 27374
NASCAR Crew V: 03/02/96

Schenk, Otto
Rudolfspltz 6
A-1010 Wein, Austria
Actor V: 01/19/96

Schiavelli, Vincent
Bauman & Hiller
5750 Wilshire Bl #512
Los Angeles, CA 90036
Actor V: 12/05/96

Schiffer, Claudia
5 Union Sq #500
New York, NY 10003
Model V: 01/14/96

Rauberstege 22
Rheinbergi D-47495 Germany
Alternate V: 11/01/96

Schiowitz/Clay/Rose Agency
1680 N Vine St #614
Los Angeles, CA 90028
Talent Agency V: 02/02/96

Schirra Jr, Walter M
NASA/LBJ Space Center
Houston, TX 77058
Astronaut V: 03/03/96

Schlesinger, John
76 Oxford St
London W1N OAX, Canada
Director V: 01/15/96

Schmelling, Max
Sonnenweg 1
Hollenstedt 21279, Germany
Boxing Star V: 01/19/96

2114 Hollenstedt
Nordheide, Germany
Alternate V: 02/10/96

Schmitt, Harrison H
PO Box 14338
Albuquerque, NM 87191
Astronaut V: 03/17/96

NASA/LBJ Space Center
Hoston, TX 77058
Alternate V: 01/19/96

Schnarr Agency
8281 Melrose Ave #200
Los Angeles, CA 90046
Talent Agency V: 03/17/96

Schnarre, Monika
11300 W Olympic Bl #870
Los Angeles, CA 90064
Actress V: 01/13/96

Schneider, John
Wm Morris Agency
151 S El Camino Dr
Beverly Hills, CA 90212
Actor V: 09/13/96

Wm Morris Agency
1325 Ave of the Americas
New York, NY 10019
Alternate V: 09/14/96

Schneider, Maria
rue du Fg St-Honore
Paris F-75008 France
Actress V: 11/01/96

Schneider, Rob
United Talent Agency
9830 Wilshire Bl
Beverly Hills, CA 90212
Actor V: 11/01/96

Schoeder, Jochen
Postfach 10 23 46
4630 Bochum 1, Germany
Actor V: 02/11/96

Schoelen, Jill
Gold/Marshak
3500 W Olive Ave #1400
Burbank, CA 91505
Actress V: 10/23/96

Schoen & Associates
606 N Larchmont Bl #309
Los Angeles, CA 90004
Talent Agency V: 03/17/96

Schoendienst, Alfred
331 Ladue Woods Ct
Crene Coeur, MO 63141
Baseball Star V: 02/10/96

Schrader, Ken
Hendrick Motor Sports
5315 Stowe Lane-PO Box 9
Harrisburg, NC 28075
NASCAR Driver V: 03/02/96

Schramm, David
Paramount Studios
555 Melrose Ave
Los Angeles, CA 90038
Actor V: 11/11/96

Schroder, Rick
Wm Morris Agency
151 El Camino Dr
Beverly Hills, CA 90212
Actor V: 02/27/96

921 N Roxbury Dr
Beverly Hills, CA 90210
Alternate V: 03/17/96

Schuck, John
c/o Borenstein
8271 Melrose Ave #110
Los Angeles, CA 90046
Actor V: 02/10/96

925 Victoria Ave
Venice, CA 90291-3933
Alternate V: 01/13/97

Schultz, Dwight
c/o CAA
9830 Wilshire Bl
Beverly Hills, CA 90212
Actor V: 01/14/96

Schumacher, Joel
Greenfield/Selvaggi
11755 Wilshire Bl #2270
Los Angles, CA 90025
Director V: 09/13/96

Schumacher, Michael
Forsthausstrasse 92
5014 Kerpen-Manheim, Germany
Race Driver V: 01/17/96

Schwartz & Associates
6922 Hollywood Bl #508
Hollywood, CA 90028
Talent Agency V: 09/16/96

Schwarzenegger, Arnold
8942 Wilshire Bl
Beverly Hills, CA 90211
Actor V: 01/14/96

PO Box 1234
Santa Monica, CA 90406
Alternate V: 02/04/96

3110 Main St #300
Santa Monica, CA 90405
Forwarded V: 01/16/96

Schwarzkopf, Norman
400 N Ashley Dr #3050
Tampa, FL 33602-4318
Military V: 03/14/96

Schweickart, Russell L
NASA/LBJ Space Center
Houston, TX 77058
Astronaut V: 03/03/96

Schwimmer, David
Gersh Ageny
232 N Canon Dr
Beverly Hills, CA 90210
Actor V: 10/10/96

Schygulla, Hanna
ZBF Agentur
Leopoldstrasse 19
8000 Munchen 40, Germany
Actress V: 01/17/96

Le Studio Canal Plus
17 rue Dumont D'Urville
Paris 75116, France
Alternate V: 02/09/96

Sci-Fi Channel
1230 Ave of the Americas
New York, NY 10020
Production Office V: 12/15/96

2255 Glades Road
Boca Raton, FL 33436
Alternate V: 02/02/96

Scialfa, Patty
11 Gimble Pl
Ocean, NJ 07712
Singer V: 01/12/96

Sciorra, Anabella
Wolf/Kasteller
1033 Gayley Ave #208
Los Angeles, CA 90024
Actress V: 10/23/96

Scofield, Paul
The Gables
Balcome, Sussex, England
Actor V: 02/28/96

Scoggins, Tracy
Gold/Marshak
3500 W Olive Ave #1400
Burbank, CA 91505
Actress V: 12/10/96

1131 Alta Loma Rd #515
Los Angeles, CA 90069
Alternate V: 01/21/96

Scorsese, Martin
146 W 57th St #75B
New York, NY 10019
Director V: 03/04/96

c/o CAA
9830 Wilshire Bl
Beverly Hills, CA 90212
Alternate V: 01/14/96

Scott, David R
NASA/LBJ Space Center
Houston, TX 77058
Astronaut V: 03/03/96

Scott, George C
11766 Wilshire Bl #760
Los Angeles, CA 90025-6535
Actor V: 11/01/96

3211 Retreat Ct
Malibu, CA 90265
Alternate V: 01/15/96

Scott, Kathryn Leigh
Pomegranate Press
PO Box 17217-3209
Beverly Hills, CA 90209
Actress V: 01/20/96

Scott, Lizabeth
PO Box 5522
Beverly Hills, CA 90210
Actress V: 03/02/96

PO Box 69405
Los Angeles, CA 90069
Alternate V: 06/17/94

Scott, Martha
14054 Chandler Bl
Van Nuys, CA 91401
Actress V: 05/15/96

Scott, Melody Thomas
20th Century Artists
15315 Magnolia Bl #429
Sherman Oaks, CA 91403
Actress V: 02/24/96

Scott, Willard
30 Rockefeller Plaza #304
New York, NY 10112
Commentator V: 06/07/96

Scott, Winston E
NASA/LBJ Space Center
Houston, TX 77058
Astronaut V: 02/02/96

Scotti Brothers
2114 Pico Bl
Santa Monica, CA 90405
Production Office V: 02/01/96

Screen Actors Guild
SAG/SEG
5757 Wilshire Bl
Los Angeles, CA 90036-3600
Guild Office V: 11/21/96

Screen Artist Agency
12435 Oxford St
N Hollywood, CA 91606
Talent Agency V: 11/11/96

Screen Gems Productions
Columbia Plaza
Los Angeles, CA 91505
Production Office V: 03/17/96

Scribner, Rick
8904 Amerigo Ave
Orangeville, CA 95662
Race Driver V: 03/12/96

Scrimm, Angus
PO Box 5193
N Hollywood, CA 91606-5193
Actor V: 02/22/96

Scuduto, Al
King Features
235 E 45th St
New York, NY 10017
Cartoonist V: 03/12/96

Seaborg, Glenn T
Lawr-Berkley Lab UC/CAL
One Cyclotron Rd
Berkely, CA 94720
Scientist V: 03/16/96

Seagal, Steven
c/o CAA
9830 Wilshire Bl
Beverly Hills, CA 90212
Actor V: 01/14/96

PO Box 727
Los Olivas, CA 93441
Alternate V: 01/16/96

2282 Mandeville Canyon
Los Angeles, CA 90049
Forwarded V: 02/02/96

Seagraves, Ralph
Rt 10, Box 413A
Winston-Salem, NC 27107
NASCAR Driver V: 03/02/96

Searfoss, Richard A
NASA/LBJ Space Center
Houston, TX 77058
Astronaut V: 03/03/96

Seattle Mariners
PO Box 4100
The Kingdome
Seattle, WA 98104
Team Office V: 02/15/96

Seattle Seahawks
11220 NE 53rd St
Kirkland, WA 98033
Team Office V: 12/15/96

Seattle SuperSonics
Box C-900911
Seattle, WA 98109-9711
Team Office V: 02/15/96

Secombe, Harry
26 St James Pl
London SW1, England
Actor V: 02/26/96

Sedaka, Neil
888 7th Ave #1600
New York, NY 10019
Singer V: 01/09/97

Seddon, Margaret Rhea
NASA/LBJ Space Center
Houston, TX 77058
Astronaut V: 03/03/96

Sedgwick, Kyra
c/o ICM
8942 Wilshire Bl
Beverly Hills, CA 90211
Actress V: 12/11/96

Sedgworth, Bill
NASCAR
1811 Volusia Ave
Daytona Beach, FL 32015
NASCAR Driver V: 03/26/96

Seeger, Pete
PO Box 431
Beacon, NY 12508
Singer V: 02/20/9

Seeger, Pete, Cont.
Rolling Blunder Review
PO Box 657
Housatonic, MA 01236-0657
Alternate V: 03/30/96

Redwood Records
6400 Hollis St-Ste 8
Emeryville, CA 94608
Forwarded V: 02/01/96

Sega, Ronald M
NASA/LBJ Space Center
Houston, TX 77058
Astronaut V: 03/03/96

Seidenspinner, Dick
Sabco Racing
5901 Orr Rd
Charlotte, NC 28213
NASCAR Crew V: 03/26/96

Seigner, Emmanuelle
Beaume & Bonnet
4 rue de Ponthieu
75008 Paris, France
Actress V: 12/01/96

Beaume Agency
201 rue Fauberg St Honore
Paris 75008, France
Alternate V: 09/14/96

Seinfeld, Jerry
Jones PR
417 S Beverly Dr
Beverly Hills, CA 90212
Actor V: 10/23/96

147 S El Camino Dr #205
Beverly Hills, CA 90212
Alternate V: 02/11/96

c/o CAA
9830 Wilshire Bl
Beverly Hills, CA 90212
Forwarded V: 01/14/96

2112 Roscomare Rd
Los Angeles, CA 90077
Forwarded V: 06/21/96

Selected Artists
3900 W Alameda Ave #1700
Burbank, CA 91505
Talent Agency V: 01/26/96

Seles, Monica
Laurel Oaks Estates
7751 Beeridge Rd
Sarasota, FL 34241
Tennis Star V: 01/14/96

Selleca, Connie
Wm Morris Agency
151 El Camino
Beverly Hills, CA 90212
Actress V: 12/12/96

14755 Ventura Bl #1-916
Sherman Oaks, CA 91403
Alternate V: 02/04/96

15030 Ventura Bl #355
Sherman Oaks, CA 91403
Forwarded V: 10/23/96

Selleck, Tom
331 Sage Lane
Santa Monica, CA 90402-1119
Actor V: 10/23/96

Serna, Pepe
Artists Agency
10000 Santa Monica Bl #305
Los Angeles, CA 90067
Actor V: 12/03/96

2321 Hill Dr
Los Angeles, CA 90041
Forwarded V: 04/06/96

Severance, Joan
c/o APA
9000 Sunset Bl #1200
Los Angeles, CA 90069
Actress V: 11/27/96

Seymour, Carolyn
Chasin Agency
8899 Beverly Bl 7th Fl
Los Angeles, CA 90048
Actress V: 12/07/96

Seymour, Jane
c/o CAA
9830 Wilshire Bl
Beverly Hills, CA 90212
Actress V: 01/14/96

PO Box 548
Agoura, CA 91376
Alternate V: 12/02/96

Seymour, Jane, Cont.
St Catherines Court
Batheaston
Bath, Avon, England
Forwarded V: 03/16/96

34800 Pacific Coast Hwy
Malibu, CA 90265
Forwarded V: 03/15/96

Seymour, Stephanie
c/o IMG
170 Fifth Ave
New York, NY 10010
Model V: 11/01/96

12626 High Bluff Dr #200
San Diego, CA 92130
Alternate V: 10/23/96

IT Model Mgmt
526 N Larchmont Bl
Los Angeles, CA 90004
Forwarded V: 01/13/96

Shaffer, Paul
1697 Broadway
New York, NY 10019
Musician V: 01/03/97

Shallert, William
14920 Ramos Place
Pacific Palisades, CA 90272
Actor V: 03/04/96

Shandling, Garry
Creative Artists Agency
9830 Wilshire Bl
Beverly Hills, CA 90212
Actor V: 12/07/96

9150 Wilshire Bl #350
Beverly Hills, CA 90212
Alternate V: 10/23/96

Shapira & Associates
15301 Ventura Bl #345
Sherman Oaks, CA 91403
Talent Agency V: 01/24/96

Shapiro-Lichtman Agency
8827 Beverly Bl
Los Angeles, CA 90048
Talent Agency V: 03/13/96

Sharif, Omar
Wm Morris Agency
31/32 Soho Square
London W1V 5DG, England
Actor V: 01/17/96

c/o Correa
18 rue Troyon
F-75017 Paris, France
Alternate V: 01/19/96

Shatner, Melanie
c/o Acme
6310 San Vicente Bl #520
Los Angeles, CA 90048
Actress V: 02/24/96

Shatner, William
Artists Agency
10000 Santa Monica Bl #305
Los Angeles, CA 90067
Actor V: 12/03/96

PO Box 7401-725
Studio City, CA 91064
Alternate V: 01/20/96

100 Wilshire Bl #1800
Santa Monica, CA 90401
Forwarded V: 01/14/96

7059 Atoll Ave
N Hollywood, CA 91605
Forwarded V: 11/01/96

Shaver, Helen
Gersh Agency
232 N Canon Dr
Beverly Hills, CA 90210
Actress V: 12/09/96

Shaw, Brewster
NASA/LBJ Space Center
Hoston, TX 77058
Astronaut V: 01/19/96

Shaw, Martin
c/o Agency
200 Fulham Rd
London SW16, England
Actor V: 03/16/96

Shea, John
Wm Morris Agency
151 El Camino
Beverly Hills, CA 90212
Actor V: 12/12/96

Shea, John, Cont.
1495 Orlando Rd
Pasadena, CA 91106
Alternate V: 01/14/96

Shear, Rhonda
CNA & Associates
1801 Ave of the Stars #1250
Los Angeles, CA 90067
Celebrity V: 12/08/96

Purrfect Productions
PO Box 430
Newbury Park, CA 91320
Alternate V: 01/13/96

317 N Palm Dr
Beverly Hills, CA 90210
Forwarded V: 10/23/96

Shearer, Harry
119 Ocean Park Bl
Santa Monica, CA 90405
Actor V: 01/03/97

Sheedy, Ally
Wm Morris Agency
151 El Camino
Beverly Hills, CA 90212
Actress V: 12/12/96

11755 Wilshire Bl #2270
Los Angeles, CA 90025
Forwarded V: 01/14/96

Sheen, Charlie
6916 Dune Dr
Malibu, CA 90265
Actor V: 06/17/96

CPC Films
353 W 57th St #2411
New York, NY 10019-3199
Forwarded V: 03/09/96

335 N Maple Dr #360
Beverly Hills, CA 90210
Forwarded V: 02/10/96

Sheen, Martin
Innovative Artists
1999 Ave of the Stars #2850
Los Angeles, CA 90067
Actor V: 12/11/96

6916 Dune Dr
Malibu, CA 90265
Alternate V: 03/15/96

Sheen, Ramon
6916 Dune Dr
Malibu, CA 90265
Actor V: 03/20/96

Shefelman, Dan
King Features
216 E 45th St
New York, NY 10017
Cartoonist V: 03/11/96

Sheldon, Sydney
10250 Sunset Bl
Los Angeles, CA 90077
Author V: 01/20/96

Shelton, Deborah
Slessinger & Associates
8271 Melrose Ave-#202W
Los Angeles, CA 90069
Actress V: 12/14/96

Shelton, Mike
King Features
216 E 45th St
New York, NY 10017
Cartoonist V: 03/11/96

Shepard, Jewel
PO Box 480265
Los Angeles, CA 90048
Actress V: 05/09/96

Shepard, Sam
c/o Berman
21 W 26th St
New York, NY 10010
Author V: 01/14/96

Shephard Jr, Alan B
1512 Bonifacio Lane
Pebble Beach, CA 93953
Astronaut V: 05/02/96

NASA/LBJ Space Center
Hoston, TX 77058
Forwarded V: 01/19/96

Shepherd, Cybill
433 N Camden Dr #500
Beverly Hills, CA 90210-4443
Actress V: 01/12/96

16037 Royal Oak Rd
Encino, CA 91436
Alternate V: 02/20/96

Shepherd, Mark Allen
Watchers of Morn
PO Box 630175
Houston, TX 77263
Actor V: 01/10/96

Shepherd, Morgan
PO Box 1456
Stow, OH 44224-0456
NASCAR Driver V: 03/14/96

McLean Marketing
9307-P Monro Rd
Charlotte, NC 28270
Alternate V: 03/02/96

Shepherd, William M
NASA/LBJ Space Center
Hoston, TX 77058
Astronaut V: 01/31/96

Sheppard, TG
TGS-FC
3341 Arlington Ave-#F206
Toledo, OH 43614-5712
Actress V: 08/28/96

Sheridan, Dinah
Jenny Hanley
30 Chalfont Ct-Baker St
London NW1, England
Actress V: 02/01/96

Sheridan, Nicolette
2131 Roscomare Rd
Los Angeles, CA 90077
Actress V: 12/15/96

c/o ICM
8942 Wilshire Bl
Beverly Hills, CA 90211
Alternate V: 03/21/96

Sherlock, Nancy J
NASA/LBJ Space Center
Houston, TX 77058
Astronaut V: 03/03/96

Sherman, Bobby
Media Artists
8383 Wilshire Bl #954
Beverly Hills, CA 90211
Actor V: 12/11/96

1870 Sunset Plaza Dr
Los Angeles, CA 90069
Alternate V: 01/13/97

Shields, Brooke
Wm Morris Agency
151 El Camino
Beverly Hills, CA 90212
Actress V: 12/12/96

2300 W Sahara Ave #630
Las Vegas, NV 89102-4352
Alternate V: 01/12/96

Shigeta, James
Sindell & Associates
8271 Melrose Ave #202
Los Angeles, CA 90046
Actor V: 12/14/96

Shimkus, Joanna
9255 Doheny Rd
Los Angeles, CA 90069-3201
Actress V: 01/12/96

Shimmerman, Armin
Silver/Kass
8730 Sunset Bl #480
Los Angeles, CA 90069
Actor V: 01/03/96

Star Trek-DS9
5555 Melrose Ave
Hollywood, CA 90036
Alternate V: 02/23/96

Innovative Artists
1999 Ave of the Stars #2850
Los Angeles, CA 90067
Alternate V: 12/11/96

Oasis/Boyne
26 Dogwood St
Jersey City, NJ 07305-4842
Forwarded V: 01/14/96

Shire, Talia
Ambrosio & Mortimer
9150 Wilshire Bl #175
Beverly Hills, CA 90212
Actress V: 12/01/96

c/o Astrim
16633 Ventura Bl #1450
Encino, CA 91436
Alternate V: 01/21/96

Shockley, William
Kohner Agency
9300 Wilshire Bl #555
Beverly Hills, CA 90212
Actor V: 12/11/96

Shore, Pauly
Creative Artists Agency
9830 Wilshire Bl
Beverly Hills, CA 90212
Actor V: 12/07/96

Short, Martin
15907 Alcoma Ave
Pacific Palisades, CA 90272
Actress V: 03/26/96

Shorter, Frank
890 Willowbrook Rd
Boulder, CO 80302
Olympian V: 10/23/96

Show, Grant
Creative Artists Agency
9830 Wilshire Bl
Beverly Hills, CA 90212
Actor V: 12/07/96

937 S Tremaine
Los Angeles, CA 90019
Alternate V: 01/13/97

Showalter, Max
8942 Wilshire Bl
Beverly Hills, CA 90211
Actor V: 02/12/96

Showbiz Entertainment
6922 Hollywood Bl #207
Los Angeles, CA 90028
Talent Agency V: 03/13/96

Showtime Network
1633 Broadway
New York, NY 10019
Network HQ V: 03/01/96

10 Universal Plaza-31st Fl
Los Angeles, CA 91608
Alternate V: 03/17/96

Shreve Talent
2665 N Palm Canyon Dr
Palm Springs, CA 92262
Talent Agency V: 02/02/96

Shrimpton, Jean
Abbey Hotel
Penzance, Cornwall, England
Actress V: 06/19/96

Shriver, Loren J
NASA/LBJ Space Center
Hoston, TX 77058
Astronaut V: 01/31/96

Shriver, Maria
3110 Main St #300
Santa Monica, CA 90405
Commentator V: 11/27/96

Shriver, Pam
133 First St NE
St Petersburg, FL 33701
Tennis Star V: 12/12/96

Shue, Andrew
Spelling TV
5700 Wilshire Bl
Los Angeles, CA 90036
Actor V: 01/14/96

9560 Wilshire Bl #500
Beverly Hills, CA 90212
Alternate V: 02/03/96

2617 Outpost Dr
Los Angeles, CA 90068
Alternate V: 01/13/97

Shue, Elisabeth
Creative Artists Agency
9830 Wilshire Bl
Beverly Hills, CA 90212
Actress V: 12/07/96

RR1-Box 820
Brooks, ME 04921
Alternate V: 05/05/96

PO Box 464
S Orange, NJ 07079
Forwarded V: 01/21/96

1146 Sierra Alta Way
Los Angeles, CA 90069
Forwarded V: 01/01/97

Shula, Don
16 Indian Creek Island
Miami, FL 33154-2904
Football Star V: 01/10/97

Shulman, Ellen L
NASA/LBJ Space Center
Hoston, TX 77058
Astronaut V: 01/19/96

Shultz, George
776 Dolores St
Stanford, CA 94305
Politician V: 01/09/97

Shumaker Talent
6533 Hollywood Bl #301
Hollywood, CA 90028
Talent Agency V: 03/13/96

Sidney, Sylvia
9744 Wilshire Bl #308
Beverly Hills, CA 90212
Actress V: 03/17/96

Siegel & Associates
7551 Sunset Bl #204
Los Angeles, CA 90046
Talent Agency V: 02/02/96

Siegfried & Roy
Mirage Hotel
3400 Las Vegas Bl South
Las Vegas, NV 89108
Performers V: 11/01/96

1639 N Valley Dr
Las Vegas, NV 89108
Alternate V: 02/11/96

Siemaszko, Casey
Gersh Agency
232 N Canon Dr
Beverly Hills, CA 90210
Actor V: 12/09/96

Sierra Talent
14542 Ventura Bl #207
Sherman Oaks, CA 91403
Talent Agency V: 02/02/96

Sikes, Cynthia
Kohner Agency
9300 Wilshire Bl #555
Beverly Hills, CA 90212
Actress V: 12/11/96

Sikking, James B
c/o MTA
4526 Wilshire Bl
Los Angeles, CA 90010
Actor V: 02/22/96

Silent Network
Box 1902
Beverly Hills, CA 90213
Production Office V: 03/17/96

Silva, Henry
Gold/Marshak
3500 W Olive Ave #1400
Burbank, CA 91505
Actor V: 12/10/96

Silver, Ron
6116 Tyndall Ave
Riverdale, NY 10471
Actor V: 03/26/94

Silver & Massetti
8730 Sunset Bl #480
Los Angeles, CA 90069
Talent Agency V: 02/19/96

Silverman, Jonathan
2255 Mountain Oak Dr
Los Angeles, CA 90068
Actor V: 10/23/96

Silverstone, Alicia
8899 Beverly Bl #510
Los Angeles, CA 90048
Actress V: 12/13/96

1638-A Marmont Ave
Los Angeles, CA 90046
Alternate V: 11/01/96

PO Box 16539
Beverly Hills, CA 90209
Forwarded V: 11/01/96

Simmons, Jason
c/o Baywatch
5433 Beethoven St
Los Angeles, CA 90066
Actor V: 09/14/96

Simmons, Jean
Smith & Associates
121 N San Vicente Bl
Beverly Hills, CA 90211
Actress V: 12/15/96

636 Adelaide Way
Santa Monica, CA 90202
Alternate V: 01/14/96

Simmons, Richard
1350 Belfast
Los Angeles, CA 90069
Fitness Expert V: 01/11/97

Simon, Carly
Arlyne Rothberg Inc
135 Central Park West
New York, NY 10023
Singer V: 08/14/94

Simon, Neil
10745 Chalon Rd
Los Angeles, CA 90024
Author V: 06/07/96

Simon, Paul
1619 Broadway #500
New York, NY 10019
Singer V: 02/03/96

Simon, Simone
5 Rue de Tilsitt
Paris, 75008 France
Actress V: 01/12/96

Simonsen, Renee
Ford Agency
344 E 59th St
New York, NY 10016
Model V: 11/01/96

Simpson, OJ
360 N Rockingham Ave
Los Angeles, CA 90049
Actor V: 04/21/96

SinBad
Wm Morris
151 El Camino Dr
Beverly Hills, CA 90212
Actor V: 01/14/96

c/o Atkins
21704 Devonshire St #13
Chatsworth, CA 91311
Alternate V: 01/11/96

Sinatra, Nancy
c/o Bootleggers
PO Box 10236
Beverly Hills, CA 90213
Singer V: 11/01/96

PO Box 69453
Los Angeles, CA 90069
Alternate V: 03/26/96

Sinatra Jr, Frank
2211 Florian Pl
Beverly Hills, CA 90210
Singer V: 03/11/96

Sindell & Associates
8271 Melrose Ave #202
Los Angleles, CA 90046
Talent Agency V: 02/02/96

Sinden, Donald
c/o Agency
60 Temple Fortune Rd
London NW11, England
Actor V: 01/18/96

Sinden, Donald, Cont.
c/o Whitehall
125 Gloucester Rd
London SW7 4TE, England
Alternate V: 03/17/96

Sinden, Jeremy
c/o Agency
388-396 Oxford St
London W1 9HE, England
Actor V: 03/17/96

Singer, Lori
c/o CAA
9830 Wilshire Bl
Beverly Hills, CA 90212
Actress V: 02/24/96

Singer, Marc
Shapira & Associates
15301 Ventura Bl #345
Sherman Oaks, CA 91403
Actor V: 12/14/96

Singleton, Penny
13419 Riverside Dr #C
Sherman Oaks, CA 91423
Actress V: 03/17/96

PO Box 174
6200 Van Nuys Bl
Van Nuys, CA 91401
Alternate V: 01/10/96

Sinise, Gary
Creative Artists Agency
9830 Wilshire Bl
Beverly Hills, CA 90212
Actor V: 12/07/96

PO Box 6704
Malibu, CA 90264-6704
Alternate V: 03/14/96

755 S Oakland Ave
Pasadena, CA 91106
Alternate V: 10/23/96

Sirola, Joseph
Henderson & Hogan Agency
247 S Beverly Dr #102
Bevery Hills, CA 90210
Actor V: 12/10/96

Sirtis, Marina
Star Trek-TNG
5555 Melrose Ave
Hollywood, CA 90038
Actress V: 03/04/96

Sirtis, Marina, Cont.
2436 Creston Way
Los Angeles, CA 90068
Forwarded V: 02/11/96

Sisti, James
21 Noe Pl
Beacon Falls, CT 06403
Magician V: 06/06/96

Sixta, George
King Features
235 E 45th St
New York, NY 10017
Cartoonist V: 03/13/96

Sixteen Magazine
233 Park Ave South
New York, NY 10003
Publisher V: 02/10/96

Sizemore, Tom
1724 N Vista St
Los Angeles, CA 90046
Actor V: 09/13/96

Skaggs, Ricky
RS Entertainment
PO Box 150871
Nashville, TN 37215
Singer V: 02/02/96

Skelton, Red
37-801 Thompson Rd
Rancho Mirage, CA 92270
Actor V: 02/04/96

Skerritt, Tom
2206 E Galer St
Seattle, WA 98112
Actor V: 12/01/96

335 N Maple Dr #360
Beverly Hills, CA 90210
Forwarded V: 03/15/96

Skye, Ione
Bresler/Kelly
15760 Ventura Bl #1730
Encino, CA 91436
Actress V: 12/06/96

Slater, Christian
150 S Rodeo Dr #220
Beverly Hills, CA 90212
Actor V: 10/23/96

Slater, Christian, Cont.
c/o CAA
9830 Wilshire Bl
Beverly Hills, CA 90212
Alternate V: 01/20/96

Slater, Helen
Innovative Artists
1999 Ave of the Stars #2850
Los Angeles, CA 90067
Actress V: 12/11/96

Slessinger & Associates
8730 Sunset Bl #220-West
Los Angeles, CA 90069
Talent Agency V: 03/11/96

Slezak, Erika
8942 Wilshire Bl
Beverly Hills, CA 90211
Actress V: 12/11/96

Slick, Grace
2548 Laurel Pass
Los Angeles, CA 90046-1404
Singer V: 03/14/96

Smith, Allison
c/o APA
9000 Sunset Bl #1200
Los Angeles, CA 90069
Actress V: 11/27/96

Smith, Allison Mary
Innovative Artists
1999 Ave of the Stars #2850
Los Angeles, CA 90067
Actress V: 01/15/97

Smith, Amber
Next Model Mgmt
23 Watts St-6th Fl
New York, NY 10013-1639
Model V: 03/14/96

Smith, Anna Nicole
200 Ashdale Ave
Los Angeles, CA 90049-2405
Model V: 11/01/96

Smith, Bubba
c/o Sindell
8271 Melrose Ave #202
Los Angeles, CA 90046
Actor V: 01/12/96

Smith, Buffalo Bob
500 Overlook Dr
Flat Rock, NC 28731
Celebrity V: 03/26/96

Smith, Charles Martin
c/o APA
9000 Sunset Bl #1200
Los Angeles, CA 90069
Actor V: 12/02/96

Smith, David
c/o Childress
PO Box 1189-Industrial Dr
Welcome, NC 27374
NASCAR Crew V: 03/12/96

Smith, Jack
850 W Main St
Spartanburg, SC 29301
NASCAR Driver V: 03/02/96

Smith, Jaclyn
10398 Sunset Bl
Los Angles, CA 90077
Actress V: 10/23/96

Smith, Kurtwood
635 Frontenac Ave
Los Angeles, CA 90065
Actor V: 02/15/96

Smith, Maggie
c/o ICM
76 Oxford St
London W1N 0AX, England
Actress V: 04/02/96

Smith, Paul L
c/o ICM
8942 Wilshire Bl
Beverly Hills, CA 90211
Actor V: 02/03/96

Smith, Roger
2707 Benedict Canyon Rd
Beverly Hills, CA 90210
Actor V: 02/17/97

Smith, Ron
Celebrity Look-Alikes
70 Hollywood Bl-PH1215
Los Angeles, CA 90028
Agency V: 03/03/96

Smith, Shawnee
5200 Lankershim Bl #260
N Hollywood, CA 91601
Actress V: 10/23/96

c/o Kincaid
43 Navy St #300
Venice, CA 90291
Forwarded V: 10/10/96

Smith, Shelley
182 S Mansfield Ave
Los Angeles, CA 90036-3019
Actress V: 01/20/96

Smith, Steven L
NASA/LBJ Space Center
Houston, TX 77058
Astronaut V: 02/02/96

Smith, Will
9830 Wilshire Bl
Beverly Hills, CA 90212
Actor V: 01/14/96

Smith, William
3250 Olympic Bl-Box 67
Santa Monica, CA 90404-5045
Actor V: 02/02/96

Smith, Yeardley
Bresler/Kelly
15760 Ventura Bl #1730
Encino, CA 91436
Actress V: 12/06/96

Smith & Associates
121 N San Vicente Bl
Beverly Hills, CA 90211
Talent Agency V: 03/11/96

Smithhart, Peggy
Paramount Pictures
5555 Melrose Ave-Wilder #214
Los Angeles, CA 90038
Actress V: 05/15/96

Smithsonian Archives
Arts/Industries Bldg-Rm2135
900 Jefferson Dr SW
Washington, DC 20560
Archive V: 03/20/96

Smits, Jimmy
Creative Artists Agency
9830 Wilshire Bl
Beverly Hills, CA 90212
Actor V: 12/07/96

Smythe, Reggie
Whitegares-96 Calidonian Rd
Hartlepool, Cleveland, England
Cartoonist V: 02/12/96

Snipes, Wesley
c/o CAA
9830 Wilshire Bl
Beverly Hills, CA 90212
Actor V: 01/14/96

Snodgrass, Carrie
Gold/Marshak
3500 W Olive Ave #1400
Burbank, CA 91505
Actress V: 12/10/96

Snow, Gene
Snowman Racing
5719 Airport Freeway
Fort Worth, TX 76117
Drag Racer V: 10/23/96

Snowden, Van
5751 Camellia
N Hollywood, CA 91601
Puppeteer V: 04/16/96

Snyder, Tom
CBS-TV
51 W 52nd St
New York, NY 10019
TV Host V: 01/14/96

1225 Beverly Estates Dr
Beverly Hills, CA 90210
Alternate V: 10/23/96

Soap Opera Digest
270 Sylvan Ave
Englewood Cliffs, NJ 07632
Publisher V: 02/10/96

c/o Editor
45 W 25th St
New York, NY 10010
Forwarded V: 06/15/96

Soap Opera Magazine
600 East Coast Ave
Lantana, FL 33462
Publisher V: 02/10/96

Soap Opera Now
c/o Editor
1767 Park Ave
New York, NY 11566
Publisher V: 06/15/96

Soap Opera People
c/o Editor
50 W 34th St
New York, NY 10001
Publisher V: 06/15/96

Soap Opera Stars
Editor/Daytime TV
355 Lexington Ave
New York, NY 10017
Publisher V: 06/15/96

Soap Opera Update
158 Linwood
New York, NY 10017
Publisher V: 06/15/96

Soap Opera Weekly
c/o Editor
41 W 25th St
New York, NY 10010
Publisher V: 06/15/96

Soles, PJ
c/o Fries
3210 De Witt #A
Hollywood, CA 90068
Actress V: 02/24/96

Somers, Suzanne
Chasin Agency
8899 Beverly Bl #713
Los Angeles, CA 90048-2412
Actress V: 12/07/96

Sommars, Julie
c/o SDB
1801 Ave of the Stars-#902
Los Angeles, CA 90067
Actress V: 02/24/96

Sommer, Elke
540 N Beverly Glen Bl
Los Angeles, CA 90024
Actress V: 12/15/96

c/o APA
9000 Sunset Bl #1200
Los Angeles, CA 90069
Alternate V: 02/24/96

Sommers, Joanie
Lawrence Int'l
10636 Santa Monica Bl #A
Los Angeles, CA 90025
Singer V: 10/23/96

Sondheim, Stephen
F Roberts
65 E 55th St #702
New York, NY 10022
Composer V: 01/14/96

300 Park Ave-17th Fl
New York, NY 10022-7402
Alternate V: 01/15/96

Sons of the Pioneers
12403 W Green Mtn
Lakewood, CO 80228
Musical Group V: 03/05/96

Sontag, Susan
470 W 24th St
New York, NY 1011
Commentator V: 10/23/96

Sorbo, Kevin
8033 Sunset Bl #920
Los Angeles, CA 90046
Actor V: 12/15/96

8924 Clifton Way #103
Beverly Hills, CA 90211
Alternate V: 09/13/96

Sorice Talent
16661 Ventura Bl #400E
Encino, CA 91436
Talent Agency V: 11/11/96

Sorvino, Mira
Wm Morris Agency
151 S El Camino
Beverly Hills, CA 90212
Actress V: 09/13/96

110 East 87th St
New York, NY 10128
Alternate V: 10/23/96

41 W 86th St
New York, NY 10024-3608
Alternate V: 08/28/96

Sorvino, Paul
Gersh Agency
232 N Canon Dr
Beverly Hills, CA 90210
Actor V: 12/09/96

Sothern, Ann
PO Box 2285
Ketchum, ID 83340
Actress V: 03/23/96

Soul, David
4337 Tioga St
Duluth, MN 55804
Actor V: 03/17/96

Spacek, Sissy
c/o CAA
9830 Wilshire Bl
Beverly Hills, CA 90212
Actress V: 01/16/96

Beau Val Farm-Rt22/#640
Cobham, VA 22929
Alternate V: 10/23/96

Spade, David
9150 Wilshire Bl #350
Beverly Hills, CA 90212
Actor V: 01/15/97

Spader, James
8942 Wilshire Bl
Beverly Hills, CA 90211
Actor V: 01/16/96

Spano, Joe
Innovative Artists
1999 Ave of the Stars #2850
Los Angeles, CA 90067
Actor V: 12/11/96

Spano, Vincent
Innovative Artists
1999 Ave of the Stars #2850
Los Angeles, CA 90067
Actor V: 01/15/97

Special Artists Agency
335 N Maple Dr #360
Beverly Hills, CA 91210
Talent Agency V: 04/01/96

Spector, Phil
1210 S Arroyo Bl
Pasadena, CA 91101
Music Executive V: 01/11/97

Spector, Ronnie
Jonathon Greenfield
39-B Mill Plain Rd #233
Danbury, CT 06811
Singer V: 10/23/96

Speed, Lake
NASCAR
1811 Volusia Ave
Daytona Beach, FL 32015
NASCAR Driver V: 03/02/96

Spelling, Aaron
c/o CAA
9830 Wilshire Bl
Beverly Hills, CA 90212
Producer V: 01/14/96

594 N Mapleton Ave
Los Angeles, CA 90077
Alternate V: 02/02/96

Spelling, Randy
Spelling Productions
5700 Wilshire Bl #575
Los Angeles, CA 90036
Actor V: 11/01/96

Spelling, Tori
Creative Artists Agency
9830 Wilshire Bl
Beverly Hills, CA 90212
Actress V: 12/07/96

Spelling Productions
1041 N Formosa Ave
Los Angeles, CA 90046
Production Office V: 03/17/96

Spencer, Bud
Mistral Film Group
24 Via Archimede
I-00187 Rome, Italy
Actor V: 01/17/96

Spencer, Jimmy
c/o Travis Racing
PO Box 588-Hwy 16 N
Denver, NC 28037
NASCAR Driver V: 02/08/96

PO Box 1626
Mooresville, NC 28115
Alternate V: 03/12/96

Spencer, John
Abrams Artists
9200 Sunset Bl #625
Los Angeles, CA 90069
Actor V: 12/01/96

Spielberg, Steven
PO Box 8520
Universal City, CA 91608
Director V: 09/20/96

c/o DreamWorks SKG
100 Universal City Plaza
Universal City, CA 91608
Alternate V: 01/14/96

c/o CAA
9830 Wilshire Bl
Beverly Hills, CA 90212
Alternate V: 01/14/96

Spillane, Mickey
General Delivery
Marrells Inlet, SC 22117
Author V: 05/22/96

PO Box 265
Murrells Inlet, SC 29576
Alternate V: 01/13/97

Spiner, Brent
6922 1/2 Paseo del Serra
Los Angeles, CA 90068
Actor V: 06/17/96

Star Trek-TNG Paramount
5555 Melrose Ave
Hollywood, CA 90038
Forwarded V: 03/04/96

Gersh Agency
232 N Canon Dr
Beverly Hills, CA 90210
Forwarded V: 01/11/97

Spock, Dr Benjamin
PO Box 1268
Camden, ME 04843-1268
Author V: 11/11/96

Sporting News
1212 N Lindburgh Bl
St Louis, MO 63132
Publisher V: 02/02/96

Sports Channel Pacific
901 Battery St #204
San Francisco, CA 94111
Production Office V: 11/11/96

Spotlight
7 Leicester Pl
London WC2H 7BP, England
Publisher V: 01/13/96

Spring, Sherwood C
NASA/LBJ Space Center
Hoston, TX 77058
Astronaut V: 01/31/96

Springer, Jerry
The Jerry Springer Show
454 N Columbus Dr-2nd Fl
Chicago, IL 60611-5502
Celebrity V: 01/12/96

Springer, Robert C
NASA/LBJ Space Center
Hoston, TX 77058
Astronaut V: 01/31/96

Springfield, Dusty
Take Out Productions
130 W 57th St #13A
New York, NY 10019
Singer V: 02/02/96

Springsteen, Bruce
1224 Benedict Canyon
Beverly Hills, CA 90210
Singer V: 01/15/96

Squire, Billy
Dera Association
584 Broadway #1201
New York, NY 10012
Singer V: 10/23/96

9903 Santa Monica Bl #517
Beverly Hills, CA 90212
Alternate V: 01/21/96

St Cyr, Lili
624 N Plymouth Bl #7
Los Angeles, CA 90004
Exotic Dancer V: 06/21/96

St John, Jill
Borinstein/Oreck
8271 Melrose Ave #110
Los Angeles, CA 90046
Actress V: 12/06/96

St Louis Blues
St Louis Arena
5700 Oakland Ave
St Louis, MO 63110
Team Office V: 02/02/96

St Louis Cardinals
250 Stadium Plaza
Busch Stadium
St Louis, MO 63102
Team Office V: 02/15/96

Stack, Robert
Blake Agency
415 N Camden Dr #121
Beverly Hills, CA 90210
Actor V: 12/06/96

321 Saint Pierre Rd
Los Angeles, CA 91602
Alternate V: 04/21/96

Stafford, Jim
c/o Blade
PO Box 1556
Gainesville, GA 32602
Singer V: 02/02/96

Stafford, Nancy
c/o MTA
4526 Wilshire Bl
Los Angeles, CA 90010
Actress V: 01/21/96

Stafford, Thomas P
NASA/LBJ Space Center
Houston, TX 77058
Astronaut V: 03/03/96

Stallone, Sylvester
c/o CAA
9830 Wilshire Bl
Beverly Hills, CA 90212
Actor V: 01/14/96

30900 Broadbeach Rd
Malibu, CA 90265-2664
Alternate V: 07/15/96

100 SE 32nd Rd
Cocnut Grove, FL 33129
Forwarded V: 09/13/96

Stamp, Terence
Duncan Heath
162 Wardour St
London W1, England
Actor V: 02/28/96

Latent Image Productions
55 Victoria St de Gaul
Potts Point, NSW 2011, Australia
Alternate V: 03/09/96

Stanley, Florence
Wm Morris Agency
151 El Camino Dr
Beverly Hills, CA 90212
Actress V: 02/26/96

Stanley, John
Creatures at Large Press
PO Box 687
Pacifica, CA 94044
Author V: 01/20/96

Stanton, Harry Dean
Bresler/Kelly
15760 Ventura Bl #1730
Encino, CA 91436
Actor V: 12/06/96

Stapleton, Jean
Bauman & Hiller
5750 Wilshire Bl #512
Los Angeles, CA 90036
Actress V: 12/05/96

635 Perugia Way
Los Angeles, CA 90024
Alternate V: 02/12/96

Stapleton, Maureen
1-14 Morgan Manor
Lenox, MA 01240
Actress V: 10/23/96

Star Talent Agency
4555 Mariota Ave
Toluca Lake, CA 91602
Talent Agency V: 02/02/96

Star Trek Official FC
Paramount Pictures
PO Box 111000
Aurora, CO 80011
Fan Services V: 03/10/96

Star Weekly
660 White Plains Rd
Tarrytown, NY 10591
Publisher V: 03/01/96

Starline Magazine
210 Route-4 East
Paramus, NY 07562
Publisher V: 02/10/96

Starr, Bart
1400 Urban Center Dr #400
Birmingham, AL 35242-2547
Football Star V: 03/14/96

Starr, Ringo
Mgmt 3
4570 Encino Ave
Encino, CA 91316
Singer V: 09/13/96

Rocca Bella
24 Ave Princess Grace
Monte Carlo, Monaco
Alternate V: 03/17/96

Starwil Talent
6253 Hollywood Bl #730
Los Angeles, CA 90028
Talent Agency V: 03/02/96

Statler Brothers
PO Box 2703
Staunton, VA 24402-2703
Musical Group V: 11/01/96

Steel, Amy
Innovative Artists
1999 Ave of the Stars #2850
Los Angeles, CA 90067
Actress V: 02/24/96

Steele, Barbara
442 S Bedford Dr
Beverly Hills, CA 90212
Actress V: 05/18/96

Steele, Danielle
PO Box 1637
Murray Hill Station
New York, NY 10156
Author V: 12/02/96

Steenburgen, Mary
1350 Ave of the Americas
New York, NY 10019
Actress V: 10/23/96

Wm Morris
151 El Camino
Beverly Hills, CA 90212
Alternate V: 03/30/96

Steiger, Rod
6324 Zumirez Dr
Malibu, CA 90265
Actor V: 03/17/96

Gold/Marshak
3500 W Olive Ave
Burbank, CA 91505
Alternate V: 02/14/96

Steinberg, David
c/o Agency
801 Westmount Dr
Los Angeles, CA 90069
Comedy Star V: 02/01/96

Stephens, Robert
Film Rights
113 Wardour St
London W1, England
Actor V: 03/01/96

Sterling, Robert
121 S Bentley Ave
Los Angeles, CA 90049
Actor V: 05/01/96

Stern, Howard
10 E 44th St #700
New York, NY 10017
Radio Star V: 02/10/96

K-ROCK-FM/WXRK
600 Madison Ave
New York, NY 10022
Alternate V: 01/14/96

Stern Agency
11766 Wilshire Bl #760
Los Angeles, CA 90025
Talent Agency V: 03/15/96

Sternbach, Rick
ST-Voyager
5555 Melrose Ave
Hollywood, CA 90036
Designer V: 02/15/96

Stevens, Andrew
c/o Schechter
9300 Wilshire Bl #410
Beverly Hills, CA 90212
Actor V: 03/18/96

Stevens, Brinke
8033 Sunset Bl #556
Hollywood, CA 90046
Actress V: 02/04/96

Stevens, Cat
Yusef Islam
3 Furlong Rd
London, N7 8LA England
Islamic Teacher V: 07/01/96

Stevens, Connie
243 Delfern
Los Angeles, CA 90024
Actress V: 02/01/96

8721 Sunset Bl-PH2
Los Angeles, CA 90069
Alternate V: 03/17/96

Media Artists
8383 Wilshire Bl #954
Beverly Hills, CA 90211
Forwarded V: 02/24/96

Stevens, Craig
1308 N Flores St
Los Angeles, CA 90069
Actor V: 09/13/96

Stevens, Fisher
Wm Morris Agency
151 El Camino Dr
Beverly Hills, CA 90212
Actor V: 03/20/96

Stevens, Shadoe
Buckwald & Associates
9229 Sunset Bl #710
Los Angeles, CA 90069
Actor V: 12/06/96

Stevens, Stella
8721 Sunset Bl-PH1
Los Angeles, CA 90069
Actress V: 03/17/96

Craig Agency
8485 Melrose Place-Suite E
Los Angeles, CA 90069
Alternate V: 12/08/96

Stevens Talent
3518 W Cahuenga Bl #301
Los Angeles, CA 90068
Talent Agency V: 11/11/96

Stevenson, Parker
Metro Talent Agency
4526 Wilshire Bl
Los Angeles, CA 90010
Actor V: 12/11/96

Stewart, Alana
c/o APA
9000 Ave of the Stars #1200
Los Angeles, CA 90069
Actress V: 02/24/96

Stewart, Catherine Mary
Gage Group
9255 Sunset Bl #515
Los Angeles, CA 90069
Actress V: 12/08/96

350 DuPont St
Toronto, ON M5R, Canada
Alternate V: 10/10/96

Stewart, Jon
Wm Morris Agency
151 El Camino Dr
Beverly Hills, CA 90212
Celebrity V: 01/14/96

Stewart, Martha
Martha Stewart Living
20 W 43rd St
New York, NY 10036
Author V: 01/14/96

10877 Wilshire Bl #900
Los Angeles, CA 90024-4341
Alternate V: 01/13/97

Stewart, Patrick
c/o ICM
8942 Wilshire Bl
Beverly Hills, CA 90211
Actor V: 12/11/96

Stewart, Patrick, Cont.
Star Trek-TNG/Paramount
5555 Melrose Ave
Hollywood, CA 90038
Alternate V: 03/04/96

c/o Boyack
9 Cork St
London W1, England
Forwarded V: 03/16/96

Stewart, Payne
390 N Orange Ave #2600
Orlando, FL 32801-1642
Golfer V: 02/04/96

Stewart, Peggy
11139 Hortense St
N Hollywood, CA 91602
Actress V: 12/12/96

Stewart, Robert L
NASA/LBJ Space Center
Houston, TX 77058
Astronaut V: 03/03/96

815 Sun Valley Dr
Woodland Park CO 80863
Alternate V: 10/23/96

Stewart, Rod
23 Beverly Park
Beverly Hills, CA 90210-1500
Singer V: 02/02/96

1435 S Ocean Bl
Palm Beach, FL 33400
Alternate V: 02/28/96

Stiers, David Ogden
Smith & Associates
121 N San Vicente Bl
Beverly Hills, CA 90211
Actor V: 12/15/96

Stiller, Ben
c/o CAA
9830 Wilshire Bl
Beverly Hills, CA 90212
Actor V: 01/14/96

Sting
The Bugle House
21A Noel St
London W1, England
Singer V: 01/14/96

Stock, Barbara
c/o MTA
4526 Wilshire Bl
Los Angeles, CA 90010
Actress V: 02/24/96

Stock-Poynton, Amy
c/o Schecter
9300 Wilshire Bl #410
Beverly Hills, CA 90212
Actress V: 01/12/96

Artists Group
10100 Santa Monica Bl #2490
Los Angeles, CA 90067
Alternate V: 12/04/96

Stockwell, Dean
PO Box 788
Ketchum, ID 83340
Actor V: 10/23/96

9630 Keokuk Ave
Chatsworth, CA 91311
Alternate V: 02/09/96

Stockwell, Guy
c/o Moss
733 N Seward St-PH
Los Angeles, CA 90038
Actor V: 02/01/96

Stoltz, Eric
Creative Artists Agency
9830 Wilshire Bl
Beverly Hills, CA 90212
Actor V: 12/07/96

Stone, Dee Wallace
Kohner Agency
9300 Wilshire Bl #555
Beverly Hills, CA 90212
Actress V: 12/11/96

Stone, Doug
Stoneage Productions
PO Box 943
Springfield, TN 37172
Singer V: 11/01/96

Stone, Hal
Sedona Shadows #273
Sedona, AZ 86336
Radio Star V: 01/20/96

Stone, Oliver
9830 Wilshire Bl
Beverly Hills, CA 90212
Director V: 01/14/96

Stone, Oliver, Cont.
1609 Georgina Ave
Santa Monica, CA 90402
Alternate V: 01/15/96

Ixtlan Corporation
201 Santa Monica Bl #610
Santa Monica, CA 90401
Forwarded V: 10/23/96

Stone, Sharon
CAA/Dorthy Stone
9830 Wilshire Bl
Beverly Hills, CA 90212
Actress V: 04/22/96

PO Box 7304
N Hollywood, CA 91603-7304
Alternate V: 01/21/96

c/o PMK
955 S Carillo Dr #200
Los Angeles, CA 90048
Forwarded V: 04/15/96

Stone, Sly
Glenn P Stone
250 W 57th St #407
New York, NY 10019-3202
Singer V: 08/28/96

Stone Manners Talent
8091 Selma Ave
Los Angeles, CA 90046
Talent Agency V: 03/13/96

Stonehenge Productions
10202 W Washington Bl
Culver City, CA 90232
Production Office V: 03/17/96

Stones, Dwight
4790 Irvine Bl #105
Irvine, CA 92620
Olympian V: 01/13/97

Storch, Larry
336 West End Ave #17F
New York, NY 10023
Actor V: 06/17/96

Storm, Gale
308 N Sycamore Ave #104
Los Angeles, CA 90036
Actress V: 03/03/96

6533 Hollywood Bl #201
Hollywood, CA 90028
Alternate V: 02/26/96

Stowe, Madeleine
c/o UTA
9560 Wilshire Bl #500
Beverly Hills, CA 90212
Actress V: 01/14/96

Strain, Julie
Purrfect Productions
PO Box 430
Newbury Park, CA 91320
Actress V: 01/13/96

Strasberg, Susan
PO Box 847
Pacific Palisades, CA 90272
Actress V: 10/23/96

Strassman, Marcia
Ambrosio/Mortimer
9150 Wilshire Bl #175
Beverly Hills, CA 90212
Actress V: 02/24/96

Streep, Meryl
c/o PMK
955 S Carillo Dr #200
Los Angeles, CA 90048
Actress V: 04/15/96

130 Paradise Cove Rd
Malibu, Ca 90265
Alternate V: 10/23/96

Streisand, Barbra
c/o CAA
9830 Wilshire Bl
Beverly Hills, CA 90212
Actress V: 01/13/96

301 N Carolwood Dr
Los Angeles, CA 90077
Alterante V: 03/26/96

Stritch, Elaine
1 Bennett St
Cambridge, MA 02138-5780
Actress V: 02/02/96

Strong, Brenda
Bauman/Hiller
5750 Wilshire Bl #512
Los Angeles, CA 90036
Actress V: 10/23/96

Stroud, Don
17020 Sunset Bl #20
Pacific Palisades, CA 90272-3212
Actor V: 11/01/96

Stroud, Don, Cont.
Bauman/Hiller
5750 Wilshire Bl #512
Los Angeles, CA 90036
Alternate V: 02/18/96

Strug, Kerri
PO Box 34-B
Balboa Island, CA 92662
Olympian V: 01/13/97

Struthers, Sally
Shapira & Associates
15301 Ventura Bl #345
Sherman Oaks, CA 91403
Actress V: 12/13/96

9229 Sunset Bl #520
Los Angeles, CA 90069
Alternate V: 12/24/96

Struycken, Carel
Sindell & Associates
8271 Melrose Ave #202
Los Angeles, CA 90046
Actor V: 12/14/96

Studio Fan Mail
1122 S Robertson Bl
Los Angeles, CA 90035
Fan Service V: 11/20/96

Stunt Action Coordinators
21828 Lassen #E
Chatsworth, CA 91311
Production Office V: 03/17/96

Stuntman's Assn
4810 Whitsett Ave
N Hollywood, CA 91607
Production Office V: 03/17/96

Stuntwoman's Assn
202 Vance St
Pacific Palisades, CA 90272
Production Office V: 03/17/96

Sturges, Shannon
Shapira & Associates
15301 Ventura Bl #345
Sherman Oaks, CA 91403
Actress V: 12/15/96

1223 Wilshire Bl #577
Santa Monica, CA 90403-5400
Alternate V: 01/10/97

Suchet, David
c/o Brunskill
169 Queen's Gate
London SW7 5EH, England
Actor V: 03/17/96

Suggs, Louise
2000 South Ocean Bl
Del Ray Beach, FL 33483
Golf Star V: 12/12/96

Sullivan, Danny
891 Washington Rd
Grosse Point, MI 48230
Race Driver V: 01/09/96

Sullivan, Kathleen
E! Entertainment TV
5670 Wilshire Bl-2nd Fl
Los Angeles, CA 90036
Correspondant V: 01/13/96

Sullivan, Kathryn
NASA/LBJ Space Center
Hoston, TX 77058
Astronaut V: 01/19/96

Sun Magazine
5401 NW Broken Sound Bl
Boca Raton, FL 33847
Publisher V: 02/10/96

Sundance Institute
PO Box 16450
Salt Lake City, UT 84116
Film Fete V: 06/15/96

Sunset-Gower Studios
1438 N Gower St
Los Angeles, CA 90028
Production Office V: 03/17/96

Super Teen Magazine
233 Park Ave South
New York, NY 10003
Publisher V: 02/10/96

Supernaw, Doug
c/o Lee
38 Music Square E #300
Nashville, TN 37203
Singer V: 02/02/96

Sutherland, Donald
Creative Artists Agency
9830 Wilshire Bl
Beverly Hills, CA 90212
Actor V: 12/07/96

Sutherland, Kiefer
10201 W Pico Bl- Bldg 15
Los Angeles, CA 90035
Actor V: 11/01/96

Sutton-Barth-Vennari
145 S Fairfax Ave #310
Los Angeles, CA 90036
Talent Agency V: 02/18/96

Suzman, Janet
Wm Morris Agency
31 Soho Square
London W1, England
Actress V: 02/28/96

Svenson, Bo
c/o Persson
1434 Princeton St #D
Santa Monica, CA 90404-3039
Actor V: 02/03/96

Swaggart, Jimmy
8919 World Ministry Ave
Baton Rouge, LA 70810
Evangelist V: 10/23/96

Swank, Hilary
3500 W Olive Ave #920
Burbank, CA 91505
Actress V: 10/23/96

Swanson, Kristy
Creative Artists Agency
9830 Wilshire Bl
Beverly Hills, CA 90212
Actress V: 12/07/96

Swayze, Patrick
Wolfe/Kasteller
1033 Gayley Ave #208
Los Angeles, CA 90024
Actor V: 12/01/96

Sweeney, DB
9560 Wilshire Bl #500
Beverly Hills, CA 90212
Actor V: 01/11/97

Sweeney, Julia
570 N Arden Bl
Los Angeles, CA 90004
Actress V: 01/03/97

Swenson, August C
1701 Azores Dr
Pflugerville, TX 78660
Actor V: 01/20/96

Swenson, Inga
Paradigm Agency
10100 Santa Monica Bl-25th Fl
Los Angeles, CA 90067
Actress V: 12/13/96

3475 Cabrillo Bl
Los Angeles, CA 90066
Alternate V: 01/11/96

Swift, Clive
c/o PTA
Bugle House-21a Noel St
London W1V 3PD, England
Actor V: 03/17/96

Swit, Loretta
6363 Wilshire Bl #600
Los Angeles, CA 90048
Actress V: 10/23/96

Artists Group
10100 Santa Monica Bl #2490
Los Angeles, CA 90067
Alternate V: 02/24/96

T

TBS SuperStation
One CNN Center
PO Box 105366
Atlanta, GA 30348
Production Office V: 12/15/96

TEKWAR
TekWar Fan Club
2522 N Sparkman Bl
Tucson, AZ 85716-2517
Fan Service V: 01/13/96

TEMPORARILY YOURS
Fox-TV
PO Box 900
Beverly Hills, CA 90213
Production Office V: 12/15/96

CBS-TV
51 W 52nd St
New York, NY 10019
Audience Services V: 01/13/97

THE CAPE
WB-TV
14238 N Gower
Hollywood, CA 90028
Audience Services V: 04/12/96

THE CITY
320 W 66th St
New York, NY 10023
Production Office V: 11/11/96

THE MARSHALL
UPN-TV
5555 Melrose Ave
Los Angeles, CA 90038
Production Office V: 01/14/96

THE NAKED TRUTH
Brillstein-Grey
9150 Wilshire Bl #350
Beverly Hills, CA 90212
Production Office V: 10/23/96

THE NANNY
Culver Studios/Bungalow R
9336 W Washington Bl
Culver City, CA 90232
Production Office V: 03/05/96

CBS-TV
51 W 52nd St
New York, NY 10019
Alternate V: 12/15/96

THE PARENT HOOD
WB-TV
1438 N Gower
Hollywood, CA 90028
Production Office V: 12/15/96

THE PRACTICE
ABC-TV
77 W 66th St
New York, NY 10023
Audience Services V: 01/13/97

THE PRETENDER
NBC-TV
30 Rockefeller Plaza
New York, NY 10112
Viewer Services V: 11/11/96

THE SENTINEL
UPN-TV
5555 Melrose Ave-Marathon 1200
Los Angeles, CA 90038
Production Office V: 12/15/96

THE SINGLE GUY
NBC-TV
30 Rockefeller Plaza
New York, NY 10112
Production Office V: 12/15/96

THE WAYANS BROTHERS
WB-TV
1438 N Gower
Hollywood, CA 90028
Production Office V: 12/15/96

THE X-FILES
Fox-TV
PO Box 900
Beverly Hills, CA 90213
Production Office V: 12/15/96

THEA
Castle Rock Entertainment
335 N Maple Dr #135
Beverly Hills, CA 90210
Production Office V: 01/16/96

THIRD ROCK FROM THE SUN
NBC-TV
30 Rockefeller Plaza
New York, NY 10112
Production Office V: 12/15/96

THIS WEEK-DAVID BRINKLEY
1717 De Sales St NW
Washington, DC 20036
Production Office V: 01/21/96

THUNDER ALLEY
Disney Studios
500 S Buena Vista St
Burbank, CA 91505
Production Office V: 01/20/96

TODAY SHOW
NBC News
30 Rockefeller Plaza
New York, NY 10112
Production Office V: 03/26/96

TONIGHT SHOW w/JAY LENO
NBC Productions
3000 W Alameda Ave
Burbank, CA 91523
Production Office V: 01/10/96

Carson Productions
9536 Wilshire Bl #300
Beverly Hills, CA 90210
Alternate V: 01/20/96

TOUCHED BY AN ANGEL
CBS Entertainment
12711 Ventura Bl #210
Studio City, CA 90206
Production Office V: 10/23/96

TOUCHED BY AN ANGEL, Cont.
Caroline Prod/Holiday Inn
999 S Main St #1792
Salt Lake City, UT 84111
Alternate V: 03/12/96

CBS-TV
51 W 52nd St
New York, NY 10019
Alternate V: 12/15/96

TOWNIES
Carsey-Werner/CBS Studios
4024 Radford Ave-Bldg 3 #103
Studio City, CA 91604
Production Office V: 11/11/96

TRUE COLORS
FOX TV
PO Box 900
Beverly Hills, CA 90213
Production Office V: 01/20/96

TSN-TV
Sports Channel
1155 Leslie St
Don Mill, Ont, M3C Canada
Production Office V: 02/09/96

TURNING POINT
147 Columbus Ave-4th Fl
New York, NY 10023
Production Office V: 01/21/96

TV Food Network
1177 Ave of the Americas
New York, NY 10036
Production Office V: 12/15/96

TV Guide
100 Matsonford Rd
Radnor, PA 19088
Publisher V: 03/01/96

TV Screen Magazine
TV/Movie Screen Magazine
35 Wilbur St
Lynbrook, NY 11563
Publisher V: 02/10/96

20/20
147 Columbus Ave
New York, NY 10023
Production Office V: 01/21/96

Tabori, Kristoffer
172 E 95th St
New York, NY 10028
Actor V: 02/01/96

Taft Entertainment
3330 Cahuenga Bl
Los Angeles, CA 90068
Network HQ V: 04/22/96

Tahoe, TC
222 N Fairview
Burbank, CA 91505
Magician V: 06/06/96

Takei, George
Stevens Talent
3518 W Cahuenga Bl #301
Los Angeles, CA 90068
Actor V: 12/15/96

3349 Cahuenga Bl #2
Los Angeles, CA 90068
Forwarded V: 11/01/96

Talbert, Billy
US Banknote Co
345 Hudson St
New York, NY 10014
Tennis Star V: 02/18/96

Talbot, Nita
3420 Merrimac Rd
Los Angeles, CA 90049
Actress V: 06/17/96

Contemporary Artists
1427 3rd St-Prominade #205
Santa Monica, CA 90401
Alternate V: 02/26/96

Talent Group
6300 Wilshire Bl #2110
Los Angles, CA 90048
Talent Agency V: 01/14/96

Tallman, Patricia
Harry Gold
3500 W Olive Ave #1400
Burbank, CA 91505
Production Office V: 01/20/96

Tamblyn, Russ
Amstel-Eisenstadt-Frasier
6310 San Vicente Bl #401
Los Angeles, CA 90048
Actor V: 12/01/96

2310 6th St #2
Santa Monica, CA 90405
Alternate V: 04/23/96

Tambor, Jeffrey
Gersh Agency
9830 Wilshire Bl
Beverly Hills, CA 90210
Actor V: 02/03/96

Tampa Bay Buccaneers
One Buccaneer Place
Tampa, FL 33607
Team Office V: 05/15/96

Tampa Bay Lightning
501 E Kennedy Bl #175
Tampa, FL 33602
Team Office V: 02/02/96

Tannen & Associates
8370 Wilshire Bl #209
Beverly Hills, CA 90211
Talent Agency V: 02/27/96

Tanner, Joseph R
NASA/LBJ Space Center
Houston, TX 77058
Astronaut V: 02/02/96

Tarantino, Quentin
A Band Apart Production
10202 W Washington Bl
Culver City, CA 90232
Director V: 10/23/96

Wm Morris Agency
151 El Camino
Beverly Hills, CA 90212
Alternate V: 01/14/96

Tarkington, Fran
Tower Place Suite 444
3340 Peachtree Rd NE
Atlanta, GA 30326
Actor V: 03/25/96

Tatler Magazine
Vogue House/Hanover Sq
London, W1R 0AD London
Publisher V: 03/03/96

Taviani, Paolo
Instituto Luce SPA
Via Tuscolana 1055
Rome, Italy 00173
Actor V: 03/14/96

Taviani, Vittorio
Instituto Luce SPA
Via Tuscolana 1055
Rome, Italy 00173
Actor V: 03/14/96

Taylor, Buck
Gerler-Stevens
3349 Cahuenga Bl W #1
Los Angeles, CA 90068
Actor V: 01/02/96

206 Via Colinas
Westlake Village, CA 91362
Alternate V: 01/02/96

20th Century Artists
15315 Magnolia Bl #429
Sherman Oaks, CA 91403
Alternate V: 12/15/96

Taylor, Christine
Metropolitan Talent
4526 Wilshire Bl
Los Angeles, CA 90010
Actress V: 12/15/96

Taylor, Elizabeth
Wm Morris
151 El Camino
Beverly Hills, CA 90212
Actress V: 01/14/96

700 Nimes Rd
Los Angeles, CA 90024
Alternate V: 02/04/96

Taylor, Holland
Gersh Agency
232 N Canon Dr
Beverly Hills, CA 90210
Actress V: 12/09/96

Taylor, Meshach
Innovative Artists
1999 Ave of the Stars #2850
Los Angeles, CA 90067
Actor V: 12/11/96

369 E Calaveras St
Altadena, CA 91001
Alternate V: 04/04/96

Taylor, Niki
c/o IMG
170 Fifth Ave
New York, NY 10010
Model V: 11/01/96

8362 Pines Bl #334
Hollywood, FL 33024
Alternate V: 01/13/97

Taylor, Regina
Wm Morris Agency
151 S El Camino Dr
Beverly Hills, CA 90212
Actress V: 10/10/96

Taylor, Rip
c/o Kjar
10653 Riverside Dr
Toluca Lake, CA 91602
Actor V: 02/22/96

Taylor, Rod
2375 Bowmont Dr
Beverly Hills, CA 90210
Actor V: 08/20/96

Taylor-Young, Leigh
12221 N Kings Rd #401
Los Angeles, CA 90069
Actress V: 05/04/96

c/o Buchwald
9229 Sunset Bl #710
Los Angeles, CA 90069
Alternate V: 02/25/96

Teague, Brad
NASCAR
1811 Volusia Ave
Daytona Beach, FL 32015
NASCAR Driver V: 03/02/96

Teen Beat Magazine
233 Park Ave South
New York, NY 10003
Publisher V: 02/10/96

Teen Machine Magazine
233 Park Ave South
New York, NY 10003
Publisher V: 02/10/96

Telemundo
1740 Broadway-18th Fl
New York, NY 10019
Network HQ V: 03/01/96

2290 W 8th Ave
Hialeah, FL 33010
Alternate V: 12/15/96

Television Arts & Sciences
3500 W Olive #700
Burbank, CA 91505
Academy Office V: 03/17/96

Temple-Black, Shirley
115 Lakeside Dr
Woodside, CA 94062
Politician V: 01/31/96

Tenuta, Judy
950 2nd Ave #101
Santa Monica, CA 90403-2438
Actress V: 03/14/96

Testi, Fabio
Via Siacci 38
00197 Rome, Italy
Model V: 01/21/96

Tewes, Lauren
1611 42nd Ave E
Seattle, WA 98112
Actress V: 08/28/96

201 Santa Monica Bl #610
Santa Monica, CA 90401
Alternate V: 10/23/96

2739 31st Ave South
Seattle, WA 98144-5531
Forwarded V: 02/25/96

Texas Rangers
PO Box 1111
Arlington Stadium
Arlington, TX 76010
Team Office V: 02/15/96

Thagard, Norman E
NASA/LBJ Space Center
Houston, TX 77058
Astronaut V: 03/03/96

Thatcher, Margaret
11 Dulwich Gate
Dulwich, London SE12, England
Politician V: 04/05/96

Chester Square, Belgravia
London, England
Alternate V: 01/13/97

Thaxter, Phyllis
Artists Agency
10000 Santa Monica Bl #305
Los Angeles, CA 90067
Actress V: 12/02/96

The Agency
1800 Ave of the Stars #400
Los Angeles, CA 90067
Talent Agency V: 11/11/96

The Byrds
9850 Sandalfoot Rd #458
Bocca Raton, FL 33428
Musical Group V: 10/23/96

The Family Channel
2877 Guardian Lane
PO Box 2050
Virginia Beach, VA 23450-2050
Production Office V: 12/15/96

The Golf Channel
7580 Commerce Center Dr
Orlando, FL 32819
Production Office V: 12/15/96

The Osmonds
PO Box 1990
Branson, MO 65616-1990
Musical Group V: 01/10/96

Theissem, Tiffani-Amber
Gold/Marshak
3500 W Olive Ave #1400
Burbank, CA 91505
Actress V: 01/12/96

Thinnes, Roy
Shapira & Associates
15301 Ventura Bl #345
Sherman Oaks, CA 91403
Actor V: 12/14/96

Thomas, Andrew
NASA/LBJ Space Center
Houston, TX 77058
Astronaut V: 02/02/96

Thomas, Blair
720 Oak Springs Rd
Rosemont, PA 19010
Football Star V: 09/10/96

Thomas, Clarence
Chief Justice Chambers
Washington, DC 20543-0001
Politician V: 01/21/96

Thomas, Donald A
NASA/LBJ Space Center
Houston, TX 77058
Astronaut V: 03/03/96

Thomas, Gareth
c/o Belfrage
60 St James's St
London SW1A 1LE, England
Actor V: 03/17/96

Thomas, Heather
c/o APA
9000 Sunset Bl #1200
Los Angeles, CA 90069
Actress V: 02/25/96

Studio Fan Mail
1122 S Robertson Bl
Los Angeles, CA 90035
Forwarded V: 10/23/96

Thomas, Jay
Buckwald & Associates
9229 Sunset Bl #710
Los Angeles, CA 90069
Actor V: 12/06/96

Thomas, John
51 Mulberry St
Brockton, MA 02402
Olympian V: 10/23/96

Thomas, Jonathan Taylor
PO Box 64846
Hollywood, CA 57896-5754
Actor V: 03/05/96

Thomas, Marlo
Wm Morris Agency
151 El Camino
Beverly Hills, CA 90212
Actress V: 12/12/96

420 E 54th St #22F
New York, NY 10022
Alternate V: 03/23/96

Thomas, Richard
Creative Artists Agency
9830 Wilshire Bl
Beverly Hills, CA 90212
Actor V: 12/07/96

4963 Los Feliz Bl
Los Angeles, CA 90027-1764
Alternate V: 01/12/96

5261 Cleon Ave
N Hollywood, CA 91601
Forwarded V: 08/20/96

400 Pelham Rd
New Rochelle, NY 10805-2202
Forwarded V: 07/14/96

Thomas Talent
124 S Lasky Dr-1st Fl
Beverly Hills, CA 90212
Talent Agency V: 02/02/96

Thomerson, Tim
Innovative Artists
1999 Ave of the Stars #2850
Los Angeles, CA 90067
Actor V: 12/11/96

Thompson, Brian
Gold/Marshak
3500 W Olive Ave #1400
Burbank, CA 91505
Actor V: 12/10/96

Thompson, Emma
c/o PMK
955 S Carillo Dr #200
Los Angeles, CA 90048
Actress V: 04/15/96

c/o Hamilton
19 Denmark St
London WC2H 8NA, England
Alternate V: 01/14/96

Thompson, Fred Dalton
US Senate
Washington, DC 20510
Senator V: 10/23/96

Abrams Artists
9200 Sunset Bl #625
Los Angeles, CA 90069
Alternate V: 02/24/96

Thompson, Lea
Gersh Agency
232 N Canon Dr
Beverly Hills, CA 90210
Actress V: 12/09/96

Thompson, Sada
Bauman & Hiller
5750 Wilshire Bl #512
Los Angeles, CA 90036
Actress V: 12/05/96

Thorne-Smith, Courtney
Paradigm Agency
10100 Santa Monica Bl-25th Fl
Los Angeles, CA 90067
Actress V: 12/13/96

Thornton, Kathryn C
NASA/LBJ Space Center
Hoston, TX 77058
Astronaut V: 01/19/96

Thornton, Sigrid
Wm Morris
151 El Camino
Beverly Hills, CA 90212
Actress V: 02/12/96

Thornton & Associates
12001 Ventura Place #201
Studio City, CA 91604
Talent Agency V: 02/27/96

Thorson, Linda
145 W 45th St #1204
New York, NY 10036
Actress V: 11/01/96

Thorton, William E
NASA/LBJ Space Center
Houston, TX 77058
Astronaut V: 03/03/96

Thuot, Pierre J
NASA/LBJ Space Center
Hoston, TX 77058
Astronaut V: 01/31/96

Thurman, Uma
c/o CAA
9830 Wilshire Bl
Beverly Hills, CA 90212
Actress V: 01/14/96

Thurmond, Nate
5094 Diamond Heights Bl #B
San Francisco, CA 94131-1653
Basketball Star V: 01/07/97

Tibbets, Paul W
5574 Knollwood Dr
Columbus, OH 43232
War Hero V: 02/01/96

Ticotin, Rachel
c/o ICM
8942 Wilshire Bl
Beverly Hills, CA 90211
Actress V: 11/27/96

Tiegs, Cheryl
2 Greenwich Plaza #100
Greenwich, CT 06830
Actress V: 06/21/96

1060 Channel Dr
Santa Barbara, CA 93108
Forwarded V: 11/01/96

Tiffany
Dick Scott
888 7th Ave #2900
New York, NY 10106
Singer V: 10/23/96

Tige, Andrew
4914 Encino Terrace
Encino, CA 91316
Actor V: 02/26/96

Tiger Beat Magazine
TV/Movie Screen Magazine
35 Wilbur St
Lynbrook, NY 11563
Publisher V: 02/10/96

Tillis, Mel
c/o Agent
PO Box 1626
Branson, MO 65616
Singer V: 02/02/96

Tillis, Pam
c/o Robertson
PO Box 120073
Nashville, TN 37212
Singer V: 02/02/96

Tilly, Jennifer
c/o ICM
8942 Wilshire Bl
Beverly Hills, CA 90211
Actress V: 04/22/96

270 N Canon Dr #1582
Beverly Hills, CA 90210-5323
Alternate V: 08/28/96

Tilly, Meg
9560 Wilshire Bl-5th Fl
Beverly Hills, CA 90212
Actress V: 10/10/96

Time Magazine
Time/Life Bldg
Rockefeller Center
New York, NY 10020
Publisher V: 02/10/96

Tisherman Agency
6767 Forest Lawn Dr #115
Los Angeles, CA 90068
Talent Agency V: 02/01/96

Titov, Vladimir
NASA/LBJ Space Center
Houston, TX 77058
Astronaut V: 02/02/96

Todd, Tony
c/o APA
9000 Sunset Bl #1200
Los Angeles, CA 90069
Actor V: 12/02/96

Tom, Heather
Savage Agency
6212 Banner Ave
Los Angeles, CA 90038
Actress V: 12/13/96

Tomei, Marisa
Altman/Greenfield
120 W 45th St #3600
New York, NY 10036
Actress V: 01/14/96

1724 N Vista St
Los Angeles, CA 90046
Alternate V: 02/26/96

7920 Sunset Bl #350
Los Angeles, CA 90046
Alternate V: 01/15/96

Wm Morris Agency
151 El Camino Dr
Beverly Hills, CA 90212
Forwarded V: 01/14/96

Tomita, Tamlyn
Artists Group
10100 Santa Monica Bl #2490
Los Angeles, CA 90067
Actress V: 12/04/96

Tomlin, Lily
PO Box 27700
Los Angeles, CA 90027
Actress V: 04/24/96

Tompkins, Angel
LA Talent
8335 Sunset Bl
Los Angeles, CA 90069
Actress V: 02/25/96

9105 Morning Glory Way
Sun Valley, CA 91532
Alternate V: 02/01/96

Tork, Peter
Moore Artists
1551 S Robertson Bl
Los Angeles, CA 90035
Actor V: 12/12/96

Torn, Rip
130 W 42nd St #2400
New York, NY 10036
Actor V: 03/26/94

Toronto Blue Jays
PO Box 7777
Adelaide St-PO
Exhibition Stadium
Toronto, Ont, Canada M5C 2K7
Team Office V: 02/15/96

The Sky-Dome
300 Bremner Bl #3200
Toronto, Ont, Canada M5V 3B3
Alternate V: 03/12/96

Toronto Maple Leafs
Maple Leaf Gardens
60 Carlton St
Toronto, Ontario, Canada M5B 1L1
Team Office V: 02/02/96

Torrence, Gwen
3606 Spring Point
Decatur, GA 30034
Olympian V: 10/23/96

Torres, Dara Gowen
Trouble in NY Agency
9 E 37th St
New York, NY 10016
Model V: 11/01/96

Torres, Liz
c/o Atkins
303 S Crescent Heights Bl
Los Angeles, CA 90048
Actress V: 02/25/96

Torrey, Rich
King Features
235 E 45th St
New York, NY 10017
Cartoonist V: 04/21/96

Totter, Audrey
Lovell & Associates
7095 Hollywood Bl #1006
Los Angeles, CA 90028
Actress V: 12/11/96

Touchstone TV & Films
5064 Fan Mail
500 S Buena Vista St
Burbank, CA 91521
Production Office V: 01/02/96

Towers, Constance
Stone Manners Talent
8091 Selma Ave
Los Angeles, CA 90068
Actress V: 12/15/96

10651 Chalon Rd
Los Angeles, CA 90077-3312
Alternate V: 02/21/96

Townsend, Robert
Creative Artists Agency
9830 Wilshire Bl
Beverly Hills, CA 90212
Actor V: 12/07/96

Tratloft, Hannes
10 Werderstrasse
757 Baden Baden, Germany
War Hero V: 03/03/96

Travanti, Daniel J
c/o Buchwald
9229 Sunset Bl #710
Los Angeles, CA 90069
Actor V: 03/29/96

Travis, Nancy
c/o UTA
9560 Wilshire Bl #500
Beverly Hills, CA 90212
Actress V: 02/03/96

Travis, Randy
Lib Hatcher Agency
1610 16th Avenue South
Nashville, TN 37212
Singer V: 11/01/96

Travolta, Ellen
Gage Group
9255 Sunset Bl #515
Los Angeles, CA 90069
Actress V: 12/08/96

Travolta, John
PO Box 20029-790
Encino, CA 91416
Actor V: 12/15/96

Treff, Alice
Bonnerstrasse 1
1000 Berlin 33
Germany
Actress V: 01/19/96

Tremayne, Les
901 S Barrington
Los Angeles, CA 90049
Radio Star V: 02/03/96

Trever, John
King Features
216 E 45th St
New York, NY 10017
Cartoonist V: 03/11/96

Trevino, Lee
5757 Alpha Rd #620
Dallas, TX 75240-4668
Golfer V: 10/23/96

14901 Quorum Dr #170
Dallas, TX 75240
Alternate V: 03/21/96

Trevor, Claire
Hotel Pierre
2 E 61st St
New York, NY 10022
Actress V: 01/19/96

22 Rue Villars
Newport Beach, CA 92660-5103
Alternate V: 01/07/97

Trickle, Dick
Moore Engines
PO Box 2916
Spartanburg, SC 29304
NASCAR Driver V: 02/08/96

Stavola Racing
PO Box 339
Harrisburg, NC 28705
Alternate V: 03/02/96

Trimark Pictures
2644 30th St
Santa Monica, CA 90405-3009
Production Office V: 02/12/96

Tripplehorn, Jean
c/o CAA
9830 Wilshire Bl
Beverly Hills, CA 90212
Actress V: 09/03/96

Tritt, Travis
c/o Kragen
1112 N Sherbourne Dr
Los Angeles, CA 90069
Singer V: 02/02/96

Trudeau, Garry
4900 Main St
Kansas City, MO 64112
Cartoonist V: 02/12/96

Truly, Richard H
NASA/LBJ Space Center
Houston, TX 77058
Astronaut V: 03/03/96

Truman, Margaret
c/o Merideth
830 Park Ave
New York, NY 10028
Author V: 03/25/96

Trump, Donald
725 5th Ave
New York, NY 10022
Executive V: 11/20/96

Trump, Ivana
c/o Mille
1100 Palm Beach Bl
Palm Beach, FL 33480
Celebrity V: 05/29/96

721 Fifth Ave
New York, NY 10022
Alternate V: 07/14/96

Tucker, Michael
Artists Group
10100 Santa Monica Bl #2490
Los Angeles, CA 90067
Actor V: 12/04/96

197 Oakdale Ave
Mill Valley, CA 94941-5301
Alternate V: 01/12/96

Tully, Susan
c/o Saraband
265 Liverpool Rd
London N1 1LX, England
Actress V: 03/20/96

Turlington, Christy
Ford Agency
344 E 59th St
New York, NY 10022
Model V: 11/27/96

Turner, Janine
Creative Artists Agency
9830 Wilshire Bl
Beverly Hills, CA 90212
Actress V: 12/07/96

Turner, Janine, Cont.
2220 Airport Fwy #440-297
Bedford, TX 76022
Alternate V: 10/23/96

8455 Beverly Bl #505
Los Angeles, CA 90048
Forwarded V: 11/01/96

Turner, Kathleen
c/o ICM
8942 Wilshire Bl
Beverly Hills, CA 90211
Actress V: 01/14/96

163 Amsterdam Ave #210
New York, NY 10023
Alternate V: 11/01/96

Turner, Ted
Turner Broadcasting
One CNN Center
Atlanta, GA 30348
Media Executive V: 01/14/96

Turner, Tina
c/o CAA
9830 Wilshire Bl
Beverly Hills, CA 90212
Singer V: 03/08/96

Turner Classic Movies
One CNN Center
PO Box 105366
Atlanta, GA 30348
Production Office V: 12/15/96

Turner Home Entertainment
Viewer Services
420 5th Ave-7th Fl
New York, NY 10018
Production Office V: 02/12/96

Turner Network TV
One CNN Center
PO Box 105366
Atlanta, GA 30348
Production Office V: 12/15/96

Turturro, John
16 N Oak St #2B
Ventura, CA 93001-2631
Actor V: 01/21/96

30-23rd Ave
Venice, CA 90291
Alternate V: 01/11/96

Turturro, Nicholas
Abrams/Rubaloff
8075 W 3rd St #303
Los Angeles, CA 90048
Actor V: 10/10/96

Twain, Shania
PO Box 1150
Timmins, Ont, P4N7H9 Canada
Singer V: 11/01/96

Tweed, Shannon
Gold/Marshak
3500 W Olive Ave #1400
Burbank, CA 91505
Actress V: 12/10/96

c/o Schechter
9300 Wilshire Bl #410
Beverly Hills, CA 90212
Alternate V: 02/25/96

Twentieth Century Artists
15315 Magnolia Bl #429
Sherman Oaks, CA 91403
Talent Agency V: 02/02/96

Twentieth Century Fox
10201 W Pico Bl
Los Angeles, CA 90035
Production Office V: 03/17/96

Twentieth Century Fox TV
PO Box 900
Beverly Hills, CA 90213
Network HQ V: 03/01/96

Tyler, Liv
Innovative Artists
1999 Ave of the Stars #2850
Los Angeles, CA 90067
Actress V: 12/11/96

Tyson, Cicely
Creative Artists Agency
9830 Wilshire Bl
Beverly Hills, CA 90212
Actress V: 12/07/96

Tyson, Mike
Don King Productions
32 E 69th St
New York, NY 10021
Boxing Star V: 01/14/96

Tyson, Richard
9000 Sunset Bl #1200
Los Angeles, CA 90069
Actor V: 03/01/96

U

U2
Wasted Talent
321 Fulham Rd
London SW10 9QL, England
Musical Group V: 03/15/96

UBU Productions
5555 Melrose Ave
Hollywood, CA 90038
Production Office V: 03/17/96

UCLA Film & TV Archive
1015 N Cahuenga Bl
Hollywood, CA 90038
Archive V: 03/13/96

UNDER SUSPICION
WB-TV
10831 SW Cascade Ave-Bldg 2
Tigard, OR 97224
Production Office V: 03/12/96

UNHAPPILY EVER AFTER
WB-TV
1438 N Gower
Hollywood, CA 90028
Production Office V: 12/15/96

UNI
9405 NW 41st St
Miami, FL 33178
Network HQ V: 03/01/96

UNSOLVED MYSTERIES
Cosgrove-Meurer Productions
4303 W Verdugo Ave
Burbank, CA 91505
Production Office V: 12/26/96

US Dept of Defense
Motion Picture Media Rec Ctr
Hq/AAVS/DOSD
Norton AFB, CA 92409
Archive V: 03/20/96

US Olympic Committee
1750 E Boulder St
Colorado Springs, CO 80909
Offices V: 03/11/96

US Skiing Association
PO Box 100
Park City, UT 84060
Team Office V: 06/14/96

US Supreme Court
1 First St NE
Washington, DC 20543
Justice Chamber V: 02/02/96

USA Network
1230 Ave of the Americas
New York, NY 10020
Network HQ V: 03/01/96

1900 Ave of the Stars #1290
Los Angeles, CA 90067
Alternate V: 03/17/96

USA Today TV
9336 W Washington Bl
Culver City, CA 90230
Production Office V: 03/17/96

Udonte, Gean Maria
c/o NC
Viale Bruno Buozzi 53
Rome 00197, Italy
Actress V: 02/28/96

Ullman, Liv
Hafrsfjordgt 7
Oslo N-0273, Norway
Actress V: 11/01/96

Ullman, Tracey
3800 La Crescenta Ave #209
La Crescenta, CA 91214-3940
Actress V: 01/12/96

c/o CAA
9830 Wilshire Bl
Beverly Hills, CA 90212
Forwarded V: 02/25/96

Umoja Talent
2069 W Slauson Ave
Los Angeles, CA 90047
Talent Agency V: 11/11/96

Underwood, Blair
5200 Lankershim Bl #260
N Hollywood, CA 91601
Actor V: 01/14/96

Unitas, Johnny
5607 Patterson Rd
Baldwin, MD 21013-9356
Football Star V: 02/07/96

United Fan Club Service
8966 Sunset Bl
Hollywood, CA 90069
Fan Service V: 02/04/96

United Fan Mail
9056 Santa Monica Bl #100
Hollywood, CA 90069
Fan Service V: 02/23/96

United Paramount Network
UPN-TV
5555 Melrose Ave-Marathon 1200
Los Angeles, CA 90038
Production Office V: 10/23/96

Media Relations
11800 Wilshire Bl
Los Angeles, CA 90025
Alternate V: 10/23/96

United Talent Agency
9560 Wilshire Bl-5th Fl
Beverly Hills, CA 90212
Talent Agency V: 03/29/96

Universal Fan Mail
7051 Rhea Ave
Reseda, CA 91335-4006
Fan Service V: 03/11/96

Universal Press Syndicate
4900 Main St
Kansas City, MO 64112
Artists V: 01/11/96

Universal Studios
100 Universal City Plaza
Universal City, CA 91608
Production Office V: 03/17/96

Universal Television
100 Universal Studios Plaza
Universal City, CA 91608
Production Office V: 03/17/96

Univision
605 3rd Ave-12th Fl
New York, NY 10158
Production Office V: 12/15/96

Unser, Bobby
7700 Central Ave SW
Albuquerque, NM 87105
Race Driver V: 01/17/96

Updike, John
The New Yorker
20 W 43rd St
New York , NY 10036
Writer V: 01/13/97

Upshaw, Dawn
Coumbia Artists Management
165 W 57th St
New York, NY 10019
Singer *V: 02/12/96*

Urban, Matt
352 Wildwood
Holland, MI 49423
War Hero *V: 02/05/96*

Urich, Robert
PO Box 5973-1006
Sherman Oaks, CA 91403
Actor *V: 02/03/96*

c/o ICM
8942 Wilshire Bl
Beverly Hills, CA 90211
Alternate *V: 03/01/96*

15930 Woodvale Rd
Encino, CA 91316
Forwarded *V: 05/11/96*

Uris, Leon
PO Box 1559
Aspen, CO 81612
Author *V: 02/13/97*

Urmson, Claire
Ford Model Agency
344 E 59th St
New York, NY 10022
Model *V: 11/01/96*

Ustinov, Peter
Wm Morris
147 Wardour St
London W1, England
Actor *V: 07/12/96*

11 Rue de Silly
92100 Boulogne, France
Forwarded *V: 05/11/96*

Utah Jazz
5 Triad Center-5th Fl
Salt Lake City, UT 84108
Team Office *V: 02/15/96*

Delta Center
301 W South Temple
Salt Lake City, UT 84101
Alternate *V: 11/11/96*

V

VH-1/Video Hits 1
1515 Broadway/MTV Network
New York, NY 10019
Production Office *V: 01/12/96*

VIP Address Book
Jim Wiggins
PO Box 489
Gleneden, OR 97388
Publisher *V: 01/31/96*

VITAL SIGNS
ABC-TV
77 W 66th St
New York, NY 10023
Audience Services *V: 01/10/97*

Vaccaro, Brenda
Kohner Agency
9300 Wilshire Bl #555
Beverly Hills, CA 90212
Actress *V: 12/11/96*

17641 Tarzana St
Encino, CA 91316
Alternate *V: 09/10/96*

Vadim, Roger
316 Alta Vista Ave
Santa Monica, CA 90402
Director *V: 10/10/96*

Valen, Nancy
Metro Talent Agency
4526 Wilshire Bl
Los Angeles, CA 90010
Actress *V: 12/11/96*

Valentine, Karen
House of Representatives
9911 Pico Bl #1060
Los Angeles, CA 90035
Actress *V: 12/10/96*

Vampira
c/o Maila Nurmi
844 1/2 N Hudson
Los Angeles, CA 90038
Actress *V: 10/23/96*

Van Arc, Joan
10950 Alta View Dr
Studio City, CA 91604
Actress *V: 01/13/97*

Van Arc, Joan, Cont.
Wm Morris Agency
151 El Camino
Beverly Hills, CA 90212
Alternate V: 12/12/96

Van Buren, Abigail
c/o Phillips-Van Buren
9200 Sunset Bl #1003
Los Angeles, CA 90069
Columnist V: 10/23/96

Van Damme, Jean-Claude
c/o ICM
8942 Wilshire Bl
Beverly Hills, CA 90211
Actor V: 01/14/96

PO Box 4149
Chatsworth, CA 91311-4149
Alternate V: 03/17/96

Van Doren, Mamie
8340 Rush St
Rosemead, CA 91770
Actress V: 05/29/96

428 31st St
Newport Beach, CA 92663
Alternate V: 03/11/96

Van Dusen, Chris
108 E Main St #2
Ayer, MA 01432-1820
Actor V: 01/21/96

Van Dyke, Barry
Wm Morris Agency
151 El Camino
Beverly Hills, CA 90212
Actor V: 12/12/96

Van Dyke, Dick
Wm Morris Agency
151 El Camino
Beverly Hills, CA 90212
Actor V: 12/12/96

23215 Mariposa de Oro
Malibu, CA 90265
Alternate V: 02/03/96

Van Dyke, Jerry
145 S Fairfax Ave #310
Los Angeles, CA 90036
Actor V: 10/23/96

Van Dyke, Jerry, Cont.
c/o Kazarian
11365 Ventura Bl #100
Studio City, CA 91604
Alternate V: 01/14/96

Van Halen, Eddie
c/o Premiere
3 East 54th St
New York, NY 10022
Musician V: 01/14/96

Van Hoften, James D
NASA/LBJ Space Center
Houston, TX 77058
Astronaut V: 03/03/96

Van Patten, Dick
Artists Agency
10000 Santa Monica Bl #305
Los Angeles, CA 90067
Actor V: 03/02/96

Van Patten, Joyce
Innovative Artists
1999 Ave of the Stars #2850
Los Angeles, CA 90067
Actress V: 02/25/96

Van Peebles, Mario
c/o UTA
15315 Magnolia Bl #429
Sherman Oaks, CA 91403
Actor V: 12/15/96

Van Shelton, Ricky
c/o Campbell
40 Music Square East
Nashville, TN 37203
Singer V: 02/02/96

Van Valkenbergh, Deborah
Epstein/Wyckoff
280 S Beverly Dr #400
Beverly Hills, CA 90212
Actress V: 12/08/96

Vancouver Canucks
Pacific Coliseum
100 N Renfrew St
Vancouver, BC, Canada V5K 3N7
Team Office V: 02/02/96

Vangelis
195 Queensgate
London W1, England
Composer V: 01/07/97

Vanity
1871 Messino Dr
San Jose, CA 95132
Actress V: 11/01/96

Wm Morris Agency
151 El Camino Dr
Beverly Hills, CA 90212
Alternate V: 12/18/96

Varney, Jim
1221 McGovock St
Nashville, TN 37203
Actor V: 05/18/96

Vaughan, Peter
c/o Agency
388-396 Oxford St
London W1 9HE, England
Actor V: 03/17/96

Vaughn, Robert
c/o APA
9000 Sunset Bl #1200
Los Angeles, CA 90069
Actor V: 12/02/96

162 Old West Mountain Rd
Ridgefield, CT 06877
Alternate V: 01/12/96

Veach, Charles Lacey
NASA/LBJ Space Center
Hoston, TX 77058
Astronaut V: 01/31/96

Vendela
c/o IMG
170 Fifth Ave
New York, NY 10010
Model V: 11/01/96

c/o Kirsebon
344 E 59th St
New York, NY 10022
Alternate V: 11/01/96

Verdon, Gwen
26 Latimer Lane
Bronxville, NY 10708-2203
Actress V: 03/14/96

PO Box 303
Quogue, NY 11959-0303
Alternate V: 02/03/96

Vereen, Ben
127 Broadway #220
Santa Monica, CA 90401
Actor V: 10/10/96

924 Westwood Bl #900
Los Angeles, CA 90024
Alternate V: 01/16/96

Verhoeven, Lis
Strenstrasse 17
8000 Munchen 22, Germany
Actress V: 01/19/96

Versace, Gianni
Versace Boutique
816 Madison Ave
New York, NY 10021
Designer V: 01/14/96

Vestron Pictures
2121 Ave of the Stars #600
Los Angeles, CA 90067
Production Office V: 03/17/96

Vetri, Victoria
7045 Hawthorn Ave #206
Los Angeles, CA 90028-6975
Actress V: 08/28/96

Viacom Productions
100 Universal Plaza-Bldg 69
Universal City, CA 91608
Network HQ V: 03/10/96

Vickers, Yvette
PO Box 292479
Phelan, CA 92329-2479
Actress V: 10/23/96

Vidal, Gore
2562 Outpost Dr
Los Angeles, CA 90068
Author V: 03/23/96

Videobrary Inc
Paul Lisy
6117 Carpenter Ave
N Hollywood, CA 91606
Archive V: 01/20/96

Vidmark Entertainment
2901 Ocean Park Bl #123
Santa Monica, CA 90405
Production Office V: 03/17/96

Viewers Choice
909 Third Ave
New York, NY 10022
Network HQ *V: 01/12/96*

Vigoda, Abe
Craig Agency
8485 Melrose Place-Suite E
Los Angeles, CA 90069
Actor *V: 12/08/96*

Village People
Just the 6 of Us
165 W 46th St #1308
New York, NY 10036
Musical Group *V: 11/01/96*

Vincent, Jan Michael
c/o Kreff
11693 San Vicente Bl #296
Los Angeles, CA 90049
Actor *V: 03/26/96*

Vincent, Vinnie
c/o ITG
729 7th Ave #1600
New York, NY 10019
Singer *V: 01/15/96*

Vincz, Melanie
PO Box 292479
Phelan, CA 92329-2479
Actress *V: 10/23/96*

Chateau/Billings
5657 Wilshire Bl
Los Angeles, CA 90036
Alternate *V: 02/25/96*

Vinton, Bobby
1905 Cold Canyon Rd
Calabasas, CA 91302
Singer *V: 01/27/96*

Visitor, Nana
Gersh Agency
232 N Canon Dr
Beverly Hills, CA 90210
Actress *V: 12/09/96*

Star Trek-DS9
5555 Melrose Ave
Hollywood, CA 90036
Alternate *V: 02/23/96*

c/o Nanites
10551 Karmont Ave
South Gate, CA 90280
Alternate *V: 12/15/96*

Visitor, Nana, Cont.
PO Box 5617
Beverly Hills, CA 90210
Alternate *V: 01/16/96*

9145 N Kings Rd #5
Los Angeles, CA 90069-4380
Forwarded *V: 11/01/96*

Vitti, Monica
Via F38-Siacci
Rome 00197, Italy
Actress *V: 02/28/96*

Voight, Jon
13340 Galewood Dr
Sherman Oaks, CA 91423
Actor *V: 10/23/96*

c/o CAA
9830 Wilshire Bl
Beverly Hills, CA 90210
Alternate *V: 03/17/96*

Volz, Nedra
Garrick Int'l
8831 Sunset Bl #402
Los Angeles, CA 90069
Actress *V: 12/08/96*

Von Gerken, Manon
Elite Model Mgmt
111 East 22nd St #200
New York, NY 10010
Model *V: 11/01/96*

Von Oy, Jenna
3 Karen Bl
Newton, CT 06470
Actress *V: 11/01/96*

Von Sydow, Max
Strandvegen B
114-56 Stockholm, Sweden
Actor *V: 11/22/96*

Voss, James S
NASA/LBJ Space Center
Houston, TX 77058
Astronaut *V: 01/31/96*

Voss, Janice E
NASA/LBJ Space Center
Houston, TX 77058
Astronaut *V: 03/03/96*

W

WALKER, TEXAS RANGER
CBS-TV
51 W 52nd St
New York, NY 10019
Production Office V: 12/15/96

CBS Entertainment
13801 Diplomat Dr
Farmers Branch, TX 75234
Alternate V: 12/15/96

CBS-TV
3939 E Hwy 80 #300
Mesquite, TX 75150
Alternate V: 03/12/96

WHEEL OF FORTUNE
Columbia TV
3400 Riverside Dr
Burbank, CA 91505-4627
Production Office V: 11/01/96

WHERE I LIVE
Disney Studios
500 S Buena Vista St
Burbank, CA 91521-2215
Production Office V: 01/20/96

WILD C.A.T.S.
Nelvana Ltd
4500 Wilshire Bl
Los Angeles, CA 90010
Production Office V: 03/12/96

WINGS
NBC-TV
30 Rockefeller Plaza
New York, NY 10112
Production Office V: 12/15/96

WORLD NEWS THIS MORNING
47 W 66th St
New York, NY 10023
Production Office V: 01/21/96

WORLD NEWS TONIGHT
47 W 66th St
New York, NY 10023
Production Office V: 01/21/96

Waggoner, Lyle
Artists Group
10100 Santa Monica Bl #2490
Los Angeles, CA 90067
Actor V: 12/04/96

Wagner, Lindsay
PO Box 188
Pacific Palisades, CA 90272
Actress V: 03/26/96

c/o ICM
8942 Wilshire Bl
Beverly Hills, CA 90211
Alternate V: 03/30/96

1111 Fiske St
Pacific Palisades, CA 90272
Forwarded V: 01/03/97

Wagner, Robert
2121 Avenue of Stars #1240
Los Angeles, CA 90093
Actor V: 10/23/96

1500 Old Oak Rd
Los Angeles, CA 90077
Alternate V: 02/04/96

PO Box 93339
Los Angeles, CA 90093
Forwarded V: 10/23/96

Wagoner, Porter
c/o Davis
PO Box 11276
Kansas City, MO 64119
Singer V: 02/02/96

Wahl, Ken
480 Westlake Bl
Malibu, CA 90265-2444
Actor V: 01/14/96

Wain Agency
1418 N Highland Ave #102
Los Angeles, CA 90028
Talent Agency V: 03/02/96

Waite, Ralph
Innovative Artists
1999 Ave of the Stars #2850
Los Angeles, CA 90067
Actor V: 12/11/96

Wakata, Koichi
NASA/LBJ Space Center
Houston, TX 77058
Astronaut V: 02/02/96

Walden, Lynette
4526 Wilshire Bl
Los Angeles, CA 90010
Actress V: 01/15/97

Waldheim, Kurt
Presseabteilung Osterrich
Hofburg, Bellariator
A-1014 Wien, Austria
Politician V: 03/16/96

Waldhorn, Gary
London Mgmt
235-241 Regent St
London W1A 2JT, England
Actor V: 03/17/96

Waldo, Janet
15725 Royal Oak Rd
Encino, CA 91436
Radio Star V: 11/11/96

Walken, Christopher
Wm Morris Agency
1325 Ave of the Americas
New York, NY 10019
Actor V: 09/13/96

142 Cedar Rd
Wilton, CT 06897
Alternate V: 02/01/96

8969 Sunset Bl
Los Angeles, CA 90069
Forwarded V: 01/15/96

Walker, Chris
c/o Agency
388 Oxford St
London W1, England
Actor V: 02/13/96

Walker, Clint
24635 Rodeo Flat Rd
Auburn, CA 95945
Actor V: 01/13/96

Walker, David M
NASA/LBJ Space Center
Houston, TX 77058
Astronaut V: 03/03/96

Walker, Doak
PO Box 77329
Steamboat Springs, CO 80477-3329
Boxing Star V: 01/10/97

Walker, Mort
61 Studio Ct
Stamford, CT 06903
Cartoonist V: 09/14/96

Walker Jr, Robert
20828 Pacific Coast Hwy
Malibu, CA 90265
Actor V: 03/26/96

Wall, Shana
c/o Cosden
3518 Cahuenga Bl W #216
Los Angeles, CA 90068
Actress V: 01/13/96

Wall Street Journal
200 Liberty St
New York, NY 10281
Publisher V: 02/10/96

Wallace, Kenny
PO Box 3050
Concord, NC 28025
NASCAR Driver V: 03/14/96

Sabco Racing
6013 Victory Ln
Harrisburg, NC 28075
Alternate V: 03/02/96

Wallace, Marcia
Artists Group
10100 Santa Monica Bl #2490
Los Angeles, CA 90067
Actress V: 12/04/96

Wallace, Rusty
PO Box 875
Manchester, MO 63021
NASCAR Driver V: 03/14/96

Penske Racing
6 Knob Hill Rd
Mooreville, NC 28115
Alternate V: 03/02/96

Wallach, Eli
Paradigm Agency
10100 Santa Monica Bl-25th Fl
Los Angeles, CA 90067
Actor V: 12/13/96

90 Riverside Dr
New York, NY 10024
Alternate V: 05/25/96

Waller, Robert James
c/o ICM
8942 Wilshire Bl
Beverly Hills, CA 90211
Author V: 01/14/96

Walley, Deborah
PO Box 1226
Sedona, AZ 86339
Actress V: 10/23/96

Wallis Agency
1126 Hollywood Way #203A
Burbank, CA 91505
Talent Agency V: 02/02/96

Walsh, Brigid Conley
Premiere Artists
8899 Beverly Bl #102
Los Angeles, CA 90048
Actress V: 02/25/96

Walston, Ray
Gold/Marshak
3500 W Olive Ave #1400
Burbank, CA 91505
Actor V: 12/10/96

423 S Rexford Dr #205
Beverly Hills, CA 90212
Alternate V: 02/03/96

Walt Disney Company
Disney Productions
500 S Buena Vista St
Burbank, CA 91521
Production Office V: 03/26/96

Walter, Jessica
c/o APA
9000 Sunset Bl #1200
Los Angeles, CA 90069
Actress V: 12/02/96

Walter, Lisa Ann
c/o Disney Studios
500 S Buena Vista
Burbank, CA 91521
Actress V: 11/11/96

Walter, Tracey
Paradigm Agency
10100 Santa Monica Bl-25th Fl
Los Angeles, CA 90067
Actor V: 12/13/96

257 N Rexford Dr
Beverly Hills, CA 90210
Alternate V: 01/04/96

Walters, Jessica
10530 Strathmore Dr
Los Angeles, CA 90024
Actress V: 10/23/96

Walton, Bill
1010 Myrtle Way
San Diego, CA 92103-5123
Basketball Star V: 01/07/97

Waltrip, Darrell
Darwal Inc
6780 Hudsdeth Rd
Harrisburg, NC 28705
NASCAR Driver V: 03/02/96

Waltrip, Michael
Wood Bros Racing
Rt 2-Box 77
Stuart, VA 24171
NASCAR Driver V: 10/23/96

Walz, Carl E
NASA/LBJ Space Center
Houston, TX 77058
Astronaut V: 03/03/96

Wang, Dr Taylor
Jet Prop Lab/Cal-Tech
4800 Oak Grove Dr
Pasadena, CA 91109
Astronaut V: 01/09/96

Wang, Garrett
ST-Voyager
5555 Melrose Ave
Hollywood, CA 90036
Actor V: 02/15/96

c/o Insiders
PO Box 13767
Sacramento, CA 95853-3767
Alternate V: 01/14/96

Wang, Wayne
c/o CAA
9830 Wilshire Bl
Beverly Hills, CA 90212
Actor V: 11/01/96

Ward, Fred
1215 Cabrillo Ave
Venice, CA 90291
Actor V: 10/10/96

Ward, Sela
c/o ICM
8942 Wilshire Bl
Beverly Hills, CA 90211
Actress V: 12/11/96

289 S Robertson Bl #469
Beverly Hills, CA 90211-2834
Alternate V: 03/14/96

2102 Century Park Ln #202
Los Angles, CA 90067-3305
Forwarded V: 10/23/96

1875 Century Park E #2647
Los Angeles, CA 90067-2501
Forwarded V: 10/23/96

Ward, Simon
c/o Agency
388 Oxford St
London W1, England
Actor V: 01/29/96

Warden, Jack
23604 Malibu Colony Dr
Malibu, CA 90265
Actor V: 01/03/97

Warfield, Marsha
c/o ICM
8942 Wilshire Bl
Beverly Hills, CA 90211
Actress V: 02/26/96

Waring, George
Joseph & Wagg
Studio 1-Tunstall Rd
London Sw9 8BN, England
Actor V: 03/17/96

Warlock, Billy
Lewis/David
2920 Maple Ave
Manhattan Beach, CA 90266
Actor V: 02/08/96

Warner, David
Buchwald Agency
9229 Sunset Bl #710
Los Angeles, CA 90069
Actor V: 03/20/96

Warner, Julie
c/o CAA
9830 Wilshire Bl
Beverly Hills, CA 90212
Actress V: 01/17/96

Warner, Malcolm-Jamal
Artists First
8230 Beverly Bl #23
Los Angeles, CA 90048
Actor V: 01/15/96

PO Box 69646
Los Angeles, CA 90069
Alternate V: 01/14/96

Warner Brothers Film
15821 Ventura Bl #685
Encino, CA 91436
Production Office V: 03/17/96

Warner Brothers Network
4000 Warner Bl-Bldg 4R
Burbank, CA 91522
Production Office V: 02/12/96

Warner Hollywood Studios
1041 N Formosa Ave
Los Angeles, CA 90046
Production Office V: 03/17/96

Warren, Jennifer
20th Century Artists
15315 Magnolia Bl #429
Sherman Oaks, CA 91403
Actress V: 12/15/96

1675 Old Oak Rd
Los Angeles, CA 90049
Alternate V: 01/15/96

Warren, Lesley Ann
Passionflower
2934 Beverly Glen Cir #372
Los Angeles, CA 90077
Actress V: 10/10/96

8730 Sunset Bl #PH-W
Los Angeles, CA 90069
Alternate V: 01/13/96

c/o ICM
8942 Wilshire Bl
Beverly Hills, CA 90211
Forwarded V: 03/20/96

Warrick, Ruth
903 Park Ave
New York, NY 10021
Actress V: 07/14/96

Abrams Artists
9200 Sunset Bl #625
Los Angeles, CA 90069
Alternate V: 02/25/96

Warwick, Dionne
1583 Lindacrest Dr
Beverly Hills, CA 90212
Singer V: 01/13/97

c/o DWFC
PO Box 343
Wind Gap, PA 18091
Alternate V: 01/13/96

Washington, Denzel
c/o ICM
8942 Wilshire Bl
Beverly Hills, CA 90211
Actor V: 01/14/96

4701 Sancola
Toluca Lake, CA 91602
Alternate V: 01/15/96

Washington Capitols
US Air Arena
Landover, MD 20785
Team Office V: 02/02/96

Washington Redskins
PO Box 17247
Dulles Int'l Airport
Washington, DC 20041
Team Office V: 05/15/96

Wass, Ted
7667 Seattle Place
Los Angeles, CA 90046
Actor V: 01/15/96

Wasson, Craig
Bloom Agency
9255 Sunset Bl #710
Los Angeles, CA 90069
Actor V: 12/06/96

Waterman, Dennis
c/o Agency
388 Oxford St
London W1, England
Actor V: 02/18/96

Waters, TA
1801 Grace Ave #72
Hollywood, CA 90028
Magician V: 03/13/96

Waterston, Sam
c/o ICM
8942 Wilshire Bl
Beverly Hills, CA 90211
Actor V: 12/06/96

Waterston, Sam, Cont.
RR Box 197-Easton St
W Cornwall, CT 06796
Alternate V: 11/01/96

Wathan, John
PO Box 419969
Kansas City, MO 64141
Baseball Star V: 01/16/96

Watson, Tom
1901 W 47th Pl #200
Shawnee Mission, KS 66205
Golfer V: 09/10/96

Watson-Johnson, Vernee
Gage Group
9255 Sunset Bl #515
Los Angeles, CA 90069
Actress V: 12/08/96

Watts, Rolanda
Rolanda Show
325 E 75th St-4th Fl
New York, NY 10021
Production Office V: 01/16/96

Waugh Talent Agency
4731 Laurel Canyon Bl #5
N Hollywood, CA 91607
Talent Agency V: 03/15/96

Wayans, Damon
12140 Summit Ct
Beverly Hills, CA 90210
Actor V: 10/23/96

Wayans, Keenan Ivory
16405 Mulholland Dr
Los Angeles, CA 90048
Actor V: 02/03/96

Wayne, Fredd
11846 Ventura Bl #100
Studio City, CA 91604
Author V: 01/16/96

Wayne, Patrick
Shapira & Associates
15301 Ventura Bl #345
Sherman Oaks, CA 91403
Actor V: 12/14/96

Weather Channel
2600 Cumberland Parkway
Atlanta, GA 30339
Production Office V: 11/11/96

Weathers, Carl
Shapira & Associates
15301 Ventura Bl #345
Sherman Oaks, CA 91403
Actor V: 12/14/96

Weaver, Dennis
Shapira & Associates
15301 Ventura Bl #345
Sherman Oaks, CA 91403
Actor V: 12/14/96

Weaver, Patty
5009 Hayvenhurst Dr
Encino, CA 91316
Actress V: 01/15/96

Weaver, Sigourney
c/o ICM
8942 Wilshire Bl
Beverly Hills, CA 90211
Actress V: 01/14/96

200 W 57th St #1306
New York, NY 10019-3211
Alternate V: 11/20/96

Webb Enterprises
13834 Magnolia Bl
Sherman Oaks, CA 91423
Talent Agency V: 03/13/96

Webber, Andrew Lloyd
P Brown
909 Third Ave-8th Fl
New York, NY 10022
Composer V: 01/14/96

725 Fifth Ave
New York, NY 10022
Alternate V: 10/23/96

Weber, Mary E
NASA/LBJ Space Center
Houston, TX 77058
Astronaut V: 02/02/96

Wedgeworth, Ann
Blake Agency
415 N Camden Dr #121
Beverly Hills, CA 90210
Actress V: 12/06/96

Weintraub, Jerry
11111 Santa Monica Bl
Los Angeles, CA 90038
Producer V: 01/16/96

Weiskopf, Tom
5412 E Morrison Lane
Paradise Valley, AZ 85253
Golfer V: 01/06/96

Weiss, Michael
Innovative Artists
1999 Ave of the Stars #2850
Los Angeles, CA 90067
Actor V: 12/11/96

Weist, Dianne
59 E 54th St #11
New York, NY 10022
Actress V: 01/15/97

Weitz, Bruce
Buckwald & Associates
9229 Sunset Bl #710
Los Angeles, CA 90069
Actor V: 12/06/96

Weitz, Paul J
NASA/LBJ Space Center
Houston, TX 77058
Astronaut V: 03/03/96

Welch, Raquel
Kohner Agency
9300 Wilshire Bl #555
Beverly Hills, CA 90212
Actress V: 12/11/96

Weld, Tuesday
8942 Wilshire Bl
Beverly Hills, CA 90211
Actress V: 11/01/96

Weller, Peter
Creative Artists Agency
9830 Wilshire Bl
Beverly Hills, CA 90212
Actor V: 12/07/96

Wells, Clyde
King Features
235 E 45th St
New York, NY 10017
Cartoonist V: 03/15/96

Wells, Dawn
Amstel-Eisenstadt-Frasier
6310 San Vicente Bl #401
Los Angeles, CA 90048
Actress V: 12/01/96

4616 Ledge Ave
N Hollywood, CA 91602
Alternate V: 11/01/96

Wells, Rachel
Chateau/Billings
5657 Wilshire Bl
Los Angeles, CA 90036
Actress V: 02/25/96

Wen, Ming-Na
Abrams Artists
9200 Sunset Bl #625
Los Angeles, CA 90069
Actress V: 12/01/96

4024 Radford Ave-Bldg 6
Studio City, CA 91604
Alternate V: 10/23/96

Wentworth, Alexandra
Creative Artists Agency
9830 Wilshire Bl
Beverly Hills, CA 90212
Actress V: 12/07/96

West, Adam
PO Box 3477
Ketchum, ID 83340-3477
Actor V: 02/28/96

c/o Chasin
190 N Canon Dr #201
Beverly Hills, CA 90210
Alternate V: 03/03/96

West, Norma
c/o Edwards
275 Kennington Rd
London SE1 6BY, England
Actress V: 02/03/96

West Side Agency
208 N Canon Dr
Beverly Hills, CA 90210
Talent Agency V: 11/11/96

Westbrook, Daniella
Young Mgmt
Rossmore Rd
London NWI 6NJ, England
Actress V: 06/26/96

Westmoreland, William
107 1/2 Tradd-Box 1059
Charleston, SC 29401
Soldier V: 01/09/97

Wetherbee, James D
NASA/LBJ Space Center
Houston, TX 77058
Astronaut V: 01/31/96

Wettig, Patricia
c/o ICM
8942 Wilshire Bl
Beverly Hills, CA 90211
Actress V: 12/11/96

5855 Topanga Canyon Bl #410
Woodland Hills, CA 91367-4621
Alternate V: 08/28/96

Whalley, Joanne
Creative Artists Agency
9830 Wilshire Bl
Beverly Hills, CA 90212
Actress V: 12/07/96

Wheaton, Wil
ST-TNG Paramount
5555 Melrose Ave
Hollywood, CA 90038
Actor V: 03/04/94

2820 Honolulu #255
Verdugo City, CA 91043
Alternate V: 11/01/96

Wheeler, HA Humpy
Charlotte Motor Speedway
PO Box 600
Concord, NC 28026-0600
NASCAR Driver V: 03/02/96

Wheeler-Nicholson, Dana
Gersh Agency
232 N Canon Dr
Beverly Hills, CA 90210
Actress V: 12/09/96

Whelan, Jill
c/o Tisherman
6767 Forest Lawn Dr #115
Los Angeles, CA 90068
Actress V: 02/25/96

Where Are They Now?
Richard Lamparski
924 Garden St-Suite D
Santa Barbara, CA 93101
Publisher V: 02/01/96

Whirry, Shannon
Stone Manners
8091 Selma Ave
Los Angeles, CA 90046
Actress V: 02/25/96

Whitaker, Forest
1990 S Bundy Dr
Los Angeles, CA 90025-5240
Actor V: 11/01/96

6409 Flagmore Pl
Los Angeles, CA 90068
Alternate V: 01/17/96

Whitaker, Johnny
12725 Ventura Bl #F
Studio City, CA 91604
Actor V: 02/04/96

Whitaker Agency
4924 Vineland
N Hollywood, CA 91601
Talent Agency V: 03/13/96

Whitcomb, Bob
Whitcomb Racing
9201 Garrison Rd
Charlotte, NC 28208
NASCAR Owner V: 03/02/96

White, Barry
3395 S Jones Bl #176
Las Vegas, NV 89102-6729
Singer V: 07/14/96

White, Betty
PO Box 3713
Granada Hills, CA 91344-0713
Actress V: 07/14/96

White, Jaleel
Wm Morris Agency
151 El Camino
Beverly Hills, CA 90212
Actor V: 12/12/96

White, Lari
c/o RCA
1 Music Circle N
Nashville, TN 37203
Singer V: 02/07/96

White, Vanna
3400 Riverside Dr
Burbank, CA 91505
Model V: 01/16/96

2600 Larmar Rd
Los Angeles, CA 90068
Forwarded V: 11/10/96

Whitelaw, Billie
Joy Jameson
7 West Eaton Place Mews
London SW1, England
Actress V: 04/03/96

Whitman, Slim
3830 Old Jennings Rd
Middleburg, FL 32086
Singer V: 09/10/96

c/o Purcell
962 2nd Ave-3rd Fl
New York, NY 10022
Alternate V: 02/02/96

Whitman, Stuart
Artists Group
10100 Santa Monica Bl #2490
Los Angeles, CA 90067
Actor V: 12/04/96

749 San Ysidro Rd
Santa Barbara, CA 93108
Alternate V: 01/20/96

9797 Easton Dr
Beverly Hills, CA 90210
Alternate V: 02/02/96

Whitmore, James
Bloom Agency
9255 Sunset Bl #710
Los Angeles, CA 90069
Actor V: 12/06/96

4990 Puesta del Sol
Malibu, CA 90265
Alternate V: 03/20/96

Whitmore Jr, James
Paradigm Agency
10100 Santa Monica Bl-25th Fl
Los Angeles, CA 90067
Actor V: 03/12/96

Whitney, Grace Lee
PO Box 69
Coursegold, CA 93614-0069
Actress V: 02/03/96

Whitten, Janet
c/o Hubert
10061 Riverside Dr #204
Toluca Lake, CA 91602-2515
Actress V: 06/22/96

Whittmore, Jack
NASCAR
1811 Volusia Ave
Daytona Beach, FL 32015
NASCAR Official V: 03/14/96

Wiest, Dianne
127 W 79th St
New York, NY 10024
Actress V: 10/23/96

Wilby, James
Marmont Mgmt/Langham House
302/308 Regent St
London W1R 5AL, England
Actor V: 03/02/96

Wilcox, Larry
Shapira & Associates
15301 Ventura Bl #345
Sherman Oaks, CA 91403
Actor V: 12/14/96

Bell Cyn-10 Appaloosa Ln
Canoga Park, CA 91307-1002
Alternate V: 11/01/96

Wilcutt, Terrence W ˜
NASA/LBJ Space Center
Houston, TX 77058
Astronaut V: 03/03/96

Wilder, Billy
10375 Wilshire Bl
Los Angeles, CA 90024
Director V: 01/15/96

Wilder, Don
King Features
235 E 45th St
New York, NY 10017
Cartoonist V: 04/01/96

Wilder, Gene
10930 Chalon Rd
Los Angeles, CA 90077
Actor V: 11/01/96

Wilder, James
8601 Wilshire Bl #801
Beverly Hills, CA 90211
Actor V: 01/11/97

Wilkinson, June
1025 N Howard St
Glendale, CA 91207
Model V: 11/01/96

Wilkenson, June, Cont.
c/o Atkins
303 S Crescent Hts Bl
Los Angeles, CA 90048
Alternate V: 02/25/96

3653 Fairesta St
La Crescenta, CA 91423
Forwarded V: 11/02/96

Williaims, Esther
9377 Read Creste
Beverly Hills, CA 90210
Actress V: 11/01/96

Williams, Andy
161 Berms Circle #3
Branson, MO 65616
Singer V: 01/04/97

Williams, Barry
Artists Group
10100 Santa Monica Bl #2490
Los Angeles, CA 90067
Actor V: 12/04/96

Williams, Billy Dee
Shapira & Associates
15301 Ventura Bl #345
Sherman Oaks, CA 91403
Actor V: 12/14/96

2114 Beech Knoll Rd
Los Angeles, CA 90046-1518
Alternate V: 01/13/96

Williams, Cindy
Shapira & Associates
15301 Ventura Bl #345
Sherman Oaks, CA 91403
Actress V: 12/13/96

7023 Birdview Ave
Malibu, CA 90265-4106
Alternate V: 01/12/96

Williams, Don
Moress/Nanas/Shea
1209 16th Ave
Nashville, TN 37212
Singer V: 10/23/96

PO Box 422
Branson, MO 65615-0422
Alternate V: 01/13/96

Williams, Donald E
NASA/LBJ Space Center
Houston, TX 77058
Astronaut V: 03/03/96

Williams, Edy
1638 Bluejay Way
Los Angeles, CA 90069
Actress V: 03/02/96

c/o Webb
7500 Devista Dr
Los Angeles, CA 90046
Alternate V: 02/25/96

Williams, Emlyn
123 Doverhouse St
London SW3, England
Actor V: 03/01/96

Williams, Esther
9377 Readcrest
Beverly Hills, CA 90210
Actress V: 12/21/96

Williams, Greg
1680 Vine St #604
Hollywood, CA 90028
Puppeteer V: 03/17/96

Williams, Hershal W
Rt 1-Box 38C
Ona, WV 25545
War Hero V: 03/01/96

Williams, JoBeth
Wm Morris Agency
151 El Camino
Beverly Hills, CA 90212
Actress V: 12/12/96

Williams, John
1560 E Valley
Santa Barbara, CA 93108
Composer V: 05/03/96

Boston Pops Orchestra
301 Massachusettes Ave
Boston, MA 02115
Alternate V: 01/12/97

PO Box 7531
Ann Arbor, MI 48107
Alternate V: 01/15/96

333 Loring Ave
Los Angeles, CA 90024
Forwarded V: 01/11/97

Williams, Kelli
Innovative Artists
1999 Ave of the Stars #2850
Los Angeles, CA 90067
Actress V: 01/15/97

Williams, Montel
Wm Morris Agency
151 El Camino Dr
Beverly Hills, CA 90212
TV Host V: 01/15/96

Williams, Paul
Stone Manners Talent
8091 Selma Ave
Los Angeles, CA 90068
Actor V: 12/15/96

8545 Franklin Ave
Los Angeles, CA 90069-1401
Alternate V: 01/15/96

Williams, Robin
c/o CAA
9830 Wilshire Bl
Beverly Hills, CA 90210
Actor V: 02/18/96

Williams, Roger
c/o Alkahest
Northside Station
PO Box 12403
Atlanta GA 30324
Composer V: 01/15/96

Williams, Stacy
Next Model Mgmt
23 Watts St-6th Fl
New York, NY 10013-1639
Model V: 03/14/96

Williams, Steven
Geddes Agency
1201 Greenacre Bl
W Hollywood, CA 90046
Actor V: 12/08/96

Williams, Ted
PO Box 581
Islamorda, FL 33036
Baseball Star V: 01/16/96

Williams, Treat
215 W 78th St #A-1804
New York, NY 10024
Actor V: 01/20/96

Williams, Van
PO Box 4758
Ketcham, ID 83340
Actor V: 03/26/96

Williams, Vanessa
Wm Morris Agency
151 El Camino Dr
Beverly Hills, CA 90212
Singer V: 03/16/96

50 Old Farm Rd
Chappaqua, NY 10514-3729
Alternate V: 01/13/97

Williams III, Clarence
Flick East-West
9057 Nemo St-Suite A
W Hollywood, CA 90069
Actor V: 03/03/96

Williams Jr, Hank
Hwy 79 East-PO Box 850
Paris, TN 38242
Singer V: 11/01/96

Williamson, Fred
Moss & Associates
733 N Seward St #PH
Los Angeles, CA 90038
Actor V: 12/12/96

Williamson, Nicol
c/o Agency
388 Oxford St
London W1, England
Actor V: 02/02/96

Willis, Bruce
Ruflen Films
1453 Third St #420
Santa Monica, CA 90401
Actor V: 11/01/96

Wm Morris Agency
151 El Camino
Beverly Hills, CA 90210
Alternate V: 12/17/96

Wilson, August
P Weiss
1285 Ave of the Americas
New York, NY 10019
Playwrite V: 01/14/96

Wilson, Brian
14042 Aubrey Rd
Beverly Hills, CA 90210-1064
Singer V: 01/12/96

Wilson, Don
849 S Broadway-#750
Los Angeles, CA 90014
Actor V: 03/11/96

Wilson, Elizabeth
c/o Paradigm
10100 Santa Monica Bl-25th Fl
Los Angeles, CA 90067
Actress V: 02/25/96

Wilson, Flip
Starwil
6253 Hollywood Bl #730
Los Angeles, CA 90028
Actor V: 01/21/96

Wilson, Frank
NC Motor Speedway
PO Box 500
Rockingham, NC 28379
NASCAR Official V: 03/02/96

Wilson, Gahan
919 Michigan Ave
Chicago, IL 60611
Artist V: 08/23/96

Wilson, Jeannie
20th Century Artists
15315 Magnolia Bl #429
Sherman Oaks, CA 91403
Actress V: 02/25/96

Wilson, John
Sabco Racing
5901 Orr Rd
Charlotte, NC 28213
NASCAR Crew V: 03/26/96

Wilson, Mara
3500 W Olive #1400
Burbank, CA 91505
Actress V: 01/11/97

Wilson, Mary
163 Amsterdam Ave #125
New York, NY 10023
Singer V: 09/10/96

1601 E Flamingo Rd
Las Vegas, NV 89110
Alternate V: 10/10/96

Wilson, Nancy
Levine/Schneider
433 N Camden Dr
Beverly Hills, CA 90210
Singer V: 09/10/96

Wilson, Peta
USA-Audience Services
1230 Ave of the Americas
New York, NY 10020
Actress V: 12/12/96

Wilson, Pete
State Capitol Bl
Sacramento, CA 95814
Politician V: 11/02/96

Wilson, Rick
Petty Entertainment
311 Branson Mill Rd
Randleman, NC 27317
NASCAR Driver V: 03/02/96

Wilson, Rita
PO Box 1650
Pacific Palisades, CA 90272
Actress V: 09/10/96

Creative Artists Agency
9830 Wilshire Bl
Beverly Hills, CA 90212
Alternate V: 12/07/96

Wilson Agency
5410 Wilshire Bl #227
Los Angeles, CA 90036
Talent Agency V: 02/18/96

Wincott, Jeff
Agency For Performing Arts
9000 Sunset Bl #1200
Los Angeles, CA 90069
Actor V: 12/02/96

Windom, William
6535 Langdon Ave
Van Nuys, CA 91406
Actor V: 03/14/96

Windsor, Marie
9501 Cherokee Lane
Beverly Hills, CA 90210
Actress V: 01/10/97

Winfield, Paul
Artists Agency
10000 Santa Monica Bl #305
Los Angeles, CA 90067
Actor V: 12/03/96

5693 Holly Oak Dr
Los Angeles, CA 90068
Alternate V: 03/26/96

Winfrey, Oprah
Harpo Inc
PO Box 909715
Chicago, IL 60690
Celebrity V: 02/10/96

Harpo Inc
110 N Carpenter
Chicago, IL 60607
Alternate V: 03/03/96

Wing, Toby
PO Box 1197
Lake Elsinore, 92531
Actress V: 01/10/97

Winger, Debra
20220 Inland Ave
Malibu, CA 90265
Actress V: 11/27/96

Wingert, Dick
King Features
235 E 45th St
New York, NY 10017
Cartoonist V: 02/28/96

Winkler, Henry
PO Box 49914
Los Angeles, CA 90049-0914
Actor V: 03/14/96

c/o ICM
8942 Wilshire Bl
Beverly Hills, CA 90211
Alternate V: 03/09/96

Winkler Productions
5555 Melrose Ave
Hollywood, CA 90038-3197
Production Office V: 02/21/96

Winngham, Mare
Wm Morris Agency
151 El Camino
Beverly Hills, CA 90212
Actress V: 12/12/96

PO Box 19
Beckwourth, CA 96122
Alternate V: 01/17/96

Winnipeg Jets
Winnipeg Arena
15-1430 Maroons Rd
Winnipeg, Man, Canada R3G 0L5
Team Office V: 02/02/96

Winslet, Kate
Wm Morris Agency
31/32 Soho Square
London W1V 5DG, England
Actress V: 12/15/96

Winter, Edward
Henderson & Hogan Agency
247 S Beverly Dr #102
Bevery Hills, CA 90210
Actor V: 12/10/96

Winters, Jonathan
Abrams/Rubaloff
8075 W 3rd St #303
Los Angeles, CA 90048
Actor V: 01/04/96

4310 Arcola Ave
Toluca Lake, CA 91602
Alternate V: 06/17/96

Winters, Shelley
c/o ICM
8942 Wilshire Bl
Beverly Hills, CA 90211
Actress V: 12/11/96

457 N Oakhurst Dr
Beverly Hills, CA 90210-3911
Alternate V: 11/01/96

c/o Gladys Hart
1244 11th St #A
Santa Monica, CA 90401
Forwarded V: 01/03/96

Wirth, Billy
Slessinger & Associates
8271 Melrose Ave #202
Los Angeles, CA 90069
Actor V: 12/14/96

Wisdom, Norman
19 Denmark St
London W2, England
Actor V: 02/28/96

Wise, Robert
315 S Beverly Dr #214
Beverly Hills, CA 90212
Film Producer V: 01/20/96

Wisenthal, Simon
Dokumentationszentrum
1010 Wien, Saltztorgasse
Austria 6/IV/5
Nazi Hunter V: 07/02/96

Wisoff, Peter J
NASA/LBJ Space Center
Houston, TX 77058
Astronaut V: 03/03/96

Witt, Alicia
c/o ICM
8942 Wilshire Bl
Beverly Hills, CA 90211
Actress V: 12/15/96

Witt, Katarina
Zwechaur Str 12
Karl Marx Stadt, Germany
Olympian V: 02/21/96

Witt\Thomas\Harris Agency
846 N Cahuena Bl
Hollywood, CA 90038
Production Office V: 03/17/96

Witter, Karen
Innovative Artists
1999 Ave of the Stars #2850
Los Angeles, CA 90067
Actress V: 02/25/96

Wm Morris Agency
151 El Camino Dr
Beverly Hills, CA 90212
Talent Agency V: 01/24/96

31/32 Soho Sq
London W1V 5DG, England
Alternate V: 01/20/96

Wolf, David A
NASA/LBJ Space Center
Houston, TX 77058
Astronaut V: 03/03/96

Wolf, Scott
Gersh Agency
232 N Canon Dr
Beverly Hills, CA 90210
Actor V: 12/15/96

Wolfe, Tom
21 E 79th St
New York, NY 10021
Author V: 12/01/96

Women in Film
6464 Sunset Bl #660
Hollywood, CA 90028
Production Office V: 03/17/96

Women in Show Business
PO Box 2535
N Hollywood, CA 91602
Production Office V: 03/17/96

Women's Tennis Assn
133 1st St NE
St Petersburg, FL 33701
League Office V: 12/01/96

Wonder, Stevie
4616 Magnolia Bl
Burbank, CA 91505
Singer V: 04/01/96

Wong, BD
c/o APA
888 7th Ave
New York, NY 10106
Actor V: 12/01/96

Woo, John
20th Century Fox
10201 W Pico Bl
Los Angeles, CA 90038
Director V: 02/02/96

Wood, Eddie
McLean Marketing
9307-P Monro Rd
Charlotte, NC 28270
NASCAR Crew V: 03/02/96

Wood, Elijah
Wm Morris Agency
151 El Camino Dr
Beverly Hills, CA 90212
Actor V: 02/12/96

760 N La Cienega Bl #200
Los Angeles, CA 90069
Alternate V: 02/28/96

Wood, Glen
McLean Marketing
9307-P Monro Rd
Charlotte, NC 28270
NASCAR Owner V: 03/02/96

Wood, Judith
1745 N Gramercy Pl #517
Los Angeles, CA 90028-5859
Actress V: 05/06/96

Woodard, Alfre
c/o STE
9301 Wilshire Bl #312
Beverly Hills, CA 90210
Actress V: 01/17/96

Woods, James
8942 Wilshire Bl
Beverly Hills, CA 90211
Actor V: 12/11/96

760 La Cienega Bl
Los Angeles, CA 90069
Alternate V: 11/10/96

Woodward, Joanne
1120 Fifth Ave #1C
New York, NY 10128-0144
Actress V: 02/03/96

40 West 57th St
New York, NY 10019
Alternate V: 10/23/96

Woodward, Morgan
Gerler-Stevens
3349 Cahuenga Bl #2
Los Angeles, CA 90068
Actor V: 03/15/96

Wooley, Sheb
Circuit Rider
123 Walton Ferry Rd
Hendersonville, TN 37075
Singer V: 02/02/96

Rt3-Box 231
Sunset Island Trail
Gallantine, TN 37066
Alternate V: 03/20/96

Wopat, Tom
Bloom Agency
9255 Sunset Bl #710
Los Angeles, CA 90069
Actor V: 12/06/96

2614 Woodlawn Dr
Nashville, TN 37212
Alternate V: 01/17/96

Worden, Alfred M
129 Commodore
Jupiter, FL 334777
Astronaut V: 01/04/96

NASA/LBJ Space Center
Hoston, TX 77058
Forwarded V: 01/19/96

World Championship Wrestling
1 CNN Center
PO Box 740124
Atlanta, GA 30374
League Office V: 02/09/96

World Class Sports
880 Apollo St #337
El Segundo, CA 90245
Talent Agency V: 02/02/96

World Wide Acts
23233 Saticoy St #140
Canoga Park, CA 91304
Talent Agency V: 11/11/96

World Wrestling Federation
Titan Sports
81 Holy Lane
Greenwich, CT 06830
League Office V: 02/09/96

Worley, Jo Anne
Sutton/Barth & Vennari
145 S Fairfax Ave #310
Los Angeles, CA 90036
Actress V: 12/15/96

Woronov, Mary
Stone Manners Talent
8091 Selma Ave
Los Angeles, CA 90068
Actress V: 12/15/96

Wray, Fay
2160 Century Park E #1901
Los Angeles, CA 90067
Actress V: 06/16/96

Wright, Jenny
245 W 104th St
New York, NY 10025-4249
Actress V: 11/26/96

Wright, Teresa
140 Transylvania Rd
Roxbury, CT 06783
Actress V: 02/09/96

Wright Talent Agency
6513 Hollywood Bl #210
Hollywood, CA 90028
Talent Agency V: 01/14/96

Writers & Artists Agency
924 Westwood Bl #900
Los Angeles, CA 90024
Talent Agency V: 02/02/96

Writers Society of America
11684 Ventura Bl #868
Studio City CA 91604
Production Office V: 12/17/96

Wyatt, Jane
Wm Morris Agency
151 El Camino
Beverly Hills, CA 90212
Actress V: 12/12/96

651 Siena Way
Los Angeles, CA 90024
Alternate V: 10/23/96

Wyman, Bill
H Siegel
410 Park Ave-10th Fl
New York, NY 10022-4407
Musician V: 08/28/96

Wyman, Jane
56 Kavendish Dr
Rancho Mirage, CA 92270
Actress V: 10/23/96

Wynette, Tammy
c/o TWIFC
PO Box 121926
Nashville, TN 37212-1926
Singer V: 12/15/96

Wynn, Early
PO Box 3969
Venice, FL 34293-0130
Baseball Star V: 01/10/97

X

X-FILES
X-Files FC
411 N Central Ave #300
Glendale, CA 91203
Fan Service V: 01/13/96

Studio Fan Mail
1122 S Robertson Bl
Los Angeles, CA 90035
Forwarded V: 11/01/96

North Shore Studios
110-555 Brooksbank Bl
N Vancouver, BC, V7J 3S5
Canada
Forwarded V: 01/13/97

XENIA: WARRIOR PRINCESS
WB-TV
1438 N Gower
Hollywood, CA 90028
Audience Services V: 04/12/96

Y

YBA Enterprises
8391 Beverly Bl #339
Los Angeles, CA 90048
Talent Agency V: 11/11/96

YOUNG & RESTLESS
7800 Beverly Bl #3371
Hollywood, CA 90036
Fan Service V: 11/20/96

Yamaguchi, Kristi
3650 Montecito Dr
Fremont, CA 94530
Ice Skater V: 10/23/96

Yanni
c/o Chryssomallis
6714 Villa Madera Dr SW
Tacoma, WA 98499
Composer V: 10/10/96

5443 Beethoven St
Los Angeles, CA 90066
Forwarded V: 01/16/96

Yarborough, Cale
Yarborough Racing
9617 Dixie River Rd
Charlotte, NC 28270
Alternate V: 03/02/96

Yarborough, William
1801 Volusia Ave
Dayton Beach, FL 32015
Race Driver V: 03/01/96

Yarbrough, Glenn
2835 Woodstock Rd
Los Angeles, CA 90046
Singer V: 01/21/96

Yarlett, Claire
1540 Skylark Lane
Los Angeles, CA 90069
Actress V: 01/14/96

Yates, Cassie
520 Washington Bl #175
Marina del Rey, CA 90292-5442
Actress V: 03/14/96

Yeager, Bunny
9301 NE 6th Ave #C-311
Miami, FL 33138
Model V: 09/10/96

Yeager, Chuck
PO Box 128
Cedar Ridge, CA 95924
Test Pilot V: 04/21/96

Yeager, Jeana
Voyager Aircraft
Hanger 77
Mojave, CA 93501
Test Pilot V: 02/02/96

Yearwood, Trisha
c/o Kragen
1112 N Sherbourne Dr
Los Angeles, CA 90069
Singer V: 02/02/96

Yedid, Meir
PO Box 2566
Fair Lawn, NJ 07410
Magician V: 03/13/96

Yeltsin, Boris
4 Straya Ploschad
Moscow, USSR
Politician V: 03/03/96

Yoakam, Dwight
c/o Borman
9220 Sunset Bl #320
Los Angeles, CA 90069
Singer V: 02/02/96

York, Michael
Gold/Marshak
3500 W Olive Ave #1400
Burbank, CA 91505
Actor V: 12/10/96

Duncan Heath
162 Wardour St
London W1, England
Alternate V: 02/28/96

9100 Cordell Dr
Los Angeles, CA 90069
Forwarded V: 05/23/96

York, Susannah
J Altaras
2 Goodwins Ct
London WC2N 4LL, England
Actress V: 11/01/96

York, Susannah, Cont.
Smith & Associates
121 N San Vicente Bl
Beverly Hills, CA 90211
Alternate V: 12/15/96

Yost, Ed
48 Oakridge Rd
Wellesley, MA 02181
Baseball Star V: 02/08/96

Young, Alan
Artists Group
10100 Santa Monica Bl #2490
Los Angeles, CA 90067
Actor V: 12/04/96

Young, Dean
King Features
235 E 45th St
New York, NY 10017
Cartoonist V: 01/07/96

Young, Jesse Colin
c/o Keauhou
PO Box 325
Pt Reyes Station, CA 94956
Singer V: 04/22/96

Young, John W
NASA/LBJ Space Center
Houston, TX 77058
Astronaut V: 01/19/96

Young, Neil
1515 S Doheny Dr
Los Angeles, CA 90035
Singer V: 05/22/96

PO Box 130
Pt Reyes Station, CA 94956
Alternate V: 02/04/96

Young, Paul
c/o ITG
729 7th Ave #1600
New York, NY 10019
Singer V: 10/10/96

Young, Sean
PO Box 20547
Sedona, AZ 86341
Actress V: 03/01/96

Z

ZBF Agentur
Jenfelder Allee 80
22045 Hamburg, Germany
Talent Agency V: 02/27/96

Leopoldstrasse 19
8000 Munchen, Germany
Alternate V: 02/27/96

Ordensmeisterstrasse 15-16
12099 Berlin, Germany
Alternate V: 02/27/96

Zabitowsky, Fred W
PO Box 660
Pembroke, NC 28372
War Hero V: 02/05/96

Zadeh & Associates
11759 Iowa Ave
Los Angeles, CA 90025
Talent Agency V: 02/27/96

Zadora, Pia
9560 Wilshire Bl
Beverly Hills, CA 90212-2427
Singer V: 02/25/96

Zane, Billy
c/o CAA
9830 Wilshire Bl
Beverly Hills, CA 90212
Actor V: 01/16/96

450 N Rossmore Ave #1001
Los Angeles, CA 90004
Alternate V: 11/01/96

Zapata, Carmen
Artists Group
10100 Santa Monica Bl #2490
Los Angeles, CA 90067
Actress V: 12/04/96

Zappa, Moon
Ambrosio & Mortimer
9150 Wilshire Bl #175
Beverly Hills, CA 90212
Actress V: 12/01/96

Zealous Artists
139 S Beverly Dr #222
Beverly Hills, CA 90212
Talent Agency V: 02/02/96

Zeigler, Heidi
150 E Olive Ave #304
Burbank, CA 91502
Actress V: 01/16/96

Zeman, Jacklyn
Stone Manners Talent
8091 Selma Ave
Los Angeles, CA 90046
Actress V: 12/15/96

Zemeckis, Robert
9830 Wilshire Bl
Beverly Hills, CA 90212
Director V: 01/14/96

PO Box 5218
Santa Barbara, CA 93150-5218
Alternate V: 11/20/96

Zerbe, Anthony
Smith & Associates
121 N San Vicente Bl
Beverly Hills, CA 90211
Actor V: 12/15/96

245 Chateaux Elise
Santa Monica, CA 93109
Alternate V: 10/23/96

Ziegler, Bill
King Features
235 E 45th St
New York, NY 10017
Cartoonist V: 02/20/96

Zierling, Ian
9000 Sunset Bl #1200
Los Angles, CA 90069
Actor V: 12/15/96

Zimbalist, Stephanie
151 El Camino
Beverly Hills, CA 90212
Actress V: 12/12/96

Sharon Leigh
PO Box 487
Sunland, CA 91041-0487
Forwarded V: 02/20/96

Zimbalist Jr, Efrem
3518 Cahuenga Bl W #216
Los Angeles, CA 90068
Actor V: 03/11/96

4750 Encino Ave
Encino, CA 91316
Alternate V: 04/27/96

Zinc, Tom
c/o WCW/Turner
One CNN Center-Box 105366
Atlanta, GA 30348-5366
Wrestler V: 03/26/95

Zmed, Adrian
22103 Avenida Morelos
Woodland Hills, CA 91364
Actor V: 01/17/95

Henderson/Hogan
247 S Beverly Dr #102
Los Angeles, CA 90210
Alternate V: 03/16/95

Zmievskaya, Galina
Int'l Skating Center
1375 Hopmeadow St
Simsbury, CT 06070
Ice Skating Coach V: 01/09/96

Zucker, Richard
c/o Sony
10202 W Washington Bl
Culver City, CA 90232
Producer V: 01/16/95

Zuckerman, Pinchas
711 W End Apt #5K-NN
New York, NY 10025-6843
Musician V: 11/20/96

Zumwalt, Admiral Elmo
100 Wilson Bl #3105
Arlington, VA 22209-3901
Soldier V: 01/13/97

Zuniga, Daphne
c/o ICM
8942 Wilshire Bl
Beverly Hills, CA 90211
Actress V: 12/11/96

c/o Murphy
2401 Main St
Santa Monica, CA 90405
Alternate V: 01/14/96

c/o Constellation
PO Box 1249
White River Jct, VT 05001
Forwarded V: 06/29/96

Zydeco, Buckwheat
Ted Fox
PO Box 561
Rhinebeck, NY 12572
Singer V: 11/27/96

REFERENCE AND RESOURCE LISTINGS

We list these dealers and publishers as a service to our readers and assume no responsibility for their business in part or whole. In the past they have been known to give excellent customer service and we presume they have continued to do so.

RECOMMENDED HOT WEBSITES & E-MAIL ADDRESSES:

Celebrity Access Publications
Party with the Movie Guy. Have fun. Hollywood/Collectors Information clearing house. Movie reviews, autograph collecting info, and reference books, links, and much more. Mention you found the site in this book.
Website: http://members.aol.com/accessstar/index.html

E-mail: 103632.156@compuserve.com
CelebrityAccess@compuserve.com
AccessStar@aol.com

Autograph Collector Magazine
The #1 Hollywood collectors magazine goes on line with this one. They have a lot to offer here. This should be on your "must see" list.
Website: http//:www.AutographCollector.com
E-mail: Odysgroup@aol.com

Celebrity Connection
Looking for unsigned photos? Want to find out where to look in collecting? This is the place. Check out their hot links.
Website: http://www.celebrityconnection.com
E-mail: photos@goodnet.com

Magazines/Newsletters:

Autograph Collector Magazine
510-A South Corona Mall, Corona, CA 91719-1420 / (909) 734-9636
This is a premiere autograph magazine. We've been subscribers since their first issue. They are always bringing a new level of learning with every issue. It features celebrity articles, follows collecting trends, gives celebrity addresses, auctions, and much more. Look for their website at Http://www.AutographCollector.com

V.I.P. Autogramm-Magazin
PO Box 15 68, D-63456 Maintal, Germany, Phone:49-6181/4928
Celebrity contacts worldwide, articles, photos, and merchandising. Please, include 2 post office International Reply Coupons for info. This awesome colorful international magazine has thousands of celebrity address listings of all your favorite stars, sports heroes, you name the occupation. You really have to see this to believe it. We were happily pleased and surprised. Published six times a year.

Autograph and Manuscript Organizations:

Universal Autograph Collectors Club
Penn and Quill Magazine, PO Box 6181, Washington, DC 20044-6181
Internationally recognized association with a magazine for its members and governed by the tops in autograph collecting. If you collect autographs or learn as you collect, you owe it to yourself to be informed.

The Manuscript Society
350 N Niagara St, Burbank, CA 91505
Here is where you look, when you want the most serious approach to historical autographs and manuscripts. The membership consists of top professionals with a passion for the rare and wonderful.

Newspapers(Magazine):

Autograph Times
1125 W Baseline Rd, #2-153, Mesa, AZ 85210-9501
Packed with articles, in-person celebrity interviews, collecting tips, who's hot and who's not. An international newspaper for collectors. We enjoy the easy to read format. Loaded with helpful information.

The Autograph Review
305 Carlton Rd, Syracuse, NY 13207
This fantastic mini-magazine, is full of current information leaning heavily towards sports with some information on film stars. Sports interviews are here as well. This is certainly worth the subscription.

Movie Collectors World
PO Box 309, Frazier, MI 48026 / (810) 774-4311
This is a "super huge" monthly paper which contains information on where to fulfill all your film collecting needs. Aside from the articles, one will find the largest assortment of dealers anywhere.
The paper is a huge two section, cornucopia for collectors. This is for serious collectors. We use it ourselves.

Paper Collectors Marketplace
PO Box 128, Scandinavia, WI 54977-0128 / (715) 467-2379
Reach collectors and dealers of Hollywood collectibles. Almost anything you can think of are offered here. Thousands of entries and listings.

The Big Reel
PO Box 1050, Dubuque, IA 52004-9986 / (800) 334-7165
This is a movie, video, and Hollywood collectibles magazine which has been around for over 20 years. Awesome listing. Assembled here is a massive listing of Movie Posters, lobby cards, photos, and everything else you can think of. If its Hollywood, its here.

Collecting Hollywood
PO Box 2512, Chattanooga, TN 37409 / (615) 265-5515
A collectors paradise for items offered in advertising. Loaded with movie Posters, prices, and Hollywood collectibles.

Collecting
510-A S Corona Mall, Corona, CA 91719-1420 / (909) 734-9639
Provides a first class source of information including feature stories, auctions & more. Autographs*Movie Posters*Props*movie memorabilia.

Celebrity Address Resources:

Jim Weaver's Address Lists
322 Mall Bl, #345, Monroeville, PA 15146-2229
This list comes out several times a year with addresses and a unique category listing (Sports, Hollywood, Horror, Sex Symbols), including updated addresses, bad address warnings, deaths, and new additions. Worth having to complete your reference library. Easy to read and follow.

Christensen's Ultimate Directory/Christensen's Address Additions/
Christensen's Address Updates
Cardiff by the Sea Publishing, PO Box 900189, San Diego, CA 92190
Here is the ultimate movie, TV, Rock & Roll, and celebrity address directory. This is one of the most comprehensive celebrity address directories ever made. It was the first one on our shelves years ago, and has remained there in current edition since. If you are looking for the hard to find or old timers, this is the book. Over 30,000 total listings.

"V.I.P. Address Book"
PO Box 489, Gleneden Beach, OR 97388
This award winning book has a place on our shelves. Unlike the others, it covers famous people in all areas of interest, with an easy to read and follow text. Hollywood, sports, science, military, the arts--almost everything. We recommend it often as a companion to the others we have listed. Also published are their 6 annual updates. A truly superior work. Over 20,000 listings.

Autograph Research Newsletter/Space Autograph News/Celebrity Home Address Newsletter

862 Thomas Ave, San Diego, CA 92109 / (619) 483-8632
If you want some great reference quotes on anything to do with autographs, look here first. They list every mention in every publication they can find on the subject, with where to find it. Also celebrity addresses, articles, signature examples, forgery alerts, and more. There are three publications. First one is research of autographs in general. Second is for any collector interested in space exploration in connection with autographs. Third says it all. For all you collectors who insist on home addresses, look no further.

Autograph Price Guide:

Sanders Price Guide to Autographs
PO Box 685, Enka, NC 28728
This is considered a standard in industry. Prices of autographs on cards, letters, typed letters, and photo's in all fields. A huge reference tool. Don't get caught selling your autographs too quickly. Be informed.

Fan Clubs and Fans:

Fandom Directory
7761 Astrella Ct, Springfield, VA 22152-3133 / (703) 913-5575
If you are a collector, dealer, publisher, convention organizer, or just a fan, you can be listed FREE! This directory is huge. Loaded with collectors and cross-referenced with their

areas of interest. They've been around serving the collector for a long time, and used by all sorts of professionals.

National Association of Fan Clubs
c/o Linda Kay, PO Box 7487, Burbank, CA 91510

Join the only International Fan Club Association representing all fan clubs, in all fields of entertainment, The benefits are many, including the sharing of information with other fan clubs, helpful suggestions a fan club which meets your needs, how to start your own fan club, and much more. Annually they publish an incredible fan club directory. Please write for membership fees, and include a self-addressed stamped envelope.

Video, Film, and Music Dealers:

The Incredibly Strange Filmworks
PO Box 28404, Las Vegas, NV 89126-2404

The strange---the bizarre---the unusual. These are words that come easy when describing there catalog of film titles. Were you unsuccessful finding a film that came and went before you could get a copy? Or a film that showed years ago and never returned. They have everything. Sci-fi...easy, Hot Rod or Biker films...no sweat. Blacksploitation...you bet. You've got to see their catalogs. It's awesome. They're the best.

Village Music
9 E Blithedale Ave, Mill Valley, CA 94941

Is there an album of any type you are looking for. New, used, rare? This is a resource where you can find the album of your dreams.

Soundtrack Video
PO Box 800704, Santa Clarita, CA 91380

The Science Fiction Video Collection
100 Fusion Way, Country Club Hills, IL 60478

Unsigned Celebrity Photographs, Books, Posters, and Memorabilia:

Photo Classics
PO Box 14410, Phoenix, AZ 85063-4410 / (602) 846-5734

A #1 selection of unsigned, high quality, reasonably priced photos.

S & P Parker's Movie Market, PO Box 1868, Laguna Beach, CA 92652

The Bijou Collectibles & Photos PO Box 201, Fullerton, CA 92632

Collectors Book Store 1708 N Vine St, Hollywood, CA 90028

Cinema Collectors Store 1507 Wilcox Ave, Hollywood, CA 90028

Hollywood Book & Poster 6349 Hollywood Bl, Hollywood, CA 90028

Rare Collector Movie Posters
105 S Wall St, PO Box 369, Benson, NC 27504

A superior selection of lobby cards & posters, in original and reprint.

Reference Books:

The Bare Facts Video Guide, by Craig Hosoda
PO Box 3255, Santa Clara, CA 95055 / (415) 249-2021
   The Bare Facts Video Guide. This unusual book helps the researcher and fan alike, to find the scenes, films, and magazines where their favorite actor or actress can be found with little or no clothing on. This oversized paperback which has already caught the attention of Playboy Magazine, is completely updated annually. This is a really a gold mine of thorough information. At 450+ pages, a it's a must.

"Creature Features Movie Guide Strikes Again" by John Stanley
PO Box 687, 1082 Grand Teton Dr, Pacifica, CA 94044
   An excellent book for cross-referencing horror stars and their movies.

"Wanted To Buy" by Collector Books, PO Box 3009, Paducah, KY 42001
   An excellent guide to help the collector find those "hard to find items."

"I'll Buy That" Dr. Tony Hyman, PO Box 699, Claremont, CA 91711
   This book is sought after by those who want a great resource. This lists the best buyers of Autographs, antiques, and collectibles, with info. on how to sell them.

"Who's Who in Hollywood" by David Ragan

"Where Are They Now?" Lamparski

"Total Television" by Alex McNeil

"Halliwell's Filmgoer's Companion"

"The Film Encyclopedia" by Ephraim Katz, A four star "who's who."

"The Complete Directory To Prime Time Network TV Shows/The Complete Directory To Prime Time Stars" by Brooke & Marsh

"Motion Picture Guide-Horror and Science Fiction"
ScanRom Publications, PO Box 72, Cedarhurst, NY 11516

MANY COLLECTING BOOKS ARE AVAILABLE IN YOUR PUBLIC LIBRARY

Autographs:

Celebrity Access Productions
20 Sunnyside Ave, Suite A 241, Mill Valley, CA 94941 (415) 389-8133
   Buy/Sell Autographs & Collections, Authentication & Appraisal Service.

CELEBRITY CLOTHING

A Star Is Worn
7303 Melrose Ave, Los Angeles, CA 90046 (800) 545-0524
   Clothing worn previously by stars can be purchased here.